Andrew Johnson, Benjamin Perley Poore, United States Congress

Trial of Andrew Johnson

President of the United States, before the Senate of the United States, on

Impeachment by the House of Representatives for High Crimes and Misdemeanors

Andrew Johnson, Benjamin Perley Poore, United States Congress

Trial of Andrew Johnson
President of the United States, before the Senate of the United States, on Impeachment by the House of Representatives for High Crimes and Misdemeanors

ISBN/EAN: 9783337155346

Printed in Europe, USA, Canada, Australia, Japan

Cover: Foto ©ninafisch / pixelio.de

More available books at **www.hansebooks.com**

TRIAL

OF

ANDREW JOHNSON,

PRESIDENT OF THE UNITED STATES,

BEFORE THE SENATE OF THE UNITED STATES,

ON

IMPEACHMENT

BY THE HOUSE OF REPRESENTATIVES

FOR

HIGH CRIMES AND MISDEMEANORS.

PUBLISHED BY ORDER OF THE SENATE.

VOLUME III.

INDEX.

INDEX.

[The Roman numerals indicate the volumes.]

A.

Able, Barton. (See *Testimony*.)
Acquittal on Article XI..II—486, 487
    II..II—496
    III...II—497
  judgment of, entered...II—498
Adjournment *sine die*...II—498
Admissibility of testimony. (See *Evidence*.)
Admissions to the floor, order (in Senate) that, during the trial, no person besides those who have the privilege of the floor, &c., shall be admitted except upon tickets issued by the Sergeant-at-arms—[*By Mr. Anthony;*] agreed to...I—10
Alta Vela letter..II—144, 262, 289, 306
  remarks on, by—
    Manager Butler...II—262, 267, 268, 281, 282, 284
    Mr. Nelson..................................II—144, 265, 266, 267, 268, 280, 281, 282, 283, 284, 307
    Manager Logan..II—268
Answer, application of counsel for forty days to prepare....................................I—19
  discussed by—
    Manager Bingham...I—20, 22
    Mr. Curtis...I—20
    Mr. Stanbery...I—21
    Manager Wilson..I—20
  denied..I—24
  orders offered fixing day for respondent to file, by—
    Mr. Edmunds..I—24, 35
    Mr. Drake..I—35
    Mr. Trumbull...I—35
  order that respondent file, on or before 23d March—[*By Mr. Trumbull.*]
    offered and agreed to...I—35
    read and filed..I—37
  exhibits accompanying—
    A, message of President, March 2, 1867, returning with objections tenure-of-office bill.............I—53
    B, message of President, December 12, 1867, announcing suspension of Secretary Stanton...........I—58
    C, address to President, by Hon. Reverdy Johnson, August 18, 1866, communicating proceedings of National Union Convention...I—66
Anthony, Henry B., a senator from Rhode Island..I—11
  orders by—
    (in Senate,) that during the trial no persons besides those who have the privilege of the floor, &c., shall be admitted except upon tickets issued by the Sergeant-at-arms. Agreed to....................I—10
    that no senator shall speak more than once, nor to exceed fifteen minutes during deliberation on final question, except by leave of Senate, to be had without debate, as provided by Rule xxiii, offered...II—471
    tabled, (yeas 28, nays 20)...II—474
    that on Wednesday, (May 13,) at 12 o'clock, the Senate shall proceed to vote, without debate, on the several articles, &c.; offered and rejected, (yeas 13, nays 27)...........................II—476
  remarks by......................................I—16, 247, 301, 370, 425, 490, 498, 634, 700, 726, 728, 738, 741
                              II—13, 307, 389, 470, 471, 472, 476, 486. III—368
Application of counsel for forty days to prepare answer....................................I—19
  denied...I—24
  for thirty days to prepare for trial...I—69
    denied, (yeas 12, nays 41)...I—82
  for three days to prepare proofs..I—367, 369
    granted...I—371
  for adjournment in consequence of illness of Mr. Stanbery...............................I—533
Argument, right of counsel making motion to open and close, thereon........................I—77
  final, orders offered to fix the number of speakers on, by—
    Manager Bingham..I—450
    Mr. Frelinghuysen...I—451
    Mr. Sumner..I—491, 497, 532
    Mr. Sherman..I—495, 741. II—6
    Mr. Conness..I—535. II—5, 8
    Mr. Doolittle..I—536
    Mr. Stewart..I—741
    Mr. Vickers..II—3, 4
    Mr. Johnson..II—5
    Mr. Corbett..II—7
    Mr. Henderson...II—8
    Mr. Trumbull...II—11
    Mr. Buckalew..II—12
    Mr. Cameron...II—12
    Mr. Yates..II—12

IV   INDEX.

Argument, final—Continued.
   order that as many of managers as desire be permitted to file, or address Senate orally, the conclusion of oral argument to be by one manager—[*By Mr. Trumbull.*]
      offered ....II—11
      adopted, (yeas 28, nays 22) ....II—14
Argument on the case by—
   Manager Butler ....I—87
   Mr. Curtis..I—377, 390, 397
   Manager Logan ....II—14
   Manager Boutwell ....II—67, 84, 99
   Mr. Nelson ....II—118, 141
   Mr. Groesbeck ....II—189
   Manager Stevens ....II—219
   Manager Williams...II—230, 249
   Mr. Evarts ....II—269, 284, 308, 336
   Mr. Stanbery..II—359, 360
   Manager Bingham ....II—389, 447
Armstrong, William W. (See *Testimony*.)
Articles of impeachment exhibited by House of Representatives...........................I—6
   vote on. (See *Question*.)

B.

Bayard, James A., a senator from Delaware ....I—11
   remarks on the competency of the President *pro tempore* to sit as a member of the court...........III—372
   order by—
      that no senator shall speak more than once, nor to exceed thirty minutes, during deliberations on final question; offered and rejected, (yeas 16, nays 34) ....II—218
   remarks by..II—7, 218
Bingham, John A., of Ohio, a manager, chairman...................................I—4, 17
   motions by—
      that upon filing replication the trial proceed forthwith; offered and denied, (yeas 25, nays 26)....I—25
      to amend Rule XXI, so as to allow such of managers and counsel as desire to be heard to speak on final argument..I—450
   argument by—
      on application of counsel for forty days to prepare answer........................I—20, 22
      for thirty days to prepare for trial..I—69, 77, 78
      on motion to fix day for trial to proceed....................................I—32, 33
      on right of managers to close debate on interlocutory questions................I—77
      on authority of Chief Justice to decide questions of evidence............I—180, 181, 183
      on motion in regard to rule limiting argument on final question.............I—450, 534
      on right of Counsel to renew examination of a witness recalled by court........I—524, 525, 527
   on admissibility—
      of Adjutant General Thomas's declarations to Mr. Burleigh, February 21, 1868 ....I—202, 206
      to clerks of War Department...I—213
      of President's letter to General Grant, unaccompanied with enclosures..........I—244
      of appointment of Edmund Cooper, to be Assistant Secretary of the Treasury ....I—262
      of President's declarations to Adjutant General Thomas, February 21.............I—425
      prior to March 9...I—430
      of question, Whether General Sherman gave President an opinion, &c ....I—498, 505, 506
      of President's message to Senate, February 24.....................I—540, 541, 542, 543
   final, on the case..II—389, 447
Blodgett, Foster. (See *Testimony*.)
Boutwell, George S., of Massachusetts, a manager....................................I—4, 17
   argument by—
      on application of counsel for thirty days to prepare for trial ....I—78
      on authority of Chief Justice to decide questions of evidence................I—181, 184
   on admissibility—
      of telegrams relating to the reconstruction of Alabama.......................I—274
      of extracts from records of Navy Department................................I—567
   final, on the case ....II—67, 84, 99
   remarks on the case of the removal of Timothy Pickering....................I—367
   on motion relating to the number of speakers on final argument..............I—405
Brief of authorities upon the law of impeachable crimes and misdemeanors—[*By Hon. William Lawrence, M. C., of Ohio*] ....I—123. III—355
Buckalew, Charles R., a senator from Pennsylvania...................................I—11
   remarks on the competency of the President *pro tempore* to sit as a member of the court ......III—383, 385
   order by—
      that the conclusion of the oral argument be by one manager, as provided in Rule XXI; offered and agreed to...II—12
      prescribing form of final question; offered...................................II—178
      that the views of Chief Justice on the form of putting final question be entered on the journal; offered and agreed to...II—480
   remarks by...I—431, 738, 740, 741. II—5, 12, 478, 480, 483, 489
   opinion on the case ....III—218
Burleigh, Walter A. (See *Testimony*.)
Butler, Benjamin F., of Massachusetts, a manager....................................I—117
   argument by—
      on motion to fix a day for trial to proceed....................................I—25
      on motion relating to the number of speakers on final argument ....I—406
      on application of counsel for thirty days to prepare for trial ....I—4
      opening, on the case..I—87
      on authority of Chief Justice to decide questions of evidence........I—176, 177, 181, 184
      on right of counsel to renew examination of a witness recalled by court..........I—523
   on admissibility—
      of Adjutant General Thomas's declarations to Mr. Burleigh, Feb. 21, 1868......I—187, 192, 193, 195, 2, 7
      to clerks of War Department..I—213
      of appointment of Edmund Cooper to be Assistant Secretary of Treasury ....I—250, 260, 262, 264, 265

INDEX   V

Butler, Benjamin F., of Massachusetts, argument by, on admissibility—Continued.
  of telegrams relating to the reconstruction of Alabama ....I—270, 271, 273, 275, 276
  of Chronicle's report of President's speech in reply to Hon. Reverdy Johnson......I—286, 289, 297, 301
  of Leader's report of President's speech at Cleveland.......................................I—322, 323, 324
  of President's declarations to Adjutant General Thomas, Feb. 21.......................I—420, 421, 422
    prior to March 9, as to use of force...I—429, 430
  of conversations between President and General Sherman, Jan. 14...I—462, 463, 465, 468, 469, 470, 471
                                                                                          472, 473, 475, 479
  of question respecting Department of the Atlantic...I—481, 482
  of tender of War Office to General Sherman..I—482, 483, 484
  of President's purpose to get the question before the courts...................................I—485, 486
  of question, Whether General Sherman formed and gave President an opinion, &c.....I—500, 501, 574
  of affidavit and warrant of arrest of Lorenzo Thomas........................I—510, 511, 512, 513, 514
  of President's message to Senate, Feb. 24....................................I—538, 539, 540, 541, 542, 543
  of extracts from records of Navy Department......................I—561, 562, 563, 564, 565, 566
  of employment of counsel by President to get up test case.................................I—597, 600, 604
  of President's declarations to Mr. Perrin, Feb. 21...I—625, 627
    to Secretary Welles..I—667, 671
  of advice to President by Cabinet touching constitutionality of tenure-of-office act......I—676, 677, 678
    touching construction of tenure-of-office act..I—694, 695
  of cabinet consultations in regard to obtaining a judicial decision, &c........................I—698, 699
  of papers in Mr. Blodgett's case...I—722, 723, 724, 725
  remarks on application of counsel for adjournment..I—628, 629
  on the Alta Vela letter...II—262, 267, 268, 281, 282, 284

C.

Cameron, Simon, a senator from Pennsylvania..I—11
  order by—
    that all the managers and counsel be permitted to file arguments by eleven o'clock, April 23;
      offered and rejected..II—12
  order by—
    that Senate hereafter hold night sessions from eight until eleven p. m.; offered..............II—283
      tabled, (yeas, 32; nays, 17)..II—308
  remarks by.......I—184, 240, 266, 267, 370, 371, 632, 726. II—12, 268, 283, 469, 470, 473, 481, 482, 487, 491, 497
  question by...II—267
Cattell, Alexander G., a Senator from New Jersey..I—11
  opinion on the case..III—178
Chandler, William E. (See *Testimony*.)
Chandler, Zachariah, a senator from Michigan..I—11
  remarks by...I—674, II—482, 483
Chew, Robert S. (See *Testimony*.)
Chief Justice, attendance of, requested as presiding officer in the trial...............................I—10
  oath administered to..I—11
  casting vote given by..I—185, 276
  resolution denying authority of, to vote on any question during the trial—[*By Mr. Sumner*.]
    offered and rejected, (yeas, 22; nays, 26)...I—185
  order denying privilege of, to rule questions of law—[*By Mr. Drake*.]
    offered and rejected, (yeas, 20; nays, 30.)...I—186
  order denying authority of, to give casting vote—[*By Mr. Sumner*.]
    offered and rejected, (yeas, 21; nays, 27)...I—187
  order that the ruling of, upon all question of evidence, shall stand as the judgment of the Senate unless
    a formal vote be asked, &c.—[*By Mr. Henderson*.]
    offered..I—185
    agreed to, (yeas, 31; nays, 19)...I—186
  views of, on form of putting final question...II—491
  appeals from decisions of..II—488, III—394
  opinion of Mr. Sumner on the question, Can the, presiding in the Senate, rule or vote?...........III—384
Clarke, D. W. C. (See *Testimony*.)
Clephane, James O. (See *Testimony*.)
Cole, Cornelius, a senator from California...I—11
  remarks by..I—508, II—479
Committee (in House) to communicate to Senate the action of the House directing an impeachment of
  Andrew Johnson; ordered..I—2
  appointed..I—3
  appear at bar of Senate..I—5
  report to House..I—3
(in House) to prepare articles of impeachment against Andrew Johnson; ordered.......................I—2
  appointed..I—3
  report of..I—3, 6
(in Senate) to consider and report on the message of the House relating to the impeachment of Andrew
  Johnson; ordered and appointed..I—5
  report of...I—5, 13
(in Senate) to request the attendance of the Chief Justice as presiding officer in the trial; ordered and
  appointed..I—10
Competency. (See *Evidence*.)
Conkling, Roscoe, a senator from New York..I—11
  orders by—
    that Rule XXIII be amended by inserting "subject to operation of Rule VII."
      offered and agreed to..I—18
    that, unless otherwise ordered, trial proceed immediately after replication filed; offered........I—30
      agreed to, (yeas, 40; nays, 10)..I—31
    that the Senate commence the trial 30th March instant; agreed to, (yeas, 28; nays, 24).........I—85
    prescribing form of final question; offered..II—478
    that Senate proceed to vote on remaining articles; rejected, (yeas, 26; nays, 28)..............II—492
  remarks by.........I—17, 18, 24, 31, 32, 33, 85, 179, 180, 208, 210, 236, 216, 267, 297, 301, 324, 359, 370, 390, 450,
                           451, 452, 490, 497, 521, 537, 565, 671, 676, 689, 716.
        II—5, 6, 99, 152, 203, 250, 306, 322, 470, 471, 472, 474, 475, 476, 477, 478, 479, 492, 493, 494
  questions by...I—246, 504

INDEX.

Conness, John, a senator from California .... I—11
  remarks on the competency of the President *pro tempore* to sit as a member of the court .... III—367, 395
  orders by—
    that Rule XXI be amended to allow as many of managers and counsel to speak on final argument
      as choose, four days to each side, managers to open and close; offered and rejected, (yeas, 19;
      nays, 27) .... I—535
    that hereafter Senate meet at eleven a. m.; offered .... I—631
      adopted, (yeas, 29; nays, 11) .... I—639
    that such of managers and counsel as choose have leave to file arguments before April 24; offered
      and disagreed to, (yeas, 24; nays, 25) .... II—5
    prescribing form of final question; offered .... II—178
  remarks by .....I—30, 161, 185, 207, 246, 247, 268, 276, 298, 325, 367, 370, 371, 414, 462, 507, 514, 519, 532, 535, 58).
                         611, 612, 628, 631, 633, 666, 673, 679, 699, 706, 7.6
    II—3, 4, 5, 6, 8, 10, 11, 83, 84, 413, 469, 470, 471, 472, 473, 474, 476, 478, 481, 483, 484, 488, 492, 493, 494, 498
  question by .... I—727
Conversations. (See *Evidence; Testimony.*)
Corbett, Henry W., a senator from Oregon .... I—11
  order by—
    that two of counsel have privilege of filing written or making an oral address, &c.; amendment
      offered .... II—7
      withdrawn .... II—8
  remarks by .... II—7, 8, 11
Counsel for respondent .... I—18, 19, 34
Cox, Walter S. (See *Testimony.*)
Cragin, Aaron H., a senator from New Hampshire .... I—11
  remarks by .... I—673
Creecy, Charles E. (See *Testimony.*)
Curtis, Benjamin R., of Massachusetts, counsel .... I—19
  motion by—
    for an allowance of three days to prepare proofs; offered .... I—367, 369
    granted .... I—371
  argument by—
    on application for forty days to prepare answer .... I—20
    for time to prepare proofs .... I—367, 369
    opening, for the defence .... I—377, 390, 397
    on admissibility—
      of Adjutant General Thomas's declarations to Mr. Burleigh February 21, 1868 .... I—198, 199
      of President's letter to General Grant, unaccompanied with enclosures .... I—244
      of telegrams relating to the reconstruction of Alabama .... I—270, 271, 272
      of President's message to Senate February 21 .... I—537, 538
      of extracts from records of Navy Department .... I—562, 563, 564, 565, 566, 567, 568
      of employment of counsel by President to get up test case .... I—602, 604
      of President's declarations to Secretary Welles .... I—669
      of advice to President by cabinet touching constitutionality of tenure-of-office act... I—677, 678, 689, 692

D.

Davis, Garrett, a senator from Kentucky .... I—11
  remarks on the competency of the President *pro tempore* to sit as a member of the court .... III—363, 366
  order by—
    that a court of impeachment cannot be legally formed while senators from certain States are
      excluded; offered and rejected, (yeas, 2; nays, 49) .... I—36
  remarks by .... I—35, 487, 587, 519, 598. II—219, 282, 469, 482, 485
  opinion on the case .... III—156
Dear, Joseph A. (See *Testimony.*)
Declarations. (See *Evidence; Testimony.*)
Dixon, James, a senator from Connecticut .... I—11
  remarks on the competency of the President *pro tempore* to sit as a member of the court .... III—388, 389,
                                  390, 391, 392, 393, 394, 395, 396
Documents. (See *Evidence.*)
Doolittle, James R., a senator from Wisconsin .... I—34
  order by—
    that on final argument managers and counsel shall alternate, two and two; managers to open and
      close; offered and indefinitely postponed, (yeas, 31; nays, 15) .... I—536
  remarks .... I—250, 276, 486, 489, 535, 436. 611, 632, 740, 711. II—9, 487, 492, 493
  opinion on the case .... III—244
Drake, Charles D., a senator from Missouri .... I—11
  remarks on the competency of the President *pro tempore* to sit as a member of the court ...... III—389, 389,
                                           390, 393
  orders by—
    that respondent file answer on or before 20th March; agreed to, (yeas, 28; nays, 20) .... I—35
    reconsidered, (yeas, 27; nays, 23) .... I—35
    that Chief Justice presiding has no privilege of ruling questions of law on the trial, but all such
      questions should be submitted to Senate alone; offered and rejected, (yeas, 20; nays, 30) ...... I—186
    that votes upon incidental questions shall be without a division, unless requested by one-fifth of
      members present, or presiding officer; (amendment to Rule VII,) offered .... I—230
    agreed to .... I—277
    that any senator shall have permission to file his written opinion at the time of giving his vote;
      offered .... II—476
    rejected, (yeas, 12; nays, 38) .... II—477
    that the fifteen minutes allowed by Rule XXIII shall be for the whole deliberation on final question,
      and not to final question on each article; offered .... II—471
    adopted .... II—478
  remarks by ......I—33, 82, 145, 176, 179, 186, 207, 238, 246, 230, 247, 255, 276, 277, 278, 280, 298, 325, 336, 424, 480,
                485, 489, 496, 497, 50c, 516, 519, 520, 529, 533, 535, 536, 545, 605, 634, 680, 693, 696
                          II—84, 1ee, 472, 471, 476, 477, 484, 487, 491, 497, 498
  question by .... I—533

E.

Edmunds, George F., a senator from Vermont..I—17
  orders by—
    that answer be filed April 1, replication three days thereafter, and the matter stand for trial April 6,
      1868; offered..I—21
    that when the doors shall be closed for deliberation upon final question, the official reporters shall
      take down debates to be reported in proceedings: offered................................II—141
      not indefinitely postponed, (yeas 20, nays 27)..II—188
      read...II—218, 471
      tabled, (yeas 28, nays 20)..II—474
    that the standing order of the Senate, that it will proceed at twelve o'clock noon to-morrow to vote
      on the articles, be rescinded—[May 11, 1868:] offered..................................II—482
      agreed to..II—483
    that the Senate now proceed to vote upon the articles, according to the rules of the Senate offered
      May 16..II—485
      agreed to..II—486
  remarks by.......................................I—24, 85, 86, 208, 211, 277, 336, 390, 451, 519, 534, 537, 566, 597, 660, 741
                II—3, 10, 11, 12, 14, 141, 188, 218, 268, 471, 474, 475, 476, 479, 482, 483, 484, 485, 490, 493
  questions by...I—566, 597
  opinion on the case...III—82
Emory, William H. (See *Testimony*.)
Evarts, William M., of New York, counsel...I—19
  motions by—
    that after replication filed, counsel be allowed reasonable time to prepare for trial: offered........I—83
    for an adjournment in consequence of illness of Mr. Stanbery................................I—533
  argument by—
    on application for thirty days to prepare for trial...I—68, 71
    on authority of Chief Justice to decide questions of evidence....................................I—184
    on right of counsel to renew examination of a witness recalled by court.................I—523, 524, 526
  on admissibility—
    of Adjutant General Thomas's declarations to Mr. Burleigh, February 21, 1868..............I—206, 207
    to clerks of War Department..I—212
    of President's letter to General Grant, unaccompanied with enclosures......................I—244, 245
    of appointment of Edmund Cooper to be Assistant Secretary of the Treasury........I—258, 263, 264
    of telegrams relating to the reconstruction of Alabama..........................I—270, 271, 272, 273
    of Chronicle's report of President's speech in reply to Hon. Reverdy Johnson.......I—286, 288, 289
    of Leader's report of President's speech at Cleveland.........................I—322, 323, 324
    of President's declarations to Adjutant General Thomas, February 21........................I—424
      prior to March 9...I—429, 430
    of President's conversations with General Sherman, January 14.............................I—470, 475
    of tender of War Office to General Sherman..I—482, 484
    of question whether General Sherman gave President an opinion, &c.................I—501, 504, 506
    of affidavit and warrant of arrest of Lorenzo Thomas.........................I—510, 511, 514
    of President's message to Senate, February 24..............................I—538, 539, 542, 543
    of extracts from records of Navy Department...I—566, 568
    of employment of counsel by President to get up test case..............................I—599, 603
    of President's declaration to Mr. Perrin......................................I—625, 626, 627
    to Secretary Welles..I—668, 672, 673
    of advice to President by his cabinet touching constitutionality of tenure-of-office act.......I—676, 672
    touching construction of tenure-of-office act..I—694, 696
    of cabinet consultations in regard to obtaining a judicial decision, &c........................I—699
    of papers in Mr. Blodgett's case..I—722, 723, 724, 725
    final, on the case..II—269, 284, 308, 336
  remarks announcing illness of Mr. Stanbery..................................I—533, 590, 716
  on order in regard to limiting argument on final question....................I—497, 534. II—7, 9
  on application for adjournment...I—628, 629, 631
Evidence, question, whether objections to, should be decided by Chief Justice, or, in first instance, submitted to Senate—[*By Mr. Drake*]..I—175, 179
  discussed by—
    Manager Butler...I—176, 177, 181, 184
    Manager Bingham..I—180, 181, 183
    Manager Boutwell..I—181, 184
    Mr. Evarts..I—184
  presiding officer may rule all questions of, which ruling shall stand as the judgment of the Senate,
    unless a vote be asked, &c.; or he may, in first instance, submit such questions to Senate—[*By
    Mr. Henderson*]—offered; I—185; agreed to; (yeas 31, nays 19).........................I—186
  admissibility of—
    declarations of Adjutant General Thomas, as to the means by which he intended to
      obtain possession of War Department: (objected to by *Mr. Stanbery*)...............I—175, 188
    discussed by—
      Manager Butler..I—187, 192, 193, 195, 207
      Mr. Stanbery...I—188, 192, 193, 195, 206, 207
      Mr. Curtis..I—198, 199
      Manager Bingham..I—202, 206
      Mr. Evarts...I—206, 207
    admitted; (yeas 39, nays 11)..I—209
    declarations of Adjutant General Thomas to clerks of War Department, antecedent to his appointment as Secretary of War *ad interim*, as to his intention when he came in command: (objected
      to by *Mr. Evarts*)..I—212
    discussed by—
      Mr. Evarts..I—212
      Manager Butler..I—212
      Manager Bingham...I—213
    admitted; (yeas 28, nays 22)..I—214
    letter of President to General Grant, February 10, 1868, unaccompanied by other letters referred
      to therein: (objected to by *Mr. Stanbery*)..I—243

VIII INDEX.

Evidence, admissibility of—
 President's letter to General Grant—Continued.
  discussed by—
   Mr. Stanbery...I—244, 245
   Manager Wilson..I—244, 246
   Mr. Evarts...I—244, 246
   Manager Bingham..I—244
   Mr. Curtis...I—244
  objection not sustained: (yeas 20, nays 29)...I—247
 appointment of Edmund Cooper, private secretary of President, as Assistant Secretary of
  Treasury; (objected to by *Mr. Evarts*)...I—258
  discussed by—
   Mr. Evarts...I—258, 263, 264
   Manager Butler..I—259, 260, 263, 264, 265
   Mr. Stanbery...I—260, 261, 262, 264
   Manager Bingham...I—262
  not received; (yeas 22, nays 27)..I—263
 telegrams between President and Lewis E. Parsons, January 17, 1867, in relation to constitutional
  amendment and reconstruction of Alabama; (objected to by *Mr. Stanbery*)...............I—270
  discussed by—
   Manager Butler...I—270, 271, 272, 273, 275, 276
   Mr. Evarts..I—270, 271, 272, 273
   Mr. Stanbery..I—270
   Mr. Curtis..I—270, 271, 272
   Manager Boutwell..I—274
  admitted; (yeas 27, nays 17)...I—276
 Chronicle's report of President's speech, August 18, 1866, in reply to Hon. Reverdy Johnson;
  (objected to by *Mr. Evarts*)...I—286
  discussed by—
   Mr. Evarts...I—286, 288, 289
   Manager Butler..I—286, 289, 297, 301
  withdrawn..I—301
 Leader's report of President's speech at Cleveland, September 3, 1866; (objected to by *Mr. Evarts*)..I—322
  discussed by—
   Mr. Evarts...I—322, 323, 324
   Manager Butler..I—322, 323, 324
  admitted; (yeas 35, nays 11)...I—325
 declarations of President to Adjutant General Thomas, February 21, 1868, after order for removal
  of Mr. Stanton, to show an absence of purpose to use force; (objected to by *Manager Butler*)..I—420
  discussed by—
   Manager Butler...I—420, 421, 422
   Mr. Stanbery..I—421
   Mr. Evarts..I—424
   Manager Bingham..I—425
  admitted; (yeas 42, nays 10,)...I—426
 declarations of President to Adjutant General Thomas prior to 9th March, in respect to use of force
  to get possession of the War Office; (objected to by *Manager Butler*)..............I—429
  discussed by—
   Manager Butler...I—429, 430
   Mr. Evarts...I—429, 430
   Manager Bingham...I—430
  admitted..I—430
 conversations between President and Lieutenant General Sherman, January 14, 1868, in regard to
  removal of Mr. Stanton ; (objected to by *Manager Butler*)..........................I—462
  discussed by—
   Mr. Stanbery..I—462, 463, 465, 468, 469, 471, 472
   Manager Butler..............................I—462, 463, 465, 468, 469, 470, 471, 472, 473, 475, 479
   Mr. Evarts...I—470, 475
   Manager Wilson...I—478, 479
  not admitted, (yeas 23, nays 28)...I—481
 question in regard to creation of department of the Atlantic; (objected to by *Manager Butler*)....I—481
  discussed by—
   Manager Butler...I—481, 482
   Mr. Stanbery...I—481, 482
  not admitted..I—482
 tender to General Sherman of appointment as Secretary of War *ad interim*; (objected to by *Manager Butler*)..I—482
  discussed by—
   Manager Butler...I—482, 483
   Mr. Evarts..I—482
   Mr. Stanbery..I—482
  admitted..I—483
 question, Whether at the first offer of War Office to General Sherman anything further passed in
  reference to the tender or acceptance of it; (objected to by *Manager Butler*).......I—484
  discussed by—
   Manager Butler...I—484
   Mr. Evarts..I—484
  not admitted, (yeas 23, nays 29)..I—485
 President's declaration of purpose of getting Mr. Stanton's right to office before the courts; (objected
  to by *Manager Butler*)...I—485
  discussed by—
   Manager Butler...I—485, 486
   Mr. Stanbery..I—486
   Mr. Evarts..I—486
  not admitted, (yeas 7, nays 44)...I—487
 President's declaration of purpose in tendering General Sherman the appointment of Secretary of
  War *ad interim*; (objected to by *Manager Bingham*)................................I—488
  not admitted, (yeas 25, nays 27)..I—489

INDEX. IX

Evidence, admissibility of—Continued.
 President's declarations to General Sherman in reference to use of threats or force to get possession
  of the War Office; (objected to by *Manager Butler*) .... I—489
  not admitted .... I—490
 question, Whether General Sherman gave President an opinion as to advisability of a change in the
  War Department; (objected to by *Manager Butler*) .... I—498
  discussed by—
   Manager Bingham .... I—498, 505, 506
   Mr. Stanbery .... I—499, 501, 501
   Manager Butler .... I—500, 501, 504
   Mr. Evarts .... I—501, 504, 506
  not admitted, (yeas 15, nays 35) .... I—507
 advice to President to appoint some person in place of Mr. Stanton; (objected to by *Manager Butler*)... I—507
  not admitted, (yeas 18, nays 32) .... I—508
 affidavit of Edwin M. Stanton and warrant of arrest of Lorenzo Thomas; (objected to by *Manager
  Butler*) .... I—510
  discussed by—
   Manager Butler .... I—510, 511, 512, 513, 514
   Mr. Evarts .... I—510, 511, 514
   Mr. Stanbery .... I—512, 513, 514
  admitted; (yeas 34, nays 17) .... I—515
 question, Whether President stated to General Sherman his purpose in tendering him the office of
  Secretary of War *ad interim*; (objected to by *Manager Bingham*) .... I—517
  admitted, (yeas 26, nays 22) .... I—518
 President's declaration of purpose in tendering General Sherman the office of Secretary of War *ad
  interim*; (objected to by *Manager Bingham*) .... I—518
  admitted; (yeas 26, nays 25) .... I—520
 message of President to Senate, February 24, 1868, in response to Senate resolution of February 21,
  1868; (objected to by *Manager Butler*) .... I—538
  discussed by—
   Manager Butler .... I—538, 539, 540, 541, 542, 543
   Mr. Curtis .... I—537, 538
   Mr. Evarts .... I—538, 539, 542, 543
   Manager Bingham .... I—540, 541, 542, 543
  not admitted .... I—544
 extracts from records of Navy Department, exhibiting practice in respect to removals; (objected to
  by *Manager Butler*) .... I—561
  discussed by—
   Manager Butler .... I—561, 562, 563, 564, 565, 566
   Mr. Curtis .... I—562, 563, 564, 565, 566, 567, 568
   Mr. Evarts .... I—566, 568
   Manager Boutwell .... I—567
  admitted; (yeas 36, nays 15) .... I—568
 employment of counsel by President to raise question of Mr. Stanton's right to hold the office of
  Secretary of War against authority of President; (objected to by *Manager Butler*) .... I—597
  discussed by—
   Manager Butler .... I—597, 600, 604
   Mr. Evarts .... I—598, 603
   Mr. Curtis .... I—602, 604
   Manager Wilson .... I—602
  admitted; (yeas 29, nays 21) .... I—605
 acts toward getting out *habeas corpus* in the case of Lorenzo Thomas; (objected to by *Manager Butler*) I—608
  admitted; (yeas 27, nays 23) .... I—609
 acts, after failure to obtain *habeas corpus*, in pursuance of President's instructions to test the right of
  Mr. Stanton to continue in office; (objected to by *Manager Butler*) .... I—610
  admitted; (yeas 27, nays 23) .... I—612
 declarations of President to Mr. Perrin, February 21, 1868, in reference to removal of Mr. Stanton,
  and nomination of a successor; (objected to by *Manager Butler*) .... I—625
  discussed by—
   Manager Butler .... I—625, 627
   Mr. Evarts .... I—625, 626, 627
   Manager Wilson .... I—626
  not admitted; (yeas 9, nays 37) .... I—628
 President's declarations to Secretary Welles, February 21, in relation to removal of Mr. Stanton;
  (objected to by *Manager Butler*) .... I—667
  discussed by—
   Manager Butler .... I—667, 671
   Mr. Evarts .... I—668, 672, 673
   Mr. Curtis .... I—669
  admitted; (yeas 26, nays 23) .... I—674
 advice to President by cabinet touching constitutionality of tenure-of-office act; (objected to by
  Manager Butler) .... I—676
  discussed by
   Manager Butler .... I—676, 677, 678
   Mr. Evarts .... I—676, 678
   Mr. Curtis .... I—677, 678, 680, 692
   Manager Wilson .... I—681
  not admitted; (yeas 20, nays 29) .... I—693
 advice to President by cabinet in regard to construction of tenure-of-office act, and its application to
  Secretaries appointed by President Lincoln; (objected to by *Manager Butler*) .... I—694
  discussed by—
   Mr. Evarts .... I—694, 696
   Manager Butler .... I—694, 695
  not admitted; (yeas 22, nays 26) .... I—697
 cabinet consultations in regard to obtaining a judicial decision on constitutionality of tenure-of-office
  act; (objected to by *Manager Butler*) .... I—698
  discussed by—
   Manager Butler .... I—698, 699
   Mr. Evarts .... I—699
  not admitted; (yeas 19, nays 30) .... I—700

Evidence, admissibility of—Continued.
   question, Whether any suggestions were made in cabinet looking to the vacation of any office by
      force; (objected to by *Manager Butler*)... I–705
      not admitted; (yeas 18, nays 26).. I–701
   opinions given to President by cabinet on question, Whether the Secretaries appointed by President
      Lincoln were within the provisions of tenure-of-office act; (objected to by *Manager Bingham*). I–715
      not admitted; (yeas 20, nays 26).. I–716
   answer of Foster Blodgett to Postmaster General's notice of his suspension from the office of post-
      master at Augusta, Ga.; (objected to by *Mr. Evarts*)... I–722
      discussed by—
        Mr. Evarts.. I–722, 723, 724, 725
        Manager Butler.. I–722, 723, 724, 725
      not admitted... I–726
   nominations of Lieutenant General Sherman, February 13, 1868, and of Major General George H.
      Thomas, February 21, 1861, to be Generals by brevet; (objected to by *Mr. Evarts*)......... I–736
      not admitted; (yeas 14, nays 35).. I–738
Evidence, documentary, for the prosecution—
   copy of oath of Andrew Johnson, President of the United States, April 15, 1865, with accompanying
      certificates... I–147
   copy of President Lincoln's message to Senate, January 13, 1862, nominating Edwin M. Stanton to be
      Secretary of War... I–148
   copy of Senate resolution in executive session, January 15, 1862, consenting to appointment of Edwin
      M. Stanton to be Secretary of War... I–148
   copy of President's message to Senate, December 12, 1867, announcing suspension of Edwin M. Stanton
      from the office of Secretary of War, and designation of General Grant as Secretary of War *ad
      interim*... I–148
   copy of Senate resolution, January 13, 1868, in response to message of President announcing suspen-
      sion of Edwin M. Stanton, and non-concurring in such suspension............................... I–155
   copy of Senate order, January 13, 1868, directing Secretary to communicate copy of non-concurring
      resolution to President, to Edwin M. Stanton, and to U. S. Grant, Secretary of War *ad interim*.... I–155
   copy of President's message to Senate, February 21, 1868, announcing removal of Edwin M. Stanton
      from office, and designation of the Adjutant General of the army as Secretary of War *ad interim*.. I–156
   copy of President's order, February 21, 1868, removing Edwin M. Stanton from the office of Secretary
      of War... I–156
   copy of President's letter of authority to Lorenzo Thomas, February 21, 1868, to act as Secretary of
      War *ad interim*, and directing him immediately to enter upon duties........................... I–156
   copy of Senate resolution, February 21, 1868, that President has no power to remove the Secretary
      of War and to designate any other officer to perform duties of that office *ad interim*........... I–157
   copy of Senate order, February 21, 1868, directing Secretary to communicate copies of foregoing
      resolution to President, to Secretary of War, and to Adjutant General of the army............. I–157
   copy of President Lincoln's commission to Edwin M. Stanton as Secretary of War, January 15, 1862. I–157
   commission of Edmund Cooper as Assistant Secretary of Treasury, November 20, 1867............ I–163
   letter of authority to Edmund Cooper, December 2, 1867, to act as Assistant Secretary of Treasury... I–164
   copy of General Orders No. 15, March 12, 1868, requiring all orders relating to military operations
      issued by President or Secretary of War to be issued through General of the army............. I–237
   copy of Brevet Major General W. H. Emory's commission, July 17, 1866............................ I–239
   Special Orders No. 426, August 27, 1867, assigning General Emory to command of department of
      Washington.. I–240
   order of President, February 13, 1868, that Brevet Major General Thomas resume duties as Adjutant
      General.. I–240
   letter of General Grant, January 24, 1868, requesting to have in writing order given him verbally by
      President to disregard orders of E. M. Stanton as Secretary of War, &c........................ I–240
   President's instructions to General Grant, January 29, 1868, not to obey orders from War Depart-
      ment, unless, &c... I–240
   letter of President to General Grant, February 10, 1868, in regard to his having vacated the office of
      Secretary of War *ad interim*.. I–241
   copy of President's letter of authority to Lorenzo Thomas to act as Secretary of War *ad interim*... I–248
   copies of order removing Edwin M. Stanton, and letter of authority to General Thomas with indorse-
      ments thereon, forwarded by President to Secretary of Treasury for his information............ I–248, 249
   copy of General Orders No. 17, March 14, 1867, requiring all orders relating to military operations to
      be issued through General of the army... I–249
   copy of order of General of army to General Thomas to resume duties as Adjutant General........ I–256
   message of President communicating report of Secretary of State, showing proceedings under concur-
      rent resolution of the two houses requesting President to submit to legislatures of States an addi-
      tional article to the Constitution... I–278
   report of President's speech, August 18, 1866, in reply to Hon. Reverdy Johnson, as sworn to by
      Francis H. Smith.. I–288
   report of President's speech, August 18, 1866, revised by William G. Moore, his secretary......... I–301
      at Cleveland, September 3, 1866, in Cleveland Leader.. I–325
      at Cleveland, September 3, 1866, by D. C. McEwen.. I–328
      at Cleveland, September 3, 1866, in Cleveland Herald.. I–333
      at St. Louis, September 8, 1866, in Missouri Democrat... I–340
      at St. Louis, September 8, 1866, in St. Louis Times.. I–348
   forms of various commissions as issued by President before and after passage of civil-tenure act.... I–353
   list of removals of heads of departments at any time by President during session of Senate......... I–358
   list of appointments of heads of departments at any time by President without advice and consent of
      Senate and while Senate was in session.. I–358
   correspondence between President John Adams and Timothy Pickering, May 1800, relating to re-
      moval of Mr. Pickering from office of Secretary of State... I–362
   copy of President John Adams's message, May 12, 1800, nominating John Marshall to be Secretary
      of State in place of Timothy Pickering removed, and action of Senate thereon.................. I–365
   letter from President, August 14, 1867, notifying Secretary of Treasury, "in compliance with re-
      quirements" of tenure-of-office act, of suspension of Edwin M. Stanton........................ I–364
   letter of Secretary of Treasury, August 15, 1867, notifying heads of bureaus, in compliance with
      requirements of tenure-of-office act, of suspension of Edwin M. Stanton....................... I–366
   executive messages of President communicating information of suspension of several officers....... I–369
   communication from Secretary of State, December 19, 1867, reporting to President, in compliance
      with provisions of tenure-of-office act, the suspension of the consul at Brunel, Borneo........... I–369

INDEX.

XI

Evidence, documentary, for the prosecution—Continued.
copy of letter from Adjutant General Thomas to President, February 21, 1868, reporting delivery of President's communication to Edwin M. Stanton removing him from office, and accepting appointment of Secretary of War *ad interim* .... I—376

Evidence, documentary, for the defence—
affidavit of Edwin M. Stanton, and warrant of arrest of Lorenzo Thomas, February 22, 1868 .... I—515
docket of entries as to disposition of case of United States *vs.* Lorenzo Thomas......................... I—531
President's nomination of Thomas Ewing, sen., to be Secretary of War, February 22, 1868 .... I—537
copy of Senate proceedings, May 13, 1800, on nomination of John Marshall to be Secretary of State, in place of Timothy Pickering, removed... I—555
copy of President Tyler's order, February 29, 1844, appointing John Nelson, Attorney General, to discharge duties of Secretary of State *ad interim*.. I—557
copy of Senate resolution, March 6, 1844, confirming nomination of John C. Calhoun as Secretary of State, vice A. P. Upshur.. I—558
copy of President Fillmore's order, July 23, 1850, designating Winfield Scott to act as Secretary of War *ad interim*.. I—558
copy of Senate resolution, August 15, 1850, confirming nomination of Charles M. Conrad as Secretary of War.. I—558
copy of President Buchanan's order, January 10, 1861, appointing Moses Kelley to be Acting Secretary of Interior... I—559
copy of President Lincoln's commission, March 5, 1861, to Caleb B. Smith as Secretary of Interior .. I—559
copy of letters of Acting Secretary of Treasury, August 17, 1842, relating to removal of collector and appraiser in Philadelphia... I—560
extracts from records of Navy Department exhibiting practice in respect to removals................... I—569
list of civil officers of Navy Department, appointed for four years under act of May 15, 1829, and removable at pleasure, who were removed, their terms not having expired............................. I—573
copies of documents from State Department, showing practice of government in removal of officers during session of Senate, during recess, and covering all cases of vacancy............................ I—574, 590
copies of documents from Post Office Department, showing removals of postmasters during session of Senate and *ad interim* appointments... I—581
message of President Buchanan, January 15, 1861, in answer to Senate resolution respecting vacancy in the office of Secretary of War.. I—583
list of persons who discharged duties of cabinet officers, whether by appointment made in recess and those confirmed by Senate, as well as those acting *ad interim*, or simply acting....................... I—595
statement of beginning and ending of each legislative session of Congress from 1789 to 1868 .... I—594
statement of beginning and ending of each special session of Senate from 1789 to 1868 .... I—595
copy of President Adams's commission to George Washington, July 4, 1798, constituting him Lieutenant General of the army.. I—653
tables from Department of Interior, showing removals of officers, date, name, office, and whether removal was during recess or during session of Senate... I—654
list of consular officers appointed during session of Senate where vacancies existed when appointments were made... I—662
form of navy agent's commission... I—705
official action of Post Office Department in removal of Foster Blodgett................................... I—709

Evidence, documentary, for the prosecution, in rebuttal—
Journal of first Congress, 1774-'75, exhibiting report of committee to draft commission to General George Washington.. I—718
letter of James Guthrie, Secretary of Treasury, August 22, 1855, as to practice of government in appointing officers during recess to fill vacancies existing before adjournment......................... I—719
copy of indictment in case of Foster Blodgett in district court of United States for southern district of Georgia... I—720
list of the various officers in United States affected by President's claim of right to remove at pleasure and appoint *ad interim*, their salaries, &c.. I—722

Ewing, Thomas, sen., nomination of, to be Secretary of War......................... I—508, 516, 537, 555, 556

F.

Ferry, Orris S., a senator from Connecticut... I—11
orders by—
that the hour of meeting be at 11 a. m., and that there be a recess of thirty minutes each day at 2 p. m.: offered and rejected, (yeas 24, nays 26).. I—536
that tabular statements presented by Manager Butler be omitted from published proceedings:
offered.. I—633
adopted.. I—634
remarks by .... I—186, 197, 336, 536, 602, 632, 633, 701, 716. II—I, 495. III—394
question by .... I—602
opinion on the case.. III—121

Ferry, Thomas W. (See *Testimony*.)

Fessenden, William P., a senator from Maine... I—11
remarks on the competency of the President *pro tempore* to sit as a member of the court...III—366, 367, 391, 401
remarks by .... I—176, 266, 267, 268, 336, 478, 479. II—6, 7, 195, 469, 473, 483, 485
questions by .... I—267, 268
opinion on the case... III—16

Fowler, Joseph S., a senator from Tennessee... I—11
remarks by .... I—175, 276. II—7
opinion on the case... III—193

Frelinghuysen, Frederick T., a senator from New Jersey... I—11
remarks on the competency of the President *pro tempore* to sit as a member of the court ....III—380, 385
order by—
that as many of managers and counsel as shall choose be permitted to speak on final argument,
offered and laid over.. I—451
discussed... I—491
modified... I—495
tabled, (yeas 38, nays 10).. I—496
remarks by .... I—188, 451, 491, 495. II—13, 471
question by .... I—188
opinion on the case.. III—206

G.

Grimes, James W., a senator from Iowa... I—11
  remarks on the competency of the President *pro tempore* to sit as a member of the court .... III—382, 394, 401
  order by—
    that hereafter the hour of meeting shall be 12 o'clock m. each day, except Sunday:
      offered .... II—99
      adopted, (yeas 21, nays 13) .... II—141
  remarks by .... I—17, 78, 179, 298, 315, 618, 701, 709.   II—6, 8, 13, 90, 217, 268, 322, 360, 469, 485
  question by .... I—315
  opinion on the case .... III—328
Groesbeck, William S., of Ohio, counsel .... I—34
  argument, final, on the case .... II—189

H.

Harlan, James, a senator from Iowa... I—11
  opinion on the case .... III—233
Henderson, John B., a senator from Missouri .... I—11
  orders by—
    that application for thirty days to prepare for trial be postponed until after replication filed ; offered
      and not agreed to, (yeas 25, nays 26) .... I—81
    that presiding officer may rule all questions of evidence, which ruling shall stand as the judgment
      of the Senate, unless some member shall ask a formal vote, in which case it shall be submitted to
      the Senate ; or he may submit any such question to a vote in the first instance, (amendment to
      Rule VII:)
      offered .... I—185
      agreed to, (yeas 31, nays 19) .... I—186
    that, subject to Rule XXI, all managers not delivering oral arguments may file written arguments
      before April 24, and counsel not making oral arguments may file written arguments before April 27 ;
      offered .... II—8
  remarks by .... I—81, 185, 247, 265, 266, 450, 488, 529, 530, 699.   II—8, 9, 10, 11, 336, 488, 491, 494
  questions by .... I—265, 529, 699
  opinion on the case .... III—245
Hendricks, Thomas A., a senator from Indiana... I—11
  remarks on the competency of the President *pro tempore* to sit as a member of the court...... III—360, 364,
                                                                                                               392, 399, 401
  order by—
    that trial proceed with all convenient despatch ; amendment offered and agreed to .... I—86
    prescribing form of final question : offered .... II—458
  remarks by .... I—86, 186, 231, 565, 633.   II—13, 262, 263, 473, 474, 478, 483, 484, 487, 488, 489
  opinion on the case .... III—85
Hour of meeting, order fixing, at 11 a. m.—[*By Mr. Conness.*]
  offered .... I—631
  adopted, (yeas 29, nays 14) .... I—633
order fixing, at 12 o'clock m. each day, except Sunday—[*By Mr. Grimes.*]
  offered .... II—99
  adopted, (yeas 21, nays 13) .... II—141
Howard, Jacob M., a senator from Michigan .... I—11
  remarks on the competency of the President *pro tempore* to sit as a member of the court ...... III—361, 367,
                                                                                                                  382, 383, 388, 389, 390, 392, 393, 401
  orders by—
    (in Senate,) that the message of the House, relating to the impeachment of Andrew Johnson, be
      referred to a select committe of seven, to consider and report thereon ; agreed to............... I—5
    (in Senate,) that the Senate will take proper action on the message of the House in relation to the
      impeachment of Andrew Johnson ; reported and agreed to... I—6
    (in Senate,) that at 1 o'clock to-morrow afternoon, the Senate will proceed to consider the impeach-
      ment of Andrew Johnson, &c. ; agreed to March 4 .... I—9
    that a summons do issue to Andrew Johnson, returnable on Friday, March 13, at 1 o'clock p. m. ;
      adopted .... I—16
    that no senator shall speak more than once, nor to exceed 15 minutes on one question, during final
      deliberations ; offered and rejected, (yeas 19, nays 30) .... II—218
  remarks by .. I—5, 9, 12, 16, 17, 34, 36, 60, 77, 78, 82, 166, 180, 188, 214, 235, 265, 276, 324, 325, 346, 367, 370, 451, 486,
                497, 514, 530, 566, 606, 612, 673, 680, 683, 716, 738.   II—5, 10, 14, 218, 219, 262, 330, 446, 472, 485, 498
  questions by .... I—276, 530, 566, 680
  opinion on the case .... III—31
Howe, Timothy O., a senator from Wisconsin .... I—11
  remarks on the competency of the President *pro tempore* to sit as a member of the court........... III—380
  remarks by .... I—36, 490, 508, 520, 533, 608, 611, 740.   II—12, 282, 283, 475
  opinion on the case .... III—58
Hudson, William N.   (See *Testimony*.)

I.

Impeachable crimes, definition of... I—88, 123, 147, 476.   II—286.   III—355
Impeachment of Andrew Johnson, President of the United States—
  resolution (in House) providing for the, [*By Mr. Covode, Feb. 21, 1868* ;] referred .... I—1
    reported .... I—1
    adopted, (yeas 126, nays 47).. I—2
  Committee (in House) to communicate to Senate its action directing an—
    ordered .... I—2
    appointed .... I—3
    appear at bar of Senate.. I—5
    report to House .... I—3
  Committee (in House) to prepare articles of—
    ordered .... I—2
    appointed .... I—3
    report of .... I—3, 4, 6

INDEX.   XIII

Impeachment of Andrew Johnson—Continued.
  order (in House) limiting debate, and directing proceedings when articles of, are reported to House—
    adopted, (yeas 106, nays 37) .... I—3
  managers elected and Senate notified .... I—4
    directed to carry articles to Senate .... I—4
    House informed that Senate is ready to receive .... I—4
    House in Committee of the Whole to attend .... I—4
    appear at bar of the Senate with articles .... I—6
    demand that the Senate take process, &c .... I—16
  articles of .... I—6
  rules of procedure on the trial of .... I—6, 13
  answer of respondent .... I—37
  replication .... I—84
  opening arguments .... I—87, 377
  evidence .... I—147, 415
  arguments .... II—14–417
  final vote .... II—486, 487, 496, 497
  opinions III

J.

Johnson, Andrew, President of the United States—
  articles of impeachment .... I—6
  summons issued to .... I—16
  returned .... I—18
  called by proclamation .... I—18
  appearance entered and counsel named .... I—19
  forty days asked to prepare answer .... I—19
  answer to articles .... I—37
  oath of office, April 15, 1865 .... I—147
  suspension of Edwin M. Stanton, Secretary of War, and designation of General Grant Secretary ad
    interim communicated to Senate December 12, 1867 .... I—148
    Senate's non-concurrence in, communicated .... I—155
  removal of Edwin M. Stanton, Secretary of War, and designation of Lorenzo Thomas Secretary ad
    interim, February 21, 1868 .... I—156, 248
    Senate's denial of power to remove and appoint communicated .... I—157, 158
  appointment of Edmund Cooper Assistant Secretary of Treasury .... I—163, 164
  order that Adjutant General Thomas resume his duties .... I—240
  instructions to General Grant not to obey orders from War Department, unless, &c .... I—240
  letter to General Grant in regard to his having vacated the office of Secretary ad interim .... I—241
  telegram to Governor Parsons .... I—272
  message communicating report relating to amendment of the Constitution .... I—278
  reports of speech August 18, 1866, in reply to Hon. Reverdy Johnson .... I—294, 301
    at Cleveland, September 3, 1866 .... I—325, 328, 333
    at St. Louis, September 8, 1866 .... I—340, 348
  notification to Secretary of Treasury, August 14, 1867, of suspension of Mr. Stanton .... I—361
  conversation with General Emory .... I—233, 236
    with General Wallace .... I—253, 256
    with Mr. Wood .... I—372
    with Mr. Blodgett .... I—375
    with Adjutant General Thomas .... I—417, 418, 426, 427, 428, 430, 437, 438, 439, 452, 453
    with Lieutenant General Sherman .... I—461, 481, 483
    with Mr. Cox .... I—597, 605, 609, 613
    with Mr. Merrick .... I—617, 623
    with Mr. Perrin .... I—623, 624
    with Secretary Welles .... I—664, 671, 675
  tender of War Office to Lieutenant General Sherman .... I—461, 483, 485, 517, 518, 521, 528, 529
  nomination of Mr. Ewing Secretary of War, February 22, 1868 .... I—508, 516, 537, 555, 556
  instructions to test Lorenzo Thomas's right to office .... I—605, 609, 620
  acquittal on article XI .... II—486, 487
    II .... II—496
    III .... II—497
Johnson, Reverdy, a senator from Maryland .... I—11
  remarks on the competency of the President pro tempore to sit as a member of the court. III—361, 366, 369,
                                                                                                                                        390, 392, 401
  orders by—
    that trial proceed at the expiration of 10 days, unless for causes shown to the contrary: offered ... I—83
      considered .... I—84
    that Senate commence the trial 2d of April: offered .... I—85
    that two of managers be permitted to file printed arguments, &c.; amendment offered and adopted, II—5
  remarks by ...... I—18, 33, 78, 82, 83, 84, 85, 147, 154, 160, 161, 176, 206, 208, 209, 236, 237, 247, 265, 270, 298, 312,
            325, 362, 365, 368, 370, 372, 387, 452, 486, 487, 495, 507, 515, 517, 518, 519, 520, 521, 522,
            523, 524, 528, 529, 532, 534, 537, 562, 563, 564, 566, 568, 573, 583, 589, 590, 612, 620, 621,
            626, 644, 654, 661, 669, 675, 676 680, 692, 709, 711, 714, 716, 717, 718, 721, 722, 738, 739,
            740, 741. II—5, 6, 13, 118, 166, 189, 216, 262, 281, 282, 283, 306, 389, 469, 475, 479, 483,
            484, 485, 487, 490, 498.
  questions by .... I—236, 265, 507, 517, 680
  opinion on the case .... III—50
Jones, J. W. See Testimony.
Judgment of acquittal entered .... II—498

K.

Karsner, George W. (See Testimony.)
Knapp, George. (See Testimony.)

L.

Lawrence, William, a representative from Ohio—
  brief of authorities upon the law of impeachable crimes, by .... I—123. III—355

Legislative business. (See *Practice*.)
Logan, John A., of Illinois, a manager .... I—4, 17
 argument by—
  on application of counsel for thirty days to prepare for trial .... I—69
  final, on the case .... II—14
 remarks on the Alta Vela letter .... II—268

M.

Managers on the part of the House elected, and Senate notified .... I—4
 directed to carry articles to Senate .... I—4
 House informed that Senate is ready to receive .... I—4
 House in Committee of the Whole to attend .... I—4
 appear at bar of Senate with articles .... I—6
 demand that the Senate take due process, &c .... I—16
McCreery, Thomas C., a senator from Kentucky .... I—11
 motion by .... II—489
McDonald, William J. (See *Testimony*.)
McEwen, Daniel C. (See *Testimony*.)
Meigs, R. J. (See *Testimony*.)
Merrick, Richard T. (See *Testimony*.)
Moore, William G. (See *Testimony*.)
Moorhead, James K. (See *Testimony*.)
Morgan, Edwin D., a senator from New York .... I—11
Morrill, Justin S., a senator from Vermont .... I—11
 order by—
  that Senate meet on Monday next (May 11) at 11 a. m., for deliberation, and on Tuesday at 12 m. proceed to vote without debate on the several articles—each senator to be permitted to file his written opinion within two days after the vote: offered .... II—476
  agreed to .... II—478
 remarks by .... I—390, II—249, 476, 478
 opinion on the case .... III—136
Morrill, Lot M., a senator from Maine .... I—11
 remarks on the competency of the President *pro tempore* to sit as a member of the court .... III—364, 394
 order by—
  that Senate proceed on Monday next to take the yeas and nays on the articles without debate; any senator to have permission to file a written opinion; offered .... II—476
 remarks by .... I—185, 442, II—470, 476, 483, 494, 495
 opinion on the case .... III—126
Morton, Oliver P., a senator from Indiana .... I—11
 remarks on the competency of the President *pro tempore* to sit as a member of the court .... III—367, 387
 remarks by .... I—24, 86, 674, II—219, 485

N.

Nelson, Thomas A. R., of Tennessee, counsel .... I—19
 argument by—
  on motion to fix a day for trial to proceed .... I—28
  on motion to fix the number and order of speakers on final argument .... I—534, II—9
  final, on the case .... II—118, 141
 remarks on the Alta Vela letter .... II—144, 265, 266, 267, 268, 280, 281, 282, 283, 284, 307
Norton, Daniel S., a senator from Minnesota .... I—11
Nye, James W., a senator from Nevada .... I—11

O.

Oath administered to Chief Justice .... I—11
 to senators .... I—11, 12, 17, 34
Question. Whether it is competent for the President *pro tempore* of the Senate to take the, and become thereby a part of the court—(*By Mr. Hendricks*)—discussed .... III—360
 withdrawn .... III—400
Officers, territorial and executive, list of, with their tenures .... I—548
Opinion; order, that each senator shall be permitted to file, within two days after the vote shall have been taken, to be printed with the proceedings [*By Mr. Morrill of Vermont*] .... II—476
 agreed to .... II—478
 filed by—
  Mr. Buckalew .... III—218
  Mr. Cattell .... III—178
  Mr. Davis .... III—156
  Mr. Doolittle .... III—244
  Mr. Edmunds .... III—82
  Mr. Ferry .... III—121
  Mr. Fessenden .... III—16
  Mr. Fowler .... III—193
  Mr. Frelinghuysen .... III—208
  Mr. Grimes .... III—328
  Mr. Harlan .... III—243
  Mr. Henderson .... III—296
  Mr. Hendricks .... III—95
  Mr. Howard .... III—31
  Mr. Howe .... III—58
  Mr. Johnson .... III—50
  Mr. Morrill, of Maine .... III—126
  Mr. Morrill, of Vermont .... III—136
  Mr. Patterson, of New Hampshire .... III—309
  Mr. Pomeroy .... III—340
  Mr. Sherman .... III—3
  Mr. Stewart .... III—152

INDEX.   XV

Opinion, filed by—
  Mr. Sumner..III—247
  Mr. Tipton...III—188
  Mr. Trumbull..III—319
  Mr. Van Winkle..III—147
  Mr. Vickers..III—116
  Mr. Williams..III—247
  Mr. Wilson...III—214
  Mr. Yates...III—102

P.

Patterson, James W., a senator from New Hampshire...I—17
  opinion on the case..III—309
Patterson, David T., a senator from Tennessee..I—11
  remarks by...I—160
Perrin, Edwin O. (See *Testimony*.)
Pomeroy, Samuel C., a senator from Kansas...I—11
  remarks on the competency of the President *pro tempore* to sit as a member of the court......III—379, 390,
   394, 401
  order by—
    (In Senate,) that the notice to Chief Justice to meet the Senate in the trial and request his attendance be delivered by a committee of three, &c.; agreed to..I—10
  remarks by...I—10, 451. II—4, 358, 490
  opinion on the case..III—340
Practice. (See *Rules*.)
  right of counsel making motion to open and close argument thereon...................................I—77
  the limitation of argument on interlocutory questions to one hour, by rule XX, has reference to the whole number of persons to speak on each side, and not to each person severally..............I—207, 208
  it is not in order to call up business transacted in legislative session...I—301
  objections to putting question to witness by a member of the court must come from the court itself...I—507, 519
  but after question is asked, it is competent for managers to state objections to its being answered....I—519
  it is competent for Senate to recall any witness...I—518, 523
  if managers desire to cross-examine they must cross-examine before dismissing witness............I—534
  an application for an order of Senate to furnish a statement from its records can only be addressed to Senate in legislative session...I—529
  the general rules of the Senate in its legislative session govern proceedings of the court, so far as applicable..I—451, 530
President. (See *Johnson, Andrew*.)
President *pro tempore* of the Senate—
  question, Whether it is competent for the, to take the oath and become thereby a part of the court—
    [By Mr. *Hendricks*]..III—360
  discussed by—
    Mr. Anthony...III—385
    Mr. Bayard..III—372
    Mr. Buckalew..III—383, 385
    Mr. Conness...III—367, 395
    Mr. Davis...III—363, 366
    Mr. Dixon......................................III—388, 389, 390, 391, 392, 393, 394, 395, 396
    Mr. Drake..III—386, 389, 390, 393
    Mr. Ferry...III—394
    Mr. Fessenden...III—366, 367, 394, 401
    Mr. Frelinghuysen..III—380, 385
    Mr. Grimes..III—388, 394, 401
    Mr. Hendricks...III—360, 364, 392, 399, 401
    Mr. Howard...........................III—361, 367, 382, 383, 388, 389, 390, 392, 393, 401
    Mr. Howe..III—380
    Mr. Johnson...III—361, 366, 369, 390, 392, 401
    Mr. Morrill, of Maine...III—364, 394
    Mr. Morton...III—367, 387
    Mr. Pomeroy..III—379, 390, 394, 401
    Mr. Sherman..III—360, 371, 391, 392, 401
    Mr. Stewart..III—395
    Mr. Sumner..III—375
    Mr. Thayer..III—381
    Mr. Williams..III—365, 366
  withdrawn..III—400

Q.

Question, final, order that when doors shall be closed for deliberation upon, the official reporters shall take down debates, to be reported in proceedings—[By Mr. *Edmunds*.]
  offered..II—141
  read..II—188, 218, 471
  tabled, (yeas 28, nays 20)..II—474
  order, that Senate proceed to vote on the several articles at twelve o'clock on day after the close of arguments—[By Mr. *Sumner*.]
    offered...II—189
    called up..II—474, 476
  order, that the Senate meet on Monday next (May 11) at 11 a. m., for deliberation on, and on Tuesday, at 12 m., proceed to vote without debate on the several articles, &c.—[By Mr. *Morrill, of Vermont*.]
    offered...II—476
    agreed to..II—478
  orders offered prescribing form of, by—
    Mr. Buckalew..II—478
    Mr. Conkling..II—478

Question, final—Continued.
  orders offered prescribing form of, by—
    Mr. Conness..II—478
    Mr. Hendricks...II—479
    Mr. Sumner...II—189, 219, 474
  views of Chief Justice on form of putting..II—480
  order that the views of Chief Justice be entered on the journal—[*By Mr. Buckalew.*]
    offered and agreed to..II—480
  order that, he put as proposed by presiding officer, and each senator rise and answer "Guilty" or "Not guilty" only—[*By Mr. Sumner.*]
    offered and agreed to..II—481
  order, that the standing order of the Senate that it will proceed to vote on the articles at 12 o'clock m. to-morrow be rescinded. [*By Mr. Edmunds.*]
    offered May 11, 1868...II—482
    agreed to...II—483
  order, that the Senate now proceed to vote upon the articles, according to the rules of the Senate—[*By Mr. Edmunds.*]
    offered May 16..II—485
    agreed to...II—486
  order that, shall be taken on eleventh article first, and thereafter on the other ten successively as they stand—[*By Mr. Williams.*]
    agreed to, (yeas 34, nays 19)..II—484, 485
  taken on—
    Article XI: That he attempted to prevent the execution of the tenure-of-office act by unlawfully devising means to prevent Mr. Stanton from resuming the functions of his office, and to prevent the execution of the clause in the appropriation act of 1867 requiring that all orders should pass through the General of the army, and the reconstruction acts of March 5, 1867; (yeas 35, nays 19)..II—486, 487
  order that, be now taken on remaining articles—[*By Mr. Conkling.*]
    offered and rejected, (yeas 26, nays 22)...II—492
    that the several orders heretofore adopted as to order of voting on, be rescinded—[*By Mr. Williams.*]
    offered..II—490, 491
    agreed to...II—495
  taken on—
    Article II: That he issued a letter of authority to Lorenzo Thomas to act as Secretary of War *ad interim*, with intent to violate the Constitution and the tenure-of-office act; (yeas 35, nays 19)...II—496
  taken on—
    Article III: That he appointed Lorenzo Thomas to be Secretary of War *ad interim*, with intent to violate the Constitution, (yeas 35, nays 19.)...II—497
Questions. (See *Practice.*)

R.

Ramsey, Alexander, a senator from Minnesota...I—11
  remarks by..I—276
Randall, Alexander W. (See *Testimony.*)
Replication, read and filed...I—84
Ross, Edmund G., a senator from Kansas..I—11
  motion by..II—495
Rule VII, order amending, in respect to submitting questions of evidence, &c., to Senate—[*By Mr. Henderson.*]
  offered, I—185; agreed to, (yeas 31, nays 19)...I—186
VII, order amending and requiring votes upon incidental questions to be without division, unless demanded, &c.—[*By Mr. Drake.*]
  offered, I—230; agreed to..I—277
XX, construction of...I—207, 208
XXI, motion to amend, so as to allow such of managers or counsel as desire to be heard, to speak on final argument—[*By Manager Bingham*]..I—450
XXI, motion to remove limit fixed by, as to number who may participate in final argument—[*By Mr. Frelinghuysen.*]
  offered...I—451
  discussed by—
    Manager Williams..I—491
    Manager Stevens...I—494
    Manager Boutwell..I—495
    Mr. Stanbery..I—495
    Manager Butler..I—496
    Mr. Evarts..I—497
  tabled, (yeas 38, nays 10)...I—498
XXIII, order amending, to subject it to operation of Rule VII—[*By Mr. Conkling.*]
  offered, and agreed to...I—18
amendment, that the fifteen minutes allowed by, shall be for the whole deliberation on final question, and not to final question on each article—[*By Mr. Drake.*]
  offered, II—471; adopted..II—478
Rules. (See *Practice.*)
  order (in House) limiting debate and directing proceedings when articles are reported to House—[*By Mr. Washburne, of Illinois:*] adopted; (yeas 106, nays 37)...I—3
  of procedure and practice...I—6, 13
  of Senate sitting in legislative session, adopted for guidance of court, as far as applicable......I—451, 532
Rulings. (See *Evidence; Practice.*)

S.

Saulsbury, Willard, a senator from Delaware...I—12
Senators, oath administered to..I—11, 12, 17, 34
Seward, Frederick W. (See *Testimony.*)
Sheridan, James B. (See *Testimony.*)
Sherman, John, a senator from Ohio..I—11
  remarks on the competency of the President *pro tempore* to sit as a member of the court.....III—360, 371, 391, 392, 401

Sherman, John—Continued.
  orders by—
    that trial proceed on 6th of April; offered and discussed .... I—25
    that under the rules all questions other than of order should be submitted to Senate; offered ...... I—185
    that additional time allowed by amendment to Rule XXI shall not exceed three hours; offered .... I—495
    that managers and counsel have leave to file written or printed arguments before oral argument
      commences; offered .... I—741
    that managers be permitted to file printed or written arguments; amendment offered .... II—6
  remarks by .... I—25, 82, 83, 154, 155, 181, 185, 264, 363, 449, 451, 494, 496, 537, 565, 568, 589, 608, 611, 673, 676,
                        709, 715, 716, 741. II—5, 6, 83, 84, 188, 280, 281, 359, 403, 469, 471, 473, 475, 479, 480, 487
  questions by .... I—181, 264, 508
  opinion on the case .... III—3
Sherman, William T. (See *Testimony*.)
Smith, Francis H. (See *Testimony*.)
Sprague, William, a senator from Rhode Island .... I—11
  remarks by .... I—477. II—8, 493
Stanbery, Henry, of Kentucky, counsel .... I—19
  motions by—
    for an allowance of forty days to prepare answer .... I—19
      denied .... I—24
    for an allowance of thirty days to prepare for trial .... I—69
      denied, (yeas 12, nays 41) .... I—82
  argument by—
    on application for forty days to prepare answer .... I—21
    for thirty days to prepare for trial .... I—75
  on admissibility—
    of Adjt. Genl. Thomas's, declarations to Mr. Burleigh, February 21, 1868 ... I—188, 192, 193, 195, 206, 207
    of President's letter to General Grant, unaccompanied with enclosures .... I—244, 245
    of appointment of Edmund Cooper to be Assistant Secretary of Treasury .... I—260, 261, 262, 264
    of telegrams relating to the reconstruction of Alabama .... I—270, 275
    of President's declarations to Adjutant General Thomas, February 21 .... I—421
    of conversations between President and Gen'l Sherman, January 12 ...I—462, 463, 465, 468, 469, 471, 472
    of question respecting department of the Atlantic .... I—481, 482
    of tender of War office to General Sherman .... I—482
    of President's purpose to get the question before the courts .... I—485
    of question, Whether General Sherman formed and gave the President an opinion, &c. ...I—499, 501, 504
    of affidavit and warrant of arrest of Lorenzo Thomas .... I—512, 513, 514
    on motion to remove limit to number of speakers on final argument .... I—495
    on right of counsel to renew examination of a witness recalled by court .... I—524
    final, on the case .... II—359, 360
Stanton, Edwin M., Secretary of War—
  nomination of .... I—148
  confirmation of .... I—148
  commission of .... I—157
  suspension of, communicated to Senate .... I—148
  Senate's non-concurrence in .... I—155
  removal of, order for .... I—156, 248
  communicated to Senate .... I—156
  Senate resolution on .... I—157
  interviews of, with Adjutant General Thomas, demanding possession .... I—164, 174, 220, 223, 232
  letter of, denying General Thomas's authority .... I—420
  affidavit of, for arrest of General Thomas .... I—515
Stark, Everett D. (See *Testimony*.)
Stewart, William M., a senator from Nevada .... I—11
  remarks on the competency of the President *pro tempore* to sit as a member of the court .... III—395
  orders by—
    that Manager Logan have leave to file written argument:
      offered .... I—741
      amended .... I—741
      read .... II—3
  remarks by .... I—489, 491, 532, 561, 632, 680, 717, 740, 741. II—11
  opinion on the case .... III—152
Stevens, Thaddeus, of Pennsylvania, a manager .... I—4, 17
  remarks on order relating to final argument .... I—494. II—7
  argument, final, on the case .... II—219
Summons ordered .... I—16
  return of, read and verified .... I—18
Sumner, Charles, a senator from Massachusetts .... I—11
  remarks on the competency of the President *pro tempore* to sit as a member of the court .... III—373
  orders by—
    that Senate proceed with trial from day to day unless otherwise ordered:
      offered .... I—85
      withdrawn .... I—86
    that Chief Justice presiding has no authority to vote on any question during the trial, &c.:
      offered and rejected, (yeas 22, nays 26,) .... I—185
    that where the Senate were equally divided, and Chief Justice gave a casting vote, such vote was
      without authority under the Constitution:
      offered and rejected, (yeas 21, nays 27,) .... I—187
    that trial proceed without delay on account of removal of limit provided by Rule XXI:
      amendment offered and accepted .... I—491
    that on final argument the several managers who speak shall close:
      offered .... I—497
    that under rule limiting argument to two on a side, such others as choose may file arguments at any
      time before the argument of the closing manager:
      laid over .... I—532
      amended .... I—534
      indefinitely postponed, (yeas 34, nays 15,) .... I—536

2 IP

XVIII   INDEX.

Sumner, Charles, orders by—Continued.
    that all evidence offered not trivial or obviously irrelevant be received without objection, to be
        open to question at the bar to determine its value, and to be sifted and weighed in the final
        judgment:
        offered..I—529
        tabled, (yeas 33, nays 11)...I—590
    that Senate sit from 10 a. m. to 6 p. m. :
        offered..I—631
        rejected, (yeas 13, nays 30)..I—633
    that Senate proceed to vote on the several articles of impeachment at twelve o'clock on the day
        after close of arguments:
        offered...II—189
        called up..II—474, 476
    that after removal, which follows conviction, any further judgment shall be determined by a majority
        of members present :
        offered and laid over..II—249
    that Mr. Nelson, one of counsel, having used disorderly words, has deserved the disapprobation of
        the Senate :"
        offered..II—280
        tabled, (yeas 35, nays 10)..II—307
    that Senate will sit from 10 a. m. to 6 p. m. :
        offered and tabled, (yeas 32, nays 17)...II—308
    denying permission to each senator to file written opinion, &c :
        offered and rejected, (yeas 6, nays 42)..II—477
    that the question be put as proposed by presiding officer, and each senator shall rise in his place
        and answer "Guilty" or "Not guilty" only :
        offered and agreed to..II—481
  rules by—
    XXIII. In taking the votes of Senate on the articles, presiding officer shall call each senator by
        name, and upon each article propose the question of "Guilty or not guilty ?" whereupon each
        senator shall rise in his place and answer:
        proposed April 25...II—189
        laid over...II—219
        called up...II—478
    XXIV. on a conviction by Senate it shall be the duty of presiding officer forthwith to pronounce the
        removal from office of the convicted person ; any further judgment shall be on the order of
        Senate :
        proposed April 25...II—189
        laid over...II—219
        called up...II—481
  remarks by....I—24, 25, 85, 86, 154, 155, 185, 186, 187, 265, 298, 367, 370, 371, 489, 491, 496, 497, 532, 534, 536, 561,
                  589, 631, 632, 633, 673. II—99, 141, 188, 189, 203, 218, 219, 249, 250, 281,
                                307, 308, 471, 475, 477, 478, 479, 481, 490, 493
  opinion on the case..III—247
  on the question, Can the Chief Justice, presiding in the Senate, rule or vote.....................III—231

T.

Testimony for the prosecution—
  William J. McDonald: service of Senate resolutions at office of President..........................I—158
  J. W. Jones: service of Senate resolution on Adjutant General Thomas..............................I—159
  C. E. Creecy: form of commission before and after tenure-of-office act, I—160, 161, 162; commission of
    Edmund Cooper, as Assistant Secretary of Treasury, I—163; date of change in form of commis-
    sion, I—164; President's notification to Secretary of Treasury of Secretary Stanton's suspen-
    sion, I—363, 364; notification of Secretary of Treasury to heads of bureaus, I—366.
  Burt Van Horn: Adjutant General Thomas's demand for possession of War Department........I—164-170
  James K. Moorhead: Adjutant General Thomas's demand for possession of War Department....I—170-174
  Walter A. Burleigh: Adjutant General Thomas's account of interview with Secretary Stanton, I—
    174; his intentions, I—188; his declarations to clerks, I—211, 214, 215, 219, 220; means by which he
    intended to obtain possession, I—175, 188, 210, 211, 218, 219.
  Samuel Wilkeson: Adjutant General Thomas's account of interview with Secretary Stanton ....I—220
  George W. Karsner: conversations with Adjutant General Thomas, I—223-230; his intentions, I—224,
    227; interview with Secretary Stanton, I—231.
  Thomas W. Ferry: occurrences at War Department, February 22..................................I—232
  William H. Emory: conversations with President in reference to troops, I—233-236; Orders No. 15
    and 17, I—235, 238.
  George W. Wallace: conversation with President in regard to garrison at Washington and movement
    of troops..I—253-256
  William E. Chandler: process of drawing money from Treasury Department, I—256, 265, 266; course
    of issuing commission to an officer confirmed by Senate, I—257; authority of Assistant Secretary
    of Treasury to sign warrants, I—266; the practice, I—267.
  Charles A. Tinker: telegrams between Lewis E. Parsons and President relating to reconstruction in
    Alabama, I—268-272; President's speech, August 18, 1866, as telegraphed, I—280, 281, 289, 290.
  James B. Sheridan: President's speech, August 18, 1866, in reply to Hon. Reverdy Johnson, I—281-
    283; manner of reporting it, I—282, 283, 291; corrections by President's secretary, I—281, 290, 291.
  James O. Clephane: President's speech, August 18, 1866, in reply to Hon. Reverdy Johnson, I—283,
    284; revision by President's secretary, I—284, 294; verbatim report rewritten for Chronicle, I—284,
    285, 286.
  Francis H. Smith: President's speech, August 18, 1866, I—292, 293; revision by President's secretary,
    I—292.
  William G. Moore: corrections of report of President's speech, August 18, 1866...............I—294, 297
  William N. Hudson: President's speech at Cleveland, September 3, 1866, reported for Cleveland
    Leader, I—301-310; cries of the crowd, I—310-315.
  Daniel C. McEwen: President's speech at Cleveland, September 3, 1866........................I—316-318
  Everett D. Stark: President's speech at Cleveland, September 3, 1866, reported for Cleveland
    Herald..I—318-321
  L. L. Walbridge: President's speech at St. Louis, September 8, 1866..........................I—337-340
  Joseph A. Dear: President's speech at St. Louis..I—345-348

INDEX.   XIX

Testimony for the prosecution—Continued.
  Robert S. Chew; change in form of commissions after passage of civil-tenure act, I—351, 357; change
    in place for printing forms, I—352; list of appointments of heads of departments, I—353, 360, 361;
    appointments of acting Secretaries of State, I—359; from whom, I—360, 361.
  H. Wood; interview with President, September, 1866, I—372; President and Congress, I—373; pat-
    ronage, I—373; statement to Mr. Koppel, I—373, 374, 375.
  Foster Blodgett; suspension from office of postmaster at Augusta, Georgia............................I—375
Testimony for the defence—
  Lorenzo Thomas; service, I—415, 432; restoration to duty as Adjutant General, I—416, 417, 433;
    appointment as Secretary of War *ad interim*, I—418, 433, 434, 435, 436; letter of Mr. Stanton, I—420;
    arrest, I—427, 441; interviews with Secretary Stanton, I—417, 418, 419, 428, 429, 437, 460; with Pres-
    ident, I—417, 418, 426, 427, 428, 430, 437, 438, 439, 452, 453; with Mr. Burleigh, I—431, 439, 440, 442, 452;
    with Mr. Karsner, I—431, 432, 448, 449, 453; with Mr. Wilkeson, I—439; with R. B. Johnson, I—
    454, 455; use of force, I—420, 429, 430, 431, 440, 441, 442, 443, 444; testimony before House commit-
    tee, I—433, 442, 443, 457, 458, 459; would obey President's orders, I—434, 435, 437, 443; address to
    clerks, I—450; corrections of testimony, I—452.
  William T. Sherman; duties in Washington, December, 1867, I—460, 461; interviews with President,
    I—461, 481, 483; tender of appointment as Secretary of War *ad interim*, I—461, 483, 485, 517; Pres-
    ident's declarations of purpose in making tender, I—485, 517, 518, 521, 528, 529; use of force, I—529,
    530.
  R. J. Meigs; warrant of arrest of Lorenzo Thomas, I—508, 516; docket of entries, I—517, 531.
  D. W. C. Clarke; nomination of Thomas Ewing, sen., to be Secretary of War, February 22, 1868,
    I—537; when received, I—537, 55.).
  William G. Moore; nomination of Mr. Ewing to be Secretary of War, I—556; when received, I—556;
    and delivered, I—557.
  Walter S. Cox; counsel for Adjutant General Thomas, I—595, 596; employed by President, I—597,
    613; President's instructions, I—605, 609; proceedings and their purpose, I—606-609, 612-617; appli-
    cation for *habeas corpus*, I—606-609; preparation of *quo warranto*, I—612; making a test case, I—
    605, 611, 612; J. H. Bradley, I—614; discharge of Thomas, I—609, 617.
  Richard T. Merrick; employment in case of General Thomas, I—617-623; report to President, I—618;
    President's instructions, February 22, in respect to obtaining *habeas corpus*, I—620; acts in refer-
    ence thereto, I—620, 621; discharge of Thomas, I—622.
  Edwin O. Perrin; interview with President, February 21 ....I—623, 624
  Wm. W. Armstrong; President's speech at Cleveland..I—634-637
  Barton Able; President's speech at St. Louis...I—637-640
  George Knapp; President's speech at St. Louis...I—640-643
  Henry F. Zider; President's speech at St. Louis, I—643; corrections, I—643, 644; differences in re-
    ports, I—646-653.
  Frederick W. Seward; practice in appointments of vice-consuls ....I—660, 661
  Gideon Welles; date of commission, I—663, 701; movements of troops, February 21, 1868, I—663,
    702, 703; conversation with President, I—664, 674, 675; removal of Mr. Stanton, I—666, 667, 674;
    appointment of Mr. Ewing, February 22, I—664, 702; consideration of civil-tenure act in cabinet,
    I—675, 693, 697, 700.
  Edgar T. Welles; form of navy agent's commission, I—704; movement of troops, I—705, 706.
  Alexander W. Randall; date of commission, I—707; suspension of Foster Blodgett, I—707-715; law
    by which he was suspended, I—711; indictment, I—712, 713, 714, 719; explanation, I—726, 727.
Thayer, John M., a senator from Nebraska..I—11
  remarks on the competency of the President *pro tempore* to sit as a member of the court............III—381
  remarks by..I—184, 208, 489, 490, 536, 606. II—8, 472, 493
Thomas, Lorenzo—
  rank and service of..I—415, 432
  restoration of, to duty as Adjutant General, February ....I—210, 256, 416, 417, 433
  appointment of, Secretary of War *ad interim*..I—156, 248, 418, 433, 434, 435, 436
  Senate resolution on, communicated to..I—157, 158
  letter of, accepting ....I—369
  demand of, for possession............I—164, 165, 166, 167, 168, 169, 170, 171, 172, 173, 174, 220, 221, 222, 223, 232
  conversations of—
    with President..I—417, 418, 426, 427, 428, 430, 437, 438, 439, 452, 453
    with Secretary Stanton...I—417, 418, 419, 428, 429, 437, 460
    with Mr. Burleigh..I—174, 220, 431, 439, 440, 442, 452
    with Mr. Wilkeson..I—223, 439
    with Mr. Karsner..I—223, 431, 432, 448, 449, 453
    with Mr. R. B. Johnson ....I—454, 455
  declarations of, to clerks of the War Office..I—211, 214, 215, 219, 220, 450
  intentions of, as to obtaining possession.................................I—175, 188, 210, 211, 218, 219, 431, 440, 441, 442, 443, 444
  arrest of, and proceedings thereon...I—427, 441, 515
Tickets, order, (in Senate,) that during the trial, no persons besides those who have the privilege of the
  floor, &c., shall be admitted except upon, issued by the Sergeant-at-arms.—[*By Mr. Anthony.*]
  agreed to..I—10
Tinker, Charles A. (See *Testimony*.)
Tipton, Thomas W., a senator from Nebraska...I—11
  remarks by...I—297. II—187, 289, 483
  opinion on the case ....III—189
Trial, motion to fix a day for, to proceed—
  discussed by—
    Manager Butler..I—25
    Mr. Nelson..I—28
    Manager Bingham..I—32, 33
  order that, unless otherwise ordered, the, proceed immediately after replication filed—[*By Mr. Conkling.*]
    offered...I—31
    agreed to, (yeas 40, nays 10) ....I—33
  application of counsel for thirty days to prepare for ....I—69
    discussed by—
      Mr. Evarts...I—68, 71
      Manager Bingham..I—69, 77, 78
      Manager Logan..I—69
      Manager Wilson...I—73
      Mr. Stanbery...I—75

XX   INDEX.

Trial, motion to fix a day for, to proceed—Continued.
  discussed by—
    Manager Boutwell..I—78
    Manager Butler..I—81
  denied, (yeas 12, nays 41)..I—82
  orders offered to fix time for, to proceed by—
    Mr. Edmunds...I—24
    Manager Bingham...I—25
    Mr. Sherman...I—25
    Mr. Conkling..I—31, 32, 85
    Mr. Johnson...I—83, 84, 85
    Mr. Hendricks.
    Mr. Sumner..I—85
  application of counsel for reasonable time, after replication filed, to prepare for..............I—83
  order fixing the 30th of March for commencement of—[*By Mr. Conkling.*]
    offered and agreed to, (yeas 28, nays 24)..I—83
Trumbull, Lyman, a senator from Illinois...I—11
  orders by—
    that respondent file answer on or before 23d March; agreed to............................I—35
    that as many of managers as desire be permitted to file arguments or address Senate orally; but
      the conclusion of oral argument shall be by one manager, as provided by rule XXI:
      offered..II—11
    adopted, (yeas 28, nays 22)..II—14
  remarks by..............................I—81, 160, 187, 188, 208, 209, 297, 451, 489, 528, 547, 631, 632, 673
                                          II—7, 11, 12, 281, 308, 469, 470, 473, 475, 476, 488, 490, 492, 493, 495
  opinion on the case..III—319

                                         V.

Van Horn, Burt. (See *Testimony*.)
Van Winkle, P. G., a senator from West Virginia.......................................I—11
  opinion on the case..III—147
Vickers, George, a senator from Maryland..I—17
  orders by—
    that any two of managers, except those who open and close, and who have not addressed Senate,
      may file written arguments before adjournment or make oral addresses after the opening by one
      of managers and first reply of counsel, and that other two of counsel who have not spoken may
      reply, but alternating with said two managers, leaving closing argument for President and mana-
      gers' final reply under original rule; offered, II—3; disagreed to, (yeas 20, nays 26,) II—4.
    that one of managers may file printed argument before adjournment, and that after oral opening by
      a manager and reply by one of counsel another counsel may file written or make oral address, to
      be followed by closing speech of one of counsel and final reply of a manager: offered...........II—4
  remarks by..II—3, 4
  opinion on the case...III—116
Votes. (See *Chief Justice*; *Evidence*; *Question*; *Rules*.)

                                         W.

Wade, Benjamin F., a senator from Ohio..I—12
  (See *President pro tempore*.)
Walbridge, L. L. (See *Testimony*.)
Wallace, George W. (See *Testimony*.)
Welles, Edgar T. (See *Testimony*.)
Welles, Gideon. (See *Testimony*.)
Wilkeson, Samuel. (See *Testimony*.)
Willey, Waitman T., a senator from West Virginia..I—12
Williams, George H., a senator from Oregon..I—12
  remarks on the competency of the President *pro tempore* to sit as a member of the court.......III—365, 366
  orders by—
    that consideration of respondent's application for time be postponed until managers have sub-
      mitted their evidence: offered...I—85
    not agreed to, (yeas 9, nays 42)...I—86
    that no senator shall speak more than once, nor to exceed fifteen minutes during deliberations on
      final questions; offered...II—218
    postponed...II—219
    tabled, (yeas 22, nays 23)..II—474
    that the question shall be taken on the eleventh article first, and thereafter on the other ten suc-
      cessively as they stand; agreed to, (yeas 34, nays 19)............................II—484, 485
    that the several orders heretofore adopted as to the order of voting upon the articles be
      rescinded: offered...II—490
    agreed to...II—495
  remarks by.........I—85, 86, 187, 267, 497, 522, 524, 528, 634, 692, 706. II—218, 472, 473, 484, 487, 490, 492, 495, 496, 4,7
  questions by..I—522, 692, 706
  opinion on the case...III—347
Williams, Thomas, of Pennsylvania, a manager..I—4, 17
  argument, final, on the case...II—230, 249
  remarks on motion relating to the number of speakers on final argument..............I—491. II—6
Wilson, James F., of Iowa, a manager...I—4, 17
  argument by—
    on application of counsel for forty days to prepare answer.........................I—20
    for thirty days to prepare for trial...I—73
  on admissibility—
    of President's letter to General Grant, unaccompanied with enclosures.............I—244, 246
    of President's conversation with General Sherman..................................I—478, 479
    of employment of counsel by President to get up test case.........................I—602
    of President's declarations to Mr. Perrin...I—626
    of advice to President by cabinet touching constitutionality of tenure-of-office act.........I—681

INDEX. XXI

Wilson, Henry, a senator from Massachusetts..I—12
   remarks by..I—25, 31, 32, 86, 181, 184, 740. II—6, 141, 434, 473
   opinion on the case..III—214
Witness. (See *Practice*.)
   question, Whether counsel can renew examination of a, recalled by court—[*By Mr. Williams*]......I—522
   discussed by—
     Mr. Evarts..I—522, 524, 526
     Manager Butler..I—523
     Manager Bingham..I—524, 525, 527
     Mr. Stanbery...I—524
     withdrawn..I—528
Witnesses for the prosecution. (For analysis of testimony see *Testimony*.)
   Blodgett, Foster, suspension from office..I—375
   Burleigh, Walter A., conversations with Thomas.......................................I—174, 188
   Chandler, William E., drawing money from treasury..I—256
   Chew, Robert S., form of commissions...I—351, 357
   Clephane, James O., President's speech, August 18, 1866............................I—283, 294
   Creecy, Charles E., form of commission..I—160, 363
   Dear, Joseph A., President's St. Louis speech..I—345
   Emory, William H., conversations with President; troops.................................I—233
   Ferry, Thomas W., demand of War Office...I—152
   Hudson, William N., President's Cleveland speech...I—304
   Jones, J. W., service of Senate resolution...I—159
   Karsner, George W., conversations with Thomas.....................................I—223, 231
   McDonald, William J., service of Senate resolutions.......................................I—158
   McEwen, Daniel C., President's Cleveland speech...I—316
   Moore, William G., corrections President's speech, August 18, 1866........................I—294
   Moorhead, James K., demand of War Office..I—170
   Sheridan, James B., President's speech, August 18, 1866............................I—281, 290
   Smith, Francis H., President's speech, August 18, 1866..................................I—292
   Stark, Everett D., President's Cleveland speech...I—318
   Tinker, Charles A., telegrams..I—268, 280, 289
   Van Horn, Burt, demand of War Office..I—164
   Walbridge, L. L., President's St. Louis speech...I—337
   Wallace, George W., conversations with President; troops.................................I—253
   Wilkeson, Samuel, conversations with Thomas..I—220
   Wood, H., interview with President...I—372
Witnesses for the defence—
   Able, Barton, President's St. Louis speech...I—637
   Armstrong, William W., President's Cleveland speech....................................I—634
   Clarke, D. W. C., nomination of Mr. Ewing..I—537, 555
   Cox, Walter S., test case...I—595
   Knapp, George, President's St. Louis speech..I—610
   Meigs, R. J., arrest of Thomas..I—508, 534
   Merrick, Richard T., case of Thomas; *habeas corpus*......................................I—617
   Moore, William G., nomination of Mr. Ewing...I—556
   Perrin, Edwin O., conversations with President...I—623
   Randall, Alexander W., Foster Blodgett's case.......................................I—707, 719
   Seward, Frederick W., practice in appointments..I—660
   Sherman, William T., tender of War Office...I—460, 498, 517
   Thomas, Lorenzo, appointment; acts; conversations..................................I—415, 452
   Welles, Edgar T., form of commission; troops..I—704
   Welles, Gideon, troops; cabinet counsels..I—663
   Zider, Henry F., President's St. Louis speech..I—643

Y.

Yates, Richard, senator from Illinois..I—12
   remarks by..I—610, 718, 739. II—3, 12, 13, 140, 266, 479
   order by—
     that four of managers and counsel be permitted to make printed, written, or oral arguments, the
       manager to have opening and closing, subject to Rule XXI; offered.......................II—12
       disagreed to, (yeas, 18, nays 31)...II—13
   opinion on the case..III—102
Yeas and nays on—
   adjournment...I—276, 298, 390, 489, 490
   adjournment over...I—336, 371. II—471, 488, 489, 494, 495
   admissibility of Adjutant General Thomas's declarations to Walter A. Burleigh, (yeas 39, nays 11)..I—209
     to clerks of War Department, (yeas 28, nays 22)..I—214
     of President's letter to General Grant, without enclosures, (yeas 29, nays 20)...............I—247
     of testimony relating to appointment of Edmund Cooper, (yeas 22, nays 27)................I—268
     of telegrams between President and Lewis E. Parsons, (yeas 27, nays 17)..................I—276
     of Leader's report of President's speech at Cleveland, (yeas 35, nays 11)...................I—325
     of President's declarations to Adjutant General Thomas, February 21, (yeas 42, nays 10).....I—426
     of President's conversation with General Sherman, (yeas 23, nays 28).....................I—481
       in regard to tender of War Office, (yeas 23, nays 29).................................I—484
     of President's declarations to General Sherman—
       of purpose to get case before the courts, (yeas 7, nays 44)............................I—487
       of purpose in tendering him the War Office, (yeas 25, nays 27)........................I—488
     of Whether General Sherman gave President an opinion as to advisability of a change in the War
       Office, (yeas 15, nays 35)...I—507
     of advice by General Sherman to President to appoint, &c., (yeas 18, nays 32)..............I—508
     of affidavit and warrant of arrest of Lorenzo Thomas, (yeas 34, nays 17)...................I—515
     of Whether President stated to General Sherman his purpose in tendering him the office of Secre-
       tary of War *ad interim*, (yeas 26, nays 26)...I—518
     of President's declaration of purpose to General Sherman in tendering him the office of Secretary
       of War *ad interim*, (yeas 26, nays 25)..I—521
     of extracts from records of Navy Department, (yeas 36, nays 15)..........................I—503

XXII   INDEX.

Yeas and nays on admissibility—
    of employment of counsel by President to get up test case, (yeas 29, nays 21)...................I—605
    of acts by counsel toward getting out *habeas corpus* in the case of Thomas, (yeas 27, nays 23).....I—609
    of acts done subsequently to test Mr. Stanton's right, &c., (yeas 27, nays 23)..................I—612
    of President's declarations to Mr. Perrin, February 21, (yeas 9, nays 37)......................I—628
        to Secretary Welles, February 21, (yeas 26, nays 23)...I—674
    of advice to President by cabinet as to constitutionality of tenure-of-office act, (yeas 20, nays 29)..I—683
    of advice as to construction of tenure-of-office act, (yeas 22, nays 26).......................I—697
    of cabinet consultations in regard to obtaining a judicial decision, &c., (yeas 19, nays 30).....I—700
        in regard to use of force, (yeas 18, nays 26)...I—701
    of opinions given to President by cabinet as to scope of tenure-of-office act, (yeas 20, nays 26)...I—710
    of nominations of Lieutenant General Sherman and Major General Thomas to be generals by
        brevet, (yeas 14, nays 35)..I—738
appeals from decisions of Chief Justice......................................II—488, III—391
application of counsel for thirty days to prepare for trial, (yeas 12, nays 41).....................I—82
argument, rule prescribing order of..II—4, 5, 8, 12, 13, 14
censure of Mr. Nelson, tabling order of, (yeas 32, nays 17)...................................II—307
Chief Justice, authority of, to rule questions of evidence.....................................I—186
    authority of, to vote..I—185
consultation, motion to retire for...I—85, 185
court of impeachment, unconstitutionality of, (yeas 2, nays 49).................................I—36
impeachment of Andrew Johnson, resolution (in House) for the, (yeas 126, nays 47)...........I—2
    resolution (in House) to prepare articles of, (yeas 126, nays 42)..............................I—2, 3
    rule (in House) limiting debate, when articles of, are reported, (yeas 106, nays 37)............I—3
order for trial to proceed forthwith upon filing replication, (yeas 25, nays 26)...................I—25
    immediately after replication filed, (yeas 40, nays 10).......................................I—34
    for respondent to file answer before 20th March, (yeas 28, nays 20; and yeas 23, nays 27)....I—35
    in respect to unconstitutionality of court of impeachment, (yeas 2, nays 49)..................I—36
    postponing application for thirty days to prepare for trial, (yeas 25, nays 28; and yeas 9, nays 42).I—81, 80
    directing trial to commence 30th March, (yeas 28, nays 24)..................................I—85
    denying authority of Chief Justice to vote, (yeas 22, nays 26)...............................I—185
    denying authority of Chief Justice to give casting vote, (yeas 22, nays 27)...................I—187
    denying privilege of Chief Justice to rule questions of law, (yeas 20, nays 30)...............I—186
    directing questions to be submitted to Senate, on request, (yeas 31, nays 19)................I—86
    mode of procedure on final argument.................................I—498, 535, 536. II—4, 5, 8, 12, 13, 14
    fixing hour of meeting..I—536, 637. II—141, 308
    proposing to receive all evidence, not trivial, without objection.............................I—536
    for reporting deliberations on final question...II—188, 474
    fixing day for final vote...II—476, 477
    for filing opinions...II—477
    prescribing form of final question..II—478, 479
    directing vote to be taken on eleventh article first, (yeas 34, nays 19)...................II—484, 485
question, final, of "Guilty" or "Not guilty"—
    on Article XI, (yeas 35, nays 19)...II—486, 487
    II, (yeas 35, nays 19)...II—496
    III, (yeas 35, nays 19)..II—497

Z.

Zider, Henry F. (See *Testimony*.)

IMPEACHMENT OF THE PRESIDENT.

OPINIONS OF SENATORS,

FILED AND PUBLISHED BY ORDER OF THE SENATE SITTING ON THE TRIAL OF THE IMPEACHMENT OF ANDREW JOHNSON, PRESIDENT OF THE UNITED STATES.

Opinion of Mr. Senator Sherman.

This cause must be decided upon the reasons and presumptions which by law apply to all other criminal accusations. Justice is blind to the official station of the respondent and to the attitude of the accusers speaking in the name of all the people of the United States. It only demands of the Senate the application to this cause of the principles and safeguards provided for every human being accused of crime. For the proper application of these principles we ourselves are on trial before the bar of public opinion. The novelty of this proceeding, the historical character of the trial, and the grave interests involved, only deepen the obligation of the special oath we have taken to do impartial justice according to the Constitution and laws.

And this case must be tried upon the charges now made by the House of Representatives. We cannot consider other offences. An appeal is made to the conscience of each senator of guilty or not guilty by the President of eleven specific offences. In answering this appeal a senator cannot justify himself by public opinion or by political, personal, or partisan demands, or even grave considerations of public policy. His conscientious conviction of the truth of these charges is the only test that will justify a verdict of guilty. God forbid that any other should prevail here. In forming this conviction we are not limited merely to the rules of evidence, which by the experience of ages have been found best adapted to the trial of offences in the double tribunal of court and jury, but we may seek light from history, from personal knowledge, and from all sources that will tend to form a conscientious conviction of the truth. And we are not bound to technical definitions of crimes and misdemeanors. A wilful violation of the law, a gross and palpable breach of moral obligations tending to unfit an officer for the proper discharge of his office or to bring the office into public contempt and derision, is, when charged and proven, an impeachable offence. And the nature and criminality of the offence may depend on the official character of the accused. A judge would be held to higher official purity, and an executive officer to a stricter observance of the letter of the law. The President, bound as a citizen to obey the law, and specially sworn to execute the law, may properly in his high office as Chief Magistrate, be held to a stricter responsibility than if his example was less dangerous to the public safety. Still to justify the conviction of the President there must be specific allegations of some crime or misdemeanor involving moral turpitude, gross misconduct, or a wilful violation of law, and the proof must be such as to satisfy the conscience of the truth of the charge.

The principal charges against the President are that he wilfully and purposely violated the Constitution and the laws, in the order for the removal of Mr. Stanton, and in the order for the appointment of Gen. Thomas as Secretary of War *ad interim*. These two orders were contemporaneous—part of the same transaction—but are distinct acts, and are made the basis of separate articles of impeachment.

Their common purpose, however, was to place the Department of War under the control of Gen. Thomas, without the advice and consent of the Senate.

On these charges, certain leading facts are either admitted, or are so clearly proven that they may be assumed to be admitted. It thus appears that during the session of the Senate, and without the advice and consent of the Senate, the President did make these orders, with the avowed purpose of gaining possession of the Department of War. That he knew that his power to remove Mr. Stanton was denied and contested both by the Senate and Mr. Stanton; that this act was committed after full deliberation, and with the expectation that it would be effective in expelling Mr. Stanton from the Department of War, and that this act of removal was in no way connected with the power of the President to appoint or remove a Secretary of War by and with the advice and consent of the Senate, but was the act of the President alone, done by him under claim that it was within his power, under the Constitution and the laws. It is, therefore, not so much a question of intention, as a question of lawful power.

If the President has the power, during the session of the Senate, and without their consent, to remove the Secretary of War, he is not guilty under the first, fourth, fifth, and sixth articles presented by the House; while, if the exercise of such a power is in violation of the Constitution and the laws, and was done by him wilfully, and with the intent to violate the law, he is guilty, not only of malfeasance in office, but of a technical crime, as charged by the first article, and upon further proof of the conspiracy alleged, is guilty, as charged by the fourth, fifth, and sixth articles.

The power to remove Mr. Stanton is claimed by the President—*first*, under the Constitution of the United States, and, *second*, under the act of 1789 creating the Department of War.

First. Has the President, under and by virtue of the Constitution, the power to remove executive officers?

The question involved is one of the gravest importance. It was fully discussed in the first session of the first Congress; and latterly has been so often discussed in the Senate, that it is only necessary for me to state the general principles upon which my own judgment in this case rests.

The power to remove officers is not expressly conferred upon the President by the Constitution. If he possesses it it must be—1st. From his general duty to see that the laws are faithfully executed; or, 2d. As an incident to his appointing power; or, 3d. By authority from time to time conferred upon him by law. Is it derived from his general executive authority? The first section of the second article of the Constitution provides that "the executive power shall be vested in the President." Section three of the same article provides "that he shall take care that the laws be faithfully executed." This duty to execute the laws no more includes the power to remove an officer than it does to create an office. The President cannot add a soldier to the army, a sailor to the navy, or a messenger to his office, unless that power is conferred upon him by law; yet he cannot execute the laws without soldiers, sailors, and officers. His general power to execute the laws is subordinate to his duty to execute them with the agencies and in the mode and according to the terms of the law. The law prescribes the means and the limit of his duty, and the limitations and restrictions of the law are as binding upon him as the mandatory parts of the law.

The power of removal at his will is not a necessary part of his executive authority. It may often be wise to confer it upon him; but, if so, it is the law that invests him with discretionary power, and it is not a part, or a necessary incident, of his executive power. It may be and often is conferred upon others.

That the power of removal is not incident to the executive authority, is shown by the provisions of the Constitution relating to impeachment. The power of removal is expressly conferred by the Constitution only in cases of impeachment, and then upon the Senate, and not upon the President. The electors may elect a President and Vice-President, but the Senate only can remove them. The President and the Senate can appoint judges, but the Senate only can remove them. These are the constitutional officers, and their tenure and mode of removal is fixed by the Constitution. All other offices are created by law. Their duties are defined, their pay is prescribed, and their tenure and mode and manner of removal may be regulated by law.

The sole power of the President conferred by the Constitution as to officers of the government is the power to appoint, and that must be by and with the advice and consent of the Senate. Does the power of appointment imply the power of removal? It is conferred by two clauses of section two of article two of the Constitution, as follows:

He shall have power, by and with the advice and consent of the Senate, to make treaties, provided two-thirds of the senators present concur; and he shall nominate, and, by and with the advice and consent of the Senate, shall appoint ambassadors, other public ministers and consuls, judges of the Supreme Court, and all other officers of the United States whose appointments are not herein otherwise provided for, and which shall be established by law; but the Congress may by law vest the appointment of such inferior officers as they think proper in the President alone, in the courts of law, or in the heads of departments.

The President shall have power to fill up all vacancies that may happen during the recess of the Senate, by granting commissions which shall expire at the end of their next session.

If the power to remove is incident to the power to appoint, it can only be co-extensive with the power to appoint. In that case, during the session of the Senate the removal must be "by and with the advice and consent of the Senate." By any other construction, the implied power would defeat the express power. In all arguments on this subject it is assumed that the power to remove an officer must exist somewhere; that removal by impeachment could not have been intended to be the only mode of removing an officer, and therefore the power to remove must, from the necessity of its exercise, be held to exist in some department of the government, and must be implied from some express grant of power. By this reasoning some have implied the power to remove from the power to appoint, and a distinction has been made between a removal during the session of the Senate and one made during the recess. If the power to remove is derived from the power to appoint, then the President during the recess may exercise it, and may then fill the vacancy by a temporary appointment. But if this argument is tenable, he cannot remove an officer during the session of the Senate without they consent. Then they share with him in the power to appoint, and in all the power that is derived from the power to appoint. Therefore, the removal of one officer during the session of the Senate, except in an by the appointment of another, or by the consent of the Senate, would be clearly unconstitutional, unless the power to remove is derived from some other than the appointing power.

In this case the removal of Mr. Stanton is not claimed by the President to be derived from the appointing power; but it is asserted as a distinct exercise of an independent constitutional and legal power incident to his executive office, or conferred upon it by law. In the early discussions on this subject, especially by Mr. Madison, the alleged power of the President to remove all officers at pleasure was based upon the general clauses already quoted conferring executive authority. If this is tenable all limitations upon his power of removal are unconstitutional. A constitutional power can only be limited by the Constitution, and yet Congress has repeatedly limited and regulated the removal of officers. Officers of the army and navy can only be removed upon conviction by court martial, in some cases the assent of the Senate is required, and in others the tenure of office is fixed for a term of years. A careful examination of the debate of 1789 on the organization of the executive departments will show that while a majority of the House decided that the power of removal was with the President yet they were not agreed upon the basis of this power. The debate was only as to heads of departments, as to whom there are peculiar reasons why they should only hold their offices at the pleasure of the President. The government was new; the President commanded the entire confidence of all classes and parties, and the wisest could not then foresee the rapid and vast extension in territory and population of the new nation, making necessary a multitude of new offices, and increasing to a dangerous degree the power, patronage, and influence inherent in the executive office. Who can believe that if the great men who were then willing that Washington should remove his heads of departments at pleasure, could have foreseen the dangerous growth of executive power, would have been willing by mere inference to extend his power so as to remove at pleasure all executive officers. This power unrestricted and unlim'ted by law is greater and more dangerous than all the executive authority conferred upon the President by express grant of the Constitution. His command of the army and navy is limited by the power of Congress to raise armies and navies, to declare war, and to make rules and regulations for the government of the army and navy. His power to pardon is limited to cases other than of impeachment. His power to appoint officers and to make treaties is limited by the consent of the Senate. Surely when these express powers, far less important, are so carefully limited by the Constitution, an implied power to remove at pleasure the multitude of officers created by law cannot be inferred from that instrument. If so the implied power swallows up and overshadows all that are expressly given. What need he care for the Senate when he may remove in a moment, without cause, all officers appointed with their consent. What need he care for the law when all the officers of the law are instruments of his will, holding office, not under the tenure of the law, but at his pleasure alone. The logical effect of this power, if admitted to exist under and by virtue of the Constitution, is revolution. However much respect is due to the decision of the first Congress, yet the actual working of civil government is a safer guide than the reasoning of the wisest men unaided by experience.

Their judgment that the head of a departmant should be removable by the President may be wise, but the power to remove is not conferred by the Constitution, but like the office itself, is to be conferred, created, controlled, limited, and enforced by the law. That such was the judgment of Marshall, Kent, Story, McLean, Webster, Calhoun, and other eminent jurists and statesmen, is shown by their opinions quoted in the argument; but they regarded the legislative construction as controlling for the time the natural and proper construction of the Constitution. The legislative construction given by the first Congress has been gradually changed. Army and navy officers have long been placed beyond the unlimited power of the President. Postmasters and others have a fixed term of office. Various legislative limitations have been put upon the power and mode of removal. The Comptroller of the Currency holds his office for five years, and can only be removed by the President upon reasons to be communicated to the Senate. Finally, when the derangement of the revenue service became imminent, and the abuse of the power of removal produced a disgraceful scramble for office the legislative authority asserted its power to regulate the tenure of civil offices, by the passage, on the second of March, 1867, of the tenure-of-civil-office act. That this measure is constitutional, and that it is in the highest degree expedient, we have asserted by our vote for the law. The President had the right to demand of us a review of this opinion under the sanction of the special oath we have taken. Aided by the very able argument in this cause, and by a careful review of the authorities, I am still of the opinion that the Constitution does not confer upon the President as a part of or as incident to his executive authority the power to remove an officer, but that the removal of an officer like the creation of an office is the subject of legislative authority to be exercised in each particular case in accordance with the law.

I therefore regard the tenure-of-office act as constitutional and as binding upon the President to the same extent as if it had been approved by him. He has no more right to disregard the law passed according to the Constitution without his assent, than a senator could disregard it if passed without his vote. The veto power is a vast addition to executive authority, and experience has shown the necessity to limit rather than extend it. But, if in addition to his veto power, he may still disregard a law passed over it, or discriminate against such a law, his veto becomes absolute. No such doctrine is consistent with a republican form of government. The law, when passed in the mode prescribed, must be binding on all or on none. He who violates it violates it at his peril. If, therefore, the removal of Mr. Stanton is within the penal clauses of that act the President is guilty not only of an impeachable but an indictable offence. He cannot excuse himself by showing that he believed it unconstitutional, or that he was advised that it was unconstitutional. If a citizen assumes that an act is unconstitutional and violates it he does it at his peril. He may on his trial assert its unconstitutionality, and if the court of last resort in his case pronounces the law unconstitutional he will be acquitted. He takes that risk at his peril. If the law is held constitutional his belief to the contrary will not acquit him. Ignorance of the law does not excuse crime, and he who undertakes to violate it on the pretence that it is unconstitutional—thus setting up his opinions against that of the law-making power—must take the consequences of his crime.

The same rule applies much stronger to the President when he violates a law on the claim that it is unconstitutional. He is not only bound to obey the law, but he is sworn to execute the law. In resisting it he violates his duty as a citizen and his oath as an officer. If he may protect himself by an honest opinion of its unconstitutionality, then all his responsibility ceases. He may assert it on his trial like all other persons accused of crime, but the court having final jurisdiction of his case, must decide this question like all others, and if that court affirms the law, his guilt is complete.

In this case the President knew that a breach of this law by him could only be tried by the Senate. His pardoning power exempts him from all punishment, except by and after impeachment. His case can only be tried by the Senate, and it is a court of last resort. His violation of this law might enable others to get the opinion of the Supreme Court, by creating rights or claims to office; but his offence could not be tried before the Supreme Court, but must be tried before a court that in its legislative and executive capacity had already thrice considered this law and held it valid. A violation of it then, on the pretext of its unconstitutionality, would be in the face of these well-considered judgments of the court that alone was competent to try his cause, and would be in the highest sense wilful, deliberate, and premeditated.

It remains to consider whether, under the law as it existed on the 21st of February, 1868, the removal of Mr. Stanton was authorized, and this involves only the construction of two acts, viz:

1st. The act entitled "An act to establish an Executive Department, to be denominated the Department of War," approved August 7, 1789, and

2d. The act of March 2, 1867, entitled "An act regulating the tenure of certain civil offices."

The second section of the act of 1789, provides—

That there shall be in the said department an inferior officer, to be appointed by the said principal officer, to be employed therein as he shall deem proper, and to be called the chief clerk in the Department of War, and who, whenever the said principal officer shall be removed from office by the President of the United States, or in any other case of vacancy, shall, during such vacancy, have the charge and custody of all records, books, and papers appertaining to the said department.

This was copied from the act organizing the Department of Foreign Affairs, which was the subject of the debate so often quoted in this cause. Whatever differences of opinion existed as to the constitutional power of the removal by the President, no one questioned the purpose of this act to declare and affirm the right of the President to remove the Secretary of War. Some who denied the constitutional power were willing to confer it by law as to heads of departments, and the first draught of the bill expressly conferred the power of removal on the President. This was changed so as to declare the power to exist and to provide for the vacancy caused by its exercise. This act stands unaltered and unrepealed, unless it is modified by the tenure-of-office act. Under it the power of removal by the President of a cabinet officer has been conceded by each branch of the government during every administration—though disputes have existed as to the origin of the power—some deriving it from the Constitution and others from the plain intent of the act of 1789. The power to remove cabinet officers since the passage of that act was repeatedly recognized by all who took part in the debate in the Senate on the tenure-of-office bill—the only question being as to the propriety of continuing the power. I do not understand the managers to question the correctness of this construction, but they claim—

1st. That the power of removal was limited to during the recess of the Senate, and did not exist during the session of the Senate, and

2d. That the power to remove Mr. Stanton was taken from the President by the tenure-of-office act.

Does the act of 1789 make a distinction between removals during the session and during the recess of the Senate? Upon this point, at the opening of this trial, I had impressions founded upon a distinction that I think ought to have been made in the law; but a full examination of the several acts cited, and the debates upon them, show that in fact no such distinction was made. If such had been the intention of the framers of the act of 1789, instead of stating the unlimited power of removal, they would have provided for a removal or vacancy "during the recess of the Senate." The debates show that no such distinction was claimed, and that the majority held that the unlimited power of removal was with the President by virtue of the Constitution.

The subsequent acts of 1792, and 1795, in providing for vacancies, made no distinction between vacancies during the session and during the recess, and in the numerous acts cited by counsel, providing for the creation and tenure of offices, passed prior to March 2, 1867, no distinction is made between a removal during the session and during the recess. The practice has corresponded with this construction. In two cases the power to remove heads of departments has been exercised; the one, by John Adams, in the removal of Timothy Pickering; the other, by Andrew Jackson, in the removal of Mr. Duane. The first case occurred during the session, and the latter during the recess. In compliance with this construction, the commissions of heads of departments declare their tenure to be during the pleasure of the President, and the commission under which Mr. Stanton now holds the Department of War, limits his tenure "during the pleasure of the President of the United States for the time being." This form of commission, used without question for 70 years through memorable political contests, is entirely inconsistent with a construction of the act of 1789, limiting the power of removal to the recess of the Senate.

The distinction made by the managers between *removals* during the session and during the recess is derived from the distinction made by the Constitution between *appointments* made during the session and during the recess; but this claim is inconsistent with the foundation upon which the tenure-of-office act rests. If removals are governed by the constitutional rule as to appointments, then the President may remove at pleasure during the recess, for he may then appoint temporarily without the consent of the Senate, and Congress may not limit this constitutional power. But Congress has wisely, as I have shown, rejected this claim. It has repeatedly dissevered removals from appointments, and has treated the power of removal, not as a constitutional power, but as one to be regulated by law in the creation, tenure, pay, and regulation of offices and officers; and therefore, in ascertaining whether the law makes a distinction between a removal during the session and during the recess, we must ascertain the intention of the law as gathered from its language, history, and construction, and from these we can derive no trace of such a distinction. Nor can this distinction be derived from the rarity of removals of cabinet officers during the session of the Senate, for the argument applies as well to removals during the recess. Removals of heads of departments are rare indeed; for when the tenure-of-office bill was pending, it was not considered possible that a case would occur where a head of a department would decline to resign when requested to by his chief. The multitude of cabinet ministers who have held office recognized this duty with but two exceptions. I do not question the patriotism of Mr. Stanton in declining to resign during the recess; but cases of that kind must be of rare occurrence and dangerous example. It was held by us all that the public safety and the public service demands unity, efficiency, and harmony between the heads of departments and the President. To legislate against this, and yet hold the President responsible for their acts, would be unexampled in our history, and therefore the law always gave the President the power to remove at his pleasure these and most other executive officers until we were compelled, by the evil example of a bad President, to limit this power. I therefore conclude that, prior to the 2d of March, 1867, the law invested the President with the power at his pleasure to remove Mr. Stanton both during the session and during the recess, and the question remains whether by the tenure-of office act that power was taken away from him.

To determine the proper construction of this act we must examine its history and the particular evil it was intended to remedy. It was introduced on the 3d day of December, 1866, being the first day of the second session of the thirty-ninth Congress. The President having formally abandoned the political party that elected him, undertook, by general removals, to coerce the officers of the government to support his policy. The revenue service especially was deranged, and widespread demoralization threatened that branch of the public service. At that time nearly all civil officers of the government held at the pleasure of the President; some by the express provision of law; others under this general practice of the government.

The President, for political reasons during the then last recess, created vacancies by removal, and filled them by temporary appointments. It was to check this evil that Congress undertook to regulate the tenure of civil offices, and to protect officers in the discharge of their duties. The bill originated in the Senate, and, as introduced, excepted from its operation the heads of departments. The bill was referred to a committee, and as reported, the first section was as follows:

That every person (excepting the Secretaries of State, of the Treasury, of War, of the Navy, of the Interior, the Postmaster General, and the Attorney General) holding any civil office to which he has been appointed by and with the advice and consent of the Senate, and every person who shall hereafter be appointed to any such office, and shall become duly qualified to act therein, is, and shall be, entitled to hold such office until a successor shall have been in like manner appointed and duly qualified, except as herein otherwise provided.

On the 10th of January, 1867, a motion was made to strike out the exception of the heads of departments, and was discussed at length. The exception did not rest upon any want of power in Congress to extend the operation of the bill to the heads of departments, but upon the necessity of giving the President control over these officers in order to secure unity and efficiency to his executive authority. Nearly all the duties of heads of departments are by law required to be performed "as the President of the United States shall from time to time direct." They are rarely prescribed by law. This is especially so as to the Secretary of War, who issues all orders "by command of the President," and by virtue of his office is invested by law with less power than an accounting officer. His duty prescribed by the Constitution is to give his opinion in writing when called for by the President. His prescribed legal duty is to make requisitions upon the Secretary of the Treasury for the service of the army. All his other duties rest upon the discretion, order, and command of the President. As the President is responsible for the acts of heads of departments, as they exercise a part of his executive authority, as their duties are not defined by law, as is the case with most civil officers, it was deemed unwise to take from the Presidential office the power to remove such heads of departments as did not possess his confidence. After debate the motion to strike out the exception was lost without a division. At a subsequent stage of the bill the motion was renewed and was lost by the decisive vote of 13 yeas and 27 nays, and the bill was then passed.

In the House of Representatives the motion to strike out the exception was made and lost, but was subsequently reconsidered, and the motion was carried, and with this amendment the bill passed the House.

The question again came before the Senate upon a motion to concur with the House in striking out the exception of the heads of departments, and was fully debated, and again the Senate refused to concur with this amendment by a vote of 17 yeas to 28 nays. In this condition the disagreement between the two houses came before a committee of conference, where it was the bounden duty of the conferees to maintain as far as possible the view taken by their respective houses. The usual course in such a case, where the disagreement does not extend to the whole of the bill, or to the principle upon which it is founded, is to report an agreement upon so much as has been concurred in by both houses, thus limiting the change in existing law to those provisions which meet the concurrence of both houses; therefore, the Senate conferees might properly have declined to extend the change of the law beyond the vote of the Senate, and certainly would not have been justified in agreeing to a proposition thrice defeated by the vote of the Senate. The difference between the two houses was confined to the sole question whether that bill should regulate the tenure of office of the heads of departments. The Senate left them subject to removal at the pleasure of the President. The House secured their tenure subject to removal only at the pleasure of the Senate. After a long conference, the act as it now stands was reported. The first section is as follows:

That every person holding any civil office to which he has been appointed by and with the advice and consent of the Senate, and every person who shall hereafter be appointed to such office, and shall become duly qualified to act therein, is and shall be entitled to hold such office until a successor shall have been in like manner appointed and duly qualified, except as herein otherwise provided: *Provided*, That the Secretaries of State, of the Treasury, of War, of the Navy, and of the Interior, the Postmaster General, and the Attorney General, shall hold their offices respectively for and during the term of the President by whom they may have been appointed and for one month thereafter, subject to removal by and with the advice and consent of the Senate.

What is a fair and legal construction of this section? First. That the tenure of civil offices generally should be left as in the original bill, but a special provision should be made for the tenure of heads of departments. Second. That the President appointing a head of a department should not, during his term, without the consent of the Senate, remove him. Third. That after thirty days from the expiration of the term of the President who appointed a head of a department, the office of the latter would expire by limitation. To this extent, and to this extent alone, did the Senate conferees agree to change the existing law. The general clause prohibiting removals of civil officers is confined to those who have been appointed by and with the advice and consent of the Senate. The special clause prohibiting removals of cabinet officers is that those who have been appointed by a President during his term shall not be removed without the consent of the Senate.

The distinction is kept up between heads of departments and other civil officers, and the only limitation upon the power of the President already conferred by law, is, that having appointed such an officer he shall not remove him during his term, without the advice and consent of the Senate. In all other respects the law of 1789 remains unaltered.

Was, then, Mr. Stanton appointed by the President during his term of office? If not, he holds his office under his original commission and tenure, and not under this act. If he is included in this act its effect is to declare his office vacant April 4, 1865, for that was thirty days after the expiration of the term of the President who appointed him. No such absurd purpose was intended. The plain purpose was to leave him to stand upon his then tenure and commission and to allow each President for each term to appoint his heads of departments, with the consent of the Senate, and to secure them in their tenure during that term and thirty days thereafter, unless the Senate sooner consented to their removal. If the purpose was to protect Mr. Stanton against removal why select the language that excludes him? He was not appointed by this President, nor during this presidential term. How easy, if such was the purpose, to say that "heads of departments holding office or hereafter appointed should hold their offices, &c." To hold that the words inserted were intended to warn the President not to remove Mr. Stanton upon peril of being convicted of a high misdemeanor, is to punish the President as a criminal for the violation of a delphic oracle. It impugns the capacity of the conferees to express a plain idea in plain words.

I can only say, as one of the Senate conferees under the solemn obligations that now rest upon us in construing this act, that I did not understand it to include members of the cabinet not appointed by the President, and that it was with extreme reluctance and only to secure the passage of the bill that, in the face of the votes of the Senate I agreed to the report limiting at all the power of the President to remove heads of departments. What I stated to the Senate is shown by your records. One of your conferees (Mr. Buckalew) refused to agree to the report. Another (Mr. Williams) thought that a case of a cabinet officer refusing to resign when requested by the President was not likely to occur. I stated explicitly that the act as reported did not protect from removal the members of the cabinet appointed by Mr. Lincoln, that President Johnson might remove them at his pleasure; and I named the Secretary of War as one that might be removed. I yielded the opinion of the Senate that no limitation should be made upon the power of the President to remove heads of departments solely to secure the passage of the bill. I could not conceive a case where the Senate would require the President to perform his great executive office upon the advice and through heads of departments personally obnoxious to him, and whom he had not appointed, and, therefore, no such case was provided for. You did not expressly assent to this construction, but you did not dissent. If either of you had dissented I leave to each senator to say whether in the face of his previous vote he would have approved the report. This construction of the law, made when this proceeding could not have been contemplated, when the President and each member of his cabinet were supposed to believe the act unconstitutional, made here in the Senate as an explanation for my yielding so much of your opinions, is binding upon no one but myself. But can I, who made it and declared it to you, and still believe it to be the true and legal interpretation of those words, can I pronounce the President guilty of crime, and by that vote aid to remove him from his high office for doing what I declared and still believe he had a legal right to do. God forbid!

A Roman emperor attained immortal infamy by posting his laws above the reach of the people and then punishing their violation as a crime. An American senator would excel this refinement of tyranny, if, when passing a law, he declared an act to be innocent, and then as a judge punished the same act as a crime. For this reason I could not vote for the resolution of the 21st of February, and cannot say "guilty" to these articles.

What the President did do in the removal of Mr. Stanton he did under a power which you repeatedly refused to take from the office of the President—a power that has been held by that officer since the formation of the government, and is now limited only by the words of an act, the literal construction of which does not include Mr. Stanton. This construction was put upon the act by the cabinet when it was pending for the approval of the President. In my judgment it is not shaken by the ingenious arguments of the managers.

The original exception was in the body of the section, it was inserted by the conferees in a modified form, as a proviso at the close of the section. The first clause relates to all civil officers, except heads of departments. The second clause relates to heads of departments and no other officers. The first clause expressly excepts the officers named in the proviso, and also those described in the fourth section. To consider both classes of officers as within both clauses of the section is, it seems to me, an unnatural and forced construction of language, and certainly, when construed on a criminal trial, is too doubtful upon which to base criminal guilt.

It follows, that as Mr. Stanton is not protected by the tenure-of-civil-office act, his removal rests upon the act of 1789, and he, according to the terms of that act and of the commission held by him, and in compliance with the numerous precedents cited in this cause, was lawfully removed by the President, and his removal not being contrary to the provisions of the act of March 2, 1867, the 1st, 4th, 5th, and 6th articles, based upon his removal, must fail.

The only question remaining in the first eight articles is whether the appointment of General Thomas as Secretary of War *ad interim*, as charged in the 2d, 3d, 7th, and 8th articles is in violation of the Constitution and the laws, and comes within the penal clauses of the tenure-of-office act, and was done with the intent alleged, if so, the President is guilty upon these articles. This depends upon the construction of the clauses of the Constitution already quoted and of the several acts approved February 13, 1795, February 20, 1863, and the tenure-of-office act.

Under the Constitution no appointment can be made by the President during the session of the Senate, except by and with the advice and consent of the Senate, unless of such inferior officers as Congress may by law invest in the President alone.

By the act of February 13, 1795, it is provided—

That in case of vacancy in the office of Secretary of State, Secretary of the Treasury, or of the Secretary of the Department of War, or of any officer of either of the said departments, whose appointment is not in the head thereof, whereby they cannot perform the duties of their said respective offices; it shall be lawful for the President of the United States, in case he shall think it necessary, to authorize any person or persons, at his discretion, to perform the duties of the said respective offices, until a successor be appointed, or such vacancy be filled. *Provided*, That no one vacancy shall be supplied, in manner aforesaid, for a longer term than six months.

A grave question might arise whether this act is constitutional; whether the head of a department is an officer whose appointment even for a time might be delegated to the President alone during the session of the Senate. Its existence unrepealed would relieve the President from all criminal fault in acting upon it, but it is in derogation of the plain constitutional right of the Senate to participate in all important appointments, and if abused would utterly destroy their power. This act applied only to the three departments then existing, and was only intended to apply to vacancies existing, and not to vacancies to be made.

Its sole purpose was to provide for a temporary vacancy until the constitutional mode of appointment could be exercised, and could not infringe upon or impair the right of the Senate to participate in appointments. In the Statutes at Large it is designated as "obsolete," and is, in fact, superseded by the act approved February 20, 1863—volume 12, page 656. This act in its title shows its plain object and purpose. It is entitled "An act temporarily to supply vacancies in the executive departments in certain cases."

It provides—

That in case of the death, resignation, absence from the seat of government, or sickness of the head of any executive department of the government, or of any officer of either of the said departments whose appointment is not in the head thereof, whereby they cannot perform the duties of their respective offices, it shall be lawful for the President of the United States, in case he shall think it necessary, to authorize the head of any other executive department, or other officer in either of said departments, whose appointment is vested in the President, at his discretion, to perform the duties of the said respective offices until a successor be appointed, or until such absence or inability by sickness shall cease: *Provided*, That no one vacancy shall be supplied in manner aforesaid for a longer term than six months.

SEC. 2. *And be it further enacted*, That all acts or parts of acts inconsistent with the provisions of this act are hereby repealed.

This act, together with the clause of the Constitution providing for vacancies during the the recess provides for all cases of vacancy except the one of removal during the session of the Senate, and that is left to be exercised as a part of the constitutional power of appointment by and with the advice and consent of the Senate. This act is complete in itself, and by its second section repeals the act of 1795, and all other acts providing for temporary appointments. It is in harmony with the Constitution for it avoids the doubtful power conferred by the act of 1795, of appointing a new officer without the consent of the Senate, but delegates to another officer already confirmed by the Senate the power temporarily to perform the duties of the vacant place. Under the authority of this act in the case of the vacancies provided for the President might have authorized the head of any other executive department to perform temporarily the duties of Secretary of War, and the country would have had the responsibility of a high officer already approved by the Senate. In that event no new officer would have been appointed, no new salary conferred, no new agent of unauthorized power substituted in the place of an officer of approved merit, no mere instrument to execute executive will would have been thrust in the face of the Senate during their session—to hold the office in spite of the constitutional power of the Senate and against their advice and consent. Under this act the President had no more power to appoint General Thomas Secretary of War *ad interim* than he had to appoint any of the leaders of the late rebellion. General Thomas is an officer of the army, subject to court-martial, and not an officer of the department, or in any sense a civil or department officer.

Did the act of March 2, 1867, confer this authority? On the contrary, it plainly prohibits all temporary appointments except as specially provided for The third section repeats the constitutional authority of the President to fill all vacancies happening during the recess of the Senate by death or resignation—and that if no appointment is made during the following session to fill such vacancy, the office shall remain in abeyance until an appointment is duly made and confirmed—and provision is made for the discharge of the duties of the office in the meantime. The second section provides for the suspension of an officer during the recess, and for a temporary appointment *during the recess*. This power was exercised and fully exhausted by the suspension of Mr. Stanton until restored by the Senate, in compliance with the law. No authority whatever is conferred by this act for any temporary appointment during the session of the Senate, but, on the contrary, such an appointment is plainly inconsistent with the act, and could not be inferred or implied from it. The sixth section further provides:

That every removal, appointment, or employment, made, had, or exercised, contrary to the provisions of this act, and the making, signing, sealing, countersigning, or issuing of any commission or letter of authority for or in respect to any such appointment or employment, shall be deemed, and are hereby declared to be, high misdemeanors, and, upon trial and conviction thereof, every person guilty thereof shall be punished by a fine not exceeding $10,000, or by imprisonment not exceeding five years, or both said punishments, in the discretion of the court.

This language is plain, explicit, and was inserted not only to prohibit all temporary appointments except during the recess, and in the mode provided for in the second section, but the unusual course was taken of affixing a penalty to a law defining the official duty of the President. The original bill did not contain penal clauses; but it was objected in the Senate that the President had already disregarded mandatory provisions of the law, and would this; and therefore, after debate these penal sections were added to secure obedience to the law, and to give to it the highest sanction.

Was not this act wilfully violated by the President during the session of the Senate?

It appears from the letter of the President to General Grant, from his conversation with General Sherman, and from his answer, that he had formed a fixed resolve to get rid of Mr. Stanton and fill the vacancy without the advice of the Senate. He might have secured a new Secretary of War by sending a proper nomination to the Senate. This he neglected and refused to do. He cannot allege that the Senate refused to relieve him from an obnoxious minister. He could not say that the Senate refused to confirm a proper appointee for he would make no appointment to them. The Senate had declared that the reasons assigned for suspending Mr. Stanton did not make the case required by the tenure-of-office act, but I affirm as my conviction that the Senate would have confirmed any one of a great number of patriotic citizens if nominated to the Senate. I cannot resist the conclusion, from the evidence before us, that he was resolved to obtain a vacancy in the Department of War in such a way that he might fill the vacancy by an appointment without the consent of the Senate and in violation of the Constitution and the law. This was the purpose of the offer to General Sherman. This was the purpose of the appointment of General Thomas. If he had succeeded as he hoped, he could have changed his temporary appointment at pleasure and thus have defied the authority of the Senate and the mandatory provisions of the Constitution and the law. I cannot in any other way account for his refusal to send a nomination to the Senate until after the appointment of General Thomas. The removal of Mr. Stanton by a new appointment, confirmed by the Senate, would have complied with the Constitution. The absolute removal of Mr. Stanton would have created a temporary vacancy, but the Senate was in session to share in the appointment of another. An *ad interim* appointment without authority of law, during the session of the Senate, would place the Department of War at his control in defiance of the Senate and the law, and would have set an evil example, dangerous to the public safety—one which, if allowed to pass unchallenged, would place the President above and beyond the law.

The claim now made that it was the sole desire of the President to test the constitutionality of the tenure-of-office act, is not supported by reason or by proof. He might, in August last, or at any time since, without an *ad interim* appointment, have tested this law by a writ of *quo warranto*. He might have done so by an order of removal, and a refusal of Mr. Stanton's requisitions. He might have done so by assigning a head of a department to the place made vacant by the order of removal. Such was not his purpose or expectation. He expected by the appointment of General Sherman at once to get possession of the War Department, so when General Thomas was appointed there was no suggestion of a suit at law until the unexpected resistance of Mr. Stanton, supported by the action of the Senate, indicated that as the only way left.

Nor is this a minor and unimportant violation of law. If upon claim that the tenure-of-office act was unconstitutional, he might remove an officer and place his instrument or agent in possession of it, he might in the same way and by the same means take possession of all the executive departments, of all the bureaus, of the offices of the Auditors, Comptrollers, Treasurer, collectors and assessors, and thus control, by his will, the purse and the sword. He knew that his power was contested, and he defied it. It is clearly shown that his purpose was deliberately formed and deliberately executed, and the means for its execution were carefully selected. I, therefore, conclude that the appointment of General Thomas was a wilful violation of the law, in derogation of the rights of the Senate, and that the charges contained in the second, third, seventh and eighth articles are true.

The criminal intent alleged in the 9th article is not sustained by the proof. All the President did do in connection with General Emory is reconcilable with his innocence, and therefore I cannot say he is guilty as charged in this article.

The 10th article alleges intemperate speeches improper and unbecoming a chief magistrate, and the seditious arraignment of the legislative branch of the government. It does not allege a specific violation of law, but only personal and political offences for which he has justly forfeited the confidence of the people.

Am I, as a senator, at liberty to decide this cause against the President even if guilty of such offences. That a President in his personal conduct may so demean himself by vice, gross immorality, habitual intoxication, gross neglect of official duties, or the tyrannous exercise of power, as to justify his removal from office is clear enough; but the Senate is bound to take care that the offence is gross and palpable, justifying in its enormity the application of the strong words "high crime or misdemeanor." And above all, we must guard against making crimes out of mere political differences, or the abuse of the freedom of speech, or of the exhibition of personal weakness, wrath, or imbecility. We do not confer the office of President, and may not take it away except for crime or misdemeanor. The people alone may convict and condemn for such offences. The Senate may not trespass upon the jurisdiction of the people without itself being guilty of usurpation and tyranny. Better far to submit to a temporary evil than to shake the foundations of the civil superstructure established by the Constitution by enlarging our jurisdiction so as to punish by removal from office the utmost latitude of discussion, crimination and recrimination, which, so long as it is unaccompanied by unlawful acts, is but the foolish vaporing of liberty.

The House of Representatives of the 39th Congress refused to rest an accusation upon these speeches, and so of the present House, until other acts of a different character induced these articles of impeachment. We must pass upon this article separately, and upon it my judgment is that it does not allege a crime or misdemeanor within the meaning of the Constitution.

The great offence of the President consists of his opposition, and thus far successful opposition, to the constitutional amendment proposed by the 39th Congress, which, approved by nearly all the loyal States, would, if adopted, have restored the rebel States, and thus have strengthened and restored the Union convulsed by civil war. Using the scaffoldings of civil governments, formed by him in those States without authority of law, he has defeated this amendment, has prolonged civil strife, postponed reconstruction and re-union, and aroused again the spirit of rebellion overcome and subdued by war. He, alone, of all the citizens of the United States, by the wise provisions of the Constitution, is not to have a voice in adopting amendments to the Constitution; and yet, he, by the exercise of a baleful influence and unauthorized power, has defeated an amendment demanded by the result of the war. He has obstructed as far as he could all the efforts of Congress to restore law and civil government to the rebel States. He has abandoned the party which trusted him with power, and the principles so often avowed by him which induced their trust.

Instead of co operating with Congress, by the execution of laws passed by it, he has thwarted and delayed their execution, and sought to bring the laws and the legislative power into contempt. Armed by the Constitution and the laws, with vast powers, he has neglected to protect loyal people in the rebel States, so that assassination is organized all over those States, as a political power to murder, banish, and maltreat loyal people, and to destroy their property. All these he might have ascribed to alleged want of power, or to difference of opinion in questions of policy, and for these reasons no such charges were exhibited against him, though they affected the peace and safety of the nation. When he adds to these political offences the wilful violation of a law by the appointment of a high officer during the session of the Senate, and without its consent, and with the palpable purpose to gain possession of the Department of War, for an indefinite time, a case is made not only within the express language of the law a high misdemeanor, but one which includes all the elements of a crime, to-wit: a violation of express law, wilfully and deliberately done, with the intent to subvert the constitutional power of the Senate, and having the evil effect of placing in the hands of the President unlimited power over all the officers of the government.

This I understand to be the substance of the 11th article. It contains many allegations which I regard in the nature of inducement, but it includes within it the charge of the wilful violation of law more specifically set out in the second, third, seventh, and eighth articles, and I shall therefore vote for it.

The power of impeachment of all the officers of the government, vested in the Senate of the United States, is the highest trust reposed in any branch of our government. Its exercise is indispensable at times to the safety of the nation, while its abuse, especially under political excitement, would subordinate the executive and the judiciary to the legislative department. The guards against such a result are in the love of justice inherent in the people who would not tolerate an abuse of power, and also in the solemn appeal each of us have made to Almighty God to do impartial justice in this cause. We dare not for any human consideration disregard this oath, but guided by conscience and reason will, no doubt, each for himself, render his verdict upon these charges according to the law and the testimony, and without bias from personal, political, or popular influence. This done we may disregard personal consequences and leave our judgment and conduct in this great historical trial to the test of time.

OPINION OF MR. SENATOR FESSENDEN.

The House of Representatives have, under the Constitution of the United States, presented to the Senate eleven distinct articles of impeachment for high crimes and misdemeanors against the President. Each senator has solemnly sworn, as required by the Constitution, to "do impartial justice, according to the Constitution and the laws," upon the trial. It needs no argument to show that the President is on trial for the specific offences charged, and for none other. It would be contrary to every principle of justice, to the clearest dictates of right, to try and condemn any man, however guilty he may be thought, for an offence not charged, of which no notice has been given to him, and against which he has had no opportunity to defend himself. The question then is, as proposed to every senator, sitting as a judge, and sworn to do impartial justice, "Is the President guilty or not guilty of a high crime or misdemeanor, as charged in all or either of the articles exhibited against him?"

The first article of the series substantially charges the President with having attempted to remove Edwin M. Stanton from the office of Secretary of War, which he rightfully held, in violation of law and of the Constitution of the United States. Granting that an illegal and unconstitutional attempt to remove Mr. Stanton in the manner alleged in the article, whether successful or not, is a high misdemeanor in office, the first obvious inquiry presents itself, whether under the Constitution and the laws the President had or had not a right to remove that officer at the time such attempt was made, the Senate being then in session. To answer this inquiry it is necessary to examine the several provisions of the Constitution bearing upon the question, and the laws of Congress applicable thereto, together with the practice, if any, which has prevailed since the formation of the government upon the subject of removals from office.

The provisions of the Constitution applicable to the question are very few. They are as follows:

Article II, section 1. The executive power shall be vested in a President of the United States of America.

Article II, section 2. He (the President) * * * shall nominate, and, by and with the advice and consent of the Senate, shall appoint ambassadors, other public ministers and consuls, judges of the Supreme Court, and all other officers of the United States, whose appointments are not herein otherwise provided for, and which shall be established by law.

Same section. The President shall have power to fill up all vacancies that may happen during the recess of the Senate by granting commissions which shall expire at the end of their next session.

Article II, section 4. The President, Vice-President, and all civil officers of the United States shall be removed from office on impeachment for and conviction of treason, bribery, or other high crimes and misdemeanors.

The whole question of removals from office came under the consideration of the first Congress assembled after the adoption of the Constitution, and was much discussed by the able men of that day, among whom were several who took a prominent part in framing that instrument. It was noticed by them that the only provision which touched in express terms upon the subject of removals from office was found in the clause which related to impeachment; and it was contended that, consequently, there was no other mode of removal. This idea, however, found no favor at that time, and seems never since to have been entertained. It is quite obvious that as such a construction would lead to a life tenure of office, a supposition at war with the nature of our government, and must of necessity involve insuperable difficulties in the conduct of affairs, it could not be entertained. But it was equally obvious that a power of removal must be found somewhere, and as it was not expressly given except in the impeachment clause, it must exist among the implied powers of the Constitution. It was conceded by all to be in its nature an executive power; and while some, and among them Mr. Madison, contended that it belonged to the President alone, because he alone was vested with the executive power, and, from the nature of his obligations to execute the law and to defend the Constitution, ought to have the control of his subordinates, others thought that as he could only *appoint* officers "by and with the advice and consent of the Senate" the same advice and consent should be required to authorize their removal. The first of these constructions finally prevailed, as those who have read the debates of that period well know. This was understood and avowed at the time to be a legislative construction of the Constitution, by which the power of removal from office was recognized as exclusively vested in the President. Whether right or wrong, wise or unwise, such was the decision, and several laws were immediately enacted in terms recognizing this construction of the Constitution.

The debate referred to arose upon a bill for establishing what is known as the Department of State. And in accordance with the decision of that first Congress the right and power of the President to remove the chief officer of that department was expressly recognized in the second section, as follows:

"SEC. 2. *And be it further enacted,* That there shall be in the said department an inferior officer," &c., * * * "*who, whenever the said principal officer shall be removed from office by the President of the United States,* or in any other case of vacancy shall, during such vacancy, have the charge," &c., * * * act approved July 27, 1789. The same provision is found *in totidim verbis* in the act establishing the Department of War, approved August 7, 1789; and terms equally definite are found in the act to establish the Treasury Department, approved September 2, 1789. These several acts have continued in force to the present day; and although the correctness of the legislative construction then established has more than once been questioned by eminent statesmen since that early period, yet it has been uniformly recognized in practice; so long and so uniformly as to give it the force of constitutional authority. A striking illustration of this practical construction arose in the administration of John Adams, who, when the Senate was in session, removed Mr. Pickering from the office of Secretary of State without asking the advice and consent of the Senate, nominating to that body for appointment on the same day John Marshall, in the place of Timothy Pickering, *removed.* No question seems to have been made at the time of this exercise of power. The form of all commissions issued to the heads of departments, and to other officers whose tenure was not limited by statute, has been "during the pleasure of the President for the time being." And the right to remove has been exercised without restraint, as well upon officers who were appointed for a definite term as upon those who held during the pleasure of the President.

It has been argued that even if this right of removal by the President may be supposed to exist during the recess of the Senate, it is otherwise when that body is in session. I am unable to perceive the grounds of this distinction, or to find any proof that it has been recognized in practice. The Constitution makes no such distinction, as it says nothing of removal in either of the clauses making distinct provisions for appointment in recess and during the session. Probably this idea had its origin in the fact that in recess the President could appoint for a definite period without the advice and consent of the Senate, while in the other case no appointment could be made without that advice and consent. It has been uniformly held that a vacancy occurring in time of a session can only be filled during session by and with the advice and consent of the Senate, and cannot be lawfully filled during recess. But I am not aware that the President's power of removal during the session has ever been seriously questioned while I have been a member of the Senate. The custom has undoubtedly been to make the nomination of a successor the first step in a removal, so that the two acts were substantially one and the same. But instances have not unfrequently occurred during session where the President thought it proper to remove an officer at once, before sending the name of his successor to the Senate. And during my time of service previous to the passage of the act of March 2, 1867, I never heard his right to do so seriously questioned. The passage of that act is, indeed, in itself an admission that such were understood to be the law and the practice.

I will not attempt to discuss the question here whether the construction of the Constitution thus early adopted is sound or unsound. Probably it was thought that while the restraining power of the Senate over appointments was a sufficient protection against the danger of executive usurpation from this source, the President's responsibility for the execution of the laws required a prompt and vigorous check upon his subordinates. Judging from the short experience we have had under the act of March 2, 1867, the supervising power of the Senate over removals is poorly calculated to secure a prompt and vigorous correction of abuses in office, especially upon the modern claim that where offices are of a local character the representative has a right to designate the officer; under which claim this branch of executive authority, instead of being lodged where the Constitution placed it, passes to one of the legislative branches of the government

Such as I have described was the legislative construction of the Constitution on the subject of removals from office, and the practice under it, and such was the statute establishing the Department of War, distinctly recognizing the President's power to remove the principal officer of that department at pleasure, down to the passage of the act regulating the tenure of certain civil offices, which became a law March 2, 1867. Although that act did not receive my vote originally, I did vote to overrule the President's veto, because I was not then, and am not now, convinced of its unconstitutionality, although I did doubt its expediency, and feared that it would be productive of more evil than good. This is not the occasion, however, to criticise the act itself. The proper inquiry is, whether the President, in removing, or attempting to remove, Mr. Stanton from the office of Secretary of War, violated its provisions; or, in other words, whether, if the President had a legal right to remove Mr. Stanton before the passage of that act, as I think he clearly had, he was deprived of that right by the terms of the act itself. The answer to this question must depend upon the legal construction of the first section, which reads as follows, viz:

Be it enacted, &c., That every person holding any civil office, to which he has been appointed by and with the advice and consent of the Senate, and every person who shall hereafter be appointed to any such office, and shall become duly qualified to act therein, is, and shall be, entitled to hold such office until a successor shall have been in like manner appointed and duly qualified, *except as herein otherwise provided: Provided*, That the Secretaries of State, of the Treasury, of War, of the Navy, and of the Interior, the Postmaster General, and the Attorney General shall hold their offices respectively for and during the term of the President by whom they may have been appointed, and for one month thereafter, subject to removal by and with the advice and consent of the Senate.

In considering how far these provisions apply to the case of Mr. Stanton, the state of existing facts must be carefully borne in mind.

Mr. Stanton was appointed by President Lincoln during his first term, which expired on the 4th of March, A. D 1865. By the terms of his commission he was to hold "during the pleasure of the President for the time being." President Lincoln took the oath of office, and commenced his second term on the same 4th day of March, and expired on the 15th day of the succeeding April. Mr. Johnson took the oath of office as President on the day of the death of President Lincoln. Mr. Stanton was not reappointed Secretary of War by either, but continued to hold under his original commission, not having been removed. How, under these circumstances, did the act of March 2, 1867, affect him?

A preliminary question as to the character under which Mr. Johnson administered the office of President is worthy of consideration, and may have a material bearing.

The fifth clause of section 1, article 11, of the Constitution provides as follows, viz: "In case of the removal of the President from office, or of his death, resignation, or inability to discharge the powers and duties of the said office the same shall devolve upon the Vice-President." * * * What shall devolve upon the Vice-President? The powers and duties of the office simply, or the office itself? Some light is thrown upon this question by the remainder of the same clause, making provision for the death, &c., of both the President and Vice-President, enabling Congress to provide by law for such a contingency, as to declare "what officer shall *act as President*," and that "such officer shall *act* accordingly"—a very striking change of phraseology. The question has, however, in two previous instances received a practical construction. In the case of Mr. Tyler, and again in that of Mr. Fillmore, the Vice-President took the oath as President, assumed the name and designation, and was recognized as constitutionally President of the United States, with the universal assent and consent of the nation. Each was fully recognized and acknowledged to be President; as fully and completely, and to all intents, as if elected to that office.

Mr. Johnson then became *President.* Did *he* have a term of office? Was he merely the tenant or holder of the term of another, and that other his predecessor, President Lincoln? Did Mr. Lincoln's term continue after his death, as has been argued? It is quite manifest that two persons cannot be said to have one and the same term of the Presidency at the same time. If it was Mr. Lincoln's term, it was not Mr. Johnson's. If it was Mr. Johnson's, it was not Mr. Lincoln's. If Mr. Johnson had no term, when do the Secretaries appointed by him go out of office, under the act of March 2, 1867? When does the one month after "the expiration of the term of the President by whom *they* have been appointed" expire? A President without a term of office would, under our system, be a singular anomaly, and yet to such a result does this argument lead. I am unable to give my assent to such a proposition.

If Mr. Stanton was legally entitled to hold the office of Secretary of War on the 21st of February, 1868, as averred in the first article, he must have been so entitled by virtue of his original appointment by President Lincoln, for he had received no other appointment. If the act of March 2, 1867, terminated his office, he must, to be legally in office on the 21st of February, 1868, have been again appointed and confirmed by the Senate. He must, therefore, be assumed to have held under the commission by the terms of which he held "during the pleasure of the President for the time being." After the death of President Lincoln, then, he held at the pleasure of President Johnson, by his permission, up to the passage of the act of March 2, 1867, and might have been removed by him at any time. Did that act change his tenure of office without a new appointment, and transform what was before a tenure at will into a tenure for a fixed period? Granting that this could legally be done by an act of Congress, which may well be questioned, the answer to this inquiry must depend upon the terms of the act itself. Let us examine it.

It is obvious to my mind that the intention was to provide for two classes of officers; one, the heads of departments, and the other comprising all other officers, appointed by and with the advice and consent of the Senate. The act provides a distinct tenure for each of these classes; for the heads of departments a fixed term, ending in one month after the expiration of the term of the President by whom they were appointed; for all others an indefinite term, ending when a successor shall have been appointed and duly qualified. These two provisions are wholly unlike each other. Both are intended to apply to the present and the future, and to include all who may come within their scope. Does Mr. Stanton, by any fair construction, come within either? How can he be included in the general clause, when the Secretary of War is expressly excepted from its operation? The language is, "Every person holding any civil office, &c., shall be entitled to hold such office," "*except as herein otherwise provided.*" Then follows the proviso, in which the Secretary of War is specifically designated, and by which another and a different tenure is provided for the Secretary of War. Surely, it would be violating every rule of construction to hold that either an office or an individual expressly excluded from the operation of a law can be subject to its provisions.

Again, does Mr. Stanton come within the proviso? What is the term therein fixed and established for the Secretary of War? Specifically, the term of the President by whom he was appointed, and one month thereafter. *He* was appointed by President Lincoln, and the term of President Lincoln existing at the time of his appointment expired on the 4th of March, 1865. Can any one doubt that had a law been in existence on that day similar to that of March 2, 1867, Mr. Stanton would have gone out of office in one month thereafter? The two terms of Mr. Lincoln were as distinct as if held by different persons. Had he been then reappointed by Mr. Lincoln, and confirmed, and a law similar to that of March 2, 1867, been then in existence, is it not equally clear that he would have again gone out of office in one month after the expiration of Mr. Lincoln's second term? If so, the only question would have been whether Mr. Lincoln's term expired with him, or continued, notwithstanding his death, until the 4th day of March, 1869, although he could no longer hold and execute the office, and although his successor, elected and qualified according to all the forms of the Constitution, was, in fact and in law, President of the United States. How could all that be, and yet that successor be held to have no term at all? To my apprehension such a construction of the law is more and worse than untenable.

The word "term," as used in the proviso, when considered in connection with the obvious design to allow to each person holding the presidential office the choice of his own confidential advisers, must, I think, refer to the period of actual service. Any other construction might lead to strange conclusions. For instance, suppose a President and Vice-President should both die within the first year of the term for which they were elected. As the law now stands, a new election must be held within thirty-four days preceding the first Wednesday of December then next ensuing. A new term of four years would commence with the inauguration of the new President before the term for which the preceding President was elected had expired. Do the heads of departments appointed by that preceding President hold their offices for three years of the term of the new President and until one month after the expiration of the term for which such preceding President was elected? Such would be the consequence of giving to the word "term" any other meaning than the term of actual service. It must be evident, therefore, that the word "term" of the President, as used in the proviso, is inseparable from the individual, and dies with him.

If I am right in this conclusion, Mr. Stanton, as Secretary of War, comes neither within the body of the section nor within the proviso, unless he can be considered as having been *appointed* by Mr. Johnson.

Words used in a statute must, by all rules of construction, be taken and understood in their ordinary meaning, unless a contrary intention clearly appears. As used in the Constitution, *appointment* implies a designation— an act. And with regard to certain officers, including the Secretary of War, it implies a nomination to the Senate and a confirmation by that body. A Secretary of War can be *appointed* in no other manner. This is the legal meaning of the word *appointed*. Is there any evidence in the act itself that the word *appointed* as used in the proviso was intended to have any other meaning? The same word occurs three times in the body of the section, and in each case of its use evidently has its ordinary constitutional and legal signification. There is nothing whatever to show that it had, or was intended to have, any other sense when used in the proviso. If so, then it cannot be contended that Mr. Stanton was ever appointed Secretary of War by Mr. Johnson, and he cannot, therefore, be considered as included in the proviso. The result is, that he is excluded from the general provision because expressly excepted from its operation, and from the proviso by not coming within the terms of description.

It not unfrequently happens, as every lawyer is aware, that a statute fails to accomplish all the purposes of those who penned it, from an inaccurate use of language, or an imperfect description. This may be the case here. But when it is considered that this proviso was drawn and adopted by eminent lawyers, accustomed to legal phraseology, who perfectly well knew and understood the position in which certain members of Mr. Johnson's cabinet stood, not appointed by him, but only suffered to remain in office under their original commissions from President Lincoln; and when it is further considered that the object of that proviso was to secure to each President the right of selecting his own cabinet officers, it is difficult to suppose the intention not to have been to leave those officers who had been appointed by President Lincoln to hold under their original commissions, and to be removable at pleasure. Had they intended otherwise it was easy so to provide. That they did not do so is in accordance with the explanation given when the proviso was reported to the Senate, and which was received with unanimous acquiescence.

It has been argued that Mr. Johnson has recognized Mr. Stanton as coming within the first section of the act of March 2, 1867, by suspending him under the provisions of the second section. Even if the President did so believe, it by no means follows that he is guilty of a misdemeanor in attempting to remove him, if that view was erroneous. The President is not impeached for acting contrary to his belief, but for violating the Constitution and the law. And it may be replied that, if the President did entertain that opinion, testimony was offered to show that his cabinet entertained a different view. Whatever respect the opinion of either may be entitled to, it does not settle the question of construction. But a sufficient answer to the argument is that, whether Mr. Stanton comes within the first section of the statute or not, the President had a clear right to suspend him under the second section. That section applies to all civil officers, except judges of the United States courts, "appointed as aforesaid;" that is, "by and with the advice and consent of the Senate;" and Mr. Stanton was such an officer, whatever might have been his tenure of office. The same remark applies to the eighth section, in relation to the designation of General Thomas. That section covers every "person" designated to perform the duties of any office, without the advice and consent of the Senate. Both of these sections are general in their terms and cover all persons coming within their purview, whether included in the first section or not.

I conclude, then, as Mr. Stanton was appointed to hold "during the pleasure of the President for the time being," and his tenure was not affected by the act of March 2, 1867, the President had a right to remove him from office on the 21st of February, 1868, and, consequently, cannot be held guilty under the first article.

Even, however, if I were not satisfied of the construction given herein of the act of March 2, 1867, I should still hesitate to convict the President of a high misdemeanor for what was done by him on the 21st of February. The least that could be said of the application of the first section of that act to the case of Mr. Stanton is that its application is doubtful. If, in fact, Mr. Stanton comes within it, the act done by the President did not remove him, and he is still Secretary of War. It was, at most, an attempt on the part of the President, which he might well believe he had a right to make. The evidence utterly fails to show any design on the part of the President to effect his purpose by force or violence. It was but the simple issuance of a written order, which failed of its intended effect. To depose the constitutional chief magistrate of a great nation, elected by the people, on grounds so slight, would, in my judgment, be an abuse of the power conferred upon the Senate, which could not be justified to the country or the world. To construe such an act as a high misdemeanor, within the meaning of the Constitution, would, when the passions of the hour have had time to cool, be looked upon with wonder, if not with derision. Worse than this, it would inflict a wound upon the very structure of our government, which time would fail to cure, and which might eventually destroy it.

It may be further remarked that the President is not charged in the first article with any offence punishable, or even prohibited, by statute. The *removal* of an officer contrary to the provisions of the act of March 2, 1867, is punishable, under the sixth section, as a high misdemeanor. The *attempt* so to remove is not declared to be an offence. The charge is, that the President issued the order of February 21, 1868, *with intent* to violate the act, by removing Mr Stanton. If, therefore, this attempt is adjudged to be a high misdemeanor, it must be so adjudged, not because the President has violated any law or constitutional provision, but because, in the judgment of the Senate, the attempt to violate the law is in itself such a misdemeanor as was contemplated by the Constitution, and justifies the removal of the President from his high office.

The second article is founded upon the letter of authority addressed by the President to General Lorenzo Thomas, dated February 21, 1868. The substantial allegations of the article are, that this letter was issued in violation of the Constitution and contrary to the provisions of the "act regulating the tenure of certain civil offices," without the advice and consent of the Senate, that body being then in session; and without the authority of law, there being at the time *no vacancy* in the office of Secretary of War.

In the view I have taken of the first article there was legally a vacancy in the Department of War, Mr. Stanton having been removed on that same day, and the letter of authority states the fact, and is predicated thereon. It is a well-established principle of law that where two acts are done at the same time, one of which in its nature precedes the other, they must be held as intended to take effect in their natural order. The question then is whether, a vacancy existing, the President had a legal right to fill it by a designation of some person to act temporarily as Secretary *ad interim*. The answer to this question will depend, to a great extent, upon an examination of the statutes.

The first provision of statute law upon this subject is found in section eight of an act approved May 8, 1792, entitled "An act making alterations in the Treasury and War Departments."

That section empowers the President, "in case of the *death, absence from the seat of government, or sickness*," * * * of the Secretaries of State, War, or the Treasury, "or of any officer of either of said departments, whose appointment is not in the head thereof, in case he shall think it necessary, to *authorize* any person or persons, at his discretion, to perform the duties of the said respective offices until a successor be appointed, or such absence or inability by sickness may cease."

It will be noticed that this act provides for one case of vacancy and two of temporary disability, making the same provision for each case. In neither case does it require any consent of the Senate, or make any allusion to the question whether it is or is not in session. It is viewed as a mere temporary arrangement in each case, and fixes no specific limit of time to the exercise of authority thus conferred. Nor does it restrict the President in his choice of a person to whom he may confide such a trust.

By an act approved February 13, 1795, chapter xxi, to amend the act before cited, it is provided "*that in case of vacancy*" in either of the several Departments of State, War, or the Treasury, or of any officer of either, &c., "it shall be lawful for the President," * * "in case he shall think it necessary, to *authorize* any person or persons, at his discretion, to perform the duties of the said respective offices until a successor be appointed, or such vacancy be filled, provided that no one vacancy shall be supplied in manner aforesaid for a longer term than six months."

This act, it will be observed, applies only to vacancies, and does not touch temporary disabilities, leaving the latter to stand as before, under the act of 1792. It still leaves to the President his choice of the person, without restriction, to supply a vacancy; and while it provides for all vacancies, arising from whatever cause, like the law of 1792, it makes no allusion to the Senate, or to whether or not that body is in session. But this act differs from its predecessor in this, that it specifically limits the time during which any one vacancy can be supplied to six months.

Thus stood the law down to the passage of the act of February 20, 1863. (Stat. at Large, vol. 12, page 656.) In the mean time four other departments had been created, to neither of which were the provisions before cited applicable. And yet it appears from the record that almost every President in office since the creation of those departments had, in repeated instances, exercised the same power and authority in supplying temporary vacancies and disabilities in the new departments which he was authorized to exercise in those originally created, without objection, and even without remark.

The act of February 20, 1863, provides, "that in case of the death, resignation, absence from the seat of government, or sickness of the head of any executive department, or of any officer of either of said departments," &c., "it shall be lawful for the President * * * to *authorize* the head of any other executive department, or other officer in either of said departments whose appointment is vested in the President," "to perform the duties * * until a successor be appointed, or until such absence or disability shall cease: *Provided*, That no one vacancy shall be supplied in manner aforesaid for a longer term than six months." Section two repeals all acts or parts of acts inconsistent, &c.

This act, it will be observed, covers, in terms, the cases provided for in the act of 1792, and one more—a vacancy by *resignation*. It limits the range of selection, by confining it to certain specified classes of persons. It limits the time for which any *vacancy* may be supplied to six months, and it extends the power of so supplying vacancies and temporary absence and disability to all the departments. Clearly, therefore, it repeals the act of 1792, covering all the cases therein enumerated, and being in several important particulars inconsistent with it. There was nothing left for the act of 1792 which was not regulated and controlled by the act of 1863.

How was it with the act of 1795? That act covered all cases of vacancy. Had it repealed the prior act of 1792? It had applied the limitation of six months for any one *vacancy*, and to that extent was inconsistent with the act of 1792, so far as a vacancy by death was concerned. But it left the cases of sickness and absence untouched. The power conferred by the act of 1792 in those cases remained, and was exercised, without question, in a multitude of cases, by all the Presidents, down to the passage of the act of 1863.

In like manner, the act of 1863, while it took out of the operation of the act of 1795 the case of vacancy by resignation, and made a new provision for it, left untouched vacancies by removal and by expiration of a limited tenure of office. Suppose the act of 1863 had provided in terms for only the two cases of absence and sickness specified in the act of 1792, will it be contended that in such a case the power conferred in that act in case of death would have been repealed by the act of 1863? If not, by parity of reason, the enumeration of a vacancy by *resignation* in the act of 1863 would extend no further than to take that case out of the act of 1795, leaving the cases of removal and expiration of term still subject to its operation. The conclusion, therefore, is, that whatever power the President had by the act of 1795 to appoint any person *ad interim*, in case of removal, remains unaffected by the act of 1863.

It has been argued that the authority vested in the President by the act of 1795 is repealed by the sixth section of the act of March 2, 1867, which prohibits and punishes "the making, signing, sealing, countersigning, or issuing of any commission, *or letter of authority*, for or in respect to any such appointment or employment." If the act of 1795 is repealed by this section, it must operate in like manner upon the act of 1863. The consequence would be that in no case, neither in recess nor in session, neither in case of vacancy, however arising, absence or sickness, would the President have power, even for a day, to authorize any person to discharge the duties of any office, in any of the departments, which is filled by presidential appointment. All must remain as they are, and all business must stop, during session or in recess, until they can be filled by legal appointment. This could not have been intended. The words above cited from the sixth section of the act of 1867 are qualified by the words "contrary to the provisions of this act." The language is "commission or letter of authority for or in respect to any *such* appointment or employment;" to wit, a "removal, appointment, or employment made, had, or exercised contrary to the provisions of this act." If, therefore, the removal is not contrary to the act, neither is the designation of a person to discharge the duties temporarily; and a letter of authority issued in such a case is not prohibited.

In confirmation of this view it will be noticed that the eighth section of the act of March 2, 1867, expressly recognizes the power of the President, "without the advice and consent of the Senate," to "designate, authorize, or employ" persons to perform the duties of certain offices temporarily—thus confirming the authority conferred by the preceding acts.

My conclusion, therefore, is, that as the President had a legal right to remove Mr. Stanton, notwithstanding the act of March 2, 1867, he had a right to issue the letter of authority to General Thomas to discharge the duties of the Department of War, under and by virtue of the act of 1795.

It has been urged, however, that the six months' limitation in the act of 1795 had expired before the 21st of February, 1868, in consequence of the appointment of General Grant as Secretary of War *ad interim* on the 12th day of August, 1867. I am unable to see the force of this argument. Whatever may have been the opinion of the President as to his power of suspending an officer under the Constitution, (and I am of the opinion that he had no such power,) he clearly had the right to suspend Mr. Stanton under the second section of the act of March 2, 1867, and must be held in law to have acted by virtue of the lawful authority thereby conferred; more especially as he saw fit to conform in all respects to its provisions. The action of the Senate upon that suspension restored Mr. Stanton to his office of Secretary of War. This suspension cannot be considered as a removal, and the subsequent removal on the 21st of February created a vacancy in the office from that date. The designation of General Thomas cannot, therefore, be considered as a continuation of the original designation of General Grant on the 12th day of August, 1867.

But even if I am wrong in this conclusion, and the President had no power by existing laws to appoint a Secretary of War *ad interim*, yet, if Mr. Stanton did not come within the first section of the act of 1867, the second article fails. The gravamen of that article is the violation of the Constitution and the act of March 2, 1867, by issuing the letter of authority, with intent to violate the Constitution, &c., "there being no vacancy in the office of the Secretary of War." If a legal vacancy existed, the material part of the accusation is gone. A letter of authority, such as that issued to Thomas, is in no sense an appointment to office as understood by the Constitution. If it be, then the power to issue such a letter in any case without the assent of the Senate cannot be conferred by Congress. If it be, the acts of 1792, 1795, and 1863 are unconstitutional. The sixth section of the act of March 2, 1867, recognizes the distinction between an appointment and a letter of authority. The practice has been frequent and unbroken, both with and without the authority of statute law, to issue letters of authority in cases of vacancy and temporary disability, almost from the formation of the government. It has been called for by the necessity of always having some one at the head of a department. There is no law prohibiting such a designation in case of a vacancy in a department. If the President had no authority to issue the letter in this individual case, it was, at most, a paper having no force, and conferring no power. It was no violation either of the Constitution or the law. The fact that on the very next day a nomination was actually sent to the Senate, though, as the Senate had adjourned, it was not communicated until the succeeding day, goes to show that there might have been no design to give anything but the most temporary character to the appointment. To hold that an act of such a character, prohibited by no law, having the sanction of long practice, necessary for the transaction of business, and which the President might well be justified in believing authorized by existing law, was a high misdemeanor justifying the removal of the President of the United States from office, would, in my judgment, be, in itself, a monstrous perversion of justice, if not of itself a violation of the Constitution.

The first two articles failing, the third, fourth, fifth, sixth, seventh, and eighth must fail with them.

The third differs from the second only in the allegation that the President *appointed* Lorenzo Thomas Secretary *ad interim* without the assent of the Senate, that body being then in session and there being no vacancy in said office. The answer to this allegation is, first, it was not an appointment requiring the assent of the Senate, but a simple authority to act temporarily; and, second, there was a legal vacancy in the office existing at the time.

Of article four it is sufficient to say that there is no evidence to sustain it. There is nothing bearing upon it except the idle vaporing of Thomas himself of what he intended to do; and he testifies, under oath, that the President never authorized or suggested the use of force. What was said by Thomas was said out of doors, not to Mr. Stanton, nor communicated to him by message. The interviews between General Thomas and Mr. Stanton were of the most pacific character. The reply of Mr. Stanton when the letter of the President was delivered to him was of a nature to repel the idea of resistance, and the testimony of General Sherman shows that the President did not anticipate resistance.

It is essential to the support of this fourth article, and also of article sixth, that *intimidation and threats* should have been contemplated by the parties charged with the conspiracy, under the act of July 31, 1861. These failing, the charge fails with them in both articles.

As to the fifth and seventh articles, the attempt is made to sustain them under a law of Congress, passed February 27, 1804, extending the criminal laws of Maryland over so much of the District as was part of that State. Inasmuch as the common law was, so far as it had not been changed by statute, the law of Maryland, and conspiracy a misdemeanor, the President is charged with a misdemeanor by conspiring with Thomas to do an act made unlawful by the act of March 2, 1867. This is the only interpretation which I am able, with the aid of the arguments of the managers, to place upon these articles. Granting the positions assumed as the foundation for the charges in these articles, they must fail, if the act which the President proposed to do was a lawful act, and he did not propose to accomplish it by unlawful means. The removal of Mr. Stanton is the means proposed in order to prevent him from holding his office, as charged in the fifth, and to take and possess the property of the United States in his custody, as charged in the seventh article. The right to remove him, therefore, disposes of both articles.

Outside of any of these considerations, I have been unable to look upon either of these four articles as justifying a charge of conspiracy. The legal idea of a conspiracy is totally inapplicable to the facts proved. The President, if you please, intends to remove a person from office by an open exercise of power, against the provisions of a law, contending that he has a right so to do, notwithstanding the law, and temporarily to supply the vacancy thus created. He issues an order to that effect, and at the same time orders another person to take charge of the office, who agrees to do so. How these acts, done under a claim of right, can be tortured into a conspiracy, in the absence of any specific provision of law declaring them to be such, is beyond my comprehension.

Article eight is disposed of by what has been said on the preceding articles.

Article nine is, in my judgment, not only without proof to support it, but actually disproved by the evidence.

With regard to the tenth article, the specifications are sufficiently established by proof. They are three in number, and are extracts from speeches of the President on different occasions. It is not pretended that in speaking any of the words the President violated the Constitution, or any provision of the statute or common law, either in letter or spirit. If such utterance was a misdemeanor, it must be found in the nature of the words themselves.

I am not prepared to say that the President might not, within the meaning of the Constitution, be guilty of a misdemeanor in the use of words. Being sworn "to preserve, protect, and defend the Constitution," if he should in words persistently deny its authority, and endeavor by derisive and contemptuous language to bring it into contempt, and impair the respect and regard of the people for their form of government, he might, perhaps, justly be considered as guilty of a high misdemeanor in office. Other cases might be supposed of a like character and leading to similar results. It remains to inquire what was the character of the words proved.

Those spoken on the 18th day of August, 1866, contained nothing calculated to impair the confidence of the country in our form of government, or in our cherished institutions. They did contain severe reflections upon the conduct of a co ordinate branch of the government. They were not an attack upon Congress as a branch of the government, but upon the conduct of the individuals composing the 39th Congress. He did not speak of *Congress* generally as "hanging upon the verge of the government, as it were," but of a particular Congress, of which he spoke as assuming to be "a Congress of the United States, while in fact it is a Congress of only a part of the States;" and which particular Congress he accused of encroaching upon constitutional rights, and violating the fundamental principles of government.

It may be remarked that those words were not official. They were spoken in reply to an address made to him by a committee of his fellow-citizens—spoken *of* the Congress, and not *to* it. The words did not in terms deny that it was a constitutional Congress, or assert that it had no power to pass laws. He asserted what was true in point of fact, that it was a Congress of only a part of the States. Granting that the words spoken would seem to imply that he had doubts, to some extent, of the true character of that Congress, and the extent of its powers, so long as several States were excluded from representation, he did not, in fact or in substance, deny its constitutional existence; while in all his official communications with that Congress he has ever treated it as a constitutional body. Is there another man in the republic, in office or out of office, who had not on that day a perfect right to say what the President said? Would any one think of punishing any member of Congress for saying out of doors precisely the same things of the body of which he was a member? Is the President alone excluded from the privilege of expressing his opinions of the constitution of a particular Congress, and of denouncing its acts as encroachments upon "constitutional rights" and the "fundamental principles of government?" In process of time there might possibly be a Congress which would be justly liable to the same criminations of a President. In such a case, is he to remain silent, and is he forbidden by the Constitution, on pain of removal from office, to warn the people of the United States of their danger?

It is not alleged that the President did not believe what he said on this occasion to be true. Whether he did or not is a question between him and his conscience. If he did, he had a perfect moral right so to speak. If he did not, his offence is against good morals, and not against any human law. There is, in my judgment, nothing in these words to prove the allegation that the President's intent in speaking them was to impair and destroy the respect of the people for the legislative power of Congress, or the laws by it duly and constitutionally enacted, or to set aside its rightful authority and powers. If the words were designed to bring that particular Congress into contempt, and to excite the resentment of the people against it, however much I may disapprove both words and intention, I do not think them an impeachable offence.

The remarks contained in the second and third specifications present themselves to my mind in the same light. They, too, contain severe reflections upon the thirty-ninth Congress; nothing more. I have not been able to discover any menaces or threats against Congress, unless they are found in the declaration that he would veto their measures; and this, I think, must, in fairness, be taken as applying to measures of a certain character, of which he had been speaking. The speeches at Cleveland and St. Louis, though highly objectionable in style, and unbecoming a President of the United States, afford nothing to justify the allegation that they were menacing towards Congress or to the laws of the country. To consider their utterance a high misdemeanor, within the meaning of the Constitution, would, in my view, be entirely without justification.

So highly did the people of this country estimate the importance of liberty of speech to a free people, that, not finding it to be specifically guaranteed in the Constitution, they provided for it in the first amendment to that instrument. "Congress shall make no law" * * * "abridging the freedom of speech." Undoubtedly there are great inconveniences, and perhaps positive evils, arising from the too frequent abuse of that freedom; more, perhaps, and greater from an equally protected freedom of the press. But the people of the United States consider both as essential to the preservation of their rights and liberties. They, therefore, have chosen to leave both entirely unrestrained, subjecting the abuse of that liberty only to remedies provided by law for individual wrongs. To deny the President a right to comment freely upon the conduct of co-ordinate branches of the government would not only be denying him a right secured to every other citizen of the republic, but might deprive the people of the benefit of his opinion of public affairs, and of his watchfulness of their interests and welfare. That under circumstances where he was called upon by a large body of his fellow-citizens to address them, and when he was goaded by contumely and insult, he permitted himself to transcend the limits of proper and dignified speech, such as was becoming the dignity of his station, is matter of deep regret and highly censurable. But, in my opinion, it can receive no other punishment than public sentiment alone can inflict.

If I rightly understand the accusation contained in the eleventh article, it is substantially this : "That, on the 18th day of August, 1866, the President, by public speech, declared, in substance, that the thirty-ninth Congress was not a Congress of the United States, authorized to exercise legislative power, thereby intending to deny that the legislation of said Congress was valid or obligatory on him, except so far as he saw fit to approve the same, and thereby denying, and intending to deny, the power of said thirty-ninth Congress to propose amendments to the Constitution ;" and, "*in pursuance of said declaration,*" the President, on the 21st day of February, 1868, attempted to prevent the execution of the act of March 2, 1867:

First. By unlawfully attempting to devise means to prevent Mr. Stanton from resuming the functions of Secretary of War, after the Senate had refused to concur in his suspension.

Second. By unlawfully attempting to devise means to prevent the execution of the appropriation act for the support of the army, for the fiscal year ending June 30, 1868.

And that further, in pursuance of said declaration, he unlawfully attempted to prevent the execution of the so-called reconstruction act of March 2, 1868.

Whereby he was guilty of a high misdemeanor in office on the 21st day of February, 1868.

I have already stated, in commenting on the tenth article, that I do not consider the President's declaration, on the 18th of August, 1866, as fairly liable to the construction there put upon it and repeated in this article. There were no such words said, nor can they be fairly implied. The words were that it was not a Congress of the United States, but only of a part of the States. Taken literally, these words were true. But a Congress of a part of the States may be a constitutional Congress, capable of passing valid laws, and as such the President has uniformly recognized the thirty-ninth Congress. The declaration being perfectly susceptible of an innocent meaning, and all his official acts being consistent with that meaning, it would be unjust to suppose a different one, which he did not express.

In this view the foundation of the article fails.

But whether in pursuance of that declaration or not, did he *unlawfully* devise means to prevent the execution of the law of March 2, 1867, in the manner charged ?

The first specification rests, if upon anything, upon the letter to General

Grant, dated February 10, 1868. This letter must be taken as a whole, and not considered by detached parts.

From that letter I am satisfied that the President expected General Grant, in case the Senate should not concur in the suspension of Mr. Stanton, to resign the office to him, so that he might have an opportunity to fill the office before Mr. Stanton resumed the performance of its duties, with a view of compelling Mr. Stanton to seek his remedy in the court. If the President had such a design, it could only be carried out legally by removing Mr. Stanton before he should have time to resume the functions of Secretary of War, if the President had a right to remove him. It has been seen, by my remarks upon the first article, that I think the President had such right. The design, then, if the President entertained it, was not unlawful.

As to the second specification, it has not, that I can see, any proof to sustain it; and if it had, it is not quite apparent how an attempt to prevent the execution of the act for the support of the army can be considered as proof of an intention to violate the civil-tenure act, which seems to be the gravamen of this article.

No evidence whatever was adduced to show that the President had devised means, or in any way attempted, to prevent the execution of the "act to provide for the more efficient government of the rebel States."

It has been assumed in argument by the managers that the President, in his answer, claims not only the right under the Constitution to remove officers at his pleasure, and to suspend officers for indefinite periods, but also to fill offices thus vacated for indefinite periods—a claim which, if admitted, would practically deprive the Senate of all power over appointments, and leave them in the President alone. The President does claim the power of removal, and that this includes the power of suspension. But a careful examination of his answer will show that he claims no other power than that conferred by the act of 1795, to fill vacancies in the departments temporarily, and for a period not exceeding six months, not by appointment without the consent of the Senate, but by designation, as described in the act—a power conferred by Congress, and which can be taken away at any time, if it should be found injurious to the public interest.

Even, however, if the claim of the President did go to the extent alleged, it is not made a charge against him in the articles of impeachment. And however objectionable and reprehensible any such claim might be, he cannot be convicted of a high misdemeanor for asserting an unconstitutional doctrine, if he has made no attempt to give it practical effect, especially without a charge against him and a trial upon it.

I am unwilling to close the consideration of this remarkable proceeding before adverting to some other points which have been presented in the argument.

The power of impeachment is conferred by the Constitution in terms so general as to occasion great diversity of opinion with regard to the nature of offences which may be held to constitute crimes or misdemeanors within its intent and meaning. Some contend, and with great force of argument, both upon principle and authority, that only such crimes and misdemeanors are intended as are subject to indictment and punishment as a violation of some known law. Others contend that anything is a crime or misdemeanor within the meaning of the Constitution which the appointed judges choose to consider so; and they argue that the provision was left indefinite from the necessity of the case, as offences of public officers, injurious to the public interest, and for which the offender ought to be removed, cannot be accurately defined beforehand; that the remedy provided by impeachment is of a political character, and designed for the protection of the public against unfaithful and corrupt officials. Granting, for the sake of the argument, that this latter construction is the true one, it must be conceded that the power thus conferred might be liable to very great abuse, especially in times of high party excitement, when the passions of the people are inflamed against a perverse and obnoxious public officer. If so it is a power to be exercised with extreme caution, when you once get beyond the line of specific criminal offences. The tenure of public offices, except those of judges, is so limited in this country, and the ability to change them by popular suffrage so great, that it would seem hardly worth while to resort to so harsh a remedy, except in extreme cases, and then only upon clear and unquestionable grounds. In the case of an elective Chief Magistrate of a great and powerful people, living under a written Constitution, there is much more at stake in such a proceeding than the fate of the individual. The office of President is one of the great co-ordinate branches of the government, having its defined powers, privileges, and duties; as essential to the very framework of the government as any other, and to be touched with as careful a hand. Anything which conduces to weaken its hold upon the respect of the people, to break down the barriers which surround it, to make it the mere sport of temporary majorities, tends to the great injury of our government, and inflicts a wound upon constitutional liberty. It is evident, then, as it seems to me, that the offence for which a Chief Magistrate is removed from office, and the power intrusted to him by the people transferred to other hands, and especially where the hands which receive it are to be the same which take it from him, should be of such a character as to commend itself at once to the minds of all right thinking men as, beyond all question, an adequate cause. It should be free from the taint of party; leave no reasonable ground of suspicion upon the motives of those who inflict the penalty, and address itself to the country and the civilized world as a measure justly called for by the gravity of the crime, and the necessity for its punishment. Anything less than this, especially where the offence is one not defined by any law, would, in my judgment, not be justified by a calm and considerate public opinion as a cause for removal of a President of the United States. And its inevitable tendency would be to shake the faith of the friends of constitutional liberty in the permanency of our free institutions, and the capacity of man for self-government.

Other offences of the President, not specified in the articles of impeachment, have been pressed by the managers as showing the necessity for his removal. It might be sufficient to reply that all such were long prior in date to those charged in the articles, have been fully investigated in the House of Representatives, were at one time decided by a majority of the learned Committee on the Judiciary in that body to present no sufficient ground for impeachment, and were finally dismissed by the House, as not affording adequate cause for such a proceeding, by a vote of nearly, if not quite, two to one. But it is enough to say that they are not before the Senate, and that body has no right to consider them. Against them the President has had no opportunity to defend himself, or even to enter his denial. To go outside of the charges preferred, and to convict him because, in our belief, he committed offences for which he is not on trial, would be to disregard every principle which regulates judicial proceedings, and would be not only a gross wrong in itself, but a shame and humiliation to those by whom it was perpetrated.

It has been further intimated by the managers that public opinion calls with a loud voice for the conviction and removal of the President. One manager has even gone so far as to threaten with infamy every senator who voted for the resolution passed by the Senate touching the removal of Mr. Stanton, and who shall now vote for the President's acquittal. Omitting to comment upon the propriety of this remark, it is sufficient to say, with regard to myself, that I not only did not vote for that resolution, but opposed its adoption. Had I so voted, however, it would afford no justification for convicting the President, if I did not, on examination and reflection, believe him guilty. A desire to be consistent would not excuse a violation of my oath to do "impartial justice." A vote given in haste and with little opportunity for consideration would be a lame apology for doing injustice to another, after full examination and reflection.

To the suggestion that popular opinion demands the conviction of the President on these charges, I reply that he is not now on trial before the people, but before the Senate. In the words of Lord Eldon, upon the trial of the Queen, "I take no notice of what is passing out of doors, because I am supposed constitutionally not to be acquainted with it." And again, "it is the duty of those on whom a judicial task is imposed to meet reproach and not court popularity." The people have not heard the evidence as we have heard it. The responsibility is not on them, but upon us. They have not taken an oath to "do impartial justice according to the Constitution and the laws" I have taken that oath. I cannot render judgment upon their convictions, nor can they transfer to themselves my punishment if I violate my own. And I should consider myself undeserving the confidence of that just and intelligent people who imposed upon me this great responsibility, and unworthy a place among honorable men, if for any fear of public reprobation, and for the sake of securing popular favor, I should disregard the convictions of my judgment and my conscience.

The consequences which may follow either from conviction or acquittal are not for me, with my convictions, to consider. The future is in the hands of Him who made and governs the universe, and the fear that He will not govern it wisely and well would not excuse me for a violation of His law.

OPINION OF MR. SENATOR HOWARD.

ABSTRACT OF CHARGES.

ARTICLE I. That Johnson issued the order of removal with intent to violate the tenure-of-office act and to remove Mr. Stanton.

ART. II. That he issued the letter of authority to Thomas with intent to violate the Constitution and the tenure-of-office act.

ART. III. That he appointed Thomas Secretary of War *ad interim*.

ART. IV. That he conspired with Thomas and others unknown, unlawfully to *hinder* and *prevent* Mr. Stanton from exercising the office of Secretary of War.

ART. V. That he conspired with Thomas and others to prevent and hinder the execution of the tenure-of-office act, and in pursuance of said conspiracy did attempt to prevent Mr. Stanton from holding his office.

ART. VI. That he conspired with Thomas and others to seize by force the property of the United States in the War Department, contrary to the conspiracy act of 1861, and the tenure-of office act.

ART. VII. That he conspired with Thomas with intent to seize and take such property, contrary to the tenure-of-office act.

ART. VIII. That with intent to control the disbursements for the War Department, and contrary to the tenure-of-office act, and in violation of the Constitution, he issued the order appointing Thomas.

ART. IX. That he instructed Emory that the clause in the appropriation act of 1867, requiring that all orders should pass through the General of the army, was unconstitutional and in contravention of Emory's commission, with intent to induce Emory to accept orders directly from him, and with intent to violate the tenure-of-office act.

ART. X. That with intent to bring into disgrace, ridicule, hatred, contempt, and reproach, the Congress of the United States and the several branches thereof, and to impair and destroy the respect of the people for them, he made the speeches at the Executive Mansion, at Cleveland, and St. Louis.

ART. XI. That he attempted to prevent the execution of the tenure-of-office act by unlawfully devising means to prevent Mr. Stanton from resuming the functions of his office, and to prevent the execution of the said clause in the appropriation act of 1867, and the reconstruction acts of March 2, 1867.

It has never been claimed that the power of the President to remove an incumbent from office is granted expressly, that is, in plain terms, by the Constitution All admit, all have from the first admitted, that if it exists in him it exists by implication; in other words, that it is derived from and is necessary to the execution of powers or duties granted or imposed in plain terms by the instrument; that it is an induction from express clauses. Only three clauses have ever been relied upon as foundations of this induction or implication.

They are the clause in the second section of the second article giving him the power to nominate, and, by and with the consent of the Senate, to appoint all officers of the United States whose appointments are not therein otherwise provided for; the clause in section one of article two, declaring that "the executive power shall be vested in a President of the United States," and section three of the same article, imposing upon him the duty to "take care that the laws be faithfully executed."

I shall speak of these in their order.

I assert, then, that the appointing clause I have mentioned does not imply the power of removal by the President alone and without the consent of the Senate.

Here I hold the advocates of the power to the concession upon which alone their reasoning proceeds, viz: that the power of removal is an incident to or rather a part of the power of appointment. This concession is as old as the controversy. It is an historical element in the debate coeval with its origin. It is founded upon the uncontroverted and incontrovertible principle that the author of an agency, the constituent, may revoke and annul it at pleasure. It rests upon the freedom of the will and the right of every man to act for himself in matters pertaining to him. This concession arises from common sense, from necessity, and is irrevocable. It is the rule not only of the common law, but of the civil law and of universal law, that the constituent may revoke the power he has granted.

But who, under this clause, is the constituent? From whom does the power, the official power created by law, proceed? Whose will imparts the agency, confers the office? Not the President's alone; his sole will cannot confer the office; but the will, that is, the "advice and consent of the Senate," must unite with the will and purpose of the President. Without this advice, this consent, concurring with this will of the President, the office cannot be conferred. The appointment thus becomes the joint act of the Senate and the President. There are thus created by the Constitution two constituents instead of one. Two wills must concur in the appointment to an office. It is plain that one was intended as a check upon the other against imprudent appointments. This check is in the hands of the Senate, to whom the name of the person selected for the office by the President is first to be submitted in the shape of a nomination, before the office can be conferred upon him. Their advice and consent must first be obtained, as an indispensable prerequisite. This check was intended for the public good, for the public safety; and was doubtless suggested by the monstrous abuses practiced in the colonies by the unchecked power of the Crown in appointing unworthy favorites to office among them, who, in the language of the Declaration of Independence, had been licensed to "eat out their substance." At any rate, it was a measure of wise and sound precaution against the tyranny of an irresponsible appointing power, and the corruption and favoritism of uncontrolled, unexamined secret appointments to office. Against these, "the advice and consent of the Senate" were esteemed sufficient safeguards.

The "appointment" is then the joint act of the Senate and the President; I say joint act, because that act which, to become complete and effectual, requires the concurrence of two wills, is, in morals as in law, a joint act.

It follows, logically, that if, as is conceded and undeniable, the power of removal is an incident to or a part of the power of appointment, the appointment cannot be revoked; the office cannot be recalled; the officer cannot be removed, but by the concurrence of the same wills that acted in the appointment. The revocation must, in point of authority, be coextensive with the authority that granted the power; or, to speak more correctly, the authority must be the same.

It follows that the President has no power of removal without the consent of the Senate; because the power of removal is necessarily the same power that made the appointment. No distinction can in the nature of things be drawn between the former and the latter. They are not two powers, but one and the same. The division of them, and some have divided or sought to divide them, is a mere metaphysical subtlety, a mere play upon words. The words "appointment" and "by and with the consent of the Senate," are intended for practical use, and are addressed to us in a practical sense, for the purpose of conferring a public benefit; not as a theme of metaphysical disputation and wrangling. They are of no utility whatever unless they are held to mean that the constituent power necessary to an appointment to a public office is made up of the will of the President and the will of the Senate; and as it is this double consent, this joint, concurrent will, that gives the appointment, it cannot be revoked without the exercise of exactly the same concurrent will, this double consent.

To say that one of the two joint constituents can undo an act which it required both to do, is to give to one the power of both, which is a contradiction in terms; for an act which requires the concurrence of two parties cannot be undone by one of them without yielding to the one the power of both, which is absurd.

It is no answer to this to say that, after the consent of the Senate has been given, it rests with the President alone whether he will appoint the person nominated and consented to. This is literally true, but it is equally true that he can make no appointment whatever without that consent. He may change his mind as to the first nomination and may refuse to appoint the person named; but whoever is in the end appointed by him must receive the consent of the Senate. This consent is, by the terms of the clause, as indispensable as the consent of the President. An appointment cannot be made without the consent of both. The power to invest the person with the office is lodged in both by the plain terms of the instrument, and the Senate might as well assume to appoint without the consent of the President as the latter to appoint without the consent of the Senate.

The power claimed is not, then, derived from the appointing clause of the Constitution.

The next provision relied upon is the clause contained in section one of article two, declaring that "the executive power shall be vested in a President of the United States of America." This clause is generally appealed to as implying a grant of the power of removal from office. It is said that the power of removal is in its nature an executive power. But the first question arising here is one of definition. What is here meant by the executive power? The surest mode of obtaining a true meaning is undoubtedly to show what the expression cannot be presumed to mean. Was this expression used in reference to the so-called executive power of the English government? Surely not. For at that time, as in all former and in all subsequent times, there was not and has not been anything deserving of the name of a definition or classification of the executive powers of that government. Nor can there be; for so long as the theory remains true that the British Parliament possess unlimited power, such a classification is, of course, impossible. By that theory and by the practice of the Parliament, as history shows, there is no power, faculty, or prerogative of the British Crown which may not be modified, limited, or even taken away by act of Parliament. Indeed, that body possesses the unquestioned power both of directing the descent of the Crown and of deposing the sovereign at will. And it is practically true that all political power in England is vested in Parliament. It is true that, in administration, the King is to attend to the execution of the laws by commissioning agents or officers for that purpose; but he cannot claim it as a legal right against an act of Parliament. He might complain of such an act as an encroachment upon his prerogatives, but should Parliament appoint the officers by direct act of legislation, no one will pretend that this mode of constituting them would be illegal and void.

The very omnipotence of Parliament is a standing denial that the executive powers of our own Constitution are to be defined by reference to those of the British King; and all explanations of the expression sought for in the governments of France, Austria, or any other continental nation, afford, if possible, less light by way of definition than that of Great Britain. The reason is that none of those governments possesses a written constitution by which the political authority of the people is parcelled out among the various functionaries. With us the case is different. Here the people, the source and fountain of all political power, have seen fit to write down in their own Constitution what political powers or bundles of powers may be exercised by the three departments or faculties of the government, namely, the legislative, the executive, and the judicial. They carefully declare that "all legislative powers herein granted shall be vested in a Congress of the United States." Then follows a list or enumeration of all these legislative powers and of the subjects upon which they may be exercised. Nobody doubts that an attempt to legislate beyond these powers, or upon subjects not embraced in the enumeration, would be void and inoperative. Why? Because the power thus to legislate is not granted, and the object is not within the reach of Congress. Their legislation ceases, withers, and dies, the moment it passes the line of constitutional limitation.

Another department or faculty of the government is called in the Constitution the "judicial power." The extent of its application is in like manner laid down in the instrument, and all the cases to which it can be applied are therein carefully made known, and the restrictions upon this attribute of the government are equally perceptible in the language of the Constitution.

Thus it appears that the framers, under the respective heads of legislative power and judicial powers, were careful to enumerate and designate the legislative and the judicial attributes of the government, and to insert terms of limitation and exclusion so as to bind up those two departments specifically, to the duties imposed upon them. It was the *policy of the Constitution* to delegate, define, and limit the powers of those two branches. This is admitted by all. It is a fundamental principle, a postulate. Now, this being the case in reference to the legislative and judicial branches, who would think of deriving unrestricted executive power from that clause of the Constitution declaring that the "executive power shall be vested in a President?" No one will deny that this language is a general grant of the executive power. But it is, of course, a grant—a grant not of all or of any imaginable executive power—not a grant of royal prerogatives, or of unlimited despotic power—but a grant of powers which in their nature were as easily defined and ascertained, and were, to say the least, as deserving of designation and description as the other powers; and no reason can be devised why the convention should have so carefully defined the powers of the other two branches and left the executive branch undefined and unlimited. Such an omission would be contrary to the very genius of constitutional government, and would argue a culpable inattention and neglect on the part of the convention. This reproach cannot be cast upon them, for we find them equally assiduous and watchful in defining all the powers they delegate to the President of the United States. They grant to him no undefined powers. They had granted none to the other two branches, and the reasons for definition and restriction were and are of equal stringency in each of the three.

If, therefore, the other two branches are to look for their powers in the Constitution, and among the enumerated powers, and out of and regardless of the two general phrases "all legislative powers" and "the judicial power of the United States," which are in their nature and office mere captions or headings of chapters, we must by parity of reasoning look for the executive powers in the chapter or clauses enumerating them. And among these there is not to be found any such power as the power of removal from office. It is not there set down. It is not at all implied from that which is set down, and it is mere assumption and not a logical deduction to derive it from what is expressed.

Again, it is insisted that the power is derivable from the clause of section 3 of article II, which declares that "he shall take care that the laws be faithfully executed;" and it is said he cannot do this unless he has the power of removal.

This clause creates no power. Its language implies no grant of authority. To "take care" means to be vigilant, attentive, faithful. The language imports nothing more than an admonition to him to keep himself informed of the manner public officers entrusted with legal duties perform them, and, in cases of delinquency, to apply any corrective in his power. Laws cannot be put in force without agents, incumbents. The power and duty of nominating them are cast upon him. He must designate them to the Senate, in the first instance; and in order that the laws may be faithfully executed he must nominate faithful and competent officers. Should a vacancy happen in an office during the recess of the Senate, this clause requires him to fill it by a temporary commission to some other faithful and competent man, as provided in the next preceding clause. He does not execute the laws personally, and there is neither a word nor an intimation in the whole instrument that he is expected to do so; but he is only to *take care* that they are executed; that is, he is to use vigilantly and faithfully the power of nomination given to him separately and the power of appointment given to him jointly with the Senate, and the power to fill vacancies so happening, given to him solely for the purpose of causing the laws to be faithfully executed for the good of the people.

The doctrine, asserted broadly and unconditionally in Mr. Johnson's answer, that he has as a separate and independent power under the Constitution, the power of removal, leads to the most fatal consequences. It directly subverts the popular character of the government. If, by virtue of the clause I am considering, he can remove an officer, he may, of course, leave the office without an incumbent for an indefinite period of time, thus leaving its duties wholly unperformed; thus wholly defeating the commands of the law, and the people in the mean time may be deprived of the benefits of the law.

It is absurd to call this taking care that the laws be faithfully executed; it is the exact reverse of it, and proves the futility of the claim.

Again, if this clause gives him the power of thus rendering an office vacant and continuing it vacant, (no matter under what pretext,) it gives him full, complete, and unlimited power to constitute and create, of his own will, the agents by whom the laws shall be executed; for, if the clause imparts any power whatever, it is unlimited and undefined. The language is, "shall take care that the laws be faithfully executed." The means are not mentioned, and if they are not to be looked for in the other clauses relating to the President, then, I repeat, if the clause grants any power whatever, it is without limitation and supreme. He may resort to any means he chooses. He may give a letter of authority to any person to do the acts required by the law, and this without any reference to the Senate. He may appoint as well as remove at will; and he becomes, so far as the execution of the laws is concerned, an autocrat and the government an absolutism. The mode of constituting the officers of the law, pointed out by the appointment clause, becomes a positive superfluity, a dead letter; and he may totally, and without incurring the least responsibility, disregard it. And this is what he has done in ten distinct instances in appointing provisional governors for the rebel States, the boldest invasion of the power of Congress ever before attempted, tending directly to a one man despotism.

It is no reply to say that the claim of power under this clause is confined, or should be confined, merely to the power of removing an officer, and that it does not or should not be extended to creating an officer or agent. If it grants to him the power of *causing* the laws to be faithfully executed—which is the whole claim in its essence and reality, as no one can deny—it is impossible to make any distinction between a removal and an appointment or authorization. Both are in their nature equally necessary, equally incidental, indispensable to that end. I am in error: an appointment or an authorization is by far the more necessary.

And if this claim is well founded, why can he not of his own motion levy and collect taxes, under pretence of taking care that the laws are executed? It is a most obvious means of so doing.

Again, it is of the nature of legislative power to prescribe by what instruments the commands of the law shall be performed. But for the power of appointment specifically laid down in the Constitution, the legislative power, granted wholly to the two houses, might have been employed in creating the officers as well as the offices. The appointment alone is withheld from the category of legislative powers granted by the Constitution to the two houses. The President has no particle of these powers, but only the power of naming and commissioning incumbents. The functions to be performed, the modes and manner of performing them, the duration of the term of tenure, all the duties and liabilities belonging to the office, are created and defined by the legislative power solely. All admit this: the office and all its duties, all its functions, all its responsibilities, are purely and exclusively the creations of the law, and lie within the legislative power granted to Congress. The mode, the agencies, the instrumentalities of carrying into effect the law, are but a part of the law itself.

Now, if the President can, by virtue of the clause requiring him to take care that the laws be faithfully executed, constitute and appoint agents to carry the laws into effect, and may do this without the concurrence of the Senate; if he may do it, even, in cases where Congress has omitted to create an office for that purpose, why may he not declare and define the functions, duties, and liabilities of such agents and the duration of their terms? Of course he may; and thus all that portion of the legislative power relating to the creation of offices and of officers to execute the laws is surrendered to him—completely abstracted from the general mass of legislative powers granted to Congress by the first section of article one of the Constitution; thus making the clause requiring him to take care that the laws be faithfully executed utterly repugnant to and contradictory of the terms of that general grant of legislative powers.

Such a mode of interpreting the Constitution—a mode that annuls and destroys one part in order to give a favorite meaning to another—is contrary to all the established rules of interpretation, and is suicidal and absurd to the last degree. *It is, indeed, a total overthrow of the system of government under which we live. It seeks by cunning glosses and jesuitical constructions to establish and maintain absolutism—the one-man power*—when the fathers of the Constitution fondly imagined they had put up firm barriers against it.

It is true that the first Congress in 1789 did, as the President's answer sets up, by the act organizing the Department of State, recognize and admit the power of removal in the President. But it must not be forgotten that this legislative construction of the Constitution was sanctioned by a majority of only 12 in the House, while the Senate was equally divided upon it, the casting vote being given by John Adams, the Vice-President. This state of the vote shows plainly that the *opinion* thus expressed by the two houses was but an opinion, and that it was contested and resisted by a very powerful opposition. The dispute has continued from that day, and the ablest intellects of the country have been ranged on the respective sides; Sherman, Alexander Hamilton, Webster, Clay, and others of the highest eminence as jurists against the power; Madison and numerous others of great ability in favor of it. *It has never been a settled question.* Mr. Webster tells us that, on the passage of the act of 1789, it was undoubtedly the great popularity of President Washington and the unlimited confidence the country reposed in him, that insured the passage of the bill by moderating the opposition to it; and the history of the times confirms the comment. It was the beginning of the *lis motu*. And so doubtful has the power ever since been considered that there seems to have been no distinct case of removal by the President during the session of the Senate but by making to them a new nomination. In a speech made by Mr. Webster in the Senate in 1835, on this same question, he says:

> The power of placing one man in office necessarily implies the power of turning another out. If one man be Secretary of State and another be appointed, the first goes out by the mere force of the appointment of the other, without any previous act of removal whatever. And this is the practice of the government, and has been from the first. In all the removals which have been made, they have generally been effected simply by making other appointments. I can find not a case to the contrary. *There is no such thing as any distinct official act of removal.* I have looked into the practice, and caused inquiries to be made in the departments, and I do not learn that any such proceeding is known as an entry or record of the removal of an officer from office.

I have shown that this power of removal by the President solely is unauthorized by any clause of the Constitution, and that the claim has never been acquiesced in by the country. The Supreme Court has never passed upon it As a distinct question, it has never been passed upon by any court. It is, therefore, without judicial sanction—whatever such a sanction may be worth, for it should be remembered that judges are but fallible men, and courts often overrule their own opinions on the same question. The peace of society requires that in questions of private right the decisions of courts should be respected, and should be uniform; but in a purely political question like the present—a question relating solely to the respective powers of the various branches of the government—the great and final arbiter must be enlightened reason, drawing its conclusions from the intentions and objects of the framers of the Constitution, to be gathered from the language they employ, and the historical circumstances which inspired their work.

In this light I cannot regard what is called the legislative construction of 1789 as of any weight in the discussion. The public mind has been equally divided upon it ever since. Is not the legislation of 1867, therefore, entitled to at least equal respect as a legislative construction? The house and the Senate of 1867 were equally enlightened, equally capable of forming a correct opinion, far more numerous, and expressed their opinion with far greater unanimity. Is not this precedent even of greater weight than the former, as a legislative construction? And why may not one legislative construction be as potent to settle a disputed constitutional question as another? And why may it not completely set aside that other? The authority is the same in both cases, and if the one opinion is entitled to more weight than the other, it can only be because of the greater numbers and greater unanimity.

The next question which arises is, if the President has not the power in question, and it belongs jointly to the President and the Senate, can Congress by statute regulate its exercise, as they have assumed to do in the tenure-of-office act of 1867?

But little time need, I think, be spent upon this inquiry.

The President and Senate have, as I have shown, the power to remove. The investing this power in them is investing it "in the government of the United States," as fully and completely as if it were vested in the three branches, viz., the legislative, the executive, and the judicial, altogether; and this brings the case within the clause which declares that "Congress shall have power to pass all laws necessary and proper for carrying into execution the foregoing powers, and all *other* powers vested by this Constitution in the government of the United States, or in any department or officer thereof." This power of legislation was manifestly intended to cover every power granted by the instrument, whether express or implied. No one can read the Constitution without coming to the conclusion that the power of legislation thus to be exercised in furtherance of powers granted was intended to be, and is, in fact, coextensive with those powers. A naked power granted to the government, (that is, to any department or officer of the government, for both expressions mean the same thing,) without the means of carrying it into effect by legislation, would, indeed, be preposterous. It would be forever a dormant, inefectual power, as useless as if it had never been delegated.

There is no ground here to dispute about the words of this important clause. They are "vested in the government of the United States, or in any department or officer thereof." A power vested in either of the two houses, in both jointly, in the President, in the courts, the judges, or in individuals, is as much "vested in the government of the United States" as if conveyed "to the government" in so many words; for they would, *quo ad hoc*, represent and act for the whole government—indeed, would be the government in using the power. Hence the grant of the power of removal to the President and Senate is a grant to the government. The addition of the words "or in any department or officer thereof" cannot therefore be held to confer any power not embraced in the preceding words, "vested in the government," but is only made from abundant caution, and to give, if possible, greater clearness, certainty, and comprehensiveness to the expression. It was to make sure that Congress should legislate for the purpose of carrying into execution *all* the powers granted, whether granted to one person or set of persons, or to another.

It is believed that this principle has never been denied. The whole current of federal legislation proceeds from this fountain; and it is evident that the clause was inserted to remove the difficulties which should perpetually be raised by cavillers as to the extent of the field of legislation conceded to Congress.

The authority of Congress, then, to prescribe in what manner this power, vested in the President and Senate, shall be exercised; its authority to direct how it shall be used in order to subserve the public interests, to prevent injustice and abuses, is indisputable.

The act of 1867 forbids removals from office at all, except upon evidence of unfitness, satisfactory both to the President and the Senate, and requires him to lay the evidence before the Senate for their action thereon. If unsatisfactory to them, the officer is not to be removed, but restored to his place; if satisfactory, he is removed, and his place is to be filled by another.

This is surely a most reasonable, kindly, and salutary mode of exercising the power.

The act then is fully warranted by the Constitution, and as valid and obligatory as any other act of Congress.

The next question is, whether Secretary Stanton came within its provisions?

It is literally true that the first clause of the first section of the act prohibits the removal of every officer, high or low, who had been or should be appointed by and with the consent of the Senate. The clause declares that every such officer shall hold his office until his successor shall be appointed by and with their advice and consent. He shall be entitled to hold the office until that time.

The first section directs that all civil officers then in existence shall be entitled to hold their offices thus: "Except as herein otherwise provided: *Provided*, That the Secretaries of State, of the Treasury, of War, of the Navy, and of the Interior, the Postmaster General, and the Attorney General, shall hold their offices respectively for and during the term of the President by whom they may have been appointed, and for one month thereafter, subject to removal by and with the advice and consent of the Senate."

The first clause, by its terms applies to *all* civil officers, judicial as well as executive. But the Constitution itself takes out of the category the judges of the United States courts by declaring that they "shall hold their offices during good behavior;" so that it could not affect their tenure.

But the clause was discussed and passed in presence of the fact that there was a multitude of offices in the tenure of which there was a limitation of time to a certain number of years. The general language of the clause would have had the effect to extend these fixed and limited terms beyond the legal period. Foreseeing this, Congress guarded against it by declaring that *all* such officers should hold *except as otherwise provided in the act*. The exception guarding against this extension is found in section 4, which declares that "nothing in this act contained shall be construed to extend the term of any office, the duration of which is limited by law." Such is one of the exceptions out of the general language of the first clause.

But there were other offices whose duration was not limited by law. Among these were the offices of those same members of the cabinet. The then members had all been appointed by Mr. Lincoln during his first term, and no limit existed upon their tenure. Mr. Johnson found them in legal possession of their offices when he became President. They had a right to continue to hold indefinitely, unless removed. Mr. Lincoln's first term had passed, and he and those cabinet officers were holding their offices in his second term.

The tenure-of-office act was passed while all these facts were immediately before Congress. They knew that Mr. Stanton, like his colleague, held by virtue of that appointment, and that he had a legal right so to continue to hold. And they declare that he "shall hold his office for and during the term of the President by whom he *may have been (not shall be)* appointed." Nothing can be plainer than that the expression "the President by whom he (they) may have been appointed," is a mere *descriptio personæ*, or mode of pointing out the person from whom the appointment proceeded.

The proviso does not say that the cabinet officers shall have been appointed *during* any particular term of the President making the appointment, but only that they shall hold their offices during his term. It does not require that the appointment shall be or shall have been made during the first, second, or any subsequent term for which the President is elected; and he may, by the Constitution, be elected an indefinite number of times. They are to hold *during his term*, if he has appointed them, and for one month thereafter, no matter whether he continues to hold his term or not. It is sufficient that it is *his term*, that is, the term "for which he was elected," in which a Secretary appointed by him is found holding the office.

No one can deny that the expression, "may have been appointed," applies as well to past time as to future time. Such is the genius of our language. It covers, grammatically, both the past and the future, as we all know from constant, daily, hourly use; and it here applies with equal and unerring certainty to appointments that had been made and were unexpired at the time it was used, and to those to be afterwards made.

Uttered on the 2d of March, 1867, the language covered, unmistakably, in my judgment, the case of Mr. Stanton and his colleagues. Their appointments were within its terms and within the purposes of the act. I do not consider there was left any room for reasonable doubt or debate. The office and aim of the proviso were to change the indefinite period to a definite period in the tenure of those offices from a tenure at the will of the President, as had been formerly understood and practiced, to a tenure that was absolutely to terminate one month after the end of the President's term by whom the appointment was or should be made.

This was another exception out of the general language of the first clause, and to remove all suspicion that the general language of the first clause "is and shall be entitled to hold such office until a successor shall have been in like manner appointed and duly qualified," might leave it still to the President alone to remove them, the proviso adds that they should be "subject to removal by and with the consent of the Senate," thus expressly requiring the consent of the Senate if removed before that time.

As to all other civil officers included in section one, they cannot be removed but upon sufficient cause, to be reported to the Senate as required by section two, and after a formal suspension. And here was another exception to the term of the tenure asserted in the general language of the first clause.

The ground now taken by the counsel for the accused is that this language, covering, as I have shown and as is perfectly manifest, both the existing and all future heads of departments, applies only to future heads, leaving the existing heads wholly unaffected by it, and that such was the intention of Congress, deducible from the act.

This construction not only denies to the words "the President by whom they may have been appointed" their natural, plain, etymological meaning and application, but is, as to those Secretaries, in direct contradiction of the first clause, which by its general language authorizes them to hold until their successors are appointed with the consent of the Senate, which was exactly their former right. It wrests from the operation of the act without any apparent motive, and against the perfectly notorious wishes of both houses of Congress, the existing heads, and applies the act to those whom Mr Johnson and his successors may appoint, and is thus totally inconsistent with the meaning and effect of the words "may have been appointed." No rule of construction is better settled than that words shall have their natural and popular meaning, unless the statute itself shall imply a different meaning, and here the statute contains no such intimation. The construction is plainly at variance with the very language.

No one will deny that the necessity of including those heads of departments was as great at least as that of including future secretaries, unknown to Congress. Why should they be left to be turned out at the will of Mr. Johnson without consulting the Senate, while their successors for all time, and all other civil officers, high and low, were protected? Why was a special exemption enacted for his benefit in reference to Mr. Lincoln's appointees whom he had continued in his cabinet for two years, and one, at least, of whom, Mr. Stanton, he was, he says, aiming to turn out? *No one can answer this question!* But if, as is contended by the President's counsel, this exception applies only to future cabinets, and does not apply at all to the then cabinet, then it follows logically and irresistibly that they fall within the first clause, which expressly declares that "every person holding any civil office to which he has been appointed by and with the consent of the Senate, and every person who shall *hereafter* be appointed to any such office and shall become duly qualified to act therein, *is* and *shall be* entitled to hold such office until a successor shall have been in like manner appointed and duly qualified."

Can this proposition be made clearer by argument? If the case of those cabinet officers is not included in the special clause or exception, it must be embraced in this. There is no escape, unless it can be made out that the words "every person holding any civil office" do not mean what they say.

But this construction is a mere afterthought with Mr. Johnson. It was too clearly untenable for Mr. Johnson to act upon it in the course of administration. His own common sense rejected it, and it makes its appearance only as the refuge of his despair at a late period.

When he suspended Mr. Stanton he had no idea of this novel construction. He then treated Mr. Stanton's case as within the act. In his message of December 12 last, he openly and frankly tells us that he had *suspended* Mr. Stanton—a term hitherto unknown to our laws, and a proceeding equally unknown in our history. Suspension was a new power created solely by this statute. He says:

On the 12th of August last I suspended Mr. Stanton from the exercise of the office of Secretary of War.

The statute says:

The President may *suspend* such officer and *designate* some suitable person, &c.

The President, still using the language of the statute, says:

On the same day I *designated* General Grant as Secretary of War *ad interim*.

But this is not all. The statute provides that the President may *revoke* such suspension; and he tells us the *suspension has not been revoked*. The statute required him to report the fact to the Senate within a given time. He did so.

All this shows conclusively that at that time he regarded Mr. Stanton as coming within the act—a sound conclusion, but directly at variance with the construction he now sets up.

Thus it appears that the exceptions to the general language "*is and shall be entitled to hold such office until a successor is in like manner appointed,*" relate to the duration of the offices of the various classes of incumbents and to the peculiar modes of removal; one mode being the immediate action of the President and Senate in case of the heads of departments; the other the preliminary suspension of all other officers by the President. The statute, it is true, nowhere asserts, in terms, the joint power of the Senate in removals, but it is easy to see that the theory upon which it goes is, that this power is lodged by the Constitution in the President and Senate jointly—the true doctrine. It was plainly assumed as a postulate by the committee who draughted the bill. They regarded it as settled doctrine needing no special recognition, though it is clearly recognized in the second section, requiring the President to report the causes of a suspension, and the action of the Senate upon them, before the suspension can result in a removal.

Such, I say, was the theory of the bill; the fundamental idea upon which it was framed was that the power of removal belonged by the Constitution to the President and the Senate, exclusively, and not to the President alone. If it belongs to the President alone, then the first section, including the proviso, and the second section, providing for a suspension before removal, are totally void for unconstitutionality, for Congress cannot meddle with a power that belongs solely to him.

Such being manifestly the theory of the bill, such the undoubted opinion of both houses, it would have been strange indeed for them to abandon the very principle upon which the bill was framed and to recognize in the proviso the odious claim of the President to exercise the sole power of removal of the then existing heads of department. It was an uncalled for renunciation of the very power under which they could act, if they could act at all, on the subject.

I cannot give any weight to the remarks made by members in debate on the passage of the tenure-of-office act. The question is now before us for *judicial* solution, and we must be governed by the language of the act and the mischief which led to its passage. We are to construe it as judges, acting on our judicial oath, not as legislative debaters. Nothing is more unsafe than to look to the legislative debates for the true judicial interpretation of a statute. They are seldom harmonious, and this case fully illustrates the truth. One honorable member of the conference committee viewed this proviso as not applicable to the existing cabinet officers, while the gentleman—Manager Williams, of Pennsylvania—who actually drew it tells us the language embraces them and that such was his intention.

A reference to two adjudged cases will probably be sufficient on the question of the value of such opinions. In Eldridge *vs.* Williams, (3 Howard's Report, pp. 23 and 24,) Chief Justice Taney observed—

In expounding this law—the compromise act of 1833—the judgment of the court cannot in *any degree*, be influenced by the construction placed upon it by members of Congress in the debate which took place on its passage, nor by the motives or reasons assigned by them for supporting or opposing amendments that were offered. The law as it passed is the will of a majority of both houses, and the only mode in which that will is spoken is in the act itself. And we must gather their intention from the language there used, comparing it when any ambiguity exists with the laws upon the same subject, and looking, if necessary, to the public history of the times in which it was passed.

In The Bank of Pennsylvania *vs.* The Commonwealth, (19 Pennsylvania State Reports, page 156,) Judge Black, one of the counsel for the accused upon this record, delivering the opinion of the court, adopts the same view. "The court," he observes, "in construing an act will not look to what occurred when it was on its passage through the legislature; such evidence is not only valueless, but delusive and dangerous."

I am, and ever have been, fully convinced of the constitutionality of the act, and that it embraces by its terms and was intended to embrace the case of Mr. Stanton; and therefore that he could not be removed by Mr. Johnson. The attempt so to do was a misdemeanor, as was the appointment of General Thomas. It is too late for Mr. Johnson to claim the benefit of any doubt that might arise upon the construction of the act. The act is too plain to admit of reasonable doubt; and that he himself entertained none is shown by the fact that he adopted and recognized the true meaning in suspending Mr. Stanton. He cannot, after the commission of the offence, set up a doubt of the correctness of his former construction of it by way of removing the criminal intent. In other words, he cannot in this tribunal insist that he is to have the benefit of being himself the judge of the law. He is brought before us that we may determine that question for him.

The next question is, whether the accused has committed the offence charged in article first of the impeachment?

That offence is that on the 21st of February, 1868, while the Senate was in session, he issued the order to Secretary Stanton, declaring in so many words that the latter was "removed" from his office of Secretary of War, and directing him to turn over the records &c., of his office to General Lorenzo Thomas, who he says, in the same letter, "has this day been authorized and empowered to act as Secretary of War *ad interim*."

Mr. Stanton did not obey, and though General Thomas made two attempts to obtain possession and failed in both, the proof is that the accused has had no official communication whatever with Mr. Stanton since that time, and that he has, on the contrary, recognized Thomas as Secretary of War until now; and further, that it is the settled purpose of Thomas still to obtain possession of the office, under a direction given him by the accused on the 21st of February, and under the order.

The charge here is not that Mr. Johnson actually and legally removed Secretary Stanton. This he could not do, either by the order or the use of force, against the will of the Secretary; for the first section of the statute protected him and prohibited such a removal. It was, in law, an impossibility. Mr. Stanton could not in law be removed without the consent of the Senate. The charge, therefore, is, that the order was issued *with intent* to remove him and contrary to the provisions of the act,—not an actual and legal ouster from and vacation of the office, although the respondent, in his answer, (p. 27,) treats the order as having that precise effect, claiming that it worked an actual and legal removal. And, so far as it has been possible for him to give it that decisive character, it was a removal; for the proof is clear and uncontradicted that he has since that time in no way whatever recognized Mr. Stanton as Secretary of War, but has recognized General Thomas.

Section six of the statute declares, that "every removal," &c., "contrary to the provisions of this act," * * "shall be deemed and is hereby taken to be a high misdemeanor," punishable by "fine not exceeding $10,000, or by imprisonment not exceeding five years," &c.

It is certain that the accused could not, by any lawful means, have removed Mr. Stanton, because the law forbade it; and the law does not sanction, much less furnish, means for its own violation; and as the law prohibited and made, criminal the end which the order of removal and appointment had in view, it prohibited and made criminal the use of any and all means for the accomplishment of that end. It rendered all acts naturally calculated, and all attempts, to commit the specific offence of "removal" criminal. The order of removal and the order appointing General Thomas were alike criminal; the delivery of the paper containing them to General Thomas on the 21st of February; the direction to him (p. 414) to deliver it to Mr. Stanton; the delivery of it to him; the direction given by the accused to General Thomas on the same day to "*go on and take charge of the office and perform the duties,*" (p. 422.) after Mr. Stanton had expressly refused to surrender it, as the accused was informed by Thomas, (p. 433;) the continued refusal of the accused to recognize Mr. Stanton officially as the lawful Secretary of War; and his open recognition of an intruder vested with no legal authority as such—these facts, fully in proof, constitute a deliberate attempt to consummate the offence of removal mentioned in section 6 of the act. He has used all the means in his power, short of actual violence, to turn Mr. Stanton out, and the proof is strong that he meditated force, should other means fail; for it is indeed a tax upon our credulity to ask us to acquit him of that purpose, while we know the unqualified direction he gave to Thomas, to "go on and take charge of the office and perform the duties," and the repeated threats of the latter to "break down the door," to "kick that fellow out," and his scheme of obtaining a military force for the purpose from General Grant. Considering the very intimate relations then and *still* existing between the accused and General Thomas, it can hardly be supposed that these high-handed proceedings, contemplating actual bloodshed, could have been wholly without the knowledge and sanction of the accused, whose feelings were wrought up to a high pitch of resentment and hatred towards Mr. Stanton.

But the proof is perfectly clear and convincing that, so far as was practicable for him, short of a violent expulsion of Mr. Stanton from his office, he had already incurred—boldly, audaciously, defiantly all the guilt of removing and putting the Secretary out of his office. And I cannot doubt that under an indictment for the specific crime of *removing* him contrary to the provisions of the act he would be held to have committed the offence. For, having done all in his power to commit it, proving by his own acts that he has, so far as he is concerned, committed it, and confessing in his plea, as he not only confesses but claims in his answer to the impeachment, (p. 27,) that his two orders actually accomplished it and installed the intruder, would not a court of justice hold that the crime was complete? Would it not hold that inasmuch as *title* to the office rests in and wholly consists of the law, that it cannot be dissolved and destroyed but in accordance with the law? and that therefore no person can be, technically and strictly speaking, "*removed*" at all by any other person so as to divest him of his title. Would it not hold that the word "removal" in the sixth section must not be construed as implying a legal divestiture of the title, as it was understood in former statutes and the old practice of the Executive, but any act, done with or without force, evincing a purpose to prevent the incumbent from holding and enjoying his office during its fixed term as provided in section four of the act, or until a successor shall have been appointed by and with the advice and consent of the Senate as provided in section one? If the word "removal" is to be taken in the sense of "amotion from office" by which the title is dissolved, then it is obvious the crime cannot be committed; for as it is the law alone that binds or attaches the office to the incumbent, the ligament cannot be severed but by the law, and no man can make or annul a law, nor, consequently, commit this technical crime of "removal."

Surely the expressions, "appointment, employment, made, had, or exercised, contrary to the provisions of this act, and the making, signing, sealing, countersigning or issuing of any commission or letter of authority for or in respect to such appointment or employment," connected with the term removal in the same section, cannot be construed as implying legal and effectual appointments, &c., but must imply mere attempts in those forms to confer the legal title to an office. It is too plain for argument that the attempt merely to confer it is punishable, not the actual, legal bestowment, which is rendered impossible by the penal clause prohibiting it, and section one, which also prohibits it.

If, then, the words "appointment," "commission," equally technical, must be construed as mere attempts to expel an officer contrary to the statute, it is equally obvious that the word "removal" must have the same meaning and effect, for if the meaning I am resisting be adopted the whole statute becomes nugatory.

The construction I am combatting makes the act self-contradictory, for while the first section says "every person shall continue to hold his office," &c., the sixth section is made practically to say that he may be removed; that is, he may be divested of the office, and lose it by a removal before the allotted time.

It seems to me, therefore, that the true practical construction to be given the term is such as I have above indicated. That such is its popular sense I need not take time to argue. What has ever been understood to be a removal from office has been nothing more than the issuing of a formal order for that purpose by some officer having or claiming, as the accused now does, to have the power, and I cannot doubt but that the offence under the statute was complete the moment the order was served on Mr. Stanton. The Senate assuredly so thought, when in their resolution of February 21, p. 148, they declared in answer to Mr. Johnson's message announcing that he had removed Mr. Stanton, "that under the Constitution and laws of the United States the President has no power to remove the Secretary of War, and designate any other officer to perform the duties of that office *ad interim*." It was that order of removal that the Senate thus condemned, as being contrary to the Constitution and laws of the United States, not the legal and actual removal of the Secretary, for we held that he was in office, notwithstanding the order, holding in virtue of the Constitution and of the tenure-of-office act of March 2, 1867.

I think, therefore, the House of Representatives might properly and legally have charged Mr. Johnson with having "removed" Mr. Stanton, describing the offence in the language of the statute, instead of charging him with having unlawfully issued the order with intent to violate the act and the further intent to remove Mr. Stanton, as is done in the first article.

The first article may, in my opinion, and should, be regarded as charging that the accused actually committed the offence of a removal from office of Mr. Stanton; for his order and other acts, in proof, are, in the popular mind, all that is meant by the term "removal" in the statute; and I therefore regard this article as framed directly upon the statute, charging that the accused removed Mr. Stanton contrary to it.

I add that, even without the statute, I look upon the act as a plain violation of the Constitution of the United States, a violation of his oath to take care that the laws be faithfully executed, and therefore an impeachable offence. Committed under the grave circumstances in evidence, I need go no further to find him guilty of the highest crime and misdemeanor he can commit, for it is an undisguised attempt to subvert the legal, constitutional, and popular character of our government—one which no true friend of the government can wink at— a step towards autocracy and absolutism—an effort to strip the Senate of all effectual power over appointments to office, and carrying with itself, if unrebuked and unpunished, imminent danger of further fundamental changes towards corruption and despotism. The power of impeachment alone is left to the people to ward off the peril and to vindicate the popular character of their government. Never, in my judgment, was there, in our country, an occasion so imperatively demanding its exercise.

But if the first article be regarded only as an *attempt* to commit the crime mentioned in the sixth section of the act, it is obviously sustainable by the rules of law. No principle is better settled than that an attempt—not, indeed, a mere intention not evinced by any act—but any act or endeavor to accomplish and bring about the commission of an offence, is itself a misdemeanor. Professor Greenleaf, in his excellent Treatise on Evidence, (vol. 3, p. 4,) lays down the principle, derived from numerous adjudged cases, that "the attempt to commit a crime, though the crime be but a misdemeanor, is itself a misdemeanor. And to constitute such an attempt there must be an intent that the crime shall be committed by some one, and an act done in pursuance of that intent."

This doctrine is fully sustained by the following English and American cases: Reg. vs. Meredith, 8 C., and P. 589; Rex vs. Higgins, 2 E., 5, 17; 21; Commonwealth vs. Harrington, 3 Pick., 26; Rex vs. Vaughan, 4 Burr., 2494; State vs. Avery, 7 Conn., 266.

Many other cases might be cited affirming the same salutary doctrine. Mr. Russell, in his Treatise on Crimes, (vol. 1, pp. 45–'6,) lays down the same doctrine, and it is of daily application in the administration of justice.

Commenting upon and vindicating it from doubts and objections, Lord Kenyon said in one of the cases cited that he regarded a denial of it as a "slander upon the law."

Did, then, Mr. Johnson cherish the intention to turn Mr. Stanton out of office contrary to the provisions of the act? In his answer he tells us that he did, and that he issued the orders in question with that intent. The other acts of his, not evidenced in writing, prove the same thing. He entertained that intention and did those acts, tending to and designed for that sole purpose, in order to remove Mr. Stanton from his office against his will and contrary to the plain commands of the law.

There can be but one conclusion. He incurred the guilt, and under the first article I therefore pronounce him guilty, whether the article he regarded as founded directly upon the statute or as charging the common law misdemeanor of attempting to commit the statutory offence.

The second article of the impeachment charges the accused with having issued and delivered to General Thomas the order of February 21, authorizing and empowering him to act as Secretary of War *ad interim*, and directing him "immediately to enter upon the discharge of the duties pertaining to that office," there being no vacancy in the office.

This was too plainly to be debated, a "letter of authority" to Thomas, and an obvious violation of the sixth section of the tenure-of-office act. No one can doubt it. The section provides that the "making, signing, sealing, countersigning or issuing of any * * * letter of authority"—not conferring the office but—"for or in respect to any such appointment or employment, shall be deemed and is hereby declared to be a high misdemeanor."

This was an open, deliberate, undisguised commission of the offence; and if this statute is not totally void and inoperative for unconstitutionality, mere waste paper, the accused must be found guilty under this article.

The idea, so strongly pressed upon us by the counsel for the accused, that this letter of authority as well as the order removing Mr. Stanton are to be treated as innocent acts, on the pretence that they were done merely to obtain the decision of the Supreme Court as to the constitutionality of the statute, is out of place on this trial. Notwithstanding such intention, if it existed, the offence was nevertheless actually committed, and the sole issue the Senate has to try is whether it was in fact knowingly committed, not whether the motives that led to it were one thing or another. To excuse or justify the intelligent commission of an offence on the ground that the motive was good would be monstrous indeed. It would be to set aside the whole penal code at once and permit every bad man and many good men to be judges in their own case. Society could not exist under such a puerile and capricious system. Besides, this motive, which the evidence places rather in the light of an after-thought than a ruling design accompanying and coeval with his resolution to remove Mr. Stanton, was properly to be addressed to the House of Representatives in order to prevent the finding of the impeachment. It was, if of any weight at all, matter of mitigation and excuse for committing the offence, and naturally addressed itself to the discretion of that body upon the question whether upon the whole it was worth while to bring him to trial; for surely it has no tendency to prove that he did not knowingly and wilfully commit the offence. We cannot, therefore, sitting in our judicial capacity and acting on our oath to decide "according to law," give this pretence any weight in determining the issue.

The House had the constitutional right to bring the accused before us for trial. We are to try him according to the law and the evidence which the law makes applicable; and the House and the people in whose behalf they come before us have a right to demand of us that he shall be so tried; and our own oath makes it equally imperative upon us.

The third article charges that Mr. Johnson issued the order to General Thomas without authority of law while the Senate was in session, no vacancy having happened during the recess of the Senate, with intent to violate the Constitution of the United States.

This article distinctly raises the question whether, while the Senate is in session and not in recess, the President can lawfully under the Constitution appoint to an office without the advice and consent of the Senate.

I have already shown that under the naked Constitution he cannot do this, and that the attempt is a violation of his oath.

But the tenure-of-office act forbids it, by declaring in the first section that an officer appointed by and with the advice and consent of the Senate "shall be entitled to hold his office until a successor shall have been in like manner appointed and duly qualified."

This provision of course renders Thomas's appointment unlawful, for there cannot be two incumbents lawfully in possession of the office of Secretary of War at the same time.

But it is sufficient under this article to say that the Constitution itself prohibited this appointment of Thomas, for the President could not make it during the session of the Senate without their advice and consent. It was a wilful attempt to usurp the powers of the Senate, and therefore a gross violation of a high public duty attached to him by his oath of office, and a high crime tending towards and designed to accomplish a fundamental and dangerous revolution of the government in this respect.

The design here was to pass the office absolutely into the hands of Thomas for him to hold for an indefinite period of time, and independently, and to enable him to exercise all its functions as freely as if he had held a formal commission with the consent of the Senate; and the useless Latin phrase *ad interim* imparts to the act no qualification and imposes no restraint on his powers. Under the then existing circumstances no temporary appointment could be made. There was no law whatever that provided for it. Mr. Stanton was not absent but present in the office; he was not disabled by sickness but was in full health; he had not resigned but had refused to do so; he was not dead but alive. And it is impossible to see what magic significance was attached, or could be attached, to the words *ad interim*. If the appointment made Thomas Secretary of War, as the accused claims, then his tenure was at the President's pleasure and he needed no confirmation, and was to hold until turned out by him; no law forbade it, and the Constitution, as construed by Mr. Johnson, allowed it.

I cannot, therefore, hesitate to find him guilty under the third article.

The fourth, fifth, sixth, and seventh articles charge substantially but one offence—that of conspiring with Thomas unlawfully to prevent Mr. Stanton from remaining in the office of Secretary of War and exercising its functions, and unlawfully to seize and get possession of the property of the United States in the office.

I think this corrupt and unlawful agreement between Mr. Johnson and Thomas is fully made out by the evidence. The averment of the means by which the object was to be accomplished—whether by force, fraud or intimidation—is not material. It is the agreement entered into between them to do the *unlawful act*—to accomplish the forbidden end—that constitutes the crime. And it is not easy to see how this agreement could be more clearly proved. The delivery of the letter of authority to Thomas, and his acceptance of the same; the delivery to him of the order removing Mr. Stanton and the delivery thereof by Thomas to Mr. Stanton; the demand made by Thomas for possession; Mr. Stanton's peremptory refusal and order to Thomas to depart; his written order to Thomas, forbidding him to issue any orders as Secretary of War; the report of this demand and refusal and prohibitory order made by Thomas to Mr. Johnson, and the deliberate direction given by the latter, after hearing this report from Thomas, to "go on and take charge of the office and perform its duties,"—all which things happened on the 21st of February—and the second, and menacing, demand for the office by Thomas on the next day—all show, as clearly as human conduct can show, that just such an agreement was entered into by the accused and Thomas.

And it is made perfectly clear by the evidence that, but for the resolute firmness of Mr. Stanton, that agreement would have been carried into complete performance, and all the public property belonging to the office seized and possessed by Thomas, a mere intruder. I therefore find the accused guilty under the fourth, fifth, sixth, and seventh articles of the impeachment.

The eighth article differs from the second and third only in the averment that the order appointing Thomas was issued "with intent unlawfully to control the disbursements of moneys appropriated for the military service and for the Department of War."

I think such an intention fully made out by the proofs. General Thomas himself swears in his direct examination (page 414) that when the accused appointed him he remarked that he (Mr. Johnson) was "determined to support the Constitution and laws." This was a very gratuitous, idle remark, unless it implied a design to do something unusual, some dash against the legislation of Congress, which he so much disliked, and was, of course, uttered with reference to the tenure-of-office act, which was the only means by which Mr. Stanton kept the place he then designed to give to Thomas. He was resolved to "support," &c., against this act, and the declaration was an invitation to Thomas to aid him in trampling on that statute.

On his cross-examination (page 432) General Thomas swears the President said in this interview, "I shall uphold the Constitution and the laws, and I expect you to do the same;" and adds, "I said, certainly, I would do it, and *would obey his orders.*"

This, he says, was, as he supposes, "very natural, speaking to his commander-in-chief."

I think not. To my mind, this strange colloquy, which could not have taken place but in pursuance of Johnson's unlawful and audacious design, a design well understood by Thomas, evinces unmistakably, on the part of Thomas, the supple and reckless spirit of a dependant and flatterer, ready and willing to obey the slightest signal of the hand that feeds him. It is an assurance to Johnson that he is his tool, and will obey his wishes in all things. Contrast this low sycophancy with the manly and soldierly demeanor of General Emory when he repelled the suggestion of Mr. Johnson that he should accept orders from him directly, and that the requirement of the act of 1863 to send them through the General of the army was unconstitutional and contrary to the terms of his commission! The contrast is indeed striking. Thomas is already debauched, and bows pliantly to the will of a master! and had he got possession of the War Office no one can doubt for a moment that he would have disbursed the moneys of the department in obedience to Johnson's orders. Of course, the employment of such a person would effectually subject the public moneys to the will of the employer; and there seems to be no other reason or motive for employing him except to give such control to the accused. He is not so ignorant as not to have foreseen, from all he heard and observed at that critical moment, that a military force would have to be employed and paid in order to carry out his design of ejecting Mr. Stanton and getting control of his office; and he claimed the right to control it in all respects. Such a provision naturally and necessarily suggested to his designing mind the acquisition of money to pay the expenses of the tremendous experiment he meditated; and I cannot doubt that the employment of Thomas, willing as he was *to obey Mr. Johnson's orders*, had, in direct object the control of those moneys. I therefore find him guilty under the eighth article.

As to the ninth article, I do not think the proof sufficiently clear to justify me in saying that the accused pronounced the act of 1863, requiring him to transmit all orders through the General of the army, unconstitutional, "*with intent* thereby to induce said Emory, in his official capacity as commander of the department of Washington, to violate the provisions of said act, and to take and receive, act upon and obey," the orders of Mr. Johnson not thus transmitted. The conduct of Mr. Johnson towards General Emory was highly censurable; but I do not think that particular intention is fully made out. The evidence raises a suspicion that such may have been the case, but is consistent with the supposition of the absence of such an intention, and the doubt must go to the benefit of the accused.

As to the tenth article, the evidence is conclusive that the accused made the popular harangues therein set forth. The essence of the charge is that these discourses were "intended to set aside the rightful authority and powers of Congress, and to bring the Congress of the United States into disgrace, ridicule, hatred, contempt, and reproach, and to destroy the regard and respect of all the people of the United States for their authority."

Mr. Johnson was the lawful President of the United States; one of his sworn duties was to "take care that the laws be faithfully executed." The thirty-ninth Congress was a lawful Congress, as much so as any that ever sat. They were elected by exactly the same constituency who elected Mr. Johnson Vice-President in 1864. Under their legislation the rebellion was put down, and Mr. Johnson himself, as military governor of Tennessee, had aided actively in carrying it out, and had had the benefit of the joint resolution of February, 1865, excluding from the count of electoral votes for President and Vice-President those cast in certain of the States in rebellion. It did not, therefore, lie in his mouth to deny, directly or indirectly, that the thirty-ninth Congress was a valid, constitutional Congress. None but such as contended that the government was broken up by the secession and rebellion of the eleven States—that is, none but a traitor, could consistently and decently make such a declaration. And yet he says, in his 18th of August speech, (referred to in the first specification,) made in the Executive Mansion, and addressed to the honorable senator from Maryland (Mr. Johnson) and others, and without rebuke or reply from that learned senator, "We have seen hanging upon the verge of the government, as it were, a body called, or which assumes to be, the Congress of the United States, while, in fact, it is a Congress of only a part of the States;" plainly intimating that that Congress had no power to pass laws for the government of the rebel States, and were, in fact and in law, incompetent to legislate for the whole country; a doctrine that openly encouraged sedition and disobedience to the laws in at least those States, if not in all others—the laws which he alone, of all the people of the United States, was expressly bound by oath and the Constitution to see "faithfully executed." Suppose a judge of a State court, charged with administering the laws, should go about among the people and tell them thus openly in public speech that the legislation of the State was no legislation—that their laws were all void, and that the citizens were not under obligation to obey them—would not the power of impeachment be at once brought to bear upon him? And why? Because, entertaining such opinions, he desecrates his office, and is therefore UNFIT longer to remain in it. Did we not sustain the impeachment against Judge Humphreys, of Tennessee, for that which was the exact equivalent of this charge, namely, inculcating in a public speech the right of secession from the Union and of rebellion? What did he say, but that the government of the United States was in law no government for the seceded States? He had committed no act of treason, and the only proof was that he had thus spoken. And we convicted and removed him because he had thus spoken.

The second and third specifications contain like matter. The vulgar harangues therein recited are in denial of the legal constitutional validity of the statutes passed by the 39th Congress, and tend directly to excite sedition and insubordination to, and disobedience of, those laws, the speaker being himself specially and solely charged by the Constitution with the official duty of taking care that those laws shall be "faithfully executed." He assumes a position in direct antagonism to his oath and his duty. He himself was setting the example of disobedience to the laws, and encouraging others to imitate his wicked example. Does the law impose no responsibility for wanton conduct like this? May a public magistrate deny, contemn, and deride the duties of his office with impunity? His counsel say yes. I say no. Society must be protected by law, and in order that that protection may exist the laws must be respected by those charged with their execution, not aspersed and trampled upon.

No question of the "freedom of speech" arises here. It is not because he speaks scoffingly and contemptuously of Congress as a body; not because he dissents from their legislation merely and expresses that dissent; not because he utters against them the false and malicious calumny that the New Orleans riot, which he calls "another rebellion," "had its origin in the radical Congress;" not because he descends to the low business of lying about and scandalizing them, that the House has preferred this article against him, but because he inculcates the idea that their statutes are no laws and not to be respected by the people as laws, and because he openly threatens (in his St. Louis speech) to "kick them out; to kick them out just as fast as he can;" thus distinctly conveying the threat to use revolutionary violence against that Congress and to disperse them. It was an open threat to commit treason. And yet his counsel tell us that it was innocent and harmless.

To my mind the tenth article charges one of the gravest offences contained in the impeachment. The feelings of the whole country were shocked and disgusted by the lawless speeches of this bully President. Men and women all over the land hung their heads in shame, and the wise and reflecting saw in him a coarse, designing, and dangerous tyrant.

I vote him guilty under the tenth article, and under each of the three specifications.

As to the eleventh article, it charges in substance that he attempted to prevent the execution of the tenure-of-office act, by unlawfully devising means to prevent Mr. Stanton from resuming the functions of his office, and to prevent the execution of the said clause in the appropriation act of 1867, and the reconstruction act of March 2, 1867.

In finding him guilty under this whole article I only consult his official record, his official history, and the other facts clearly in proof. His whole policy has been that the reconstruction act was both improper and unconstitutional, and he has detested the thirty-ninth and fortieth Congresses, because they have been of an opposite opinion. This trouble has grown out of his determination to govern the rebel States by his executive decrees in defiance of the wishes of the people of the United States expressed through the legislation of Congress; in other words, to be himself the ruling power in this regard. This is usurpation and tyranny, and I think it ought to be thus met and branded. Our position as the first free nation of the world demands it at our hands; and whatever may chance to be the result of this trial, whatever may be the future fortunes of those who are now sitting in judgment, I can desire no better authenticated claim to the free and enlightened approval of future ages than that I gave my vote against him on this article; nor do I think myself capable of any act that would shed greater honor on my posterity than thus to endeavor to vindicate for them and their posterity the rights of a free and independent people governing themselves within the limits of their own free Constitution.

OPINION OF MR. SENATOR JOHNSON.

Time does not permit an examination in detail of the several articles of impeachment. I content myself, therefore, with considering the legal questions upon which the most of them depend.

I. For what can the President be impeached? If the power was given without assigning the causes, it is obvious that he would be almost wholly dependent upon Congress, and that was clearly not designed. The Constitution consequently provides that impeachment can only be for "treason, bribery, or other high crimes and misdemeanors." For no act which does not fall within the legal meaning of those terms can impeachment be maintained. Political opinions, whatever they may be, when not made crimes or misdemeanors, are not the subjects of the power. If any such opinions can be legally declared crimes or misdemeanors, what are spoken, no matter by whom, when no force is used disturbing the public peace, certainly cannot be, such legislation being prohibited, not only by reason of the absence of any delegated authority to Congress, but because that department is expressly prohibited from so legislating by the very terms of the first of the amendments of the Constitution, providing that "Congress shall make no law" "abridging the freedom of speech." This guarantee extends to every citizen, whether he be in public or private life. Whatever a private citizen can say without responsibility to Congress, the President or any other official can say. The provision is intended to secure such freedom to all without regard to official station. The right is a personal one, for the exercise of which there is no responsibility. It is secured as absolutely to every person as the right of freedom of speech is secured to members of Congress by the sixth section of the first article of the Constitution, which says that "for any speech or debate in either house they shall not be questioned in any other place." Both provisions are upon the theory, proved to be correct by history, that a free government is ever best maintained (if indeed it can be maintained without it) by such unfettered freedom. Its possession by others than members of Congress is a necessary restraint upon that department, whilst its possession by its members is equally necessary to a proper exercise of their power. In both instances the right is placed beyond restraint.

If members of Congress in debate assail the President in disparaging and vituperative language—if they charge him with treason—a violation of every duty—a want of every virtue, and with every vice; if they even charge him with having been accessory to the murder of his lamented predecessor—charges calculated to bring him "into disgrace," "hatred," "contempt, and reproach"—they are exempt from responsibility by any legal proceeding, because "freedom of speech and debate" is their right—how can it be that the President is responsible for the speeches alleged to have been made by him at the places and times referred to in the tenth and eleventh articles, when freedom of speech is equally secured to him? That such speeches, whether made by members of Congress or the President, are in bad taste, and tend to disturb the harmony which should prevail between the two departments of the government, may be conceded, but there is no law making them crimes or misdemeanors. This was attempted to be done, as far as printed publications were concerned, by the second section of the act of the 14th of July, 1798, (the sedition act.) The constitutionality of that law was denied by many of the most eminent men of the day, and the party which passed it was driven from power by an overwhelming majority of the people of the country, upon the ground that it palpably violated the Constitution. By its own terms, it was to continue but for a brief period, and no one in or out of Congress has ever suggested its revival. But the passage of the act proves that without such a law oral speeches or written publications in regard to any department of the government are not criminal offences.

If these views be sound, the articles which charge the President with having committed a high misdemeanor by the speeches made in Washington, St. Louis, and Cleveland, in 1862, are not supported—first, because there is no law which makes them misdemeanors; and, second, because if there was any such law it would be absolutely void.

II. That the terms crimes and misdemeanors in the quoted clause mean legal crimes and misdemeanors (if there could be any doubt upon the point) is further obvious from the provision in the third section of the first article of the Constitution, that, notwithstanding the judgment on impeachment, the party is liable to "indictment, trial, judgment, and punishment according to law." This proves that an officer can only be impeached for acts for which he is liable to a criminal prosecution. Whatever acts, therefore, could not be criminally prosecuted under the general law cannot be the grounds of an impeachment. Nor is this doctrine peculiar to the United States. It was held in the case of the impeachment of Lord Melville, as far back as 1806, and has never since been judicially controverted in England. The charges in that case were the alleged improper withdrawal and use of public funds intrusted to him as treasurer of the navy. By the managers it was contended that these were by law crimes and misdemeanors, and denied by his lordship's counsel. The impeachment evidently turned upon the decision of the question. The opinion of the judges was requested by the House of Lords, and their answer was, that they were not crimes or misdemeanors, and his lordship, on a vote, in the aggregate upon all the articles, of 1,350, was acquitted by a majority of 824.

III. Are, then, the acts alleged in the first eight articles crimes and misdemeanors?

1. Are they so independent of the actual intent with which they were done?
2. If not, are they without criminality because of such actual intent?

I. The acts charged are the orders of the President of the 21st of February, 1868, removing Mr. Stanton as Secretary of War, and appointing General Thomas as Secretary *ad interim*. The President's authority for the first, his counsel contend, is vested in him by the Constitution, and not subject to the power of Congress; and that if it was, and Congress had a right to pass the act of the 2d of March, 1867, "regulating the tenure of certain civil offices," that act did not take from him the power to remove Mr. Stanton. I will consider the second question first. What, then, in regard to Mr. Stanton is the true construction of that act? Did it leave the President's right to remove him as he possessed it before the act was passed? With all respect to the contrary opinion, I think that it clearly did.

Without referring now to the different views entertained by the House of Representatives and the Senate as to the propriety of including cabinet officers within the restriction which the law imposes upon the President in relation to other civil officers, it seems to me to be perfectly clear, from the language of the act itself, that Mr. Stanton's case is not within such restriction. In the first place, the title of the act is the regulation of the tenure of *certain* (not of *all*) civil offices. In the second, the tenure prescribed in the body of the first section is, that every person holding a civil office under an appointment made by the President, with the advice and consent of the Senate, and who has duly qualified, is to hold his office until his successor shall in like manner be appointed and qualified. If the law stopped here, the cabinet would be embraced and hold by the same tenure. But from this tenure certain exceptions are made. The concluding part of the section is in these words: "except as herein otherwise provided." These latter words mean the same thing as if they were in the beginning, instead of the close of the section. Place them in the beginning and no one could doubt their meaning.

It would then be clear that it was not the purpose to prescribe the tenure of all officers appointed by the President with the consent of the Senate, and that in regard to some a different one was to be provided. If this be right, and I do not see that it can be questioned, it follows that whatever tenure is differently prescribed as to other offices, these are not to be held by the tenure in the first section. Immediately succeeding the words of exception before quoted, follows the provision to which the exception refers, "that the Secretaries of State, of the Treasury, of War, of the Navy, and of the Interior, the Postmaster General, and the Attorney General," are to hold by a different tenure from that before defined. And this is, that they are to "hold their offices respectively for and during the term of the President by whom they may have been appointed, and for one month thereafter," subject, of course, to removal by the President, with the approval of the Senate. That this proviso withdraws the offices specially enumerated from the operation of the enacting clause cannot be doubted. It has the same effect in this regard as if it had been the first section of the act instead of a proviso to that section. If it had been itself the first section, and what is now the first section without the proviso had been the second, then all would admit that the tenure of office provided by the first section as it stands would have nothing to do with the tenure of cabinet officers. In other words, that it was the object of the act to assign to these offices a tenure entirely distinct from that assigned to other civil offices.

The only inquiry that remains is, what is the tenure by which cabinet officers hold their places? That they are not to hold them for an unlimited period is evident. What, then, is the limitation of their title?

I. It commences, necessarily, with the date of their appointments.

II. It expires at "the end of the term of the President by whom they may have been appointed," and one month thereafter. Mr. Stanton was appointed by President Lincoln during his first term, by and with the advice and consent of the Senate. By virtue of that appointment, and by that alone, he was commissioned. He never received any other appointment or commission. If the act of the 2d of March, 1867, had passed during Mr. Lincoln's first term, and was constitutional, Mr. Stanton's term of office would have expired at the end of one month succeeding the termination of Mr. Lincoln's first term, with no other right afterwards to the office than in the nature of a tenancy at sufferance.

The title which he could claim under the act of 1867 has long since ended. To enable him to hold the office against the wish of the President, by whom he was not appointed, in my judgment, would be a palpable violation of the law, equally inconsistent with its language and its object. Inconsistent with its language, because that says that the office is to be held "for and during the term of the President by whom" he was appointed, and Mr. Lincoln's term necessarily terminated with his life. Inconsistent with its object, because that clearly is to leave a President who comes into office at the termination, by whatever cause, of the term of his predecessor, the unfettered right at the end of one month after such termination to select his own cabinet.

If the propriety (conceding Congress to have the power) be admitted of denying to the President the right exercised by all of his predecessors of removing a cabinet officer at pleasure, it would seem to be most improper and impolitic in regard to any such officer not appointed by himself. Responsible for the preservation of the Constitution, and the faithful executions of the laws, nothing could be more unjust and unwise than to force upon him a cabinet in whom he might have no confidence whatever, either for want of integrity or capacity, or both, and in whose selection he had no choice.

III. If there could be any doubt that the construction I give to the act is correct, it would be removed by the explanation of Senators Sherman and Williams, members of the committee of conference on the part of the Senate, when making their report. The Senate had by two votes decided that cabinet officers should, as always before, hold their places at the pleasure of the President, and that such was evidently the design of Congress when organizing the several departments. The Senate, therefore, excluded them altogether from the provisions of the bill; but the House insisted upon including them. It was this difference between the two houses which the conference committee was appointed to settle. In making the report, Mr. Sherman stated that to include them would in his opinion be practically unimportant, because "*No gentleman, no man with any sense of honor, would hold a position as a cabinet officer after his chief desired his removal; and, therefore, the slightest intimation on the part of the President would always secure*" his resignation. And he added, that by the proposition of the committee, such an officer would hold "*his office during the life or the term of the President who appointed him*," and that "*if the President dies the cabinet goes out; if the President is removed for cause by impeachment, the cabinet goes out; at the expiration of the term of the President's office the cabinet goes out; so that the government will not be embarrassed by an attempt by a cabinet officer to hold on to his office despite the wish of the President or a change in the presidency.*" And that this provision obviated "*the great danger that might have arisen from the bill as it stood amended by the House.*"

Mr. Williams said that the House by its amendment had placed "the heads of departments on the same footing with other civil officers, and provided that they should not at any time be removed without the advice and consent of the Senate;" that this was objected to, *because when* "*a new President came into office he might be compelled to have a cabinet not of his own selection;*" and that the amendment proposed by the committee was, "*that when the term of office expires the offices of the members of the cabinet shall also expire,*" at the end of one month thereafter. He further added, that "the report of the committee is intended to put the heads of departments upon the same footing with all the other officers named in the bill, *with this exception, that their terms shall expire when the term of office of the President by whom they were appointed expires; that is the effect of the provision*" Relying upon these statements, the Senate adopted the report of the committee, and the bill passed with the proviso. No senator intimated that these gentlemen had not placed a proper construction upon the proviso and consequently no senator suggested that the then members of the cabinet of the President who were not appointed by him, but by Mr. Lincoln, were either within the protection of the body of the section or of the proviso, and I do not think I am mistaken in the impression that the bill could not have been passed by the Senate without the understanding that Messrs. Sherman and Williams were right in their interpretation of it.

It also appears by the President's message of the 12th of December, 1867, given in evidence by the managers, that it was construed in the same way by every member of the cabinet, Mr. Stanton included. That gentleman being appointed by Mr. Lincoln and not by Mr. Johnson, his tenure of office ended one month succeeding the death of the former. In the language of Mr. Sherman, when the President who appoints a cabinet officer "dies," the officer "goes out." How, then, can the Senate convict the President of having criminally violated the act in question, when what he did in relation to Mr. Stanton was not within the prohibition of the act, according to the interpretation put upon it at the time it was being passed by the Senate itself; and yet this they will do if they find him guilty upon the articles which relate to his attempt to remove Mr. Stanton on the 21st of February, 1868.

IV. Did the President commit a crime or misdemeanor by his order of the 21st of February, 1868, appointing General Thomas Secretary *ad interim?* That appointment forms the subject of the charges in the second, third, and eighth articles. If I am right, that Mr. Stanton was, not within the protection of the act of 1867, and could be removed at pleasure by the President, then the legal effect of his order of the 21st of February worked a removal, and of course made a vacancy in that department.

There being a vacancy, had not the President a right to fill it by an *ad interim* appointment? If he had, the articles in question are unsupported. 1. Independent of legislation, the President being, with a few exceptions, vested with the executive power of the government and responsible for the faithful execution of the laws, he must have the power by implication to provide against their temporary failure. And if this be so, then, upon the occurrence of a vacancy in office, which, if not at once supplied, will cause such a failure, he must have the right to guard against it. 2. But there is legislation which, in my judgment, clearly gives him the power to make the appointment.

On the contingency " of the death, absence from the seat of government, or sickness of the Secretary of State, Secretary of the Treasury, or of the Secretary of War," &c., the President, by the act of the 8th of May, 1792, section eighth, was authorized to appoint any person or persons to perform the duties of the said offices respectively "until a successor be appointed, or until such absence or inability by sickness shall cease."

This act provided for a vacancy caused by death in either of the three departments named, and not for one produced by any other cause. A vacancy, therefore, arising from resignation or removal or expiration of term of office was not provided for. The omission was supplied by the act of the 13th of February, 1795, which gives the President the same authority in the case of a vacancy, however produced. Like the act of 1792, it is confined to the State, Treasury, and War Departments, and differs from it in limiting the authority to a period of six months succeeding the vacancy. Both laws left unprovided for vacancies occurring in the other departments. But it appears by the evidence that such appointments were made by all the predecessors of Mr. Johnson in the departments not included within the acts referred to, as well as in those that were included. And there is nothing to show that their validity was at any time questioned by Congress. On such an appointment by President Buchanan of Judge Holt to the War Department, made during the session of the Senate, a resolution was passed calling upon him to state the authority under which he acted. This he did by the message of January 15, 1861. In that message many instances are mentioned of appointments of the kind in all the departments, as well during the session as in the recess of the Senate; and from that time to this impeachment the authority of the President had been considered established.

For the appointment of Thomas, then, the President had the example of all of his predecessors.

To hold that he committed a crime or misdemeanor in making it would, I think, shock a proper sense of justice, and impute to every President, from Washington to Lincoln, offences for which they should have been impeached and removed from office. Such an imputation could not fail to meet the severe rebuke and condemnation of the country. But it is said that the act of 1795 was repealed by that of the 20th of February, 1863. This seems to me a palpable error. That act contains no words of express repeal, nor even of reference to the one of 1795.

If it does repeal that act, it is only because its provisions are so inconsistent with it that the two cannot in any particular stand together. If they can, upon a well settled rule of interpretation, they must so stand. Are they so inconsistent that this cannot be done? 1. The legal presumption is that Congress, when they passed the latter act, had the former one before them, and that they intended only to repeal the former in the particulars for which the latter provides. The policy of such legislation was adopted in 1789 by the act organizing the several departments. By the second section of the one relating to the War Department, (and the same provision is made as to the other departments,) on the removal from office by the President of the Secretary, or a vacancy arising from any cause, the chief clerk was to have charge and custody of all the papers, &c., of the office. It was also adopted in 1792, 1795, and 1863, and is in words recognized by the eighth section of the act of the 2d of March, 1867, itself, in the provision that "whenever the President shall, without the advice and consent of the Senate, designate, authorize, or employ any person to perform the duties of any office," he shall inform the Secretary of the Treasury. This provision evidently implies that the President had the right to make such an appointment, and subject it to no other qualification (and that was unnecessary, as it was always done before) than that he advise the Secretary.

This policy is not only conducive, but absolutely necessary to the good of the public service. The act of 1863 does not embrace the case of vacancy arising from removal or expiration of term. These two cases, therefore, if the act of 1795 is not in force, and the President has not the power independent of legislation, are without remedy, and the office, although the event may occur the day after the termination of a Congress, must remain in abeyance, and all business connected with it so remain until the commencement of a succeeding Congress, which, when the act of 1863 was passed, would have been a period of eight months. The disastrous condition in which this might place the country is of itself sufficient to prove that the act of 1795, by which such a condition would be averted, was not intended to be repealed by the one of 1863. And this court, as well as any other court before whom the question may arise, is bound to rule against such an appeal.

V. Thus far I have considered the act of 1867 as constitutional. I will now examine that question. As regards this case, the inquiry is only material upon the assumption (which I have endeavored to show is unfounded) that Mr. Stanton was within the act so as to deprive the President of the power to remove him. Is the act constitutional? The Constitution is framed upon the theory (the correctness of which no political student will deny) that a free constitutional government cannot exist without a separation of legislative, executive, and judicial powers, and that the complete success of such a separation depends upon the absolute independence of each. Under this conviction, the legislative department, within the limits of its delegated powers, is made supreme; and the executive department, with a few exceptions, not necessary to be mentioned, is also made supreme; and the same is true of the judicial department.

The object of the supremacy of each would be defeated if either were subordinate to the others. To avoid this each must necessarily have the right of self-protection. This is obvious. To put it in the power of the Executive to defeat constitutional laws passed by Congress in due form would be to destroy the independence of that department; and to put it in the power of Congress to take away or limit the constitutional powers of the Executive would likewise be to destroy the complete independence of that department. How, then, are they to maintain their respective rights? To submit would be to abandon them, and be a violation of duty. If the Executive interferes with the rightful authority of Congress, that body must defend itself; and for this purpose it may resort to impeachment, if the interference be a high crime and misdemeanor.

I. Has the President, by the Constitution, the power to remove officers apppointed with the advice of the Senate? Whatever doubts were originally entertained upon the point, the power is too firmly established to be shaken, if a constitutional question can be settled by the authority of time and precedent. It was clearly held to exist when the departments were established in 1789 by the laws creating them, and by the congressional debates of the day. Until lately this was conceded. Every commentator upon the Constitution has so stated. The Supreme Court of the United States have also so held.

In a letter of Mr. Madison to Edward Coles, of the 15th of October, 1834, (4 Madison's Writings, 368,) in referring to the question of the right of the Senate to participate in removals, that distinguished statesman writes thus:

The claim on CONSTITUTIONAL ground to a share in the removal as well as appointment of officers is in direct opposition to the uniform practice of the government from its commencement. It is clear that the innovation would not only vary essentially the existing balance of power, but expose the Executive, occasionally, to a total inaction, and, at all times to delays fatal to the due execution of the laws.

And on the 16th of February, 1835, in a speech in the Senate, Mr. Webster, whilst questioning the correctness of the decision of '89, says:

I do not mean to deny "that at the present moment the President may remove these officers at will, because the early decision adopted that construction, and the laws have since uniformly sanctioned it."

If any supposed doubtful constitutional question can be conclusively solved, is not this so solved? Mr. Madison, in his message of January 30, 1815, adverting to the power of Congress to incorporate a Bank of the United States, which he, whilst a member of Congress, with great ability had denied, said he waived the question as "precluded in (his) judgment by repeated recognitions under varied circumstances of the validity of such an institution in acts of the legislative, executive, and judicial branches of the government." Are not these observations even more applicable to the present question than to the one before him?

VI. Admitting, however, for argument sake, that I am in error as to the construction of the act of the 2d of March, 1867, or its constitutionality, this can hardly be disputed—that differences of opinion in regard to each may be honestly entertained. Conceding this, it necessarily follows that there can be no criminality in the holding of either opinion. The President thought and still thinks, as he tells us, that Mr. Stanton is not so within the act as to be beyond his right to remove him; or, if he is, that the act in that respect is unconstitutional. As to the first, he has the express sanction of Senators Williams and Sherman, announced when the law was being passed, and the implied sanction of every member of the Senate who voted for it, without questioning the construction given to it by the two senators. And as to the second, he has the sanction of the doctrine established in 1789, and acted upon by every one of his predecessors from Washington to Lincoln—admitted as established by Mr. Webster in 1835, and vindicated as essential to the public service by Mr. Madison in 1834. Entertaining these opinions, what were his rights and his duty?

If by the Constitution the power of removal was vested in him, he was bound by the very terms of his official oath to maintain it. Not to have done so would have been to violate the obligation of that oath to "preserve, protect, and defend the Constitution." But two courses were left open to him—that of forcible resistance, or of a resort to the judiciary. The first might have produced civil commotion, and that he is proved never to have contemplated. The judicial department of the government was established for the very purpose, among others, of deciding such a question, it being given jurisdiction in "all cases in law and equity arising under (the) Constitution." It was to this tribunal that the evidence shows that he intended to resort. Was that a crime? He believed, and had a right to believe, that the constitutional authority of the Executive was violated by the act, if Mr. Stanton was protected by it; and he sought to have that question peaceably settled by the judgment of the very tribunal created for such a purpose. And there was no one else who could appeal to it with that view. It was the authority of the executive department of the government, not any individual right of his own, which was assailed. He, and no one else, represented that department and could institute legal proceedings for its vindication. This, therefore, was not only his right, but his sworn duty. The doctrine that the President is forced to execute any statute that Congress may pass according to the forms of law, upon subjects not only not within their delegated powers, but expressly denied to them, is to compel him to abandon his office and submit all its functions to the unlimited control of Congress, and thus defeat the very object of its creation.

Such a doctrine has no support in the Constitution, and would, in the end, be its destruction.

It has been contended on the part of the managers that the President has no right to question the constitutionality of an act of Congress, because of his duty faithfully to execute the laws. But what is the law which he is to execute, if the act is in conflict with the Constitution? Is not that also a law? The Constitution declares it not only to be one, but to be the supreme law, and prescribes no such supremacy to acts of Congress, except to such as are passed in "pursuance thereof." The execution, therefore, by him of an act not passed in pursuance of the Constitution, but in violation of it, instead of being a duty would be a breach of his sworn obligation to preserve the Constitution. Nor is there any inconsistency between his duty to protect the Constitution, and to see to the faithful execution of the laws; the Constitution itself prohibiting the enactment of any law which it does not authorize Congress to pass. Were it otherwise the Constitution might become a dead letter, as its effect from time to time would depend upon Congress; in other words, that body would be the government, possessing practically all powers, legislative, executive, and judicial, a result clearly destructive of liberty.

VII. Each of the articles charged that the enumerated acts were done by the President "with intent" "to violate" the acts of Congress specially mentioned, and were "contrary to the provisions of the Constitution," and that he was therefore "guilty of a high misdemeanor in office."

The alleged offences, then, are made to consist of acts and intent. The latter is as material as the former. Now, what doubt can reasonably be entertained that the President had not the intent imputed? On the contrary, is it not manifest that his purpose was to preserve both from violation? This is certainly true, unless it be supposed that he believed that the Supreme Court of the United States would aid him in such a violation. Assuming that he believed that tribunal to be honest and capable, the very fact of his wishing to obtain its decision upon the questions before him demonstrates that his design was not to subvert, but to uphold the Constitution, and obtain a correct construction of the act of March, 1867.

VIII. I deem it wholly unnecessary to consider the fourth, fifth, sixth and seventh—the conspiracy articles—or the ninth, the Emory article, no evidence whatever having been offered even tending, as I think, to their support.

IX. It has been said that the Senate by their resolution of February, 1868, having declared that the President's removal of Mr. Stanton was contrary to the Constitution and the law, the senators voting for it are concluded upon both points. This is a great error. That resolution was passed by the Senate in its legislative capacity, and without much deliberation. The questions were scarcely debated. To hold that any senator who voted for it is not at perfect liberty to reconsider his opinion on this trial is to confound things entirely district. That resolution the Senate at any time, in its legislative character, can reverse when convinced of its error. But this is not so in relation to any error of law or fact into which this court may now fall. It is now acting in a judicial character. The judgment which it may pronounce as regards the respondent will be final. To suppose, then, that a senator, when he is satisfied that his former opinion upon the legal questions now before him is erroneous, may not correct it, but is bound to pronounce a judgment which he is convinced would be illegal, is to force him to violate the oath he has taken to decide the case impartially, according to law and justice.

The resolution of February was not a law. That everybody will admit. To act in virtue of it, disregarding what he is convinced is the law, would be a gross abandonment of duty. It has also been said by some inconsiderate persons that our judgment should be influenced by party consideration. We have been told in substance that party necessity requires a conviction; and the same is invoked to avoid what it is madly said will be the result of acquittal—civil commotion and bloodshed. Miserable insanity; a degrading dereliction of patriotism! These appeals are made evidently from the apprehension that senators may conscientiously be convinced that the President is innocent of each of the crimes and misdemeanors alleged in the several articles, and are intended to force him to a judgment of guilt. No more dishonoring efforts were ever made to corrupt a judicial tribunal. They are disgraceful to the parties resorting to them, and should they be successful, as I am sure they will not, they would forever destroy the heretofore unblemished honor of this body, and inflict a wound upon the Constitution itself which perhaps no time could heal.

OPINION OF MR. SENATOR HOWE.

One of the questions involved in the consideration of this cause is, whether the President is or is not intrusted by the Constitution with the power to remove the heads of the executive departments. Those who now assert he has such power, instead of attempting to prove it from the text of the Constitution, generally prefer to rely upon the debate which took place in the House of Representatives of 1789, and the act of July 27th, of that year, "for establishing an executive department, to be denominated the Department of Foreign Affairs." Now I insist that what powers are or are not in the Constitution cannot be proved by reference to the annals of debates or to the Statutes at Large. The Constitution speaks for itself. What its framers intended must be gathered from the clauses to which they agreed, and not from clauses agreed to by any Congress whatever.

But if the debate and the statutes were both evidence upon the point, they would not prove the power in question to be in the Constitution. That debate commenced on the 19th of May, 1789, upon the proposition to make the Secretary for Foreign Affairs "removable at the pleasure of the President." It was objected that, by the terms of the Constitution, an officer could only be removed by impeachment before the Senate. On the contrary, Mr. Madison said "he believed they would not assert that any part of the Constitution declared that the only way to remove should be by impeachment. The contrary might be inferred, because Congress may establish offices by law; *therefore most certainly it is in the discretion of the legislature to say upon what terms the office shall be held, either during good behavior or during pleasure.*" During that debate no less than twenty-five speeches were made. Throughout the debate the issue was, can Congress authorize the President to remove from office, or is impeachment the only method of removal allowed by the Constitution?

Nearly a month later, on the 16th of June following, the debate was renewed upon a bill to establish a Department of Foreign Affairs. The first section provided that the Secretary should "be removable at the pleasure of the President." Mr. White, of Virginia, moved to strike out these words. Upon that motion a long debate ensued, running through several days. In the course of it Mr. Madison assumed a new ground of defence. In the former debate he had asserted that Congress could fix the tenure of the office as it pleased; that that power was a necessary incident of the power to create the office. In this debate he started the idea, for the first time, that the President could control the tenure as an incident of executive power.

The idea was broached cautiously and with evident hesitation. He acknowledged it was an afterthought. And he introduced it in these words:

> I have, since the subject was last before the House, examined the Constitution with attention, and I acknowledge that it does not perfectly correspond with the idea I entertained of it from the first glance. I am inclined to think that a free and systematic interpretation of the plan of government will leave us less at liberty to abate the responsibility than gentlemen imagine.

* * * * * * * *

> By a strict examination of the Constitution on what appears to be its true principles, and considering the great departments of the government in the relation they have to each other, I have my doubts whether we are not absolutely tied down to the construction declared in the bill.

Of those who affirmed and those who denied the power of removal to be in the President, during the debate, the numbers were about equal. Upon taking the vote on the motion to strike out, the noes were 34, while the ayes were but 20.

But it is evident from the nature of the question, that the majority numbered all those who believed the Constitution conferred the power of removal on the President, and all those, also, who thought Congress could and ought to confer it on him.

Mr. Sedgwick, of Massachusetts, called attention to this fact at the time. He said:

> If I understand the subject rightly there seem to be two opinions dividing the majority of this House. Some of these gentlemen seem to suppose that, by the Constitution, and by implication and certain deductions from the *principles* of the Constitution, the power rests in the President. Others think that it is a matter of legislative determination, and that they must give it to the President on the principles of the Constitution.

The minority do not seem to have been satisfied with the victory achieved by that combination of forces. Accordingly, on the 22d of June, Mr. Benson, of New York, who was of the majority, proposed once more to strike out those words in the first section which were equivalent to an express grant of the power of removal, and in lieu thereof to insert in the second section, which provided for a chief clerk, who in case of "vacancy" should have custody of the books, papers, &c., the words "whenever the said principal officer shall be removed from office by the President of the United States, or in any other case of vacancy," shall, during such vacancy, have custody, &c. He explained that "he hoped his amendment would succeed in reconciling both sides of the House to the decision and quieting the minds of gentlemen."

He seems to have persuaded himself that as the law in that form would not assert either that the President *could* remove, under the Constitution, or that he *might* remove under the act, but only mildly suggested "removed by the President" as an event possible to happen without specifying whether it was likely to happen from an exercise of constitutional or statutory authority, no one would have any particular objection to it. This expectation does not seem to have been realized. The amendment to the second section was carried by even a less majority than was obtained against amending the first section. The vote was 30 ayes to 18 noes.

Then the question was renewed to strike out from the first section the words "to be removable," &c., and it was carried by 31 ayes to 19 noes. Thus amended, the bill went to the Senate and passed that body by the casting vote of the Vice President.

Such is in brief the character of the debate of 1789, and such the conclusion in which it issued. It has frequently been cited as a legislative interpretation of the Constitution, as a legislative decision, that the Constitution vested in the President the power of removal. But it ought not to be so regarded, for it is impossible to ascertain from the records how many supported the bill because they regarded it as a declaration that the President had the power to remove; or how many supported it as a declaration that he ought to have it; or how many supported it for the sake of according with the majority, and because it declared neither one thing nor the other.

The idea that the President had the power of removal under the Constitution was not advanced for nearly a month after the debate commenced, and there is not the slightest reason for believing that the bill received a single vote for its passage in either house which it would not have received if that idea had never been conceived.

But if the act of 1789 ever had authority as a legislative decision upon the true meaning of the Constitution, that authority has been annulled by repeated decisions of the same tribunal to the contrary.

First in order of time I cite the act of May 15, 1820, entitled "An act to limit the term of office of certain officers therein named and for other purposes." The first section of that act is in the following words, to wit:

That from and after the passage of this act, all district attorneys, collectors of the customs, naval officers and surveyors of the customs, navy agents, receivers of public moneys for lands, registers of the land offices, paymasters in the army, the apothecary general, the assistant apothecaries general, and the commissary general of purchases, to be appointed under the laws of the United States, shall be appointed for the term of four years, but shall be removable from office at pleasure.

That section asserts the precise authority claimed for Congress by Mr. Madison on the 19th of May, 1789, the authority to determine when and how official tenure should end.

It was superfluous for Congress to enact that the President might remove officers if he had the same authority under the Constitution. And it was useless for Congress to attempt to limit the tenure of an office to four years if the President may extend it to twenty years, as he clearly can if the Constitution has vested in him alone the power of removal.

By that act Congress assumed to grant to the Executive the power of removal. Six years later a committee of the Senate, of which Mr. Benton was chairman, made an elaborate report, assuming the right of Congress to restrict the power of removal. It does not appear to have been considered by the Senate.

In 1835 another committee, of which Mr. Calhoun was chairman, reported a bill which practically denied the constitutional authority of the President to remove from office. As such it was received and considered by the Senate. It led to a protracted and exhaustive discussion. The debate of 1789 was thoroughly reviewed. Among those who denied the power now claimed by the President were Mr. Calhoun, Mr. Clay, Mr. Webster, Mr. Benton, and Mr. Ewing, of Ohio, whose name the President recently sent to the Senate as the successor of Mr. Stanton, whom he claimed to have removed from office under the very authority Mr. Ewing then vehemently denied and ably controverted. Upon the passage of the bill the vote of the Senate was as follows:

YEAS—Messrs. Bell, Benton, Bibb, Black, Calhoun, Clay, Clayton, Ewing, Frelinghuysen, Goldsborough, Kent, King of Georgia, Leigh, McKean, Mangum, Moore, Naudain, Poindexter, Porter, Prentiss, Preston, Tyler, Waggaman, Webster, White—31.

NAYS—Messrs. Brown, Buchanan, Cuthbert, Hendricks, Hill, Kane, King of Alabama, Knight, Linn, Morris, Robinson, Ruggles, Shipley, Talmadge, Tipton, Wright—16.

But this vote, although a very emphatic expression of the opinion of that Senate upon the power in question, and very suggestive of the opinion of that age, cannot strictly be considered a decision of that Congress, since the bill did not pass, and was not considered by the House of Representatives.

But in 1863 Congress passed an act to provide a national currency. The first section provided for a Comptroller of the Currency, and enacted as follows:

He shall be appointed by the President, on the nomination of the Secretary of the Treasury, by and with the advice and consent of the Senate, and shall hold his office for the term of five years, unless sooner removed by the President by and with the advice and consent of the Senate.

Of course, if the Constitution confers upon the President the power to remove from office, this provision was in palpable conflict with it, and yet both houses agreed to it, and President Lincoln approved the act, as President Monroe approved the act of 1820, above referred to.

Congress again asserted the same control over the power of removal in the first section of "An act to provide a national currency secured by a pledge of United States bonds, and to provide for the redemption thereof," which act was also approved by the President, on the 3d of June, 1864. (See Statutes at Large, vol. 13, p. 100.)

Again, the 5th section of the act making appropriations for the support of the army, for the year ending June 30, 1867, contains the following provision:

And no officer in the military or naval service shall, in time of peace, be dismissed from the service except upon and in pursuance of the sentence of a court-martial to that effect or in commutation thereof.

The legislative history of this provision is brief. It is strikingly suggestive of how much of this clamor against the constitutionality of the tenure-of-office act is attributable to partizan zeal, and how much to real conviction. For this reason I refer to that history here.

The army appropriation bill being under consideration in the Senate on the 19th of June, 1866, Mr. Wilson offered an amendment in the following words, to wit:

And be it further enacted, That section 17 of an act entitled "An act to define the pay and emoluments of certain officers of the army," approved July 17, 1862, and a resolution entitled "A resolution to authorize the President to assign the command of troops in the same field or department to officers of the same grade without regard to seniority," approved April 4, 1862, be and the same are hereby repealed: and no officer in the military or naval service shall be dismissed from service except upon and in pursuance of the sentence of a court-martial to that effect, or in commutation thereof. (See Congressional Globe, 1st session 39th Congress, p. 3454.)

The amendment as offered was agreed to without division and without objection. When the bill was returned to the House of Representatives it was committed, together with the Senate amendment, to the Committee on Appropriations. On the 25th of June the amendments were reported back from that committee, with the recommendation that the House non-concur in that amendment among others. (Ibid., p. 3405.)

The bill subsequently was referred to a committee of conference, consisting on the part of the Senate of Messrs. Sherman, Wilson, and Yates; and on the part of the House of Messrs. Schenck, Niblack, and Thayer.

That committee reported that the House agree to the amendment of the Senate, with an amendment inserting the words "in time of peace," after the word "shall."

In that form the amendment was accepted, without a dissenting vote in either house.

The Senate which passed that act with such unanimity was composed substantially of the same individuals who now compose this tribunal. Moreover the act was approved by the respondent himself on the 12th of July, 1866.

In his answer filed in this cause the respondent dwells upon the reluctance he felt to surrendering any one of the prerogatives which the Constitution had intrusted to the presidential office. Such a reluctance, if sincere, becomes a President always. But the respondent's professions of reluctance in 1867 were surely ill timed, admitting they were sincere. He had already surrendered this prerogative in the most solemn manner possible.

No one *has* asserted, and no one *will* assert, that the Constitution vests in the President any sort of control over the tenure of civil offices that he does not possess over that of military and naval offices.

If under the Constitution he can dismiss a postmaster, he can dismiss also the General of the army and the admiral of the navy; and a statute forbidding the dismissal of either is but idle words.

If Congress can lawfully forbid the President to remove any military or naval officer, as was done in the act above mentioned, surely it cannot be denied that Congress may prohibit the removal of any civil officer, as was subsequently done by the tenure-of-office bill.

Either, then, the respondent *now* asserts power which he *believes* to be unconstitutional, or he *then* approved a statute which he *believed* to be unconstitutional. For myself I cannot help thinking the judgment of 1866 was the most candid and unbiased. He was then under every obligation to defend the Constitution that rests upon him now. But he is now manifestly under a necessity of defending himself, which he was not under then.

If the respondent were proved to have claimed to own an estate which he had by deed conveyed to another, he would be held guilty of slandering the title of his grantee. And when he is heard, in answer to a charge of usurping power, to assert an authority which he has solemnly abjured, he must be held guilty of slandering the Constitution and the prerogatives which that Constitution vests in Congress.

Following the act of 1866 came the act of March 2, 1867, entitled "An act regulating the tenure of civil officers."

In substance it prohibits the President from removing certain civil officers, except upon certain conditions, as the act of the preceding year prohibited him from removing military and naval officers, except upon certain conditions. The principles of the two acts are precisely the same. The power to pass them must be the same. There may be considerations of expediency opposed to one which cannot be urged against the other. But the President, who approved the first act, so far as I know, without hesitation, vetoed the second, upon the ground of unconstitutionality. This will be thought strange; but it will not be thought strange that Congress, adhering to a principle so often asserted in former acts, passed this act by a majority of more than two-thirds of each house, the President's objections to the contrary notwithstanding.

Upon all these instances, I conclude that the constitutional power to remove from office cannot be proved by the decisions of Congress. Congress has never in terms affirmed its existence once. On the contrary, it has, as I have shown, denied it repeatedly and explicitly. It can as little be proved by reference to the text of the Constitution itself.

Those who, in the debate of 1789 or in subsequent discussions, have ventured to seek for this baleful authority in the text of the Constitution have claimed to find the warrant for it in the first section of the second article. They assume that the power of removal is an executive power, and therefore that it is conferred upon the President by that section. The terms of the section are these:

The executive power shall be vested in a President of the United States of America.

In my judgment, the sole office of that clause is to fix the style of the officer who is to possess executive authority, and not to define his jurisdiction—to prescribe what the Executive shall be called, and not what he may do. It seems to bear the same relation to the executive department that the first clause of the first article does to the legislative department, and the first clause of the third article to the judicial department. To ascertain what is executive power, we must examine other provisions of the Constitution.

But when you have searched the Constitution through, you do not find this of removal from office enumerated among executive powers, nor any other power like it. The one duty charged upon the President which is most like, or rather which is least unlike the duty in question, is this: "He shall take care that the laws be faithfully executed." He is not to execute the laws, but to "take care that the laws be * * executed." It is very little he can lawfully do to execute them. If, because he is charged to see that the laws are executed, he may provide any one of the means or methods, or instruments of their execution, he may provide all not otherwise expressly provided for. If, because he is to see that the laws be executed, he may remove any officer who may be employed in their execution, why should he not select all officers to be employed? Why not contrive and establish the offices they are to fill? Why not define the duties they are to discharge—the parts they are severally to perform? Why not fix the compensation which they may receive?

No one will pretend that either of these powers belongs to the President, though each one is as much executive in its nature as is the power of removal. No office not established by the Constitution can be created but by an act of Congress. Congress alone can determine the manner of filling it, define its duties, and fix its emoluments. And yet it is strangely claimed that when the legislative power has done all this, the executive power may practically defeat it all; not by abolishing the office or changing the duties, or the rate of compensation, but by creating a vacancy in the office whenever he chooses. And so his duty to see the law faithfully executed is transformed into a power absolutely to defeat the whole purpose of the law. He is charged by the Constitution to see that the laws are faithfully executed, and yet he cannot transfer an old musket from one citizen to another without making himself liable as a trespasser.

The President of the United States recently commanded an army of more than a million of men; but with all that force at his command he could not lawfully eject from his cabin the humblest squatter on the public domain. Possession is stronger, in the eye of law, than the President, and before that naked possession the commander-in-chief must halt, no matter what the physical force he commands. Only when the wrongfulness of that possession has been determined by the judicial power in a procedure prescribed by the legislative power; not until the national precept has issued, attested not by the President, but by a judge, can that possession be disturbed. And even that writ must be executed by the very person to whom Congress requires it to be directed. Whoever else attempts to serve it is a trespasser, although it be the President himself.

And yet it is strangely asserted that this officer, who is so impotent to redress so palpable a wrong, may, at his own pleasure, without judicial inquiry, without writ, in a moment by a command, in defiance of a statute, remove from the duties, the labors, the honors and emoluments of official position, the army of officers employed in the civil, the military, and naval service of the United States, not because the Constitution anywhere says he may do so, but because the Constitution charges him with the duty of seeing the laws faithfully executed.

This power of removal is, then, not vested in the President by anything said in the Constitution, nor by anything properly implied from what is said. It seems to me, on the contrary, it is positively denied by the manifest purpose of the Constitution. That manifest purpose is, that the principal offices shall be held by those in whose appointment the Senate has concurred. The plain declaration is that, "He (the President) shall nominate and, by and with the advice and consent of the Senate, *appoint* ambassadors," &c. But this purpose may be wholly defeated if the President have, by the Constitution, the unrestricted power of removal. For it is as plainly declared that "the President shall have power to fill all vacancies that may happen during the recess of the Senate, by granting commissions which shall expire at the end of their next session." If, then, the President has also the power, during the recess of the Senate, to *make* vacancies at his pleasure by removal, his choice is supreme and the Senate is voiceless. He is only to remove all officers in whose appointment the Senate has concurred, immediately upon the adjournment of that body, and commission others in their places. They will hold until the end of the next session. Just before that event he must nominate again to the Senate the officers he removed, or some others whom the Senate will confirm, and when the Senate has confirmed them and adjourned, the President may again remove them all and restore his favorites once more, to hold until the end of another session, when the same ceremony must be repeated.

A deed which should grant a house to "A" and his heirs and to their use forever, but should also declare that "B" and his heirs should forever occupy it free of rent, would probably be held void for repugnancy. I do not think the Constitution a nullity; and so I cannot concede that the President has in it a power implied so clearly repugnant to a power plainly declared to be in the Senate.

But it is urged that it is necessary to the well-being of the public service that the President should be clothed with this extraordinary power. It is urged that unless he have it unfaithful men may be obtruded upon the public service, and it would take time to displace them. It is true, incompetent or dishonest men may get into the custom-houses or the marshalships. It would be folly to deny that. And so dishonest men may get possession of other men's property and refuse to make restitution; and dishonest men may refuse to pay their just dues on demand. I readily confess that some governmental contrivance by which official positions could be instantly taken from *unfaithful* hands and placed in *faithful* ones, and by which all wrongs could be redressed and all rights enforced, instantly, and without the necessity of trial, or deliberation, or consultation, is a desideratum. But the men who made our Constitution did not provide any such contrivance. I do not think they tried to. It seems to me they studiously avoided all such effort. I think they believed what the world's whole history most impressively teaches: that while the administration of law is entrusted to fallible men, deliberation is safer than expedition.

Absolute monarchies are the handiest of all governments for that very reason; because they can execute justice and punish rascality so promptly. But the men who made our Constitution, looking back upon the experience of a few thousand years, came to the conclusion that absolute monarchs could just as promptly execute injustice and punish goodness. They resolved to discard the whole system. I am not yet satisfied they were mistaken, and am not therefore willing to see their decision reversed.

I readily concede that if we were sure the President would always be an honest, wise, unselfish, unprejudiced man, it might promote the efficiency of the public service to entrust him with the delicate and responsible duty of removing a bad officer and replacing him by a good one.

But the men who made our Constitution did not act upon any such hypothesis. They knew it was possible not only for bad men to become assessors of internal revenue, but to become Presidents as well, else they would not have provided this august tribunal for the trial and deposition of a delinquent President. I grant that when you have a true man for President it is convenient and not dangerous that he have the power of removal, for thereby he may be able to replace an incompetent district attorney with a competent one, or a dishonest inspector of customs with an honest one, without waiting to consult the Senate or with the law-making power. But if, instead, you happen to have a false man for President, then if he have the power of removal it is a power which removes all honesty from the public service, and fills it throughout with rottenness and corruption.

My conclusion is that the President derives no authority from the Constitution to dismiss an officer from the public service. A lawyer is not warranted in asserting it. A member of the 39th Congress, who assented to the act of July 12, 1866, cannot be justified in asserting it. The respondent, who approved that act, cannot be excused for asserting it. Whatever authority the President had on the 21st of February last to dismiss the Secretary of War, he derived, not from the Constitution, but from statute. The only authority he derived from the statute is found in the second section of the act of 1789, creating the office of Secretary of War.

That section is in the words following:

> That there shall be in the said department an inferior officer, to be appointed by the said principal officer, to be employed therein as he shall deem proper, and to be called the chief clerk in the Department of War; and who, whenever the said principal officer shall be removed from office by the President of the United States, or in any other case of vacancy, shall, during such vacancy, have the charge and custody of all records, books, and papers appertaining to the said department.

It was copied from the act to establish a Department of Foreign Affairs, which had been passed by the same Congress at the same session. It is evidently to be construed as the same words used by the same men in the former act are to be construed.

And whether we look at the terms employed in the section, or at the terms employed in the debate which preceded the enactment, it is very evident that the power conferred is something very different from that arbitrary and irresponsible power of removal claimed by the President in his answer—"the power, at any and all times, of removing from office all executive officers for cause to be judged of by the President alone."

On the contrary, the power contained in this section is insinuated rather than asserted, implied rather than expressed, allowed rather than conferred. It is not a power granted him to be wielded wantonly and according to his own pleasure, but a power entrusted to him in confidence that it will be sacredly employed to promote the public welfare, and not to promote his personal interests or to gratify his personal spites.

In the debate to which I have referred Mr. Goodhue urged that "the *community would be served* by the best men when the Senate concurred with the President in the appointment; but if any oversight was committed, it could best be corrected by the superintending agent."

Mr. Madison, in reply to the suggestion that if the President were empowered to remove at his pleasure he might remove meritorious men, said, "In the first place he will be impeachable by this house before the Senate for such an act of maladministration; for I contend that the wanton removal of meritorious officers would subject him to impeachment and removal from his own high trust."

How delicate the power was felt to be is apparent from the fact that from the passage of the act down to the 20th of February last it is certain the power had never been exerted *but* once, and it is not certain that it was ever exerted even once. Often Secretaries have been nominated to the Senate in place of others then in office, and upon receiving the assent of the Senate the new Secretaries have displaced the former ones. It is claimed that in 1800 a Secretary of State was removed by President Adams without the assent of the Senate. It is certain that he issued an order for the removal of Mr. Pickering before Mr. Marshall was confirmed; but as Mr. Marshall was nominated to the Senate on the same day the order for Mr. Pickering's removal was dated, and as the former was confirmed by the Senate promptly on the following day, it is evident the President acted in full confidence that the Senate would assent, and it is not certain that the order for the removal of Mr. Pickering was enforced or even served upon him before the Senate had assented.

Indeed, I am of opinion the people of this country have not delegated any such irresponsible power to any agent or officer of theirs as is claimed by the President. Every officer is held responsible in some form for the manner in which he employs every power conferred upon him. Some are responsible to the courts of law; some to the tribunals of impeachment; and all, even the members of this high court, are responsible to the people by whom and for whose use all power is delegated.

In addition to all the precautions which have been mentioned to prevent abuse of the executive trust in the mode of the President's appointment, his term of office and the precise and definite limitations imposed upon the exercise of his power, the Constitution has also rendered him directly amenable by law for mal-administration. The inviolability of any officer of the government is incompatible with the republican theory as well as with the principles of retributive justice. (1 Kent's Com., 289.)

But fairly construed I think the act above referred to does imply in the President the power to remove a Secretary of War in a proper case. I think also he is primarily the judge of what is or is not a proper case. But he is not the sole or the final judge. This court may review his judgment. For a wanton, corrupt, or malicious exercise of the power, he may, and in my judgment should be, held responsible upon impeachment. Or if he wantonly or corruptly refuse to exercis the power, he may also make himself liable to impeachment. If a President wickedly remove an officer known to be faithful, or wickedly refuse to remove one known to be corrupt, undoubtedly he may be impeached.

And this suggests the inquiry as to the offences for which an officer may be impeached.

Only for "treason, bribery, and other high crimes and misdemeanors." Such is the language of the Constitution. But what are "high crimes and misdemeanors?"

They are, say the counsel for the respondent, "only high criminal offences against the United States, made so by some law of the United States existing when the acts complained of were done." That rule is clearly stated and easily understood, and it must be correct, or the other rule is absolutely correct, to wit: that those are high crimes and misdemeanors which the triers deem to be such. By one or the other of these standards every officer when impeached must be tried. Either high crimes and misdemeanors are those acts declared to be such by the law, or those held to be such by the court.

Against the first construction we have the protest of all the authority to be found in judicial, legislative, or political history.

If opinions or precedents are to have any weight with us, they are wonderfully accordant. They are against the rule contended for by the respondent, and they are abundant. A collection of them prepared for this record occupies more than twenty-five pages.

I will cite here but one precedent and one authority:

Although an impeachment *may* involve an inquiry whether a crime against any positive law has been committed, yet it is not necessarily a trial for crime; nor is there any necessity in the case of crimes committed by public officers for the institution of any special proceeding for the infliction of the punishment prescribed by the laws, since they, like all other persons, are amenable to the ordinary jurisdiction of courts of justice in respect of offences against positive law. The purposes of an impeachment lie wholly beyond the penalties of the statute or the customary law. The object of the proceeding is to ascertain whether cause exists for removing a public officer from office. Such a cause may be found in the fact that either in the discharge of his office or aside from its functions he has violated a law or committed what is technically a crime. But a cause for removal from office may exist where no offence against positive law has been committed, as where the individual has, from immorality, or imbecility, or maladministration, become unfit to exercise the office. (Curtis's History of the Constitution of the United States, vol. 2, p. 260.)

Such is the opinion of that learned commentator as to offences for which an officer may be impeached. Not alone for what the law defines to be a crime, but for what the court think such immorality, or imbecility, or maladministration as makes him unfit to exercise the office.

In 1804 a judge of the United States district court for the district of New Hampshire was impeached and removed from office. There were four articles in the impeachment; three of them presented the defendant for maladministration in making certain orders in court; the fourth charged him with the immorality of drunkenness. Neither charged an indictable offence.

The respondent's counsel brushes all precedents and all authority aside. Ignoring the unanimous judgment of 200 years, he insists upon a new interpretation of the old words employed in our Constitution, an interpretation which seems to me invented for and adapted to this particular case. His words are:

> In my apprehension the teachings, the requirements, the prohibitions of the Constitution of the United States prove all that is necessary to be attended to for the purposes of this trial. I propose, therefore, instead of a search through the precedents, which were made in the time of the Plantagenets, the Tudors, and the Stuarts, *and which have been repeated since*, to come nearer home and see what provisions of the Constitution of the United States bear on this question, and whether they are not sufficient to settle it. If they are it is quite immaterial what exists elsewhere." (Curtis's argument, p. 404.)

This appeal from the agreement of centuries is so boldly made that I cannot forbear to present the respondent's theory of the constitutional remedy by impeachment, with a single comment upon it.

The Constitution declares:

> The President, Vice-President, and all civil officers of the United States, shall be removed from office on impeachment for, and conviction of, treason, bribery, or other high crimes and misdemeanors.

Clearly the President may be impeached for any cause for which a Secretary may be. Judgment in case of impeachment *may* not extend beyond removal from office. It cannot "extend further than to removal from office and disqualification to hold and enjoy any office of honor, trust, or profit *under the United States.*"

The Constitution declares that the House of Representatives "shall have the sole power of impeachment."

> The Senate shall have the sole power to try all impeachments.
> No person shall be convicted without the concurrence of two-thirds of the members present.

As we have seen, there is not one word in the Constitution which in terms authorizes the President to remove a Secretary for any cause whatever.

It was the opinion of many learned jurists and able statesmen in the commencement of this government, that no civil officer could be removed during his term except by impeachment; that impeachment was the only mode sanctioned by the Constitution for ridding the civil service of incapacity, of dishonesty, or of crime.

But, according to this new rendering of the Constitution, we are asked to say that whatever may be the opinion of the merits of a Secretary entertained by the House of Representatives, they cannot hope, and must not ask, to remove him by impeachment, until they can convince, not a majority, but two-thirds of the Senate; not upon probable cause, but upon legal proofs; not of official incapacity however gross, or of official delinquency however glaring, but of official misconduct such as the law has anticipated and has forbidden under heavy penalties; yet that the President may remove at will, upon his own motion, without trial or notice, the same Secretary, simply because he is distasteful to him, and thereby renders their personal relations unhappy, although he may be the ablest and the purest statesman who ever held a portfolio. Thus the power of impeachment, expressly conferred upon the two houses by the Constitution, is loaded with conditions which render it useless to the republic except against the most daring criminals; and we are asked to accept in its place an irresponsible power of removal, resting upon no express grant, but only upon an unreasonable and violent implication, to be exerted by a single man, which, in its practical operation, confounds all distinctions between official merit and official demerit, and which, in my judgment, upon the experience of half a century, has done vastly more to debauch the public service than to protect it.

If this most anomalous interpretation of the Constitution is defended upon any theory of the transcendent importance of the presidential over the ministerial office, I reply that no such distinction is warranted by the law or the facts.

In law the functions of a Secretary are as important to the nation as those of the President; and in practical administration the labors of each one of the seven heads of executive departments are worth seven-fold more to the public than the labors of the President.

I cannot, therefore, accept this new interpretation of the laws of impeachment. I hold, with the elder authorities, with the late authorities, with all the authorities, that impeachment is a process provided not for the punishment of crime, but for the protection of the state. And so holding, I must give judgment not as to whether the acts proved upon the respondent are declared by the criminal code to be crimes, but whether I think them so prejudicial to the state as to warrant his removal. When the written law refuses to guide me, my own conscience must. I cannot accept the opinions of another man. The state must furnish me with the rule of judgment or my own convictions must supply one. There can be no other umpire.

What, then, are the acts charged upon the President? how far are they proved? and to what extent are they criminal?

I believe I am not mistaken in saying that the specific acts charged against the respondent in the first eight articles are, that on the 21st day of February last he issued an order removing Edwin M. Stanton from the office of Secretary of War, and that on the same day he issued another order authorizing Lorenzo Thomas to act as Secretary of War *ad interim*. These two acts are charged in different articles, in various forms, as done with various intendments and with various legal effects. They are relied upon as specific violations of the Constitution and as violations of different laws. They are relied upon as evidences of a conspiracy to prevent Mr. Stanton from holding the office of Secretary of War, and as evidences of an attempt to drive him from office by threats, intimidation, and force.

That the respondent issued both orders is fully proved by the evidence and fully admitted by the answer.

It only remains for me to consider the circumstances under which they were issued, in order to determine whether they constitute an impeachable offence.

The respondent justifies the order of removal under the double warrant of constitutional authority and of authority conferred by the 2d section of the act of 1789 creating the Department of War.

The first claim I have already considered and rejected. The second claim is resisted upon the ground that the authority given in the act of 1789 is revoked by the act of March 2, 1867; and accordingly in the first article the order of removal is charged specifically as a violation of the last-mentioned act, known as the tenure-of-office act.

Of course, with the views I have already expressed of the true construction of the Constitution, I can entertain no doubt of the entire validity of the tenure-of-office act. I earnestly supported its passage in the Senate. With whatever ability I had I endeavored to extend its protection to the heads of the executive departments.

But while the action of the House accorded with my own views, the Senate, by three different votes, rejected those views. That disagreement between the two houses led to a committee of conference.

The committee reported the first section as it now stands in the law, in the following words:

> That every person holding any civil office to which he has been appointed by and with the advice and consent of the Senate, and every person who shall hereafter be appointed to any such office, and shall become duly qualified to act therein, is and shall be entitled to hold such office until a successor shall have been in like manner appointed and duly qualified, *except as herein otherwise provided: Provided,* That the Secretaries of State, of the Treasury, of War, of the Navy, and of the Interior, the Postmaster General, and the Attorney General, shall hold their offices respectively for and during the term of the President by whom they may have been appointed, and for one month thereafter, subject to removal by and with the advice and consent of the Senate.

This section was explained to the Senate by members of the committee at the time it was reported as not designed to affect the power of the President to remove the Secretary of War. Upon examining the provisions then it was my own opinion that it did not affect his authority in that regard. And after all the debate I have heard upon the point since, I have not been able to change that opinion.

If Mr. Stanton had been appointed during the present presidential term, I should have no doubt he was within the security of the law. But I cannot find that, either in fact or in legal intendment, he was appointed during the present presidential term. It is urged that he was appointed by Mr. Lincoln, and such is the fact. It is said that Mr. Lincoln's term is not yet expired. Such I believe to be the fact. But the language of the proviso is, that a Secretary shall hold, not during the term of the *man* by whom he is appointed, but during the *term* of the President by whom he may be appointed. Mr. Stanton was appointed by the President in 1862. The term of that President was limited by the Constitution. It expired on the 4th of March, 1865. That the same incumbent was re-elected for the next term is conceded, but I do not comprehend how that fact extended the former term.

Entertaining these views, and because the first article of the impeachment charges the order of removal as a violation of the tenure-of-office act, I am constrained to hold the President not guilty upon that article.

But even if the tenure-of-office act had never been passed, it does not follow that the respondent would not be guilty of a high crime in issuing the order of removal. The order might conclude Mr. Stanton. But it does not follow that the people could not resent it and impeach the President for issuing it.

Two of the articles in the impeachment of Judge Pickering charged him with making certain orders in a judicial procedure pending before him. He had undoubted jurisdiction to make the orders, and they were binding upon the parties until reversed. But the Senate found him guilty upon both articles, not because the making them was a usurpation of authority, but because it was an abuse of authority. I cannot find, for reasons already stated, that the respondent's order removing Mr. Stanton was a usurpation of authority, but was it not an abuse of authority? If Mr. Stanton was a meritorious officer, and yet the respondent sought wantonly to remove him, he committed the precise offence which Mr. Madison declared in the debate of 1789 to be impeachable.

The cause assigned by the President for the order of removal is—

> That the relations between the said Stanton and the President no longer permitted the President to resort to him for advice, or to be, in the judgment of the President, safely responsible for his conduct of the affairs of the Department of War as by law required, in accordance with the orders and instructions of the President; and thereupon by force of the Constitution and laws of the United States, which devolve on the President the power and the duty to control the conduct of the business of that executive department of the government, and by reason of the constitutional duty of the President to take care that the laws be faithfully executed, this respondent did necessarily consider and did determine that the said Stanton ought no longer to hold the said office of Secretary for the Department of War.

The cause for these unhappy personal relations is explained by the respondent in a message sent to the Senate on the 12th of December, 1867, and which is made a part of the answer in this cause.

That explanation is as follows:

The subsequent sessions of Congress developed new complications when the suffrage bill for the District of Columbia, and the reconstruction acts of March 2 and March 23, 1867, all passed over the veto. It was in cabinet consultations upon these bills that a difference of opinion upon the most vital points was developed. Upon these questions there was perfect accord between all the members of the cabinet and myself, except Mr. Stanton. He stood alone, and the difference of opinion could not be reconciled. That unity of opinions, which upon great questions of public policy or administration is so essential to the Executive, was gone.

The respondent does not allege that Mr. Stanton would not advise him and advise him honestly, but only that he, the respondent, "could not resort to him for advice." If the fact was so, and if the advice of the Secretary was essential to the proper discharge of the President's duty, as I have no doubt it was, it would seem to show disqualification on the part of the Executive, rather than on the part of the Secretary, and to demand the resignation of the former, rather than the removal of the latter.

But the reason urged why the President could not resort to the Secretary for advice is, that the latter differed from him upon three points of public policy— the suffrage bill for the District of Columbia, and the reconstruction acts of March 2 and March 23, 1867—" Unity of opinion was gone."

If unity of opinion had still existed, it is difficult to understand of what advantage Mr. Stanton's advice could have been to the President.

I do not readily perceive of what importance it was to the President to resort to a minister for advice, if the advisory authority of the latter was to be limited to echoing the President's own opinions.

But it is very suggestive in this connection, that the points of difference between the respondent and the Secretary were upon three public statutes. The President is known to have disapproved them all. They were, in fact, passed over his veto.

The inference seems irresistible that the Secretary approved them. But since they had all been passed into solemn laws, of what importance were the opinions of either, unless, indeed, the respondent had resolved to defeat their execution, and demanded a change in the War Office, not to aid him more efficiently in the execution of the laws, but to aid him in defeating their execution?

But another reason for wishing to get rid of the Secretary urged by the President is, that he could not "safely be responsible for his conduct of the affairs of the department." Perhaps that was so; although the evidence is not apparent. But the sufficient reply to that is, that he was *not* responsible for his conduct any further than he directed or sanctioned it. The suggestion that any President is responsible for the conduct of subordinate officers is a groundless pretext by whomsoever urged. If a President were responsible for the conduct of his subordinates, the respondent would not only have been impeachable, but would probably have been in the penitentiary long before this time; and few of his predecessors would have fared any better.

But upon this whole question, of the cause assigned for the exclusion of Mr. Stanton, the Senate has already passed. The President himself, by his message of the 12th December last, called for the judgment of the Senate upon them. I then voted them insufficient. Nevertheless the respondent issued the order of removal; and if I am now to say that that act does not constitute an impeachable offence, I must either reverse the decision I then made upon the cause of removal, or I must reverse the decision of Mr. Madison upon the nature of an impeachable offence.

I perceive no reason for reversing either. But upon the question of Mr. Stanton's merits as an officer, I am not left to rely upon my own judgment alone. Of course my own judgment must guide my own decision, since there is no authoritative law upon the subject. But I am glad to remember that my opinion was then in accord with that of a large majority of the Senate, and also manifestly in accord with what the opinion of the respondent himself had been, and with that of his predecessor, attested by both in the most solemn manner. President Lincoln employed Mr. Stanton as Secretary of War during the last and the larger part of his administration. Mr. Johnson also employed him from the time of his accession to the presidency for nearly two years before the tenure-of-office bill was passed. And after its passage he continued to employ him until Congress had adjourned, had reassembled, and adjourned again. Not until August, 1867, did he commence the labor of excluding him from office. Of course the respondent cannot be allowed to say now in his own justification that he was employing in a high trust during all that time an incompetent or an unfaithful man. He must assign some reason for wishing to exclude him from the service which did not exist before he commenced the attempt. This the respondent does. He assigns three such reasons. They were found in the fact that the Secretary approved of three different statutes, of which the President disapproved.

So an American President pleads before the Senate, as a justification for his dismissal of a minister, that the minister approved of certain public laws! A British minister leaves office the moment a law passes which he cannot approve. And if a British sovereign were to assign such a reason for the dismissal of a minister, he would not be impeached indeed, because the British constitution does not warrant such a proceeding; but there is no question he would have to quit the throne, by the authority not conferred upon but inherent in the Parliament as the representatives of the people of the realm.

Commissioned as I am, by the express letter of the Constitution, to pass judgment upon the conduct of this respondent, and sworn as I am to give true judgment, I cannot hesitate to say, that the attempt to drive an American minister from the public service because he approved the public laws, is of itself a high crime against the state.

It is urged that his only purpose in issuing the order was to raise the question of his power to remove, and obtain the judgment of the courts of law upon it. But when there was no just cause for removal, why should the President have been so anxious to vindicate his power to remove? But I dismiss this allegation with the remark that I cannot believe it. All the testimony in the case contradicts it. There is not a syllable to support it. If when he issued the order of removal he intended only a lawsuit, why did he not so say to General Thomas, to whom he gave the order? Why did he leave the Adjutant General to believe, as he told Dr. Burleigh, that he was to gain possession not by suit, but by force? Why did he leave him to suppose, as he told Mr. Wilkeson, that he should overcome the objection of Mr. Stanton, not through the aid of the Attorney General, but by help of the General of the armies; or, as he told Karsner, that he was to use kicks and not writs? If he intended no more than a lawsuit, why did he not so inform Lieutenant General Sherman when he offered him the place of Secretary *ad interim* some days before? At that time the General invited his attention to the propriety of a lawsuit, and the President repudiated the suggestion as impracticable. But above all, if he intended nothing more than a lawsuit, why has he not had one? The courts have been always open to him. No lawyer needs to be told that the Attorney General could have proceeded to try the title to the office upon an information filed upon the relation of General Thomas as well as upon the relation of Mr. Stanton. It has been suggested that the respondent's hopes of a lawsuit were frustrated by the discontinuance of some criminal proceedings taken against General Thomas upon complaint of Mr. Stanton, soon after the order was issued.

The President, however, does not in his answer urge that explanation. And it is hardly credible that the President relied upon getting into court in that particular way. Every other way has been, and still is, open to him, except one. He does not seem to have been able, so far, to get into the law courts as defendant, and that seems to have been regarded by him as a *sine qua non* to any litigation. At liberty at all times for nearly a quarter of a year to sue upon the right of General Thomas to recover possession, he has failed to do so. But he leaves us to infer that, if he could have succeeded in putting General Thomas once in possession, he would have been content to contest a suit by Mr. Stanton, even had it taken a year to determine it.

So far, I discover absolutely nothing to relieve the respondent from the guilt of having issued an order for the removal of an able and faithful officer, long trusted by himself and by his predecessor, and still trusted by a large portion of the country, charged with no fault, but that he approved of certain laws which the President condemned, and of removing him against the advice of a large majority of the Senate. On the contrary, it seems to me this guilt is greatly aggravated by the disposition the respondent sought to make of the office.

To remove a meritorious public officer, Mr. Madison declared, constituted an impeachable offence. To remove such an officer and leave the office vacant, with no one to discharge the duties, would doubtless be held to enhance the guilt. To remove a faithful and competent officer, and supply his place with an incompetent and dishonest one, would enhance it still more.

To remove a good man from office, and to replace him with a bad man, without any advice and without any sort of legal authority, seems to me an offence against the public interests, which, if it go unrebuked, will excuse any possible offence that leaves the President outside of a penitentiary.

That the respondent attempted to do all this is charged upon him, and, in my judgment, is proved upon him.

At the same time that he issued the order of removal he issued another order, authorizing the Adjutant General of the army to act as Secretary *ad interim*. The fitness of General Thomas for the office of Secretary is not fairly in issue in this cause, and consequently we can know but little about it. A few things, however, are disclosed in the evidence. It is shown that the same position was tendered, a few days before, to Lieutenant General Sherman, and he declined it. But when it was offered to General Thomas, he not only accepted it promptly, but he addressed a letter of thanks to the President for the "honor done him." When the Adjutant General gives thanks for a trust so high, so delicate, so solemn that Lieutenant General Sherman shrinks from and declines it, it suggests the inference that the former is not exactly the man for the place.

It does appear also from the testimony that the General of the army had recommended his retirement from the military service altogether. One whom General Grant thinks no longer fitted for the post of Adjutant General does not afford the highest evidence of fitness for the post of Secretary of War.

But the respondent's legal right to put General Thomas in possession of the War Office is put in issue by the *second* and by some other articles in the impeachment.

The respondent claims authority under the act of February 13, 1795. That is as follows:

That in case of vacancy in the office of Secretary of State, Secretary of the Treasury, or of the Secretary of the Department of War, or of any officer of either of said departments, whose appointment is not in the head thereof, whereby they cannot perform the duties of their said respective offices, it shall be lawful for the President of the United States, in case he shall think it necessary, to authorize any person or persons, at his discretion, to perform the duties of the said respective offices until a successor be appointed, or such vacancy be filled: *Provided*, That no one vacancy shall be supplied in manner aforesaid for a longer term than six months.

I cannot admit the claim for three reasons: First. There is reason to suppose that the statute of 1795 was never regarded as a valid law. Second. It seems to me to have been clearly repealed by the act of 1863. And third, if it were in full force it did not authorize the order issued to General Thomas.

If a vacancy occur in the office of the Secretary during a session of the Senate it may, under the Constitution, be filled immediately by a new nomination and confirmation. If the vacancy occur during the recess of the Senate the Constitution empowers the President to fill it by a new commission, to hold until the Senate convenes and can act upon a nomination. That commission can be issued under the Constitution as promptly as a person may be authorized under the act. The commission and the authorization have the same practical effect; so that the provision made by the Constitution for cases of "*vacancy*" would seem to be ample and render legislation unnecessary.

But if a Secretary be absent or sick it is evident there is no one to discharge the duties of the office; nor does the Constitution provide any mode of supplying the want. The office is not "vacant," but the incumbent is disabled.

To provide for such a case was, as I suppose, the main purpose of the eighth section of the act of May 8, 1792, entitled "An act making alterations in the Treasury and War Departments." In fact the section does a little more than provide for cases of disability. It provides for one kind of *vacancy*. The language is, " in case of *death*, absence from the seat of government, or sickness of the Secretary of State, Secretary of the Treasury, or of the Secretary of the War Department," &c., "whereby they cannot perform the duties of their said respective offices, it shall be lawful for the President of the United States, in case he shall think it necessary, to authorize any person or persons, at his discretion, to perform the duties of the said respective offices until a successor be appointed, or until such absence or inability by sickness shall be removed."

Thus the law stood until 1795. All vacancies were provided for by the Constitution; and temporary disabilities and vacancy by *death* were provided for by the law 1792.

Then the law was passed the whole of which is quoted above. It is entitled "An act to amend the act of 1792." In terms it provides for all cases of vacancy, whether by death, resignation or otherwise; and it provides for no case of disability. What the Constitution had done well, the act does over again; what the Constitution had not done at all the act omits to do.

But it is evident from every part of that short statute that the draughtsman had no definite idea of the mischiefs he wished to remedy. He does not even seem to have considered what a "vacancy" was, or to have been conscious that a vacancy differed from a disability. Hence the act attempts to qualify a *vacancy in an office* by the circumstance that it shall prevent the *incumbent* of the office from discharging its duties—as if there were some vacancies which did not prevent the regular discharge of duty.

Again, it limits, in terms, the duration of the *ad interim* appointment "until a successor be appointed or such a vacancy be filled," as if two sorts of vacancy were provided for, one of which was to determine by the appointment of a "successor," and the other by "being filled." The main purpose of the act seems to be to limit the extreme duration of an *ad interim* appointment. And in this endeavor it collides hopelessly with the Constitution.

The Constitution says the President may supply a vacancy occurring during the recess of the Senate by commissioning a person to act until the end of the next session. The act says that no vacancy shall be supplied longer than six months. It would seem that an act so incongruous ought not to be relied upon as authority for anything. I can find no evidence that it ever was quoted as authority before. In Little & Brown's edition of the Statutes at Large it is marked "obsolete." But if it ever was a living law, it seems to me indisputable that both the acts of 1792 and of 1795 are repealed by the act of February 20, 1863.

It has been seen that neither of the former acts made provision for cases out of the three Departments of State, War, and Treasury. In 1863 it was found that no provision had been made for temporary disabilities in either of the other departments. There was evidently occasion for further legislation, and it seems to me to have been made the occasion for revising the whole subject and of embodying in a single act not only all the provision to be made, but all the cases to be provided for. The title of the act and the purview of the act alike prove this. The title shows that the act is not amendatory of, or supplementary to, the former acts; but that its aim is to do *effectually* just what the other acts did *partially.*

It is entitled "An act *temporarily to supply vacancies in the executive departments in certain cases.*"

The body of the act shows unmistakably that the draughtsman had both the former acts before him. He copied from both. The act provides for cases of death, absence and sickness, as did the act of 1792. It provides for cases of resignation, and provides the six months' limitation, as did the act of 1795. Every case provided for by both the former acts is embraced within the terms of the act of 1863, unless the case of removal be an exception.

It is argued that the act of 1795, as it authorized an *ad interim* appointment in all cases of vacancy, authorized one in case of vacancy by removal. That is conceded. But it should be remembered that the power to supply a vacancy caused by removal with an *ad interim* appointment is a power not named in the statute of 1795, since the power so to create a vacancy is not in that statute. The power to *make* a vacancy by removal is found in the acts of 1789 and 1820. So, one in looking at the act of 1795 does not see the specific authority which the respondent asserted on the 21st of February. Those who drew the statute of 1863 could have seen it only by collating the act of 1795 with the acts of 1789 and 1820. The act of 1795 had been on the books for more than 70 years. The archives of the government have been ransacked and fail to show that in that whole period a single removal was ever by any President followed with an *ad interim* appointment. Every power, therefore, which could be seen by reading the act of 1795 was copied into the act of 1863; every power which had ever been exerted under that act was also copied. All provisions in former laws inconsistent with the provisions of the last-mentioned act are expressly repealed. And yet it is gravely argued that this power of supplying a vacancy caused by removal with an *ad interim* appointment still survived; not only that it survived the act of 1863, but the act of March 2, 1867, also, which deprives the President of all power to create a vacancy by removal except in the case of a head of department where no such vacancy ever was created more than once, if at all. So, in spite of the acts of 1863 and of 1867, we are asked to express, from the mere husks of that poor, misshapen statute of 1795—denounced as obsolete in the code where it stands—the authority to follow the removal of a Secretary, made when the Senate is in session, with an *ad interim* appointment. For one I cannot consent to torture the laws in order to extort from them permission for the respondent to strip the high trust of Secretary from Edwin M. Stanton and place it in the hands of Lorenzo Thomas.

It is said that repeals by implication are not favored by the courts. That is true. Nevertheless, a statute may be repealed without naming it.

It is a well-settled rule that where any statute is revised or one act framed from another, some parts being omitted, the parts omitted are not to be revived by construction but are to be considered as annulled. To hold otherwise would be to impute to the legislature gross carelessness or ignorance, which is altogether inadmissible. (Wilde, J., Ellis *vs*. Paige *et al.*, 1st Pickering, 44; 5th English, 588; 3d Greenleaf, 22; 3d Howard, 615; 12 Mass., 545; 14 Ill., 334.)

Encouraged by these authorities, I venture to conclude that when Congress embodied in the act of 1863 every single power which ever had been seen in the act of 1795, and every use which ever had been made of it, they did not intend to preserve the act just to sustain a power which never had been seen in or a use which never had been made of it.

But if the act of 1795 had been in full force on the 21st of February last, it would not have authorized the order given by the respondent to General Thomas.

Manifestly it was the purpose of all these laws (that of 1792, of 1795, and 1863) to enable the President to supply some one to discharge the duties of an office temporarily when, by reason of a vacancy in the office or the disability of the incumbent, the duties could not otherwise be discharged. It was not intended he should use either of these laws to replace a regular officer with a provisional one. Yet such is the use the respondent attempted to make of the act of 1795. There was no vacancy in the office of Secretary of War on the 21st of February last. Mr. Stanton was in the regular discharge of its duties, neither sick nor absent.

But it is urged that the President had power to remove Mr. Stanton, and, as he issued an order for that purpose, there was a "vacancy in law."

If there is any such thing as a "vacancy in law" it is excluded from the operation of the act of 1795 by its very terms. That authorizes an *ad interim* appointment only in cases of such rational vacancies as prevent the incumbents from discharging the duties of their offices. This "legal vacancy" was not of that kind. It did not prevent Mr. Stanton from discharging the duties of his office. On the contrary he continued to discharge them regularly in spite of the alleged "vacancy," and on the trial of this very cause copies of records have been read in evidence, certified by him as Secretary to be true copies, which certificates were made many weeks after the "legal vacancy" is said to have occurred, and were read without objection to their competency from any quarter. But when General Thomas was authorized to act as Secretary *ad interim* there was no "legal vacancy," nor any pretence of one. Mr. Stanton not only had not retired from the War Office, but he had received no notice to retire.

The testimony shows that while Mr. Stanton was in the regular discharge of his duties as Secretary, at the War Office, without notice of an order for his removal or of a purpose to remove him, General Thomas was called to the White House, and there presented with a warrant making him Secretary *ad interim*. As such he was at once assigned to duty. And the first duty assigned to him was that of making a vacancy by executing the order for the removal of Mr. Stanton.

It seems to me that any one who will open his eyes may plainly see that the authorization to General Thomas was issued, not as a means of supplying a vacancy, but as a means of making one; not to provide for the discharge of the duties of Secretary, but to prevent Mr. Stanton from discharging them. If the respondent had believed his simple order of removal would have made a vacancy in the office he would have proceeded to fill it by nomination, as President Adams did in 1800, and as sooner or later the respondent knew he must; and as in fact he did proceed, the next day, when he found the order of removal did *not* make a vacancy. But he did not expect Mr. Stanton would obey his order of removal. He knew Mr. Stanton had other views of the law. He thought to surprise him into acquiescence by confronting him suddenly with another pretender to the office. I believe this, because it is the only rational interpretation of his conduct, and because it is the very explanation he himself gave to General Sherman.

In his answer the respondent denies that he used or intended to use intimidation or threats, as is charged in some of the articles. But it seems to me he must either intend to deceive us by that denial, or he meant to deceive General Sherman when he offered him the appointment of Secretary *ad interim*, for he then tried to persuade him that Mr. Stanton was a coward, and would be intimidated by it. I do not suspect him of an attempt to deceive General Sherman; but, on the contrary, I hold him upon his own declarations guilty of an attempt to drive Mr. Stanton from office by threats and intimidations, as is charged against him.

I hold also that he conspired with General Thomas to do this, as is charged in article 4.

I hold that the testimony discloses every fact necessary to constitute a crime against the act of July 31, 1861.

If, instead of being arraigned before a court of impeachment, the respondent was on trial before a criminal court, I do not see how a jury could fail to convict him. Surely it will not be denied that the office of Secretary of War is such an office as is described in that act. It will not be denied that on the 21st of February last Mr. Stanton was holding it. It will not be denied that it was the purpose of both the respondent and of General Thomas to prevent him from holding it longer. To that end they conspired together. Both were unfriendly to Mr. Stanton. The respondent avows it in his answer. The Adjutant General does not avow it, but it is clearly inferable from the facts stated by him, that for several years he had been relieved from the post of Adjutant General by the Secretary, and that he had been but recently restored by the direct order of the President, and against the wishes of the Secretary.

It does not appear that any other human being was advised of this purpose common to those two individuals. On the contrary, there is strong presumptive evidence that no other person was advised of it.

It would seem natural that upon a measure of so much gravity the President should have consulted his cabinet. The gentlemen composing that cabinet were severally produced in court. The counsel for the respondent offered to prove by them what advice they gave the President upon some questions of law, but no intimation was given that they were consulted; or that they advised upon the expediency of this attempt to place the War Office in the hands of General Thomas, to the exclusion of Mr. Stanton. The means selected for that purpose were, as we have seen, two written orders, the one directing Mr. Stanton to turn over the office to the Adjutant General, and the other ordering the Adjutant General to take possession and discharge the duties. It may be said such methods were not calculated to intimidate Mr. Stanton. The result shows they did not intimidate him. But the testimony shows that the respondent reasoned otherwise. He told General Sherman that just such papers in his hands would intimidate the Secretary. If it be said that the President had the legal authority to issue the orders, and might, therefore, calculate on the obedience of Mr. Stanton, I reply that he did not revoke the orders when he found Mr. Stanton denied his authority and did not obey. If it be said no force was employed to compel obedience, I reply that force was threatened by the Adjutant General, both to Dr. Burleigh and Mr. Wilkeson.

If it be said that those threats were not sanctioned by the respondent, I reply that the Adjutant General, while he says the President did not specifically direct the employment of force, yet did authorize it by the order commanding him to take possession, and that on Friday, on Saturday, on Monday, and on Tuesday when told by the Adjutant General that Mr. Stanton refused to surrender, the respondent's uniform reply was substantially, "Go on ; take possession and discharge your duties ; " that he never once cautioned him against the use of force, and never once directed him to resort to the courts. And finally General Thomas says he abandoned the idea of force, not because he doubted his authority to use it, but because he did not wish to cause bloodshed.

And it cannot be allowed to the respondent to urge that he is not responsible for what General Thomas did, and what he threatened to do, within the scope of the warrant given him by the respondent himself, in furtherance of the common purpose. One of the reasons assigned by him for wishing to get rid of Mr. Stanton, was that he could not safely be responsible for his conduct. And yet he now protests that he is not responsible for the conduct of his successor, even when going right from his presence to prosecute a specific purpose with plenary instructions to execute it, and with no sort of restriction as to the means to be employed in the execution of it.

A few words of comment upon some considerations urged in defence upon this part of the case.

And first, it is said his attempt to eject Mr. Stanton and install General Thomas, did not succeed, and so he ought not to be punished. I cannot think the position is well taken. Whatever he could do to insure success, he did. If his orders were illegal, he cannot plead Mr. Stanton's lawful disobedience in his own justification. If his orders were legal, he cannot plead Mr. Stanton's unlawful resistence in his own justification. Mr. Stanton's conduct cannot make *his* acts either guilty or innocent. If one aim a blow at another, he is not held innocent because the intended victim wards it off, and so is not felled by it.

Again it is said the unlawfulness of his order is not clear, and the respondent might have been mistaken, and that it would be hard to impeach him for a mere mistake of law. Certainly it would. No reasonable man would think of doing so.

In my opinion the respondent has made graver mistakes as to his constitutional powers than are proved in this record. Many of his predecessors have made as grave and palpable ones. But I do not hold that either should have been impeached for them. When a President, faithfully striving to promote the public good, exerts a power which the law does not vest in him, a just people would not permit him to be punished for it. If the end aimed at be good, the means will be generously criticised.

But the respondent was aiming to do what the Senate advised should not be done, and what the Lieutenant General of the army, a man animated by great courage and great candor, and inspired by no party or personal attachments, admonished him not to do. I cannot help believing he was moved, not by any regard for the public welfare, but by the hope of gratifying his personal resentments. When malice dictates the end, judgment must not mistake the means.

But I see no reason for excusing the acts of the respondent upon the ground of mistake. If he was mistaken on the 21st of February, he is mistaken still. He has not recalled his orders. He is impeached by the representatives of the people because of them, and the issue he tenders is not that he was innocently mistaken, but that he was *right*, and that what he did, he would have done if he had known that his *conviction* was certain. He still employs General Thomas at the meetings of his cabinet as Secretary *ad interim*, while Mr. Stanton discharges the duties of Secretary at the War Office. And the astounding spectacle is exhibited of two rival claimants to that high office, the one recognized by the legislature, and by every other executive officer, and actually discharging the duties, but excluded from cabinet meetings; while the other is recognized by the President, and entertained at ministerial consultations, but is disowned everywhere else. And yet, for almost three months, the President has not taken the first legal step to terminate the pretensions of either.

If one is indicted for the larceny of a coat, and appears in the dock with the coat on his back, urges his title to it in his defence, and proclaims to the court that he would have taken it if he had been sure of going to the penitentiary for it, a jury would not be apt, after finding all the facts against him, to acquit, upon the assumption that he might have appropriated the coat under mistake.

I see nothing criminal in the interview between the respondent and General Emory. Nor am I satisfied it was prompted by any sinister purpose. And, therefore, upon the ninth article I must find the respondent not guilty.

The tenth article is of different purport from anything heretofore considered. In it the respondent is presented for certain utterances made by him on different occasions. I cannot reproduce here the language attributed to him. It is set forth at length in the article, and there is no dispute, I believe; that is proved substantially as avowed.

The representatives of the people present these speeches as official misconduct. For the defence, it is said the issue involves nothing more than a question of personal taste. However improper the words were, it is argued that the respondent must be protected in the use of them, because the Constitution guarantees freedom of speech to all men. To this the reply is that speech is not, and never was designed to be, *free*. Unrestrained speech is as fatal to freedom as the old restraints of despotism. Speech is not free in this country, nor in any country where there is both liberty and law. The Constitution has indeed commanded, in stern rebuke of an old form of despotism, that Congress shall make no law abridging the freedom of speech. Thereby fell the star-chamber and all government censorship. The clamps were struck from the organs of articulation. Thereby the tongue was made free as any other member. But no more so. Violent patients in a retreat for the insane are often put in straitjackets to avoid the possibility of mischief. But sane men are permitted to walk about in society with arms free and unconfined. But it does not follow that because they are unfettered they may use their arms as they will, and with impunity. The law still lays its imperious command upon every citizen, that he use not his freedom of limb to the injury of any man's person or property, or to the injury of the state. Whoever disregards the command must answer for the wrong. The same command is laid upon human speech. Whoever speaks to defame the character of his fellow, or to injure his property, or to incite to crime against the state, may be held responsible for so doing.

"Every freeman has an undoubted right to lay what sentiments he pleases before the public; to forbid this is to destroy the freedom of the press. But if he publishes what is improper, mischievous, or illegal, he must take the consequences of his own temerity." That sentiment is quoted from the Commentaries of William Blackstone by Justice Story, and with his hearty approval. (Story's Commentary on the Constitution, section 1878.)

And Chancellor Kent instructs us that "it has become a constitutional principle in this country, that every citizen may freely speak, write, and publish his sentiments on all subjects, being responsible for the abuse of that right; and that no law can rightfully be passed to restrain or abridge the freedom of the press." (1st Kent's Com., section 241.)

Speech is not therefore of necessity innocent because it is not muzzled.

Is the respondent amenable for the speeches attributed to him in the tenth article?

We are admonished that to hold him so would be to repeat upon him the wrong which the so-called sedition law of 1798 inflicted upon the people of the country. Clearly there is no analogy between the offence charged against the President in this article and the offences proscribed by the second section of the act of 1798. That was a proposal by the government to punish citizens for too free criticism upon the conduct of their own servants. The House of Representatives propose no more than to remove a servant of the people from office which they say he disgraces by his conduct and his speech. Counsel have treated this article as if it were an attempt to punish a citizen for animadverting upon the policy of a Congress. The purpose, if I understand it, is widely different from that. The article, after setting out the words of the respondent, used on the occasions referred to, concludes as follows: "Which said utterances, declarations, threats, and harangues, highly censurable in any, are peculiarly indecent and unbecoming in the Chief Magistrate of the United States, by means whereof said Andrew Johnson has brought the *high office of the President of the United States* into contempt, ridicule, and disgrace, to the great scandal of all good citizens, whereby said Andrew Johnson, President of the United States, did commit and was then and there guilty of a high misdemeanor in office."

The principle of the tenth article is precisely the reverse of the law of 1798. That law proposed to punish the *people* for criticising the ill conduct of their servants in the government. By the tenth article the people propose to remove one of their servants for ill conduct.

Because the servants may not tell their masters, the people, what to say, it does not follow that the people may not tell their servants what to say.

A law which should prohibit a man under penalties from tearing the siding from the house he owns, to make repairs, might be thought rather harsh, and yet it might not be thought unreasonable to prohibit a tenant from splitting up the floors and bedaubing the frescoes in the house he hires.

The people of the United States own the office of President. They built it. It is consecrated to their use. In it they thought to crystallize and employ the excellence of the republic. They claim the right to protect it from desecration. Their representatives aver that Andrew Johnson has disgraced that office. They tell us wherein. And the simple question presented in the tenth article is whether the language and the conduct proved under it are or are not degrading to the office of Chief Magistrate.

It is urged in reply that if it is disgraceful the Senate ought not to condemn it, because the representatives who prosecute have sometimes used language quite as bad, and that even in the Senate, which tries the case, words have been heard at times not much better. This defence is ingenious, but hardly good in law. The law of set-off is not unfamiliar to the practice of the courts. But I have never known it extended beyond settling of debts between the immediate parties to the record. I have never heard a defendant, sued for the amount of his grocer's bill, object that the court could not give judgment against him because the judge himself owed a bill at the same shop. I fear the respondent's counsel do not justly appreciate the Presidential office when they gravely plead in justification of the harangues set out in this article, the worst specimens of discussion found in the debates of the two houses of Congress. Much might be urged in palliation of those precedents, but all I care to say is, that, instead of being a justification for anything, they cannot be justified of themselves.

Were those utterances disgraceful to one holding the Presidential office?

It has been urged that he did not speak as a magistrate, but as a citizen. That, I apprehend, is a mistake. From the time one assumes that high office until he retires from it, he is always President. Not all he does is necessarily official, but all he does should be consistent with the exalted character of the office. The office of Chief Magistrate is not a garment to be laid off or put on at the pleasure of the incumbent. When once those high responsibilities are assumed they must be maintained. If the incumbent weary of them, he may resign. If he abuse them, he may be removed.

But, on the occasion referred to in the article, the respondent was acting semi-officially. He was not discharging any duty imposed on him as President, but he was exercising a high privilege belonging to him as such. Not as a citizen of Tennessee, but avowedly as President of the United States of America, was he then visiting and being visited by his great constituency.

Was his conduct such as became his character? I cannot find any rules in the law by which to try those utterances. I cannot consent to try them by the models furnished from the proceedings of the houses of Congress. I can try him only by my own estimate of what the bearing of a Chief Magistrate should be, when I say that in my judgment the conduct and the language proved against the respondent was wholly unbecoming the office he filled, and such as, if often repeated, would be fatal to the respect with which the people have hitherto cherished it. That judgment I believe is in strict accord with the opinion of the great majority of the American people as expressed at the time. I do not mean to speak figuratively when I say the people then hung their heads in mortification—not his political enemies alone, but his political friends as well. And of those friends, I doubt if there is one in the Senate who has not often declared his belief that but for the very matters charged in the tenth article, the people would have sanctioned the policy which the respondent then urged upon them, and which his friends professed to believe was vital to the peace and welfare of the country. How they can now vote conduct to be innocent to which they then ascribed such disastrous results, they can doubtless explain; I cannot. Many a lieutenant has been cashiered for "conduct unbecoming an officer and a gentleman." Is it possible the people cannot remove a President for the same offence, and that, too, exhibited on great public occasions?

The eleventh article alone remains to be noticed. In that the respondent is presented for having, on the 18th day of August, 1866, denied that the 39th Congress was a legitimate body authorized to enact laws for the United States, but that it was only a Congress of a part of the States; and for having, in pursuance of such declarations, set himself against the execution of several of its enactments—the acts fixing the tenure of civil offices and reconstructing the rebel States, among them. The respondent denies that he said the 39th Congress was a Congress of only part of the States, "in any sense or meaning other than that ten States of the Union were denied representation therein." No worse meaning than that could be imparted to the words he used.

"Ten States of the Union were excluded from the body. But the Constitution requires that Congress should be composed of two senators and a given number of representatives from *every* State; consequently this body was not the Congress of the United States." That was the doctrine he meant to teach. But he says free speech is secured to him, and he had a right so to teach. Of course. His right so to teach is as unquestionable as the right of the people to impeach him for it; but I cannot conceive of teachings more mischievous than these. He is sworn to see the *laws* executed. If that body was the Congress of the United States, its enactments were *laws*; if not, they were not laws. One of two conclusions, then, is inevitable. Either he meant to instruct the people that the enactments of that body might be disregarded, because not passed by a Congress, or he meant to tell them they must submit to enactments of a body which *was not*, but only *assumed* to be a Congress. Either conclusion, in my judgment, shows a criminal purpose. The article avers the first to be the true conclusion, and that in pursuance of that conclusion he himself undertook to obstruct the execution of the tenure-of-office act and some other enactments of that Congress.

The case shows that on the 12th of August, 1867, the respondent, in accordance with the provisions of the tenure-of-office act, suspended Edwin M. Stanton from the office of Secretary of War; that, in accordance with the same, he made General U. S. Grant Secretary *ad interim;* that, in accordance with the same, on the 12th of December, he communicated his reasons for the suspension to the Senate. All this was in strict *accord* with the provisions of the act, if not in *pursuance* of them. All these steps were authorized by the act of March 2, 1867, above referred to.

But that act also required that if the Senate did not approve the reasons for which the suspension was made the office should be restored.

Now, the case shows that the respondent designed and contrived to prevent that restoration in spite of the act. His letter to General Grant, on page 234 of the record, shows that, beyond all possibility of mistake. True he does not confess to have designed his exclusion longer than to try the right of Mr. Stanton in the courts of law; but that right could not be so determined during the remainder of this presidential term. But what was the question to be tried? Not the question of his right to remove Mr. Stanton, for he had not removed Mr. Stanton; he had only suspended him. Not the constitutionality of the tenure-of-office act, for the validity of that act could not be put in issue in a suit between Mr. Stanton and General Grant; for if the act was valid, it commanded Mr. Stanton to be restored, because the Senate had found the reasons for his suspension insufficient. If it was invalid, the order of suspension itself was without authority, and General Grant never had any right in the office. So, in such a suit, the respondent would have been exhibited in the attitude of asserting the validity of the tenure-of-office act, in order to get Mr. Stanton out of the office, and of denying it to prevent his getting back.

To avoid this monstrous predicament the respondent, in his answer, asserts what seems to me, if possible, still more monstrous. He asserts that he did not suspend Mr. Stanton by virtue of authority conferred by the act of March 2. True every step he took was a step prescribed by that act, and yet he avers, in his answer, that he did not suspend Mr. Stanton in pursuance of that act "until the next meeting of the Senate, or until the Senate should have acted upon the case, but by force of the power and authority vested in him by the Constitution and laws of the United States *indefinitely* and *at the pleasure of the President*."

It has come to that. The respondent, to justify his acts, not only asserts authority under the Constitution to *remove* all officers appointed by the joint act of himself and the Senate, in spite of laws to the contrary, and to replace them with others *commissioned* by himself alone, but he also claims the power to *suspend* them all and fill their places with *ad interim* appointments. The first is a power which gives the President absolute control of one incumbent for each office known to the laws. The last is a claim which gives him the right to duplicate the number.

So far as I know, this extraordinary power was never heard of until the respondent's answer was filed. I never saw a syllable in the Constitution to warrant the claim. No possible exigency of the service could require it; and to my mind the whole pretence, instead of excusing the respondent's acts, only aggravates their guilt.

Because, therefore, the testimony in this case compels me to believe that the respondent, in order to punish Edwin M. Stanton for his fidelity to the laws, did seek to remove him from the office of Secretary of War, in which he had long and ably served his country; and because he perverted to that purpose the solemn trust reposed in the Executive by the act of August 7, 1789, therein acting in wanton disregard of the public welfare; and because he attempted to do it against the advice of the Senate, without consultation with his cabinet, and without previous notice to the people; and because, in furtherance of that unlawful purpose, he sought to commit the powers of that high office to Lorenzo Thomas, and did, without any authority of law, issue his warrant to that effect, before said Stanton had surrendered those powers, and when he had no just reason to believe said Stanton would surrender them; and because he did intend and contrive thereby to intimidate said Stanton into a surrender of those powers by making him believe that force would be employed to compel his surrender; and because I believe he did use the language charged upon him by the representatives of the people, and that such utterances are of evil example, of pernicious tendency, and calculated to degrade the office of President in the estimation of the people; and because he did publicly teach that the 39th Congress was not a body whose enactments had the authority of law; and because he did himself set the example of disobeying the enactments of that Congress by endeavoring to induce the General of the army to retain possession of the office of Secretary of War, after the Senate had decided, in pursuance of one of the laws of that Congress, that said Stanton should and ought to repossess the same; therefore I find the respondent guilty of high crimes and misdemeanors respectively charged in articles 2, 3, 4, 5, 7, 8, 10, 11.

OPINION OF MR. SENATOR EDMUNDS.

I had hoped that the formal consideration of the subject would be officially reported in order that the world might know, without diminution or exaggeration, the reasons and views upon which we proceed to our judgment. But as the Senate has, for causes satisfactory to itself, decided otherwise, I have reduced to writing all that I expected to have said here, that it may be, so far as of any interest to them, exposed to the examination of my countrymen.

I can only, within the time allotted by the rules, state briefly the grounds upon which my judgment in this case rests. All the arguments on either side cannot be reviewed in detail, and they must therefore be dismissed with the general observation that in those respects in which they are not in harmony with the reasons or conclusions I now state, they appear to me to be unsound.

As my duties are clearly judicial, "impartially" to try the respondent upon the accusations contained in the articles of impeachment, and to decide "according to the constitution and the laws," I have only conscientiously to discharge that duty, and so doing I have no concern with, or responsibility for the consequences, political or other, that may flow from my decision. If the respondent has been guilty of a violation of law, the representatives of the people in the House of Representatives, like a grand jury in ordinary cases, are the sole judges whether that violation of law is of such enormity, or of such consequence as a precedent, if permitted to pass without notice, as to require the prosecution of the offender. As they have presented the cause for our action, we have only to apply the law as it is to the facts proved. We have no discretion to say guilty or not guilty according to our views of expediency, or our personal wishes. Whatever they may be they can have no tendency to show that the respondent is either innocent or guilty. These propositions are fundamental elements in all civilized systems of jurisprudence. Any other would be a mockery of justice, and soon result in the destruction of liberty and free government. The truth and the law are the only stable foundations of society, and whoever, for any cause or motive, however worthy apparently, departs from these, commits a great wrong upon what all good men unite in wishing to preserve.

The statement of these principles would have been a work of entire supererogation, but for the fact that the appeals and remonstrances of the press of the country, touching our disposition of the case, have been urgent, and which, if extended to all trials, would poison the fountains of justice.

The first three articles, taken collectively, charge the respondent with an illegal removal of Mr. Stanton from office as Secretary of War, and the illegal appointment of Adjutant General Thomas *ad interim* in his place. These articles also aver that these acts were done with intent to violate the Constitution and the law. The answer asserts that although the acts charged were designedly done, they are justifiable; because,

1. If the act of March 2, 1867, prohibited them, it was in conflict with the Constitution, and therefore void.

2. The Constitution and the laws under it in force prior to March 2, 1867, conferred the power of removal upon the respondent, and that act did not in this instance purport to take it away.

3. If Mr. Stanton was lawfully removed, the power to appoint General Thomas was conferred by the act of 1795, which for that purpose was still in force.

4. If either the removal or appointment was in violation of law, still it was done in good faith, under a sincere claim of right, and therefore, it could not be the basis of, or amount to a crime or misdemeanor.

Upon the allegations and proofs, the commission of the acts charged is indisputable, and hence the main question is, do either of them constitute a high crime or misdemeanor?

The Constitution made express provision for the *appointment* of officers, as follows:

> And he [the President] shall nominate, and by and with the advice and consent of the Senate, shall appoint ambassadors, other public ministers, and consuls, judges of the Supreme Court, and all other officers of the United States, whose appointments are not herein otherwise provided for, and which shall be established by law; but the Congress may, by law, vest the appointment of such inferior officers as they shall think proper in the President alone, in the courts of law, or in the heads of departments.

And power was also conferred upon the President "to fill up all vacancies that may happen during the recess of the Senate, by granting commissions which shall expire at the end of their next session."

"*The* executive power" named as to be vested in the President, must of necessity be *that* power and no other, which the Constitution grants to him. So speaking, it proceeds at once to define and describe it. All the *powers* of the President are specifically enumerated, with apparently the utmost precision, even those most clearly within the general definition of "executive power." Two of these, namely, the power to be commander in-chief and the power to grant reprieves and pardons, are perfect illustrations of this. On the other hand, his *duties* are partly detailed, as to "receive ambassadors," and partly generalized, as "to take care that the laws be faithfully executed." This difference arose from the nature of things. The limited *powers* which the framers of the Constitution thought fit to grant to the person who was to take the place of kings and emperors in systems of government hostile to liberty, could be easily named, and ought to be jealously defined. The *duties* relating to seeing the *laws* faithfully executed could not all be foreseen in detail, and from them there could scarcely arise any danger to the republic, for he was not to execute the laws himself, but to "take care" that they *be* "faithfully executed." This could only be done by just such, and only the methods and agencies provided for that purpose by the laws themselves. He could not, rightfully, violate the laws in order to enforce them. This is, I believe, unquestioned; and it was perfectly stated by Attorney General Black, on the 20th of November, 1860, in advising President Buchanan touching his duties relating to some of the first acts of the rebellion, as follows:

> To the Chief Executive Magistrate of the Union is confided the solemn duty of seeing the laws faithfully executed. That he may be able to meet this duty with a power equal to its performance, he nominates his own subordinates and removes them at pleasure. For the same reason, the land and naval forces are under his orders as their commander-in-chief. *But his power is to be used only in the manner prescribed by the Legislative Department. He cannot accomplish a legal purpose by illegal means, or break the laws himself to prevent them from being violated by others.* (9. Op. Att'y Gen. 516.)

The Constitution expressly provides, on the other hand, that *Congress* shall have power "to make all laws which shall be necessary and proper for carrying into execution the foregoing powers, and all other powers vested by the Constitution in the government of the United States, *or in any department thereof.*"

In view of these provisions, I cannot doubt that the regulation of the tenure of the offices to be established by law was not confided by the Constitution to the President, but was left to be provided for by legislation.

The scheme, plainly, was to leave the *selection* of persons to fill offices to the President, acting with the advice and consent of the Senate, and to leave to the *whole* government—that is to the law-making power—full discretion as to the establishment of offices, and as to the terms upon which, and the tenure by which, they should be held by the persons so selected. Any other construction would defeat, as for several years prior to the recent act it has defeated in many instances, entirely, the express declaration of the Constitution that the offices shall be filled by such persons as shall be advised by the Senate; for temporary commissions could be issued from session to session, even to the very persons rejected by the Senate, as has been the case. And if officers by the Constitution are removable at the will of the President, why, when once appointed, should they not hold at his pleasure, and if so, how can the law put a period to their holding, as has been done in various instances from the first, without question from any source?

Certainly if, when the Constitution is silent, the legislative power may declare that whoever is appointed to a particular office shall *cease* to hold it at the end of four years, it may also declare that the appointee shall enjoy it during that time. The two things are complementary to each other, and logically inseparable.

These views as to what in general belongs to legislative power are fully sustained by many decisions of the Supreme Court, among which, Martin v. Hunter's lessee, 1 Wheat., 326; Wayman v. Southard, 10-1; 16 Peters, 89; Jones v. Van Zandt, 5 How., may be read with profit.

It was to establish a reign of law, the only safeguard of society, and the only means of liberty, that the Constitution was formed. We must, therefore, suppose that the cases not specifically provided for, and the implied powers generally were intended to be left to the provisions of law, in making which both the President and Congress must always participate, and usually concur, and not to the uncontrolled will of the executive. Indeed, the counsel for the respondent do not seem very seriously to question this interpretation of the Constitution considered independently of a construction, which they insist has been by legislative discussion and enactment, and by long practice of executives put upon it.

I will dispose, very briefly, of this construction, as it is called. Extended examination, for which there is not time, would make the fallacy of it clear to demonstration. So far as legislative discussion is concerned, (although that is no safe or admissible guide to the construction of law as law, for no member is bound by the opinions or words of any other, and so his silence is no acquiescence,) the pretension has been from the beginning the subject of dispute between adherents of a President and the representatives of the States and people, not as to the right of a President to resist a legislative rule, which has rarely if ever before been asserted, but as to the propriety of enacting one; and even Mr. Madison himself, whose opinions are so much relied upon by the counsel for the respondent, was at different times on both sides of the question, and Mr. Adams, whose casting vote in the Senate passed the act of 1789, was strongly opposed to the provision of the Constitution requiring the Senate to confirm any appointment, and he was by the public so generally supposed to have been influenced by his expectation of becoming President himself, that he thought it necessary to repel the accusation of (to use his own words) "deciding in favor of the powers of the prime because I look up to that goal."

An analysis of the debates and votes upon the act of 1789, creating the department of foreign affairs, will demonstrate the inconclusiveness of tests of this sort. Of the fifty-four members of the House of Representatives present, those who argued that the power of removal was, by the Constitution, in the President, were Sedgwick, Madison, (who had maintained the opposite,) Vining, Boudinot, Clymer, Benson, Scott, Goodhue, and Baldwin. These who contended that the President had not the power, but that it might be conferred by law, but ought not to be, were Jackson, Stone, and Tucker.

Those who believed that the President had not the power, and that it could not be conferred, were White, Smith of South Carolina, Livemore, and Page.

Those who maintained that the President had not the inherent power, but that it might be bestowed by law, and that it was expedient to bestow it, were Huntington, Madison at first, Gerry, Ames, Hartly, Lawrence, Sherman, Lee, and Sylvester—twenty-four in all, speaking. Of these, fifteen thought the Constitution did not confer this power upon the President, while only nine thought otherwise. But those who thought he had the power and those who thought the law ought to confer it were seventeen.

Thirty did not speak at all, and in voting upon the words conferring or recognizing the power, they were just as likely to vote upon the grounds of Roger Sherman as upon the reasons of those who merely intended to admit the power. On the motion to strike out the words "to be removable by the President," the ayes were twenty, and the noes thirty-four; but no guess, even, can be formed that this majority took one view rather than the other. Indeed, adding only the eight who spoke against the inherent power, but for the provisions of law, to the twenty opponents of both, and there is a clear majority adverse to any such inherent power in the President. And when on the next day it was proposed to change the language to that which became the law, among the ayes are the names of White, Smith of South Carolina, Livemore, Page, Huntington, Gerry, Ames, and Sherman, all of whom, as we have seen, were of opinion against the claim of an inherent power of removal in the President. All this, with a possible error as to one or two persons, arising from the vagueness or contradictory character of their language, is in the record of the proceedings, obvious to any one who will undergo the labor of its examination.

The construction, then, claimed to be derived from this source ceases to have any foundation in point of fact.

On the other hand, a select committee of the Senate, of which Thomas H. Benton was chairman, and having among its members Mr. Van Buren and Mr. Hayne, made a report in 1826, in which they say, "Not being able to reform the Constitution in the election of President, they must go to work upon his powers, and trim down these by statutory enactments whenever it can be done by law, and with a just regard to the proper efficiency of the government. For this purpose they have reported six bills," &c. One of these bills was a bill entitled "A bill to prevent military and naval officers from being dismissed the service at the pleasure of the President;" and it prohibited any dismissal except on the sentence of a court-martial, or on address of both Houses of Congress. The substance of this bill became a law by the approval of the respondent himself, on the 13th day of July, 1866. In 1835, on the favorable report of a select committee of which Mr. Calhoun, Mr. Webster and Mr. Benton were members, on the same subject of executive patronage, analagous measures were agitated, but I have not space to detail them. Aside from actual legislation appearing in the statutes, there has been no general recognition of these claims, but a constant protest by all parties, in their turn, against them.

As to the supposed recognition by the laws themselves, and a practice under them, it need only be said that the whole course of legislation, comprised in more than twenty statutes, has until 1863, *authorized* the President to make removals; and hence *they furnish no evidence of his powers, independently of the law, but the contrary.* It needs no argument to show that what the laws have *authorized* they may *forbid.* No law can become so old that the legislative power cannot change it; and even as to legislative construction it is the same. A later Congress has just as much power in that respect as an earlier.

The acts of 1792, 1795, and 1863, relating to *ad interim* appointments, which have always been acquiesced in without question from any source, are decisive utterances, so far as legislative action can possibly be so, of the power of the *law* to regulate the exercise of powers and duties *expressly conferred* by the Constitution upon the President and Senate. Our own statutes, and those of all states having written constitutions, are full of similar or analogous instances.

Can it be said, then, that where the letter of the Constitution is silent upon another branch of the same subject, the law has no power to speak, and that behind that veil of silence sleeps a kingly prerogative of the President?

The act of 1863, providing for a national currency, expressly declared that the comptroller of the currency should hold his office for five years, and should not be removed without the advice and consent of the Senate. It was passed by votes irrespective of party, receiving, among others, that of the honorable senator from Wisconsin who sits furthest from me, (Mr. Doolittle), without any objection, from any source; to this feature of it. It was approved by President Lincoln. The law and practice of the government was thus changed, and, in that instance, restored to the letter and true spirit of the Constitution, with the concurrence of all parties, full five years before this case arose. And, as I have said, substantially, and indeed, identically, the same principle was, with the official approval of the respondent himself, applied to military and naval officers by the act of July 13, 1866, relating to the army, prohibiting their removal without the sentence of a court-martial, which power had been exercised during the war, *under the authority of law*, and not under claim of prerogative. (Act of July 17, 1862.)

The judicial decisions and opinions touching this subject support the same view.

Marbury vs. Madison, 1 Cranch, is, as I understand it, expressly in point; and in the late case of Mr. Guthrie, (17 How.,) the only judge whose views of jurisdiction made it proper for him to speak, upheld the same doctrine.

For these reasons, and many others that the time does not permit me to state, I conclude that the act of March 2, 1867, is perfectly constitutional.

Does the act apply to the case of Mr. Stanton, and forbid his removal at the will of the President?

It is conceded that the leading clause of the section does include him, but it is claimed that he is taken out of it by a proviso which not only effects that, but which also excludes him from the proviso itself or fails to mention him at all! In construing a statute it is always necessary to look at the whole scope of the law in all its sections, and at the state of facts existing at the time of its passage, in order to make a proper application of the law, and to search through the language of the act for the design to which it was devoted.

These facts are that Mr. Stanton was then the Secretary of War, subject to removal from office under the act of 1789 at the pleasure of the respondent. On that state of facts the proviso said that "the Secretary of War," &c., "*shall hold their offices*, respectively, for and during the term of the President by whom they may have been appointed," &c. Now, as Mr. Stanton was then Secretary of War, he must be the person included in that description. That Secretary is (with the others) by name the very subject of which the proviso speaks. And it will be noticed that the language as to the appointment is in the past tense, "*may have been* appointed" are the words. That the proviso declared something touching the tenure of Mr. Stanton cannot truly be denied. But if it did not declare *anything* as to him, then, confessedly, the leading and sweeping opening clause embraces him, for then, as to him it is not "otherwise provided." Having ascertained, then, that the proviso speaks of Mr. Stanton, we find that it says that he "*shall hold*" his office, &c., for a described period. These words, it will be seen, apply only to the *future*, and import, if language has any meaning, that he shall, after the passage of the act, *continue and remain in office by force of the law*. The respondent's counsel insist, however, that the real meaning of this language is (if applicable to him) that he shall *not* hold the office at all!

If, as we have shown, when the act passed, he was the Secretary of War named in and affected by the proviso, the question is, was he, on the 21st day of February, 1868, holding office in the same way and under the same tenure that he was at the passage of the act, which said he *should hold*, and not that he should not? It is not disputed that he was. Was he then, at the passage of the act, holding his office "during the term of the President by whom he was appointed?" He was appointed by President Lincoln. Then was

March 2, 1867, the time of the passage of the act, during the term of Mr. Lincoln, who was, so far as relates to Mr. Stanton, the President named in the proviso?

The Constitution says the President " shall hold his office during the *term of four years*," and that the Vice-President shall be " chosen for the same term." It creates and permits no other term or period whatever, but provides only, in case of death, &c., for the devolution of " duties" or " *office*," not the term, upon the Vice-President.

Mr. Lincoln began a regular term on March 4, 1865, and died in April of that year, when the office devolved on the respondent. Now, if the respondent became thereby invested with a constitutional " *term*" *of his own* as President, he must be in for *four years* from April 15, 1865, which is not pretended by any one. Hence, he must take the office for the *unexpired term of Mr. Lincoln,* his predecessor. It was the *office* and not the *term*, which are distinct things, that Mr. Lincoln held when he died. The *office* did not die with him, but survived in all its current identity and force to his successor, the respondent, measured by precisely the same " *term*" that it was before. When, therefore, the statute speaks of " the term of the President," it does not refer to ownership or possession, which a man cannot be said to have after his death, but it plainly refers to the term *for and in relation to which* that President was elected, and which, by the Constitution, was attributed to him. A reference to any lexicon will show that this is the principal and most frequent meaning of the word " of."

To claim that at the death of Mr. Lincoln the " term" applicable to him thereby expired and ended, would be as erroneous as to claim that the death of a tenant for a term of years not yet expired, produces an end of the term, and that his legal representative either takes a new term or none at all.

But it is truly said that Mr. Lincoln had a prior term *in which*, in the language of counsel, Mr. Stanton was appointed, which had expired two years before the passage of the law; and it is claimed that that *first term* is the one named in the act, and that it meant therefore that Mr. Stanton should hold for one month after March 4, 1865, instead of one month after March 4, 1869. The answer (if any be needful) is that the act passed in the middle of Mr. Lincoln's second *and then existing term*, and to reject that term, and apply the words of the statute to a past and completed term, which had then no existence either in law or fact, would be contrary not only to any supposable intention of the law makers, but in direct violation of the words of the statute, which declare that he " shall hold" (instead of not holding) not during the term " in which" he " may have been appointed," as counsel use the words, but " during the term of the President *by whom* he may have been appointed." Any other construction would involve the gross absurdity that Congress by that act, on the 2d of March, 1867, legislated out of office virtually, as of April 4, 1865, those Secretaries who had been appointed by Mr. Lincoln, and intended to declare that officers then legally holding should go out of office two years before the passage of the act!

This result was sought to be avoided by the distinguished counsel who opened the defence, if I rightly understood him, by advancing the idea that the proviso should be construed to read and apply to *future* Secretaries, &c., and to have no reference to the then present ones. This is, perhaps, sufficiently answered already. I know of no rule of construction by which that word can be interpolated into the statute, and if it were, the proviso would be made thereby to have no reference at all to the present Secretaries, who would then fall within the very letter and protection of the body of the section.

The proviso cannot fairly be made to take the case out of the general clause of the section, on the ground that this is a case therein "otherwise provided" for, as is claimed, and then be construed not to affect the case itself, and to leave it under the act of 1789, on the ground that it does not apply to the case at all! That would be saying that it did and did not speak of the case.

The idea that the proviso does not speak of the present Secretary of War arises, on the very reasoning of those who maintain it, out of the fallacy of confounding the *subject* of the proviso, (the Secretary of War,) with what is *affirmed of that subject,* thus: " What is declared or affirmed in the proviso of the Secretary of War is, under the circumstances, erroneous or non-existing; therefore nothing is declared of the subject, (the Secretary of War;") which is absurd. The second section plainly points out, also, the *only* way of removal of *all* officers, but with my views of the first it is not necessary to enlarge upon it.

It is said that this was not the intention in fact when the law passed; and to prove this the expression of one or two senators, made upon the spur and in the hurry of the moment, are cited. I dissent entirely from any such inference, and from any such rule of interpreting or administering law, as law. With the exception of certain questions appealing to the will of the whole law-making power, and not necessary to be now enumerated, the body is responsible for, and its will is found in, what it declares in its laws, and not for, or in the opinions of its individual members. The journals of the houses, even, cannot be resorted to for any such purpose. This is the rule in all civilized countries, and is, with the solid reasons for it, known to every lawyer.

It is urged, as touching in some degree the probable intent of this proviso, that the construction I have put upon it would work an inequality in the duration of the offices of the various Secretaries, some having been appointed by Mr. Lincoln, and some by Mr. Johnson. If that were the effect, it could not alter the plain construction of the law as applied to the first-named Secretaries. But no such result follows. The evident meaning of the word "of," used in the phrase "during the term of the President by whom they may have been appointed," being "relating, or having reference to," the word "*term*" as there used and applied. under the circumstances existing, to *all the Secretaries*—which embraced both classes—related both to Mr. Lincoln and Mr. Johnson. It related, as I have shown, to Mr. Lincoln primarily and expressly, and it related to Mr. Johnson *sub'modo*, who, as Vice-President, was chosen for, and who succeeded as President for, the "*same* term," and who was, under the qualifications of the Constitution, filling out the unexpired term relating to Mr. Lincoln. Thus, and in no other way, can all the words of the proviso be made effective, and a rational and just result be reached. It appears to me, therefore, without any doubt, that the law in question covers the case.

The act, then, prohibited the removal of Mr. Stanton and the appointment of General Thomas, and it declared such removal or appointment to be a high misdemeanor, and denounced a punishment against it.

But it is contended that, as the articles charge not only an intentional doing of the acts forbidden—which the respondent admits—but also an intent thereby to violate the law and the Constitution—which he denies—he cannot be found guilty unless it is also proved that such intent existed in point of fact. I do not understand that to be the law, and I think no authority for such a proposition can be found anywhere. Certainly the cases cited by the counsel for the respondent do not maintain it, unless it be conceded that the discretion therein spoken of as existing in the course of exercising constitutional executive powers, or authority delegated by law, means a discretion to decide what powers are executive, and what authority is delegated, in spite of the Constitution that measures and defines the powers, and the law that confers the authority; a proposition so contrary to justice and reason and so subversive of government that it carries its own refutation.

The philosophy and experience of ages concur in the propriety of the maxim that "ignorance of the law excuseth no man." For obvious reasons a government of laws could not exist if any man or officer were to be left to put his own construction upon, or to form and act upon his own views of the validity of the laws framed for the benefit and protection of all. Every citizen, either in or out of office, acts in the peril of the law. If the respondent really believed that this case was not within the act of Congress, or that the act was unconstitutional, he could do what he did at the risk of being condemned if he proved to be wrong, or of being justified if he proved to be right, in the judgment of the tribunal of last resort before which he might be brought for trial, and to which tribunal, the same Constitution, which he claims the right to judge of for himself, has committed by express command the high duty to try *him* for such acts, upon the same principles of law impartial and immutable, as apply to the humblest citizen in the land.

In general, it is only when the motive or intention is an element in the description or definition of the very act forbidden that it becomes material on the trial of a person accused of crime. Murder, larceny, and robbery, like the case cited by Mr. Evarts, are instances of this kind. Treason, violations of the fugitive slave laws, and the liquor laws, are illustrations of the other class of cases, which embraces so much of this one as relates to removal and appointment, the unlawful doing of which the statute declares to be a misdemeanor, and punishes as such. All that is required in such cases is the voluntary commission of the act forbidden. An erroneous belief that it was lawful is no defence. Upon this all writers upon criminal law, all decisions, all systems of jurisprudence, and the practice of all countries, agree. It is true that the morally innocent sometimes suffer from this necessary rule, but in such cases the hardship necessary to the stability of society is usually mitigated by a remission of penalties.

In this case there is no penalty in the legal or constitutional sense to be inflicted by this tribunal. *Punishment* by impeachment does not exist under our Constitution. The accused cannot thereby be deprived of life, liberty, or property. He can only be removed from the office he fills and prevented from holding office, not as a punishment, but as a means merely of protection to the community against the danger to be apprehended from having a criminal in office. It merely does what the respondent himself claims the power to do, at his own pleasure, in respect to Mr. Stanton and every other officer in the land. The only difference is, that this body does it under oath, upon a trial, under an authority expressly conferred, while the respondent claims it and has done it without any such sanctions of justice and at his mere will.

The "indictment, trial, judgment, and punishment" of the respondent are, by the Constitution, expressly reserved to the ordinary criminal courts.

It has been said that there is injustice in condemning an officer for infractions of law committed under the supposition that they were legal acts. There may be hardship, but there can be no injustice, in vindicating the supremacy of the law. We do not make the law, we only adjudge what it is. It is the law that speaks to the offender through us, and the same law imposes upon us the duty to declare it. Were it material, however, to inquire into the motive and purposes of the respondent in these transactions, it would be an easy task to show that they are not above criticism, resting, as they seem to do, upon his dislike to a system of laws which he wished to overthrow, but which the Secretary was unwilling to assist in. It is enough, for the present, to say that if the respondent be legally guilty, to acquit him upon any such grounds as are claimed would be to sanction a disregard of law and to invite him, as well as future Presidents, to try more forcible and dangerous experiments upon the government, instead of teaching the great lesson that, in some form, all nations must learn at last, that its highest officers ought to be most careful and scrupulous in the observance of its laws.

I conclude, then, that the intents charged in these three articles are either immaterial, or such as the law conclusively infers from the acts proved, although I should have no hesitation in finding, as a matter of fact, that in the removal of Mr. Stanton, the respondent did intend to violate the act of March 2, 1867, if not the Constitution. While it is probable that he and many of the heads of departments thought at the time the act passed, as did some members of Congress, that the Secretaries appointed by Mr. Lincoln were not within it, I am fully satisfied that, either upon or without advice, he thought, when he suspended Mr. Stanton in August, 1867, and has since thought that the statute covered the case. His conduct is, to my mind, reconcilable with no other hypothesis. He had then determined (as he says himself) that he could no longer tolerate Mr. Stanton in the office; yet, instead of removing him, as he had, if he acted with a view to the faithful execution of the laws, a perfect legal right to do under the act of 1789, if the act of March 2, 1867, did not protect him, he *suspended* him, as that act permitted, designated another to act, for which designation, upon a suspension, there was no pretence or color of law, save that same act, and reported his action to the Senate within the time and in the manner required by it. And, as he now claims, he also took these and subsequent steps, in order to test in the courts the validity of this law, which he believed to invade the constitutional rights of the executive, and which he was, therefore, bound to test judicially. If he thought the case was not within the law, why did he not remove Mr. Stanton in August? And how could he think that the case could be made to try the validity of a law that did not apply to it?

But the respondent insists that, although the law may be valid and cover the case, inasmuch as his act of dismissal of Mr. Stanton was illegal and void, it was no removal of Mr. Stanton, and no violation of the law prohibiting removals. If this novel notion could be popularized into all criminal trials it would be of vast benefit to offenders. The result would be that, as no act in violation of law changes the rights of innocent persons, all such acts must be guiltless, because void. The statute does not forbid or punish *legal* acts of removal, (it would be strange if it did,) but *illegal* ones like this, which, so far as anything the respondent could do, was complete; for, had it been legal, Mr. Stanton by that act alone would have been out of office. The respondent's position put in the forms of logic would stand thus : the statute punishes all removals ; illegal removals are void and not removals at all ; therefore the statute punishes no illegal removals.

It has been made a question in respect to the appointment of Thomas, (supposing Mr. Stanton had been lawfully removed so as to create a vacancy,) whether that appointment was lawful. No power for that appointment is claimed under the Constitution ; but the act of 1795 is relied upon as authority for it. It is so if it be still in force; but it seems clear to my mind, after a careful investigation of the three acts on the same subject, and the decisions of courts upon analogous questions, that the act of 1863 is a substitute for both the act of 1792 and 1795, and that it was intended to take the place of both these acts entirely. In statutes, as in contracts, the intention of the framers, drawn from the words of the acts and the facts to which they apply and under which they were made, is the pole star of construction.

The act of 1792 applied to cases of "death," "absence," and "sickness," in the three then existing departments, and provided for temporary appointment, without limitation as to the choice of persons, till the cause therefor should cease.

The act of 1795 provided in the same way for cases of "vacancy" in the same three departments only, but limited the supply to six months. These might happen in four modes, as the law then stood ; by death, expiration of term, removal from office, and resignation.

The act of 1863 covered *all* the departments, and described two cases of vacancy, those by death and by resignation, and also sickness and absence, and required the temporary service to be performed by some officer of some department other than the one in which the case might arise, and for six months only. The last act, therefore, is on the same subject as both the former ones, and changes the provisions of each. It provides for all the *classes* of cases embraced in both those acts, though not for every *instance* in each class, and it requires a *totally different* and *restricted method of supply*. It is impossible to imagine any reason for requiring a vacancy caused by death or resignation, both of which must be independent of the President's will, and fortuitous as to him, to be supplied in a particular and limited manner, while a vacancy caused by removal at the will of the President, or expiration of term, neither of which could be fortuitous, should be left to be filled at the mere pleasure of the President, without any guard or limitation whatever. It must be presumed, therefore, that the intention was to substitute a more carefully guarded and limited system, in the place of the old one, and not to allow vacancies made by the law or the will of the President to be so filled. This is made the more probable when we consider that even this is going to the utmost verge of legislative power in such cases.

The law upon the subject of repeals, by implication, is well summed up by the supreme court of Massachusetts, in Bartlett *vs.* King, (12 Mass., 563,) as follows:

"A subsequent statute revising the whole subject matter of a former one, and evidently intended as a substitute for it, although it contains no express words to that effect, must, on the principles of law, as well as in reason and common sense, operate to repeal the former."

And in Leighton *vs.* Walker, (9. N. H, 61,) it is decided that—

"When the design to revise a statute clearly appears, the former statutes are to be considered as no longer in force, though not expressly repealed."

I am of opinion, therefore, that the respondent is guilty, as charged in the first three articles. There is another view of this removal and appointment not necessary, as I construe the law, to a decision, but which is of too much importance to be passed by in silence. It is this, whether if the case stood upon the acts of 1789 and 1795 alone, one of which authorizes a removal at pleasure, and the other an appointment *ad interim*, the respondent can justify his conduct upon the evidence before us. The inducing and controlling *motive* of these acts of the respondent was displeasure because the Secretary of War was not so subservient to him in his avowed and determined opposition to the laws of the land respecting the southern States as some other heads of departments; and the undisputed *design* of the respondent, in his efforts to displace Mr. Stanton, was to replace him by some one more pliant to his wishes and less earnest in his administration of the laws. This was the "harmony" desired in the "cabinet." These were the "public considerations of a high character" which made Mr. Stanton's resignation desirable to the respondent, and which have led him to commit the acts appearing in the evidence. The case then is, a removal of a faithful officer, neither accused nor suspected of any other wrong than adherence to the duty the law imposed upon him, *because* of that faithfulness and adherence to duty, by a President of the United States who was determined thereby to counteract and defeat the law, because he believed or professed to believe in a different "policy" of his own! In my opinion no higher crime, no graver violation of constitutional duty, no act more dangerous to law, or to the liberties of the nation, can be found within the reach of the executive. Surely, the opinion of Mr. Madison, so much referred to by the counsel, cannot be questioned on this point. He says:

"The danger then consists merely in this: The President can displace from office a man whose merits require that he should be continued in it; what will be the motive which the President can have for such abuse of his power, and the authority that operates to prevent it? In the first place he will be impeachable by the House for such an act of maladministration, &c." (Annals Congress VI, p. 517.)

It is, perhaps, proper in this connection that I should say expressly, what is implied in what I have stated, that I entirely disagree with the doctrine advanced in the argument, that we may find the respondent guilty, although the statute he has violated, affecting his rights, is itself a nullity, and in violating it he has only done what the Constitution, the supreme law, permitted. If such be the law the Constitution, instead of being a guard, guide, and warning to officers, is a snare.

The fourth article is denied by the answer, and I do not think that it is proved.

The fifth article charges an unlawful conspiracy to prevent the execution of the act of March 2, 1867, and an unlawful attempt to prevent Mr. Stanton from holding the office. The conspiracy is denied, but the act is admitted, with a claim of its legality. This article is, I think, embodied within the same principles as the first, and I am of opinion, upon the grounds already stated, that the respondent is guilty; for, although the mere attempt to do an unlawful act is not within the penal section of that act, I think that an attempt to commit an unlawful act of such grave character as this, is in law, a high misdemeanor.

The Supreme Court of the United States (United States vs. Quincy, 6 Pet., 465) has correctly defined a criminal attempt as follows:

"To attempt to do an act does not, either in law or in common parlance, imply the completion of the act or any definite progress towards it. Any effort or endeavor to effect it will satisfy the terms of the law."

The sixth and seventh articles allege a conspiracy to seize (the sixth) by force, (the seventh,) unlawfully, the War Department, property, &c. This is denied by the answer. It seems to be properly conceded by the defence, even if the respondent had a lawful right to remove Mr. Stanton and to appoint General Thomas, that if that right was in honest dispute he could not justify resorting to force instead of the law to dispossess an officer from an office which he had legally held, and which he still claimed in good faith to hold legally.

The question then on this article is purely one of fact. Did the respondent, upon the facts proved, and what we may lawfully notice of public history in connection with those facts, combine with Thomas to get possession of the War Office at the expense of resorting to violence, or physical power, if that should be needful to reach the result? At the expense of repetition, to a certain extent, I will state the case upon this question. It is matter of history that prior to the July session of Congress in 1867, the opposition of the respondent to the laws relating to the rebel States was so great that every obstacle that legal ingenuity could suggest was, under his sanction, thrown in the way of their operating in the spirit intended by Congress, and that their effect was thus almost paralyzed. It is also historic that Mr. Stanton, through whose department these laws were to be carried into execution or to be obstructed, was earnestly in favor of carrying them out according to the manifest will of Congress and the fair meaning of the laws themselves. Nevertheless, obstructive interpretations and orders were issued which led to the session of July, 1867, and the explanatory act of that session. The personal relations of the respondent and Mr. Stanton had been theretofore always friendly, and it has never been suggested even, that Mr. Stanton had or has committed any wrong toward the President personally or otherwise, save in his conduct before mentioned, and in his refusal to resign. "Public consideration," alone, as the President himself stated, were the cause of the difference. The difference as to these laws, then, existed at that session. The respondent, in his answer, says that prior to August 5, 1867, which was only two weeks after the adjournment, "he became satisfied that he could not allow the said Stanton to continue to hold the office without hazard to the public interest." In other words the President was opposed to the law in all its parts, and determined to defeat it. Mr. Stanton was for it. This was the sole *casus belli*. There was a clear opportunity to resort to legal means to displace the Secretary then by nominating another suitable person in his place. It may be said that the President knew that there would be no hope of the confirmation of any one who would not disagree with him about the full execution of laws as greatly as Mr. Stanton, and hence it was useless for him to resort to that method of relief. This is doubtless true, and it places the respondent in the position of refusing to take a clear legal method of change because it would not answer his purpose. This necessarily leads to the presumption that if the respondent was in earnest he would try some other way. He did so. No sooner had Congress adjourned than he "suspended" Mr. Stanton, as he had a legal right to do under the act of 1867, provided he acted in good faith in so doing, and not as a mere cover to get rid of an obstacle in the way of his own opposition to law. Had he believed in his power of removal, he could have exercised it then, and if Mr. Stanton would not yield, he could have instantly resorted to the courts of law. This he did not do, but on the contrary excluded Mr. Stanton from the office *under the law* for nearly six months, and then endeavored to arrange for defeating the same law, by preventing Mr Stanton from resuming possession under the vote of the Senate of January, 1868. At that time, then, his design was plainly to *prevent* Mr. Stanton, not, by law, but by some other expedient, from holding the office, and forcing *him*, if he could, to resort to legal measures for redress.

During all this period down to the 21st of February, when the act in question was committed, no one was nominated to succeed Mr. Stanton ; and from the vote of January to that date, no step whatever was taken to resort to any legal mode to procure the change he was determined to bring about. There was no need to make an *ad interim* appointment if the sole object was to put things in process of judicial decision, for the order of dismissal alone, if not obeyed, would do that ; and if obeyed, there would be no further steps in that respect for the President to take ; the desired end would be accomplished. In this state of things, with the Senate in session and presumably ready to confirm an irreproachable man, he turns his back upon it and makes overtures to General Sherman to take the office under his fiat. This is declined. Then General Thomas, a man who, judging from his appearance in court, must have been known to the respondent not to be suited to the place of Secretary of War, is suddenly restored to place as adjutant general, the principal executive officer in the army, and is then at once appointed Secretary *ad interim*, with instructions to "enter immediately upon the discharge of the duties," &c., which General Thomas agrees to do, with a formal mutual *salvo* that "the Constitution and the laws" under which the President had professed at the same time to dismiss Mr. Stanton, should be maintained. I cannot believe that the respondent expected that Mr. Stanton would yield to anything less than force. He had been formally notified in writing in August by Mr. Stanton himself that he denied his power to remove him, or to suspend him without legal cause, and that he would only yield when he had "no alternative but to submit, under protest, to superior force." Thomas confesses on the stand that at some time in the course of the effort to get possession, he expected to use force. In view of all these circumstances I cannot resist the conclusion that the sixth and seventh articles are proved, and that the respondent is guilty, as therein charged.

The gravamen of the eighth article seems to be the alleged attempt, by certain means alleged, to get unlawful control of the public moneys. If this be the meaning of that article, and I think it is, I think the proof does not sustain the charge, and that the respondent is not guilty upon that article.

The ninth article appears to me also to be wholly unsustained by proof.

The tenth and eleventh articles, so far as they relate to the sayings and speeches of the respondent, require for their support under the rule I have before adverted to, an unlawful and criminal design and intent. However disgraceful these speeches may be—and they certainly do not need any comment in that respect—fairly considered they were, I think, only intended to appeal to the political prejudices of the people, and to induce them to overturn the party of Congress by a revolution at the polls, and not by illegal violence. As such, I think them, in a legal sense, within the liberty of speech secured by the Constitution and by the spirit of our institutions; a liberty so essential to the welfare and permanency of a free government in a state of peace and under the rule of municipal law, that it were better to tolerate a considerable abuse of it, rather than to subject it to legal repression or condemnation.

Besides the accusation of criminal speech, article eleven seems to contain three charges: a contriving of means to defeat the act of March 2, 1867; to defeat the army appropriation bill of 1867; and to defeat the act for the more efficient government of the rebel States. The first and third of these charges, I think, for the reasons already stated, are proved by the evidence already referred to as to the causes for and the attempt to remove Mr. Stanton. The second I think is not. But upon the construction put upon this article by the Senate, that it only contains an accusation touching Mr Stanton, I feel bound to vote guilty upon it.

Much has been said in the course of the trial upon the nature of this proceeding, and the nature of the offences which can fairly be embraced with the terms of the Constitution. In my opinion this high tribunal is the sole and exclusive judge of its own jurisdiction in such cases, and that, as the Constitution did not establish this procedure for the punishment of crime, but for the secure and faithful administration of the law, it was not intended to cramp it by any specific definition of high crimes and misdemeanors, but to leave each case to be defined by law, or, when not defined, to be decided upon its own circumstances, in the patriotic and judicial good sense of the representatives of the States. Like the jurisdiction of chancery in cases of fraud, it ought not to be limited in advance, but kept open as a great bulwark for the preservation of purity and fidelity in the administration of affairs, when undermined by the cunning and corrupt practices of low offenders, or assailed by bold and high-handed usurpation, or defiance; a shield for the honest and law-abiding official; a sword to those who pervert or abuse their powers, teaching the maxim which rulers endowed with the spirit of a Trajan can listen to without emotion, that "kings may be cashiered for misconduct."

Two exceptions that go, practically, to the jurisdiction of this tribunal over such a cause as this, have been so much insisted upon in argument that their bravery challenges admiration as much as their error does condemnation. The first is that the Senate has no right to judge in what is called its own case; that such an act is contrary to the first principles of justice, &c.

In any proper sense it is not its own case. Its members have no personal interest in it. It is the case of the *law* violated by the usurpation of power under color of office. As well might it be said that a court could not try a contempt, or punish a breach of injunction, or sit in judgment in a case in which the community of which the judges were members, had an interest. To countenance such a doctrine would be to defeat this great but gentle remedy of the Constitution, almost entirely; for most of the powers capable of easy usurpation are those granted to this body.

The second is that the three great departments of the government created by the Constitution, being co-ordinate, neither has the power to bring into review the acts of the other, and each is the supreme judge for itself, of its own rights under the Constitution. If each of the departments were, in all respects the equal of the other, this would be true, and the only method of correcting the misconduct or aggression of either, would be the *ultima ratio regum*—force. But the fathers, whose wisdom has been so much and justly praised by the counsel for the respondent, foresaw that such an arbitrament would destroy the government and the liberty that the Constitution was intended to perpetuate. They, therefore, in the Constitution defined and measured, so far as was possible, the respective powers of each. To this they superadded the last and only means possible to human agency, a tribunal composed of the representatives of equal States, chosen for periods long enough to remove them from the sudden impulses of popular excitement, and short enough to make them feel responsible to the settled convictions of the community they represented. To this tribunal, sworn to impartiality and conscientious adherence to the Constitution and the laws, they committed the high powers indispensable to such a frame of government, of sitting in judgment upon the crimes and misdemeanors of the President, as well as all other officers of the United States. These faculties of the Senate fill up the measure of that description of it given by Mr. Madison, as the "great sheet anchor of the government." August, benignant, and supreme, upon the complaint of the people's representatives, it brings to its judgment seat judges and Presidents and all the ministers of the law—no station too lofty or powerful for its reach; none too low to escape its notice—and subjects them, alike, to the serene and steadfast justice of the law. The mechanism of government can do no more for society than this. These great powers, at once the emblem, the ideal, and the realization of that orderly justice which is the law, we must this day exercise without fear. And so acting, there can follow to us no possible reproach, and no detriment to the republic.

Opinion of Mr. Senator Hendricks.

In the eleven articles of impeachment the President is charged, in different forms of statement, with six acts of official misconduct, as follows:

1. The removal of Mr. Stanton from the office of Secretary of War.
2. The appointment of Lorenzo Thomas, the Adjutant General of the army, to the office of Secretary of War *ad interim*.
3. The conspiracy with said Thomas to prevent the execution of the tenure-of-office act by hindering Mr. Stanton from holding the office of Secretary of War.
4. The instructions to General Emory that the second section of the act of March 2, 1867, requiring all military orders made by the President or the Secretary of War to be issued through the General of the army, was unconstitutional.
5. The President's speeches against Congress.
6. The denial of the authority of the thirty-ninth Congress by the attempt on the part of the President to prevent the execution of the tenure-of-office act, the army appropriation act, and the act " to provide for the more efficient government of the rebel States."

The sixth charge is found in the eleventh article. The respondent in his answer has taken exception to the sufficiency of the statements contained in that article, upon the ground that the alleged acts of the President, which he did in his attempts to prevent the execution of said laws, are not stated, but it is averred only that he did unlawfully devise and contrive and attempt to devise and contrive means to prevent their execution. The exception seems to be sufficiently supported by the well-established and reasonable rule of pleading, that charges preferred against a party in any judicial proceeding shall be stated with such reasonable certainty that the accused may know the nature of the charge, its scope and limit, the character of evidence that may be brought against him, and the class of evidence that may be invoked in his defence.

Until accusations are stated with such reasonable certainty courts do not require the accused to answer. The eleventh article should have stated what means were devised and contrived or attempted to be devised and contrived, so that this court might decide whether they amount to a high misdemeanor, and if so that the respondent may know the nature of the evidence that may be brought against him, and the character of evidence he may offer in his defence. This vice in the pleading is not removed by the averment that the means were devised and contrived to prevent Mr. Stanton's return to the War Department after the decision of the Senate upon the reasons for his suspension. Reasonable certainty requires that the means devised and contrived should be stated. If the means were stated the Senate might not agree with the House of Representatives that they were "unlawfully" devised; but might hold them lawful and proper. If the device and contrivance were the appointment of a successor, or proceedings in the courts to test a right claimed on the one side and denied on the other, then the averment that it was "unlawful" would fall.

But beyond the question of pleading, the question arises whether the eleventh article defines any high misdemeanor, or even any act of official misconduct. As inducement, it is stated that as far back as August, 1866, the President in public speeches did question the lawful authority of Congress; and it is then averred that as late as February, 1868, in pursuance of that declaration he did "attempt to prevent the execution of" the said several acts, by "devising and contriving, and attempting to devise and contrive means by which he should prevent" Mr. Stanton from resuming the functions of the office of Secretary of War, and to prevent the execution of the other acts. Passing over the question whether an attempt to prevent the execution of a statute without success is a misdemeanor, when the statute does not so declare, the question arises whether it can be a crime or misdemeanor in a single person, without combination or conspiracy with others, to devise and contrive means without executing the schemes? To devise or contrive is an intellectual process, and when not executed by acts done cannot be punished as a crime, however unworthy or vicious. Can we undertake the punishment of the thoughts, opinions, purposes, conceptions, designs, devices, and contrivances of men when not carried into acts? The eleventh article does not attempt the definition of a crime, unless, indeed, we hold the vicious thoughts and evil purposes of public officers to be such, in the absence of any law so declaring.

In the presence of the provision of the Constitution of the United States which protects the right of free speech, and in the absence of any law, State or federal, declaring its exercise in any manner or by any person to be a crime, it is not necessary to examine the tenth article, which rests its charge of a misdemeanor upon the President's speeches made to the people, in response to their calls, in his capacity as a citizen and not in the exercise of his office.

In our country, so long as the Constitution stands, no legislative body can make it a crime to discuss the conduct of public officers with entire freedom, and the House of Representatives cannot by any proceeding whatever shield itself from individual criticism and popular review, and any effort to do so betrays conscious weakness and disturbs public confidence.

The ninth article rests upon the conversation between the President and General Emory. In that part of the President's conduct no fault can be found, much less a violation of law. He had been informed by a member of his cabinet that there were evidences of important changes of the military forces at and near this city. It was his right and perhaps his duty to become informed of the extent and purpose of any such movements. He sent for General Emory to make the necessary inquiries. In the course of the conversation General Emory called his attention to the order issued in pursuance of the section of the law requiring all military orders from the President to be issued through the General of the army, and then the President expressed the opinion that it was unconstitutional thus to control him in the exercise of his constitutional powers as commander-in-chief of the army. He went no further than the expression of that opinion; he gave no orders to General Emory, nor does it appear that at any time he has disregarded the said law. In any proceeding less grave than the present, it would be regarded as frivolous to charge it as a crime that an opinion had been expressed upon the constitutionality of any law.

The fourth, fifth, sixth, and seventh articles charge a conspiracy between the President and General Lorenzo Thomas to prevent Mr. Stanton's holding the office of Secretary of War, and to obtain the custody and charge of the property of the United States in the War Department. It is not necessary to notice the averments, in two of these articles, of a purpose to resort to intimidation and threats, and to use force, inasmuch as the evidence wholly fails to show that the President, at any time, contemplated a resort to either; and it does appear that there was no resort to either. In the absence of intimidation, threats, and force, in the purpose and conduct of the President and General Thomas, no case is made within the conspiracy act of July 31, 1861. But it appears to me that it cannot be said that the President and General Thomas conspired together when the former issued to the latter the *ad interim* appointment, and the latter accepted it. It is plain that the President issued the orders under a claim of legal right, and that General Thomas received them because, as a subordinate officer, he thought it was his duty. Such conduct does not define a conspiracy.

It only remains for me to consider the conduct of the President in issuing the order for the removal of Mr. Stanton from the office of Secretary of War, and the *ad interim* appointment of General Thomas. The force and effect of the *ad interim* appointment must depend upon the validity of the order for the removal of Mr. Stanton. If the removal did not in law take place upon the issue of the order, then, as Mr. Stanton did not surrender the office, the appointment did not clothe General Thomas with any authority—it was a blank, without legal force or meaning. If Mr. Stanton's commission did not become revoked, the appointment of General Thomas was of no more force or consequence than a second deed by the same grantor.

Had the President the authority to remove Mr. Stanton? According to the provisions of the act of August 7, 1789, creating the War Department, and the terms of his commission, Mr. Stanton held the office "during the pleasure of the President of the United States for the time being." That act expressly recognized the power of the President to remove the Secretary of War at any time. It did not confer the power, but recognized it as already possessed, the provision being that "whenever the said principal officer (the Secretary) shall be removed from office by the President of the United States, and in any other case of vacancy," the chief clerk of the department shall, for the time being, have charge of the records, books, &c. Under that law, Mr. Stanton received his commission from President Lincoln, January 15, 1862, "to hold the said office, with all the powers, &c., during the pleasure of the President of the United States for the time being." Has that law been repealed or amended in that respect? The tenure-of-office act of March 2, 1867, has no repealing clause, and therefore repeals or modifies the act of 1789 only so far as the two acts cannot stand together. Mr. Stanton's term of office, as fixed by the law and his commission, was during the will of the President, and I think a proper construction of the first section of the tenure-of-office act leaves that unchanged. He was appointed during Mr. Lincoln's first term, which expired on the 4th March, 1865, and therefore it is unnecessary to consider the question which has been discussed, whether Mr. Johnson is filling the office for Mr. Lincoln's unexpired term, or whether he has his own term of office; for it is quite certain that he is not in the term during which Mr. Stanton was appointed. The first and second terms of the presidential office for which Mr. Lincoln was elected, were as distinct, under the Constitution, as if another had been elected in his stead for the second. If the tenure of Mr. Stanton's office be changed by the tenure-of-office act, it is by the proviso to the first section, and clearly the proviso has no such effect. The proviso is that the cabinet officers "shall hold their offices respectively for and during the term of the President by whom they may have been appointed, and for one month thereafter." Not having been appointed during the existing presidential term, Mr. Stanton has no new term bestowed upon him, but he still holds, in the language of his commission, "during the pleasure of the President." This obvious construction of the language is strengthened by a consideration of the history of the tenure-of-office bill. It first passed the Senate in such form as expressly to exclude all cabinet officers. In the House, it was so amended as to include them. The Senate disagreed to that amendment. A committee of conference was the result of this disagreement between the two houses. In this condition of the measure, it will be observed that the Senate insisted that cabinet officers should not be included at all, and the House insisted that they should be included, just as other officers are. The conference committee considered this question of disagreement, and settled it upon the proposition, then supposed to be just, that each President shall have the selection of his own cabinet officers, and shall not be required to continue the Secretaries of his predecessor. The Senate conceded that a President, having selected his own cabinet, shall continue them during his term, and the House conceded that he shall not be required to continue the cabinet of his predecessor, or any member thereof. Upon that adjustment, the bill passed. This construction was then put upon the proviso in the Senate—for when the bill came back from the committee with the proviso as the compromise between the two houses, Mr. Sherman, of the committee, said—

That this provision does not apply to the present case is shown by the fact that its language is so framed as not to apply to the present President. The senator [Mr. Doolittle] shows that himself, and argues truly that it would not prevent the present President from removing the Secretary of War, the Secretary of the Navy, and the Secretary of State.

This construction of the bill was then acquiesced in by the silence of the other members of the conference committee, and not disagreed to by any senator, and thereupon the Senate agreed to its passage. And now, by adhering to that construction, we have just what the Senate then intended, what is plainly just and right—that each President shall select his own constitutional advisers—and what will promote the harmony and efficient action of the executive department, and we avoid a question of serious difficulty. If the act be so construed as to include Mr. Stanton's case, the constitutional question arises, whether Congress can by law extend the term and change the tenure of an office, after the appointment has been made with the consent of the Senate. Such construction would allow that, after the appointing power under the Constitution had bestowed the office, the legislative department, having no power of appointment, might bestow an additional term upon the officer, and thus become an appointing power. It is gratifying that the language of the act, the history of its enactment, the legislative construction, the obvious intention of the Senate, and the highest interests of the public service all allow me so to construe the act as to avoid this grave question. Mr. Stanton's case not being within the tenure-of-office act, the power of the President to make the removal is beyond doubt; and the only question remaining is, did he have the power to make the appointment of General Thomas *ad interim?* There is great force in the opinion that has been expressed, that the constitutional obligation upon the President to see that the laws be executed carries with it the power to use such agencies as may be clearly necessary, in the absence of legislative provision. In that view, it would appear that, in the case of a vacancy in an office and until it could be filled, in the case of sickness, absence from the post of duty, or other disability of an officer to discharge the duties, the President might designate some person to discharge them in the mean time, to the end that the laws might be executed and the public service suffer no harm. And this opinion seems to have been entertained by our most eminent and revered Presidents, for they made very many such *ad interim* appointments, without the pretence of legislative authority. But in the case now before this court we need not consider this question, for, in my judgment, the authority of the President to make the *ad interim* appointment, as well during the session as the recess of the Senate, is clearly established by law.

Section 8 of the act May 8, 1792, provides as follows:

That in case of the death, absence from the seat of government, or sickness of the Secretary of State, Secretary of the Treasury, or of the Secretary of the War Department, or of any officer of either of the said departments whose appointment is not in the head thereof, whereby they cannot perform the duties of their said respective offices, it shall be lawful for the President of the United States, in case he shall think it necessary, to authorize any person or persons at his discretion to perform the duties of the said respective offices until a successor be appointed, or until such absence or inability by sickness shall cease.

It will be observed that this section authorized *ad interim* appointments only in three of the departments, that is, in the Departments of State, Treasury, and War, and only in three cases, that is, in the cases of death, absence from the seat of government, and sickness of the head of the department or other officer. It fails to provide for the temporary supply of the service in the case of any vacancy occurring otherwise than by death. That omission was in part supplied by the act of February 13, 1795, but only as to the same three departments. That act is as follows:

Be it enacted by the Senate and House of Representatives of the United States of America in Congress assembled. That in case of vacancy in the office of Secretary of State, Secretary of the Treasury, or of the Secretary of the Department of War, or of any officer of either of the said departments whose appointment is not in the head thereof, whereby they cannot perform the duties of their said respective offices, it shall be lawful for the President of the United States, in case he shall think it necessary, to authorize any person or persons, at his discretion, to perform the duties of the said respective offices until a successor be appointed or such vacancy be filled: *Provided,* That no one vacancy shall be supplied, in manner aforesaid, for a longer term than six months.

It will be observed that this act of 1795 provides a temporary supply of the service in all cases of vacancies whether caused by death, resignation, removal from office, or expiration of the term, but makes no provision for the cases of temporary disability already provided for by the act of 1792, and therefore does not repeal that act. Both acts remained in force, without further legislation on the subject, until the passage of the act of February 20, 1863, which is as follows:

That in case of the death, resignation, absence from the seat of government, or sickness, of the head of any executive department of the government, or of any officer of either of the said departments whose appointment is not in the head thereof, whereby they cannot perform the duties of their respective offices, it shall be lawful for the President of the United States, in case he shall think it necessary, to authorize the head of any other executive department, or other officer in either of said departments, whose appointment is vested in the President, at his discretion, to perform the duties of the said respective offices until a successor be appointed, or until such absence or inability by sickness shall cease: *Provided,* That no one vacancy shall be supplied, in manner aforesaid, for a longer term than six months.

The legislative purpose in the enactment of this law was not to repeal the act of February 13, 1795, but to extend the provisions of the act of May 8, 1792, to the other departments. During the previous month President Lincoln had called the attention of Congress to the subject in the following message:

WASHINGTON, *January 2, 1863.*

To the Senate and House of Representatives:

I submit to Congress the expediency of extending to other departments of the government the authority conferred on the President by the eighth section of the act of the 8th of May, 1792, to appoint a person to temporarily discharge the duties of Secretary of State, Secretary of the Treasury, and Secretary of War, in case of the death, absence from the seat of government, or sickness of either of those officers.

ABRAHAM LINCOLN.

It was in response to that message that the act of 1863 was passed, and it does not appear that the attention of Congress was at all called to the act of 1795. Neither its history nor the provisions of the act of 1863 justify us in believing that it was the intention of Congress thereby to repeal the act of 1795. The acts are not inconsistent; both can stand; both must remain, for the act of 1795 provides for two cases of vacancy—by removal and by expiration of the term—not provided for in the act of 1863. It is not questioned that the act of 1795, if unrepealed, confers upon the President the power to provide temporarily for the service in the case of a removal, and therefore I need not further consider this part of the case, except to add that the tenure-of-office act does not in terms or by implication repeal either the act of 1795 or the act of 1863. It has no repealing clause, and there is no such inconsistency in the provisions of the acts as to cause a repeal by implication. There is the same necessity for a supply of the temporary service by *ad interim* appointments, in cases of vacancy, sickness, absence, or other disability, as before the passage of the tenure-of-office act, and Congress cannot be understood to have intended to leave such cases unprovided for.

Whoever proposes to convict the President, as of a crime, for the *ad interim* appointment of General Thomas, should stop to consider the many cases in which his illustrious predecessors exercised the same power during the session of the Senate, as well as during the recess, under the Constitution, and without the pretence of legislative authority. In this opinion but a few of the many cases proven can be cited. It will be borne in mind that the acts of 1792 and and 1795, authorizing temporary appointments, did not include the Navy, Interior, and Post Office Departments, and that until 1863 no law extended the authority over them, and, therefore, appointments made by the President, in those departments, to supply the temporary service, were made under the constitutional duty and authority to see that the laws be executed, and not under any statute.

On the 9th July, 1836, President Jackson appointed John Boyle, the chief clerk of the Navy Department, to discharge the duties of Secretary during the absence of the Secretary. The Senate had then adjourned five days.

On the 6th October, 1838, President Van Buren made the same appointment.

On the 19th March, 1841, President Harrison appointed John D. Simmes to be acting Secretary of the Navy, during the absence of the Secretary.

On the 13th May, 1851, President Fillmore appointed C. M. Conrad, the Secretary of War, to be "acting Secretary of the Navy *ad interim*" during the absence of the Secretary, and on the 3d August, 1851, the same President appointed W. A Graham, the Secretary of the Navy, to be the acting Secretary of the Interior.

And on the 22d September, 1862, President Lincoln appointed John B. L. Skinner, then the acting First Assistant Postmaster General, to be acting Postmaster General *ad interim*, the Postmaster General being absent.

On the 29th June, 1860, four days after the adjournment of the Senate, the postmaster at New Orleans was removed, and the office placed in the hands of a special agent, by President Buchanan, Joseph Holt being Postmaster General.

On the 10th day of May, 1860, the Senate then being in session, President Buchanan removed Isaac V. Fowler, the Postmaster at New York, and placed the office in the hands of a special messenger.

And on the 21st January, 1861, the Senate being in session, he took the Milwaukee post office out of the hands of the postmaster and placed it in the charge of a special agent. Hon. Joseph Holt was then Postmaster General.

On the 20th June, 1864, the Senate being in session, President Lincoln removed Isaac Henderson from the office of navy agent at New York, and instructed a paymaster of the navy to take charge of the office.

On the 26th day of December, 1864, the Senate being in session, President

Lincoln removed James S. Chambers from the office of navy agent at Philadelphia, and placed Paymaster Watson in charge. These two offices were highly important, both in view of the duties to be discharged and the emoluments received by the incumbents.

On the 19th December, 1840, Thomas Eastin, the navy agent at Pensacola, was, by order of President Van Buren, "dismissed from the service of the United States," and Purser Dudley Walker appointed to take charge of the office. The Senate was then in session.

These are but a few of the hundreds of cases that might be cited to show that, the practice of making *ad interim* appointments has been uniform, whether authorized by statute or not.

I cannot concur in the opinion that has been expressed, that if a technical violation of law has been established, the Senate has no discretion, but must convict. I think the Senate may judge whether in the case a high crime or misdemeanor has been established, and whether in the name of the people the prosecution ought to be made and sustained. Van Buren was not impeached for the removal of the Pensacola navy agent and the designation of Purser Walker to take charge of the office. President Jackson was not impeached for the *ad interim* appointment of Boyle as Secretary of the Navy under a claim of constitutional authority, without any statute allowing it. Presidents Harrison and Fillmore were not impeached for making *ad interim* appointments of Secretary of the Navy, with no statute authorizing it. President Buchanan was not impeached for removing the postmaster at New Orleans and filling the place *ad interim*, nor for removing Fowler, the postmaster at New York, during the session of the Senate, and supplying the service *ad interim*, with no statutory authority; nor was he impeached for authorizing Joseph Holt to discharge the duties of Secretary of War *ad interim* upon the resignation of John B. Floyd, though the Senate called upon him for his authority, and in his reply he cited one hundred and seventy-nine precedents, not going back of Jackson's administration. Mr. Lincoln was not impeached for the appointment of General Skinner Postmaster General *ad interim* without any statute authorizing it, nor for the removal of Isaac Henderson, navy agent at New York, during the session of the Senate, and the *ad interim* appointment of Paymaster Gibson to the office; nor for the removal of Chambers, the navy agent at Philadelphia, during the session of the Senate, and the appointment of Paymaster Watson *ad interim* to the office, there then being no statute authorizing it. He was not impeached for continuing Major General Frank P. Blair in command long after the Senate had declared by resolution that in such case the office could not be held "without a new appointment in the manner prescribed by the Constitution;" nor for appointing at one time many more generals in the army than the laws allowed.

Supported by a long line of precedents, coming through our whole history, unchallenged and unrebuked by Congress, President Johnson stands before us upon these charges; and I ask my brother senators what answer we will make to the people when they ask us why we selected him for a sacrifice for doing just what was always recognized as right in his predecessors? Upon my oath I cannot strike such a blow.

The judgment of the first Congress was, that the President has the right under the Constitution to remove the Secretaries, and that judgment is supported by the uniform practice of the government from that day till the meeting of the 39th Congress. The evidence shows that Mr. Johnson was advised by every member of his cabinet, including Mr. Stanton, that he had that right under the Constitution, and that Congress could not take it from him, nor impair it, and therefore it was his duty to veto the tenure-of-office bill; and that the bill did not include the appointments made by Mr. Lincoln; and that notwithstanding the passage of the bill he would have the right to remove the Secretaries of War, of State, and of the Navy. This advice was given by the members of the cabinet under the obligations of the Constitution and of their oaths; and now, if we say that he, being so informed and advised, was guilty of a crime in demanding the right to select his own constitutional advisers, as it has been conceded to all the Presidents, and for that drive him from his office and give it to a member of this body, it does seem to me that we will do an act of such flagrant injustice and cruelty as to bring upon our heads the indignant condemnation of all just men, and this impeachment will itself stand impeached before the civilized world.

Opinion of Mr. Senator Yates.

It is difficult to estimate the importance of this trial. Not in respect merely to the exalted position of the accused, not alone in the fact that it is a trial before the highest tribunal known among us, the American Senate, upon charges preferred by the immediate representatives of the sovereignty of the nation, against the President of the United States, alleging the commission by him of high crimes and misdemeanors; it is not alone in these respects that the trial rises in dignity and importance, but because it presents great and momentous issues, involving the powers, limitations and duties of the various departments of the government, affecting the very form and structure of the government, and the mightiest interests of the people, now and in the future.

It has been aptly termed the trial of the Constitution. Constructions of our Constitution and laws here given and precedents established by these proceedings will be quoted as standard authorities in all similar trials hereafter. We have here at issue, before this highest judicial tribunal, in the presence of the American people, and of the civilized world, whether our Constitution is to be a landmark to the citizen, a guide to the statesman, and authoritative over the magistrate, or whether this is a land of anarchy, crime and lawless usurpation. It is a trial which challenges the broadest comprehension of the statesman, the highest intellect and clearest discrimination of the jurist, and the deepest solicitude of the patriot. Its issues are to be determined by clearly ascertaining the duties and powers of the co-ordinate branches of the government, all jealous of encroachments upon their functions, and all in danger if one shall usurp powers which by virtue of the Constitution and laws belongs to others.

Although it seems to me that no man of honest judgment and true heart can have a possible doubt as to the guilt of the respondent in this cause, and although he has long since been indicted and found guilty in the judgment and conscience of the American people of a giant apostacy to his party—the party of American nationality and progress—and of a long series of atrocious wrongs and most daring and flagrant usurpations of power, and for three years has thrown himself across the path of the country to peace and a restored Union, and in all his official acts has stood forth without disguise, a bold, bad man, the aider and abettor of treason, and an enemy of his country; though this is the unanimous verdict of the loyal popular heart of the country, yet I shall strive to confine myself, in the main, to a consideration of the issues presented in the first three articles. Those issues are simply: whether in the removal of Edwin M. Stanton, Secretary of War, and the appointment of Lorenzo Thomas Secretary of War *ad interim*, on the 21st day of February, 1868, the President wilfully violated the Constitution of the United States, and the law entitled "An act regulating the tenure of certain civil offices," in force March 2, 1867.

Upon the subject of appointments to civil office the Constitution is very explicit. The proposition may be definitely stated that the President cannot, during the session of the Senate, appoint any person to office without the advice and consent of the Senate, except *inferior* officers, the appointment of whom may, by law, be vested in the President. The following is the plain letter and provision of the Constitution defining the President's power of appointment to office:

> He shall have power, by and with the advice and consent of the Senate, to make treaties, provided two-thirds of the senators present concur; and he shall nominate, and *by and with the advice and consent of the Senate shall appoint*, ambassadors, other public ministers and consuls, judges of the Supreme Court, and *all other officers of the United States, whose appointments are not herein otherwise provided for, and which shall be established by law;* but the Congress may by law vest the appointment of such inferior officers as they think proper in the President alone, in the courts of law, or in the heads of departments.

Is it not plain, very plain, from the first clause above set forth, that the appointment of a superior officer, such as a Secretary of War, or the head of any department cannot be made during the session of the Senate without its advice and consent? It is too clear for argument that the Constitution does not confer the prerogative of appointment of *any* officer upon the President alone during sessions of the Senate, and that he can only appoint *inferior* officers even, by virtue of laws passed by Congress, so that the appointment of a head of a department cannot be made without the concurrence of the Senate, unless it can be shown that such appointment is, in the words of the Constitution, "otherwise provided for;" and it is not pretended that any such other provision can be shown.

The framers of the Constitution wisely imposed this check upon the President to secure integrity, ability, and efficiency in public officers, and to prevent the appointment of men who, if appointed by the President alone, might be his mere instruments to minister to the purposes of his ambition.

I maintain that *Congress itself* cannot pass a law authorizing the appointment of any officer, excepting inferior officers, without the advice and consent of the Senate, it being *in session* at the time of such appointment. It is just as competent for Congress, under the clause which I have read, to invest the President with the power to make a treaty without the concurrence of two-thirds of the Senate, which is, as all agree, inadmissible. Any law authorizing the class of appointments just mentioned, without the Senate's concurrence, would be just as much a violation of the constitutional provision which I have read, as would a law providing that the President should not *nominate* the officer to the Senate at all. No appointment is complete without the two acts, nomination by the President, and confirmation by the Senate.

I think my colleague, (Mr. Trumbull,) had not well considered when he made the statement in his argument, that "the Constitution makes no distinction between the power of the President to remove during the recess and the sessions of the Senate."

The clause of the Constitution which I shall now quote shows very clearly that the power of the President to fill vacancies is *limited to vacancies* happening during the *recess* of the Senate:

> The President shall have power to fill up all vacancies that may happen during the recess of the Senate, by granting commissions which shall expire at the end of their next session.

His power to fill vacancies during the recess, without the advice and consent of the Senate at the time, proceeds from the necessity of the case, because the public service would suffer unless the vacancy is filled; but even in this case the commission of the temporary incumbent is to expire at the end of the next session of the Senate, unless the Senate, during said next session, shall have consented to his appointment. The reason of this limitation upon the President to the filling of vacancies happening during the recess, and why he cannot appoint during the session of the Senate without consent, is clearly because the Senate being in session may at the time of the nomination give its advice and consent. The provision that "the President shall have power to fill all vacancies *during the recess* of the Senate by granting commissions which shall expire at the end of the next session," excludes the conclusion that he may create vacancies, and fill them during the session and without the concurrence of the Senate. If this view is not correct, it would seem that the whole provision of the Constitution on this point is meaningless and absurd.

The conclusion of the whole matter is, that if the President issued an order for the removal of Mr. Stanton and the appointment of Thomas, without the advice and consent of the Senate, it being then in session, then he acted in palpable violation of the plain letter of the Constitution, and is chargeable with a high misdemeanor in office. The production of his own order removing Stanton, and of his letter of authority to Thomas, commanding him to take possession of the War Office, are all the proofs necessary to establish his guilt. And when it appears, as it does most conclusively in the evidence before us, that he not only did not have the concurrence of the Senate, but its absolute, unqualified dissent, and that he was notified of that dissent by a certified copy of a resolution to that effect, passed by the Senate, under all the forms of parliamentary deliberation, and that he still wilfully and defiantly persisted, and does still persist in the removal of Mr. Stanton, and to this day stubbornly retains Thomas as a member of his cabinet, then who shall say that he has not wickedly trampled the Constitution under his feet, and that he does not justly deserve the punishment due to his great offence?

That the facts stated are proved, and substantially admitted in the answer of the President to article first, will not be denied by the counsel for the respondent, nor by his apologists on the floor of the Senate.

The next question to which I invite attention is whether the President has intentionally violated the *law*, and thereby committed a misdemeanor. Blackstone defines a misdemeanor thus:

A crime or misdemeanor is an act committed or omitted in violation of a public law either forbidding or commanding it.

Misdemeanor in office, and misbehavior in office, or official misconduct, mean the same thing. Mr. Madison says in Elliott's Debates that:

The wanton removal of meritorious officers would subject him (the President) to impeachment and removal from his own high trust.

Chancellor Kent, than whom no man living or dead ever stood higher as an expounder of constitutional law, whose Commentaries are recognized in all courts as standard authority, and whose interpretations are themselves almost laws in our courts, says, in discussing the subject of impeachment:

The Constitution has rendered him [the President] directly amenable by law for maladministration. The inviolability of any officer of the government is incompatible with the republican theory as well as with the principles of retributive justice.

If the President will use the authority of his station to violate the Constitution or law of the land, the House of Representatives can arrest him in his career by resorting to the power of impeachment. (1 Kent's Com., 289.)

Story, of equal authority as a commentator on the Constitution, says:

In examining the parliamentary history of impeachments, it will be found that many offences not easily definable by law, and many of a purely political character, have been deemed high crimes and misdemeanors worthy of this extraordinary remedy.

Judge Curtis, one of the distinguished counsel for the respondent in this case, said in 1862:

The President is the commander-in-chief of the army and navy, not only by force of the Constitution, but under and subject to the Constitution, and to every restriction therein contained, and to every law enacted by its authority, as completely and clearly as the private in the ranks. *He is general-in-chief; but can a general-in-chief disobey any law of his own country? When he can he supersedes to his rights as commander the powers of a usurper, and that is military despotism;* * * * * *the mere authority to command an army is not an authority to disobey the laws of his country.*

Besides, all the powers of the President are executive merely. He cannot make a law. He cannot repeal one. He can only execute the laws. He can neither make nor suspend nor alter them. He cannot even make an article of war.

Section 3, article 1 of the Constitution says:

The Senate shall have the sole power to try all impeachments.

I was present on the 15th day of April, 1865, the day of the death of the lamented Lincoln, when you, Mr. President, administered to Andrew Johnson the oath of office as President of the United States. He then and there swore that he would "preserve, protect, and defend the Constitution of the United States," and "take care that the laws should be faithfully executed."

On the 2d day of March, 1867, Congress passed a law, over the veto of the President, entitled "An act to regulate the tenure of certain civil offices," the first section of which is as follows:

Be it enacted by the Senate and House of Representatives of the United States of America in Congress assembled, That every person holding any civil office to which he has been appointed by and with the advice and consent of the Senate, and every person who may hereafter be appointed to any such office and shall become duly qualified to act therein, is and shall be entitled to hold such office until a successor shall have been in like manner appointed and duly qualified, except as herein otherwise provided: *Provided,* That the Secretaries of State, of the Treasury, of War, of the Navy, and of the Interior, the Postmaster General, and the Attorney General, shall hold their offices respectively for and during the term of the President by whom they may have been appointed, and for one month thereafter, subject to removal by and with the advice and consent of the Senate.

This law is in entire harmony with the Constitution. "Every person appointed or to be appointed" to office with the advice and consent of the Senate, shall hold the office until a successor shall "in *like manner,*" that is, "by the advice and consent of the Senate" be appointed and qualified. This is obviously in pursuance of the Constitution.

Now, if we construe this section independently of the proviso, we shall see that the removal of Mr. Stanton without the advice and consent of the Senate, and before his successor was appointed with the advice and consent of the Senate, was a misdemeanor, and was so declared and made punishable by the 6th section of the same act. And, again, if Mr. Stanton's case is excepted from the body of the act, and comes within the proviso, then his removal without the concurrence of the Senate, was a violation of the law, because, by the terms of the proviso, he was only subject to removal by and with the advice and consent of the Senate.

But my colleague (Mr. Trumbull) contends that Mr. Stanton was not included in the body of the section, because there is a proviso to it which excepts him and other heads of departments from "every other civil officer," and yet he argues that he is not in the proviso itself, which certainly is strange logic. He argues that his tenure of office was given under the act of 1789, and that by that act the President had a right to remove him. If this be so, why did not the President remove him under that act, and not suspend him under the tenure-of-office act, and why did my colleague act under the tenure-of-office law in restoring Mr. Stanton?

It is claimed that Mr. Stanton is not included within the civil-tenure-of-office act, because he was not appointed by Mr. Johnson, in whose term he was removed; that he was appointed by Mr. Lincoln, and that Mr. Stanton's term expired one month after his (Mr. Lincoln's) death, and that Johnson is not serving part of Mr. Lincoln's term.

The true construction of the whole section, including the proviso, is that every person appointed and to be appointed, with the advice and consent of the Senate, is to hold the office until his successor shall have been in like manner appointed and qualified, *except* the heads of departments, who are to hold their offices, not till their successors are appointed, but during the term of the President by whom they may have been appointed and for one month longer, and always "subject to removal by and with the advice and consent of the Senate."

Now, the only object of the proviso was to confer upon the Secretary of War, and other heads of departments, a definite tenure of office, and a different term from that given in the body of the act. Can anything be plainer than that the case of Stanton is embraced in the meaning of the section, and that he is entitled either to hold until his successor shall have been appointed, by and with the advice and consent of the Senate, or during the term of the President, not "in which he was appointed," but "during the term of the President *by whom he was appointed?*"

At the time of the passage of the act of March 2, 1867, Mr. Stanton was holding the office of Secretary of War for, and in the term of, Mr. Lincoln, by whom he had been appointed, which term had commenced on the 4th of March, 1865, and will end March 4, 1869. The Constitution defines the President's term thus: "He shall hold his office during the term of four years." It further says that the term of the Vice-President shall be four years. In case of death or vacancy "the duties of his office shall devolve on the Vice-President." When Mr. Lincoln died, Mr. Johnson's term was not a new one, but he succeeded to Mr. Lincoln's office and performs its duties for the remainder of Mr. Lincoln's term. Mr. Stanton was appointed by Mr. Lincoln, and, according to the proviso, holds for the term of the President "by whom he was appointed, and one month thereafter," and can be removed only by the appointment of a successor, with the advice and consent of the Senate, before the expiration of his term.

If, as contended by the President, Mr. Stanton's term expired with the death of Lincoln, and Mr. Johnson did not reappoint or commission him, then from the death of Mr. Lincoln until the commencement of this trial there was no legal Secretary of War, and the President permitted Stanton to act without authority of law, to disburse millions of public money, and to perform all the various functions of Secretary of War without warrant of law, which would of itself be a misdemeanor. I believe it was the senator from Maine (Mr. Fessenden) who said "dead men have no terms." When that senator was elected for six years to the Senate, does it not remain his term though he should die or resign before its expiration, and would not his successor chosen to fill the vacancy serve simply for the remainder of *his* term, and not a new term of his own for six years? I could consent to the construction of the senator from Maine if, instead of limiting the presidential term to four years, it had provided that his term should be four years or till the death of the President, in case of his decease before the expiration of the four years; but it does not so provide.

The meaning of the word "vice" in Vice-President is, "instead of" or "to stand in the place of; "one who stands in the place of another." Therefore, Mr. Johnson succeeded, not to his own, but to Mr. Lincoln's term, with all its conditions and incidents. Death does not terminate a man's *term* of office. If a tenant of a farm for a term of seven years dies at the end of his first year, the remainder of the lease vests in his legal representatives; so the remainder of Mr. Lincoln's term at his death vested in his successor, Mr. Johnson. It follows that Mr. Stanton's term, ascertained by the act of March 2, 1867, does not expire till one month after the 4th of March, 1869, and that his removal, and the appointment of an officer in his place, without the advice and consent of the Senate, was a violation of the law.

The second section provides that when the Senate is not in session, if the President shall deem the officer guilty of acts which require his removal or suspension, he may be suspended until the next meeting of the Senate; and that within twenty days after the meeting of the Senate the reasons for such suspension shall be reported to that body; and if the Senate shall deem such reasons sufficient for such suspension or removal, the officer shall be considered removed from his office; but if the Senate shall not deem the reasons sufficient for suspension or removal, the officer shall forthwith resume the functions of his office, and the person appointed in his place shall cease to discharge such duties.

That is to say, when any officer, appointed in manner and form as provided in the first section—that is, by and with the advice and consent of the Senate—

is suspended, and the Senate does not concur in the suspension, such officer shall forthwith resume the functions of his office. Mr. Stanton having been appointed, by and with the advice and consent of the Senate, was suspended, but the Senate refused to concur in his suspension. According to the law, he was then entitled to resume the functions of his office, but the President does not permit him to do so, and refuses to have official relations with him, and has appointed and recognized as a member of his cabinet another Secretary of War. Is not this a palpable violation of the very letter of the law? By what technical quibble can any senator avoid the conviction of the culprit who thus defies a tatute? If it is admitted that the President can legally "*remove*" Mr. Stanton, that proves too much, because the second section of the act in question declares that the President shall only "suspend" the officer, and in the case of suspension and *that only*, and during *recess*, may an *ad interim* appointment be made. An *ad interim* appointment upon a removal is absolutely prohibited. As was well said by the senator from Oregon, (Mr. Williams:)

Vacancies in office can only be filled in two ways under the tenure-of-office act. One is by temporary or *ad interim* appointment during the *recess of the Senate*; the other is by appointment, by and with the advice and consent of the Senate, *during the session*.

Let us see—the Senate being the sole tribunal to try impeachments, and to decide upon the validity and violation of this law—what action the Senate has already taken.

On the 12th day of August, 1867, the Senate then not being in session, the President suspended Edwin M. Stanton, Secretary of the Department of War, and appointed U. S. Grant, General, Secretary of War *ad interim*. On the 12th day of December, 1867, the Senate being then in session, he reported, according to the requirements of the act, the causes of such suspension to the Senate, which duly took the same into consideration, and by an overwhelming vote of 35 to 6 refused to concur in the suspension, which action, according to the tenure-of-office act, reinstated Mr. Stanton in office. The President, bent upon the removal of Stanton, in defiance of the Senate and of the law, on the 21st day of February, 1868, appointed one Lorenzo Thomas, by letter of authority or commission, Secretary of War *ad interim*, without the advice and consent of the Senate, although the same was then in session, and ordered him (the said Thomas) to take possession of the Department of War and the public property appertaining thereto, and to discharge the duties thereof, and notified the Senate of his action. The Senate considered the communication, and, after debate, by a vote of 29 to 6, passed the following resolution:

Resolved by the Senate of the United States, That under the Constitution and laws of the United States the President has no power to remove the Secretary of War and to designate any other officer to perform the duties of that office *ad interim*.

And now, after such action under our oaths, are we to stultify ourselves, and swallow our own words and resolutions passed in the most solemn manner? Can we say that the President did not violate the law? that he did not become liable to conviction for violating the provisions of the tenure-of-office act, after he has admitted, in his answer upon this trial, that he tried to rid himself of Stanton by complying with the act; and after he has acknowledged that he was acting under the law of March 2, 1867, as shown by his letter to the Secretary of the Treasury, dated August 14, 1867, as follows:

Sir: In compliance with the act entitled "An act to regulate the tenure of certain civil offices," you are hereby notified that, on the 12th instant, Hon. Edwin M. Stanton, Secretary of War, was suspended from his office as Secretary of War, and General Grant authorized and empowered to act as Secretary *ad interim?*

To show also how trifling is the plea of the President that the law did not apply to this case; after he had acted upon it, as above stated by himself, and after he had reported the reasons for suspension, within the 20 days as required by the act, there is the further and still more conclusive proof, that the forms of commissions and official bonds were altered to conform to the requirements of the same tenure-of-office act, and under his own sign manual issued to his appointees commissioned since its passage. If it be admitted, then, that Mr. Stanton's case did not come within the provisions of the first section of the act, yet is the President clearly guilty under the second section.

I shall now ask attention to the sixth section of the act, which is as follows:

That every removal, appointment, or employment made, had, or exercised contrary to the provisions of this act, and the making, signing, sealing, countersigning, or issuing of any commission or letter of authority for or in respect to any such appointment or employment, shall be deemed, and are hereby declared to be, high misdemeanors; and upon trial and conviction thereof every person guilty thereof shall be punished by a fine not exceeding $10,000 or by imprisonment not exceeding five years, or both said punishments, in the discretion of the court.

If this section stood alone, who can deny that by his order to Thomas appointing him Secretary of War *ad interim*, and commanding him to turn Mr. Stanton out of office and take possession of the same, its books and papers, he did commit a misdemeanor, especially when, by the very terms of this section, the issuing of such an order is expressly declared to be a high misdemeanor, and punishable by fine and imprisonment?

The second article charges that the President violated this law by issuing to General Thomas a letter of authority as Secretary of War *ad interim*. How, then, can my colleague use the following language:

Considering that the facts charged against the President in the second article are in no respect contrary to any provision of the tenure-of-office act, they do not constitute a misdemeanor, and are not forbidden by any statute.

How can he justify such a statement, when he admits that the letter of authority was issued, and it is specifically declared in the act to be a misdemeanor?

Again, it is said that the prosecution is bound to prove criminal intent in the President. Such is not the law. The act itself proves the intent, if deliberately done by the party committing it. Such is the construction and the practice in all courts. If any person voluntarily commits an unlawful act the criminal intent is presumed. The principle is as old as our civilization, recognized in all courts of our own and other countries, that any unlawful act, voluntarily committed by a person of sound mind and mature age, necessarily implies that the person doing it, intends all the consequences necessarily resulting therefrom. The burglar who breaks into your house in the night, with revolver in hand, may plead for the burglary, larceny, and even murder itself, the not unworthy motive, that his only purpose was to procure subsistence for his starving wife and little ones. Booth, the vilest of assassins, declared, while committing the bloodiest crime in time's frightful calendar, that he murdered a tyrant for the sake of humanity, and in the sacred name of patriotism.

But it is not necessary to insist upon the technical rule that the criminal intent is to be presumed on proof of the act, for if there is one thing that is directly proved, that stands out in bold relief, that is plain as the sun at noonday, it is, that the President wilfully, wickedly, and defiantly *violated* the law; and that, after due notice and admonition, he wickedly and with criminal perverseness persisted in violating the Constitution and the laws, and in bold usurpations of power, unsettling the proper checks, limitations, and balances between the departments of the government; with malice aforethought striving to eject from office a faithful servant of the people, whose only crime was his loyalty, and substituting in his stead a man who was to be his willing instrument in thwarting the policy and legislation of the people's representatives, and in placing the government again in the hands of rebels, who with corrupt hearts and bloody hands struck at the nation's life.

Edwin M. Stanton, Mr. Lincoln's faithful minister and friend, whom the people learned to trust and lean upon in the dark hours of the republic, who wielded that mighty enginery by which our army of more than a million of men was raised, clothed, armed, and fed; who with the genius of a Napoleon comprehended the vast field of our military operations and organized war and victory with matchless skill—a man of unstained honor, spotless integrity, unquestioned loyalty, having the confidence of all loyal hearts in the country—this was the man who incurred the bitter hatred of Johnson, because he opposed his usurpations and his policy and acts in the interest of traitors, and because, like a faithful sentinel upon the watchtower of liberty, he gave the people warning against Johnson's schemes of mad ambition.

In proof of the respondent's malicious intent to violate the law, I refer you to his attempt to induce General Grant to aid him in open, avowed violation of the law, as proved in his letter to Grant dated January 31, 1868. He therein declared his purpose to eject Stanton "*whether sustained in the suspension or not.*" and upbraided Grant because, as he alleges, Grant agreed, but failed to help him keep Stanton out by refusing to restore the office to Stanton, as by the second section of the act of March 2, 1867, he was required to do. He says:

You had found in our first conference "that the President was desirous of keeping Mr. Stanton out of office, *whether sustained in the suspension or not.*" You knew what reasons had induced the President to ask from you a promise; you also knew that in case your views of duty did not accord with his own convictions it was his purpose to fill your place by another appointment. Even ignoring the existence of a positive understanding between us, these conclusions were plainly deducible from our various conversations. It is certain, however, that even under these circumstances you did not offer to return the place to my possession, but, according to your own statement, placed yourself in a position where, could I have anticipated your action, I would have been compelled to ask of you, as I was compelled to ask of your predecessor in the War Department, a letter of resignation, or else to resort to the more disagreeable expedient of suspending you by a successor.

That he intended to violate the law by preventing Mr. Stanton from resuming the functions of his office, as provided by law, should the Senate non-concur in his suspension, is clearly proved by his other letter to General Grant of February 10, 1868, from which I quote as follows:

First of all, you here admit that from the very beginning of what you term "the whole history" of your connection with Mr. Stanton's suspension, you intended to circumvent the President. It was to carry out that intent that you accepted the appointment. This was in your mind at the time of your acceptance. It was not, then, in obedience to the order of your superior, as has heretofore been supposed, that you assumed the duties of the office. You knew it was the President's purpose to prevent Mr. Stanton from resuming the office of Secretary of War.

If you want intent proved, how can you more clearly do it than to use his own words that it was his " purpose to do the act, and that Grant knew that was his purpose from the very beginning when Stanton was suspended?"

Is it necessary to dwell upon the subject of intent when in his own answer he confesses to having violated the law which expressly says that the officer, for good reasons only, should be suspended until the next session of the Senate, and coolly tells us that he "did not suspend the said Stanton from office until the next meeting of the Senate," as the law provided, " but by force and authority vested in him by the Constitution he suspended him *indefinitely*, and at the pleasure of the President, and that the order was made known to the Senate of the United States on the 12th day of December, 1867." In other words, he says to the Senate with most complacent effrontery: " Your law says I shall only suspend Stanton to the end of 20 days after the beginning of your next session. I *have* suspended him *indefinitely*, at the pleasure of the President, and I defy you to punish or hinder me." With all this, the respondent's counsel ask for proof of criminal intent. He tells the law-making power of the sovereign people that he sets up his pleasure against the positive mandates of law. He tells the Senate, " I do not acknowledge your law, which you, by your votes on your oaths, adopted and declared constitutional. I think it unconstitutional, and so said in my veto message, and I will not execute the law, but I will execute my veto; the reasons of my veto shall be my guide. I understand the constitutionality of the law better than Congress, and although my message vetoing the bill was overruled by two-thirds of Congress, and though you have declared by law that I can only suspend Stanton, I choose, of my own sovereign will, which is above law, to remove him indefinitely. Furthermore, your law says, that in case his suspension is not concurred in by the Senate, Mr. Stanton shall forthwith resume the functions of his office, and you have by resolution, a copy of which I confess to have received, refused to concur with me in suspending him. I shall not, however, suffer him to hold the office, and I have appointed Lorenzo Thomas Secretary of War, not with your advice and consent, but contrary to the same." This is the offence of the President which, in the judgment of the President's apologists, is so "trifling" that we ought to pass it by in silence, or rather excuse, by approving it in our verdict.

But what shall we say of the President's crime, when to the violation of law he adds falsehood and deception in the excuses he gives for its violation? His plea that he violated the law because of its unconstitutionality, and his desire to refer it to the Supreme Court, is shown to be a mere subterfuge—an afterthought—by the fact that, in August last, when he designated Grant to perform the duties of the War Office, he distinctly avowed that he was acting under the act of March 2, 1867; by the fact that he had caused the departments to so alter the forms of commissions and bonds as to make them conform to this very statute; by the fact that he reported reasons for the suspension, as required in the act, in an elaborate message to the Senate; and finally by the fact that nowhere in said message does he intimate that he does not recognize the validity of the act, but argues distinctly that he proceeds *under* the same. He did not tell senators in that message that the act was unconstitutional and that he had suspended Stanton *indefinitely*. And I assert that every senator was led to believe that it was the purpose of the President to regard the act valid, and to abide the judgment of the Senate. It was not until the ghost of impeachment, the terrors of a broken oath, and removal from the high trust which he has abused, as a punishment for violated law, rose up to confront him, that he resorted to the technical subterfuges of his answer that the law was unconstitutional, and the specious plea that his purpose in resisting the law was to test its validity before the Supreme Court.

In the whole history of these transactions, he has written as with a pen of steel in dark and imperishable lines his criminal intent to violate the law: First, he attempted to seduce General Grant to his purpose, but he indignantly refused; then General G. H. Thomas; then General Sherman; then General Emory; and finally he selected General Lorenzo Thomas, a man who was willing, as he testifies, "to obey the President's orders;" and who in pursuance of those orders threatened to "kick Stanton out;" and "if the doors of the War Office were barred against him," he would "break them down by force;" and who says on his oath that he would have executed his threats on the following day but for his arrest, after his return from the masquerade ball.

And now, as senators, we are exhorted to find him guiltless in violating a law which we have often declared constitutional and valid, upon the subterfuge, the afterthought of the criminal, the excuse of a lawbreaker caught in the act, the plea born of fear and the terrors of impeachment, and shown by the record made by his own hands to be utterly false. For one I cannot be so false to convictions, so regardless of fact, so indifferent to consistency, so blind to evidence, so lenient to crime, so reckless of my oath and of my country's peace.

Ours is a land of law. The principle of submission to the authority of law is canonized in the hearts of the American people as a sacred thing. There are none too high to be above its penalties, none too low to be beyond its protection. It is a shield to the weak, a restraint to the strong, and is the foundation of civil order and peace. When the day comes that the laws may be violated with impunity by either high or low, all is lost. A pall of darkness will shut us in with anarchy, violence, and blood as our portion, and I fear the sun of peace and liberty will never more illumine our nation's path. The nation looks for a most careful observance of the law by the highest officer known to the law, because he has an "oath registered in heaven" that he "will take care that the laws shall be faithfully executed." If the President of the United States, who should be the high exemplar to all the people, shall violate his oath with impunity, at his mere pleasure dispense with, or disregard, or violate the law, why may not all do the same? Why not at once sweep away the Constitution and laws, and level to the earth our temples of liberty and justice; resolve society into its original elements, where brute force, not right, shall rule, and chaos, anarchy, and lawless violence dominate the land?

The Constitution and the laws passed in pursuance thereof are "the supreme law of the land." The President admits in his answer, and in his defence, that he acted in violation of the provisions of a statute, and his strange and startling defence is, that he may suspend the operation of a law; that is to say, in plain terms, violate it at his pleasure, if, in *his opinion*, the law is unconstitutional; "that being unconstitutional it is void, and that penalties do not attach to its violation."

Mr. President, I utterly deny that the President has any such right. His duties are ministerial, and in no sense judicial. It is not his prerogative to exercise judicial powers. He must execute the laws, even though the legislature may pass acts which, in his opinion, are unconstitutional. His duty is to study the law, not with the purpose to set it aside, but that he may obey its injunctions strictly. Can a sheriff, sworn to execute the laws, refuse to hang a convicted murderer, because, in his judgment, the law under which the criminal has been tried is unconstitutional? He has no remedy but to execute the law in manner and form as prescribed, or resign to a successor who will do so.

I quote from the Constitution to show how laws become such, and that when certain prescribed forms are complied with the requirements of a law must be observed by all as long as it remains on the statute-book unrepealed by the Congress which made it, or is declared of no validity by the Supreme Court, it of course having jurisdiction upon a case stated:

Every bill which shall have passed the House of Representatives and the Senate shall, before it becomes a law, be presented to the President of the United States; if he approve, he shall sign it, but if not, he shall return it with his objections to that house in which it shall have originated, who shall enter the objections at large on their journal and proceed to reconsider it. If, after such reconsideration, two-thirds of that house shall agree to pass the bill, it shall be sent, together with the objections, to the other house, by which it shall likewise be reconsidered, and if approved by two-thirds of that house it shall become a law. * *

If any bill shall not be returned by the President within ten days (Sundays excepted) after it shall have been presented to him, the same shall be a law in like manner as if he had signed it, unless the Congress by their adjournment prevent its return, in which case it shall not be a law.

Every bill which has passed the House of Representatives and the Senate, and been approved by the President, "shall become a law." If not approved by him, and it is again passed by two-thirds of each house, "it shall become a law;" and if he retains it more than ten days, whether he approve or disapprove, it shall still "*become a law.*" No matter how pertinent may be his objections in his veto message; no matter with how much learning or law he may clothe his argument; no matter how vividly he may portray the evil which may result from its execution, or how flagrantly it may, in his view, conflict with the Constitution, yet if it is passed over his veto by two-thirds of the Senate and House of Representatives, his power ceases and his duties are at an end, and it *becomes a law*, and he is bound by his oath to execute it and leave the responsibility where it belongs, with the law-makers, who must answer to the people. If he then refuses to execute it, what is this but simple resistance, sedition, usurpation, and, if persisted in, revolution? Is it in his discretion to say it is not a law when the Constitution says, in the plain English vernacular, it is a law? Yes, Mr. President, it is a law to him *and to all* the people, to be obeyed and enforced throughout all the land.

It is a plain provision of the Constitution "that all legislative power granted by this Constitution shall be vested in a Congress, which shall consist of a Senate and House of Representatives." The President is no part of this legislative power. His veto message is merely suggestive, and if his reasons are deemed insufficient he is overruled, and the bill becomes a law "in like manner" as if he had approved it. The doctrine contended for by the President is monstrous, and if admitted is the end of all free government. It presents the question whether the people of the United States are to make their own laws through their representatives in Congress, or whether all the powers of the government, executive, legislative, and judicial, are to be lodged in a single hand? He has the executive power, and is Commander-in-chief of the army and the navy. Now, if it is his province to judicially interpret and decide for himself what laws are constitutional and of binding validity upon him, then he has the judicial power, and there is no use for a Supreme Court; and, if having decided a law, in his opinion, to be unconstitutional, he may of his own will and sovereign pleasure set aside, dispense with, repeal, and violate a law which has passed over his veto, then he has the legislative power, and Congress is a myth, worse than "an excrescence hanging on the verge of the government." Thus the purse and the sword, and all the powers which we heretofore considered so nicely balanced between the various departments of the government, are transferred to a single person, and the government is as essentially a monarchy or a despotism as it would be if the Constitution and Congress were obliterated and the whole power lodged in the hands of the President. When such questions as these are involved shall we wonder that the pulse of the popular heart of this nation beats, and heaves with terrible anxiety as we hear the final judgment on this great trial, in which the life of the nation hangs trembling in the scale, as much so as when it was struggling for existence in the perilous hours of the war through which it has recently passed. Am I, as a senator and one of this high court of impeachment, called upon to register, not that the Constitution and the laws shall be the supreme law, but that the will of one man shall be the law of the land?

Let us look at another point in the defence. The President says he violated the law in removing Stanton for the purpose of making a case before the Supreme Court, and thus procuring a decision upon the constitutionality of the law. That is, he broke the law in order to bring the judiciary to his aid in resisting the will of the people. I would here commend to his careful attention the opinion of Attorney General Black, his whilom constitutional adviser. He says, in 1860:

> But his (the President's) power is to be used only in the manner prescribed by the legislative department. He cannot accomplish a legal purpose by illegal means, or break the laws himself to prevent them from being violated by others. (9 Op. Att'ys Gen., 516.)

It is to be regretted that considerations of great gravity prevented the President from appearing here by counsel thus committed to a view of the extent of executive authority at once so just and so acceptable to the candid patriot.

Inasmuch as it has already been shown that good intentions do not justify the violation of known law, I am unable to see the propriety of stopping the wheels of government and holding in abeyance the rights of many individuals, and paralyzing the usefulness of our army, until the President sees fit to proceed through all the formalities and tedious delays of the Supreme Court, or any other court. If the President can do this, why may not any and all parties refuse compliance with the requirements of inconvenient laws upon the same plea? To oppose such a view with argument, is to dignify an absurdity.

One other point of the defence I wish to notice before closing. It is argued at length, that an offence charged before a court of impeachment must be an indictable one, or else the respondent must have a verdict of acquittal. Then why provide for impeachment at all? Why did not the Constitution leave the whole matter to a grand jury and the criminal courts? Nothing can be added to the arguments and citations of precedents by the honorable managers on this point, and those most learned in the law cannot strengthen that view which is obvious to the most cursory student of the Constitution, viz: that impeachment is a form of trial provided for cases which may *lack* as well as those which do contain the features of indictable crime. Corresponding to the equity side of a civil court, it provides for the trial and punishment, not only of indictable offences, but of those not technically described in rules of criminal procedure. The absurdity of the respondent's plea is the more manifest in this case, because, not the Supreme Court, but the Senate of the United States is the only tribunal to try impeachments, and the President's vision should rather have been directed to what the Senate, sitting as a court of impeachment, would decide, than to have been anticipating what some future decision of a court having no jurisdiction in the case might be.

Impeachable misdemeanors partake of the nature of both political and criminal offences. Hence the Constitution has wisely conferred upon the people, through their representatives in Congress, the right and duty to become the prosecutors of great offenders for violations of laws, and crimes tending to the destruction of social order, and the overthrow of government, and has devolved the trial of such cases upon the Senate, composed of men supposed to be competent judges of law and facts, and who are allowed larger latitude of rulings than pertains to courts. With this view I have tried to weigh impartially the testimony in this case. I would not wrong the respondent, nor do I wish harm to come to the institutions of this land by his usurpations. I also desire to be consistent with myself so far as I may justly do so. I voted, not in haste, but deliberately, that the action of the President in removing or attempting to remove Stanton, was unconstitutional and in violation of law.

Is it possible that there is some newly discovered "*quirk*" in the law, not understood on the 24th February last, which renders Johnson's act less criminal than it then appeared? Did not senators believe the act of March 2, 1867, constitutional when they voted for it? After the President had arrayed all conceivable objections against it in his veto, did not two-thirds of this and of the other house still vote it constitutional and a valid law? Did they not by solemn resolution declare that the President had violated it and the Constitution in removing Stanton and appointing Thomas? How can we say, while under oath we try this man, that he is innocent? Is it not trifling with the country, a mockery of justice, an insult to the representatives of the people, and a melancholy instance of self-stultification, for us to solemnly declare the President a violator of law, thus inviting and making it the duty of the House of Representatives to prosecute him here, and after long investigation, at large expense of the people's money, with both confession of the criminal, and large and conclusive proofs of the crime—all this and more—for us to declare him not guilty?

The position in which senators are placed by the votes which they have heretofore given is so well stated in an editorial of a leading newspaper of my own State, the Chicago Tribune of May 7, 1868, that I extract from it as follows:

Johnson disregarded the constitution and the law, and broke them both by appointing a Secretary of War without the consent of the Senate when no vacancy existed.

* * * * * * * * * *

No man can tell how black-letter lawyers may be influenced by hair-splitting niceties, legal quirks, and musty precedents. * * * * * *

Now, to acquit Andrew Johnson is to impeach the Senate, to insult and degrade the House and to betray the people. If Johnson is not guilty of violating the law and the constitution, the Senate is guilty of sustaining Stanton in defiance of the constitution; is guilty of helping to pass an unconstitutional law; is guilty of interfering with the executive prerogatives Every senator who voted for the tenure-of-office bill, who voted that Johnson's removal of Stanton was in violation of that law, who voted to order the President to replace Stanton, and who now votes for the acquittal of Johnson, stultifies and condemns himself as to his previous acts, and the whole country will so understand it.

The Senate knew all the facts before the House impeached; the Senate's action made impeachment obligatory on the part of the House, and on the heads of the senators rest, the responsibility of defeating a verdict of guilty against a criminal who stands self-confessed as guilty of breaking the law and disregarding the Constitution. No matter what personal antipathy senators may feel for the man who will become Johnson's successor, no matter about the plots and schemes of the high-tariff lobby, the Senate has a solemn duty to perform, and that is to punish a wilful and malicious violation of the law. If the President, in disregard of his oath, may trample on the law, who is bound to obey it? If the President is not amenable to the law, he is an emperor, a despot; then what becomes of our boasted government by law, of our lauded free institutions?

My colleague is certainly in error when he says:

It is known, however, that the resolution coupled the two things, the removal of the Secretary of War and the designation of an officer *ad interim*, together, so that those who believed either without authority were compelled to vote for the resolution.

Just the reverse of that is the true doctrine. If a senator believed one branch of the proposition to be true, and the others false, he was bound by his oath to vote *against* the resolution.

Where two allegations are made, one of which is true and the other false, there is no obligation to affirm both.

Mr. President, I ought, in justice to those who may vote for acquittal, to say that I do not judge them. Nor do I think it a crime to vote in a minority of one against the world. When I have taken an oath to decide a case according to the law and the testimony, I would patiently listen to my constituents, and be willing, perhaps anxious to be convinced by them, yet no popular clamor, no fear of punishment or hope of reward, should seduce me from deciding according to the conviction of my conscience and my judgment; therefore I judge no one. Our wisest and most trusted men have been often in a minority. I speak for myself, however, when I say it is very hard for me to see, after what seems to me such plain proof of wilful and wicked violation of law, how any senator can go back upon himself and his record, and upon the House of Representatives and the country, and set loose the greatest offender of modern times, to repeat at pleasure his acts of usurpation, and to plead the license and warrant of this great tribunal for his high crimes and misdemeanors.

In the eleventh article, among other things, it is charged that the President did attempt to prevent the execution of the act of March 2, 1867, providing for the more efficient government of the rebel States. It is plain to me from his veto messages, his proclamations, his appointments of rebels to office, his indiscriminate use of the pardoning power, his removal of our most faithful military officers from their posts, that he has been the great obstacle to the reconstruction of the Union.

With his support of Congress in its measures every State would long since have resumed its friendly and harmonious relations to the government, and our 40,000,000 of people would have rejoiced again in a restored and happy Union. It is his perverse resistance to almost every measure devised by Congress which retarded the work of reconstruction, reanimated the hopes and reinflamed the virus of rebellion in the southern States. The Freedmen's Bureau bill, the civil-rights bill, and the various reconstruction bills were remorselessly vetoed by him and every obstacle thrown in the way of their proper and efficient execution. His unvarying purpose seems to have been to save the rebel oligarchy from the consequences which our victory pronounced upon it, and to enable it to accomplish by his policy, and abuse of his power, what could not be accomplished by the power of the sword. The rebellion lives in his vetoes and acts. If some daring usurper, backed by a powerful faction, and the army and navy subject to his call, should proclaim himself king or dictator, would not the blood leap in the heart of every true American? and yet how little less than this is the condition of our public affairs, and who has not seen on the part of Andrew Johnson a deliberate purpose to override the sovereign power of the nation, and to usurp dangerous, dictatorial and kingly powers? And what true patriot has not felt that in such conflicts of power there is eminent peril to the life of the republic, and that if some check by impeachment or otherwise be not put upon these presidential usurpations, the fruits of the war will be lost, the rebellion triumph, the last hope of a permanent reunion of the States be extinguished forever?

For reasons such as these, and for proof of which there is much of evidence in the documents and records of this trial, but more especially for the violation of the Constitution and of positive law, I cannot consent that with my vote the President shall longer work his treacherous and despotic will unchecked upon my suffering countrymen.

Mr. President, this is a tremendous hour for the republic. Gigantic interests and destinies concentrate in the work and duties of the eventful moments through which we are passing.

I would do justice, and justice requires conviction; justice to the people whom he has so cruelly wronged. I would be merciful, merciful to the millions whose rights he treacherously assails by his contempt for law. I would have peace; therefore I vote to remove from office this most pestilent disturber of public peace. I would have prosperity among the people, and confidence restored to capital; therefore I vote to punish him whose turbulence makes capital timid and paralyzes our national industries. I would have economy in the administration of public affairs; therefore I vote to depose the promoter and cause of unheard of official extravagance. I would have honesty in the collection of the public revenues; therefore I vote to remove this patron of the corruptionists. I would have my government respected abroad; therefore I vote to punish him who subjects us to dishonor by treating law with contempt. I would inspire respect for law in the youth of the land; I therefore vote to impose its penalties upon the most exalted criminal. I would secure and perpetuate liberty, and I therefore vote to purge the citadel of liberty of him who, through murder, succeeded to the chief command, and seeks to betray us to the enemy.

I fervently pray that this nation may avoid a repetition of that history, in which apostates and usurpers have desolated nations and enslaved mankind. Let our announcement this day to the President, and all future Presidents, and all conspirators against the liberties of this country, be what is already the edict of the loyal millions of our land, "You shall not tear this temple of liberty down." Let our warning go down the ages that every usurper and bold violator of law who thrusts himself in the path of this republic to honor and renown, whoever he may be, however high his title or proud his name, that, Arnold-like, he shall be gibbeted upon every hilltop throughout the land as a monument of his crime and punishment, and of the shame and grief of his country.

We are not alone in trying this cause. Out on the Pacific shore a deep murmur is heard from thousands of patriot voices; it swells over the western plain, peopled by millions more; with every increasing volume it advances; on by the lakes and through the busy marts of the great north, and re-echoed by other millions on the Atlantic strand, it thunders upon us a mighty nation's verdict, *guilty.* While from out the smoke and gloom of the desolated south, from the rice fields, and along the great rivers, from hundreds of thousands of persecuted and basely betrayed Unionists, comes also the solemn judgment, *guilty.*

The criminal cited before this bar by the people's representatives is, by his answer and the record, *guilty.*

Appealing for the correctness of my verdict to the Searcher of all hearts, and to the enlightened judgment of all who love justice, and in accord with this "cloud of witnesses," I vote, guilty.

Standing here in my place in this mighty temple of the nation, and as a senator of the Great Republic, with all history of men and nations behind me, and all progress and human happiness before me, I falter not, on this occasion, in duty to my country and to my State.

In this tremendous hour of the republic, trembling for life and being, it is no time for me to shrink from duty, after having so long earnestly supported those principles of government and public policy which, like Divine ordinances, protect and guide the race of man up the pathway of history and progress. As a juror, sitting on this great cause of my country, I wish it to go to history and to stand upon the imperishable records of the republic, that in the fear of God, but fearless of man, I voted for the conviction of Andrew Johnson, President of the United States, for the commission of high crimes and misdemeanors.

OPINION OF MR. SENATOR VICKERS.

The Constitution secures to the President of the United States the nomination of civil officers, and their appointment, if the Senate shall advise and concur. He is the initiating and acting power, and gives character and form to the proceeding before it is presented to the consideration of the Senate, which body has no power to present the name of any one to the President as an object of official favor. The act of 1789, which created the Department of War, does not limit the tenure of the office of the Secretary of that department, but assigns such duties as shall be enjoined upon and entrusted to him by the President, agreeably to the Constitution.

Soon after the government went into operation, the power of removal from office was exercised by the Executive during the session as well as in the recess of the Senate; the commissions to the Secretaries and many other officers contained the statement that they held at the pleasure of the President. A practice immediately arose and prevailed, and was continued down to the year 1867, of removal from office by the Executive; the power of removal was claimed as an incident to that of appointment, and as essential to a faithful execution of the laws, on the ground that unless the President possessed it he could not remove a faithless officer who might be engaged in obstructing the execution of the laws or in embezzling the public funds; the duty of the President under the Constitution, to take care that the laws should be faithfully executed, could not be efficiently discharged unattended by the power of removal. Although differences of opinion may have existed upon this as well as other provisions of that instrument, yet the practice uninterruptedly continued, with the implied assent of the legislature, for upwards of 75 years, and constituted a legislative construction which was affirmed by different Attorney Generals of the United States, whose attention had been specially called to the subject.

The acquiescence by Congress in that construction, whether originally correct or not, was fully sufficient to justify President Johnson in its exercise. Although it may be termed an implied power, it is as valuable and essential to a co-ordinate department as an express grant. The power to create banks, and of erecting custom and light-houses, is derived by implication. The concurrent authorities of Kent and Story refer to the power of removal of officers by the President, as established by usage and acquiescence, as well as by the opinions of the most eminent lawyers, judges, and statesmen, as the settled construction of the Constitution. It was advocated and practiced by Jefferson, Madison, Monroe, Jackson, Van Buren, and other Presidents, down to Mr. Johnson. The elder Adams removed Mr. Pickering, Secretary of State, during the session of Congress, and without consulting it; he requested Mr. Pickering to resign, and on his refusal removed him by a peremptory order, and nominated John Marshall his successor. The right of Mr. Adams does not seem to have been questioned. The act of 1789, in its second section, provides for the appointment of a chief clerk in the Department of War, who, whenever the principal officer, the Secretary, shall be removed by the President, or in any other case of vacancy, shall have the charge and custody of all the records and papers in the office. The language of this act recognizes an existing right in the President, under the Constitution, to remove a Secretary at his discretion. The debates in Congress in 1789, by the ablest men of the nation, show that the power of removal from office was conceded to be in the President, and the bills establishing the departments and regulating the duties to be performed were framed purposely to conform to that construction of the Constitution. Thus, in the act relating to the Treasury Department, the seventh section provides that the assistant shall take charge of the records, books, and papers "whenever the Secretary shall be removed from office by the President of the United States, or in any other case of vacancy." In the same year the Department of Foreign Affairs was created, and in the second section of the act it is declared that there shall be appointed an inferior officer, to be called the chief clerk, and who, "whenever the said principal officer shall be removed from office by the President of the United States, or in any other case of vacancy, shall, during such vacancy, have the charge and custody of the records," &c. These three statutes do not confer the power of removal, but they treat it as existing in the executive department, and were designed and draughted to exclude the presumption of implication of a grant of that power to the President by legislative authority

The act of the 2d March, 1867, regulating the tenure of civil offices, and passed over the President's veto, was intended to alter and change the settled construction of the Constitution, and to empower the Senate to continue a cabinet officer in commission against the will and wishes of the Executive, and to restrain and check his wonted power of removal; the statute trenched upon and materially impaired what the President and his legal advisers, including the Secretary of War, believed and declared to be a constitutional right and prerogative of the executive department The President having sworn to "preserve, protect, and defend the Constitution of the United States," considered it to be his duty, as custodian of the executive department, to treat the act as unconstitutional and to exert the power claimed and exercised by all his predecessors. The statute of 2d March, 1867, essays to create an offence of a high misdemeanor in any one who may attempt to violate it, and for this effort of the President to maintain the integrity of his department until the judiciary, the only arbiter to determine a question of such magnitude in the last resort, should decide, the impeachment is predicated.

If one department shall attempt or do what another department shall believe to be an essential and vital encroachment upon its high powers or functions, the law of self-defence is as applicable as it would be to a personal attack by one upon another. It cannot be expected that the executive department is to be the agent for executing a statute upon itself which is to dismember and deprive it of half its vigor or vitality; the duty enjoined upon the President to see that the laws are executed was not designed to operate in such a case, for the practical recognition of such a principle might be used to work the destruction of the whole frame of the government and make the Constitution its own destroyer. The allegation that if the President shall be permitted to contravene a statute which he and his cabinet believe invades and infracts the constitutional limits and powers of the department over which he presides, and feels bound to preserve, that he may be at equal liberty to disregard any law of a different character and object, has no more force than that the right of self-defence may be extended to justify an individual in assaulting every person he may chance to meet. If it is in the lawful competency of Congress to punish the infraction of every law by pains and penalties, and to deprive the courts of the United States of their jurisdiction over the same, Congress would soon become omnipotent, the co-ordination of the departments be destroyed, and the structure and genius of our government be changed by the action of one department.

It may well be questioned if the cabinet officers who were appointed by a former President, and not reappointed in a second term, either by that President or by Mr. Johnson, his successor, were intended to be embraced by the act of 2d March, 1867; if it were a matter of doubt the accused would be entitled to the benefit of it. From a careful examination of the act, taken in connection with the avowed purpose of it, as declared in the Senate and House of Representatives, by the committees of conference, at the time of its final passage, my opinion is that such officers were not, nor intended to be, included in it. Entertaining the views I have expressed, I do not consider that the first and eighth articles of impeachment are sustained.

The act of Congress of 1795, ch. 21, provides for the filling of all vacancies by the President, by appointments *ad interim* for a period not exceeding six months. The power of removal or suspension necessarily carries with it the right to fill the vacancy temporarily on the ground of public necessity; the exigency may exist at any time, whether during the session or in the recess of the Senate, and the public interest and service may require the promptest action by the President. The acts of 1863 and 1867 do not, by implication, repeal the cases provided for and covered by the act of 1795, which embraces all cases of vacancy from whatever cause, and authorizes *ad interim* employments, but only such as are occasioned by death, resignation, absence or sickness, leaving the vacancies occasioned by removal and expiration of commission unrepealed. The act of 1867 regulating the tenure of certain civil offices, by its second section, empowers the President to fill vacancies which may happen during the recess of the Senate, by reason of death or resignation, and in such cases to grant commissions, which shall expire at the end of the next session thereafter, but makes no provision for filling vacancies which may occur during the session of the Senate, leaving such to be filled under existing laws and the usages of the department. The eighth section of the tenure-of-office act declares that whenever the President shall, without the advice and consent of the Senate, designate, authorize or employ any person to perform the duties of any office, he shall notify the Secretary of the Treasury, &c. This recognizes the right of the President to make *ad interim* appointments without the consent of the Senate. This class of appointments is not the same mentioned in the third section of that act, because he is authorized by that section to issue commissions to expire at the end of the next session; but in the eighth section it is stated to be a mere designation or employment of some person to perform the duties of an office. According to usage, from the necessity of the case, and the act of 1795, unrepealed in part by 1863 or the act of 1867, the President had the power to designate General Thomas to perform, for a brief period, the duties of the Department of War. To avoid circumlocution I have sometimes used the word appointment, instead of designation or employment in connection with *ad interim* duties, but an appointment to office, legally and technically, has three essential elements: 1. A nomination by the President. 2. A confirmation or approval by the Senate. 3. A commission signed, sealed, and delivered to the appointee. A concurrence of all is necessary to its consummation. The designation of a person to take possession and fulfil the duties is but for a temporary purpose, till a suitable successor can be found and his nomination sent to the Senate; the public interest may demand such a course of action.

The proceedings in this case abound with instances of *ad interim* employments, directed by all the Presidents from Mr. Adams (the elder) to Mr. Johnson, including President Lincoln. The designation of General Thomas was on the 21st February, and the nomination of Mr. Ewing was sent to the Senate on the 22d February, but in consequence of an early adjournment, and the next day being the Sabbath, it was not actually received by the Senate till Monday, the 24th of that month. But if the President, the Attorney General, and other cabinet officers were mistaken in their construction of the law, which I do not think, such an error was a venial one, and cannot properly be considered a high crime or high misdemeanor.

But if none of the laws alluded to authorized the *ad interim* appointment of General Thomas, yet, if Mr. Stanton's case is not covered by the first section of the act of March 2, 1867, called the tenure-of-office law, the 2d article and others into which it enters are not subjects of impeachment. Mr. Stanton was appointed by Mr. Lincoln in 1862, during the first term of his Presidency; his term expired with Mr. Lincoln's, as definitively as if the latter had not been re-elected; he was not reappointed either by Mr. Lincoln or by President Johnson, and only held by courtesy and sufferance. The month allowed to the cabinet officers appointed by Mr. Johnson and confirmed by the Senate does not apply to officers appointed by Mr. Lincoln, and who held no legal term under President Johnson. The latter, therefore, committed no misdemeanor in designating General Thomas to perform the duties till a regular nomination could be made: first, because Mr. Stanton's case is not protected by the first section of the act of 1867, all the subsequent sections having reference to the cases only which are included in that section—the sixth section, relating to *ad interim* appointments, expressly declaring them to be "contrary to the provisions of this act," and if not within the first section, it cannot be within the sixth; secondly, because no other act forbids such appointments; and thirdly, because it was in conformity to the settled practice of the executive department since its formation, acquiesced in by all the departments, and necessary to a proper and faithful execution of the laws. In any aspect of the case the second and third articles are not maintainable. With the views already expressed, that the President is not guilty of the principal charge, which is modified and extended over other articles, it follows that he is not punishable on the charge for conspiring to do the acts mentioned in the fourth, fifth, and seventh articles, and especially not in the absence of all proof of any such conspiracy. The sixth article charges a conspiracy to seize and take by force the property of the United States in violation of the conspiracy act of July, 1861. This statute does not, in my opinion, apply to the removal of an officer under claim of constitutional right; besides, no proof was offered of any authority from the President to use force, (none was used,) and no legitimate inference of such an intention can be drawn under an act penal in its character when the presumptions are favorable to the citizen, and especially to a high public functionary of the government in the discharge of official duty. The ninth article, which alleges an attempt to seduce an officer of the army from his duty to promote sinister purposes of the President, appears to be wholly unsupported by proof. The commander-in-chief has an undoubted right to consult with his subordinates, to inquire into the disposition of the military forces, and to express opinions; the relation between them precludes the presumption of an unlawful purpose in making proper inquiries and communications. In such a case the charge should be expressly proved; but there was not only no evidence offered tending to prove it, but a laudable motive was proved by the Secretary of the Navy, who suggested to the President the propriety of making the investigation.

The tenth supplemental article is in reference to certain public speeches of the President, and charges that they are high misdemeanors in office. These speeches were made in a private, and not in an official, capacity, and however injudicious some may think portions of them, and to be regretted, I know of no law which can punish Mr. Johnson with a removal from office because they were made. As we have no law to punish those who may indulge in political discussions, it cannot reasonably be expected that the President should be removed for exercising a privilege enjoyed by every American citizen; the first amendment to the Constitution declares that Congress shall pass no law abridging the freedom of speech or of the press.

The eleventh article is anomalous, indefinite, and liable to the objection of multiplicity. If it were possible to put it in the form of an indictment or of a declaration in a civil action, it would be quashed on motion by a court of law. The first item or paragraph is not in the form of a charge, but is the recital of a speech contained in the tenth article and appears to be only introductory, or alleged as inducement to a charge which follows, viz: that the President, in pursuance of said speech made in August, 1866, attempted to prevent the execution of the tenure-of-office act, passed on the 2d March, 1867; then follows a vague allusion to the means by which he made the said attempt, to wit, on the 21st February, 1868, by unlawfully devising, contriving, and attempting to devise and contrive, means to prevent E. M. Stanton from forthwith resuming the functions of the office of Secretary of War, which had been peaceably and quietly resumed on the 13th January, 1868, about five weeks prior to the alleged contrivances, as appears by Mr. Stanton's affidavit to procure a warrant for General Thomas's arrest, and also by the first article of impeachment. The other means are to prevent the execution of the act making appropriations for the support of the army—of which no proof was offered except that in relation to the ninth article in reference to General Emory's interview with the President. The last means charged are to prevent the execution of an act to provide for the efficient government of the rebel States, passed 2d March, 1867; the only evidence introduced was a telegram to Governor Parsons, dated several weeks prior to the passage of the said act alleged to be violated. This eleventh article seems to be made up by uniting fragments or portions of other articles; if separately the articles in full are not sustained, the joining together of some of their disunited parts cannot impart to them additional strength or vitality. There is no proof of any connection between the speeches referred to and the tenure-of-office act, nor between that act or any alleged violation of it and the means and contrivances imputed to the President. It was contended on the part of the prosecution that the act of 1789, and not the Constitution, conferred upon the President the power of removal from office and separated that power from that of appointment. The act of 1867 does not essay to punish a removal under the act of 1789 unless made in the recess of the Senate, and as Mr. Stanton's removal was during the session of that body, the prohibition of the act is not applicable. The act of 1789 is general, and not confined in its operation to the recess of the Senate or to its sessions; its language is, "whenever the said principal officer (the Secretary being meant) shall be removed from office by the President of the United States," the inferior officer shall have charge of the records, books, and papers appertaining to the department.

A President and his cabinet may be called upon to examine and determine the meaning, scope, and operation of statutes they may be required to execute materially affecting the powers, duties, and practice of the executive department of the government. Judgment is necessarily involved in that examination and consideration. If, after a candid and diligent investigation and mature deliberation, the President acts upon the conclusion thus formed, can it be contended that for doing so he is guilty of a high crime or misdemeanor and punishable by removal from office? There must be some wilful and manifest abuse of authority, usurpation, or corruption in such a case to justify a proceeding so degrading in its character and consequences. If Congress, by legislation of two-thirds, after the exercise of the veto by the Executive, should assume the power of making appointments to office, irrespective of his right of nomination, of negotiating and confirming treaties, of diminishing his compensation during the term for which he was elected, can it be said that he would have no right to judge of the constitutionality of these acts? and, if he should refuse to regard them, to be subjected to impeachment and removal, as well as to fine and imprisonment, although they attempted to abstract the essential attributes of his office and reduce the department to a subordinate and inferior condition? Surely such a proposition could not be seriously advocated. But further, suppose that Congress by its acts should grant titles of nobility and require the President to issue commissions to perfect them, or pass bills of attainder or *ex post facto* laws, or lay a capitation tax without reference to the census, and devolve the execution of the statutes upon the President; shall he be bound, regardless of his oath to protect and defend the Constitution, to execute them against his own convictions and against the unanimous opinion and advice of the Attorney General and his other constitutional advisers? If in any case the right of judgment is to be exercised, no criminality can be legally imputed for its honest exercise, though the conclusion may be erroneous.

For these reasons, independent of those already assigned, and from a careful consideration of the evidence adduced and of the circumstances of the case, I do not think that the first eight and the eleventh articles can be maintained.

OPINION OF MR. SENATOR FERRY.

Eleven articles of impeachment are preferred by the House of Representatives against the President of the United States.

The first, second, third, eighth, and eleventh depend, wholly or in part, upon the validity and construction of the act of March 2, 1867, "regulating the tenure of certain civil offices," and will be considered together in a subsequent portion of this opinion.

The fourth, fifth, sixth, and seventh charge the commission of the offence technically known as "conspiracy," either as defined by statute, or by common law. It is sufficient to say, in regard to these articles, that the proof does not sustain the charge. No testimony has been adduced to show a "conspiracy" by the President with any person other than Lorenzo Thomas, and the evidence exhibited is substantially confined to the letter of authority of February 21, 1868, signed by the former, and the acceptance of the place of Secretary of War *ad interim* by the latter. The conduct of General Thomas seems to have been influenced by a mistaken idea of the obligation of military obedience, (to which, indeed, the phraseology of the letter of authority affords some countenance,) while the President treats him as a subordinate rather than as a confederate.

So, also, the proof fails to sustain the ninth article, which is based upon the conversation between the President and General Emory on the 22d of February, 1868. The only evidence before us is the testimony of General Emory himself, which discloses the declaration by the President of his opinion of the validity of an act of Congress, but affords no reason to infer that it was given as charged, "with intent thereby to induce said Emory, as commander of the department of Washington, to violate the provisions of said act," &c.

The specifications of the tenth article, as to the delivery of the speeches, are substantially proved, but the legal conclusion, that thereby "said Andrew Johnson, President of the United States, did commit, and was then and there guilty of a high misdemeanor in office," does not result from the establishment of the truth of the specifications. The speeches proved were certainly not indictable, either at common law or by statute, nor were they, in any sense, acts of official misconduct, or omissions of official duty. They were vain, foolish, vulgar, and unbecoming, but the Constitution does not provide that a President may be impeached for the exhibition of these qualities.

Contenting myself with these observations upon the fourth, fifth, sixth, seventh, ninth, and tenth articles of impeachment, I find the respondent *not guilty* upon each and all of them.

The first, second, third, eighth, and eleventh articles remain to be considered, and upon these I am constrained to arrive at a different result. I accept, preliminarily, the construction given by the Chief Justice to the eleventh article:

> The gravamen of this article seems to be, that the President attempted to defeat the execution of the tenure-of-office act. * * * The single substantive matter charged is the attempt to prevent the execution of the tenure-of-office act. * * * This single matter, connected with the other matters, previously and subsequently alleged, is charged as the high misdemeanor of which the President is alleged to have been guilty. The general question, guilty or not guilty of a high misdemeanor as charged, seems fully to cover the whole charge. (Remarks of the Chief Justice, Impeachment Trial, p. 1236.)

If an actual violation of the tenure-of-office act is a high misdemeanor, as declared by the act itself, then, in my judgment, the attempt to "defeat," to "prevent" the execution of that act by the President of the United States, charged with the whole responsibility of executive duty, is a high misdemeanor in office, for whose commission the Constitution subjects him to impeachment and removal from office.

With this preliminary statement I observe that my opinion upon the second, third, eighth, and eleventh articles arises out of and must stand or fall with the opinion which I have formed upon the first. The greater portion of my remaining observations will therefore be directed to that article.

The substantive charge in the first article is the removal of Mr. Stanton, contrary to the provisions of the tenure-of-office act. It is true that the removal is alleged only indirectly, but it is familiar law that the technicality of an indictment is unnecessary in articles of impeachment. The first article states in detail what the President did and the intent with which it was done, viz: to violate the act; and the facts stated constitute in effect an actual removal, with which statement the evidence also accords.

On the 21st of February, 1868, the President sends written notice to Mr. Stanton stating to him "you are hereby removed.". On the same day the President informs Lorenzo Thomas that Mr. Stanton has "been this day removed," and appoints the Adjutant General Secretary *ad interim*. The Secretary *ad interim* is invited to take and does take his place as Secretary of War in the cabinet councils from that day to the present; is recognized there as Secretary by the President and cabinet, and Mr. Stanton is carefully excluded; and finally, two nominations of a permanent Secretary have been sent to the Senate by the President " in place of Edwin M. Stanton, removed." By these acts the President must stand or fall; according to them he is to be tried, and he accepts the issue.

Was, then, the removal of Mr. Stanton a high misdemeanor as charged? The sixth section of the tenure-of-office act is as follows:

> Every removal, appointment, or employment, made, had, or exercised, contrary to the provisions of this act, and the making, signing, sealing, countersigning, or issuing of any commission or letter of authority for or in respect to any such appointment or employment, shall be deemed, and are hereby declared to be, high misdemeanors, and, upon trial and conviction there f, every person guilty thereof shall be punished by a fine not exceeding ten thousand dollars, or by imprisonment not exceeding five years, or both said punishments, in the discretion of the court.

If the statute is valid, and Mr. Stanton is within its provisions, the character of the offence would seem to be unmistakable.

The President denies its validity, asserting "that the Constitution of the United States confers on him as part of the executive power, and as one of the necessary means and instruments of performing the executive duty expressly imposed upon him by the Constitution, of taking care that the laws be faithfully executed, *the power at any and all times of removing from office all executive officers for cause to be judged of by the President alone.*"—Answer to Article 4.

Of course this claim would extend not only to the act of March 2, 1867, but would sweep from the statute-book every act fixing any tenure-of-office except the pleasure of the President. The assertion of these extraordinary prerogatives rests upon the following words of the Constitution:

The executive power shall be vested in a President of the United States of America.

It is not pretended that there is a word in the Constitution besides these, that confers upon anybody the power of removal from office, except in cases of impeachment. It behooves us then to inquire what is this "*executive power*" which is "*vested*" in the President of the United States of America.

Executive powers differ in different nations. A Russian czar has executive power quite unlike that of a British sovereign, and we have hitherto supposed that of the latter to be equally dissimilar to the authority of a republican President. How then shall we measure the executive functions in the United States? Simply by the Constitution. Does that instrument expressly confer a power? We must submit. Is it silent, and is it necessary to place the power somewhere for the well-ordering of the state? We must search the Constitution to find the authority which is clothed with the function of creating or designating the proper depositary.

The Constitution is silent upon the power of removal; but this is a power that may be needful for the well-ordering of the state; and turning to the last clause of the eighth section of the first article of the Constitution, we find the authority given to Congress "to make all laws which shall be necessary and proper for carrying into execution all powers vested by this Constitution in the *government of the United States, or in any department or officer thereof.*"

It would certainly seem too plain for argument that the "act regulating the tenure of certain civil offices" is within the very letter of this constitutional authority. The judgment of the Senate, three times definitely expressed, has been in conformity with these views, and to that judgment I adhere.

The inquiry whether Mr. Stanton is within the provisions of the law has been complicated by the ingenuity of counsel, but, upon a fair consideration of the act, presents little difficulty. The first section is as follows:

" * * *Every person* holding any civil office to which he has been appointed by and with the advice and consent of the Senate, and every person who shall hereafter be appointed to any such office, and shall become duly qualified to act therein, is, and shall be, entitled to hold such office until a successor shall have been in like manner appointed and duly qualified, except as herein otherwise provided: *Provided*, That the Secretaries of State, of the Treasury, of War, of the Navy, and of the Interior, the Postmaster General, and the Attorney General, shall hold their offices respectively for and during the term of the President by whom they may have been appointed, and for one month thereafter, subject to removal by and with the advice and consent of the Senate.

It is claimed that the debates in Congress, and especially in the Senate, upon the passage of the act, demand a construction which shall exclude Mr. Stanton from its provisions. I remark here that these debates should not be confounded with what is termed "contemporaneous construction." I shall have occasion to consider the latter in another place. The debates may properly be examined in order to ascertain the intent of the makers of the law. I was not in Congress at the passage of the act, and must consider it in its historic and legal aspect. The counsel who opened the case for the President very truly remarked, (page 375, Impeachment Trial:)

This law, as senators very well know, had a purpose; there was a practical object in the view of Congress; and however clear it might seem that the language of the law, when applied to Mr. Stanton's case, would exclude that case; however clear that might seem on the mere words of the law, if the purpose of the law could be discerned, and that purpose plainly required a different interpretation, that different interpretation should be given.

What, now, was the practical object of this law so far as it refers to cabinet officers? I think that no candid reader of the debates in the House of Representatives can doubt that that body intended to protect all the members of Mr. Johnson's cabinet against removal by the President alone. Rightly or wrongly, they felt that it would be safer for the country to have the departments in the hands of the existing cabinet officers until the Senate should consent to their removal. I think that it is also evident that the Senate was willing to leave with the President the power of removing all cabinet officers as theretofore practiced.

Here the two houses disagreed, and in the bill as reported by the conference committee there was a compromise. I think that the House supposed that it had attained its object by the bill as reported by the conference committee, by keeping in *all* the cabinet officers until one month after the close of the current presidential term, unless the Senate should sooner consent to their removal. I think that the Senate supposed that it had gained its point so far as the Secretaries appointed by Mr. Lincoln were concerned. I am thus brought to the necessity of construing a law passed by one House with a different intention from that which animated the other. I am, of course, left to determine the true intent and meaning of the law by the law itself, giving to its language its ordinary legal scope and signification.

Coming thus to the consideration of the first section of the act, (which alone is material to this inquiry,) it will be observed that it does not deal with the incidents of *offices*, but with the franchises of *persons*. It regulates *tenures*, not *terms*, of office. It is only the opposite view, which has no sanction in the statute, that can lead to a misconception of its scope.

The word *tenure* comes to us from the law of real estate.

The thing holden is styled a *tenement*, the possessors *tenants*, and the manner of their possession a *tenure*. (2 Bla. Com., 60.)

Webster defines the word as follows:

Tenure: the act or right of holding as property. Manner of holding in general.

It is a right or title pertaining to a *person*, and as such is treated throughout the statute. The body of the section comprehends "*every person holding civil office*," and is restricted only by a single exception, viz: the persons described in the proviso as holding their offices during the term of the President by whom they were appointed. The counsel for the President (page 1,099, Impeachment Trial) quotes the proviso:

Provided, That the Secretaries of State, of the Treasury, of War, of the Navy, and of the Interior, the Postmaster General, and the Attorney General, shall hold their offices respectively, &c.

And adds:

That does not mean the men; it means the offices shall have that tenure.

This certainly sounds like absurdity. The Secretary of State, or of War, is not an *office* but an *officer;* a person holding an office. An office has no tenure; the possessor of an office has that "manner of possession," that "act or right of holding," that "manner of holding" which is a *tenure*. The absurdity becomes apparent if we read the proviso according to the construction of the counsel for the President:

The offices of Secretary of State, of War, &c., shall hold their respective offices, &c.

It follows, therefore, as suggested by one of the managers, that it is immaterial whether we consider Mr. Stanton as holding his office during the term of the President by whom he was appointed or not; all agree that he was holding the office; if within the term of the President by whom he was appointed, he is embraced in the proviso; if not within such term, he was a "person holding civil office" and protected by the body of the section.

If, now, I turn to contemporaneous construction to ascertain the meaning of the law, I find such a construction given both by the executive and legislative departments of the government. Whatever the President or his cabinet may have thought before the final passage of the act of its effect upon Mr. Stanton, a period arrived within a few months after its passage when it became necessary for Mr. Johnson to give it a practical construction. He informs us that he proceeded with great and anxious deliberation, and the evidence before us demonstrates that he arrived at the conclusion that Mr. Stanton was within the act.

On the 12th of August, 1867, the President suspended the Secretary of War from office, in conformity with the provisions of the act. By the same authority he appointed General Grant Secretary *ad interim*. He notified the Secretary of the Treasury of his action, citing the act by name as the authority for such notification. He sent in his reasons to the Senate pursuant to the law, and, as he informs us, hoped for the concurrence of the Senate and the removal of the Secretary, in accordance with the law.

It is too late now to do away with the effect of this executive construction by the assertion that a power of suspension has been discovered in the Constitution which has never been exercised, and never thought of before since the foundation of the government.

Upon the presentation of the President's reasons for the removal of the Secretary, the Senate gave a legislative construction to the statute. It proceeded in exact conformity with the terms of the law; it considered the reasons; it debated them; it refused to concur in them, and sent notice thereof to the President. I am not aware that a single senator in that debate suggested that Mr. Stanton was suspended by virtue of the Constitution, or that he was not embraced in the protection of the tenure-of-office act.

Upon, then, a fair consideration of the debates accompanying the passage of the act, upon the proper construction of the language of the act itself, and upon the contemporaneous construction given to it by the executive and legislative branches of the government, I find Mr. Stanton to be embraced within the provisions of the first section.

I find, therefore, the act to be valid, and that it includes Mr. Stanton in its protection against the presidential power of removal without the consent of the Senate.

I find that the President has deliberately broken this law, and, by its express terms, has, in so doing, committed a high misdemeanor.

It is urged, however, that the offence is not complete because the criminal intent was absent. It is said that the law was broken to test its constitutionality. To this the obvious answer is, he who breaks a law for this purpose must take the risk of its being held to be constitutional by the proper tribunals. In this case, the Senate is the proper tribunal for the trial of the question, and it affirms the constitutionality of the law.

But I do not find, in fact, that it was the intention of the President to try the constitutional question. The means adopted were not adapted to that end. Upon the removal of Mr. Stanton the latter could have no remedy in the courts, and the President, though time and opportunity have been ample since the passage of the law, has never attempted to initiate legal proceedings himself.

The evidence in this case exhibits the real intent with perfect clearness. The declarations of the President at different periods during the last two years, as proved before us; his intermeddling with the southern legislatures in opposition to Congress, as shown by the Alabama telegram; his conversation with Wood, unfolding his purpose of distributing a patronage, whose emoluments exceed twenty-one millions of dollars a year, for the purpose of creating a party hostile to the measures of Congress—all these demonstrate a fixed and unconstitutional design to "defeat" and "prevent" the execution of the laws. Grant that he was honest in all this, and that he believed that the laws ought to have been defeated. So were Charles I and James II honest in their ideas of the royal prerogative; but those ideas brought the one to the block and cost the other his crown. In this country the legislature is the organ of the people, and the laws are the people's will. For the Executive to set his own will in opposition to the will of the people, expressed through Congress, and employ the powers vested in him for other purposes to that end, is repugnant to the whole spirit of the Constitution.

Yet the evidence leaves no doubt that such has been the persistent course of the President for more than two years. In this course Mr. Stanton had become a formidable obstacle to the designs of Mr. Johnson. The message of the latter of December 12, 1867, communicating the reasons for the suspension of the Secretary, and the answer to the first article of impeachment, disclose the irreconcilable nature of their differences, and, as is evident from the President's letter to General Grant, these differences culminated soon after the passage of the supplementary reconstruction bill of March 23, 1867. From the time of the passage of that bill the possession of the Department of War would confer vast influence either in favor of or against the whole system of reconstruction adopted by Congress, according to the views of the possessor. Mr. Stanton was known to favor that system, as the President himself declares in the letter to General Grant.

And herein I find the intent of the President in this removal of the Secretary; an intent to defeat the will of the people already crystallized into law, and substitute his own will instead; an intent unlawful, unconstitutional, and revolutionary, and which, breaking out into overt act, in the removal of Mr. Stanton, gives to that act a deeper tinge of guilt than attaches to any mere violation of a penal statute.

Complaint has been made because upon this question of intent the Senate refused to hear the testimony of cabinet officers as to the advice given by them to the President. I cannot conceive of any proposition more dangerous to the stability of our institutions than that the President may shield himself from impeachment for high crimes and misdemeanors behind the advice of his Secretaries. Apart from the common-law objection of irrelevancy, such evidence should be excluded upon the gravest considerations of public policy.

Upon this review of the law and the testimony, I find that the President is guilty of a high misdemeanor as charged in the first article of impeachment.

It is a necessary result of this opinion that I also find him guilty of high misdemeanors as charged in the second, third, eighth, and eleventh articles of impeachment. I do not think it needful to elaborate the legal and logical connection, as it will be obvious to any careful reader of the articles themselves, keeping in mind that the construction suggested by the Chief Justice is applied to the eleventh article, as before stated.

OPINION OF MR. SENATOR MORRILL, *of Maine.*

The President is impeached by the House of Representatives of high crimes and misdemeanors, in that on 21st of February last he issued an order for the removal from office of Edwin M. Stanton, Secretary of War, with intent to violate the tenure-of-office act, and to remove said Stanton from office.

In that on said 21st February he issued to General Thomas a letter authorizing and empowering him to act as Secretary of War, there being no vacancy in that office, with intent to violate the tenure-of-office act.

In that on the said 21st of February he did appoint said Thomas to be Secretary for the Department of War *ad interim*, without the advice and consent of the Senate, no vacancy having happened in said office, with intent to violate the Constitution of the United States.

In that he conspired with said Thomas to hinder and prevent said Stanton from filling said office; to prevent and hinder the execution of the tenure-of-office act; to get possession of the War Office, and of the property of the United States in the Department of War.

In that, with intent to violate the tenure-of-office act, he authorized said Thomas to act as Secretary of War, there being no vacancy in said office, and the Senate then being in session.

In that he attempted unlawfully to induce General Emory to obey his orders, and not those issued by the General of the army, with intent to enable him to defeat the tenure-of-office act, with intent to prevent said Stanton from holding his office.

In that, to bring Congress into contempt, and excite the odium of the people against Congress and the laws by it enacted, he made certain public addresses, indecent and unbecoming in the Chief Magistrate, by the means whereof he brought the office into contempt, ridicule, and disgrace.

In that he attempted to prevent said Stanton from resuming the office of Secretary of War, after the refusal of the Senate to concur in his suspension; also to prevent the execution of the act of 2d March, 1867, making appropriations for the support of the army, and an act to provide for the more efficient government of the rebel States.

The President, answering, does not controvert the essential facts charged, but insists that the acts complained of are authorized by the Constitution and laws; and further, that if in any respect this plea fails of a complete justification, he should still be acquitted, as those acts were all done in good faith in the performance of public duties arising in the execution of his office, imposed upon him by the Constitution and laws and in defence and execution of them. Concurring in much of the reasoning of the senators who are of opinion that the answer and defence of the President as to several of the charges fails of such justification, I shall content myself with a statement of the grounds of my opinion upon a portion of the articles only.

The three first articles and the eleventh relate to the attempt to remove Mr. Stanton from the office of Secretary of War; the authority to General Thomas to take possession and to do the duties of the office; the appointment of General Thomas as Secretary of War *ad interim*; and the attempt to prevent Mr. Stanton from resuming the duties of his official office after his suspension had been non-concurred in by the Senate.

The question arising under these articles turns chiefly upon the question whether the tenure-of-office act is in conflict with the Constitution of the United States, and the case of Mr. Stanton was affected by it.

These are understood to be the grounds upon which the counsel for the President place the defence to these articles, and that upon which opinion divides in the Senate.

Is the tenure-of-office act unconstitutional, and is Mr. Stanton embraced in its provisions so as to be protected by it?

As to the first proposition as between the Senate and the President, it is not a new question, and it is difficult to perceive how it can properly be regarded by either as an open question. The act had been fully considered when it was first enacted in the Senate, was reconsidered after it had been returned by the President with his objections fully stated, and again passed with that unanimity necessary to give it the force of law, his objections to the contrary notwithstanding, and calculated to leave little doubt as to the confidence with which the Senate held its opinions.

The legislative and executive precedents and practice in our history touching the power of the President to remove from office, relied upon by him as authoritative interpretation of the Constitution, were known and familiar to Congress at the time. It is not suggested that the act was hastily or inconsiderately passed, as it will not be doubted that Congress had, in the recent examples of the exercise of this power by the Executive, abundant opportunity of judging of the expediency of a further continuance of this practice.

The binding force of this practice of removal by the President rests upon the interpretation given to the Constitution by the first Congress. It is not insisted that this interpretation by that Congress was authoritative and conclusive upon succeeding Congresses, and it is admitted that the extent of its authority is as a precedent only. The question was therefore open to further legislative regulation, and the practice which had obtained under the act of 1789 could properly and should necessarily be modified or reversed, as experience should dictate that the public interests demanded. The Congress of 1867, it will not be denied, had all the power over the subject that the Congress of 1789 is supposed to have had.

Besides it is well known that the Congress of 1789 were far from having been unanimous in their opinions and action. One branch was equally divided upon the measure, and it finally passed by the casting vote of the presiding officer; and that from that time to the date of the act in question the interpretation of the first Congress had been repeatedly the subject of grave debate in Congress, and was believed by the most eminent of our statesmen, jurists, and commentators upon the Constitution, to be unsound.

Indeed, the President is not understood to invoke the Senate now to declare void for conflict with the Constitution a law which had so recently received its sanction, and that after his objections to it had been fully considered, but that the argument presented is rather in extenuation of his refusal to obey and enforce it. For the purpose of these proceedings, the act in question may properly and must necessarily be regarded as valid, unless, indeed, it should be deemed advisable that Congress should repeal all laws the validity of which may be questioned by the President, which he may deem inexpedient, or to which he does not yield a willing obedience.

We are then brought to consider the question whether the case of Mr. Stanton was affected by the tenure-of-office act. The first section of that act is as follows:

That every person holding any official office to which he has been appointed by and with the advice and consent of the Senate, and every person who shall hereafter be appointed to any such office, and shall become duly qualified to act therein, is and shall be entitled to hold such office until a successor shall have been in a like manner appointed and duly qualified, except as herein otherwise provided: *Provided,* That the Secretaries of State, of the Treasury, of War, of the Navy, and of the Interior, the Postmaster General, and the Attorney General, shall hold their offices respectively for and during the term of the President by whom they may have been appointed, and for one month thereafter, subject to removal by and with the advice and consent of the Senate.

The counsel for the President contend that "out of this body of the section it is explicitly declared that there is to be excepted a particular class of officers, 'except as herein otherwise provided.'" The senator from Iowa, Mr. Grimes, in his published opinion, says: "Mr. Stanton's case is not within the body of the first section. The tenure which that provides for is not the tenure of any Secretary." Other senators, who agree with Mr. Grimes in the conclusion to which he comes, adopt the views of the counsel for the President. These views are the opposites in statement and principle, and cannot be reconciled with each other.

The construction of Judge Curtis is that the body of the section—the words "every person holding any civil office, appointed with the advice and consent of the Senate"—*necessarily includes* Mr. Stanton's case, as he was a civil officer who had been appointed with advice and consent of the Senate; and to get rid of Mr. Stanton's case he is forced to the construction that the words, "except as herein otherwise provided," "except him out of the body of the section;" while the senator from Iowa accomplishes the same result, more directly, but not less erroneously, by denying altogether that his case is included in the body of the section. It admits of no argument that this last opinion is unsound, and that conclusions drawn from such premises are untenable. The words, "every person holding any civil office," &c., by the force of the unavoidable meaning of language, it must be conceded, embrace the case of Mr. Stanton, then holding the office of Secretary of War.

But leaving this discrepancy of deduction I turn to the construction of the act of Judge Curtis, which seems to be the generally received interpretation of those who hold that Mr. Stanton's case is not provided for in the act.

He concedes that the words "every person holding any civil office," &c., include Mr. Stanton, but insists that the words "except as herein otherwise provided," taken in connection with the proviso that follows, operate to *exclude* him from this general description of persons.

The words "except as herein otherwise provided," it is plain, either standing alone or taken in connection with the proviso are not entitled to the force of terms of absolute exclusion, but rather are used in the sense of qualifying some antecedent provision in the body of the section. Now what are these antecedent words or provision to which these qualifying words relate, and which they are supposed to modify? Do they qualify the provision "every person holding any civil office," &c., "except as herein otherwise provided," or the words "is and shall be entitled to hold his said office until his successor shall in like manner be appointed and qualified?" "except as herein otherwise provided."

Do the qualifying words operate to *exclude* a portion of the *persons* from holding office under this act altogether, or do they operate to qualify the *condition of holding?* The former construction, it is submitted, does violence to the intent of the act; besides, it is an obvious misapplication of the qualifying words to a portion of the section to which they do not relate. It is clear that it was the intent of the act to regulate a tenure of office, of some sort, of all the persons described in the body of the section, that is, "every person holding any civil office," &c.; but by this construction a portion of those persons fail to be provided for altogether; while the adoption of the other view provides for them a tenure of office, but different in its conditions, and is thus in harmony with the objects of the law.

If it be accepted that the Secretaries are not excepted out of the body of the section, and that the effect of the proviso is simply to provide and determine what their tenure of office shall be, the only remaining question is whether the provision does make such tenure for Mr. Stanton. It is contended that it does not, as he was not the appointee of Mr. Johnson, and that the term of Mr. Lincoln, whose appointee he was, was determined by death. It is conceded that Mr. Stanton was appointed by Mr. Lincoln in his first term of office, by and with the advice and consent of the Senate, to hold during the pleasure of the President for the time being; that he was duly holding office under that appointment in the second term of Mr. Lincoln and up to his death. He was, therefore, the appointee of Mr. Lincoln, by original appointment in his first term, and not less so in his second term, in effect, by adoption and continuance in office under the first appointment, the person and the office being identical, and there being no limitation in the tenure of the office, except the pleasure of the President for the time being. Mr. Stanton was, therefore, properly holding office by appointment of Mr. Lincoln in his second term at his death. He continued to hold under such appointment and commission from Mr. Lincoln after the succession of Mr. Johnson, and, by his adoption and continuance in office, and was so holding at the passage of the tenure-of-office act.

But it is said that if he is to be regarded as the appointee of Mr. Lincoln in his second term, he is still not embraced in the terms of this act, as that term closed with the death of Mr. Lincoln, and that since that event he has been holding in the term of Mr. Johnson. It therefore becomes necessary to determine what was the "term" of President Lincoln. Was it an absolute period of four years, or was it that period during which he served in his office; the period for which he was elected, or the period he held and occupied his office? Was the *term* of his office subject, in the language of the counsel for the President, to a "conditional limitation?" The *term* of the presidential office, by the Constitution, is four years, and that without regard to the contingency of holding or period of actual service. It describes the period for which the office lasts, and is without limitation. The *tenure* of his office is subject to the contingencies of death, resignation, or removal; but that relates to the *condition* of actual holding or period of service, and in no way affects the *term* or period for which he was elected. Now, the language of the proviso is, "shall hold for the *term* of the President by whom appointed." Mr. Stanton was appointed by Mr. Lincoln, whose *term* of office was absolutely *four years*, under the Constitution. The statute adopts the same word *term*, and this makes the period of holding identical with the period of the presidential office, and does not subject it to the contingencies of the *tenure* of his office or the period of his service.

I pass the question whether Mr. Johnson is or not serving out his own or the term of Mr. Lincoln as unimportant in the view taken of the question. Their terms of office, as a period of time, were identical, and whether he is serving out Mr. Lincoln's term of office, as Vice-President, upon whom devolve the duties of the office of President, by death, can have no influence upon the general fact of what was Mr. Stanton's term of office. In either case his term would be the same.

But if, as is contended by counsel for the President and those who adopt his views, the proviso failed to provide a tenure for Mr. Stanton, he being conceded to be in the body of the section, then as to him the words, "except as herein otherwise provided," fail to have any effect, and leave his tenure unaffected, and the same as that provided in the body of the section for the description of persons mentioned. I conclude, therefore, that the act did not fail of its object, namely, to *regulate* the tenure of office of "every person holding any civil office to which he has been appointed by and with the advice and consent of the Senate;" that Mr. Stanton's case was not excepted out of its provisions; that the proviso does regulate for him a tenure of office; but if it do not, then it is clear that it is regulated as is provided in the body of the section for "every person holding any civil office," &c., and that his removal was a clear violation of this act.

But it is said that it is at least doubtful if the act did affect Mr. Stanton's case, and that the effort to remove him from his office on the 21st February last was an attempt on the part of the President which he might well believe he had a right to make; that the attempt did not succeed, and that it would be an abuse of power to remove him from his high office on grounds so slight.

But did the President truly believe that he had the right, that it was clear, and that the public welfare justified and demanded its exercise? He had refused his assent to the tenure-of-office act, stating in his message, among his reasons expressed for refusal so to do, that its provisions deprived him of control over his cabinet.

He had suspended Mr. Stanton under its provisions—so stated to the Secretary of the Treasury, as required by its provisions. He had communicated his reasons for this suspension, agreeably to the terms of the act, to the Senate. He had been advised of the action of the Senate upon that suspension, and of the acquiescence of General Grant in its determination of the case, and had witnessed the return of Mr. Stanton to his office and its duties in accordance with the imperative provisions of this act. With these acts and this knowledge upon the record, it is difficult to believe that the President was acting in that measure of good faith and in the presence and under the pressure of a public necessity which would justify the defiance of a law of even doubtful import;

that in this attempt to put aside a high officer of the government without charge of misconduct in office, and after his purpose had been overruled by the Senate, it is submitted there is apparent less of desire to consult the public interests and faithfully to execute the laws, than to execute his own purposes upon a public officer who had incurred his personal displeasure. Nor is it easy to adopt the opinion that the charges and proof in support of these may properly be regarded as slight or unimportant.

The President may not arbitrarily and without cause depose a high public officer with impunity independent of the act under consideration. Wantonly to do it would constitute the essence of arbitrary and unbridled power, and tend to establish that irresponsible license over the laws fatal to republican government, the first appearance of which demand to be rebuked and resisted. The officers and the office belong and are amenable to the law; they are its servants and not the "satraps" of the President. The right of removal is not an arbitrary right in any respect; and subject to removal himself, the President could have no right to complain of the enforcement of a rule against him which he could apply to those in his power. *The public interest*, and that alone, must justify the action.

The President declares in his answer that so early as August last he had determined to cause Mr. Stanton "to surrender his office of Secretary of the Department of War." To that end on the 12th of the same month he suspended him from his office, on pretence of misconduct in office, as now in his answer claimed, under the exercise of a power before unheard of, and certainly never before practiced or asserted by any of his predecessors, namely, the power to *suspend* from office indefinitely, and at his pleasure, not until meeting of the Senate, "*as incident to the right of removal*;" and having so suspended, kept that officer out of his office and out of the public service for many months, and long after Congress and the Senate had convened, and for reasons stated in his message to the Senate, wholly inadequate, unsatisfactory, and unjustifiable in the judgment of that body, and which, if not trifling, were characterized by personal rather than public considerations.

It will be observed that he at once invokes the aid of the tenure-of-office act to enable him to suspend from office a public officer who had incurred his personal displeasure, and afterwards, when that had failed, attempts to remove him in defiance of its authority and in contempt of its validity. He at once *invokes* and *violates* the act of 1795. He professes to have appointed General Grant Secretary of War *ad interim* under it, and then violated it by retaining him in office contrary to its provisions.

He invokes the judgment of the Senate on the suspension of Mr. Stanton, and after that judgment has been pronounced against him, and under it the officer had returned to his duties in obedience to the act under which he had been suspended, he defies its authority by his removal, appoints General Thomas Secretary of War *ad interim*, holds him out to the country as the rightful Secretary of War, treats him as a constituent member of his cabinet, ignores Mr. Stanton altogether, and thus subjects the conduct of the office of the Department of War to the dangers, embarrassments, and perils which may come of these conflicting pretensions, and must come if these pretensions are made good by his acquittal. If to these be added the spirit of defiance manifest in his message to the Senate of February 22 last, and his determination, at any and all hazards to the public interests, to cause a personally obnoxious public officer "to surrender his office," I am persuaded that the peril to our republican structure of government will have become imminent when such conduct in the President shall come to be regarded and tolerated as slight and trifling, and shall not, on the contrary, be held as high misdemeanors in office. Mr. Madison, in commenting upon this subject, says, "I contend that the *wanton* removal of meritorious officers would subject him (the President) to impeachment and removal from his own high office."

A different question is presented on the second and third articles. On the

21st February, assuming to have removed Mr. Stanton. the President, in writing, authorized General Thomas to act as Secretary of War, and appointed him Secretary of War *ad interim*, there being no vacancy in that office, or pretence of vacancy, except the letter to Mr. Stanton of the same date, the Senate then being in session and not being advised upon the subject.

The President, in his answer, insists that at the date of the letter and its delivery to General Thomas there was a vacancy in the office of Secretary of War caused by removal; that, notwithstanding the Senate was in session, it was lawful and in accordance with long-established usage to empower said Thomas to act as Secretary of War *ad interim*; and that if the tenure-of-office act be valid, in doing so he violated none of its provisions.

Whether there was or not a vacancy in that office will depend upon the effect given to the letter of removal addressed to Mr. Stanton, which was not acquiesced in, and under which no removal *de facto* was effected; and whether the attempted removal, or order of removal, was justified by any usage arising under any provision of law. It is not pretended that any act of Congress expressly confers this power while the Senate is in session, much less that the power is drawn from any express provision of the Constitution. No parallel in the history of the government is shown or is believed to exist. The only case at all approaching it is that of Timothy Pickering, where the removal and the nomination to the Senate of his successor were simultaneous, and were essentially one and the same act, and was in and of itself the mode adopted by the President of obtaining the advice and consent of the Senate to the removal. But in this case was an attempted removal without reference to the Senate and independent of it, and the appointment of a Secretary *ad interim*, and no nomination to the Senate of a successor. Neither by the implication of the Constitution, laws, nor usage was the removal of Mr. Stanton and the designation of General Thomas as Secretary of War *ad interim* authorized.

But it is insisted that the removal of Mr. Stanton having created a vacancy the President was authorized to fill it temporarily by the designation of General Thomas, under the act of 1795, and that that act was not repealed by the act of 1863. This latter act repeals all acts and parts of acts inconsistent with its provisions; and it is said that its provisions are not inconsistent in some one or more particulars with the former act upon the same subject, and to that extent at least is not repealed. This construction is quite too narrow. The question is not whether the repealing act in any particular negatives the former act, but whether in its object and scope it was a substantial revision of the law upon the particular subject. If so, then, by well-established rules of legal interpretation, it does operate to repeal the former laws upon that subject.

Now it is apparent from an examination of those statutes that the act of 1863 was such statute of revision. The act of 1792, upon the same subject, made provision for the case of vacancy by death, and certain temporary disabilities in the State, War, and Treasury Departments. That of 1795 provided that "in case of vacancy," &c.; and both alike in the cases contemplated, provided that the President might "authorize any person or persons, at his discretion, to perform the duties," &c. The act of 1863 provides that in case of resignation, death, absence from the seat of government, or sickness in the heads of any of the existing departments, the President *may authorize any head of any other department*, &c., to perform the duties, &c.

The act of 1863 is a revision of the law on the subject, as it embraces the objects of both prior statutes; provides for vacancy by resignation, not provided for specifically, and changes the rule of both prior statutes as to the persons to be authorized to perform the duties temporarily, and makes provision for the other departments, and adapts the existing laws to the present changed state of affairs. Can it be doubted that the act of 1863 was intended to be a revision of the whole law upon the subject; that it did provide and was intended to provide one uniform rule for all the departments; and not that in case of vacancy by death, resignation, &c., authorize the appointment of heads of departments, &c., and in case of vacancy by removal to authorize "any person or persons?" That the act of 1863 was intended to have this effect is clear, from the statement of the chairman of the Committee on the Judiciary who reported the act, Hon. Mr. Trumbull, that it was his understanding that it did repeal all former acts upon that subject.

But this precise question of the removal of Stanton and appointment of General Thomas was fully adjudicated by the Senate, and concluded by its action on the 21st February last. This is its record:

Whereas the Senate have received and considered the communication of the President, stating that he had removed Edwin M. Stanton, Secretary of War, and had designated Lorenzo Thomas to act as Secretary of War *ad interim*: Therefore

Resolved by the Senate of the United States, That under the Constitution and laws of the United States the President has no power to remove the Secretary of War and designate any other officer to perform the duties of that office ad interim.

Was that adjudication of an act done and submitted to the Senate for its consideration erroneous? The resolution finally passed the Senate without division.

To those who would weaken the force of this record, or find excuse for the President in the unimportance of the transaction, it may be replied that if the Senate would retain its self-respect, or command the respect of others, it must stand by its decrees until reversed for error, and not for the reason that the President defies them, or refuses to yield obedience to them. The President tells the Senate, in his communication upon the subject, that as early as August last he had "determined to cause Mr. Stanton to surrender the office of Secretary for the Department of War." That issue is now for the third time distinctly before the Senate, twice by the action of the President, and now by the action of the representatives of the people. A surrender of the record of the Senate is a surrender of a public officer to the predetermined purpose and personal will of the President. It is needless to say such a result would be the deposition of a high public officer without cause, a triumphant defiance of the law of the land and of the supreme legislative authority of the country.

Whoever contemplates such a result with indifference may prepare for the advent of executive usurpation totally subversive of our system of government.

It only remains to consider the proposition of the counsel for President that he should not be held guilty on an assumed innocent mistake in interpreting the law. In judging of the intent with which the President acted, the public record of the officer, his acts, speeches, and policy, the current events of history connected therewith, may properly be considered. The quality of the particular act may be reflected from the body of official reputation and public conduct, good or bad.

In determining the character of the acts complained of, touching the intent of the President, we may consider whether they relate to his antecedent official conduct, whether they were purely public and official or private and personal, whether they arose out of some real or supposed pressing public exigency, or whether, as in the case of Mr. Stanton, the real or assumed misconduct of a public officer, or from a settled determination to get rid of one who had become disagreeable to him, at all hazards, and because it was his pleasure no longer to tolerate him in his office. In this light consider some of the facts connected with the removal of Mr. Stanton and the designation of General Thomas as Secretary of War *ad interim*. In his note of 5th August last, requesting the resignation of Mr. Stanton, the President says he is constrained to do so from "public considerations of a high character." The precise nature of these *considerations* it is left to conjecture.

In his message of December 12, 1867, assigning the reason for the suspension of Mr. Stanton, he says he deemed the reply to his note above referred to as a defiance and expression of a loss of confidence in his superior, and "that it must necessarily end our most important relations."

Also, that Mr. Stanton held opinions upon the suffrage bill for the District of Columbia and the reconstruction acts of March 2 and 23, 1867, which could not be reconciled with his own or the rest of the cabinet, and that there was but one result that could solve the difficulty, and "that was the severance of official relations."

As these reasons antedate those assigned for the immediate suspension of Mr. Stanton, and are the only causes of recent occurrence, it is fair to presume that the note which is declared to have led to the suspension was induced by a pre-determination to sever the relations, rendered necessary, in his opinion, by that want of "unity of opinion" existing in the cabinet on account of the conflicting opinion of Mr. Stanton.

In his answer to article one the President says that on or prior to August 5, 1867, "he had become satisfied that he could not allow Mr. Stanton to continue to hold the office of Secretary for the Department of War without hazard to the public interests." "That the *relations* between them no longer permitted the President to resort to him for advice or be responsible for his conduct of the affairs of the Department of War," and that therefore he determined that he ought not longer to hold said office, and considered what he might lawfully do to cause him to surrender said office.

Those are understood to be the reasons for the suspension, as also for the removal, or attempted removal, of the Secretary of War.

They are, substantially, that the "relations between them" had become such in August, 1867, as not to "permit the President to resort to him for advice, or be responsible for his conduct of the Department of War as by law required;" and these "relations" are the "differences of opinion" upon the "suffrage bill," and the reconstruction acts of the 2d and 23d March, 1867, "upon which Mr. Stanton stood alone in the cabinet, and the difference of opinion could not be reconciled."

Those are the "public considerations of a high character," stated in the note of August 5, which was a request for the resignation of the Secretary, and which led to his suspension and subsequent removal, to prevent his resuming the duties of his office after the action of the Senate.

When before in the history of the government did a President hold that "differences of opinion" of a cabinet officer as to the policy of a law of Congress, or of its constitutionality, or of the propriety of its enforcement, were "public considerations of a high character," which not only "constrained" him to request his resignation of office, but impelled him to a determination to "cause him to surrender the office"—to suspend him—and, defeated in that by the adverse action of the Senate, to *remove* him, to "prevent him from resuming the duties of the office." It is certain that differences of opinion "in the cabinet" are not unknown in our history, as to the expediency, the policy, and the interpretation of laws; that they were marked in the cabinet of Washington, and that they were not supposed and were not held to be "public considerations of a character" demanding removal from office.

The present case is especially noticeable, from the fact of public notoriety, as well as declared in the President's answer and message, that the "difference of opinion" complained of was that the opinions of the Secretary of War were in harmony with those of Congress upon the acts mentioned, while those of the President were opposed, as had been expressed in his veto message, and that "difficulties" from such "differences of opinion," and which could only be solved by suspension and removal from office were such as are publicly known to have arisen on the question of the *execution* of the reconstruction acts of March 2 and 23.

It is observable that no public exigency is stated by the President to have arisen demanding action in Mr. Stanton's case; no malversation or misconduct in office; no disobedience of, or refusal or neglect to obey orders of the President, is alleged or suggested. Besides, the Senate had been recently in session, since the "relations and difference of opinion had developed," in two different periods, affording ample opportunity for the appointment of his successor, if the public interests demanded a change of that officer and were of a character to commend themselves to that body.

Some stress has been laid upon the want of "confidence" in the Secretary, which would not permit a resort to him for advice, and rendered it unsafe that the President should be responsible for his official conduct.

It is difficult to appreciate the importance which seems to be attached to this statement. The Secretary of War is certainly not the constitutional adviser of the President in his general administration, nor is the President entitled to his opinion, except in the case contemplated in the Constitution, and that upon affairs arising in his own department, and in relation thereto.

Nor is it obvious what is intended by the statement in the answer by being responsible for his conduct of the affairs of the Department of War.

What is the nature of this supposed responsibility, and how imposed? We are not informed in the answer. No such responsibility is understood to be imposed by the Constitution, and none is believed to exist in the laws creating the Department of War and defining the duties of the Secretary of War.

By no provision of the Constitution or laws is it believed that the President is chargeable with the consequences of the misconduct or neglect of duty of that officer with which he himself is not connected.

The Secretary and he alone must answer to the violated law for his misconduct and neglect of duty, and the assumption that the President is responsible for them is to assume that the War Department is under the direction and at the discretion of the President, and not under the statute creating it, and by which it is conducted.

It is difficult to believe that in the suspension of and subsequent removal of Mr. Stanton the President was actuated solely by "public considerations," and especially does he fail to make it clear that he was acting on the pressure of a state necessity or public exigency which justified him in first experimenting with a law of Congress by suspending a public officer under it, and failing of his declared purpose in that, namely, "*to cause him to surrender his*" office, then to defy its authority by disregarding it altogether, and remove the officer so suspended confessedly to prevent his resuming the duties of the office, after the adverse action of the Senate upon the case, submitted to it for its consideration.

The doubts which are invoked to shield the President fail to protect him, as he fails to show any case or public necessity for the exercise of doubtful power under the Constitution and laws, while his official conduct plainly shows a spirit of hostility to the whole series of acts of Congress designed for the reconstruction of the late insurrectionary States and the pacification of the country, and an intent to obstruct rather than faithfully to execute these laws.

If, therefore, doubts arise on the record, they belong to the country and to the violated laws, and presumption of innocence cannot obtain where the sinister purpose is apparent. It is impossible to withhold a conviction of the President's guilt under the articles presented by the House of Representatives for usurpations of power not delegated by the Constitution, and for violation and obstruction of the laws of the land, and so guilty of high crimes and misdemeanors in his office, which, as a remedy for the present disorders which afflict the nation consequent upon them, and for the future security against the abuse of executive authority, demand, in harmony with the provisions of the Constitution, his removal from office.

OPINION OF MR. SENATOR MORRILL, *of Vermont.*

An explanation of a vote in the Senate may be desirable and sometimes useful, but no explanation can ever rise in value above that of the record of the vote itself; and there is no vote which can be taken under any circumstances from which the consciences of senators can be separated from an oath. In an impeachment trial the obligation is more impressive by being made special instead of general. The duty is changed, and a corresponding change is made in the form of the oath. That change freshly requires of us impartiality according to law and the facts. Our votes upon the articles of impeachment will stand for all coming time as the embodiment of our view of the merits of the whole case. It is that upon which I hope to justify a clear conscience, and not upon making a better argument than has yet been made upon one side or the other.

I shall not attempt an exhaustive examination of any one of the articles of impeachment, but shall give my opinions upon some of the topics raised by the questions at issue, and the results of those opinions when applied to the several articles.

The guilt or innocence of President Johnson, as charged in the eleven articles presented by the House of Representatives, largely rests upon facts standing upon the record. In their nature the proofs are irrefragable, and we must take them as we find them. The written Constitution, the written law, the written order to Secretary Stanton to surrender his office, and the written authority to Lorenzo Thomas to take possession of the office of Secretary of War, with its papers and effects, are all before us, and the issue on trial depends chiefly, as it appears to me, upon a correct interpretation which we may be expected to give to these documents. In addition to this there is much documentary evidence and the testimony of living witnesses, and especially that of General Lorenzo Thomas, who testifies that he has acted as Secretary of War so far as to meet with the President at meetings of his cabinet, and was there recognized as Secretary of War. Such is the support upon which the main burden of the larger portion of the articles of impeachment rests.

The first article charges in substance that, on the 21st day of February, 1868, Andrew Johnson, President of the United States, in violation of the Constitution and laws of the United States, did unlawfully issue an order in writing for the removal of Edwin M. Stanton from the office of Secretary for the Department of War, without the advice and consent of the Senate, then and there being in session, and against the provisions of "An act regulating the tenure of certain civil offices," passed March 2, 1867.

The second article charges that, in violation of the Constitution and the law, as mentioned in the first article, on the same day the President issued and delivered a letter of authority to Lorenzo Thomas, empowering him to act as Secretary of War *ad interim*, and to immediately enter upon the discharge of the duties of that office, there being no vacancy therein.

The 3d article varies from the 2d article by charging the same acts to have been done in violation of the Constitution and without authority of law.

To ascertain whether the Constitution has been violated it is necessary, after finding that the principal facts as alleged have been proved or admitted, to carefully examine what are its provisions, and we find that the President shall have power to "nominate, and, by and with the advice and consent of the Senate, shall appoint ambassadors, other public ministers and consuls, judges of the Supreme Court, and all other officers of the United States whose appointments are not herein otherwise provided for, and which shall be established by law; but Congress may by law vest the appointment of such inferior officers as they think proper, in the President alone, in the courts of law, or in the heads of departments. The President shall have power to fill all vacancies that may happen during the recess of the Senate by granting commissions which shall expire at the end of their next session."

The power of removal being nowhere expressly given to the President, it is only an implied power, resulting from the power to appoint, and the power to appoint is confided to the President by and with the advice and consent of the Senate, including the latter as substantially as the former, except in the case of inferior officers, which Congress may think proper by law to vest in the President alone, in the courts, or heads of departments.

As an implied power, derived from that of appointment, it must attach to those having the power to appoint. It cannot be claimed that the office of Secretary of War is an inferior office, nor that any existing law vests authority in the President alone to appoint a Secretary of War during the session of the Senate, nor yet that the power to nominate carries with it the power to confer upon any such nominees the right to take and hold office with all the emoluments without an appointment by and with the advice and consent of the Senate.

It is true the President may temporarily fill vacancies which happen during the recess of the Senate; but it is going too far to assume that he may first do an act not allowed by the Constitution in order to open the door so that he may do another thing which is allowed; that he may empty under the power only to fill; or that he may make a vacancy to happen with a view to an exercise of the power to fill a vacancy: Things *happen* by chance—as by death, resignation, absence—not by previous contrivance. An insurance policy is valid when the ship happens to get foundered, not when it is designedly scuttled and sunk by the owner. The power to create vacancies at will, to fill them with A, and then to come to the Senate for advice and consent to fill them either with A or with B, is an absurdity. The faithful daughter asks parental advice and consent before she gets married, not after. The power claimed by President Johnson to create vacancies at will would blot out one of the most important functions of the Senate, designed to be one of the highest safeguards of the Constitution against executive indiscretions and usurpations, as even appointments consented to during the session of the Senate, if the claim of unlimited power of removal by the President were to be tolerated, might be set aside the moment after the adjournment of the Senate for other and different appointments never advised, and never consented to by the Senate. All stability would be lost, and all officers of the government would hold their places at the mere will and caprice of the President. It would enthrone the one-man power against all else. Such a power in a free government would be neither prudent nor safe, though placed in the most scrupulous hands; and if, by chance, in other hands, it would be dangerous.

Yet President Johnson, in face of the plain provision of the Constitution, not only deliberately makes a removal of the Secretary of War, but officially authorizes another man, an obedient subordinate, to discharge the duties of the office. It matters little by what name the President designated him, or for how long a time, or whether as Secretary *ad interim*, for one day or indefinitely, he intended that Lorenzo Thomas should be for the time the actual Secretary of War, so to be recognized by himself, and so to be recognized by all the executive departments of the government, and to immediately enter upon the discharge of the duties of the office, although there is no more lawful power to *authorize* than to *appoint* to office, or to issue a letter of authority, than to make an actual appointment, and no more power to appoint an *ad interim* Secretary than a Secretary *in full*. Nothing but the illegality of the act of the President now keeps Thomas *out* and Stanton *in* office as Secretary of War. If the Senate decide to-day that the President has not transcended his lawful authority in the removal of Mr. Stanton, by force of that decision Adjutant General Thomas may take possession of the office to-morrow. If that be so, then Senators who by their votes reinstated Mr. Stanton in his office inflicted a great wrong upon him, and have given to Congress and the country a very unnecessary excitement. It seems to me that there was no constitutional authority for the removal of Stanton by the President, and still less for the appointment of Thomas as Secretary *ad interim.*

The next thing I propose to consider is the act regulating the tenure of certain civil offices, passed March 2, 1867, as follows, viz:

That every person holding any civil office to which he has been appointed by and with the advice and consent of the Senate, and every person who shall hereafter be appointed to any such office, and shall become duly qualified to act therein, is and shall be entitled to hold such office until a successor shall have been in like manner appointed and duly qualified, except as herein otherwise provided: *Provided,* That the Secretary of State, of the Treasury, of War, of the Navy, and of the Interior, the Postmaster General, and the Attorney General, shall hold their offices respectively for and during the term of the President by whom they may have been appointed, and one month thereafter, subject to removal by and with the advice and consent of the Senate.

As its title declares, this act regulates the tenure of certain civil offices—authorizing all persons in office, whether for fixed or indefinite terms, to hold the same until their successors "shall have been appointed by and with the advice and consent of the Senate," (as contemplated by the Constitution,) except that the heads of the executive departments are to "hold their offices respectively for and during the *term of the President by whom they may have been appointed,* and one month thereafter, subject to removal by and with the advice and consent of the Senate."

This is not an unusual exercise of legislative power. The subject is one that has been legislated upon by Congress both early and late, and whatever laws may be on the statute book of a prior date in conflict with the latest act, must be held to be superseded, and need not be considered so far as this case is concerned. I understand this to be the legal view, and it is certainly a common-sense view of the rules of construction. The law of March 2, 1867, holds the President and Senate simply to the requirements of the Constitution, and fixes the term of office. The question whether it includes members of the cabinet appointed by President Lincoln is the only one deserving consideration. Intended as a permanent statute, it was provided that the term of the heads of the executive departments should expire one month after the term of the President by whom they were appointed had expired. The term of the President under the Constitution is four years—no more and no less—fixed by law to commence on the 4th of March next after the presidential election; and, though the President may die, or become insane, and his place be filled by another, the term will expire at precisely the same time it would had he lived or remained sane. When the Vice-President becomes President by accident by death, or otherwise, he serves out the remainder of the term for which his predecessor was elected, and no more, be the fraction longer or shorter. Neither legally nor nominally has he any term. The time of service is purely accidental, and cannot be foreseen nor fixed by law. It has been even questioned whether the person so acting as President, though not so elected, should receive the official title of President; but it has not been doubted that the term of his official existence was that of the deceased President, and to be terminated at the end of the four years for which the latter had been elected. A senator or a member of the House of Representatives dies during his term of service, and another is elected to fill out the vacancy, but the new senator or new member has no term of office himself; he serves out the remainder of the term to which he has succeeded of his predecessor. The presidential term must be analogous to that of senator or member of the House. If this be deemed a fair conclusion it will be seen that the proviso, as well as the body of the act of March 2, 1867, prevents the removal of Mr. Stanton without the advice and consent of the Senate. Contemporary construction of the language of a statute cannot be held to set aside its plain meaning; but when it sustains that plain meaning it is not unfair to consider it. The House of Representatives, it is well known, in framing the tenure-of-office act, strenuously contended that the members of the cabinet should be included and protected; but the Senate only proposed to prevent the sweeping removal of all civil officers except cabinet officers.

The minister of war had rendered conspicuous service, and whether he needed or desired protection against sudden removal without the consent of the Senate or not, the House was urgent to have it awarded. Beyond all doubt they so intended to have it, and with reason believed they had accomplished their purpose. As a member of the House I so understood the language of the act then, and I am unable to give it a different construction now. On its final passage General Schenck, of the committee of conference, said : " It is in fact an acceptance by the Senate of the position taken by the House." Could anything be more emphatic? The Senate manager, (Mr. Williams, of Oregon,) who had most to do with the language of the bill in the committee of conference, where it took its final shape and form, had no doubt then, and, as I understand, has none now, that it did and does include all members of the cabinet. Nor is there anything wrong in such a conclusion as applicable to President Johnson. When the presidential office fell upon him the tenure-of-office act had not been passed, and he might undoubtedly have changed his cabinet officers at his pleasure; whether wisely or not it is unnecessary to consider. By not doing so he both legally and morally adopted them as his own as much as he could have done by actual appointment. He has daily so recognized the fact officially in all possible forms. When the act was before him for approval he clearly comprehended its provisions, as appears by his veto message. He also admits in his message to the Senate, December 12, 1867, referring to his cabinet, that "if any one of these gentlemen had then said to me that he would avail himself of the provisions of that bill in case it became a law, I should not have hesitated a moment as to his removal," showing that he had not failed to understand its full import. It is also worthy of notice, from this declaration of President Johnson, that no head of any of the executive departments, whatsoever might have been his merits or demerits otherwise, could then have given an opinion in favor of the bill but at the peril of instant ejection from office; and if all gave opinions against it, as has been intimated, the President might very well feel safe from any embarrassments in the future in retaining them. But when Secretary Stanton came to consider laws not affecting himself so much as the nation, and failed to second President Johnson in his policy of obstruction to the reconstruction acts, passed in July, 1867, then President Johnson sought to crush out the Secretary as promptly as he undoubtedly would have succeeded in doing had no such law as the tenure-of-office act been passed. After the bill became a law Mr. Stanton obeyed it, even though it be true that, not foreseeing the full extent of the President's perverse policy and purposes, he had not favored its passage; but the President determined not to obey it. Even when, in compliance with the letter of the law, he suspended Mr. Stanton in August, 1867, informing other departments that he had so suspended him, and reported the reasons for the suspension to the Senate, (in strict accordance with the law,) within 20 days after the commencement of the next session, it would only seem to have been done in good faith, provided the Senate consented to the suspension; but if the Senate should not so consent, *it was the President's purpose to prevent Mr. Stanton from resuming the office of Secretary of War*, according to his own confession, in his letter to General Grant, February 10, 1868; or, in other words, if he could not bend the Senate to his will, he had already determined to defy the law. The suspension of Mr. Stanton in August would have been lawful had there been, instead of mere pretexts, any valid charges of misbehavior or disability against him worthy of the just consideration of the Senate, but there were no such charges, and he was properly restored by the Senate. President Johnson could now, while the Senate is in session, by obtaining its advice and consent, oust Mr. Stanton at any moment, or any other civil officer, by only nominating a fit and proper person for his successor; but solitary and alone he cannot legally remove him, nor does it even appear probable that the Secretary of War *ad interim*, Lorenzo Thomas, to use his most energetic words, can "kick him out." The constitutional power of the President has not been invaded by Congress, but the joint power of the Senate has been solemnly asserted and ought not now to be surrendered to any President, and especially not to one who manifests so much avidity to monopolize the political control of the government as does the present incumbent. Without passing upon the question as to whether the tenure-of-office act is in every respect expedient or not, I see no reason to question its expediency now, nor its constitutionality at any time. That question has been twice solemnly decided by more than two-thirds of each branch of Congress, and recently by a still larger proportion of the Senate. Not one of these legislators, under their oath of office, could have voted for this law believing it was unconstitutional, and it would be pitifully absurd to suppose that they have suddenly changed their opinions, or that the country will be very swift to accept the opinions of President Johnson and his advisers as of more weight than the combined authority of more than two-thirds of both houses of Congress.

Precedents have been cited to sustain the action of the President, and it should be noted, first, that they all, such as they are, bear date prior to the passage of the tenure-of-office act, when there might have been some lawful authority to justify the same; but it is hardly too much to claim that there is not one valid precedent in the whole history of our government where a President has positively removed a cabinet officer while the Senate was in session without its consent. The case of Timothy Pickering, under President Adams, was no exception, for on the same day the Senate advised and consented to the appointment of John Marshall in the place of Pickering. Admit President Johnson's pretensions and he might at once, and without any barrier, remove McCulloch or F. E. Spinner and put any general of the army into power as Secretary of the Treasury *ad interim* or as Treasurer *ad interim*. He has certainly as much power over the purse as over the sword of the nation, and no more.

Sanction this pretension of the Executive and our republic would be no more a free government than that of the French empire.

I shall cite one more significant fact that fully confirms the views already expressed. As is well known, every outgoing President, some weeks prior to the close of his term, as an act of official courtesy due to his successor, issues a proclamation to convene the Senate at 12 o'clock m., on the 4th of March next succeeding, " to receive and act upon such communications as may be made to it on the part of the Executive," and this is done to give the incoming President a chance to have a new cabinet, by and with the advice and consent of the Senate. This has been the universal practice. Franklin Pierce issued such a proclamation on the 16th day of February, 1857, for the Senate to convene at 12 o'clock m., on the 4th of March, 1857, and it did so convene and remain in session for 10 days. James Buchanan issued a like proclamation in the same words, February 11, 1861. Now, if the President can make removals and appointments of cabinet officers or manufacture any *ad interim* substitutes without the advice and consent of the Senate, why do these extraordinary executive sessions of the Senate so regularly appear and reappear in our history?

The main facts set forth against the President in the first, second, and third articles are confessedly true, and they are, in my opinion, without any constitutional or lawful justification. That they come within the range of impeachable offences there can be no reasonable doubt.

The fourth article charges that the President did unlawfully conspire with Lorenzo Thomas and other persons with intent, by intimidation and threats, to hinder Edwin M. Stanton from holding the office of Secretary of War, in violation of the provisions of "An act to define and punish certain conspiracies," passed July 31, 1861.

It does not appear to me that sufficient proof has been produced to sustain the charge of "intimidation and threats," as alleged. The President told General

Sherman that Stanton "was cowardly," but it does not appear that he has yet acted on the idea of trying to operate upon him through his fears, nor does it appear that he authorized General Thomas so to operate.

The fifth article charges that the President did unlawfully conspire with Lorenzo Thomas and other persons to prevent and hinder the execution of the tenure-of-office act, passed March 2, 1867, and did unlawfully attempt to prevent Edwin M. Stanton, then Secretary of War, from holding said office.

It is very evident that President Johnson was ready to accept aid, and that he sought it from various quarters, to prevent and hinder the execution of the tenure-of-office act, and that he did attempt to prevent Mr. Stanton from holding the office of Secretary of War by making an unlawful agreement or by conspiring with Lorenzo Thomas. It is clear, also, that at last the President found General Thomas grateful for his recent restoration to the office of Adjutant General of the army, who with the *Constitution and the laws* on his lips agreed and was ready to carry out his unlawful orders, designs and purposes. If any further proof was required beyond his many abortive struggles to accomplish his ends, the admissions of the President in his letter to General Grant, February 10, 1868, would be conclusive on this point.

The sixth article varies from the fourth in charging that the President conspired by force to seize, take, and possess the property of the United States in the Department of War, in violation of the conspiracy act of July 31, 1861, and of the tenure-of-office act of March 2, 1867.

That Adjutant General Thomas had revolved in his own mind the idea of force, if it should be necessary, to get possession of the War Department, there is no doubt from his own testimony, as well as that of others, especially that of Samuel Wilkeson; but the President appears to have pocketed the order suggested by Thomas for a call upon General Grant for a military order, and it hardly seems right to make President Johnson responsible for the utterances or the acts of this frivolous old man, Adjutant General Thomas, notwithstanding he was the President's trusted agent, and, perhaps, as liable to put on a coat of mail as any more peaceful mask. Furthermore, it does not appear to me that the act of July 31, 1861, "to define and punish certain conspiracies," one of the legislative necessities arising during the war, was intended to apply or can properly be made to apply to the present case.

The seventh article varies from the fifth in charging the President with unlawfully conspiring with Lorenzo Thomas to unlawfully seize, take, and possess *the property* of the United States in the Department of War, in disregard of the act of March 2, 1867.

The facts and reasons touching the fifth article are applicable to the seventh, and the same conclusions follow.

The eighth article charges the President with intent unlawfully to control the disbursements of the moneys appropriated for the military service and the Department of War, contrary to "An act regulating the tenure of certain civil offices;" and, without the advice and consent of the Senate, then being in session, did on the 21st day of February, 1868, issue and deliver a letter of authority to Lorenzo Thomas, empowering him to act as Secretary of War *ad interim.*

This article is controlled by most of the facts and arguments belonging to article second. I shall only add that the main purpose of wresting the office of Secretary of War from the hands of Edwin M. Stanton could not have been to deprive him of the barren honor of the official title, but to get the control of its departmental power. The control of the disbursements of moneys for the preservation of the public peace in the rebellious States, or for the maintenance of the Freedmen's Bureau, by which much or nothing may be done, according to the discretion of those in authority, would be no barren sceptre within the grasp of one whose profoundest hatred seems to be excited when beholding such disbursements made for the protection of the Union men of the south, now more than ever struggling for life and liberty, and who are seeking to restore rebellious States to their practical relations with the Union on the basis of freedom, equality, and justice.

The ninth article charges that the President on the 22d day of February, 1868, brought before him General William H. Emory, the commander for the department of Washington, and sought to instruct him that a certain law, requiring military orders from the President or Secretary of War to be issued through the General of the army, was unconstitutional, with intent to induce the said Emory to violate the same, and with further intent thereby to enable the President to prevent the execution of the tenure-of-office act, and to prevent Mr. Stanton from holding the office of Secretary of War.

The particular subject of conversation here censured appears to have been first introduced by General Emory, and not by the President. Each expressed frank opinions, and those of General Emory being the most commendable, the President appears to have been, and ought to have been, quite as much instructed as was General Emory. If any guilty purpose was entertained on the part of the President it did not ripen into a disclosure in the presence of the main witness, General Emory.

The tenth article charges President Johnson with having in various speeches made declarations, threats, and scandalous harangues, intended to excite the contempt and odium of the people against Congress, and the laws of the United States duly enacted thereby.

The facts here alleged seem to have been abundantly proved, and there is no doubt of the stain brought upon the country and upon the President by these intemperate and indecent utterances. They are evidences of bad taste and violent temper, such as are not infrequently exhibited in political discussions, and sometimes, it is to be regretted, have appeared as foul blots in legislative discussions. It would be hardly just to give these presidential harangues any interpretation beyond their political significance. We may regret them because of the stigma and scandal thereby brought upon the nation. If these discreditable speeches had been made with a view to excite armed rebellion, or had been made in time of war, the charge would be far more serious. I do not, however, think it a stretch of charity to suppose the President when making them had no other than a political object in view. To President Johnson it will be a cruel and unavoidable punishment, unparalleled in our history, that such speeches are to be perpetuated as a prominent feature of his future presidential fame. I do not desire to place any greater burden on his back.

The eleventh article charges, first, that the President declared by public speech that the 39th Congress was not a Congress, intending to deny its power to propose amendments to the Constitution; in pursuance of this declaration, that the President attempted to prevent the execution of the tenure-of-office act by devising means whereby to prevent Mr. Stanton from forthwith resuming the functions of the office of Secretary of War, notwithstanding the refusal of the Senate to concur in his suspension; and further, devised means to prevent the execution of the act making appropriations for the army for the year ending June 30, 1868; and also to prevent the execution of "An act to provide for the more efficient government of the rebel States," passed March 2, 1867.

There are not less than four distinct charges here made, any one of which, if proved, affords sufficient foundation to sustain this article, and so far as the facts are similar to those embraced in several of the preceding articles, the argument need not be repeated. Some of the charges appear to have been sustained by the proof, and that is sufficient to determine the proper vote, though other allegations contained in the article may or may not be sustained by proper proof. After saying this it may be useless to pursue the subject further; but, among the independent charges here clustered together, there is one of the gravest in the whole series made against the President in relation to the execution of the act for the more efficient government of the rebel States, upon which a brief comment may not be inappropriate.

Nearly all of the other unlawful acts charged upon President Johnson have been done by him in order to enable him to accomplish his great crowning purpose of defeating the legislation of Congress for the rebel States. Proof in relation to any other allegations, therefore, to the end contributes to the support of this charge, as well as whatever proof may be found on the record particularly relating to it. Evidence in relation to such a charge to a large extent must necessarily be circumstantial, where the party, while ostensibly executing the law, predetermines its miscarriage, and must be surrounded by difficulties, but it does not seem easy to dismiss the matter as having no foundation whatever.

The *animus* of the President has been made offensively conspicuous in his assignments and changes of the commanders of the several military departments, and especially by the removal of General Sheridan and the appointment of General Hancock in Louisiana, whose action in that department, regarded as a dread calamity by Union men, so enraptured the President that he even ventured upon the official impudence of asking Congress to tender to the new commander a vote of thanks, well knowing that Congress could have no other feeling than that of painful solicitude, if not of disgust, in regard to the part which the President had persuaded one of our veteran generals to assume in the execution of the reconstruction acts; but all such facts, which have not been formally offered in evidence, may be excluded from our view of this article, and there will enough remain of substance in other charges of the article to justify the conclusion that it should be considered as having been conclusively supported by the proof.

The various charges in the articles of impeachment raise the question whether the President can do certain acts with impunity. Can he, in violation of his oath, refuse to take care that the laws be faithfully executed? Can he, in violation of the Constitution, exercise an exclusive power to remove and appoint to office? Can he, in violation of the laws of the land, disobey such parts of the laws as he pleases, and when he pleases? With so much he appears to have been justly charged, and such acts would not seem to be improperly characterized when called high misdemeanors. If they are not, what are they? Certainly they are not innocent acts. What is a misdemeanor? The definitions given in Webster's dictionary are as follows:

1. Ill behavior; evil conduct; fault; mismanagement.
2. (*Law.*) Any crime less than a felony. The term applies to all offences for which the law has not furnished a particular name.

If we limit the term to the law definition, it would still be a very modest name for the offences.

If the President is guilty, he cannot be guilty of anything less than a misdemeanor. If the facts charged do not amount to a misdemeanor, then the power to impeach the President might as well forever be abandoned.

But the issues immediately involved in the articles of impeachment only thinly cover other and graver matters, identical in character with some of the great questions raised by the recent rebellion. It is a serious question whether the executive department of the government shall be permitted to absorb some of the most important powers conferred upon Congress by the Constitution; but it is an aggravation of the question when this absorption is struggled for in the interest of disloyal citizens, and in behalf of the fallen fortunes of slavery. It is as much the duty of Congress to maintain its own rights as it is its duty not to trench upon the just powers of the Executive; but the maintenance of the rights of Congress looms up to higher importance when it is seen that just now hereon hangs the right of ten States to a republican form of government, to freedom and the protection of equal laws. To concede that laws made by a vote of two-thirds of each branch of Congress, the President's objections to the contrary notwithstanding, may be litigated or disregarded and set at defiance by a vetoing President, would be to yield a plain provision of the Constitution.

Even to allow such laws to be evaded, or to wink at a halting execution of such laws, would soon undermine and destroy the check which it was intended should be placed upon an ambitious and self-willed executive. If the President can make and unmake, remove and appoint the chief officers of the government at his own will and pleasure—having in view no other consideration than whether they are or are not subservient to *his policy*—then, instead of being the agent of the Constitution to "take care that the laws be faithfully executed," he becomes the agent of governmental patronage, to bend both the law-makers and the people to his will. If the Senate has the right to be consulted as to appointments, this right cannot be abrogated by Congress, nor nullified by the President. In time of war the power of the executive stretches out its strong arm over a new and vast field; but even in time of war, and over military and naval officers, the power of the President does not extend to the latitude which President Johnson claims in time of peace in regard to officers in the civil service.

It would be wrong to convict President Johnson upon a merely technical violation of the law, without violence to substance, and harming nobody, and it would be equally wrong to exonerate him upon a mere technicality while the practical breach of the law was flagrant. If he has been substantially guilty of the unlawful offences charged, then our duty to the government and the people requires his conviction. If through inadvertence, or compelled by any haste, he made a mistake in his interpretation of the law, acting with entire good faith, a mistake that he would gladly repair on the first opportunity, then he perhaps might be forgiven. But this is no such case, and the President of the United States, of all men, should not ask to be excused on account of ignorance of the law. It is, however, rather an obstinate adherence of the President to his own predetermined will. He does not think he has made a mistake. His veto message of the 2d of March, 1867; the suspension of Mr. Stanton, August 5, 1867, under the act, with the appointment of General Grant as Secretary *ad interim;* and his report to the Senate of December 12, 1867, of the reasons for the suspension of Mr. Stanton, all prove that the President fully comprehended the law, and he must have acted with deliberation when he exercised his constitutional right to withhold his assent from the bill before it became a law, and with equal deliberation when he subsequently conformed to the strict letter of the law in the suspension of Stanton, though giving unsatisfactory reasons therefor. When he flatly disobeyed the law by removing Stanton, February 21, 1868, and authorized Thomas to fill his place, he did not act inadvertently—he had pondered long how to break the law with personal impunity—and, although it is not pretended that this last move of President Johnson was devised or advised by any of his constitutional advisers, it cannot have been made through a mere blunder as to the meaning of the law, but it appears more like a bold attempt to trample the law under the heels of executive power.

If the intent of the President was good, that should mitigate and possibly shield him from the extreme penalty hanging over him for the offences charged and either proved or admitted. A positive breach of the law carries on its face a bad intent, and there is little or no proof of good intent other than the offer of proof through members of his cabinet of what the President had at some time said to them, or what they had at sometime said to him. Suppose this be admitted: that his cabinet, one and all, pronounced the law unconstitutional; that it did not include the Secretary of War; and that the question as to the validity of the law ought to be carried to the Supreme Court. All this would only show that the President gave and received bad advice, which, to say the least, is not the best evidence of good intent, and, instead of diminishing the offence, theoretically increases it; for, after all, the President, by whomsoever advised, must be held responsible for his own acts, and, in addition thereto, to some extent, for the acts of his ministers. If he choose to break the law he must do it at his own peril and take the consequences. The advice of his cabinet, if good, would only shield the President if practically adopted, but it would be monstrous to shield him from the fact that bad advice had been given to him when it is too plain that the tender of good advice, if unpalatable, would be at the peril of the instant removal of the party by whom given. It is quite plain that the President intended to oust Mr. Stanton at all hazards—by fair means if he could, but at any rate to oust him—and he did not intend himself, whatever others might do, to resort to any law suit in the process. The testimony of General Sherman shows that the President believed Mr. Stanton would yield because, as he said, he was "cowardly;" so when General Thomas brought to the White House the account of his doings on the 21st of February, the President said, "Very well; go and take charge of the office and perform the duties." There was then no hint of disappointment at the lack of a law suit. It was not until the next day, when the masquerade was over and Adjutant General Thomas found himself in the clutches of the law, that the President again said, according to General Thomas, "Very well; that is the place I want it, in the courts." Though others might litigate the question, it is not clear that he ever sought to initiate any legal proceedings himself. But the assumption on the part of the President that it was his privilege, if not his duty, to violate the law rather than to faithfully execute it, in order to make up a case for the decision of the courts, instead of showing good intent, exhibits an obstinate purpose not to yield to a law passed by a constitutional majority of Congress against his objections. And the pretence that the courts would decide against the constitutionality of the law is sheer assumption. Even if there had been reasonable doubt as to its constitutionality, it was the law of the land until decided otherwise by the Supreme Court, the only tribunal having authority to stay the force of any law for a single moment. Certainly the President, who swears to maintain the Constitution which makes it one of his chief duties to take care that the laws be faithfully executed, cannot at his own will elect what laws he will execute and what he will ignore. But there is hardly more reason to suppose the Supreme Court would decide the tenure-of-office act unconstitutional than any other law among our statutes.

Nor can good intent be found in the mode pursued by the President in striving to get rid of the hated war minister. When he suspended Mr. Stanton, in August, 1867, in order to prevail upon the Senate to consent to the suspension he made General Grant Secretary of War *ad interim*—entirely an unexceptionable appointment. But after he quarrelled with General Grant because he did not, when the Senate refused to consent to the suspension, aid and abet him in placing the office in the lap of the President before Mr. Stanton could repossess it, then he proposed to act independently of the law and of the Senate, and took General Thomas, so utterly unfit that his very designation impeaches the judgment if not the integrity of the appointing power. Later nominations are open to criticism either as bad, or when otherwise, they appear too evidently extorted in the nature of a propitiation to the Senate sitting on the trial of the impeachment of Andrew Johnson. The general history of the conduct and manner of the President, in his various attempts to remove Mr. Stanton, certainly fail to furnish evidence of any good intent; nor is it to be believed, if the field had been opened for a wider search, that it would have been attended by any happier result.

Having been among those who were originally for living down the administration of President Johnson, rather than to attempt to bring it to an abrupt close by an impeachment, although admitting his culpability, I have yet had no other desire than to be able to render a just and impartial verdict. Summoning to my aid all the light with which the case has been illuminated, and at the close of the trial the culpability still appearing no less, I cannot, under the solemnities of an oath, declare the President innocent. The example of President Johnson, were it possible so gross a wrong could have passed unheeded, might have been comparatively harmless; but when solemnly adjudicated, with the eyes of the world fixed upon it, establishing, as it will, a precedent to be quoted and followed in all future time, I cannot consent to ignore or waive it as a light matter, and thereby engraft the idea into the republican Constitution of the United States that the executive is paramount and may dominate at will over the legislative branch of the government.

Mr. Stanbery, counsel for the President and late Attorney General, has made a feeling appeal to us in behalf of his client. He has seen him *often tempted by bad advice* and knew that *evil counsellors were around him* more than once, but never discovered anything in him *but loyalty to the Constitution and the laws*. "Yes, senators," says Mr. Stanbery, "with all his faults, the President has been more sinned against than sinning. Fear not to acquit him. The Constitution of the country is as safe in his hands from violence as it was in the hands of Washington."

This appeal would be more apt not to go unheeded if Mr. Stanbery himself could be considered an impartial judge as to what course the President ought to pursue, and had not heretofore failed to *discover anything in that man but loyalty;* but it is painful to be obliged to presume that Mr. Stanbery, as one of the chief advisers of the President's most obnoxious measures, is entitled to some share of the doubtful honor of our Chief Magistrate's present position.

Neither the facts surrounding this case, nor those making up the history of President Johnson's administration, show evidences of good intent or justify future confidence. Ever since Andrew Johnson reached the Presidency, more or less pressure has been felt that it was necessary for Congress to remain in session—adjourning late to meet early and at extraordinary and inconvenient seasons—lest grave evils and perplexing complications should be precipitated upon the country by his headstrong, if not treacherous, action in the absence of the legislative branch of the government. Decide the charges here in his favor now; say that he has done no wrong; admit that the House of Representatives are all at fault, and Congress or the Senate never more need to remain here as the guardians of law and of a representative form of government, or as a bulwark against the encroachments of executive power. President Johnson and all future Presidents may break laws or make appointments at will, and do anything which goes to make up the character of an uncurbed despot.

I am glad to remember that at the commencement of the late rebellion Andrew Johnson took a bold, outspoken stand in behalf of the Union, and that fact shall protect him, so far as my vote is concerned, from any other penalty for his recent great offences, than a simple removal from office. I would not deprive him of the poor privilege of being a candidate for the suffrages of any portion of the people who may think him worthy, whether for President or alderman. But his appointment to office of men supposed corruptly to be putting more money into their own pockets than into the treasury; his discreditable use of the pardoning power; his unmasked threat in his last annual message that it might become proper for him to "adopt forcible measures or such as might lead to force" in opposing an unconstitutional act of Congress; his appointment, in violation of law, to places of honor and trust, rebels not able to take the oath of office, in preference to loyal men; his malign attempts to foist upon the country his policy of restoring the rebellious States without security for the future and against the measures of salutary reform proposed by Congress; and his bitter and active efforts to defeat the adoption of the constitutional amendment proposed by the 39th Congress, known as article 14, and known, also, as the great seal of security for the broad principles of national freedom and human rights; these facts, and such as these, do not allow me to gratuitously credit the President with good intent in the past, nor can I, notwithstanding his counsel's appeal, in the face of such a record, by a verdict of acquittal, become responsible for his conduct in the future.

OPINION OF MR. SENATOR VAN WINKLE.

In the following remarks I have endeavored to state the conclusions to which I have arrived, with some reasons for them, and not to review the whole case. I have, therefore, omitted the consideration of all questions raised in the course of the proceedings which do not affect those conclusions:

Conceding the constitutionality of the tenure-of-office act of March 2, 1867, there yet remain some questions to be disposed of before an intelligent answer can be given to the accusation or charge contained in the first article of impeachment. Senators are to pronounce upon this, as well as the charges in the other articles, by replying, under the oaths they have respectively taken, to the question, "Is the respondent, Andrew Johnson, President of the United States, guilty or not guilty of a high misdemeanor, (or crime, as the case may be,) *as charged in this article?*" I have, therefore, in each case, where I deemed it at all necessary, endeavored to present the charge stripped of immaterial verbiage, in order to ascertain more readily and certainly whether it describes a misdemeanor or crime.

The first article alleges that the respondent did, unlawfully and in violation of the Constitution and laws, issue an order in writing for the removal of Edwin M. Stanton from the office of Secretary *for* the Department of War, with the intent to violate the act above referred to, and with the further intent, contrary to and in violation of the provisions of the said act, and contrary to the provisions of the Constitution, and without the advice and consent of the Senate, then in session, remove the said Stanton from his said office.

The Constitution is silent on the subject of removals from office, unless a rule on the subject may be inferred from the provisions it contains relating to offices and officers. The only authoritative interpretation of its meaning in this relation previous to the passage of the tenure-of-office act is found in an act of Congress passed in 1789, and this concedes to the President alone the right to remove. The provisions of the tenure-of-office act must therefore be examined in order to determine whether what is charged to have been done by the respondent was a violation of that act and of the Constitution.

The plain and evident intention of the act just referred to is that no person appointed to any office by and with the advice and consent of the Senate shall be removed therefrom, although he may be suspended in certain specified cases, without the like advice and consent. There is no question that Mr. Stanton was so appointed to the office of Secretary of War, and was duly qualified to act therein. In order to prevent a removal from any such office the act provides, in effect, that the incumbent shall hold it until his successor is in like manner appointed and duly qualified, unless the time is limited by law, and shall expire before such an appointment and qualification. The proviso in the first section does not, in my opinion, except any of the cabinet officers from the operation of the preceding clause of the same section, although, for the first time, it specifically limits their respective terms. If, as is alleged, the proviso leaves it doubtful as to the duration of Mr. Stanton's term, it is, in my opinion, certain that at the time the said order in writing was issued his tenure was protected by the preceding clause. In its very language he was, and is still, "holding *a* civil office to which he had been appointed by and with the advice and consent of the Senate," and the order in writing not only addresses him as Secretary *for* the Department of War, but asserts that his "functions as such will terminate on receipt of that communication."

The sixth and only penal section of the act which refers to a case like that under consideration provides that every removal, appointment, or employment made, had, or exercised contrary to the provisions of that act shall be deemed, and is thereby declared to be, a high misdemeanor. It therefore appears that the act of the respondent complained of, if it was criminal, must be obnoxious to the provisions of this section.

The charge made by the first article is, that the respondent did "issue an order in writing (which is set out at full length) for the removal of Edwin M. Stanton from the office of Secretary *for* the Department of War." This is the whole of it, so far as the acts as distinguished from the intentions of the respondent are concerned. There is not even an allegation that the order in writing was ever delivered to, or served on, Mr. Stanton, or ever directed to be so delivered or served, or that any attempt was made to deliver or serve it; or, in fact, that Mr. Stanton ever saw or heard of it.

As the order in writing is neither an appointment or employment it must have effected a removal, or have been, at least, an attempt to remove, in order to constitute a violation of the act; but no removal or attempt to remove is charged, and consequently the respondent could not have been guilty "of a high misdemeanor, as charged in this (first) article." Had an attempt to remove been charged there was still no averment of even attempted delivery or service of the order in writing. "To issue," which means simply to send forth, cannot imply a delivery or service; and if there is evidence of a delivery to be found in the proceedings it cannot be applicable to this article, in which there is no charge or averment. This objection may seem technical, but a consideration of the whole article will show that it is substantial, and that a service or delivery was, in fact, necessary to complete the alleged offence, especially if it is observed that the order in writing addressed to Mr. Stanton says, " Your functions as such (Secretary of War) will terminate upon receipt of this communication," and consequently not till then. It is, therefore, evident that the delivery to and receipt by Mr. Stanton of the order in writing was necessary to complete his removal from office, if any mere writing could have that effect.

Admitting that the intents of the respondent in issuing the order in writing were precisely as charged, it may be questioned whether they, together with the act done, constitute a high misdemeanor. Of course the intent alone does not. It merely qualifies or characterizes the act, and however reprehensible the former may be the latter must be of itself unlawful. There is no clause in the act that forbids or denounces the mere issue, without some further act, of such a paper as the order in writing, and such an issue could not be even an attempt to remove from office. By the very terms of the order any intention to remove Mr. Stanton until he had received it is negatived, and there is no charge or allegation that he did receive it.

It has been suggested that the answer of the respondent to the first article contains confessions which cure the defects above indicated. To this I reply that the answer cannot confess what is not charged.

The second article is based upon the letter of authority issued and delivered by the respondent to General Lorenzo Thomas. It charges that the respondent, with intent to violate the Constitution and the tenure-of-office act, the Senate being then in session, and there being no vacancy in the office of Secretary of War, did issue and deliver to the said Thomas the aforesaid letter of authority, which is set out at full length. Referring to some remarks made above on the first article, it is plain that the issue and delivery of the letter of authority cannot be a violation of the Constitution unless it is also a violation of the tenure-of-office act, which is charged. In order, therefore, to ascertain whether the charge made in the second article covers a misdemeanor the act itself must be reviewed.

The most rigid examination of that act will fail to disclose that its provisions anywhere refer to an *ad interim* appointment, except in its second section, where, in case of a suspension, such an appointment is authorized. The language, after stating what offence or misconduct will authorize a suspension, is that " in such case, and in no other," " the President may suspend such officer, and designate some suitable person to perform temporarily the duties of such office," &c. Here the suspension is the principal thing, and the temporary designation the subordinate. This justifies the construction that the words "in such case, and no other," mean that only such cases as are specified in the beginning of the section, occurring in a recess of the Senate, will authorize suspension. They do not and cannot mean that in no other case shall there be a temporary designation or appointment. Such a conclusion is forbidden by the fact that temporary designations were, at the passage of the act, and still are, authorized by both law and custom.

Turning to the penal sections of the tenure-of-office act it will be seen that the fifth applies only to those who accept, hold, or exercise any office or employment contrary to the provisions of that act; and, as General Thomas is not upon trial, its further consideration may be dismissed. If, then, the respondent committed a misdemeanor under this article, the act or acts done by him must have been such as are described in the sixth section.

That section declares that "every removal, appointment, or employment made, had, or exercised, contrary to the provisions of this act, and the making, signing, sealing, countersigning, or issuing of any commission or letter of authority, for or in respect to any such appointment or employment," shall be deemed a high misdemeanor. Leaving out of consideration the word removal, which is not involved in the charge, the section includes only appointments and employments made, had, or exercised, contrary to the provisions of the tenure-of-office act, and certain acts relating to such appointments and employments. As the latter are a consequence of the former, and as if the former was legal, the latter, in the same case, would be legal also; and, in fact, there could be no employment without a previous appointment—the former may be considered as included in the latter—so that if the appointment of General Thomas was legal, or the reverse, his employment would bear the same character.

It may be fairly questioned whether the authority conferred on General Thomas was in its nature an appointment, in the strict legal sense of that term. The letter set out in the article simply empowers and authorizes him to act, and does not use the word appoint, or any equivalent term. In the case of a suspension, authorized by the second section, it is not said that the President may appoint, but that he may "designate some suitable person," &c. The term appointment may be familiarly used in such cases; but what is questioned is whether such is its proper legal application. Conceding this, however, it remains to inquire whether the appointment of General Thomas was, in the language of the penal sections, "contrary to the provisions of the act." It is very evident that the act refers everywhere to appointments made by and with the consent of the Senate, except in the second section, and there so far only as the same relates to the designation of a person to act *ad interim* in the case of a suspension, which has been already noticed. It is very certain that an *ad interim* appointment, designation, or authorization has never been held, or, so far as I am informed, even supposed to require the advice and consent of the Senate. It does not seem, therefore, that the letter of authority, as it is called in the article, is contrary to the provisions of the tenure-of-office act. As the making, signing, &c., of any letter of authority, made penal by the sixth section, must be for or in respect to such an appointment, &c., as is contrary to the provisions of the act, and it has been shown that the letter of authority to General Thomas did not relate to such an appointment, the issue and delivery of it did not constitute a misdemeanor, as charged in the second article.

The third article is also based upon the letter to General Thomas, which is set forth at length, but is not here called a letter of authority, but an appointment. It is not charged to have been issued contrary to the tenure-of-office act; but the remarks on the preceding article may properly be referred to here. The charge is that, under circumstances precisely similar to those stated in the second article, the respondent did, without authority of law, the Senate being in session, appoint one Lorenzo Thomas to be Secretary for the Department of War *ad interim*, without the advice and consent of the Senate, with intent to violate the Constitution, no vacancy having happened in the said office during the recess of the Senate or existing at the time.

It will be observed that it is not charged that the Secretary was not temporarily absent from the office, or sick, in which cases the so-called appointment would have been legal. The act of the respondent is alleged to have been done without authority of law, with intent to violate the Constitution. If it can be deemed a full appointment it was such a violation, for such appointments require the advice and consent of the Senate; but as the letter, the only evidence on the subject, shows it to have been only *ad interim*, and the Constitution makes no mention of such appointments, it does not appear that it can be such a violation. As to its being done "without authority of law," it can hardly be intended to assert that every act for which a special or general permission of law is not shown is unlawful and a misdemeanor. Yet this is the only ground on which the alleged act of the respondent is charged to be the latter.

The fourth, fifth, sixth, and seventh articles are severally based on an alleged conspiracy of the respondent and General Thomas. It is sufficient to say as to these that there is no evidence before the Senate which furnishes proof of even a technical conspiracy.

As to the eighth article, it may be remarked that the evidence relating to its subject clearly shows that the *ad interim* appointment of General Thomas, or of any other person, would not have enabled the respondent "to control the disbursements of the moneys appropriated for the military service and the Department of War" any further than he legally might with Mr. Stanton or any other acceptable person in the office. This negatives the alleged criminal intent.

The ninth article is supported by evidence, and the alleged intents may be said to be disproved.

The tenth article charges, in substance, that the respondent, designing and intending to set aside the rightful authorities and powers of Congress, attempts to bring Congress and its several branches into disgrace, ridicule, hatred, contempt, and reproach; to impair and destroy the respect of the people for Congress and its legislative power and to excite the odium and resentment of the people against Congress and the laws enacted by it; in pursuance of such design and intent, openly and publicly made and delivered, with a loud voice, certain intemperate, inflammatory, and scandalous harangues, the particulars of which are set forth in the three specifications found in this article. It is pleasant to learn, as is disclosed at the end, that this design and intent of the respondent was in some manner frustrated, for it is there said that by means of the said utterances, declarations, threats, and harangues, the respondent had brought, not Congress, but "the high office of the President of the United States into contempt, ridicule, and disgrace, to the great scandal of all good citizens." There may be more truth than poetry in this; and if so, it is not the first case of an engineer "hoist by his own petard." It may, nevertheless, be difficult to determine whether the ineffectual design and intention, or the accomplished result, constitutes the alleged misdemeanor.

The difficulty, however, may be obviated by remembering that several of the original States, almost as a condition of their respective ratifications of the Constitution, insisted that certain amendments of that instrument should be adopted which, as to the most of them, was speedily done. The first provides that "Congress shall make no law abridging the freedom of speech." This remains in the Constitution, and is unquestionably of universal application. It seems, therefore, that no such misdemeanor as is charged in this article can be committed in this country.

The eleventh article alleges in substance that the respondent, by public speech, declared and affirmed that the 39th Congress was not a constitutional Congress, authorized to exercise legislative power, but a Congress of only part of the States, thereby denying and intending to deny that its legislation was valid or obligatory upon him, except in so far as he saw fit to approve the same, and also thereby denying and intending to deny the power of the said 39th Congress to propose amendments to the Constitution of the United States.

I do not perceive or admit that these alleged intentions are proved, and in my remarks on the preceding article have expressed the opinion that declarations and affirmations made by public speech cannot constitute a criminal offence. This, however, is of little importance, as the whole is merely introductory, and does not constitute or greatly, if at all, affect the charge which follows, on which the judgment of the Senate must be predicated.

Giving to the language used its ordinary meaning and construction, it is somewhat difficult to state the charge with entire certainty, as when stated it will be seen to involve the apparent anomaly of asserting that the respondent attempted to prevent the execution of an act of Congress by attempting to prevent the execution of two other acts of Congress, or rather by devising and contriving, and attempting to devise and contrive, means so to do. But I will endeavor to state in terms what the charge is, as it appears to me, after a careful and critical examination of the language used.

The charge, in effect, is that, in pursuance of the said declaration, the respondent did unlawfully, and in disregard of the requirements of the Constitution, that he should take care that the laws be faithfully executed, attempt to prevent the execution of the tenure-of-office act by unlawfully devising and contriving, and attempting to devise and contrive, means by which he should prevent Mr. Stanton from forthwith resuming the functions of his office, notwithstanding the refusal of the Senate to concur in his suspension; and also attempted to prevent the execution of the said act by further unlawfully devising and contriving, and attempting to devise and contrive, means to prevent the execution of the army appropriation act of 1867, and also to prevent the execution of the reconstruction act of the 2d of March, in the same year.

As there is no specification of any "means" so devised and contrived, and no sufficient proof of any attempt to interfere with the execution of the two last-mentioned acts, their further consideration may be dismissed. The only specific charge remaining is the devising and contriving, and attempting to devise and contrive, means by which he should prevent Mr. Stanton resuming his office under the circumstances stated; and, in fact, as the *attempting to attempt* to commit a misdemeanor is rather too remote to be in itself a misdemeanor, the naked charge is that the respondent attempted to prevent the execution of the tenure-of-office act by devising and contriving means, which are nowhere specified or described, by which he should prevent Mr. Stanton from forthwith resuming the functions of his office. The proof of this charge rests wholly upon the respondent's correspondence with General Grant, which is in evidence, and by which it appears that the respondent endeavored to induce the General, at a time previous to the correspondence, but while that officer was authorized to perform, and was performing, the duties of Secretary of War *ad interim*, to keep possession of that office, and thereby prevent Mr. Stanton's resumption of it, or to surrender it in time to permit the induction of a successor for that purpose.

This evidence, as far as it goes, is sufficiently explicit, but it remains to be determined whether the respondent is, in the words of the question to be proposed to every senator, and to be answered by him under the oath he has taken, "guilty or not guilty of a high misdemeanor, as charged in this article." It is, therefore, necessary to consider whether the charge it contains described a high misdemeanor; and, if so, whether the respondent is guilty as charged.

There can be no doubt that an actual prevention of the execution of a law by one whose duty it is to take care that the laws be faithfully executed is a misdemeanor, and it may be conceded that an attempted prevention by such a person is also a misdemeanor; but it may be doubted whether merely devising and contriving means by which such prevention might be effected is an attempt to commit the act which constitutes the offence. "Devising" is simply a mental operation, and while "contriving" may have a broader signification, the connection in which it is used here seems to restrict it. Even with the light thrown upon these words by the evidence, as above cited, they appear to imply nothing more than an intention to effect the alleged prevention. An intention, not followed by any act, cannot constitute an attempt to commit a misdemeanor, and the question to be proposed must be answered negatively.

It may be remarked that the evidence further discloses that the object of the respondent in his proposal to General Grant was to compel Mr. Stanton to institute legal proceedings, by which his right to the office, denied by the respondent, could be tested. This would not have justified the alleged attempt had it been actually made, but it would have qualified the intention, by showing that the object was not primarily to violate the law, and thus have at least tended to diminish the criminality involved in the illegal act.

OPINION OF Mr. SENATOR STEWART:

A brief examination of the law will determine the character of the President's conduct in removing Stanton and appointing Thomas *ad interim*. The act to regulate the tenure of certain civil offices supercedes all former legislation on the questions involved in that removal and appointment. The 6th section of the act declares:

"That every removal, appointment, or employment made, had, or exercised contrary to the provisions of this act, and the making, signing, sealing, countersigning, or issuing of any commission or letter of authority for or in respect to any such appointment or employment, shall be deemed, and are hereby declared to be, high misdemeanors, and, upon trial and conviction thereof, every person guilty thereof shall be punished by a fine not exceeding ten thousand dollars, or by imprisonment not exceeding five years, or both said punishments, in the discretion of the courts."

The same penalties are imposed for issuing orders or giving letters of authority for or in respect to removals and appointments which are prohibited by law that are imposed in cases of actual removals and appointments. It matters not whether Stanton was actually removed or Thomas actually appointed *ad interim*, the issuance of the order for the removal and the giving the letter of authority to Thomas are admitted. If the power was wanting either to remove Stanton or to appoint Thomas, the President is guilty of a high misdemeanor, on the admitted facts. The questions, then, to be determined are, was the removal of Stanton and the appointment or employment of Thomas, or either of them, unlawful? The body of the first section declares:

"That every person holding any civil office to which he has been appointed by and with the advice and consent of the Senate, and every person who shall hereafter be appointed to any such office and shall become duly qualified to act therein, is, and shall be, entitled to hold such office until a successor shall have been in like manner appointed and duly qualified, except as *herein otherwise provided*."

This language, if unqualified by any other provisions of the act, would extend the term of all officers therein described (including Mr. Stanton, Secretary of War,) until a removal by the appointment and qualification of a successor as *therein provided*. It also prescribes the manner in which removals and appointments may be effected, and prohibits all other modes of removals and appointments. The term of office and the mode of vacating and filling office are the three distinct propositions of the body of the first section of the act. There must be no departure from these propositions, except as therein (that is, in that act,) otherwise provided. All former acts of Congress providing a different term or a different mode of appointment or removal are by this section repealed

Any practice of the government inconsistent with the provisions of this law is prohibited. This dispenses with the necessity of examining former acts or former practice concerning any matter within the scope and meaning of this section. There can be no qualification to this language not found in the act itself. It does not read, except as the practice of the government or former acts of Congress may prescribe, but it does read, *except as herein otherwise provided.* Can the legislative will, in repealing former acts or changing existing practice, be more clearly expressed than to declare a rule and also to declare that it shall be the only rule? The body of the first section clearly prohibited the removal of Stanton and the appointment of Thomas *ad interim.* If these acts were not in violation of law, it was because they were authorized by other provisions in the act itself. The interpretation of the act, then, so far as it effects the President, depends upon the question, what is *therein otherwise provided?* Is it *therein provided* that he may do the acts complained of? If so, he obeyed the law; if not, he violated it. The limitations or exceptions upon the first section are four. One relates to removals, one to appointments, and two relate to the term of office. The former are contained in the second section, and the latter are found in the fourth section and the proviso to the first. The second section reads as follows:

"That when any officer appointed as aforesaid, excepting judges of the United States courts, shall during a recess of the Senate, be shown, by evidence satisfactory to the President, to be guilty of misconduct in office, or crime, or for any reason shall become incapable or legally disqualified to perform its duties, in such case, *and in no other,* the President may suspend such officer and designate some suitable person to perform temporarily the duties of such office until the next meeting of the Senate, and until the case shall be acted upon by the Senate, and such person so designated shall take the oaths and give the bonds required by law, to be taken and given by the person duly appointed to fill such office, and in such case it shall be the duty of the President within twenty days after the first day of such next meeting of the Senate, to report to the Senate such suspension, with the evidence and reasons for his action in the case, and the name of the person so designated to perform the duties of such office. And if the Senate shall concur in such suspension and advise and consent to the removal of such officer, they shall so certify to the President, who may thereupon remove such officer, and by and with the advice and consent of the Senate, appoint another person to such office. But if the Senate shall refuse to concur in such suspension, such officer so suspended shall forthwith resume the functions of his office, and the powers of the person so performing its duties in his stead shall cease, and the official salary and emoluments of such officer, shall, during such suspension, belong to the person so performing the duties thereof, and not to the officer so suspended."

The emphatic language is "*in such case and no other*" the President may suspend and designate a person to perform the duties of said office temporarily. This suspension and temporary appointment limit two of the general propositions in the first section, first, a temporary removal may be made by the President alone at the times and in the cases therein provided, but in no other. This limits the first section so that in substance the act declares that no person now in office, or who may hereafter be in office by and with the advice and consent of the Senate, shall be removed by the President alone without the advice and consent of the Senate to the appointment of a successor, except in recess of the Senate, when the President may suspend for the causes set forth in the second section of this act, and in no other case whatever. The other general proposition of the first section which is limited by the second section relates to appointments.

Upon the question of appointment, to an office held by another, the first and second sections contain all existing statutory regulations. The substance of these two sections bearing upon the question under consideration is, that no person shall be appointed by the President alone, to an office where there is no vacancy, and which office is, by law, to be filled by and with the advice and consent of the Senate, without such advice and consent except in cases of suspension in the *recess* of the Senate arising under the provisions of the second section of this act, and in such *case and no other* the President may make temporary appointment, as therein provided. The temporary suspension and appointment are limitations upon the positive language of the first section, and are qualifications therein otherwise provided, and the only qualifications anywhere appearing in the act to the general rule requiring the advice and consent of the Senate to an appointment, and prohibiting all removals, except through such appointment. It is true the removal is not complete, but it is the first step towards it, and is an actual suspension from office without the advice and consent of the Senate to the appointment of a successor, and it is also true that the appointment is only temporary, but the appointee, contrary to the provisions of the first section, enters upon the discharge of the duties of the office without any action of the Senate.

This is all the statutory law which bears upon the question under consideration, namely the removal of Stanton and the appointment of Thomas *ad interim*, and it positively prohibits that removal and appointment by the President alone. The President recognized the binding force of this law in the suspension of Stanton and appointment of General Grant *ad interim*, and in several other cases, and his subsequent disregard of its plain provisions cannot be pleaded as an inadvertance. The two other exceptions to the first section do not relate to the mode of vacating or filling office, which is the subject of inquiry, but to the term of office. The only reason for an examination of these exceptions in this connection is to exclude any inference that provision is made in the act either for removing Stanton or appointing Thomas *ad interim*.

The fourth section reads as follows:

"That nothing in this act contained shall be construed to extend the term of any office the duration of which is limited by law."

This section leaves unchanged the term of office as fixed by law, notwithstanding the general language of the first section that such term shall extend until the appointment and qualification of a successor. The proviso contains the other limitation and relates to the term of certain designated offices, but contains no exception to the general rule as to removals or appointments. The language is "*Provided*, That the Secretary of State, of the Treasury, of War, of the Navy, and of the Interior, the Postmaster General, and the Attorney General shall hold their offices respectively for and during the term of the President by whom they may have been appointed, and for one month thereafter, subject to removal by and with the advice and consent of the Senate." Nothing is more certain than that this proviso is silent, both as to removals and appointments by the President alone. The proviso fixes a limit on the term of the offices therein named, but makes no other exception. If it be contended that the language is obscured, how does that obscurity help the President, for no possible construction can make it confer the authority to do what is prohibited in the body of the section, namely, to remove an officer and appoint another to fill his place *ad interim* without the advice and consent of the Senate. When the President found that he was prohibited from removing, suspending, or appointing, except as in said act provided, it was enough for him to know that nothing in the act authorized him to remove Stanton and appoint Thomas *ad interim*. Stanton's appointment was for an indefinite term, and he was still in office on the 21st day of February, 1868. It makes no difference what his term of office was or by whom appointed. The mode adopted to put him out was prohibited. There is no reason, in view of the conduct of the parties or the language of the law, to support the suggestion that the law was retroactive and operated to terminate Stanton's office one month after Johnson became President. Such a construction would not only be inconsistent with the whole conduct of the President in recognizing Stanton as Secretary of War, but would be in violation of the well-established rule of statutory construction that no law shall have a retroactive effect, unless the will of the law making power be so clearly expressed as to be wholly inconsistent with any other interpretation. This law, without any violation of language or principles of construction, applies to the present and to the future, and was so understood, until it became important to change or pervert its obvious meaning.

The President understood the law on the 2d of March, 1867, when he sent his veto message to Congress. (Page 38 of Record.)

He says in that message, "In effect the bill provides that the President shall not remove from their places any of the civil officers whose terms of service are not limited by law without the advice and consent of the Senate of the United States." Then it included any civil officers whatever. Now it includes some and excludes others.

I am aware that a constitutional question has been raised upon the denial of the right of the President to remove from office, which I need not discuss after the repeated votes of the Senate affirming the constitutional validity of such a law. But no one has contended or will contend that the President could make any appointment for any temporary purpose whatever, without the authority of law, and he certainly cannot do so against a plain statute. The issuance of the letter of authority for the appointment or employment of Thomas is expressly declared to be a misdemeanor. It is no answer to the admitted constitutional power of Congress to pass the law to say that cases might arise in which it might be inconvenient if the President were deprived of the right to fill temporary vacancies. That would be a matter for the legislative department to decide, and besides no such case had arisen when Thomas was appointed or employed, but on the contrary Mr. Stanton was in office and fully qualified to discharge the duties of the Department of War. It is no excuse for violating a law to say that cases may arise when the law would work inconveniences particularly when no inconvenience exists in the given case. No precedent has been found in the history of the government for the removal of Stanton and the appointment of Thomas *ad interim*. They are in direct violation of the Constitution and cannot be justified or excused by practice, if such practice has existed.

Usurpation is not to be tolerated against the express provisions of written law and against the protest of the Senate after mature consideration. I regard the removal of Stanton and the appointment of Thomas as parts of the same transaction. The two acts taken together in defiance of law and the decision of the Senate, constitute a bold and deliberate attempt to dispense with the provision of the Constitution which makes the advice and consent of the Senate necessary to the appointment to office. For if the President can remove the Secretary of War and appoint a person *ad interim* to fill the place, the advice and consent of the Senate are of no consequence. This would authorize him to remove all executive officers, civil and military, and put persons into these offices suitable to his purposes, who might remain in office indefinitely. He might or he might not nominate to the Senate. If he should condescend to do so he might nominate the persons holding *ad interim*, and the Senate could only choose whether it would confirm the nominees or let the same persons continue *ad interim*. The Senate could in that case choose as to the character of the commissions, but would have no voice as to the character of the officers. But suppose the President should nominate different persons from the *ad interim* appointees, which persons would of course be also the choice of the Executive, and in that event the Senate might confirm or allow the *ad interim* officers to continue to discharge the duties of the respective offices. In that case the Senate would have the poor privilege of choosing between two instruments of the President. If this can be done in the case of the Secretary of War, it can be done in all cases of executive offices, civil and military. The whole power of the government would then be in the hands of one man. He could then have his tools in all the offices through whom alone the civil and military power of the United States could be exercised. To acquit Andrew Johnson is to affirm this power in the present and all future presidents.

The motives of the President in deliberately violating law cannot be considered. Such a defence might be set up in every criminal case. He does not claim that he did not intend to issue the order for the removal of Stanton and issue the letter for the appointment of Thomas *ad interim*. If either of these acts was a misdemeanor, he intended to commit a misdemeanor. The question of intention or motive can only be material where doubt exists as to voluntary or deliberate character of the offence. My conclusion is that the President deliberately violated the law both in issuing the order for the removal of Stanton and in giving the letter of authority to Thomas, and that all the articles involving a charge of either of those acts ought to be sustained if we desire to preserve the just balance of the co-ordinate departments of the government and vindicate the authority of law.

OPINION OF MR. SENATOR DAVIS.

The subject of impeachment is provided for in the Constitution by several clauses, which I will quote:

The House of Representatives shall have the sole power of impeachment.

The Senate shall have the sole power to try all impeachments. When sitting for that purpose they shall be on oath or affirmation. When the President of the United States is tried the Chief Justice shall preside; and no person shall be convicted without the concurrence of two-thirds of the members present.

The President, Vice-President, and all civil officers of the United States, shall be removed from office on impeachment for and conviction of treason, bribery, or other high crimes and misdemeanors.

Judgment in cases of impeachment shall not extend further than to removal from office and disqualification to hold and enjoy any office of honor, trust, or profit under the United States; but the party convicted shall, nevertheless, be liable and subject to indictment, trial, judgment, and punishment according to law.

Our system of impeachment has not been transferred from any other government, nor was its organization confided to Congress; but the cautious statesmen who founded our government incorporated it in and built it up as part of the Constitution itself. They enumerated its essential features and made it *sui generis*. 1. No person but civil officers of the United States are subject to impeachment. 2. The Senate is constituted the court of impeachment. 3. The Chief Justice of the United States is to preside over the court when the President is under trial, and the Vice-President or President *pro tempore* of the Senate in all other cases. 4. No conviction can take place unless two thirds of the senators present concur. 5. No impeachment can be made but for treason, bribery, or other high crimes and misdemeanors against the United States. 6. Judgment of impeachment cannot extend to death or other corporal punishment, or fine or imprisonment; but is restricted to removal from and disqualification to hold office; but the party convicted, nevertheless, to be liable and subject to indictment, trial, judgment, and punishment according to law. The offenders, offences, court, and punishment are all distinctly impressed with political features.

But the prosecution has assumed two strange and untenable positions in the course of this trial. 1. That the Senate, in the performance of the present most important office and duty, is not a court. It is certainly not a *legislative* body, nor *exercising legislative* powers; it is not an advisory council connected in a common function with the President. What, then, is it? Most of the States had previously to the formation of the Constitution organized their several tribunals to try cases of impeachment, and by some they had been denominated *courts of impeachment*, and all had invested them with the powers and attributes of courts. They were universally held to be courts. The Constitution invests the Senate with the *sole* power to try all impeachments. *To try* is to examine a case judicially by the rules of law, and to apply them to the legal evidence taken in the trial, and to render the judgment of the law upon the claims of the parties according to the evidence. The phrases "to try," "tried," "convicted," "conviction," and "judgment" are all used in the Constitution in connection with impeachment and the proceedings in it. Those words, in connection with their context, establish, organize, and describe a court; and as applied to the Senate necessarily constitute it a court with jurisdiction to try all cases of impeachment.

The Senate now and for this occasion is a *court* of impeachment for the trial of the President of the United States, and, like all other courts, is bound by the law and the evidence properly applicable to the case.

The other novel position of the prosecution—that on this trial the Senate "is a law to itself"—is still more extraordinary. The power conferred by the Constitution on the Senate when trying impeachment is limited and wholly judicial, and the idea of combining with it any legislative power whatever is not only without any warrant, but is in direct hostility to the fundamental principle of our government, which separates and makes naturally impassable all its legislative and judicial power. But the position that the Senate, when trying an impeachment, is "a law to itself," is bound by no law, may decide the case as it wills, is illimitable and absolute in the performance of special, restricted, judicial functions in a limited government, is revoltingly absurd. On the trial of any impeachment the Senate has no more authority to make or disregard law than it has to make or disregard facts; and it would be as legitimate and proper and decorous for the managers, in relation to the evidence in this case, to announce to the Senate, "You are witnesses to yourselves," as "You are a law to yourselves." No court has any right or power to make or disregard either law or evidence in the trial of any case; and a court which would act upon and avow that rule of conduct would be execrated by mankind. There is a particular and emphatic contrary obligation on this court, for each one of its members has individually made a solemn appeal to God "that in all things appertaining to the trial of the impeachment of Andrew Johnson, President of the United States, now pending, he will do impartial justice according to the Constitution and the laws."

One of the leading and inflexible laws which bind this court is embodied in the Constitution in these words:

No person shall be removed from office but on impeachment for and conviction of treason, bribery, or other high crimes and misdemeanors.

That is the category of all impeachable offences, and they must be acts declared by the law of the United States to be treason or bribery, or some other offence which it denominates a "high crime or misdemeanor." The laws which define impeachable offences may be the Constitution, or acts of Congress, or the common law, or some other code, if adopted either by the Constitution or act of Congress. No common-law offence, as such merely, can sustain the impeachment of any officer; but to have that authority it must have become a part of the law of the United States by being adopted by the Constitution or some act of Congress, and would have operation and effect only to the extent that it was consistent with the provisions, principles, and general spirit of the Constitution.

No respectable authority has ever maintained that all offences merely against the common law, or merely against public morals or decency, were impeachable under our Constitution. Story has argued, in support of the position, that some offences against the common law, and not made so by act of Congress, are impeachable; but he states his premises so generally and vaguely that it is impossible to obtain a full and clear comprehension of his meaning. He neither asserts the broad proposition that all common-law offences are impeachable, nor does he attempt to define or describe generally those that are, but contents himself with the position, vaguely and hesitatingly taken and maintained, that there are common-law offences which are offences against the United States and which are impeachable; but how or where, or by what language of the Constitution or law of Congress, they become offences against the United States he does not attempt to show. But he distinctly admits that to be impeachable the offence must be against the United States.

The idea of prosecuting and punishing an act as an offence which no law has made an offence, all must reject. *Treason, bribery, high crimes and misdemeanors* are technical terms, found in the common law, and that express certain classes of offences; but the common law, in whole or part, is not *necessarily* or *per se* the law of the United States, and to become so must be adopted by the Constitution or an act of Congress, and not otherwise. There is no provision or words in the Constitution which expressly or by implication adopts the common law. When it was before the conventions of the States on the question of their ratification of it, that it did not adopt the common law was frequently and strenuously objected to, especially in the convention of Virginia; and no one denied the truth of that position. The courts, federal and State, and the profession generally, have, up to the present time, held that there is no adoption of the common law by the Constitution of the United States, and there never has been any by act of Congress.

But this precise question has been decided by the Supreme Court in the negative, and more than once. Hudson & Goodwin were indicted under the common law, in the circuit court of the district of Connecticut, for a libel against the government of the United States; and the case was taken up to the Supreme Court, which decided without any announced difference of opinion among its members, and with the full approbation of Pinckney, Attorney General, that the courts of the United States have no *common law* jurisdiction in cases of *libel* or *any other crimes* against the United States; but that, by the principles of general law, they have the power to fine for contempt, to imprison for contumacy, and to enforce the observance of their orders, &c.; that the legislative authority of the Union must first make an act a *crime*, affix a punishment to it, and declare the court that shall have jurisdiction. (7 Cranch, 32.) The court, in the case of the United States *vs.* Coolidge, (1 Wharton, 415,) being an indictment under the common law, for rescuing a prize at sea, recognized the authority of the previous case, and dismissed the indictment. Judge Story sat in both cases, and was the only judge who expressed a dissent in the latter case from the ruling of that court.

The common law, in whole or part, has been adopted by the constitutions or statutes of most of the States; but in Louisiana it has never been made to supersede the civil law, nor the Partidas in Florida. The courts of the United States recognize and adopt, not the criminal, but the civil portion of the common law, generally to the extent to which it has been appropriated by a State, in all cases arising in that State within their jurisdiction; but not as the *common law*, nor as the *law of the United States*, but as the law of the particular State. In States that have not appropriated the common law in whole or part, the United States courts adopt such other law generally as they have established for the government of cases arising in them respectively. But this adoption by the courts of the United States of the laws of the States never extends to criminal or penal cases, but is restricted to those of a civil nature. No State ever executes in any form the penal laws of another State, and the United States only their own penal laws, and they exist in no other form than acts of Congress.

The State of Maryland adopted the common law, and on the organization of the District of Columbia, Congress recognized and continued the laws of that State in so much of it as had been ceded by Maryland. But the laws so adopted by Congress were local to the Maryland portion of the District; they did not extend to the part of it ceded by the State of Virginia, in which Congress adopted and continued in the same way the laws of Virginia. As the laws of each State are local and distinctive, so are the laws of Maryland and Virginia, which were adopted by Congress for the District of Columbia on its organization, local and distinctive to the portions of the District that were ceded by those States respectively.

Treason, bribery, and other offences of the nature of high crimes and misdemeanors, to be impeachable, must be crimes against the general law of the United States, and punishable in their courts of the localities where committed. Thus, treason against the United States is an impeachable offence, whether it be committed in any State or Territory, or the District of Columbia; and so of any other act to be impeachable, it must be an offence by the laws of the United States, if perpetrated anywhere within its boundary. That an act done in the portion of this District ceded by the State of Maryland would be an impeachable offence, and a similar act done in any place beside in the United States would not be impeachable, is sustained by neither law nor reason. Such an offence would be against the District of Columbia, not against the United States. The law of impeachment is uniform and general, not various and local, and it has no phase restricted to the District of Columbia, as has been assumed by the prosecution.

Then, besides treason and bribery, which are impeachable by the Constitution, to make any other act an impeachable offence it must not only be defined and declared to be an offence, but it must be stamped as a *high crime or misdemeanor* by an act of Congress. The words "high crimes and misdemeanors" do not define and create any offence, but express, generally and vaguely, criminal nature, and of themselves could not be made to sustain an indictment or other proceeding for any offence whatever; but a law must define an offence, and affix one of those terms to it to make it a constitutional ground of impeachment. And this is not all; the offence in its nature must have the type of heinous moral delinquency or grave political viciousness, to make an officer committing it amenable to so weighty and unfrequent a responsibility as impeachment. He may have been guilty of a violation of the Sabbath or of profane swearing, or of breaches of the mere forms of law, and if they had been declared offences by act of Congress, with the prefix of "high crime" or "high misdemeanor" attached to them, they would not be impeachable offences. They would be too trivial, too much wanting in weight and State importance to evoke so grave, so great a remedy. Nor would any crime or offence whatever against a State, or against religion or morality, be a cause for impeachment, unless such an act had been previously declared by a law of Congress to be a *high crime* or a *high misdemeanor*, and was in its character of deep turpitude.

It results from this view of the law of impeachment, that as none of the articles against the President charge him with treason or bribery, which are made impeachable offences by the Constitution, they, or some one of them, must allege against him the doing of an act or acts which a law of Congress has declared to be an offence against the United States, and denominated it to be, and in its vicious nature it must be a high crime or high misdemeanor, and that the President did that act with a criminal intent to violate the law, to authorize this court to convict him and pronounce judgment that he be removed from office.

I will now proceed to the examination of the offences charged in the several articles. The first charges the President with the commission of a high misdemeanor in having sent a letter to Edwin M. Stanton, Secretary of the Department of War, dismissing him from office while the Senate was in session, in violation of the act of Congress "to regulate the tenure of certain civil offices."

Article two charges the President with the commission of a high misdemeanor in having delivered his letter to Lorenzo Thomas directing him to assume possession of the War Department and to perform its duties *ad interim*, the Senate being then in session, and without its advice and consent, there being no vacancy in the office of Secretary of the Department of War, in violation of his oath of office, the Constitution of the United States, and the act of Congress aforesaid.

Article four charges the President of unlawfully conspiring with Lorenzo

Thomas, with intent, by intimidation and threats, to prevent Edwin M. Stanton, Secretary of War, from holding said office, in violation of the Constitution of the United States and the "act to define and punish certain conspiracies," whereby he committed a high crime in office.

Article six charges the President of having conspired with Lorenzo Thomas, by force, to seize, take, and possess the property of the United States, in the Department of War, in violation of the civil office tenure act, whereby he committed a high crime in office.

The third, fifth, seventh, and eighth articles charge the same matter, in somewhat different form, as is embodied in the other four articles; and I propose to consider the charges of the whole eight as growing out of the act of the President in sending his letter to Stanton removing him from the office of Secretary of War, and his letter to Thomas to take charge *ad interim* of it. Those two letters comprehend the substance of all the offences charged against the President in the first eight articles.

The ninth article charges the President, as Commander-in-Chief of the army, of having attempted to induce General Emory, an army officer, to disobey the law of Congress requiring army orders from the President, or Secretary of War, to be transmitted through the General of the army, and was guilty thereby of a high misdemeanor in office.

To this article three answers may be made:

1. The act does not make an attempt to induce a military officer to disobey it, whether committed by the President or other person, any offence.

2. The evidence not only does not sustain, but disproves that charge against the President.

3. If the charge had been sustained by the proof, the President, as Commander-in-chief, has the absolute and unquestionable right to issue military orders directly, and without the intervention of another officer, to any officer or soldier whatever; and the provision of the act on which this article is based is an unconstitutional and flagitious attempt by Congress to subordinate, in a measure, the Commander-in chief to the General of the army.

The tenth article is based wholly on passages taken from several public speeches made by the President, not in his official character but as a private citizen, to assembled crowds of the people, by whom he was called out and urged to address them. Whatever of improper matter, manner, or spirit are in those public addresses was provoked by gross insults then offered to him, which, though not a justification, is much palliation. The President was then exercising a right which our fathers held inviolable, and which they intended should never be invaded, and for the protection of which they made this special amendment to the Constitution:

Congress shall make no law abridging the freedom of speech or the press.

For the Senate, as a court of impeachment, to set up to be "a law to itself," and impeach the President as guilty of a high crime and misdemeanor for exercising a liberty which the founders of our government deemed so valuable, so necessary to the preservation of their freedom, as to declare in their fundamental law should never be abridged, would violate that fundamental law and shock the free spirit of America. The basing of an article of impeachment on those speeches of the President is calculated to bring down upon the whole proceeding the suspicion and revulsion of a free people, and it ought to be dismissed from this court as containing no impeachable matter.

The 11th article charges that Andrew Johnson, President of the United States, was guilty of a high misdemeanor in declaring and affirming in substance "that the thirty-ninth Congress of the United States was not a Congress of the United States authorized by the Constitution to exercise legislative power under the same, but, on the contrary, was a Congress of only part of the States." This is not the language proved in the case to have been used by the President on any occasion; and if he had used it, he could not be impeached for it, because there is no law which makes the use of such language by the President, or any person, a high crime or misdemeanor or any offence, and any act of Congress declaring it to be an offence would be unconstitutional and void as abridging the freedom of speech. This article also charges—

That the said Andrew Johnson, President of the United States, did, unlawfully and in disregard of the requirement of the Constitution that he should take care that the laws be faithfully executed, attempt to prevent the execution of an act entitled "An act regulating the tenure of certain civil offices." by unlawfully devising and contriving means by which he should prevent Edwin M. Stanton from forthwith resuming the functions of the office of Secretary for the Department of War, notwithstanding the refusal of the Senate to concur in the suspension theretofore made by said Andrew Johnson of said Edwin M. Stanton from said office.

To this charge it may be answered—it is made in terms too general and vague to require any answer—that the unlawful means which the President devised and contrived to prevent Edwin M. Stanton from forthwith resuming the functions of the office of Secretary of War, are not described or set out by any language whatever; and that act or any law of Congress does not make the devising or contriving of any means to prevent Edwin M. Stanton or any other civil officer whom the President has removed from office, and in whose removal the Senate has refused to concur, from resuming the duties of the office from which he has been so removed, a high crime or misdemeanor, or any offence; and said civil-office-tenure bill, so far as it restricts the President's power to remove said Stanton, is not consistent with, but in derogation of, the Constitution, and null and void.

And the eleventh article charges also that Andrew Johnson, President of the United States, devised and contrived other unlawful means to prevent the execution of an act entitled "An act making appropriations for the support of the army for the fiscal year ending June 30, 1868, and for other purposes;" and also to prevent the execution of an act entitled "An act to provide for the more efficient government of the rebel States." Upon this last charge it may be observed—there is no description of facts setting out the means which the President devised and contrived to prevent the execution of either of the acts therein referred to—that the devising and contriving means to prevent the execution of said acts, or either of them, is not made a high crime or misdemeanor by them, or any law; that there is no evidence that he did devise and contrive any means to prevent the execution of said acts, or either of them; and that the act first referred to, in the part which the President is charged to have violated, and the last act, wholly, are unconstitutional, null and void. Thus, it is shown, on these several grounds, that there is nothing in the eleventh article on which the President can be impeached.

Some of the articles charge the President with the commission of high misdemeanors, and others of high crimes in the violation of his official oath and of the Constitution generally. The Constitution has no provision declaring a violation of any of its provisions to be a crime; that is a function of the legislative power, and it has passed no law to make violations of the Constitution, or of official oaths, by the President or any other officers, crimes.

The articles of impeachment seem to be drawn with studied looseness, duplicity and vagueness, as with the purpose to mislead; certain it is, if their matter charged to be criminal had been separately, concisely, and distinctly stated, this court, and especially its many members who are not lawyers, would have had a much more ready comprehension of it. I will not take up and consider the other articles *seriatim*, but will group their matter under three heads: 1. The removal of Mr. Stanton from the office of Secretary of War. 2. The designation of General Thomas to take charge of that office *ad interim*. 3. The alleged conspiracies of the President with Thomas to prevent, by intimidation and force, Stanton from acting as Secretary of War, and to take possession of the property of the United States in his custody. The letter of the President to Mr. Stanton, informing him that he was thereby removed from office as Secretary of War, is charged to be a high misdemeanor, and in violation of the act to regulate the tenure of certain civil offices.

The fifth and sixth sections of that act are the only parts of it which define and create any offences, and I will quote them both in their order:

If any person shall, contrary to the provisions of this act, accept any appointment to, or employment in any office, or shall hold or exercise, or attempt to hold or exercise, any such office or employment, he shall be deemed, and is hereby declared to be guilty of a high misdemeanor, &c.

This provision might apply to General Thomas, the *ad interim* employé, but cannot include the President.

The sixth section enacts:

That every removal, appointment, or employment made, had, or exercised, contrary to the provisions of this act, and the making, signing, sealing, countersigning, or issuing of any commission or letter of authority for or in respect to any such appointment or employment, shall be deemed, and are hereby declared to be, high misdemeanors, &c.

The President's letter to Mr. Stanton is not, in fact, his removal from office, though it was intended to procure it; but he refused obedience to it, persisted in holding the office of Secretary of War, and still continues in it and the actual discharge of its duties. The President's letter to him did not remove him in fact, and if the civil-office-tenure act be constitutional it did not in law; and he is now, and has been ever since, notwithstanding the President's letter dismissing him, in fact and law, in office. It is contended by the prosecution that the letter of dismission is against the Constitution and the law, and has no legal effect whatever. Stanton was at its date, in fact, in possession of the office and performing its duties, and has so continued to the present time, and on this theory of the prosecution there has been no removal of him in fact or in law. And if that theory be unsound, and the President have the power by the Constitution to remove him, and the act of Congress proposing to restrict that power is consequently void, his removal was and is *de jure* valid. In one aspect there is a removal proper and constitutional; in the other there is no removal of Mr. Stanton.

But these are the great questions in the case: Is the first section of the civil-office-tenure act in conflict with the Constitution, void, and of no effect? Does that section cover the case of the removal of Mr. Stanton? Did the President, in writing the letter of removal from office of Mr. Stanton, and the letter to General Thomas, directing him to take charge of the office *ad interim*, wilfully and with criminal intent violate the civil-office-tenure bill? These propositions comprehend the substance matter of the first eight articles.

The first section of that act is in these words:

That every person holding any civil office to which he shall have been appointed by and with the advice and consent of the Senate, and every person who shall hereafter be appointed to any such office, and shall become duly qualified to act therein, is and shall be entitled to hold such office until a successor shall have been in like manner appointed and duly qualified except as hereinafter provided: *Provided*, That the Secretary of State, of the Treasury, of War, of the Navy, and of the Interior, the Postmaster General and the Attorney General, shall hold their offices respectively for and during the term of the President by whom they may have been appointed, and for one month thereafter, subject to removal by and with the advice and consent of the Senate.

The Constitution creates a Congress, in which it vests all the legislative power of the government of the United States; a President, in whom it vests all the executive power; and a Supreme Court, and authorizes inferior courts to be established by Congress, in which it vests all the judicial power—except that it provides that the Senate shall constitute a court of impeachment, with jurisdiction to try all civil officers who might be impeached by the House of Representatives, and to adjudge amotion from and disqualification to hold office. Neither department can rightfully, or without usurpation, exercise any powers which the Constitution has vested in either of the other departments. Congress has the power, and is bound in duty to pass all laws necessary and proper to enable the President to execute the powers intrusted to him by the Constitution, and without which legislation there are many he could not execute, but it cannot confer on him any additional power, nor can it divest him of any. He forms a separate and co-ordinate department of the government, with Congress as another, and the courts as the third, and each derive all their powers from the Constitution alone. Neither is subordinate to the others, though the powers vested in Congress are the most various, extensive, vigorous, and popular, and necessarily it is the most aggressive and effective in its aggressions upon the other departments; the judiciary is the least so, though the inevitable tendency of all power, however lodged, is to augment itself.

The power of appointment to office exists necessarily in all governments, and is of an executive nature; and if the Constitution had contained no particular provision on this subject, its language, " the executive power shall be vested in a President of the United States of America," would have imparted the power of appointing to office, and by implication would have vested it wholly in the President. But the effect of this general language is qualified by a special provision:

And he (the President) shall nominate, and by and with the advice and consent of the Senate shall appoint, ambassadors, &c.

This is restrictive and exceptional of the general power of appointment, previously by implication conferred on the President, and has no other operation than what is expressed in its words. and they being exceptional no implied power results from them against the general grant of power from which they make an exception. But the power of removal from office also, as necessarily as the power of appointment, exists in all governments, and is no less an executive power. It is located somewhere in the government of the United States, but being an executive power it cannot be in Congress, for legislative powers only are vested in that body. It is not established or vested by any express or special provision of the Constitution, but is by the general language:

The executive power shall be vested in a President of the United States of America.

The Constitution leaves the power of *removal* just as this general provision vests it, with the President alone. The power of Congress to make all laws which shall be necessary and proper for carrying into execution its enumerated powers, and all other powers vested by the Constitution in the government of the United States, or any department or officer thereof, is purely a legislative power, and gives no authority to assume or interfere with any powers of the President, or the judicial department. Instead of being a power to assail them, its legitimate and literal office is to uphold their powers and to give facilities in their execution. That, or any other provision of the Constitution, gives to Congress no warrant or pretext to interfere with the executive power of removal from office, vested by the Constitution in the President alone.

The power of removal and the power of appointment to office, though both executive, are in their nature distinct and independent of each other. One, the power of appointment, was treated specially and separately from the other in the Constitution, it associating the Senate with the President in its exercise. But for this particular regulation of the power of appointment, it is most probable that no question as to the other distinct power of removal from office would ever have been made; and that all would have silently conceded that both powers being executive in their character, and all the executive power of the government having been vested by the Constitution in the President, they properly appertained to him alone, and he would never have been challenged in the sole and exclusive exercise of either. But however that may be, the truth of this proposition cannot be successfully controverted; the provision of the Constitution associating the Senate with the President in the power of *appointment*, does not invest it with the same, or any connection with the power of *removal;* or authorize Congress to pass the civil-office-tenure act, or any other act that would impair the President's sole power and right to exercise it.

But the whole subject of the power of removal from office came up for consideration in the first Congress, on the organization of the department of foreign affairs, in 1789, and elicited a debate of great ability among the ablest men of the body, many of whom had been members of the convention which framed the Constitution. Congress was much divided on the subject, but a majority of both houses sustained the position that the Constitution conferred on the President the power to remove from office, and the contending parties made a compromise, by which the act organizing the department recognized the power of the President to remove the head of this department, in this language:

The chief clerk, whenever the principal officer shall be *removed* from office by the *President* of the United States, or in any other case of vacancy, shall, during such vacancy, have the charge and custody of all records, books, and papers appertaining to the said department.

The supporters of the exclusive power of the President were opposed to any language being used in the act that *seemed to confer* this power on the President, and its opponents accepted language that conceded and recognized the President's power of removal without expressly deducing it from the Constitution.

The act establishing the Department of War, with a provision in the same language recognizing the power of the President to remove the Secretary, was passed at a subsequent day of the same session, with but little and no serious opposition.

Both those acts formally admit the sole power of the President to remove the heads of the respective departments, but neither of them contains any language to confer that power on the President. The supporters of the principle that the Constitution vested it solely in him rejected from the bill organizing the Department of Foreign Affairs all language that seemed to confer it upon the President, and claimed and determined to maintain it as one of his powers solely from the Constitution; and the opponents of this principle, being willing to concede the power to the President, if the acts did not expressly state the power to be conferred on him by the Constitution, they were passed in their existing form, recognizing it as a presidential power to remove both Secretaries. The acts were not intended to confer this power on the President; they have no language whatever to that effect, yet they concede that he possessed it; and he could derive it only from the Constitution. This was as certain an assertion and establishment of the sole constitutional power of the President to remove from office, as if it had been expressed in the most direct terms; and no attempt has ever, before the passage of the civil-office-tenure bill, been made in Congress to disturb this question as thus settled.

From that time every President has claimed and exercised the sole power of removal at all times as an executive power conferred by the Constitution. The great commentators on it, Kent, Story, and Rawle, have treated this power as belonging to the President alone by the provision and effect of the Constitution itself, settled by the acts of Congress of 1789, the uniform and unchallenged practice of the government, and the general acquiescence of the country. The Supreme Court has repeatedly, and without doubt or hesitation, recognized it as an established constitutional principle; and Chief Justice Marshall many times, in his opinions, refers to it, as he does to the other and unquestioned powers of the President. Hamilton and Madison were among its great authors and firm defenders; it was conceded to be a settled principle by Clay, Calhoun, Benton, Wright, Clayton, and all the statesmen of America down to the passage of the civil-rights bill; and Mr. Webster maintained, adhered to it, and advocated its exercise, while the Senate was in session and at all times, as Secretary of State under President Tyler. No attempt had ever before been made to arrest or qualify its unconditional exercise by the President, as well when the Senate was in session as when it was not. The reason of America, guided by principle, authority, and experience, was unwilling to divest, unsettle, or change this presidential power by act of Congress or alteration of the Constitution because of being satisfied that it was essentially of the nature of an executive power and absolutely necessary to enable the President to perform his greatest duty, to see that the laws be faithfully executed. If a controverted constitutional question can ever be settled, the power of the President to remove from office at his own will has been beyond further legitimate question.

The sixth section of the civil-office-tenure act, before quoted, declares that—

> Every removal, appointment, or employment, made, had, or exercised contrary to the provisions of this act, and the making, signing, sealing, or countersigning of any commission or letter of authority for or in respect to any such appointment or employment, shall be deemed, and are hereby declared to be, high misdemeanors, &c.

But, if the Constitution invests the President with the sole and exclusive power to remove all the officers referred to in said act, his exercise of that power at all times is legitimate and makes a vacancy in the office, which his duty requires him to fill according to the Constitution and the laws; and an act of Congress which by its terms so provides as to strip him of that power, in whole or part, and to make his performance of duty after its exercise a crime, is unconstitutional and void. The exercise of a constitutional power and the performance of constitutional duty by the President can be made neither criminal nor punishable, either by impeachment, or fine and imprisonment.

If President Johnson has from the Constitution the sole power to remove from office, his letter to Mr. Stanton dismissing him from the office of Secretary of War could not be made a crime by any act which Congress could pass; and it produced a vacancy in the office which his action, in some form, was necessary to fill; and, in the mean time, it was his duty to supply the vacancy in the office temporarily according to law.

Very soon after the government went into operation, vacancies by death and otherwise occurred in various offices; and, whether it was during the recess or session of the Senate, the President was frequently not prepared to fill them properly by appointment and commissions to terminate at the end of its next ensuing session, or to make a nomination to it for its advice and consent, from a want of a knowledge of men, and many other causes. To meet this temporary exigence Congress, in an act passed in May, 1792, made this provision:

> That in case of the death, absence from the seat of government, or sickness of the Secretary of State, Secretary of the Treasury, or of the Secretary of the Department of War, or of any officer of either of said departments whose appointment is not in the head thereof, whereby they cannot perform the duties of their respective offices, it shall be lawful for the President of the United States, in case he shall think it necessary, to authorize any person or persons, at his discretion, to perform the duties of the said respective offices until a successor shall be appointed.

This law is strictly within the power of Congress :—

> To make all laws which shall be necessary and proper for carrying into execution the powers vested by the Constitution in the President.

It confers no new power upon him; all the executive power of the government had been vested in him by the Constitution, and this act only furnished him facilities for its proper and convenient execution.

But this law was essentially defective; it was limited to the three departments first organized—State, Treasury, and War—and to vacancies in office occasioned by death, absence from the seat of government, or sickness. Other legislation was necessary, and in February, 1795, Congress passed this other law:

> That in case of vacancy in the office of Secretary of State, Secretary of the Treasury, or of the Secretary of the Department of War, or of any officer of either of the said departments whose appointment is not in the head thereof, whereby they cannot perform the duties of their respective offices, it shall be lawful for the President of the United States, in case he

shall think it necessary, to authorize *any person* or persons, at his discretion, to perform the duties of said respective offices, until a successor be appointed or such vacancy filled: *Provided*, That no one vacancy shall be supplied in manner aforesaid for a longer period than six months.

It will be observed that this second law covers the whole ground, and more, occupied by the first; it applies to the same three departments, none others being then organized; but it is extended beyond vacancies occasioned by death, absence from the seat of government, or sickness, and provides for *all vacancies, from whatever cause produced*, and limits the continuance of such supplies to six months.

But this leg'slation in time became incomplete, as it did not provide for this supply of temporary service in the Navy, Post Office, and Interior Departments, and the office of Attorney General, when vacancies should occur in them. But, nevertheless, in consideration of the special requisition of the Constitution, that the President should see that the laws be faithfully executed, that all the executive power of the government was vested in him, and, from the necessity of the case, every President from the passage of the first act of 1792 exercised the power of designating some person for the supply temporarily, when vacancies occurred, not only in the Foreign, Treasury, and War Departments, but also in all the other departments; and there are many instances of such appointments spreading over that whole period. These temporary appointments were not provided for by the Constitution, but from time to time by the laws of Congress which regulated them; and they were in truth not *appointments to office*, but a designation of persons to supply the places and perform the duties temporarily of offices in which vacancies occurred, until they could be filled by regular appointments; and their necessity and validity was questioned by no one.

But in February, 1863, Montgomery Blair, Postmaster General, resigned his office during the session of the Senate, and President Lincoln designated an Assistant Postmaster General to perform the duties *ad interim* of Postmaster General, and afterwards sent a special message to Congress, then in session, asking its attention to the fact that the laws of Congress in relation to such appointments applied only to the Foreign, Treasury, and War Departments, and recommended the passage of an act to extend them to the other departments of the government. Thereupon Congress passed the act containing these provisions:

That in case of the death, resignation, absence from the seat of government, or sickness of the head of any executive department of the government, or of any officer of either of said departments whose appointment is not in the head thereof, whereby they cannot perform the duties of their respective offices, it shall be lawful for the President of the United States, in case he shall think it necessary, to authorize the head of any other executive department, or other officer in either of said departments whose appointment is vested in the President, at his discretion, to perform the duties of the said respective offices until a successor be appointed, or until such absence or inability by sickness shall cease: *Provided*, That no one vacancy shall be supplied in manner aforesaid for a longer period than six months.

SEC. 2. *And be it further enacted,* That all acts or parts of acts inconsistent with the provisions of this act are hereby repealed.

I have embodied in this opinion the whole of the three acts of Congress, authorizing the temporary supply, or *ad interim* appointments to the several departments of the government. The last act only has express words of repeal, and they are restricted to acts or parts of acts that are inconsistent with its provisions. It provides in general language for the supply of vacancies occurring in all the departments, and the spirit and meaning of the provision will also include the office of Attorney General; it, however, does not apply to *all vacancies* that may occur in them, but only to such as are caused by "death, resignation, absence from the seat of government, or sickness." It makes no provision whatever for vacancies resulting from other causes, but, like the act of 1792, is defective in this respect; that act having provided only for vacancies produced by death, absence from the seat of government, or sickness, and this act making provision but for one additional class of vacancies by death: both omitted vacancies by removal and expiration of term of office.

The chief purpose of the act of 1795 was to supply the defect of the act of 1792, in the class of vacancies, and it was made to extend to vacancies generally, all vacancies that might occur from any cause; but, like the previous act, it extended only to the departments of Foreign Affairs, of the Treasury, and of War, being all the departments then organized. If this provision of the act of 1795 had embodied words which would have applied it to such other departments of the government as might thereafter be created, there would have been no necessity for the act of 1863, and there never would have been any thought of it. The act of 1795 comprehending vacancies from *every cause*—expiration of the term of office, removal, or any other possible cause—and the act of 1863 providing only for such as were produced by death, resignation, absence from the seat of government, and sickness, the act of 1795, so far as it provides for vacancies from expiration of official term or removal from office, is not inconsistent with the act of 1863, and therefore, to that extent, is not repealed by it, and governs the case of the removal of Stanton and the letter of the President to General Thomas directing him to take charge *ad interim* of the War Department. If there was a vacancy it was produced by presidential *removal;* and the designation by the President of General Thomas or *any other person* for the temporary performance of its duties was authorized by the law of 1795, and if there was no vacancy in the office there could be and was no appointment to or employment of Thomas in it, as Stanton was never out and he never in actually; and the letter of the President to him being neither appointment to or employment in the office, and having no validity or effect, its simple delivery to Thomas constitutes no crime for punishment by impeachment, or trial, judgment, and sentence in a criminal court. It is the *appointment* or *employment*, not the abortive effort to do either, by the President that is the offence.

It is admitted that if the President's letter to Thomas had been addressed to any officer or either of the departments, or he had filled an office in one of them, it would not have been in conflict with the act of 1863, and would have been authorized by the act of 1795. As it had no effect to put Stanton out or Thomas in office, and no more results were produced by it than if it had never been written, can statesmen, senators, and judges announce to the nation and the world that the writing of this letter is a high crime and misdemeanor, and sufficient ground for the impeachment of the President of the United States?

There is another constitutional principle which prevents the civil-office-tenure act from governing the case of Stanton. He was appointed by President Lincoln in his first term, and by the language of his commission was to hold his office during the pleasure of the President. All concede that the law, constitutional or statutory at that time, and down to the passage of the civil-office-tenure bill, authorized the President to remove Stanton from office whenever he willed to do so.

But it is contended that this act changed the tenure and conditions by which he had held his office from an indefinite term and presidential will to a certain term, and the overruling of the presidential by the senatorial will; that he held his office until the expiration of one month from the 4th of March, 1869, when the four years for which Mr. Lincoln was elected the second time would end, and Mr. Stanton's term as Secretary of War would thus continue until April 6, 1869, during which period he could not be removed by the President without the permission of the Senate. This is not the appointment, the ordination into the office of Secretary of War of Stanton as President Lincoln made it, but a new and essentially different one; and who conferred it upon him? Not the President, by and with the advice and consent of the Senate, but Congress, by the form of a legislative act. It is an indirect attempt by the legislative department of the government to strip the executive department of a material portion of the power of removal from office, and to invest one of its own branches with it, and this against the presidential veto. To give Mr. Stanton, or any officer in office, the benefits of the new conditions and tenure organized by the civil-office-tenure act, requires a new appointment to be made by the President, with the advice and consent of the Senate, and not by Congress in the form of an act of legislation. To confer on him these cumulative benefits would require a cumulative appointment and commission, in the form and by the authority prescribed by the Constitution.

But another ground of the defence against the articles based on the removal of Mr. Stanton is, that his case does not and was not intended to come within the language and operation of the civil-office-tenure act.

From the terms, provisions, and history of the passage of that act through the two houses of Congress, it is plain that that body adopted the general purpose of requiring the concurrent action of the Senate to enable the President to remove the officers designated in it; but intended so far to modify that purpose as to allow to every President, as his personal and official prerogative, to make *one* selection of *all* the members of his cabinet. No one will deny that this is the general rule established by the act; and to give it practical effect it provides that the term of office of the chiefs of the several departments shall end one month after the term of the President by whom they may have been appointed. The obvious intention was that no President should be bound to continue officers, between whom and himself such important and confidential relations must necessarily subsist, who had not been chosen by him, but that he should have one choice for each office, and be held to it until the Senate should give its consent that he might make another.

This right is accorded to him not by express language, but by implication so clear as to admit of no doubt; and he possesses it as the portion of his before general power of removal, of which this act does not attempt to deprive him—it does not confer or attempt to confer it upon him, but leaves him in possession of it. The act is framed on the concession of the then existing power of the President to remove the officers for whose cases it provides; and after declaring a general rule for them, excepts from its operation the cabinet officers, and makes for them a special rule, which is to continue to operate in relation to each one for one month after the expiration of the term of the President by whom he was appointed; and then leaves him subject to the President's sole and unqualified power of removal as it existed before the act. The President may then permit him to remain in office, or may remove him at his pleasure, whether the Senate is in session or not. After removing him the President may designate *any person* to perform the duties of the office *ad interim* for six months, by which time he must make a nomination to the Senate for its advice and consent.

The general and unrestricted power to remove from office had been exercised, without question, by every President of the United States up to the date of the civil-office-tenure act, including Tyler, Fillmore, and Johnson, Vice-Presidents, on whom the Constitution had devolved the office of President.

The first section of the civil-office-tenure act embodies all of it that bears upon the question whether the case of Mr. Stanton is comprehended by it. By this law each cabinet officer holds his place for one month after the expiration "of the term of the President by whom he was appointed;" it is, therefore, necessary to know what is meant by the words, "the term of the President."

Section one, article two, of the Constitution, is in these words:

The executive power shall be vested in a President of the United States of America. He shall hold his office during the term of four years, and, together with the Vice-President, chosen for the same term, be elected as follows.

All authorities say that "term is the time for which anything lasts." In our government no office lasts after the death of the termor, or passes to heirs, devisees, or executors, but reverts immediately to the state. The tenure of some offices is for life, others for a definite number of years, and some during the pleasure of the appointing power; but the term of all ends also inexorably upon the death of the incumbent. The term of the many marshals and other officers, who are appointed for four years, could, with as much reason and truth, be said to continue to the end of that time, though the incumbents died before its lapse, as it can be said that the term of a President, who died early in the four years for which he was elected, runs on until the expiration of the four years. When a man in office dies that closes his term; and so soon as another is appointed to it his term commences.

Mr. Lincoln was elected President and Mr. Hamlin Vice-President for a common term of four years, commencing on the 4th of March, 1861, and as both survived it the term of each ended by lapse of time, March 3, 1865. The second term of Mr. Lincoln for four years, and Mr. Johnson's term for the same time, began the 4th of March, 1865, and both ended April following; Mr. Lincoln's by his death, and Mr. Johnson's by the office of President being devolved on him, and he thereby ceasing to be Vice-President, under this provision of the Constitution:

In case of the removal of the President from office, or of his death, resignation, or inability to discharge the powers and duties of the said office, the same shall devolve on the Vice-President.

Mr. Johnson became President by having been elected Vice-President, and by the operation of the Constitution, upon the death of the President, Mr. Lincoln. He is as much the President as if he had been elected to that office instead of to the vice-presidency. His presidential term commenced when he was inaugurated into the office, and is to continue to *last* for the residue of the term for which Mr. Lincoln was elected President and he Vice-President. His presidential term, though not so long, is as definite as Mr. Lincoln's was; both by the Constitution were to continue until the 4th of March, 1869, and both, by the same law, were subject to be determined before that time by their "removal from office, death, resignation, or inability to discharge the powers and duties of the office." The presidency, while Mr. Johnson has been filling it and performing its duties under the Constitution, is as much his office as it was Mr. Lincoln's when he held the same relation to it; and the proposition that this time of Mr. Johnson in the office is not his *term* but a *continuation of Mr. Lincoln's term*, is not sustained by the Constitution, fact, or reason.

But if it were a continuation of Mr. Lincoln's term, it would be of his second, not his first term, which the Constitution inexorably closed on the 3d of March, 1865; and he having been re-elected his second term commenced the next day. If Mr. Johnson be serving out Mr. Lincoln's term, it is not his *first one*, for that is "with the years before the flood," but his second term; and Mr. Johnson would be invested with every right and power in it to which Mr. Lincoln would be entitled; and among them would be the power and the right to remove Mr. Stanton from the office of the Secretary of War. This act provides that the chief officer of the seven principal departments of the government shall respectively hold their offices according to the tenure established by it, for and during *the term* of the President by whom they may have been appointed. This is a permanent and uniform law, and the measure established by it being the term of the President by whom the officer was appointed, and one month thereafter, and Mr. Stanton having been appointed Secretary of War by Mr. Lincoln during his first term in January, 1862, and that term having expired with the 3d of March, 1865, if Mr. Lincoln had lived until the passage of this act, under it he would have had the power to remove Mr. Stanton, and any other of his cabinet officers whom he had not appointed in his second term, and this right passed to President Johnson.

There are several purposes apparent on the face of the civil-office-tenure bill:

1. That all officers appointed by and with the advice and consent of the Senate should hold their places until it should approve their removal.

2. That the cabinet officers of the President should be so far exceptional to this rule that all Presidents should have the privilege and the power to make one election for each of those offices.

3. That, having made a choice, he shall be held to it until the Senate shall have given him its consent to make another choice.

This arrangement in relation to the President and his cabinet was, doubtless, made upon some reasons; and all concede that it applies to every President chosen by the electoral college; and what reasons are there that make it necessary and proper for the administration of a President so elected that do not apply with equal force to one upon whom the Constitution has devolved the office on the death of a President with whom he was elected to the vice-presidency? The plain letter and meaning of the Constitution and this act of Congress assure this right to President Johnson, and it cannot be wrested from him without doing violence to both Constitution and law. If he had given in his adhesion, and plainly and palpably exercised this power for the benefit of the party which passed the law by removing one of his Secretaries who is opposed to that party, and had nominated to the place one of their faithful and trusted men, would his right to make the removal have been questioned?

After the best inquiry of which I am capable, I think these positions to be true beyond reasonable doubt:

1. That the President, by the well-settled principle of the Constitution, possesses, as one of his executive powers, the sole and exclusive power of removing all officers, as well when the Senate is in session as when it is not.

2. That the provision of the civil-office-tenure act, which requires the President to report to the Senate his removal of certain officers, and its advice and concurrence to make the removal complete and effective, is in derogation of that constitutional power of the President, and is, therefore, unconstitutional and void.

3. That the case of the removal of Stanton does not come within the provision, spirit, and meaning of the civil-office-tenure act.

4. That President Johnson had the power and the right to remove Stanton as Secretary of War; and having removed him, and thereby caused a vacancy, he had the power, under the act of 1795, and it was his duty, to supply that vacancy temporarily; and his designation of General Thomas to take charge of the office *ad interim* was a proper exercise of power. Consequently neither the removal of Stanton nor the *ad interim* appointment of Thomas by President Johnson was an impeachable offence, but a legitimate exercise of power.

There is then left for my examination only those articles of impeachment which embrace the matter of the conspiracies with General Thomas charged against the President. There is but one law of Congress against conspiracies, which was passed in 1861, and is in these words:

That if two or more persons within any State or Territory of the United States shall conspire together to overthrow or to put down or to destroy by force the government of the United States, or to levy war against the United States, or to oppose by force the authority of the government of the United States, or by force to prevent, hinder or delay the execution of any law of the United States, or by force to seize, take, or possess any property of the United States against the will or contrary to the authority of the United States, or by force or intimidation or threats to prevent any person from accepting or holding any office of trust or place of confidence under the United States, each and every person so offending shall be guilty of a high crime, and upon conviction thereof in any district or circuit court of the United States having jurisdiction thereof, or district or supreme court of any Territory of the United States having jurisdiction thereof, shall be punished by a fine not less than $500 and not more than $5,000, or by imprisonment, with or without hard labor, as the court shall determine, for a period not less than six months nor greater than six years, or by both such fine and imprisonment.

This was a war measure passed at the beginning of the rebellion, and was directed against rebels and traitors, and their abettors at that time and in the future. It was never intended, and is a perversion of that law to attempt to apply it to the case of removal by the President of an officer of the government, and his direction to the person whom he had designated to supply temporarily the vacancy to take possession of the office, and his application to the person removed to turn over to him the books, property, &c., appertaining to the office.

All the offences enacted by that law require, as an essential constituent of them, that the persons committing them shall conspire together to do the several acts which are made criminal with force or intimidation or threats; and in the absence of that purpose there is no crime. The charges against the President are, in the fourth article, that he did unlawfully conspire with one Lorenzo Thomas, and with other persons to the House of Representatives unknown, with intent, by intimidation and threats, unlawfully to hinder and prevent Edwin M. Stanton, Secretary of War, from holding said office; in the fifth article, that he did unlawfully conspire with one Lorenzo Thomas, and with other persons to the House of Representatives unknown, to prevent and hinder the execution of an act entitled "An act regulating the tenure of certain civil offices;" in the sixth article, that he did unlawfully conspire with one Lorenzo Thomas by force to seize, take, and possess the property of the United States in the Department of War; in the seventh article, that he did unlawfully conspire with one Lorenzo Thomas with intent unlawfully to seize, take, and possess the property of the United States in the Department of War.

As to the fifth and seventh articles, they charge no intent or purpose on the part of the President of doing the things therein specified with force, intimidation, or threats; which being of the essence of said offences and omitted, no offences are charged; and as to those articles, and also the fourth and sixth, there is no evidence that the President entered into any conspiracy with General Thomas, or any persons, to do the things set forth in said articles; or that he intended, advised, or sanctioned the use of any force, intimidation, or threats in doing them. The whole case against the President in connection with the matters charged in those four articles is, that he wrote a letter of the usual tenor to Mr. Stanton, removing him from the office of Secretary of War, and a letter to General Thomas, notifying him of his designation to supply the vacancy temporarily, and directing him to take charge of the office and enter upon its duties; all of which, by the Constitution and laws, he had the power and the right to do. There is no evidence that he intended, advised, or sanctioned the use of any force, intimidation, or threats in connection with these transactions. There is nothing in the case to sustain the fourth, fifth, sixth, and seventh articles, and with the others they all fall together.

Upon the grounds I have stated I reach the conclusion, that the defence of the President is full and complete; but there are other grave and weighty reasons why this court should not proceed to his conviction, that I will now proceed to consider.

The Senate is sitting as a court of impeachment, to try articles preferred by the House of Representatives against the President of the United States. Each member has taken a special oath prescribed by the Constitution, and in these words:

I solemnly swear that in all things appertaining to the trial of the impeachment of Andrew Johnson, President of the United States, now pending, I will do impartial justice according to the Constitution and the law: so help me God.

None of his acts can be considered but those which are set forth against him in the articles as offences, and he can be convicted only upon such as are defined and declared by the laws of the United States to be high crimes or misdemeanors, and which are in their nature and essence offences of that character. This court is bound to try these articles of impeachment by the same laws and rules of evidence, substantially, which would govern an ordinary criminal court on the trial of indictments against Andrew Johnson for the same offences—except in the matter of judgment against him, which here would be more grievous.

I will quote from Blackstone's Commentaries a fundamental principle, which is found in all works on criminal law, is recognized in every criminal court in America, and which should guide and control this court in the pending trial:

And as vicious will without a vicious act is no civil crime, so, on the other hand, an unwarrantable act without a vicious will is no crime at all. So that to constitute a crime against human laws there must be first a vicious will; and secondly, an unlawful act consequent upon such vicious will.

This principle, that to the unlawful act there must attach a criminal intent or purpose, which prompted the commission of the act, is the guiding light of all courts: a person doing the act charged to be a crime, in its absence, might be guilty, but it would be without criminality. The law generally infers the criminal intent from the unlawful act, but it always permits the accused party to show by proof the absence of the criminal intent, which is generally an easier task in relation to offences merely *mala prohibita*, than in those which are also *mala se*. All the offences charged against the President are merely and strictly *mala prohibita*.

If the civil-office-tenure bill on its face is so ambiguous and uncertain as not to inform an officer of government possessed of a good common understanding, with reasonable certainty, whether or not it did comprehend the case of Mr. Stanton, and forbid his removal from office by the President, that act being new and never having received a judicial construction; and Andrew Johnson was under trial on indictment in an ordinary criminal court for the violation of that act, in the removal of Mr. Stanton, the court on motion would instruct the jury to acquit.

If the question whether that act does not trench on a great constitutional power of the President, and is not therefore void, be one of doubt and difficulty, and President Johnson desired to have that question solved correctly, and to that end consulted the Attorney General and all the other members of his Cabinet, and their opinion was unanimous that it was unconstitutional; and he was counseled by them all, including Mr. Stanton, to veto the act upon that ground; and one of his purposes in removing Mr. Stanton was to make a case for the Supreme Court, in which its constitutionality should be decided, universal reason and justice would pronounce that, in writing his letter to Mr. Stanton dismissing him from office, the President had no criminal intent, and did not commit an impeachable offence.

The evidence on this point which the prosecution presented, and which was admitted without objection, would probably be sufficient with most minds to exculpate the President from all criminal intent; but the most satisfactory proof that could have been made upon it, and which was clearly competent, was the evidence of the members of the cabinet, which a majority of this court ruled it would not hear. A criminal court would not have excluded this evidence, or, if having done so inadvertently, on conviction by the jury, it would of its own motion award a new trial. In the face of so grave an error committed by this court, and affecting so materially the defence of the respondent, it would be a great wrong to him and the country to proceed to his conviction.

The powers of our government are carefully and wisely divided out among the three departments, and the lines of separation are in some cases so indistinct that it is difficult to avoid overstepping them. A just and patriotic President would not wilfully infringe the constitutional powers and rights of Congress;

nor would that body, if composed of such men, make any intentional aggression upon those confided to the President. I have observed no such disposition on the part of the present executive head; and the question between him and Congress, growing out of the civil-office-tenure bill, he desired to have submitted to and decided by the Supreme Court, as has been satisfactorily proved in this case. He took legal advice, and was informed that, under existing laws, he could not have any proceeding instituted to determine it, which could be taken to the Supreme Court and be tried by it until about the time or after the expiration of his presidential term. He had no remedy by which he could test the question in a reasonable time.

Congress and the President both should have desired and have sought the settlement of this, and all other questions of controverted power between them, by the judgment of that tribunal which the Constitution had designed for that purpose. In a few hours of any day, Congress could have framed and passed a law which would have enabled the Supreme Court summarily to have got possession of, and to decide promptly, this and all other questions between it and the President; and such settlement of the disputed boundaries of their respective powers would have been accepted by the people generally, and as to those questions would have given repose to the country, but instead of such wise and peaceful legislation, Congress was exhausting all its ingenuity and all its resources to make its aggressions upon the executive department successful and complete; and so to organize, fetter, and intimidate the Supreme Court, as to prevent it from interfering to perform its great office of settling such questions by the Constitution, law, and reason.

But Mr. Stanton sued out a criminal warrant against General Thomas to protect himself against intrusion into the War Office; and when the President heard of this proceeding he expressed his gratification, knowing that the question of the validity of his removal of Mr. Stanton would come up on the hearing of a writ of *habeas corpus* that might be sued out by General Thomas. The latter executed bond with surety to appear before Judge Cartter to answer the complaint of Stanton, and at the appointed time appeared before the judge with his surety, who surrendered him to the court. It was the plain duty of Judge Cartter to have ordered General Thomas into the custody of the marshal or to prison; but he did neither, because either would have been a restraint of his liberty and have made a ground for suing out a writ of *habeas corpus* for a judicial inquiry into the cause of his detention. The case, immediately after hearing by the judge before whom the writ might be returned, could be taken to the Supreme Court, heard at once, and the questions of right between Stanton and Thomas to the War Office and the constitutionality of the civil-office-tenure bill would be before the court for its decision.

This was the purpose of Thomas, and by this time it had become apparent; and the *impartial and patriotic* judge determined to defeat it by the disregard of his own official duty; and he refused to order Thomas into custody, and consequently there ceased to be any ground for Thomas to sue out a writ of *habeas corpus*. Here a corrupt judge revealed himself, and afforded to the House of Representatives an opportunity to impeach him for corruption in office, palpable and flagitious. But it was their bull that had gored the ox.

The purpose and desire of the President to have the question of the constitutionality of the civil-rights bill decided by the Supreme Court is manifest; that it and all other questions between them have not been submitted to that test is due to the default of Congress.

But the exclusion of important evidence by this court involves another and very grave error. The Constitution says of impeachment, "No person shall be convicted without the concurrence of two-thirds of the members present." *Convicted* does not mean *simply condemned*, for a man may be condemned of a crime without or against evidence; but *convicted* means *proved and determined to be guilty.* There may be *condemnation*, but cannot be *conviction* without *proof.* One of the necessary elements of *conviction* is evidence, and it might be impossible on all the evidence of the defence in a case, and yet practicable and easy upon the residue after excluding a material part of it. The exclusion of material evidence is a *part* of *conviction*, and may be *substantially* and practically the conviction.

But conviction is a totality, can exist only *in solido,* and in all its parts and processes, and as a whole, it requires two-thirds of the senators present. To demand two-thirds to *convict,* and to *permit* a majority to exclude all or a material part of the evidence which might produce conviction, would not only be a hollow mockery, but an absurdity and contradiction. The constitutional rule, which requires two-thirds to convict, by necessary implication, makes the same number necessary to rule out the defendant's evidence, in whole or part, and so produce conviction. If this court, by a majority of its members, had excluded the whole of the defendant's evidence, it would have shocked the country, and there would have been a general exclamation, that a rule of practice which would enable a bare majority indirectly to effect what a great constitutional principle required two-thirds to do, to convict in all cases of impeachment, was both mischievous and unsound. This court should correct this erroneous ruling of an important constitutional principle by its judgment in favor of the President.

There are still other cogent considerations against the impeachment of the President, one of the most weighty of which I made at the opening of the trial, and will here restate. This court is not constituted according to the requirements of the Constitution, and, therefore, is incompetent to try the case before it.

The Constitution provides that—

The Senate of the United States shall be composed of two senators from each State, chosen by the legislature thereof for six years; and each senator shall have one vote. * * * * No State, without its consent, shall be deprived of its equal suffrage in the Senate. * * * The Senate shall have the sole power to try all impeachments, &c.

Every State has an equal right to have two members of the Senate, and to choose them by her legislature, and to organize her government and elect that legislature by her own people, with whom rests her political power, without any dictation or interference by Congress. When a State has chosen her senators, and they apply at the bar of the Senate for admission as members, it is the right of the State and of her senators elect, if they have the qualifications required by the Constitution, to be admitted, and this body cannot, without violating it, keep them out. The Senate has the right to reject an applicant who does not present himself with qualifications, election, and return in conformity to the Constitution, but every one who comes so arrayed is entitled to admission.

In time of peace, when there is no rebellion or insurrection in a State against the United States, a majority or any number of the Senate or of the two houses of Congress have no right or power to deny to such or any State representation in them; and its exercise is destructive of the Constitution, and overthrows the government which it created. Such a power would at all times enable a faction, that happened to hold a majority in the two houses, to mutilate them at will, and control the whole government by excluding the senators and representatives from as many States as might be needful for their purposes. All this has been inaugurated and is in course of successful enactment by the dominant party.

When the rebellion was crushed out and those engaged in it made their submission, the Constitution, by its own force, reinstated the States involved in it *de jure* to their previous position in the Union, with all the rights and duties of the other States. They conformed their constitutions and governments, so far as they had been estranged by secession and rebellion, to the Constitution and government of the United States, and elected their senators and representatives.

Congress, by many of its laws, the Executive, by multitudinous appointments and other acts, and the Supreme Court, by hearing all cases coming up from them and allotting its members to hold circuit courts in them, recognize them as States; but still the Senate and House persisted in keeping out their senators and representatives. At length Tennessee extended the right of suffrage to her negro population, and disfranchised a large portion of her white men that had been implicated in the rebellion, and forthwith the majority in the two houses admitted her senators and representatives; but the other southern States continued to be contumacious on the vital, radical party question of negro suffrage, and therefore were continued to be denied their great constitutional right of representation in the two houses of Congress. It was thus demonstrated, that the cause of denying to the southern States representation in Congress, in violation of the Constitution, was their not having conferred the right to vote on their negro population, and that they were to continue unrepresented until they surrendered that point, or until means could be devised to fasten it upon them. A Senate from which almost one-third of its members is excluded, and who, if present, would probably differ from the majority of those here in their judgment of this important case, cannot form a constitutional court of impeachment for its trial.

The impeachment of the President of the United States is the arraignment of the executive department of the government by one branch of the legislative department and its trial by the other. The incongruity of such a responsibility had consequent danger of the ultimate subordination of the executive to the legislative department excited the gravest apprehensions of that wisest political sage, Mr. Madison, when the Constitution was being framed. Short of the sword, it is the extreme remedy, and was intended for the worst political disorders of the executive department. Nothing but treason, official bribery, or other high crimes and misdemeanors, made so by law, and also in their nature of deep moral turpitude, which are dangerous to the safety of the State, and which palpably disqualify and make unfit an incumbent to remain in the office of President, can justify its application to him. Cases that do not come up to this measure of delinquency, those who made the Constitution intended should be remedied in the frequency of our elections by the people at the ballot-box, and the public repose and welfare require that they should be referred to that most appropriate tribunal.

Impeachment was not intended to be used as an engine to gratify private malice, to avenge disappointed expectations, to forward schemes of personal ambition, to strengthen the measures or continue the power of a party, to punish partisan infidelity, to repress and crush its dissentions, to build up or put down opposing factions. By our system all that sort of work is to be done in popular canvasses; and to bring the great and extraordinary remedy of impeachment to do any of it, is the vile prostitution of what was intended to be a rare and august remedy for great evils of state.

The impeachment of a President of the United States, for a difference of political policy between him and Congress, is a monstrous perversion of power. Is the present prosecution anything but that? President Johnson and Congress agreed in their policy and measures to put down the rebellion, and they were signally successful; and after it was crushed out these departments of the government did many formal and important official acts relating to each and all of them engaged in the rebellion as States in the Union, and as having the same relations as the other States with the government of the United States.

Those States complied with conditions insisted upon both by the President and Congress, and by their constitutions and laws they respectively abolished slavery, renounced the principle of secession, repudiated their debts created by their rebellion, and ratified the 13th amendment of the Constitution, by which slavery was abolished throughout the United States. For the masses of the people of those States, the President thought all this was submission and expiation enough, and refused to insist that they should, in addition, confer on their late slaves, who in two States exceeded the whites, and in all of them were a large portion of the aggregate population, the right of suffrage, nor would he consent to unite in unconstitutional measures to force negro suffrage upon those States. This is the real head and front of the President's offending; he would not co-operate with the radicals in their scheme to get possession of and control the governments and all the political power of the southern States by the agency of voting negroes against the will of the white people, and to all their unconstitutional measures to effect it he opposed the power with which the Constitution had invested him.

A subordinate ground of their ire against the President was, that to many of the people of the southern States who were engaged in the rebellion he extended the magnanimity and clemency of the people of the United States in the exercise of the pardoning power, the noblest of all the great powers with which they have intrusted him. But there were no rebels, however vile, that were willing to become the liegemen of the radical party, whose pardon they did not favor; and they have trenched further upon the powers of the President by assuming that of pardon, in bills introduced in both houses to remove the disabilities of a great number of rebels, since become radicals. But it is time all were pardoned!

Among the many strange positions assumed by the prosecution are: 1. The President has no right to inquire into and act upon his conclusion that the civil-office-tenure act, or any other act of Congress, is unconstitutional. 2. That it was his duty to execute that act without any question of its constitutionality. 3. That this court of impeachment has no right or power to inquire into the constitutionality of that act.

The latter position is so palpably and flagitiously unsound as to deserve no other answer than a simple denial. The others are entitled to some consideration, though they are negatived by the Constitution itself, to prove which I will quote from it:

> This Constitution and the laws of the United States which shall be made in *pursuance thereof* * * * * shall be the supreme law of the land; and the judges in every State shall be bound thereby, anything in the constitutions or laws of any State to the contrary notwithstanding.
>
> The senators and representatives before mentioned, and the members of the several State legislatures, and all executive and judicial officers, both of the United States and of the several States, shall be bound by oath or affirmation to support this Constitution.
>
> The President, before he enter on the execution of his office, shall take the following oath or affirmation:
>
> I do solemnly swear (or affirm) that I will faithfully execute the office of President of the United States, and will to the best of my ability preserve, protect, and defend the Constitution of the United States.

The plain sequences of these provisions of the Constitution are some very important principles:

1. The Constitution is the paramount law of the land throughout the United States.

2. Every constitution and law of the States and every act of Congress, so far as they may be inconsistent with the Constitution of the United States, fall before its predominant authority and force, and from their origin are void and of no effect.

3. While it is the right of every citizen to oppose unconstitutional acts of Congress by every proper means, it is the especial duty of the President to make that resistance, as the chief executive officer of the government, who has taken an official oath before entering on the execution of his office that he will faithfully execute the office of President of the United States, and will to the best of his ability preserve, protect, and defend the Constitution of the United States. He has no more important duty to perform, and none more obligatory

upon him, than to preserve, protect, and defend the Constitution against all assailants, against Congress, and all comers. In doing this, he is not to make war, or any civil convulsion; but he is to resort to every appropriate means with which the Constitution and the laws have intrusted him; and none could be more fit than his removal of Mr. Stanton from office, with the purpose of making a case for the Supreme Court, in which the constitutionality of the civil-office-tenure bill should be decided by the tribunal appointed by the Constitution for the final judgment of all such questions.

The right of each department of the government to interpret and construe the Constitution for itself, and by it to determine the validity of all acts of Congress, within the scope of the performance of their respective functions in the government as to all questions not adjudged by the Supreme Court, has heretofore been a generally received principle, and has always been acted upon in the administration of the government. That a President was bound to execute an unconstitutional act of Congress without any question, until it was so decided by the Supreme Court, and by taking steps to have it subjected to that test committed an impeachable crime, is one of the absurd and mischievous heresies of this day.

In relation to this matter Mr. Madison so clearly expresses the true principles of the Constitution that I will dismiss it with a quotation from him, with the remark that the principles which he expresses have always been generally held by all the statesmen, courts, and jurists of America. Madison Papers, volume 4, page 394, dated in 1834, says:

As the legislative, executive, and judicial departments of the United States are co-ordinate, and each equally bound to support the Constitution, it follows that each must, in the exercise of its functions, be guided by the text of the Constitution according to its own interpretation of it; and consequently that in the event of irreconcilable interpretations the prevalence of the one or the other department must depend on the nature of the case as receiving the final decision from one or the other, and passing from that decision into effect without involving the functions of any other.

But notwithstanding this abstract view of the co-ordinate and independent right of the three departments to expound the Constitution, the judicial department most familiarizes to the public attention as the expositor, by the order of its functions in relation to the other departments, and attracts most the public confidence by the composition of the tribunal.

In the judicial department, in which constitutionality as well as legality generally find their ultimate discussion and operative decision; and the public deference to and confidence in the judgment of that body are peculiarly inspired by the qualities implied in its members, and by the gravity and deliberation of their proceedings, and by the advantage their plurality gives them over the unity of the executive department, and their firmness over the multitudinous composition of the legislative department.

Without losing sight, therefore, of the co-ordinate relations of the three departments to each other, it may always be expected that the judicial bench, when happily filled, will, for the reasons suggested, most engage the respect and reliance of the public as the surest expositor of the Constitution, as well in questions within its cognizance concerning the boundaries between the several departments of the government as in those between the Union and its members.

Mr. Chief Justice, I believe these propositions to be true:

1. The power of removal from office is an executive power, and is vested by the Constitution in the President solely; and, consequently, that so much of the act to regulate the tenure of certain civil offices as proposes to restrict the President's exercise of that power is unconstitutional and void.

2. That the case of Edwin M. Stanton, Secretary of War, does not come within the operation of that act, and it presented no obstruction to his removal by the President if constitutional.

3. That the removal of Stanton produced a vacancy in the office of Secretary of the Department of War, which the President was authorized by the laws of Congress to supply for six months, by the designation of any person to perform its duties for that period.

4. That there is no evidence that the President violated or attempted to violate the "act to define and punish certain conspiracies," the act which directs

"all orders and instructions relating to military operations by the President or Secretary of War to be issued through the General of the army, and in case of his inability through the next in rank," or the act "to provide for the more efficient government of the rebel States." And, moreover, I believe the two acts last referred to were in conflict with the Constitution and void and of no effect.

5. I believe the President has the same freedom of speech which the Constitution guarantees to every American citizen; and if he had not, he has been guilty of no such abuse of it as to constitute an impeachable offence.

Upon these propositions, the truth of which I do not doubt, I conclude that there is no ground whatever for the impeachment of the President, and pronounce my opinion that all the articles be dismissed.

In conclusion, I will express condemnation of the harsh spirit and flagrant violations of decorum with which this case has been prosecuted in court; and especially of the violent and unjustifiable denunciations and opprobrious epithets with which some of the managers have indulged themselves toward the respondent. Such exhibitions certainly do not commend proceedings by impeachment before the Senate of the United States to the respect and high consideration of our countrymen or the world.

OPINION OF MR. SENATOR CATTELL.

Having carefully considered the articles of impeachment preferred by the House of Representatives against Andrew Johnson, President of the United States, and the evidence adduced in support thereof, and having arrived at the conclusion that the charges contained in the leading articles are fully sustained by the proof, and that the acts therein charged and proved, being plain violations of the Constitution and of the laws of the United States, constitute a misdemeanor in office, I propose to state the grounds and reasons for the conclusion to which I have arrived.

If it may seem presumptuous for one uneducated in the law to deal with a question which has been illuminated by the discussions on either side of the most learned lawyers in the land, I may be permitted to say that, profoundly impressed with the gravity of the issue, and deeply sensible of the responsibility which rests upon each individual senator, I prefer to state for myself and in my own language the grounds upon which my verdict of *guilty* is given. I propose to confine my remarks chiefly to the consideration of the first three articles. Stripped of all technicality the following is the statement of the charges contained therein:

Article one charges the issuing of an order in writing for the removal of Edwin M. Stanton, Secretary for the Department of War, as contrary to the Constitution and laws, and especially as contrary to the act entitled "An act to regulate the tenure of certain civil offices," passed March 2, 1867.

Article two charges the issuing and delivery of a letter of authority to Lorenzo Thomas authorizing and empowering him to act as Secretary for the Department of War as a violation of the Constitution, and especially as contrary to the tenure-of-office law.

Article three charges that Thomas was appointed without authority of law, without the advice and consent of the Senate and while it was in session, when no vacancy had happened during the recess of the Senate, and no vacancy existed at the time, with intent to violate the Constitution.

The second and third articles, charging in special and general terms the appointment of Thomas as a violation of law, may, I think, be held to present two distinct aspects of criminality, namely, the unlawful appointment, and the unlawful removal which was declared in the letter, and which is implied in, and is of necessity accomplished by, the unlawful appointment; and they are sustained if it is shown that the appointment of Thomas alone is unlawful, or if it is shown that it was unlawful as including the removal of Stanton, so that the two acts taken together were criminal; for the appointment to an office thereby unlawfully vacated includes all the criminality of an unlawful removal.

But I propose to consider, first, the charge contained in the first article; viz., the issuing of the unlawful order for the removal of Mr. Stanton. The fact that the order was issued is proved, and indeed is admitted, in the answer of the respondent. The inquiry then is, Was the removal of Mr. Stanton an act contrary to the Constitution or laws of the United States? If it was, then it was clearly a misdemeanor in office.

The Constitution gives no such power of removal directly to the President, and the advocates of such a power can claim it only as derived by implication from that clause which affirms that "the executive power shall be vested in the President."

Now, if we assume that the laws regulating and restricting the power of removal, which have been passed from time to time, including the tenure-of-office act, are constitutional, and that the power is subject to legislative control, then this power cannot be held to be a quality inherent in the *executive* power as conferred on the President by the Constitution. If such a power ever existed as an element of constitutional executive power, it could not be curtailed or restricted by legislative enactment; but it is restricted by these acts; and if they are admitted to be valid laws, which hitherto has not been denied, the existence of the absolute power of removal as an essential executive quality is concluded.

All the implications of the Constitution are against the idea that this power is in the President. The fact that the power of appointment is given by the Constitution to the President and Senate jointly, would seem to deny him the power to vacate an office which he could not alone fill, and create a vacancy which he cannot alone supply. The provision that he may fill vacancies "*that may happen during the recess of the Senate,*" and then only until the next session, would seem to deny him the power to fill any vacancies other than those which *happen*, or to fill *any* at any time other than "*during the recess of the Senate.*" A thing happens, in the largest sense that can be given to that term, when it comes to pass not by the motion of the person whose action is affected by the happening. A vacancy does not *happen* when it occurs by the action of him who is to fill it.

This clause then does not provide for the filling of vacancies which are *made* by removals, but confines the President's power to other vacancies, even in recess, and implies that there shall be no removals unless the Senate is in session and advise and consent.

The President then derives *from the Constitution* no power of vacating by removal, except by the nomination, confirmation, and appointment of a successor. Whatever of other power of removal is rightfully exercised by him has been derived from the terms or implications of legislative enactment. Assumed necessity or convenience have conceded to him the power during the recess of Congress, but neither the language nor the implications of legislative enactments have extended the power; necessity or convenience do not demand, nor has precedent sanctioned, its exercise at any other time.

The case of Pickering, the only one cited which has any similarity with the case under consideration, does not make against the principle contended for. The fact that an immediate nomination to the Senate was stated in the President's letter to Mr. Pickering to be necessary, and the fact that it does not appear that the nomination of his successor did not precede the letter informing him of his removal, together with the fact that it has never, through sixty-eight years of immensely increased patronage, been drawn into a precedent for the exercise of such executive power, show that the real circumstances of the case were not such as to assert any executive claim to this power.

But even if they were such, a single act, standing alone, and never repeated, through a long lapse of years crowded with similar occasions, should have no weight as a precedent in favor of the principle which it seems to illustrate, but on the contrary it may be inferred that the act was not accepted as correct practice at the time; that the principle was disapproved of and the practice ever since discontinued. Thus it appears to me that even before the passage of the "tenure-of-office law," or even if Mr. Stanton's case is not included in it, the removal charged in the first article was an act unauthorized by the Constitution or the law, principle or precedent.

I am not unaware of the fact that the views which I have thus briefly stated, questioning the President's power of removal, as a constitutional prerogative in the absence of legislative enactment, are controverted by many. Differences of opinion on this point exist now as they did at the time of the adoption of the Constitution, and among the distinguished men of the first Congress. An examination of the debates which took place in the Congress of 1789 upon the acts establishing the several departments, will show that the eminent statesmen of that day differed widely in their construction of the Constitution as to the President's power in this regard. But whatever differences of opinion may have existed then, or may exist now upon this point, one thing is clear, the power has been considered a proper subject for legislative construction from the time of the first Congress down to the present day, and it is too late now to question the right of legislative control over the subject.

Mr. Manager Bingham quotes the authority of Webster in proof of the position that the provisions of the acts of 1789, establishing the Departments of State and War, which provide an officer to have charge of the records, &c., "*whenever the said principal officer shall be removed from office by the President,*" was a grant of power, and from that day to this, Congress has exercised the power to grant and to regulate the power of the Executive in this particular, and the right has never been seriously questioned or the constitutionality of the laws doubted.

In pursuance of this practice, the thirty-ninth Congress passed March 2, 1867, the act entitled "An act to regulate the tenure of certain civil offices," which covers the whole question of removal from and appointment to office in all cases not specially provided for by the Constitution. This law, framed to restrain the President in the exercise of the lesser power of arbitrary removal during the recess, certainly by its spirit, scope and object, intends to deny and most clearly in all its terms and implications does deny and conclude the larger power of arbitrary removal "*during the session of the Senate.*" Let us examine the provisions for a moment in their bearing on this case. The terms of the law define in strict language the limits of executive authority on this subject. Its passage over the veto of the President by two-thirds of both houses of Congress, exhausted all right to question its constitutionality by the Executive, whose duty thenceforward was to execute it as a law of the land.

I shall then assume for the purposes of this statement that it is a valid and constitutional law in all its parts, and that the President knew and understood that it had been so declared with express view to his executive action, and that he knew if he violated it he was directly attacking a legislative power which the representatives of the people claimed and meant to assert.

The only remaining inquiry upon this particular question is, does the law apply to Secretary Stanton's case?

If the removal of Mr. Stanton was against the provisions of this law the President is guilty under it, for the only *intent* in question *is the intent to break the law*, not the motive or intention with which it was done. If Mr. Stanton is included among the officers referred to in the first section of this law, then his removal without the advice and consent of the Senate was against its provisions. The language of this section is—

That *every person* holding *any* civil office to which he has been appointed, by and with the advice and consent of the Senate, and every person who shall hereafter be appointed to any such office, and shall become duly qualified to act therein, is and shall be entitled to hold such office until a successor shall have been in like manner appointed and duly qualified, except as herein otherwise provided: *Provided*, That the Secretaries of State, of the Treasury, of War, of the Navy, and of the Interior, the Postmaster General, and the Attorney General, shall hold their offices respectively for and during the term of the President by whom they may have been appointed, and one month thereafter, subject to removal by and with the advice and consent of the Senate.

Now it seems irresistible that this language, referring as it does to those in office at the time of its passage, as well as those thereafter to be appointed, includes either in the general provisions of the body of the section, or in the exception, all persons holding any civil office appointed with the consent of the Senate. The words "*every person* holding *any* civil office," are as comprehensive as language can make them, and, in the absence of any exception, would include all, and of course Mr. Stanton.

But the fact that there is an exception makes even this strong language more comprehensive than before; for when an exception is mentioned, the conclusion is strengthened that nothing is left outside of the general provisions except what is included in the exceptions. Thus the words "all" and "except," in construction include everything.

Besides, the express language of the general clause provides for *all* civil officers thus appointed, *except* such as are affirmatively otherwise provided for "herein;" that is, in the law itself. This shows that the law undertakes affirmatively to provide "therein" for *every* such officer. It thus expressly says that *all* are included and provided for in the general clause for whom there is not some other affirmative provision made in the proviso. Thus no officer or class is left out of the law by implication, for it declares substantially that every one excluded from the exception by its language or by implication, is not taken by the exception out of the effect of the general clause. To say then that Mr. Stanton's case is not provided for in the exception, is to affirm that it is included in the general clause. It matters not, for the purpose of this trial, whether the case of Mr. Stanton comes under the general clause or the exception. The reasoning is strong that the case is included in the exception. The words of the exception are: "*may have been* appointed." These words seem to contemplate, in relation to the tenure of these offices, the possible existence of the term of a President other than the one who may be actually in office when the question of removal arises. The act took effect upon offices as they existed at the time it passed, and when it referred to terms during which they were, after its passage, to expire, it referred to the term then existing and to those which should occur in the future.

By the Constitution the *term* of the President continues "during four years.". The word *term* means strictly limit or boundary. A term of office is the time which must elapse before its limit is reached. The limit of Mr. Lincoln's second term was four years from the 4th of March, 1865. When the word term was used in the act, this was the term contemplated in regard to offices filled by him, and still held by his appointees at the time of its passage. This term did not expire on the 21st of February, and has not yet expired. If Mr. Lincoln had been living when the act was passed it would certainly have been held to apply to his present term, as it then existed, and to extend the offices to the end of it. It is not the less Mr. Lincoln's term that it was also Mr. Johnson's, who was, in the language of the Constitution, chosen "for the same term." When, upon Mr. Lincoln's death, Mr. Johnson came in, the powers and duties of the office devolved upon him for the *remainder* of *Mr. Lincoln's term*. He had no other relation to the term, and no more or other power in relation to the officers he found in, than Mr. Lincoln would have had had he lived. It matters not, as I have said, whether these views prevail or not. If they do not, it only shows that Mr. Stanton's case is not provided for in the proviso, for the reason that the term of the President by whom he was appointed had already lapsed, and, therefore, the terms of the limitation of the proviso cannot be made to apply to his case, and that not being "otherwise provided for therein" is not included in the exception, and, therefore, is included in the general clause; for every case not therein otherwise provided for is covered by the general clause.

Again, the second section of the act, which applies to all officers, (except certain classes in relation to whom the Constitution prescribes otherwise, viz: the judges of the United States courts,) and contains no other exception of any officer, of course included Mr. Stanton. The very fact that this section excepts by this special exception only such officers confirmed by the Senate as are placed out of its reach, shows that it was intended to affect all within its reach. By its express terms it enacts that the President, within the limits and in the manner therein prescribed, may, "*during a recess of the Senate, suspend*" an officer, in the case therein mentioned, "and in no other." This section reads as follows:

SEC. 2. *And be it further enacted,* That when any officer appointed as aforesaid, excepting judges of the United States courts, shall, during a recess of the Senate, be shown, by evidence satisfactory to the President, to be guilty of misconduct in office, or crime, or for any reason shall become incapable or legally disqualified to perform its duties, in such case, and in no other, the President may suspend such officer and designate some suitable person to perform temporarily the duties of such office until the next meeting of the Senate, and until the case shall be acted upon by the Senate, and such person so designated shall take the oaths and give the bonds required by law to be taken and given by the person duly appointed to fill such office; and in such case it shall be the duty of the President, within twenty days after the first day of such next meeting of the Senate, to report to the Senate such suspension, with the evidence and reasons for his action in the case, and the name of the person so designated to perform the duties of such office. And if the Senate shall concur in such suspension, and advise and consent to the removal of such officer, they shall so certify to the President, who may thereupon remove such officer, and, by and with the advice and consent of the Senate, appoint another person to such office. But if the Senate shall refuse to concur in such suspension, such officer so suspended shall forthwith resume the functions of his office, and the powers of the person so performing its duties in his stead shall cease, and the official salary and emoluments of such officer shall, during such suspension, belong to the person so performing the duties thereof, and not to the officer so suspended: *Provided, however,* That the President, in case he shall become satisfied that such suspension was made on insufficient grounds, shall be authorized, at any time before reporting such suspension to the Senate as above provided, to revoke such suspension and reinstate such officer in the performance of the duties of his office.

It will be seen that this section operates in connection with the other sections of the law to prescribe the President's relations to offices which are not vacant. I say in connection with the other sections of the law, because the law must always be construed as a whole, and a particular section must be construed in relation to the other sections. It is also true, of course, that the act only operates upon what the Constitution does not itself fix, and only so far as legislative enactment may. Now, the President's relations to offices for the purpose of *absolute removal* are fixed by the first section of the act, in accordance with the provisions of the Constitution. This section provides in effect that there shall be *no absolute removal* of the officers therein included except by nomination and confirmation of a successor. This operates to confine *absolute* removals to times when the Senate is in session. This being fixed, the President's relations to officers during the recess of the Senate is provided for in the second section. This second section, in enacting "that when any officer," &c., "shall during the recess of the Senate be shown," &c., "in such case and in no other" the President may "suspend," prescribes three governing things which are each essential elements of "such case" and of the action prescribed in regard to it:

First. That "during the recess of the Senate" the President shall do nothing more in relation to any office than "*suspend*" in the manner provided for in this act.

Second. That "during the recess of the Senate" he may act in "such case" as is provided in the act, but "in no other." This is an essential element of his relations to the offices "during the recess of the Senate," as prescribed by the act.

Third. That there shall be no suspension even, except "*during the recess of the Senate*," for it is an essential element of "such case" that it shall be during recess.

Now, the fact that this second section, which does not refer to any officers other than those referred to in the first section, but assumes to prescribe for *all* officers under the circumstances not provided for in the first section—that is, during the recess—is without any exception which would exclude Mr. Stanton, seems to be conclusive that he is not omitted in the first section, which covers the time of the session; for why make the second section broader than the first, and restrain the President's power over Mr. Stanton during recess and leave him unprotected during the session of the Senate?

Then, the *third* section of the act, supplementary to the first and second sections, prescribes in respect to the filling of offices in case of the *happening of a vacancy* during the recess of the Senate, and the condition of these offices after the constitutional power of the President in relation to them has been exhausted. The third section reads as follows:

SEC. 3. *And be it further enacted*, That the President shall have power to fill all vacancies which may happen during the recess of the Senate by reason of death or resignation, by granting commissions which shall expire at the end of their next session thereafter. And if no appointment, by and with the advice and consent of the Senate, shall be made to such office so vacant or temporarily filled as aforesaid during such next session of the Senate, such office shall remain in abeyance, without any salary, fees, or emoluments attached thereto, until the same shall be filled by appointment thereto, by and with the advice and consent of the Senate; and during such time all the powers and duties belonging to such office shall be exercised by such other officer as may by law exercise such powers and duties in case of a vacancy in such office.

Thus it will be perceived that these three sections of this act, taken together, provide, subject to the provisions of the Constitution, a *general rule* of governmental action, and thus, while the letter of the first section includes, as certainly as general language can, the case of Mr. Stanton, an examination of the tenor and effect of the whole law confirms this construction. It would, upon every principle of legal construction, require an express exception to take an officer outside of the terms of a law intended as a general rule. On no principle can this be done by implication. Implication avails only where the letter of the law is doubtful, and its spirit, as derived from the law itself, would require an exception to some general provision. This law then covers, and was intended to cover, in connection with the provisions of the Constitution, every possible condition of offices, and to apply to all without exception.

If this law provides, wherever the Constitution does not, a general rule in relation to all offices, it repeals, to its extent, all former laws, and destroys the effect of all previous customs, rules, or precedents; and if it provides such general rule in relation to all conditions of offices, without exception, it covers the subject-matter of all former laws on the same subject, and overlies and repeals them.

It is apparent, then, that after the passage of this act, the whole law in relation to both removals and appointments of civil officers requiring confirmation was to be found in the Constitution and the tenure-of-office act. These together constitute the general governing rule of action on this subject, and all lawful action must be under and in accordance with it, and any official act in disregard of or contrary to it is a violation of law and a *misdemeanor in office*.

That the President understood that this was the effect of the tenure-of-

office law is conclusively apparent. His action in August last in regard to Mr. Stanton, and his suspension from office, was had under the second section of this law, otherwise it could not lawfully have been had at all, for that section prescribes when and how the suspension may be made, and *forbids* one under *all* other circumstances.• The President acted strictly under the provisions of this law: first, in the form of the suspension; second, in the authorization of General Grant; third, in the notice to the Secretary of the Treasury; fourth, in his report to the Senate. Indeed, how could he intend, as he claims that he did intend, to test in the courts the constitutionality of the law by the removal of Mr. Stanton, if he thought his case was not included in the law?

Again, by the second section, which applies without question to Mr. Stanton, the President was not authorized "during the recess of the Senate" to "remove" him; he was only authorized and only claimed to be authorized to "suspend" him, although it was during the recess. Now, upon whatever implication of constitution or law the power of removal or suspension is assumed for him, that implication is certainly, on principle and precedent, stronger in favor of the power during a recess of the Senate than during its session. Upon what principle, then, in view of the authoritative declaration of Congress that he may only *suspend* an officer "during the recess," can he claim to *remove* him during the session?

But again, this second section in terms settles the question of removal against him. The section is admitted to include Mr. Stanton within its general provisions. It provides that the President may, under certain circumstances, suspend an officer during the recess. This he did. It provides that, having done so, he shall, when the session occurs and within a limited time after its commencement, report the suspension, with his reasons, to the Senate. This he also did. It also provides that, if the Senate shall concur and advise and consent, and so certify, he may "*thereupon* remove." It will be observed that this is during the session of the Senate, and that the removal is only to be made upon the advice and consent of the Senate. He may remove him "*thereupon*," that is, *not otherwise*. In Mr. Stanton's case the Senate did not concur, and the condition of his removal being wanting, the President could not remove him, but under the provisions of this section he "forthwith resumed the functions of his office." He holds his office then by the provisions of this law, contained in a section which certainly applies to him, contrary to the will of the President, under the action of the Senate, which is thus by law made capable of preventing his removal. Why should he so hold it, and why is this power declared by law to be in the Senate, and the President's power thus restrained, if the President may the next moment remove him without the consent and despite the action of the Senate? And does not this show that this law is intended to comprehend the whole subject-matter, and to regulate in all respects the power of the President in this regard? Is it not conclusive that *all* power of suspension and removal, except by nomination and confirmation, under the Constitution, is exhausted by these proceedings? What becomes of the claimed implication of a power of removal in the President, without precedent, or even with precedent, in the face of the irresistible language and implication of this law, that the Senate must concur in all removals, and that any removal without such concurrence is a direct defiance of the legislative authority and a misdemeanor in office?

The remaining question on these three articles is, was the appointment of Thomas, as set out in the *second* and *third* articles, an act authorized either by the Constitution or by law? If not, then these articles are sustained.

A general power of appointment by the Executive, by and with the advice and consent of the Senate, a special power himself to fill vacancies "*which may happen*" during the recess, and the power to appoint inferior officers where such power has been given him by legislative enactment—these comprise all the authority of the President for this purpose, given in or to be derived from the Constitution.

Whatever rightful authority, then, was exercised by the President in making this appointment to the War Department, must have been derived from the express terms of some legislative enactment.

By the eighth section of the act of 1792, making alterations in the Treasury and War Departments, it is *made lawful* for the President, in case of the death, sickness, or absence of the Secretary, to authorize some person to perform the duties of the office until a successor is appointed in case of death, or the absence or inability from sickness shall cease. The only actual vacancy contemplated by this act is one *happening by death*.

The act of 1795, amendatory of the last mentioned act, declares, generally, that in every case of vacancy in the department "*it shall be lawful*" for the President to authorize any person to perform the duties of the office until a successor be appointed, " provided that no one vacancy shall be supplied in manner aforesaid for a longer term than six months." This act contemplates lawful vacancies only, for none other are vacancies which can be lawfully filled. We have already seen that the President could not lawfully make a vacancy without the concurrence of the Senate while it was in session to take concurrent action; and to claim that the President is authorized by this act to make an appointment to a vacancy made during a session of the Senate by his separate action, is simply begging the whole question. If there was no lawful vacancy, it could not lawfully be filled, and there is nothing in the law which makes any vacancy lawful which was not lawful before its passage. By the act of February 20, 1863, it is *made* lawful for the President, in case of the death, resignation, sickness, or absence of the head of any executive department, to authorize the head or other officer of one of the departments to perform the duties " until a successor is appointed, or such absence or inability by sickness shall cease."

This was the condition of the law before the passage of the " tenure-of-office act."

The act of 1792 had been superseded by the act of 1795, and this had been followed in turn by the act of 1863. This last act was, I doubt not, *intended* to supersede the act of 1795, as it provides that the vacancies to which it applies shall be filled with a select class of persons, and there could have been no reason why all vacancies in the same office, however produced, should not be filled by the same select class. The act appears to be intended to provide for the temporary supplying of all vacancies in the offices referred to, and, by omitting from its list of vacancies *vacancies by removal*, it seems, by its later implication, to conclude the President's power of removal, as derived from the implications of the earlier laws of 1789, creating the departments.

But if it is conceded that the President retained the power of removal, during the recess, after the passage of the act of 1863, it must also be conceded that the act of 1863 did not cover all the subject-matter of the act of 1795, and does not, therefore, completely supersede it. It will be seen that none of these laws affirmatively recognize or imply a power of removal in the President during the session of the Senate, and consequently they give him no power of appointment to a vacancy *made* by him at such time, while not one precedent can be found that goes to this extent, so that this power is claimed contrary to the necessary implications of the Constitution, and without authority either of law or precedent. But the tenure-of-office act clearly covers and regulates this whole subject-matter, and supersedes the previous laws, including the act of 1795. We have already seen that this act applies to this case.

The second section certainly does apply, and if the vacancy which is said to exist in the War Department is claimed to have been made " during a recess" in August last, it must have been under that section, for it provides that "during the recess of the Senate" vacancies shall only be made by the President by suspension, and that no suspension shall be had, except in a case made under its provisions, and that "*in such case, and in no other,*" the President may designate a suitable person temporarily to perform the duties; but if the Senate does not consent, the suspended officer shall "*forthwith resume the functions of his office*." So if the vacancy was made in vacation, that vacancy no longer existed after the refusal of the Senate to consent to it, and the appointment of Thomas was without authority of law. But the terms of the President's letter of February 21st to Mr. Stanton assume that he was then in office, and was thereby removed "during the session of the Senate." We have already seen that all removals at such times are regulated by the first section of the tenure-of-office act, and that the case of Stanton is included by its provisions; but by that section all temporary or *ad interim* appointments to the offices referred to therein are abolished, and the officer appointed by and with the advice and consent of the Senate is "entitled to hold" his office until a successor shall have been appointed "in like manner," that is, with the concurrence of the Senate. The appointment of Thomas was not "in like manner."

It will also be perceived that the words in the body of the first section, immediately preceding the proviso, are "*except as herein otherwise provided.*" This language refers to the whole act. Its meaning is except as is otherwise provided in this act. Now the term of office, and the manner of removal from and appointment to office, are distinct propositions contained in the body of the section. The proviso relates only to the term of the officers therein named; but that part of the subject-matter of the general clause which provides how the *successors* of all civil officers requiring confirmation shall be appointed, viz: by and with the advice and consent of the Senate, is not affected by the proviso.

This subject is not "*otherwise provided for*" in that proviso in relation to any officers, and the provision of the general clause in relation to it is not restricted by the terms or implications of the proviso.

To take the *officers* mentioned in the exception *wholly* outside of the provisions of the general clause, which covers other subject-matter besides that covered by the exception, the language must have been, except the *officers* hereinafter mentioned, or something of like effect. Thus whether Mr. Stanton's case, as far as relates to the tenure of his office, is within the general clause, or the exception of this section, or within neither, his *successor's* case is clearly within the general clause, and no one can be lawfully appointed to succeed him except "*in like manner,*" as he was himself appointed, that is, with the concurrence of the Senate.

Again, the reasoning on the spirit of the second section of the act is irresistible. Does it not seem a ridiculous claim that the President may "during a session of the Senate" appoint a successor or *locum tenens* of any kind for an officer whom the Senate has just, under express authority of law, refused to remove, and who has just, under like authority, resumed the functions of his office!

The appointment of Thomas, then, was unauthorized by any law, and was an unlawful attempt by the exercise of usurped executive power to seize upon and control a most important department of the government, in violation of express legislative enactment.

This crime, so clearly shown, is really a higher and more dangerous one than the removal of Stanton, for it not only includes the unlawful removal, but is in itself an affirmative, while the other is, in some sense, but a negative act of usurpation.

Whatever plea of misinformation, mistake, or absence of intent may be set up by his friends or his counsel, the President makes no such plea. He has claimed and does claim in his answer, and by the lips of his special representatives among the counsel, that he has removed Mr. Stanton and appointed Thomas by virtue of power vested in him as the Chief Executive, notwithstanding the tenure-of-office act. And it is proved that he intends to carry out his attempt should this trial result in his favor. By a verdict of acquittal, then, the Senate must either recede from their position on this act, or must submit that the President may defy its spirit and violate its express provisions with impunity.

In the consideration of this question I have assumed the constitutionality of the tenure-of-office act. I cannot consent to even consider this a debatable point. The Senate has solemnly adjudicated this question for itself on four distinct occasions, each individual senator acting under the obligation of an oath as solemn and binding as that administered at the commencement of this trial, of the solemnity of which we have been so often reminded by the counsel for the President. First, by the passage of the bill in question, after a full discussion of its provisions, by a vote of 29 yeas to 9 nays. Secondly, the bill having been submitted to the President for his approval, and returned to the Senate with his objections in an elaborate veto message arguing against the constitutionality of the measure, the Senate again passed the bill in the face of the arguments submitted, by a vote of more than two-thirds of the members present and voting. Upon the question "Shall the bill pass, the objections of the President to the contrary notwithstanding?" the vote was as follows:

YEAS—Messrs. Anthony, Cattell, Chandler, Conness, Cragin, Edmunds, Fessenden, Fogg, Foster, Fowler, Frelinghuysen, Grimes, Harris, Henderson, Howard, Kirkwood, Lane, Morgan, Morrill, Nye, Poland, Pomeroy, Ramsey, Ross, Sherman, Sprague, Stewart, Sumner, Trumbull, Van Winkle, Wade, Willey, Williams, Wilson, Yates—35.

NAYS—Messrs. Buckalew, Cowan, Davis, Dixon, Doolittle, Hendricks, Johnson, Nesmith, Norton, Patterson, Saulsbury—11.

Thirdly, the Senate recognized the validity of this law when, in response to the message of the President communicating the fact that he had "during the recess" suspended Mr. Stanton, the Senate took action, under and in accordance with the said law, and after due consideration refused to concur in the suspension of that officer, and informed the President thereof. Fourthly, when the President, after having exhausted all legal means to displace this faithful and efficient officer, and rid himself of what his counsel chooses to call "*a thorn in his heart*," deliberately, wilfully, and knowingly violated the provisions of this act by the arbitrary removal or attempted removal of Mr. Stanton and the appointment of Lorenzo Thomas, and defiantly flaunted his action in the face of the Senate, this body again reaffirmed the validity of the tenure-of-office act by declaring that the action of the President was without lawful authority.

I submit, then, that the tenure-of-office bill, having been passed over the President's veto by a vote of two-thirds of both houses, by express provision of the Constitution "*it became a law;*" *a law* to the President, and *a law* to all the people; *a law* as valid and binding as any on the statute-book; and I cannot believe that the Senate will consent to stultify itself by the admission that its oft-repeated action upon this bill was in violation of the Constitution, which each member had solemnly sworn to support.

Moreover, the President himself recognized the validity of the law by taking action under its provisions in the suspension of Mr. Stanton, as I have already shown in the course of this argument. Upon what principle may he consider a law valid and binding to-day and of no force or effect to-morrow? The law was sufficient so long as he thought he could accomplish his purpose to get rid of Mr. Stanton under it; but when he failed in this by the refusal of the Senate to concur in the proposed removal, he overrides the law, and then attempts to shelter himself, when arraigned for the offence, under the plea that it is not a constitutional law.

But admitting for the sake of argument that there were doubts as to the constitutionality of the law, who clothed Andrew Johnson with judicial power to settle that question? Under what clause of the Constitution does he presume to derive the power to decide which of the enactments of Congress are valid and binding and which are not? If he may exercise judicial functions in regard to one law, why not in regard to all laws? As I read the Constitution, the President is enjoined to "take care that *the laws* be faithfully executed." I find no provision in that instrument which clothes him with the more than regal power to decide *which* laws he will execute and *which* he will not.

If judicial power is a prerogative of the Executive, of what use is the Supreme Court? Why not abolish so useless an institution? Nay, more, if a law of Congress, though passed by the constitutional vote of two-thirds of both houses, may not "*become a law*" unless it meets the sanction of the executive—if he may suspend or virtually repeal by rendering inoperative the enactments of Congress, why not abolish the legislative department of the government?

It may be that Andrew Johnson is wiser than the Senate and House of Representatives; it may be that wisdom dwells with him, and will die with him; it may be unfortunate that the Constitution under which we live has not given to him who claims to be its especial custodian and guardian, the more than imperial power to make the laws and judicially pass upon them, as well as the duty to take care that they "be faithfully executed;" but, in my judgment, the American people will be slow in arriving at any such conclusion. So monstrous a proposition as that which virtually surrenders to one man all the power of our great government is not worthy of serious consideration.

Mr. President, for the first time in the history of our government we are confronted with a clear, decided and flagrant act of executive usurpation. For his offence against the majesty of the law the House of Representatives, in accordance with the provisions of the Constitution, and in the name of all the people of the United States, have impeached Andrew Johnson for high crimes and misdemeanors, and have brought him to the bar of the Senate to answer to the charges exhibited against him. The issues involved in these proceedings are of the gravest character, reaching down to the very foundation of our system of government, and it behooves us as the representatives of forty million of people to see to it that impartial justice is done as between the people and the accused. If this, the highest tribunal of the nation, shall render a verdict of acquittal, it will be a virtual admission of the President's assertion of "the power at any and all times of removing from office all executive officers for cause to be judged by the President alone." It will be a complete surrender of the constitutional power of the Senate over all appointments to office, for of what practical value will be the required advice and consent of the Senate to an appointment, if the person so appointed may the next hour be removed by the action of the Executive alone, regardless of, and, indeed, in despite of the wishes of the Senate?

It will, moreover, be a virtual surrender of what has been claimed from the origin of the government to this day, the right to regulate and control, by legislative enactment, the executive power over removals from office of such officers as require confirmation by the Senate, and it will give to the President the unrestrained control of the officers of the army and navy, as well as those of the civil service.

It will give license to Andrew Johnson and all future occupants of the presidential office to disregard at pleasure the enactments of the legislative department, and to plead in justification that you have so ruled by your verdict in this case.

It will tend to destroy the harmonious relations of the several departments of the government, so nicely adjusted, with checks and balances and limitations by the wisdom of the fathers of the Constitution, by increasing immensely the powers and privileges of the executive at the expense of the legislative department. Thenceforward the ruler will no longer be the servant of the people, but the people will be the servants of the ruler, and we shall not be able hereafter to say, in the sublime language of the martyred Lincoln, that ours is "a government of the people, by the people, and for the people."

Believing, as I conscientiously do, that such are the results which must follow the acquittal of Andrew Johnson by this tribunal, and believing that the House of Representatives have made good the material charges preferred against him, I cannot doubt as to my duty in the premises. I deeply regret that the necessity for these momentous proceedings has arisen. I would gladly have escaped the solemn responsibilities of this hour. But this may not be, and I must, therefore, upon the law and the evidence, in accordance with the dictates of my conscience, and in view of the solemn obligations of my oath, declare that in my judgment Andrew Johnson is guilty of high crimes and misdemeanors as charged by the representatives of the people.

OPINION OF MR. SENATOR TIPTON.

When the act regulating the tenure of civil offices passed Congress on the 2d day of March, 1867, Edwin M. Stanton was Secretary of War, having been appointed to said office by Mr. Lincoln and confirmed by the Senate January 15, 1862, and commissioned to hold the office "during the pleasure of the President of the United States for the time being." The first section of the act is as follows:

That every person holding any civil office to which he has been appointed, by and with the advice and consent of the Senate, and every person who shall hereafter be appointed to any such office, and shall become duly qualified to act therein, is and shall be entitled to hold such office until a successor shall have been in like manner appointed and duly qualified, except as herein otherwise provided: *Provided*, That the Secretaries of State, of the Treasury, of War, of the Navy, and of the Interior, the Postmaster General, and the Attorney General, shall hold their offices respectively for and during the term of the President by whom they may have been appointed, and one month thereafter, subject to removal by and with the advice and consent of the Senate.

Before the passage of the above-recited section the only limit to a Secretary's term was the *pleasure* of the President; but it was determined to make the termination definite, and hence we have a time specified beyond which it could not extend, namely, *one month* after the expiration of the term of the President by whom appointed.

The question relative to the Secretary of the Interior to be settled would be, how long will his commission run? while the answer would be just one month after the termination of the term of Mr. Johnson, by whom he was, by the advice and consent of the Senate, appointed. So his term would expire on the 4th day of April, 1869, which would be the end of one month after the expiration of Mr. Johnson's term, in case he filled the full unexpired term of Mr. Lincoln. He being in office on the 2d of March, 1867, under a commission which was a precise copy of Mr. Stanton's, I would look *forward*, not *backward*, to find the period of time when the law would put an end to his term of office, unless sooner removed by and with the advice and consent of the Senate.

To find the limit of Mr. Stanton's term I would look *forward* also, and as he is serving with the Secretary of the Interior, upon the *same term*, and under the same identical commission, I would declare him liable to removal by force of law, just as soon as one month shall have passed after the expiration of the term, which is being served out alike by himself and the Secretary of the Interior.

To the objection that the Secretary of the Interior was appointed by Mr. Johnson, and is serving out his term, while Mr. Stanton was appointed by Mr. Lincoln, whose term had expired nearly two years before the date of the act limiting terms, I reply that the terms of these Secretaries are one and the same, and there is no period of time subsequent to the date of the act which one Secretary shall retire in advance of another.

In regard to Mr. Stanton's term having expired according to the limitations of this law, one month after the death of Mr. Lincoln, I deny the proposition.

First, because the law was not in existence until about two years subsequent to that event. Second, because it could not, on the 2d day of March, 1867, act back and produce a vacancy in an office already filled, every act of which has been regarded valid by every branch of the government. Third, because Mr. Stanton has been in office ever since the date of the law, and is still performing the functions of Secretary of War. As Mr. Johnson received from Mr. Lincoln the War Office with its Secretary, just as he received each one of the other departments of government with its Secretary, each and all of them with subsequent appointments must be regarded as of his own appointment, for all purposes of the civil-tenure act; and as it is impossible to remove a portion in the past and the balance in the future, they must all share the same fate and be subject to the same limitations.

Hereafter there will be no trouble in construing the law, for one month subsequent to the termination of a President's term will vacate every secretaryship; and if this act had been in force at the time of Mr. Lincoln's death Mr. Johnson would have had all the heads of departments at his disposal one month thereafter. To claim, therefore, that Mr. Johnson can remove Mr. Stanton without the advice and consent of the Senate is to affirm an impossibility, inasmuch as the only period of time at which a President can get clear of a Secretary, independent of the Senate, is at the end of a month subsequent to the end of a President's term. And unless Mr. Johnson will receive a re-election he shall never reach that official hour in which Mr. Stanton would vacate, by force of law, one month subsequent to the expiration of Mr. Johnson's term. But if he should ever reach a second inauguration, and the month had expired, and Mr. Stanton was inclined to remain, he could demand his removal independent of the Senate, on the grounds that having received him when he received Mr. Lincoln's term, and having adopted him as the legal head of the War Department, and all departments of the government having indorsed the legality of his acts to the last hour of his previous term, the Secretary must be regarded in the light of one of his original appointments and retire accordingly.

By every reasonable rule of construction it seems perfectly plain that Mr. Stanton has not been removed by force of the civil-tenure act, and consequently is entitled to its protection, which was accorded to him by the Senate when they restored him from suspension by their vote of January 13, 1868. Having attempted to accomplish that, independent of the Senate, which he failed to secure when admitting the constitutionality of the act by yielding to its provision for suspensions, the President has certainly been guilty, as charged in the first article, of a "high misdemeanor in office."

The plea which he makes in his answer, that he does not believe the act of March 2, 1867, constitutional, cannot avail him, since, when Congress passed the act and laid it before him for his signature, he having vetoed it, it was then passed over the veto by three-fourths of each branch of Congress—the provision of the Constitution being that a bill passed by two-thirds of each house over the President's veto "shall become a law." Having thus become a law, he had no discretion but to enforce it as such; and by disregarding it, merited all the penalties thus incurred.

He is not to be shielded behind the opinions of his cabinet, although they may have advised him to disregard the law, since their only business is to enforce and obey the laws governing their several departments, and neither to claim nor exercise judicial functions.

The plea of innocent intentions is certainly not to vindicate him for having violated a law, for every criminal would be able to plead justifiable motives in extenuation of punishment, till every law was broken and every barrier of safety swept aside.

The strongest possible case that can be stated would be that of a senator who might have declared his belief of the unconstitutionality of the act of March 2,

1867, before its passage over the veto, and now being called upon to decide upon the right of the President to disregard the provisions of this same act. I hold that he would be bound by his oath of office to demand of the President obedience to its provisions until such time as, it should be repealed by Congress or annulled by the decision of a court of competent jurisdiction. The President must take care that the laws are faithfully executed.

It is very astonishing that the President should deny that Mr. Stanton is protected in office by the civil-tenure act, after having suspended him from office under that act on the 12th of August, 1867, and having reported him to the Senate under the same act as being legally suspended, and having, under a special provision of the same act, notified the Secretary of the Treasury of his action in the premises; for unless he was legally Secretary of War he was not subject to such suspension.

It has been argued that as Mr. Stanton has continued to occupy the War Office, and the removal has not been entirely completed, the penalty for removal cannot attach; but Mr. Johnson receives General Thomas as Secretary of War at his cabinet meetings, thus affirming his belief that Thomas is entitled to be accredited as such. It should be remembered in this connection, that it is a high misdemeanor to attempt to do an act which is a misdemeanor. The removal of Mr. Stanton against law would be a high misdemeanor, and a persistent effort in that direction, issuing orders, withdrawing association from him, and accrediting another, does, in my opinion, constitute a high misdemeanor.

By article two he stands charged, during the session of the Senate, with having issued a letter of authority to Lorenzo Thomas, authorizing him and commanding him to assume and exercise the functions of Secretary of the Department of War, without the advice and consent of the Senate, which is charged to have been in violation of the express letter of the Constitution and of the act of March 2, 1867.

Of his power to appoint, the Constitution, article two, section two, says:

He shall nominate, and, by and with the advice and consent of the Senate, shall appoint.

In this case he claimed a vacancy to which he might appoint *independent of the Senate*, while the Constitution affirms that the President shall have power to fill up all vacancies that may happen during "*the recess of* the Senate," not during *the session of* the Senate.

It is only necessary to quote the charge, the text of the Constitution, and his own admission in his answer, that he "did issue and deliver in writing as set forth in said second article, in order to establish the commission of an unconstitutional act." But the language of the act of March 2, 1867, is equally explicit. It affirms in section six—

That every removal, appointment, or employment made, had or exercised contrary to the provisions of this act, and the making, signing, sealing, countersigning, or issuing of any commission or letter of authority for or in respect to any such appointment or employment, shall be deemed, and are hereby declared to be, *misdemeanors;* and upon trial and conviction thereof every person guilty thereof shall be punished by a fine not exceeding $10,000, or by imprisonment not exceeding five years, or both said punishments, in the discretion of the court.

If Mr. Stanton was protected by the first clause of section one, the issuing of the letter to Thomas drew upon the author the penalty; but if he was covered by the proviso, the vacancy had not happened and the consequence was the same. And if the President, during session of the Senate, can remove one officer and appoint *ad interim*, so he may remove any or all, and thus usurp departments and offices, while the people seek in vain for the restraining and supervising power of a prostrate and insulted tribunal.

The first article, affirming the illegal removal of Secretary Stanton; the second, charging the illegal issue of the letter of authority to Thomas, and the third, affirming the *ad interim* appointment of General Thomas, admitted as facts and established by evidence, are the foundations of the whole impeachment superstructure.

The fourth, relative to an unlawful conspiracy with respect to intimidating the Secretary of War; the fifth, affirming a combination to prevent the execution of a law; the sixth, charging a conspiracy to seize and possess the property of the War Department in violation of an act of 1861; the seventh, charging a like intent in violation of an act of 1867; and the eighth, charging the appointment of Thomas with intent to control the disbursements of the War Department, are all more or less incidental acts, springing from or tending to the same criminal foundation charges, and may or may not be considered established without affecting the original article. If, however, the first three are not sustained, these will not be likely to receive more than a passing notice.

The ninth article charges the President with having instructed General Emory that part of a law of the United States, which provides that "all orders and instructions relative to military operations issued by the President or Secretary of War shall be issued through the General of the army, and, in case of his inability, through the next in rank," was unconstitutional and in contravention of the commission of said Emory, in order to induce him to violate the laws and military orders.

It appears that while General Emory was acting under a commission requiring him to observe and follow such orders and directions as he should receive from the President and other officers set over him by law, an order reached him embodying a section of law, which law had been previously approved by the President himself, but, as it provided that orders from the President and Secretary of War should be issued through the General of the army, or next in rank, and the President being engaged to remove the Secretary of War and thwart the action of the Senate, in a discussion with General Emory, as to his duty as an officer, said, "This (meaning the order) is not in conformity with the Constitution of the United States, which makes me Commander-in-chief, or with the terms of your commission." While General Emory was inclined to obey the order, the President could not command him but through General Grant's headquarters, and thus would have to make public his military orders; but, if General Emory could be made to believe the order was in conflict with his commission and the Constitution, and could be induced to disregard it, then the President could secretly issue orders to him and accomplish his designs. He could only have desired to cause General Emory to see his duty in such light as to disregard this legal order, and, if Emory had yielded to his construction of law and Constitution, he could have sheltered himself under his commission and trampled the law under foot.

This effort to tamper with an officer who was obeying the law of his government is characterized very mildly by the charge of reprehensible. It should be made a crime of serious magnitude for a President to command a military officer to violate a law which was promulgated in orders, in accordance with all the forms of national legislation. In this case the experiment upon the officer's fidelity and firmness seems to have gone no further than to discover that General Emory could not be tampered with, and then the effort was dropped on the very verge of criminality.

The tenth article charges the President with having, at Washington city, Cleveland, Ohio, and St. Louis, Missouri, indulged in language tending to bring into disgrace and ridicule, contempt and reproach, the Congress of the United States, which utterances were "highly censurable in any, and peculiarly indecent and unbecoming in a Chief Magistrate."

Under ordinary circumstances I would allow the utmost latitude of speech, and would never attempt to apply a corrective only where the crime became magnified by virtue of the peculiar surroundings. If the President had gone upon the stump with inflammatory language in order to assist in leading or driving States out of the Union, then I would hold him responsible for the character of his act. And when the very life of the nation is imperiled by the absence of ten States, and all legal efforts are making to induce their early return, if I find him denying the legal and constitutional authority of Congress, and charging disunion, usurpation, and despotism upon the representatives of the loyal people, thus strengthening the evil passions of malcontents and rebels, on account of the tendency of his teachings, I should not hesitate to declare his conduct a high misdemeanor.

For the reasons just specified I would find him guilty of a misdemeanor on the evidence sustaining the first allegation of the eleventh article, which charges him with denying the authority of Congress to propose amendments to the Constitution. I would also hold him responsible for devising means by which to prevent Edwin M. Stanton from resuming the functions of Secretary of War on the Senate having voted his restoration from the President's suspension. And of his guilt relative to impeding the proper administration of the reconstruction laws of Congress, by discouraging and embarrassing officers of the law, and using such defiant language as had all the force of commands upon rebels, I have not the shadow of a doubt.

The only matter of astonishment is that an Executive so unscrupulous and so defiant of co-ordinate power has been allowed so long to defy the people's representatives and defeat the solemnly-expressed enactments of their will.

Believing that the stability of government depends upon the faithful enforcement of law, and the laws of a republic being a transcript of the people's will, and always repealable by their instructions or change of public servants, I would demand their enforcement by the President, independent of any opinion of his relative to necessity, propriety, or constitutionality.

OPINION OF MR. SENATOR FOWLER.

The President of the United States is now on trial before the Senate of the United States for certain alleged high crimes and high misdemeanors. These charges were preferred by the House of Representatives of the United States in eleven distinct and well-considered articles.

The Senate of the United States has been organized as a court of impeachment for the decision of the case. The Chief Justice of the United States, in fulfilment of his constitutional duties, has presided over its deliberations. The character of the tribunal, the solemn oath taken by each of its members " to render impartial justice according to the Constitution and the laws," the eminent ability and the high position of its presiding officer, the office of the accused and the character of the prosecutors, all tend to impress upon the candid and thoughtful the solemn duty of the individual members of the court.

The accused is not on trial for his political opinions, nor for his general character, nor for every act of his life or his administration, but for eleven specific charges. These, and these alone, are before the court for its decision. That decision is to be made according to the Constitution and laws applicable to the facts. No opinion of my own in relation to his proper or improper policy of reconstruction, to the proper or improper, legal or illegal use of the pardoning power, to his use or abuse of the veto power, has any place in this trial. The House of Representatives have chosen to rest the case on the eleven articles they have in their wisdom, and sense of justice and duty to the Constitution and laws, considered the political and legal offences of the President.

The framers of the Constitution, more anxious for the liberty and protection of the citizen, than for the power and capacity of the government to oppress, shunned with jealousy the precedents and customs of the past. They limited the power of large majorities and endeavored to set bounds to passion, prejudice, and ambition. They defined in their great charter the offences for which a President or other officer could be impeached and divested of his office. The Constitution says that "the President, Vice-President, and all civil officers of the United States shall be removed from office on impeachment for and conviction of treason, bribery, or other high crimes and misdemeanors." They were not content to leave the term treason to any construction that party spirit or unbridled ambition might educe from the judicial or parliamentary state trials, or more properly "state murders," of England. They defined treason against the United States to consist *only* in levying war against them, or adhering to their enemies, giving them aid and comfort. They sill further guarded against the danger of parliamentary injustice and oppression, by declaring that "the trial of all crimes, except in cases of impeachment, shall be by jury." They placed additional guard around decisions for causes of treason. They have thus shown that the character and rights of the individual were objects of special care.

The present cause involves neither treason nor bribery, but high crimes and high misdemeanors. "A crime is an offence against a public law." In its limited sense it is confined to felony. The term misdemeanor includes all crimes inferior to felony. Their elements are the same. The difference consists in the magnitude of the offence, and this is determined by the consequences of the act to society and the malignity of the intention of the actor. The simple act is not in law necessarily criminal; it must be accompanied with a criminal purpose. *Actus non facit reum, nisi mens sit rea.* Lord Kenyon says: "It is a principle of natural justice and of our law, that the intent and the act must both concur to constitute the crime."

The intent itself is not punishable; indeed not the subject of human law. It must accompany in some manner an act. *Cogitationis pœnam nemo patitur.* "The intent must also be proved as alleged."

The proof both of fact and intent must establish the unlawful act, and also the criminal intent as charged in the articles exhibited.

The first article charges in substance that Andrew Johnson did on the 21st day of February, 1868, issue an order for the removal of Edwin M. Stanton, Secretary for the Department of War, with intent to violate the tenure-of-civil-office act and the Constitution of the United States.

By section 6 of the tenure-of-civil-office bill it is provided that every removal contrary to the provisions of the act is a high misdemeanor. The first question that presents itself is, was the act of issuing an order for the removal of Mr. Stanton a removal? admitting that the order was delivered, which is neither charged nor proved. If it operated a removal it must have been by force of law, for no other force was used, or attempted to be used, or intended to be used, so far as the proof shows. That conclusion would involve the legality of the order and at once destroy the idea of crime.

The issuing of an order can in no sense be regarded as a violation of the law unless it may be considered as an attempt to make a removal; and hence an attempt to commit a misdemeanor. I will, however, examine the question upon a broader basis. I will assume that the order to Mr. Stanton did effect his removal. This of course depends upon the Constitution and laws of Congress. The question which underlies the whole subject of impeachment is, had the President the right to remove Mr. Stanton from the office of Secretary for the Department of War?

Under the construction of the Constitution, as made prior to the civil-tenure-bill, commencing in the Congress of 1789, the first Congress that sat under the present Constitution, the President had the undoubted power to remove a cabinet minister and other executive officers. On this point I will quote the conclusion of Mr. Webster: "I consider it therefore a settled point, settled by the practice of the government, and settled by statute."

The civil-tenure act sought to reform certain abuses, or what was by some regarded as abuses. It must be admitted that this opinion was not uninfluenced by a violent party feeling very unfavorable to a proper decision of such questions. Indeed it is unwise legislation to attempt a construction of our Constitution under the influence of party animosity. The impelling cause of the act was to prevent the removal of revenue officers and postmasters, as well as other officers, that was supposed to be going on to the injury of the public service, and especially to the interest of those adhering to the dominant party.

The first section of the bill is set forth in the following terms:

That every person holding any civil office to which he has been appointed by and with the advice and consent of the Senate, and every person who shall hereafter be appointed to any such office, and shall become duly qualified therein, is and shall be entitled to hold such office until a successor shall have been in a like manner appointed and duly qualified, except as herein otherwise provided: *Provided*, That the Secretaries of State, of the Treasury, of War, of the Navy, and of the Interior, the Postmaster General, and the Attorney General, shall hold their offices respectively for and during the term of the President by whom they may have been appointed, and for one month thereafter, subject to removal by and with the advice and consent of the Senate.

I will call attention to the caption of the act: "An act to regulate the tenure of certain civil offices." The first exception is one of constitutional implication. The judges of the Supreme Court and all other federal courts are excepted of necessity. The fourth section of the bill is another limitation or exception. The proviso is a third exception. It is with the last that we are concerned, as it alone applies to the case in question. I will repeat the proviso, and give the reason for its insertion and its office:

Provided, That the Secretaries of State, of the Treasury, of the Navy, of War, and of the Interior, the Postmaster General, and the Attorney General, shall hold their offices respectively for and during the term of the President by whom they may have been appointed, and for one month thereafter, subject to removal by and with the advice and consent of the Senate.

The reason for this exception is this: the Senate considered the cabinet officers as the constitutional advisers of the President. They are and have always been regarded as the agents of the Executive. This is peculiarly true of the Secretary of War. The act of 1789, establishing this department provides:

There shall be a principal officer therein to be called the Secretary for the Department of War, who shall perform and execute such duties as shall from time to time be enjoined on or intrusted to him by the President of the United States.

He is thus only the President acting—the agent of his will. He could, under the Constitution, be nothing else. The President has always had the right to select his own cabinet. It is a right guaranteed to him by the Constitution. The legislative department has no power either directly or indirectly to legislate a cabinet minister upon the President, or to remove him save by impeachment. The Senate knew and appreciated this view of the case, and did not desire to touch the long-established doctrine under which the government had flourished. There were in the cabinet two classes of officers. The Secretary of State, the Secretary of the Navy, the Secretary of War, and the Secretary of the Treasury, who had been appointed by Mr. Lincoln in his first term, and who held over through the forbearance of Mr. Johnson, were the first class. The Secretary of the Interior, the Postmaster General, and the Attorney General, who had been appointed by Mr. Johnson, constituted the second class.

The Senate committee did not desire to legislate this first class of officers upon the President, and consented to the compromise by which all the cabinet officers were excepted from the body of the bill and placed in the proviso, as will be seen at once. The question now arises: Is Mr. Stanton protected in his office by the bill in any manner? If he answers the *description* of the proviso, and serves the purpose for which it was intended, he is; if not, he is left where he was before its passage under the Constitution, construed by the law of 1789, *removable* at the will of the President.

The language of the proviso is that the cabinet officers, naming each officer, "shall hold their offices respectively for and during the term of the President by whom they were appointed, and one month thereafter, subject to removal by and with the advice and consent of the Senate."

For whose term were these Secretaries commissioned? The first class were commissioned by Mr. Lincoln during his first term of office, and were to hold "during the pleasure of the President for the time being." The language of the Constitution providing for an executive term is:

The executive power shall be vested in a President of the United States of America. He shall hold his office during the term of four years, and together with the Vice-President chosen for the same term, be elected as follows:

The period of four years is assigned as the general tenure of his office. But the same instruments makes provision for a limitation of that term:

In case of the removal of the President from office, or of his death, resignation, or inability to discharge the powers and duties of said office, the same shall devolve on the Vice-President.

The President has no absolute tenure for four years. There are constitutional provisions for limitations, "conditional limitation." Death, removal, resignation, or inability to discharge his duties are limitations. In case of any of these contingencies, the Vice-President has a constitutional term. In case of the inability of both, a new election might be ordered for a new period of four years, although the former period of four years had not elapsed. The term of the President is the period of his actual service, whether four or a less number of years. The question is not a new one. Two instances before this occurred. Vice-President Tyler succeeded President Harrison, and Vice-President Fillmore President Taylor. The period during which they served was called and is now called the term of President Tyler and the term of President Fillmore. I do not know that this has ever been called in question.

On the death of the President his term vests in the Vice-President, whose term is the remainder. As well might this be called the impeachment of Mr. Lincoln as his term of service. Mr. Johnson is a real being; he is a real active officer; he is a President of the United States; he has a salary, duties, and a term of office. If this is not his term, whose term is it? What is his term? It is trifling with the use of language and a solemn mockery of justice to call it the term of Mr. Lincoln. It is an afterthought to defeat the ends of justice and force a conviction without cause. As Mr. Stanton does not come within the terms of the description of the proviso, he is left under the operation of the laws existing at the time of his appointment. Nor would his case be at all improved if this were Mr. Lincoln's second term instead of Mr. Johnson's. As Mr. Stanton was appointed during Mr. Lincoln's first term, he would no more be protected by the act under Mr. Lincoln's second term than if any other person than Mr. Lincoln had been chosen.

Mr. Stanton's case was excepted from the body of the bill and his office placed in the proviso for the purpose of classification, and he was then, by the terms of description, intentionally left under the operation of the law as it existed at the time of his appointment in order to afford Mr. Johnson one choice for his War Minister.

If any other construction were placed upon this; if he were covered by the body of the bill, the two classes of Secretaries would have different tenures. Those appointed by Mr. Lincoln would hold during the pleasure of the Senate, and might hold for life, whilst the term of those appointed by Mr. Johnson would terminate at the expiration of his term and one month thereafter. Such a result was never contemplated. The construction of the law given at the time of its passage is, to my mind, conclusive as to the interpretation I have given.

Let us now examine with some care the construction placed upon the proviso at the time of its passage. It must be borne in mind that the section was a compromise between the Senate and the House; the Senate desiring to except the cabinet from the operation of the bill, and the House to include them among other civil officers.

The Senate believed that the President had a right to the choice of his own cabinet officers. It was agreed that he should have at least the opportunity of making one selection, and that he should not remove any one of them after having made choice, during the remainder of his term, without the consent of the Senate. It must be apparent that the legislature were not legislating for any particular administration, but designed the law rather for the future than for the present, so far as respects the cabinet.

Mr. Schenck made the report of the conference committee to the House, in the following words:

I propose to demand the previous question upon the question of agreeing to the report of the committee of conference. But before doing so, I will explain to the House the condition of the bill, and the decision of the conference committee upon it. It will be remembered that by the bill as it passed the Senate it was provided that the concurrence of the Senate should be required in all removals from office, except in the case of the heads of departments. The House amended the bill of the Senate so as to extend this requirement to the heads of departments as well as to their officers.

The committee of conference have agreed that the Senate shall accept the amendment of the House. But, inasmuch as *this would compel* the President to keep around him heads of departments until the end of his term, who would hold over to another term, a *compromise* was made by which a *further amendment* is added to this portion of the bill, so that the term of office of the heads of departments shall expire with the *term* of the *President who appointed them*, allowing those heads of departments one month longer, in which, in case of death or otherwise, other heads of departments can be named. This is the whole effect of the proposition reported by the committee of conference; it is, in fact, an acceptance by the Senate of the position taken by the House. (Congressional Globe, 39th Congress, 2d session, p. 1340.)

The Senate agreed to strike out the exception of the cabinet officers from the body of the bill, and the House agreed to a compromise by which a special term was made for the cabinet officers. This is the only explanation given in the House. Mr. Williams, in the Senate, gave a similar explanation, but not so definite as that given by Mr. Sherman, one of the committee of conference on the part of the Senate, whose views are clearly conceived and clearly expressed, and were received by the Senate as the explanation of the proviso, without which explanation it could not have passed the Senate. In reply to Mr. Doolittle, of Wisconsin, Mr. Sherman said:

I do not understand the logic of the senator from Wisconsin. He first attributes a purpose to the committee of conference which I say is not true. I say that the Senate have not legislated with a view to any persons or any President, and therefore he commences by asserting what is not true. We do not legislate in order to keep in the Secretary of War the Secretary of the Navy, or the Secretary of State. (Ibid, p. 1516.)

After some further conversation, Mr. Sherman said:

That the Senate had no such purpose is shown by its vote twice to make this exception. That this provision does not apply to the present case is shown by the fact that its language is so framed as *not to apply* to the *present President*. The senator shows that himself by the fact that its *language is so framed* that it would *not prevent the present President from removing the Secretary of War*, the *Secretary of the Navy*, and the *Secretary of State*. And if I supposed that either of those gentlemen was so *wanting in manhood*, in *honor*, as to hold his place after the *politest intimation* by the President of the United States that his services were no longer needed, I certainly, as a senator, would consent to his removal at any time, and so would we all. (Ibid, p. 1516.)

This view of the case clearly establishes the construction I have given to the bill. This must be regarded as the will of the entire committee; it was expressed in open Senate and corroborated by the expression of Senators Williams and Buckalew, as far as they went. The latter, it is true, dissented from the bill on different grounds, but sustained this explanation, which was unquestioned at the time by any senator. Under all the circumstances, from the well-known rules of interpretation, from the nature and practice of our government, we may well ask if this be not the true interpretation. From all these considerations we deduce this conclusion.

Mr. Stanton's case was excepted from the body of the bill and by the proviso placed under the operation of pre-existing laws. By the authority of the Constitution under the construction given by the law of 1789, the President had an undoubted right to remove him from office. In doing so he exercised a legal right, and can in no sense be considered guilty of either crime or misdemeanor.

If the construction of this law by any means could be considered in a different light; if it might admit of a different construction, and should a forced construction forbid the exercise of such a power on the part of the President, it would neither comport with *justice* nor the *dignity* of a great people to convict their Chief Magistrate of high crimes or of high misdemeanors on such a law as this, and without any evidence of criminal purpose.

I come now to consider the second question involved in the first article: Did the President, in his act of issuing an order for the removal of Edwin M. Stanton, intentionally violate the Constitution of the United States?

The framers of the Constitution organized our government by the establishment of three separate, independent, co-ordinate departments. As far as possible they conformed to the principle laid down by Montesquieu.

They made three departures from it. The first is by a limitation of the legislative by the veto of the executive. The second is the limitation of the executive power of appointment and the treaty making power by the union of the Senate's advisory power. The third is in uniting the Chief Justice with the Senate in a court of impeachment.

These limitations are all a departure from the principle of the government, and should be, as they are, received with a jealous watchfulness, and should be subjected to a strict construction against the limitation.

The Constitution declares that "the executive power shall be vested in a President of the United States." The limit of the executive power is not well defined, and in the nature of things does not admit of it. It is a power capable of extending to all the demands of the Constitution. There are certain powers conferred specially upon him, such as that of making treaties by and with the advice and consent of the Senate, those of nomination and appointment by the same limitation, and the commanding of the army and navy.

There is another set of powers that are of a ministerial character put forth in executing the laws. Even here the executive power is derived from the Constitution. The legislative may furnish the occasion for its exercise, but can confer no power not inherent in the Constitution. The law may be and is the rule by which his authority is directed, but creates no power not already authorized when the circumstances arise for its exercise. The legislative is just as powerless to cut off a constitutional function of the executive or of the judiciary as it is to grant one to either.

It is the duty of each department to guard against the encroachments of one upon the other. The liberties of the citizen are due in a great degree to this capacity of one department to check the other in any efforts to overstep the boundaries assigned to it by the Constitution. It is not only the right but the solemn duty of each to preserve its functions complete, and to take such peaceful and lawful means as shall test the issue before the Supreme Court first and finally before the people.

The rights and powers of the executive department under the government are the questions now under consideration. The present trial may, indeed, be called, as the historian will so denominate it, *the trial of the integrity of the republic.* The personal interest of Mr. Johnson is a question of no moment compared with the real issue. Shall the three departments remain as our fathers constituted them, or shall this generation change them?

The first question that I shall consider is, what is the power of the Executive in removals from office as understood by legislation and the practice of the government?

The first Congress settled the question by a constitutional construction, acknowledging to the Executive the right of removal. I will insert the result of that debate from Marshall's Life of Washington, vol. 2, page 162:

> After an ardent discussion, which consumed several days, the committee divided and the amendment was negatived by a majority of thirty-four to twenty. The opinion thus expressed by the House of Representatives did not explicitly convey their sense of the Constitution. Indeed, the express grant of the power to the President rather implied a right in the legislature to give or withhold it at their discretion. To obviate any misunderstanding of the principle on which the question had been decided, Mr. Benson moved in the House, when the report of the Committee of the Whole was taken up, to amend the second clause in the bill, so as clearly to imply the power of removal to be solely in the President. He gave notice that if he should succeed in this he would move to strike out the words which had been the subject of debate. If those words continued, he said, the power of removal by the President might hereafter appear to be exercised by virtue of a legislative grant only, and consequently be subjected to legislative instability, when he was well satisfied in his own mind that it was by fair construction fixed in the Constitution. The motion was seconded by Mr. Madison, and both amendments were adopted. As the bill passed into a law, it has ever been considered as a full expression of the sense of the legislature on this important part of the American Constitution.

The result of that debate and the action of Congress was not to confer the power by legislative enactment, but to *declare* it the *constitutional power* of the President. Chancellor Kent, Justice Story, Rawle, Webster, all the leading statesmen down to the present time, concur in the opinion that the first Congress did so decide this question.

Twenty administrations have exercised it without doubt, and without challenging its correctness.

Thirty-eight Congresses have concurred in sanctioning the doctrine.

The concurrent decisions of the Supreme Court for eighty years have maintained the same.

The uniform decisions of the Attorneys General have sanctioned the same.

The elder Adams, whilst President of the United States, exercised the power by removing Timothy Pickering from the office of Secretary of State, and that during the session of the Senate. In this connection I desire to say that if the President has the right of removal, it makes no difference whether the Senate is in session or not. This act, although done in the presence of the Senate, was not and has not been called in question. Here is the decided official opinion of Mr. Adams, under his solemn oath of office, and that, too, during the session of the Senate:

> PHILADELPHIA, *May* 12, 1800.
>
> SIR: Divers causes and considerations essential to the administration of the government, in my judgment, requiring a change in the Department of State, you are hereby discharged from any further service as Secretary of State.
>
>   JOHN ADAMS,
>   *President of the United States.*

This power has been frequently exercised by Presidents subsequent to Mr. Adams and during the session of the Senate.

General Jackson exercised the power of removal, and his conduct has been indorsed by the American people. It is vain to quote authority for the position. The correctness of the decision has long been established by the practice of the government and the approval of every tribunal before which it has ever come.

It is now maintained that the Senate must concur in the act of removal.

There is no specific mode of removal pointed out by the Constitution, but by impeachment, in which the Senate has any place assigned by that instrument, but it is not supposed by any statesman that all removals must be by impeachment. The government could not readily be administered by such a rule. It would produce not only delay and loss to the government, but trials would become mere partisan conflicts and end in the overthrow of all sense of justice and right in the Senate. There is no party impenetrable to the seductions of power. However much of integrity they may possess in their origin, they will in time run upon the common rock on which all political parties in a republic must sooner or later be wrecked. "To the victors belong the spoils," soon becomes not only the maxim but the spirit which rules even senates when they are subjected to the making and unmaking offices. Political partisans will find ample opportunity to dodge from their personal responsibilities by distributing the guilt among the number, trusting that the people will only award to each the share to which he is entitled from a fair division among the whole number. Thus it will ever be found that the greatest number will in times of high party feeling yield to the pressure of the political demand where the opportunity of quieting any compunctions of conscience is so easily found. Wisely, then, did our fathers consider when they decided not to connect the Senate with the power of removal.

The Constitution gives the Senate an advisory power in appointments, but gives no such power in removals. It is a most dangerous step to wrest by construction such a power. In all cases, as I have already set forth, where the executive power is limited by the Senate, it should be construed strictly against the Senate. To infer a new and different power from a grant to advise and consent in cases of appointment, is an unwarranted and dangerous abuse of construction. The power to remove is by no means a consequence of the power to appoint. Both are executive powers, and the reason that the appointing power is specifically pointed out was that it was necessary to express in the Constitution in direct terms the action the Senate should take in cases of appointment. Without such a clause the Senate could have claimed no such power. As the framers of the Constitution intended that the Senate should have no such advisory power in removals, they put no word in that instrument that could give them any such control over that subject. The action of the first Congress is to my mind conclusive on this point, as they decided that the power was an executive power, and therefore one in which the Senate had no right to participate. This is sufficient, if indeed any other authority than the utter silence of the Constitution on this point were demanded.

As Mr. Stanton is not protected by the civil-tenure act, his case is fairly under the power of the Executive, and he was removable at the pleasure of the President. The President committed no violation of the Constitution in issuing an order for his removal. I could never consent to impeach a President and convict him of a high misdemeanor for the exercise of a power sanctioned by the decisions and practice of 80 years of the government. Such a decision could not fail to convict the Senate, in the judgment of posterity, of gross injustice and disregard of their solemn oaths.

I come now to consider the charge in the second article. This sets forth the fact that President Johnson did, on the 21st day of February, issue and deliver a letter of authority to Lorenzo Thomas with intent to violate the act of the 2d of March, 1867, and the Constitution of the United States.

The sixth section provides that the issuing of any commission contrary to the provisions of this act shall be a high misdemeanor.

The fifth section enacts that the President shall have power to fill all vacancies which may happen during the recess of the Senate, by reason of death or resignation, by granting commissions which shall expire at the end of their next session thereafter. "And if no appointment, by and with the advice and consent of the Senate, shall be made to such office so vacant or temporarily filled, as aforesaid, during such next session of the Senate, such office shall remain in abeyance, without any salary fees or emoluments attached thereto, until the same shall be filled by appointment thereto by and with the advice and consent of the Senate, and during such time all the powers and duties belonging to such office shall be exercised by such other officer as may by law exercise such powers and duties in case of a vacancy in such office."

It will be seen here at once that this act provides for two classes of vacancies—those occasioned by death or resignation, that happen during the recess of the Senate. And it will readily be admitted that the section should be followed if it be constitutional. The President is bound to conform to it in the two specified cases. It will be as readily conceded that if vacancies of a different class take place, he is not bound to consider a statute that makes no provision for them, but must conform to other statutes making provisions for the filling of vacancies such as may actually be.

In the early legislation, in the very act providing for a Secretary of War, it is provided that the chief clerk, "who, whenever said principal officer shall be removed by the President of the United States, or in any other case of vacancy, shall, during such vacancy, have the charge and custody of all records, books, and papers appertaining to the said department." This act was superseded by the act of 1792, which did not meet all the demands, as it applied to the State, Treasury, and War Departments alone, and did not embrace all classes of vacancies and inabilities. To meet the wants of the government in the year 1795 the following act was passed to provide for all cases of vacancy that might occur in either of the three departments then organized. (1 Statutes at Large, page 415.)

That in case of vacancy in the office of Secretary of State, Secretary of the Treasury, or of the Secretary of the Department of War, or of any officer of either of the said departments, whose appointment is not in the head thereof, whereby they cannot perform the duties of their said respective offices, it shall be lawful for the President of the United States, in case he shall think it necessary, to authorize any person or persons, at his discretion, to perform the duties of the said respective offices until a successor be appointed or such vacancies be filled: *Provided*, That no one vacancy shall be supplied, in manner aforesaid, for a longer term than six months.

This legislation lasted, notwithstanding four new departments had been created, until 1863, when a vacancy occurring in the Post Office Department not provided for by any former law, Mr. Lincoln then, without any law whatever, designated St. John B. L. Skinner to discharge the duties of the office. The subject was then brought, by a message of Mr. Lincoln, to the attention of Congress, and the law of 1863, extending the act of 1792 to all the departments, found in 12 Statutes at Large, pp. 65–66, was passed, providing as follows:

That in case of the death, resignation, absence from the seat of government, or sickness of the head of any executive department of the government, or of any officer of either of the said departments whose appointment is not in the head thereof, whereby they cannot perform the duties of their respective offices, it shall be lawful for the President of the United States, in case he shall think it necessary, to authorize the head of any other executive department, or other officer in either of said departments, whose appointment is vested in the President, at his discretion, to perform the duties of the said respective offices until a successor be appointed, or until such absence or inability by sickness shall cease: *Provided*, That no one vacancy shall be supplied in manner aforesaid for a longer term than six months.

Which provided for all the departments, embracing one case of vacancy more than the act of 1792. Let us now examine the subject-matter of the acts of 1795, 1863 and 1867.

The law of 1795 provides for filling any vacancy occurring at any time in the office of Secretary of State, Secretary of the Treasury, and the Secretary of the Department of War, or any officer of either of said departments whose appointment is not in the head thereof.

The act of 1863 provides:

That in case of the death, resignation, absence from the seat of government, or sickness of the head of any executive department of the government, or any officer of either of the said departments whose appointment is not in the head thereof.

The law of 1867 provides that the President shall have power to fill all vacancies which may happen during the *recess* of the Senate, by reason of *death or resignation* only. It will be seen here that for any vacancy in the office of Secretary of either of the Departments of State, War or Treasury, &c., the President could make an *ad interim* appointment, or give a letter of authority, or designate by such letter any person to discharge the duties, under the law of 1795. The law of 1863 does not embrace so many classes of vacancies: "death, resignation," two vacancies, "absence from the seat of government, or sickness," two inabilities; but it extends to seven departments, whilst the law of 1795 extends to three departments only.

The law of 1867 embraces two classes of vacancies, "death or resignation," and that in the *recess* of the Senate, but extends to all departments. By the law of 1867, if an inability should occur from sickness, it could not be supplied. It makes no provision for any such a case; or, if it should occur from absence, no provision is made for it. It makes no provision for expiration of office or for removals from office for any cause, or if they should occur at any other time than during *recess*. The law of 1863 makes no provision for filling vacancies by designation, by *ad interim*, or by letter of authority, which happen from expiration of term of office or from removal. It will thus be seen that when a case of vacancy should occur from expiration of term of office or from removal in either the Departments of War, State, or Treasury, the President would be compelled to resort to the law of 1795 for authority to fill it. In either of the other four departments he would have no power to fill any vacancy from removal or from expiration of term of service by any existing law. These cases are yet to be provided for.

It is manifest that neither one of these statutes entirely repeals the other. There is no repealing clause, and if there is a repeal, it must be by implication. This can only take place when the laws or any part of them cannot stand together. It is a rule of law that repeals by implication are condemned, unless the repugnancy between the statutes is clear. It will be observed that the subject-matter of the law of 1795 is vacancies however created, that of 1863 vacancies created by death or resignation and inabilities caused by absence or sickness, that of 1867 vacancies by death or resignation and that during the recess of the Senate. There is no repugnancy in these statutes. They can stand together, are necessary (except the law of 1867) to administer the government, and they must be held in full force and effect so far as the one does not conflict with the other; and whilst one—the law of 1795—embraces every known vacancy and inability, 1863 two vacancies and two inabilities; and that of 1867 two vacancies that happen *during recess*, there can be no reasonable doubt that the President was in the discharge of his duty in executing these several acts whenever an occasion should occur in his judgment for the exercise of such a discretion. That an occasion did arise, and a proper one, for the exercise of such a discretion as he undoubtedly has, we shall endeavor to show.

Let us assume that the order for the removal of Mr. Stanton operated a removal. There was then a vacancy in the War Department of the office of Secretary. That vacancy could be supplied for the time being by the authority conferred by the act of 1795 upon the President. He did, by virtue of that authority, designate Lorenzo Thomas to take charge of the War Office until a regular nomination could be forwarded to the Senate, which was made out the next day and sent to the Senate, which, not being in session, did not receive it until Monday the 24th day of February, three days, including Sunday, after the order for removal. Upon no reasonable hypothesis could it violate the law of 1867. It was to supply a vacancy not known to the law of 1867, and no violation of it.

In section eight of the act of 1867, it is enacted "that whenever the President *shall, without* the *advice* and *consent* of the *Senate, designate, authorize,* or *employ* any person to perform the duties of any office, he shall forthwith notify the Secretary of the Treasury." Thus clearly showing that the President was authorized and expected to make such designation and provision for the proper exercise of the authority he possessed. It provides for the very class of designations under consideration, and shows conclusively the intention of the legislature was not to forbid the exercise of a power so salutary and necessary for the administration of the government.

If then Mr. Stanton had been removed, or if the President so construed his order, he had a clear right to designate Lorenzo Thomas, by letter or order, to take charge of the office, to preserve the papers and other property until a successor to Mr. Stanton could be nominated and confirmed.

Under these circumstances I cannot vote to convict Andrew Johnson of a high misdemeanor. To do so would be a spectacle which neither God nor good men could approve, and which would be certain to meet the just condemnation of posterity.

If he had not the clear statute right, if upon a decision by the Supreme Court it should prove not to be the construction of the statute of 1867, I still could not vote him guilty of a high misdemeanor, for an exercise of a discretion which I believe he has under the Constitution, and for the violation of a statute of doubtful construction and still more doubtful propriety, without any evidence of criminal intent.

I come now to the charge that he violated the Constitution, and intentionally violated it, in the letter of authority or of designation to Lorenzo Thomas.

If a vacancy existed, or if the President believed that in contemplation of law a vacancy existed in the office of Secretary of War, the President had, by virtue of the authority granted to him as the Executive of the nation, the constitutional right to make such a designation. It was not only a right, but a duty to make this temporary designation. It was no appointment, for an appointment requires *a nomination, then confirmation by the Senate*, then the *signing* of a commission.

The act of designating an officer to fill a vacancy or supply temporarily an inability is in no sense an appointment. The legislature in the Congress of 1789, 1792, 1795, 1863, and again in the act of March 2, 1867, has recognized the importance of the exercise of this power of the Executive, and has, in the aforesaid acts, made provisions for its exercise, and set forth the contingencies under which it shall be. The case of Lorenzo Thomas is one that falls under the act of 1795, which has been held constitutional by all.

The fact that the Senate was in session does not change the case. An *ad interim* is only for a temporary purpose, and is designed to be made at any time that the occasion requires, whether in session or out of session, and has been so exercised by all of our Executives since the passage of the act of 1792.

There was no violation of the Constitution in this act of the President, and no misdemeanor. The practice of the government from its origin shows not only the true power of the Executive, but the construction of all the laws enacted for the purpose of designating persons to supply for short periods vacancies in certain offices.

In the year 1861 Mr. Buchanan designated Joseph Holt to perform the duties of the War Office, in place of John B. Floyd, resigned, under the act of 1795. In his message he shows that no less than 179 instances of such designations had been made since the year 1829, and that for the chief officers for the departments. These designations were made both during the session and in recess, indiscriminately. Mr. Buchanan says of this power, and says correctly:

It must be allowed that the precedents, so numerous and so long continued, are entitled to great respect, since we can scarcely suppose that the wise and eminent men by whom they were made could have been mistaken on a point which was brought to their attention so often. Still less can it be supposed that any of them wilfully violated the law or the Constitution.

The lawfulness of the practice rests upon the exigencies of the public service, which require that the movements of the government shall not be arrested by an accidental vacancy in one of the departments; upon an act of Congress expressly and plainly giving and regulating the power, and upon long and uninterrupted usage of the Executive, which has never been challenged as illegal by Congress.

This answers the inquiry of the Senate so far as it is necessary to show "how and by whom the duties of said office are now discharged." Nor is it necessary to explain further than I have done "how, when, and by what authority" the provisional appointment has been made. But the resolution makes the additional inquiry, "why the fact of said appointment has not been communicated to the Senate."

I take it for granted that the Senate did not mean to call for the reasons upon which I acted in performing an executive duty, nor to demand an account of the motives which governed me in the act which the law and the Constitution left at my own discretion.

I come now to the third article, which charges, first, that the President appointed Lorenzo Thomas to be Secretary for the Department of War *ad interim*; that it was done without the advice and consent of the Senate; that there was no vacancy having happened in the office of Secretary of War during a recess of the Senate; that no vacancy existed at the time of the appointment; that in so doing he committed a high misdemeanor in violating the Constitution. The difficulty in this charge is manifest. The President did not appoint Lorenzo Thomas. To appoint consists of three distinct acts of the Executive: first, the nomination, his sole voluntary act; second, the appointment by and with the advice and consent of the Senate; third, the signing and delivering of the commission. The act of the President was, therefore, not an appointment, but a mere designation by letter, as is shown in the article.

The second consideration is that a designation *ad interim* does not require the consent of the Senate, and never has been asked by any President.

It is alleged that no vacancy happened during the recess of the Senate. That is a matter of indifference, as the *ad interim* designation is intended for a temporary vacancy whenever it may happen or whenever the Executive may in contemplation of law believe it does exist. It has never been confined to *any time* by the practice of the government, but may be made either in session or during recess when the purpose of the President is to administer the government and not to usurp power for wicked ends. It is alleged again that there was no vacancy. Then there was no removal of Mr. Stanton; and if no removal of Mr. Stanton, there could have been no violation of the act of March 2, 1867, and all the articles based on the removal must fail, and the charge in question must fail. The act is alleged to have been a violation of the Constitution, and therefore a high misdemeanor. I cannot understand how an *ad interim* designation could have been any violation of the Constitution. The practice of the government as well as the laws of Congress from 1795 down to this time gave ample authority for the course pursued by the President. This has already been shown and needs no further consideration.

I come now to the articles known as the conspiracy articles. These are four in number. The fourth and sixth charge high crimes. They are based on the act of July 31, 1861, entitled "An act to define and punish certain conspiracies." The fifth and seventh charge conspiracy, but are founded on the violation of no law.

There is no conspiracy proved. There is no proof of any unlawful purpose, unless it may be considered as an unlawful purpose in the President of the United States to exercise authority confided to him by the Constitution and laws to remove a contumacious officer and to designate another officer to take charge of the office until a new nomination could be made; or, failing in this, to bring before the Supreme Court for its adjudication a law that invaded the functions of his office if so construed as not to allow him to remove Mr. Stanton. The whole testimony in this case tending to throw any light on the conspiracy proved that the President was endeavoring to maintain by peaceful and lawful remedies the integrity of the constitutional functions of his office.

The conduct of the Secretary of War towards General Thomas, and the disposition of his case by the judge of the court of the District of Columbia, show that neither of those parties placed any confidence in such a charge or attributed any criminality to Lorenzo Thomas. If any confidence in this charge had ever existed in the minds of either the Secretary of War or the judge of the District court, the case of Lorenzo Thomas would never have been disposed of as it was. The only reasonable conclusion is that the judge regarded such a charge as groundless, and also a charge for the violation of the sixth section of the civil-tenure bill.

The ninth is the Emory article, which not only is not sustained by the proof, but actually disproved by the witness himself, General Emory. This article belongs properly to the tenth and eleventh, and involves the freedom of speech. The effort to convict the President on such a charge, by such proof, is one of serious moment to every free man in the nation. It must in time be regarded as a dangerous invasion of a personal and constitutional right. In my judgment it will not fail to meet such a verdict from the American people, as well as from all enlightened nations. The President, acting under the advice of his Secretary of the Navy, inquired of General Emory concerning certain movements of troops that he had learned had taken place. General Emory gave him the information, which was received without comment. General Emory then brought before the President the subject of a certain order, which they discussed; the one doubting its constitutionality, and the other maintaining its authority as sanctioned by the advice of excellent counsel. This was all of it. The proof shows neither criminal conduct nor criminal purpose, but that the President was making an inquiry of an officer of the army on a subject not only his right but his duty to understand. He made a proper inquiry of the proper person and under proper circumstances.

The tenth article is one of a character differing much from any of those yet considered. It is one of those which alleges the violation of no law, but involves the propriety or impropriety of a certain style of speech. It is an article much better suited for the press than for the grave deliberation of the highest tribunal of justice in the land. It is placed before the court not for the purpose of criticism, but for the purpose of convicting the Chief Magistrate of the nation of a high misdemeanor, and depriving him of his office. It is not for the court to condemn these speeches as in bad taste, but to consider their criminality. The charge consists of three specifications, which set forth certain extracts from alleged speeches. The allegation is that Andrew Johnson did, on the 18th of August, 1866, and on divers days and times, make and deliver in a loud voice certain intemperate, inflammatory, and scandalous harangues, by which he attempted to bring into disgrace, ridicule, hatred, and contempt and reproach, and destroy the respect of all the good people of the United States, and to excite the odium of the good people of the United States against Congress.

The first specification sets forth a passage from a speech of the President made at Washington, in the Executive Mansion, on the 18th day of August, 1866, many parts of which are in bad taste, but nothing in it that is not guaranteed to him and every other citizen of this land to say.

The second specification is from a speech made at Cleveland, Ohio, on the 3d of September, 1866. The third is from a speech made in St. Louis, September 8, 1866. All these speeches contain passages condemned by the good taste and good judgment of all wise and prudent men. But it is not for any body of men to say that no speeches shall be made unless the sentiment corresponds with their sense of propriety and unless the style corresponds with their standard of elegance and refinement.

I would not pretend to say, nor do I know, how far a speech might go to be considered a high misdemeanor; in no case certainly unless it was made to another for the purpose of inducing him to commit a misdemeanor, which was committed in pursuance thereof. I am not aware of any rule of law or of any decisions of a judicial tribunal that lays down rules for abridging the exercise of the liberty of speech. Any citizen may praise or condemn the acts of Congress at pleasure, and should always preserve not only his own self-respect, but a proper decency of speech for Congress. If he does not choose to make a selection of elegant terms, can he be made to talk in a more approved style? This was once attempted by Congress in the enactment of the sedition law for two years. The American people pronounced their judgment upon that *law* and upon that *Congress*. Perhaps no measure ever met with a more signal condemnation.

However much I may condemn the style and tone of these speeches, I cannot see that Mr. Johnson did more than exercise that liberty of speech guaranteed to him by the Constitution and laws of the country.

It is very manifest that if he intended to bring Congress into disgrace he failed in his purpose, and ended by placing himself in that most unfortunate position, as the article in the end alleges.

To violate law and justice merely to establish a standard of taste by a senatorial decision for the gratification of any body of men, however cultivated and refined, would be a reproach to American liberty and justice. It could not fail to bring upon all who should participate in such an act the righteous retribution of a just and discriminating posterity. The correction for such improper and reprehensible language is the good taste of the people.

I come now to the eleventh and the final article in this list of charges. To it I have brought much labor and study in the hope of understanding this remarkable production.

The allegation appears to be this: that Andrew Johnson did, on the 18th of August, in the city of Washington, by public speech declare and affirm in substance that the 39th Congress was not a Congress of the United States, authorized by the Constitution of the United States to exercise legislative power, and in pursuance of such declaration did the following alleged things:

That he did unlawfully attempt to prevent the execution of "An act regulating the tenure of certain civil offices by unlawfully devising and contriving and attempting to devise and contrive means by which he should prevent Edwin M. Stanton from forthwith resuming the office of Secretary for the Department of War." And also by further "unlawfully devising and contriving and attempting to devise and contrive means to prevent the execution of the act of June 30, 1868." One also to prevent the execution of the "act for the more efficient government of the rebel States." To bring this into a more simple form I will express it in brief: that Andrew Johnson did declare that the 39th Congress was not a Congress having legislative power; and in pursuance thereof, he, by devising and contriving, and attempting to devise and contrive means, attempted to prevent the execution of certain laws.

Here a certain declaration of Mr. Johnson is set forth which has not been proved, viz: that the 39th Congress was not a Congress with legislative power. But admit that he did so state; then a consequence of that declaration is asserted: that he attempted to prevent the execution of certain laws by devising and contriving and attempting to devise and contrive means.

It will be here observed that no conspiracy is charged; that no other parties are connected with him, but that he, by devising and contriving and attempting to devise and contrive means to prevent the execution of certain laws, committed a misdemeanor. Admitting that an attempt to commit a misdemeanor is a misdemeanor, the devising and contriving and attempting to devise and contrive an attempt to commit a misdemeanor can scarcely be so regarded by any tribunal other than an inquisition, as a crime; that he by devising and contriving and attempting to devise and contrive an attempt can in no sense be regarded as either a crime or a misdemeanor. This view is an admission of the truth of the charge without a question of proof. If the several allegations are examined and so construed as to, admit of any reasonable meaning, they will be found unsupported in fact and in law. Suppose that the article did intend to charge the President with having attempted to prevent the execution of the civil-tenure act, instead of devising and contriving and attempting to devise and contrive means to prevent the execution of said act, how does it stand?

The proof is that the President desired to bring before the Supreme Court, for its decision, a law that he believed invaded a function of the office of the Executive. This he had a clear right to do. To that tribunal the question should have been sent, and its decision would have commanded the respect of all the people and all the departments of the government.

The correspondence between General Grant and the President, and the testimony of General Sherman, clearly establish the purpose of the President to test the constitutionality of the "act limiting the tenure of certain civil offices." This was in my judgment not only his right but his duty to do in a lawful and peaceful manner, and there is no proof that anything else was either intended or attempted. The allegation that he attempted to prevent the execution of the army appropriation has no proof in its support. The last allegation that he attempted to prevent the execution of the act for the more efficient government of the rebel States has no proof to support it, nor was any offered except a telegram to Governor Parsons, of Alabama, relative to the action of the Alabama legislature on the constitutional amendment, and that the January preceding at least two months the passage of the act in question.

I will now recall one position assumed on this trial: that this court could not take into consideration the constitutionality or unconstitutionality of a law, but is bound by the act, and that the President is bound by the same principle in the execution of the laws. I cannot but condemn such a doctrine as alike destructive to good morals, the life and spirit of the government, and the liberty and independence of the citizen. An act in violation of the Constitution is no law at all, and has no claim to obedience from either the citizen, the Executive, or the judge. Its resistance must be, it is true, made in a peaceful and lawful way. That way is by bringing the question before the proper tribunal for adjudication. The doctrine is quite as abhorrent as the assertion that the Senate are a law unto themselves; both deserve the condemnation of a free people.

I have, in coming to my conclusion, been governed by the Constitution and laws. It has been my purpose to make a faithful application of the law to the acts charged and the testimony produced.

The position of a senator as a judge in a court of impeachment is one of personal responsibility. He can neither shun it nor escape from it in any way, and is no more bound by the wishes and purposes of those outside of the court than is a juror or a judge. Any efforts to bias or influence his judgment by threats or appeals to his personal prejudices or party affiliations or demands are not less pernicious to the ends of justice than personal violence or bribery to accomplish the same results. To silence strict and impartial justice by the clamor for political ends, is at once to poison the moral sentiments of the nation and overthrow the respect of the people for the sanctity of law.

In arriving at my conclusion I have been guided by what I cannot but regard as the truth by which my decision must alone be controlled. To a discriminating public and the just judgment of posterity, I trust with confidence. The slanders of the partisan, the desertion of friends, I can endure if it shall become necessary. I cannot shun the ever-watchful presence of God, and cannot afford to disregard his voice; nor can I dare to become a fugitive from myself through time and eternity. The interests and preservation of my country and the priceless boon of liberty committed to it are objects too sacred to be trusted to the passions of the hour against the demands of conscience and the authority of law.

OPINION OF MR. SENATOR FRELINGHUYSEN.

There is no more responsible duty than that of trying the question whether the Chief Magistrate of a great nation, who holds his office under the Constitution and by the suffrages of the people, shall be deposed. On the one hand, the result of the issue is serious to the individual who is on trial, reaches to the rights of every citizen, may affect the maintenance of the checks, balances, and even the stability of the government. On the other hand, to suffer the Executive successfully to assert the right to adjudicate on the validity of laws, claimed to be inferentially, though not in terms contrary to the Constitution, and to execute such as he approves and violate such as he condemns, would be to permit the government to be destroyed. And since the issue whether the law shall be obeyed has been made before the country and before the world, to suffer the President defiantly, and to this hour persistently to disobey it, would be to surrender the supremacy of that sovereignty for the maintenance of which hundreds of thousands of loyal hearts have within the past few years ceased to beat. Walking along this narrow pathway, with perils on either side, one is only secure as he rests his hand on the firm support of duty.

We are but the agents of the people, authorized to act for them only in accordance with the Constitution and the laws. If we fail to protect the trusts committed to us, we are cowards; if we exceed our powers and assume to exercise our arbitrary will, we are usurpers. Having on questions as to the admission of evidence exercised all the liberality that was consistent with principle, and having held my opinion, subject to all legitimate influences, until the whole cause was closed, and the final vote about to be taken, I am now prepared briefly to express my views.

Senators are sworn in this case to do impartial justice according to the Constitution and the laws. The obligation thus imposed may not be disregarded. The Senate, while trying the President, are not only invested with the functions of a court and jury, but also retain their official characters as senators intrusted with the interests of the nation. Were this not so, the articles of impeachment might as well be tried before the quarter sessions of the District as before the Senate of the United States. We may not remove the President because we believe the welfare of the nation would thereby be promoted, if the charges against him are not proven, but if those charges are proven, we may, for the well-being of the republic, abstain from the exercise of that clemency which in other judicial proceedings is reposed in the court and in the pardoning power, but which in the matter of impeachment is involved in the verdict of the Senate.

There are three questions to be determined, viz:

1. Has Andrew Johnson violated the law as charged ?
2. Does such violation amount to what in the Constitution is denominated a high misdemeanor ?
3. Do the interests of the country demand the enforcement of the penalty for this violation of law, or demand the exercise of clemency ?

There are eleven articles of impeachment presented against the President. I shall confine my remarks to the first three and the eleventh.

The first article charges Andrew Johnson with violating the "Act regulating the tenure of certain civil offices" by the removal of Secretary Stanton. The second and third articles charge a violation of the same act, by appointment of General Thomas as Secretary of War *ad interim*, and the eleventh article, as construed by the Chief Justice charges that the President violated the same act by "attempting to defeat its execution."

The first, second, and sixth sections of the act entitled "An act regulating the tenure of certain civil offices," are as follows:

Be it enacted by the Senate and House of Representatives of the United States of America in Congress assembled, That every person holding any civil office to which he has been appointed by and with the advice and consent of the Senate, and every person who shall hereafter be appointed to any office, and shall become duly qualified to act therein, is and shall be entitled to hold such office until a successor shall have been in like manner appointed and duly qualified, except as herein otherwise provided: *Provided,* That the Secretaries of State, of the Treasury, of War, of the Navy, and of the Interior, the Postmaster General, and the Attorney General, shall hold their offices respectively for and during the term of the President by whom they may have been appointed and for one month thereafter, subject to removal by and with the advice and consent of the Senate.

SEC. 2. *And be it further enacted,* That when any officer appointed as aforesaid, excepting judges of the United States courts, shall, during a recess of the Senate, be shown, by evidence satisfactory to the President, to be guilty of misconduct in office, or crime, or for any reason shall become incapable or legally disqualified to perform its duties, in such case, and in no other, the President may suspend such officer and designate some suitable person to perform temporarily the duties of such office until the next meeting of the Senate, and until the case shall be acted upon by the Senate, and such person so designated shall take the oaths and give the bonds required by law to be taken and given by the person duly appointed to fill such office; and in such case it shall be the duty of the President, within twenty days after the first day of such next meeting of the Senate, to report to the Senate such suspension, with the evidence and reasons for his action in the case, and the name of the person so designated to perform the duties of such office. And if the Senate shall concur in such suspension and advise and consent to the removal of such officer, they shall so certify to the President, who may thereupon remove such officer, and, by and with the advice and consent of the Senate, appoint another person to such office. But if the Senate shall refuse to concur in such suspension, such officer so suspended shall forthwith resume the functions of his office, and the powers of the person so performing its duties in his stead shall cease, and the official salary and emoluments of such officer shall, during such suspension, belong to the person so performing the duties thereof, and not to the officer so suspended: *Provided, however,* that the President, in case he shall become satisfied that such suspension was made on insufficient grounds, shall be authorized, at any time before reporting such suspension to the Senate as above provided, to revoke such suspension and reinstate such officer in the performance of the duties of his office.

SEC. 6. *And be it further enacted,* That every removal, appointment, or employment, made, had, or exercised, contrary to the provisions of this act, the making, signing, sealing, countersigning, or issuing of any commission or letter of authority for or in respect to any such appointment or employment, shall be deemed, and are hereby declared to be, high misdemeanors, and upon trial and conviction thereof shall be punished by a fine not exceeding ten thousand dollars, or by imprisonment not exceeding five years, or both said punishments, in the discretion of the court: *Provided,* That the President shall have power to make out and deliver, after the adjournment of the Senate, commissions for all officers whose appointment shall have been advised and consented to by the Senate.

The first, second, third, and eleventh articles of impeachment charge, in effect, that Edwin M. Stanton, being then Secretary of War, Andrew Johnson, on the 12th of August, 1867, suspended him from office under the provisions of the second section of said act; that within twenty days of the next meeting of the Senate, to wit, on the 12th of December, 1867, he reported to the Senate the reason for such suspension, and also that he had appointed General Grant Secretary of War *ad interim.* That on the 13th of January, 1868, the Senate having refused to concur in said suspension and having so notified Andrew Johnson, the said Edwin M. Stanton was restored to the functions of his said office, under said act; that Andrew Johnson then devised means to prevent the execution of the said act by striving to induce General Grant to refuse to surrender the said office to Mr. Stanton; that failing in this effort, on the 21st of February, 1868, he made the following orders for the removal of Mr. Stanton and for the appointment of General Thomas as Secretary of War *ad interim:*

EXECUTIVE MANSION,
Washington, D. C., February 21, 1868.

SIR: By virtue of the power and authority vested in me as President, by the Constitution and laws of the United States, you are hereby removed from office as Secretary for the Department of War, and your functions as such will terminate upon receipt of this communication.

You will transfer to Brevet Major General Lorenzo Thomas, Adjutant General of the army, who has this day been authorized and empowered to act as Secretary of War *ad interim*, all records, books, papers, and other public property now in your custody and charge.

Respectfully, yours,

ANDREW JOHNSON.

Hon. EDWIN M. STANTON,
Washington, D. C.

EXECUTIVE MANSION,
Washington, D. C., February 21, 1868.

SIR: The Hon. Edwin M. Stanton having been this day removed from office as Secretary for the Department of War, you are hereby authorized and empowered to act as Secretary of War *ad interim*, and will immediately enter upon the discharge of the duties pertaining to that office.

Mr. Stanton has been instructed to transfer to you all the records, books, papers, and other public property now in his custody and charge.

Respectfully, yours,

ANDREW JOHNSON.

Brevet Major General LORENZO THOMAS,
Adjutant General U. S. Army, Washington, D. C.

The facts thus charged are proven beyond all dispute. There are many other facts of aggravation, and showing intent, also proven, not referred to because not necessary to the case.

If Andrew Johnson did remove Mr. Stanton and issue a letter of authority for the appointment of General Thomas Secretary of War, or do either, *contrary to the provisions of the tenure-of-civil-office act*, he, by the terms of the sixth section of that act, hereinbefore recited, is guilty of a high misdemeanor.

It is insisted that he did not remove Mr. Stanton, because he is in fact still in possession of the War Department. The removal referred to as constituting the misdemeanor in the sixth section does not mean a physical removal, but means such an act of removal as it was in the power of the President to perform. Neither does the removal spoken of in the act mean a *valid* removal, for it would be an absurdity to hold that a valid act of the President was a misdemeanor. The "removal" spoken of is just such an act as the President performed, issuing under his authority an order of removal, notifying the other departments that Mr. Stanton was removed, and informing the Senate that by his order Mr. Stanton had ceased to be Secretary of War, refusing to acknowledge him as such, and recognizing General Thomas as his successor.

It is again insisted, in defence of Mr. Johnson, that Mr. Stanton is not included within the provisions of the tenure-of-civil-office act, and is not protected in his office thereby, and that consequently his removal was legal; and that, a vacancy thus lawfully existing, the appointment of General Thomas *ad interim* thereto was not prohibited by the said act.

Let us examine whether Mr. Stanton is not protected by the act. The proviso to the first section of the act says the "Secretaries of State, Treasury, War, &c., shall hold their offices respectively for and during the term of the President by whom they may have been appointed and for one month thereafter." The Constitution makes the presidential term four years, commencing the 4th of March; and as Mr. Lincoln's term commenced March 4, 1865, this is his term, and Mr. Stanton, having been by him appointed, is protected from removal by the words of the act. But it has been insisted that the true construction of the act is that the Secretaries, to be protected under the act, must have been appointed during the existing presidential term, and that Mr. Stanton was not appointed by Mr. Lincoln after his re-election and during the existing term. There is some force in this claim, and I have only called attention to the fact that Mr. Stanton is within the words of the act for the purpose of showing that those who deny that he is under the protection of the law are obliged to resort to intendment and construction to maintain their position.

But let us look at the act again. The *pivot word* of the act is "successors." The body of the first section (as distinguished from the proviso) declares that "every person holding or who shall hold a civil office by and with the advice and consent of the Senate shall be entitled to hold such office until a *successor* shall be in like manner appointed." So that neither the President nor the President and Senate together can remove from office such civil officer, excepting by the nomination and confirmation of a successor. The act, however, makes two exceptions to this rule. It provides that the rule referred to shall exist, "*except as herein otherwise provided;*" and then we have one exception to this rule in the second section, which enacts that when the President suspends an officer he must send his reasons to the Senate; and if the Senate advise and consent to the removal of the officer, they shall so certify to the President, who may thereupon *remove* him, and this without nominating a successor. And we have another exception to the rule in the proviso to the first section, namely, that the Secretaries of State, Treasury, War, &c., shall be subject to removal by and with the advice and consent of the Senate, and this without a successor being appointed.

All civil officers, except as above excepted, hold their offices until a successor is appointed. Now, if Mr. Stanton does not come within the proviso to the first section, he comes within the body of that section; and if within the proviso, he can only be removed by and with the advice and consent of the Senate, and if he comes within the body of the act he can only be removed by a successor being appointed by and with the advice and consent of the Senate. As the President has removed Mr. Stanton without a successor being appointed by and with the advice and consent of the Senate, and without the Senate's having consented to such removal, he has violated the law.

It has been argued that if the Secretary of War is not within the proviso, he drops out of the act and is not protected by it, because, as is said, the office of Secretary of War is in the *proviso*, and the officer must remain where his office is; and as you cannot carry the office back to the body of the act, so you cannot carry the officer there. The defect in this nice argument is that the body of the act as well as the proviso speaks not of *offices*, but of *persons*—the body of the act, of every *person* holding any civil office; and the proviso, of the *Secretaries* of State, Treasury, War, &c. So Mr. Stanton, either under the body of the act or the proviso, is placed under the protection of the act.

But why should we be technical in construing a statute that is plain? The second section enacts that whenever any officer (except judges of the Supreme Court) appointed as aforesaid—that is, appointed by and with the advice and consent of the Senate—shall during a *recess* be guilty of misconduct in office, or crime, or become incapable or legally disqualified to perform his duties, in such case, and *in no other*, the President may suspend such officer; and within 20 days after the next meeting of the Senate the President shall report to the Senate the reasons for his action. If the Senate concur in such suspension, and consent to the removal of such officer, the President may remove him; but if the Senate shall refuse to concur in such suspension, such officer so suspended shall resume the functions of his office. Mr. Stanton is, beyond doubt, included within the provisions of this second section, being appointed by and with the advice and consent of the Senate, and has been treated by the President as within the section by being suspended under it.

And now, I insist that if the President can only *suspend* for *cause* during a *recess* of the Senate, *a fortiori*, he cannot *remove without cause* during the *session of the Senate*. What an absurdity to hold that, when the President wants to be rid of an officer, he has only a limited power of temporary suspension, and yet has, at the same time, an unlimited power of absolute removal! Of what possible efficacy are the guarded limitations of *suspension* if, at will, the President can arbitrarily *remove?* It is from this view that we conclude that Mr. Stanton is protected by the act, and that his removal and the appointment of General Thomas was a violation of the statute.

But may not the President have been mistaken as to the true interpretation of the law? Some senators do not now consider that Mr. Stanton is under the protection of the law. May not Mr. Johnson have fallen into the same error?

It is not possible that Andrew Johnson did not consider Mr. Stanton within the law, because, during the recess of the Senate, he suspended him under this law, and within the limited period of twenty days submitted to the Senate his reasons for such suspension; and his counsel, (Mr. Groesbeck,) in argument, stated that the suspension was made under the act. Besides, there is no other authority under which this proceeding could have been had. If the Constitution conferred upon the President the power of removal, it knows of no proceeding of suspension, trial by the Senate, and restoration to the functions of office.

There are other facts which show that the removal of Mr. Stanton was not the result of any mistake. After the President had submitted his reasons to the Senate and they had adjudicated against those reasons, and after he had informed the Senate that he had now removed Mr. Stanton and appointed General Thomas, the Senate sent the President a resolution, passed by that body, to the effect that he had acted in violation of the Constitution and the laws. The President did not annul the order of removal and appointment, but, on the contrary, at the next meeting of the Senate, on the 24th of February, 1868, sent them a message stating, in substance, that if satisfied that his removal of Mr. Stanton should involve his own removal, he still would have removed him. The House of Representatives then presented articles of impeachment against him, and since then, for a quarter of a year, Congress has been engaged in the investigation relative to this removal and appointment, but he has never annulled those orders, but stands to-day contemning, not the Senate, but the sovereign power of the nation—the law. Had Andrew Johnson at any time withdrawn from his position of defiance of that law which he is sworn to execute, he might have pleaded that he was mistaken. The Senate has spoken, the representatives of the people have spoken, and he disregards their voice. He cannot plead the views of individual senators. Neither can he plead the opinion of his Attorney General; for no offer that I know of was made to prove that the Attorney General ever officially gave any opinion to sustain the President's views; certainly no proof of such an opinion after the President suspended Mr. Stanton under this law. Before the nation and the world the question Mr. Johnson forces us to determine is, whether the law in America shall or shall not be supreme. The issue joined now to be settled is, Where is lodged the *ultimate* power of the nation—in one man or in the representatives of the people? I feel that we have no election but to stand by the doctrine that power is with the people.

Again, let us inquire whether the President's purpose may not have been to test the constitutionality of the tenure-of-civil-office act.

That act makes the consent of the Senate necessary to the removal of certain civil officers who can only be appointed by such consent. The Constitution nowhere gives the President the right to remove from office, and to hold that he has that power, even against the will of the Senate, is virtually to destroy that provision of the Constitution which makes the advice and consent of the Senate necessary to an appointment. It is the same power that appoints that has the right to remove. For eighty years the removal from office has been governed and regulated by law.

But, waiving the constitutional argument, is the President to violate laws at pleasure on the plea that he desires to ascertain their constitutionality? Does he not know that, since the formation of the government, not more than two or three general laws have ever been declared invalid? Could he not have taken some less important case for the trial? Three months have transpired since the removal, and the first step to make this test has not been taken. And if such suit was now instituted, it could not possibly be determined before March next. No, such was not the President's purpose. After the Senate refused to concur in his reasons for Mr. Stanton's suspension, his purpose was to carry out his own arbitrary will in defiance of the law and its authors.

2. Andrew Johnson having violated the law as charged, the next question is, does such violation constitute a high misdemeanor?

The tenure-of-civil-office act in its sixth section declares its violation to be a high misdemeanor; but that enactment is not conclusive on the Senate, for if it were, the legislative branch of the government, by mere statutes, might destroy the power of the executive branch. The Senate are called on to determine whether the violation is such as, *under the Constitution*, is subject-matter for impeachment and conviction.

The Constitution makes treason and bribery (crimes eminently affecting the state) and other high crimes and misdemeanors impeachable. The word "high" as qualifying misdemeanors, clearly intends to direct and restrict impeachment to such offences as derive their importance from the effect they have upon the state.

Forgery, arson, and other crimes, so far as the individual who perpetrates them is concerned, are more serious and higher crimes than the violation of a prohibitory statute like the one in question, but, so far as the government is concerned, may not be so important. If the wilful, defiant, persistent disregard of law in a chief magistrate of a great people does not constitute a high misdemeanor in office, what does? The state is infinitely less interested in the personal dereliction of the official than in a course of action, which, if tolerated, saps and destroys the government; and as, down to the present hour, the law and its authors are defied, we cannot do otherwise than declare that such conduct constitutes a high misdemeanor in office.

3. Is this a case where the Senate by its verdict should, in view of the well-being of society, pass over the transgression, or should they enforce the penalty of removal provided by the Constitution?

On this point the tribunal trying the President act not only as a court, and as jurors, but act also as senators, bound to look at the condition and to the welfare of the country.

There are considerations bearing on the question, whether the penalty of the violated law shall be enforced, which seriously affect the welfare of the nation. Among those considerations are, his desertion, at the most critical of periods, of the cherished principles of the party that confided in and elected him; his denial of the validity and constitutionality of our government as organized, which had just been rescued at a great price from the hands of treason; the repetition of that sentiment from his lips by his counsel on the trial; the declaration of his annual message that in his controversy with Congress he had contemplated a resort to force; his encouraging a spirit of discontent and disloyalty in the rebel States by his offensive denunciations of the reconstruction measures; his assuming, without right, to establish governments in the South which left the defenders of the Union unprotected; his exertion of influence against the adoption of the fourteenth amendment to the Constitution, to the ratification of which the people fondly looked for national harmony; his obstruction to the practical working of those measures of reconstruction which the rejection of the amendment referred to rendered necessary; his pardoning of rebels and his appointing them to office; the fact that the distrust of Congress in the Chief Magistrate has been such that a due regard for the republic induced them to remain in session, to convene at unusual periods of the year, and induced them to enact laws requiring all military orders to be issued by the "General of the army," and prohibiting the removal of that officer by the President; the general conviction that the unfortunate millions just relieved from bondage at the south who have been true to the Union are deprived of the much needed protection of the federal government: these, and many like considerations, force us to the conclusion that if Andrew Johnson has wilfully violated the law, its penalty should be enforced.

But we are sworn that we will do "impartial justice" in the case, and to try the question whether we may not be influenced by prejudice let us apply a severe test.

Suppose that the tenure-of-civil-office act had been in force during the administration of Abraham Lincoln, and that distinguished patriot had under the law, from some personal pique, suspended Edwin M. Stanton, a man who has organized more victories for freedom than any living civilian; suppose Mr. Lincoln to have submitted his reasons for such suspension to the Senate, and that body, after due deliberation, to have determined against the sufficiency of the alleged cause of suspension, and (as authorized by the law) to have ordered that Mr. Stanton resume the functions of his office; and that then Mr. Lincoln, having first endeavored to seduce the temporary incumbent of the office not to surrender the office, and having in this failed, should have issued an order for the absolute and unqualified removal of Mr. Stanton, and for the appointment of a successor, and that he by message should have informed the Senate of what he had done; and let us suppose that the Senate by resolution promptly informed Mr. Lincoln that in his procedure he had acted contrary to the Constitution and the laws, and that then Mr. Lincoln had sent a message to the Senate informing them that if he had known that his own removal would be the consequence of the removal of Mr. Stanton, he would nevertheless have removed him; then suppose that the representatives of the people had presented articles of impeachment against Mr. Lincoln, and the Senate had proceeded with the trial, and that for three months, with all these notifications, Mr. Lincoln had persisted in his defiant disobedience to the law and to the will of Congress, and thus made the unavoidable issue—whether the law should be supreme, and whether the *ultimate* power of government was with one intrusted only to execute law, or with the representatives of the people—would Abraham Lincoln have been entitled to an acquittal? No. If all the tenderness of feeling which now clusters around the memory of our martyred President had belonged to him while living, and the issue had been thus conspicuously forced upon us, whether he should remain in office and the law be contemned, or he be removed and its majesty vindicated, duty would have impelled an adjudication for his removal.

The case I have supposed is that proven against the respondent in these proceedings. That justice which would have been executed against Abraham Lincoln must be *impartial* when applied to Andrew Johnson, and I shall vote for conviction.

OPINION OF MR. SENATOR WILSON.

Mr. PRESIDENT: The past seven years have been to gentlemen occupying seats in this chamber, years of pressing duties and stern trials. In the trying times through which the nation has passed and is passing, it has sometimes happened that senators of large capacity, ripe experience, and eminent public service have widely differed in the interpretation of the Constitution and the construction of the laws. Whenever the high duties imposed upon senators by the exigencies of the country have pressed for action, and our deliberations have been distracted by the diverse opinions of senators learned in the law, I have striven to discharge my duty by giving whatever doubts clouded my judgment or embarrassed my action, to patriotism, to liberty, and to justice—to the security of my country and the rights of all its citizens. In glancing back over these years, I find few votes I would recall by following this rule of action.

In this great trial, imposed upon the Senate by the Constitution of our country and the representatives of the people, I shall give whatever doubts have arisen to perplex or embarrass to my country, rather than to its Chief Magistrate, now arraigned as a violator of the Constitution, a violator of the laws, and a violator of his oath to faithfully execute the laws. By a too rigid adherence to forms and technicalities the substance is often lost. Discarding forms and technicalities and looking only to the substance, I shall so vote as to secure the ends of justice.

I am not, I trust, unmindful of the gravity of the occasion, of the solemnities of my oath, nor of the obligation ever resting upon me "to be just and fear not." I know that the vote I shall give in this great trial will be criticised sharply in our age and in ages to come. The President is on trial before the Senate—the Senate is on trial before the present age and before the coming ages. I intend to vote for the conviction of the President and for his removal from his high office, and to submit my motives and my action to the judgment of the present and of the future. From the verdict of the Senate the President has no appeal; from the verdict of posterity the Senate has no appeal. I propose to state, with brevity, some of the reasons why I shall vote for the conviction of the President of the United States upon the charges preferred by the representatives of the people.

The framers of the Constitution well knew the seductive, grasping, and aggressive nature of executive power. They knew that for ages the contest had been "to rescue," in the words of Daniel Webster, "liberty from the grasp of executive power," and that "our security was in our watchfulness of executive power." They knew that the champions of human freedom in the Old World, though often baffled, had struggled for generations to limit and restrain executive power. They sought to make the executive power of the nation useful to the country, but not dangerous to the liberties of the people. They gave to the President a short term of office, and clothed the representatives of the people with power to arraign him before the Senate, not only for high crimes, but for high misdemeanors too. Jealous of executive power, the framers of the Constitution gave to the House of Representatives, a body representing the interests, the sentiments, the opinions of the people, and their passions too, complete authority to arraign the Chief Magistrate of the nation before the tribunal of the Senate. They clothed the Senate of the United States, composed of gentlemen quite as liable as are the members of the House of Representatives to be influenced by the interests, the opinions, the sentiments, and the passions of the people, with ample power to try, convict, and remove the President, not only for the commission of high crimes but for high misdemeanors.

High misdemeanors may or may not be violations of the laws. High misdemeanors may, in my judgment, be misbehavior in office detrimental to the interests of the nation, dangerous to the rights of the people, or dishonoring to the government. I entertain the conviction that the framers of the Constitution intended to impose the high duty upon the House of Representatives to arraign the Chief Magistrate for such misbehavior in office as injured, dishonored, or endangered the nation, and to impose upon the Senate the duty of trying, convicting, and removing the Chief Magistrate proved guilty of such misbehavior. Believing this to be the intention of the framers of the Constitution and its true meaning; believing that the power should be exercised whenever the security of the country and the liberties of the people imperatively demand it; and believing by the evidence adduced to prove the charges of violating the Constitution and the tenure-of-office act, and by the confessed and justified acts of the President, that he is guilty of high misdemeanors, I unhesitatingly vote for his conviction and removal from his high office.

The President is charged by the House of Representatives with violating the Constitution and the tenure-of-office act in removing Mr. Stanton from the office of Secretary of War, and in appointing Adjutant General Thomas Secretary of War *ad interim*. The removal of Mr. Stanton and the appointment of Adjutant General Thomas, and the violation of the tenure-of-office act, if Mr. Stanton be within that act, stand confessed and justified in the answer of the President to the charges of the House of Representatives. The answer of the President, without any other evidence, is to my mind conclusive evidence of his guilt. Upon his answer, confessions, assumptions, and justifications, I have no hesitation in recording my vote of "guilty." The assumptions of power put forth by the President in his defence cannot but startle and alarm all men who would maintain the just powers of all branches of the government. Had the President inadvertently violated the Constitution and the laws; had he pleaded in justification misconstruction of the Constitution and the laws, I might have hesitated to vote for his conviction. But he claims the right to remove civil officers and appoint others, *ad interim*, during the session of the Senate. If that claim of power is admitted by a vote of acquittal, the President can remove during the session of the Senate tens of thousands of civil officers with their millions of compensation, and appoint his own creatures to fill their places without the advice and consent of the Senate, and thus nullify that provision of the Constitution that empowers the Senate to give its advice and consent to appointments.

Not content with this assumption of power, the President claims the right to pronounce a law of Congress unconstitutional, to refuse to execute it, although he is sworn to do so, and to openly violate it with a view of testing its constitutionality in the courts, although no means may exist for months or years to come, to test the constitutionality of the law so violated in the judicial tribunals of the country. The President claims and has exercised the right to declare Congress an unconstitutional body, incapable of enacting laws or of proposing amendments to the Constitution; to hold the laws in abeyance; to refuse to execute them, and to defiantly violate them in order to test their constitutionality. These are the positions assumed by Andrew Johnson. These assumptions, if admitted, radically change the character of our government. If they are sustained by a verdict of acquittal, the President ceases to be the servant of the law, and becomes the master of the people; and a law-non-executing power, a law-defying power, a law-breaking power is created within the government. Instead of an executive bound to the faithful execution of the laws of Congress, the nation has an executive bound only to execute the laws according to his own caprices, whims, and sovereign pleasure. Never can I assent, by a vote of acquittal, to executive assumptions so unconstitutional, so subversive of the government, so revolutionary in their scope and tendency. These assumptions will introduce into our constitutional system, into our government of nicely adjusted parts, derangement, disorganization, and anarchy.

Criminal acts raise the presumption of wrong motives, intentions and purposes. The President's acts, claims and assumptions, made against the well-known protests of vast masses of the people, the organs of public opinion, the Congress of the United States and the laws of the land, afford ample evidence that his motives, intentions and purposes were unworthy if not criminal. We are sworn to give this arraigned President a trial as impartial as the lot of humanity will permit. But we cannot close our eyes to the records of the past three years, nor can we wholly shut out from all influences our personal knowledge of his intentions, purposes, and acts. The framers of the Constitution, when they empowered senators to sit in judgment upon an arraigned Chief Magistrate, must have presumed that senators would know something of the motives, intentions and purposes, and be familiar with the public record of him who should exercise executive power in their time. The framers of the Constitution knew, when they gave senators the power to try an arraigned Chief Magistrate, the country knows, and we know, that personal knowledge and the historic records of the country cannot but influence in some degree the feelings and judgments of men.

Four years ago eleven States were wrenched from the Union, their governments were arrayed against the country, the land was desolated with civil war, the nation was struggling to restore and maintain the unity of the country, the supremacy of the government, and the freedom of millions made free by executive proclamation and a constitutional amendment. The faith of the nation was plighted to restore the broken Union on the basis of loyalty, and to maintain the freedom of millions of emancipated bondmen. The men pledged to liberty and union accepted Andrew Johnson, supported and trusted him. Coming into power, he at once, in spite of the fears and protests of the loyal men who had confided in him, entered upon a policy that placed the conquered rebel States in the keeping of traitors, and put loyal men and the freedmen completely under the authority of men who had striven for four years on bloody fields to destroy their country, to perpetuate the slavery of the very men surrendered to their control.

To lighten the burdens and partially protect and defend the endangered rights of the freedmen, Congress passed a Freedmen's Bureau bill; the President arrested it by a veto. Congress passed another Freedmen's Bureau bill; the President endeavored to defeat it by another veto, and when it passed into law he strove to embarrass and thwart its operations. To protect the freedmen he had wickedly abandoned to the control of their enemies and the nation's enemies, Congress passed a civil-rights bill; the President attempted to arrest it by a veto; and failing in that, he has utterly neglected to enforce it. Congress endeavored by submitting an amendment to the Constitution to secure the reconstruction of the Union; the President met it by a denial of the authority of Congress to submit an amendment, and by an invocation to his governments in the rebel States to reject it. The rebel States having failed to adopt the constitutional amendment, Congress passed the reconstruction measures over executive vetoes. Those measures of restoration have encountered in their execution the hostility of the President. Faithful generals have been removed for their fidelity and efficiency, and others have been rebuked and thwarted.

The history of the past three years records it, and our personal knowledge attests it, that the President has sought to prevent the enforcement of the laws passed over his vetoes. In every form he has striven to prevent the restoration of the Union on a basis of loyalty to the country and the equal rights and privileges of the people. The evidences legally before us, the records of the country, the personal knowledge of senators, show the motives, intentions, and designs of President Johnson.

To accomplish his purposes and designs, Mr. Johnson sought, by the use of executive patronage, to corrupt the American people. When Congress, by the casting vote of Vice-President Adams, decided, in the beginning of Washington's administration, that the Senate was a part of the appointing power, but not of the removing power, the office-holders of the country were but a few hundred in number, and received a compensation amounting to but a few thousands of dollars. In our time the federal office holders are counted by tens of thousands, and their compensation amounts to many millions. To defeat the will of the people, the President, in the interests of disloyalty, inequality, and injustice, sought to use the corrupt and corrupting influences of executive patronage. The Postmaster General made the shameless declaration, that officers who ate the President's bread should support the President's policy. To maintain the cause of the country, as well as to protect honest public officers who would not betray their country, Congress enacted the civil-tenure act. It met the executive veto, the executive denunciation of unconstitutionality, and the executive violation. Mr. Williams, of the House of Representatives, who drew the proviso to the first section of the act, tells us that he intended that the act should protect Mr. Stanton. The senator from Oregon, (Mr. Williams,) who introduced the original bill, and who was on the committee of conference, and the senator from Vermont, (Mr. Edmunds,) who reported the bill from the Committee on the Judiciary, and who was also on the committee of conference, both claim that Mr. Stanton is protected by the act. A fair and logical construction of the language of the act gives its protection to Mr. Stanton. A large majority in Congress voted for the bill in the belief that it threw its protection over the great War Secretary, who stood before the country one of the foremost champions of Congress in its struggle against the anarchical, disorganizing, and unpatriotic action of the Executive. Mr. Stanton was suspended by Mr. Johnson; the reasons for his suspension were submitted to Congress; the reasons were pronounced insufficient by more than a three-fourths vote of the Senate; Mr. Stanton returned to his office; the President refused to acknowledge him; and, after several days, issued the order for his removal, and he appointed Adjutant General Thomas Secretary of War *ad interim*—all in direct violation of the tenure-of-office act.

The President refused to send a nomination to the Senate, knowing that it was the will of the Senate and of the nation that Mr. Stanton should remain at the head of the War Department. He had vainly sought to induce General Grant to be a party in thwarting the will of the Senate, by preventing the return of Mr. Stanton to the War Office. He had failed to persuade Lieutenant General Sherman to aid him in removing Mr. Stanton from his office. He then took Adjutant General Thomas, through whom all communications must go to the army, and made him Secretary of War *ad interim*. The law requires all communications to the army to go through General Grant. Might it not have been, by placing Thomas in the War Department, while holding the office of Adjutant General, the purpose of the President to have the means of communication with the army under his control, and substantially to set aside the law requiring such communications to go through the General of the army?

In support of the acts of the President, claims are made and powers asserted by Mr. Johnson and his counsel hostile to the spirit and genius of our institutions, to the integrity of the government, and to the security of public liberty. The acquittal of the President will give the sanction of the Senate to the monstrous powers assumed, claimed, and exercised by the President, and will, in my judgment, increase the lawlessness, disorder, and outrage now so prevalent in the States lately in rebellion. His conviction and removal from office will rebuke lawlessness, disorder, and crime, and inspire hope and courage among loyal and law-abiding men. I cannot contemplate without the deepest anxiety the fatal effects, the suffering and sorrow that must follow the acquittal of the President. The disastrous consequences of his acquittal seem to flash upon me whichsoever way I turn. Conscious of the responsibilities that rest upon me, I shall unhesitatingly vote for the conviction of the President, for his removal from office, and for his disqualification from hereafter holding any office under the Constitution he has violated and the government he has dishonored.

OPINION OF MR. SENATOR BUCKALEW.

THE STANTON ARTICLE.

The first article of impeachment, which charges the issuing of the order for the removal of Edwin M. Stanton from his office of Secretary of War upon the 21st February, 1868, is the most important one of the articles, and presents itself first for consideration. It is charged that that order was unlawfully issued with intent to violate the tenure-of-office act of March 2, 1867, and contrary to the Constitution of the United States, and that by issuing it the President did commit and was guilty of a high misdemeanor in office.

Was the order for the removal of Mr. Stanton authorized by the Constitution and laws of the United States, or was it in violation of either or both? The argument upon this question has been prolonged and exhaustive; but to a just conclusion it will only be necessary to examine a few points and place them in their proper relations to each other and to the general question involved.

As a constitutional question, the executive power to remove from office may be placed upon those two provisions of the Constitution of the United States which declare that the executive power of the government shall be vested in the President, and that he shall take care that the laws be faithfully executed. The power to remove being executive in its nature, and its exercise, upon fit occasions, being necessary to the due execution of the laws, it is insisted that it is vested in the President by these provisions of the Constitution. And such was the decision of Congress after full debate in 1789.

If this construction of the Constitution be a true construction, there can be no doubt that the President had due authority to issue the order for the removal of Mr. Stanton.

But the power of the President to remove a Secretary of War from office is clearly declared by the second section of the act of the 7th of August, 1789, organizing the War Department. That section reads as follows:

There shall be in said department an inferior officer, to be appointed by the said principal officer, to be employed therein as he shall deem proper, to be called the chief clerk in the Department of War, and who, *whenever the said principal officer shall be removed from office by the President of the United States*, or in any case of vacancy, shall during such vacancy have the charge and custody of all records, books, and papers appertaining to the said department.

Whether this section simply admits that the President has power to remove by virtue of the Constitution or confers the power upon him is not material to our present purpose. In either case it is a legislative declaration that he can remove the Secretary, the "principal officer" in the Department of War.

Again, it is in evidence and undenied that Secretaries of War have always been appointed and commissioned to hold their office "during the pleasure of the President of the United States for the time being," and Mr. Stanton's commission—the only one ever issued to him—is in that form.

It only remains to inquire whether recent legislation has changed the tenure of office of the Secretary of War so as to impair or destroy the President's power of removal. The first section of the tenure-of-office act of 2d March, 1867, is as follows:

That any person holding any civil office to which he has been appointed by and with the advice and consent of the Senate, and every person who shall hereafter be appointed to any such office and shall become duly qualified to act therein, is and shall be entitled to hold such office until a successor shall have been in like manner appointed and duly qualified, except as herein otherwise provided: *Provided*, That the Secretaries of State, of the Treasury, of War, of the Navy, and of the Interior, the Postmaster General and the Attorney General, shall hold their offices respectively for and during the term of the President by whom they may have been appointed and for one month thereafter, subject to removal by and with the advice and consent of the Senate.

The proviso of this section puts the heads of departments into a class by themselves, but cannot have practical effect upon four of the Secretaries who were appointed to office by Mr. Lincoln, namely, the Secretary of State, the Secretary of War, the Secretary of the Treasury, and the Secretary of the Navy. They were appointed by Mr. Lincoln in his first term and were commissioned by him, in the usual form which they obtained, to hold their offices "during the pleasure of the President of the United States for the time being." Theirs was then a tenure at will; they were to hold at the pleasure of the President who appointed them, or of his successor, whoever that successor might be.

The Secretary of the Interior, the Postmaster General, and the Attorney General had been appointed by Mr. Johnson and had received commissions in the same form. So stood the case as to the heads of departments when the tenure-of-office act was passed.

The proviso, therefore, in declaring that heads of departments should hold during the term of the President by whom they may have been appointed and for one month thereafter, could not have the practical effect of expanding or changing the tenure upon which the Lincoln Secretaries held their offices; for the term of the President who appointed them, and during which they were appointed, expired March 4, 1865, and they were never reappointed after its expiration. Besides, Mr. Johnson's term began in April, 1865, and when the law was passed, March 2, 1867, there was no term running of a President by whom they had been appointed. There can be no pretence of an appointment of them by Mr. Johnson or by Mr. Lincoln in his second term, from the fact that they held over after March 4, 1865. No new commissions were issued to them, and in fact no new appointments were possible without the advice and consent of the Senate, which was never asked for or given.

In my opinion all Secretaries, present and future, were within the descriptive words of the proviso, but the Lincoln Secretaries were not practically within the operation of the new tenure which that proviso established. They were within the words which distinguished and separated heads of departments from other civil officers of the government, but not effectually brought within the new tenure rule. For purposes of classification all heads of departments were named in the proviso and excluded from the body of the section, but the tenure of those Secretaries was not in fact changed, but was left as before.

No one can doubt the complete application of the tenure-of-office act to all heads of departments appointed by future Presidents. They will all hold during the term of the President who shall appoint them, and for one month thereafter; there will be no exceptions. If a President shall be chosen for a second term the members of his cabinet must be reappointed if they are to hold for more than one month in his new term. But suppose a President shall die, resign, or be removed from office before his term shall run out? Will his cabinet be fastened upon his successor for one month only or for the remainder of the full term? Will a Secretary appointed March 4, 1869, be entitled to hold for a fixed and indefeasible term of four years and one month, or may he lose his place sooner by the death, resignation, or removal of the President who appoints him? Now this is, in one view, an important inquiry in fixing the construction of the tenure-of-office act in its application to the case before us. For if it shall appear that upon the death, resignation, or removal of a future President his cabinet will go out at the end of one month, there is no ground left for the argument that Mr. Stanton now holds his office under the law. He can claim to hold it only upon the ground of the non-expiration of Mr. Lincoln's second term. If that term expired with Mr. Lincoln's life, he has no standing whatever in any forum of honest debate.

In my opinion, in case of the death, resignation, or removal of a future President, his cabinet will go out of office at the end of one month. A President takes a four-year term subject to the implied condition that he shall live so long and shall not resign or be removed upon impeachment. His term ends when for any cause he vacates or is removed from his office and can no longer perform its duties. The term of the Emperor Charles V ended when he resigned his crown; that of James II when Parliament declared he had abdicated the throne by withdrawing himself from the realm. In the ordinary case of an officer of the United States who holds for a term of years, if he die, resign, or be removed from office pending his term, the term ends and his successor takes a new full term. But it may be said that our present case is a peculiar one, because a Vice-President is provided to fill out the term of a President who dies, resigns, or is removed. The Constitution does not say that. It says that in case of the death, &c., of the President, the duties of the presidential office shall devolve upon the Vice-President. If it be a case of temporary disability of the President, the Vice-President will perform the duties of the office until the disability shall be removed. If it be a case of vacancy in the presidential office, the Vice-President will perform the duties of the office *during the time or term for which he was elected Vice-President.* He becomes President in fact, not for the term of another, but for his own.

The Constitution provides that when there is no President or Vice-President to discharge the duties of the presidential office, such duties shall be discharged by some other officer to be designated by law, until a new President shall be chosen. But under an existing law (act of March 1, 1792) such choice of a new President may possibly be made by electors, two or three years before the running out of the former President's term, and yet the new President will be chosen and will hold for a full four-year term. The old and the new terms will not overlap each other in such case, will not be co-existent to any extent, because the former ends with the event, whatever it may be, which causes the vacancy in the presidential office.

We may conclude, then, that the words *"the term of the President,"* mentioned in the tenure-of-office act and in the Constitution, is the actual period of service of a President—including any time of temporary disability—and that such term may end by death, resignation, or removal, as well as by the regular expiration of four years. It follows that Mr. Stanton could not claim to hold his place as Secretary of War under the tenure created by the proviso to the first section of the tenure-of-office act, even though he had been appointed in fact or constructively in Mr. Lincoln's second term of service as President of the United States. In no sense can it be said that he is holding his office in or during "the term of the President" by whom he was appointed.

But if this be granted, it becomes evident that his case is quite outside of the tenure-of-office act, and wholly unaffected by it. And the plain words of the act of 1789, and the language of his commission, declare him to be subject to removal at the pleasure of the President.

I shall not examine at length the adroit argument which places Mr. Stanton's case within the body of the first section of the tenure-of-office act upon its logical expulsion from the proviso. This is evidently an afterthought, which can derive but little support from verbal criticism, and none whatever from the history or policy of the law. Plainly the purpose of the law was to put all heads of departments in a separate class and attach them to the particular Presidents by whom they are appointed. No President shall have Secretaries imposed upon him whom he has not selected, nor (as I construe the law) shall he be compelled to retain in a second term those he had selected in his first. He may once in a term freely choose his advisers, (subject only to senatorial confirmation,) but if re-elected he is not bound to keep them, nor can he in any case impose them upon his successor. The law only binds him to retain them (when once chosen) during the term, or remainder of the term, in which they are selected, and then they retire.

But this evident policy of the law is in flat contradiction of the argument which places Mr. Stanton's case within the body of the section, and assigns to him a tenure of indefinite duration in the future. No future President (any more than the present one in case of his re-election) could shake off this Secretary without the consent of the Senate, if this argument be sound.

Not one word was uttered in either house of Congress when the act was passed indicating that the Lincoln Secretaries were included or intended to be included in the body of the first section; but a most explicit statement was made by Senator Sherman (without dissent from any quarter) that they were excluded from the protection of the act and would remain subject to removal by the President.

It is charged in the first article of impeachment as an ingredient of the offence therein alleged to have been committed by the President, or as a serious aggravation thereof, that the order for the removal of Mr. Stanton **was** issued during a session of the Senate and without senatorial advice and consent. This particular accusation was supposed by many in the outset of this controversy to be unanswerable. But it possesses no importance whatever; for neither the constitutional argument for executive power to make removals from office, nor the act of 1789 organizing the War Department, nor any other former statute relating to removals, nor the practice of the government, recognizes any distinction of time (in making removals) between session and recess. The President in all cases where he is authorized to remove an officer may remove him during a session of the Senate as well as in a recess between sessions, for aught that appears in the constitutional reasoning, in the legislation, or in the practice of the past.

Prior to 1867 all removals were to be made by the President upon his own responsibility, without senatorial advice or consent. Whether the Senate was in session or not when a removal was made, was, therefore, wholly immaterial to his exercise of his power. The presence of the Senate was of importance only when a new and complete appointment was to be made to fill a vacancy, whether produced by removal or other cause.

Upon the whole we must come to the conclusion that if Mr. Stanton holds under the tenure-of-office act he cannot be removed, either in session or in recess, without the consent of the Senate; but if he does not hold under that act, then, under the prior laws and practice of the government, he may be removed by the President at any time. In either case the charge that he was removed during a session of the Senate is unimportant, if not absurd.

The order for the removal of Mr. Stanton was in exact conformity with the precedent in the case of Timothy Pickering, Secretary of State, who was removed from office by President Adams on the 12th of May, 1800.

The first session of the sixth Congress began December 2, 1799, and ended May 14, 1800. (Trial, p. 595.) The removal was therefore during a session of the Senate. On Saturday, May 10, President Adams wrote to Mr. Pickering requesting him to resign, and stating his desire for an answer to his communication "on or before Monday morning, because the nomination of a successor must be sent to the Senate as soon as they shall sit." This last remark was obviously made with reference to the adjournment of Congress; for by resolution of the 21st of April the two houses had agreed to adjourn the session on Monday, May 12, and a resolution of the Senate to extend the session to the 14th had just been rejected by the House. (3 Senate Journal, 77, 78, 92.) It was necessary, therefore, that a nomination of a successor should be sent to the Senate "as soon as they should sit" on Monday, in order to confirmation before the final adjournment of the session.

Mr. Pickering's answer, refusing to resign, is dated on Monday, the 12th, and it is a fair if not inevitable conclusion, from the facts known to us, that it was sent to the President on the morning of that day. For the President had requested that the answer should be sent to him on or before that morning, and he took action upon the answer, which indicates that he received it at that time. He issued an order dated the 12th, peremptorily discharging Mr. Pickering from further service as Secretary of State, and as soon as the Senate met, on the same day, sent to it a message nominating "John Marshall, of Virginia, to be Secretary of State in place of Timothy Pickering, removed." (Trial, pp. 356, 357.)

On May 12, a resolution passed both houses extending the session to the 14th, (3 Senate Journal, 92, 94,) and on Tuesday, the 13th, the Senate, in executive session, confirmed the nomination of Judge Marshall as Secretary of State. (Trial, p. 359.)

It is clear, then, that Mr. Pickering was removed during a session of Congress and of the Senate; that he was removed before a nomination of his successor was transmitted to the Senate, and that his successor was confirmed and appointed on a subsequent day.

The views of the managers of the impeachment upon the Pickering case, as expressed by them to the Senate upon this trial, appear to be quite groundless. One of them [Mr. Butler] was of opinion that the nomination of Marshall was sent to the Senate before the order of dismissal was sent to Pickering, (Trial, pp. 358, 359, 360,) while another [Mr. Bingham] insisted at length that the order of removal was issued before the Senate "had commenced its session," and that President Adams "did not consider that it was proper, even under the law of 1789, for him to make that removal during the session of the Senate." (Trial, p. 1173.) Neither one of those contradictory opinions can stand. It is very evident that the removal of Pickering preceded the nomination of Marshall, and it is beyond dispute that the entire transaction was during a session of the Senate, and not in recess. The Senate had been in session for months; it sat on the preceding Saturday, (3 Senate Journal, 92,) and there can be no pretence of a vacation or recess on the Monday when Pickering was removed from office. The Pickering case is therefore a decisive authority in support of the order for the removal of Stanton.

THE THOMAS ARTICLES.

The second, third, and eighth articles of impeachment charge the designation by the President of General Thomas to perform the duties of Secretary of War *ad interim* as unlawful, and as constituting a high misdemeanor in office

I think that that act of the President was authorized by the act of 13th February, 1795, (1 *Statutes at Large*, p. 416.) But in view of the argument that the law of 1795 is no longer in force, it becomes necessary to consider, in connection, the several laws which relate to official vacancies and disability of officers in the several executive departments.

The act of 8th of May, 1792, section 8, provides:

In case of the death, absence from the seat of government, or sickness of the Secretary of State, Secretary of the Treasury, or of the Secretary of the War Department, or of any officer of either of the said departments whose appointment is not in the head thereof, whereby they cannot perform the duties of their said respective offices, it shall be lawful for the President of the United States, in case he shall think it necessary, to authorize any person or persons, at his discretion, to perform the duties of the said respective offices until a successor be appointed, or until such absence or inability by sickness shall cease. (1 Stat., 281.)

This act, it will be seen, was confined to the Departments of State, of the Treasury, and of War, which were the only ones organized when the act was passed. It will be seen, also, that the act applies only to cases of vacancy occasioned by death, and to cases of disability occasioned by sickness or absence from the seat of government.

The act of 13th of February, 1795, in its first section, makes further provision, as follows:

In case of vacancy in the office of Secretary of State, Secretary of the Treasury, or of the Secretary of the Department of War, or of any officer of either of the said departments, whose appointment is not in the head thereof, whereby they cannot perform the duties of their said respective offices, it shall be lawful for the President of the United States, in case he shall think it necessary, to authorize any person or persons, at his discretion, to perform the duties of said respective offices until a successor be appointed or such vacancy be filled: *Provided,* That no one vacancy shall be supplied in manner aforesaid for a longer term than six months.

This act has no application to cases of temporary disability, but to cases of vacancy alone; but as to such it is comprehensive and includes those of every description. It is, however, like that of 1792, confined to the Departments of State, the Treasury, and War.

Next follows the act of 20th of February, 1863. (12 Statutes at Large, p.

65.) Its passage was recommended by President Lincoln in a special message dated 2d of January, 1863, which reads as follows:

I submit to Congress the expediency of extending to other departments of the government the authority conferred on the President by the eighth section of the act of the 8th May, 1792, to appoint a person to temporarily discharge the duties of Secretary of State, Secretary of the Treasury, and Secretary of War, in case of the death, absence from the seat of government, or sickness, of either of these officers.

In pursuance of this recommendation the act was passed in the following words:

In case of the death, resignation, absence from the seat of government, or sickness of the head of any executive department of the government, or of any officer of either of the said departments whose appointment is not in the head thereof, whereby they cannot perform the duties of their respective offices, it shall be lawful for the President of the United States, in case he shall think it necessary, to authorize the head of any other executive department, or other officer in either of said departments whose appointment is vested in the President, at his discretion, to perform the duties of the said respective offices until a successor be appointed, or until such absence or inability by sickness shall cease: *Provided*, That no one vacancy shall be supplied in manner aforesaid for a longer term than six months.

It will be observed that this act follows mainly the language of the act of 1792. The particulars in which it departs from it are these:

1. It extends to all the seven executive departments instead of being confined to the three which were in existence in 1792.
2. It applies to a case of vacancy by resignation.
3. It authorizes the employment in temporary service in a department of officers of another department, instead of "any person" as in the former laws; and lastly, it borrows from the act of 1795 the limitation of six months upon the term of special service in each case provided for.

Now the question is presented, did this act of 1863 repeal by necessary implication the vacancy act of 1795? It provides for the cases of disability covered by the act of 1792, and for cases of vacancy occasioned by death covered by the same act. But it provides further for cases of vacancy occasioned by resignation which were not within the act of 1792, but would appear to be within the act of 1795.

It is clear that when a later statute entirely supplies the place of a former one it works its repeal. And so where a later statute contradicts a former one, or is plainly inconsistent with it, the former law falls. In each case supposed, there is an implied or constructive repeal of the old law.

And when the place of an old law is supplied in part by a new one, or is in part plainly inconsistent with a new one, the same result takes place as to such unnecessary or inconsistent parts of the old law.

Now, the act of 1863 makes provision only for vacancies caused by death or resignation, whereas the act of 1795 extended to all cases of vacancy, including those caused by removal or expiration of term of service. As there is no express repeal of the old law, and as the new one does not fully supply its place, the old law must remain partly in force and still apply to cases of vacancy caused by removal or expiration of term.

And this view is strengthened by considering the fact that the act of 1863 was asked for by Mr. Lincoln for no purpose of repealing former laws, but to extend the disabilities act of 1792 to all the executive departments.

It may be insisted upon further, that whereas the act of 1795 did not repeal the act of 1792, that of 1863 cannot be held to repeal the act of 1795. Now, the act of 1792 was often acted upon in the practice of the government down to recent times, and it was referred to by Mr. Lincoln as a subsisting law in his communication to Congress of 2d January, 1863. If, then, the act of 1795 did not repeal the act of 1792 because it provided for a case of vacancy by death, and thus far supplied the former law, the act of 1863 cannot be held to repeal the act of 1795 because it provides for cases of vacancy by death and by resignation. In each case the elder statute continues in force except so far as its place is filled by the younger.

The argument so far proceeds upon the ground that the act of 1863 is to some extent inconsistent with the former laws and partially displaces them. But is it clear that it is inconsistent with those laws? The former laws authorize the President to designate "*any person*" to discharge the duties of an office *ad interim* in case of vacancy therein or disability of the incumbent. Is it certain that these words, "*any person*," should be held to include any officer of the government without regard to the character of his office or the duties and responsibilities charged upon him by law? An officer under bond, if taken away from his proper office and appropriate duties, could not be held responsible upon his bond for any default caused thereby (nor his sureties either) without gross injustice; and many other difficulties might be suggested upon such construction of the law. At all events, one would think that a very clear, specific, express provision by statute would be necessary to withdraw an officer from the duties of an office to which he had been assigned by due appointment under the Constitution (upon senatorial confirmation) and assign him to duty in another office. The act of 1863 provides specifically that this may be done, and thus gave a legal sanction to a practice which had obtained to some extent before its passage. But it is very doubtful whether the disability and vacancy acts of 1792 and 1795 conferred this power of transferring officers from one office to another upon the President. If they did not, the act of 1863 may be held as additional to and not restrictive of the provisions of the former law, and all question of inconsistency between them will disappear. The former laws may then be held to stand good as to *all* cases arising under them, and to authorize *ad interim* authority to "any persons" not heads of or presidential appointees in the departments and charged with other duties by law.

The rules for the construction of statutes, cited on behalf of the defence on this trial tell very strongly against the argument for the implied repeal of the act of 1795 by the act of 1863. Repeals by implication are not favored by the law; where a later statute is not plainly inconsistent with a former one, both shall stand; remedial statutes shall be construed liberally, so as to secure fully their object. These and other rules sanctioned by the wisdom of ages fully protect the statute of 1795 against the argument of the prosecution, and give to it a complete sanction as an existing law. Assuming that that act continued in force as to vacancies occasioned by removal, it justified, beyond all question, the letter of authority to General Thomas of February 21, authorizing him to perform the duties of Secretary of War *ad interim*, and the second, third, and eighth articles of impeachment are wholly without support.

It has been said that the tenure-of-office act repeals all prior laws which authorized *ad interim* service in the executive departments, but the fact is not so. The tenure-of-office act has no repealing clause, and its eighth section does most clearly recognize the validity of *ad interim* selections for executive offices. That section is as follows:

> That whenever the President shall, without the advice and consent of the Senate, designate, authorize, or employ any person to perform the duties of any office, he shall forthwith notify the Secretary of the Treasury thereof; and it shall be the duty of the Secretary of the Treasury thereupon to communicate such notice to all the proper accounting and disbursing officers of his department.

Passing now from the general question of *ad interim* legislation, it remains to inquire whether the letter of authority to General Thomas was forbidden by any provision of the tenure-of-office act. The sixth section of that act provides—

> That every removal, appointment, or employment, made, had, or exercised *contrary to the provisions of this act*, and the making, signing, sealing, countersigning, or issuing of any commission or letter of authority, for or in respect to any *such* appointment or employment, shall be deemed, and are hereby declared to be, high misdemeanors, &c.

Now, an act done which is declared to be a high misdemeanor by this section must be one which is "contrary to the provisions" of this act. And it is evident that it must contravene some provision of the first, second, or third sections, because those alone relate to the subject-matter of removal and appointment. But it has been shown already that Mr. Stanton's case is not within the first section of the act, and that that section could not be violated by his removal and the designation of Thomas to supply his place *ad interim*. Nor have we in hand a case of suspension or temporary appointment or employment in recess, under the second section, nor the case of an office in abeyance under the third section.

The sixth section, therefore, can find no provision in any other part of the law to which it can attach itself for the purpose of charging a misdemeanor upon the President of the United States. In other words, the letter of authority to General Thomas not being "contrary to the provisions" of the tenure-of-office act, the sixth section cannot declare the act of issuing it to be a high misdemeanor, punishable by indictment or impeachment.

I shall pass the charge found in these articles, that the letter of authority to Thomas was issued during a session of the Senate and without senatorial consent, with the single remark that it is made upon a misconception of the nature of an *ad interim* order. Such order is not an appointment, (within the meaning of the Constitution,) nor is it subject to senatorial advice and consent.

But the question remains: suppose the act of 1863 did completely repeal the act of 1795, relating to vacancies in executive offices, and that there is no law which expressly authorizes the letter of authority to General Thomas, then was the issuing of that letter a high misdemeanor in office? Unquestionably it was not, unless made such by the sixth section of the tenure-of-office act, which has just been disproved. In fact the issuing of such a letter by the President, even without statutory authority, when required by the interests of the public service, may be not innocent merely, but laudable. The order issued by President Lincoln to General Skinner, to act as Postmaster General *ad interim*, although without authority of law, was not a criminal offence. It was a justifiable order to meet an emergency in the public service. A large number of similar orders for *ad interim* service in the several executive departments, wholly unauthorized by any statute, have been put in evidence on the present trial. They were made by President Jackson and by his successors in the presidential office frequently and without question.

THE CONSPIRACY ARTICLES.

The fourth, fifth, sixth, and seventh articles of impeachment charge, in various forms, a conspiracy between the President and General Thomas on 21st of February, 1868, and are, when condensed and freed from verbiage, in substance as follows:

ARTICLE IV. That the President conspired with Thomas and others unknown with intent by intimidation and threats unlawfully to prevent Mr. Stanton from holding his office as Secretary of War, thus violating the Constitution and the conspiracy act of July 31, 1861, and thereby committing a high crime in office.

ARTICLE V. That he conspired with Thomas and others to prevent the execution of the tenure-of-office act, and, in pursuance of that conspiracy, unlawfully attempted to prevent Mr. Stanton from holding his office of Secretary of War, thereby committing a high misdemeanor in office.

ARTICLE VI. That he conspired with Thomas to seize by force the public property in the Department of War, whereof Stanton had custody, contrary to the conspiracy act of 1861, and with intent to violate the tenure-of-office act, whereby he did commit a high crime in office.

ARTICLE VII. That he conspired with Thomas unlawfully to seize the public property in the Department of War, in Stanton's custody, with intent to violate the tenure-of-office act, whereby he did commit a high misdemeanor in office.

The charges in the fourth and sixth articles, of conspiracy to use intimidation, threats, and force to prevent Mr. Stanton from holding his office, and to obtain possession of the public property in the War Department, contrary to the conspiracy act of 1861, are not sustained but disproved by the evidence upon the trial; and it is, therefore, unnecessary to subject them to particular examination.

The charges in the fifth and seventh articles, of conspiracy to violate and to prevent the execution of the tenure-of-office act, as well as those in the fourth and sixth articles, are founded upon the order for the removal of Mr. Stanton and the letter of authority to General Thomas of 21st of February, 1868, and have no support whatever if those papers were lawfully issued.

It is difficult to see how the simple issuing of an official executive order or letter under a claim of right, and its acceptance or peaceful action under it by a subordinate officer, can constitute a conspiracy in point of law. The confederating together—the mutual agreement or plot between the parties—which is an essential element of conspiracy, would in such case seem to be wanting. But, certainly, if the order and letter of authority were issued to accomplish a lawful purpose, there is an end of all the conspiracy articles, and of all the other articles down to and including the eighth. The allegations about intimidation, threats, and force in the fourth and sixth articles being unproved or disproved, all the first eight articles rest upon the assertion that Mr. Stanton's case is within the tenure-of-office act, and his tenure defined and protected by it. If that assertion be refuted, all those eight articles, unsupported, fall into ruin.

THE EMORY ARTICLE.

But few words are necessary upon the ninth article, which recites the conversation between the President and General Emory on the 22d February, 1868, in which the President expressed the opinion that the second section of the army appropriation act of March 2, 1867, which required that all orders and instructions relating to military operations issued by the President or Secretary of War should be issued through the General of the army, &c., was unconstitutional. The article charges the President with an intent to induce General Emory to violate said act, and to receive and obey his orders in contravention thereof, with the further intent thereby to enable him (the President) to prevent the execution of the tenure-of-office act, and to prevent Mr. Stanton from holding the office of Secretary of War.

The testimony, instead of sustaining these averments of intent, repels them, and it explains in a satisfactory manner how the interview between the President and General Emory was brought about, and how the conversation concerning the army appropriation act arose. It is not necessary to consider the legal sufficiency of this article in form or substance as an article of impeachment when its material averments are disproved.

THE BUTLER ARTICLE.

The tenth article charges the utterance of certain public speeches by the President as a high misdemeanor in office. The first was delivered at the Executive Mansion, in Washington, on the 18th day of August, 1866; the second at Cleveland, on the 3d September; and the third at St. Louis, on the 8th of September of the same year; and extracts from them are set forth in the specifications of this article. They are charged to have been indecent and unbecoming, and made with intent to bring the Congress of the United States into contempt and disgrace, and to excite the resentment of the people against it and against the laws by it duly enacted.

The sufficient answer to this article is, that it charges no offence against the laws of the United States, and that it calls in question that privilege of freedom of speech which is the common birthright of the American people. The President in those speeches denounced the thirty-ninth Congress for its course on the subject of reconstruction, and imputed to some of its members responsibility for the New Orleans massacre. He said also that it was a Congress of but a part of the States, a remark which was perfectly true, and did not necessarily import a denial of its constitutional powers. But, neither these nor any other observations made by him can be brought within the prohibitions of any law of the United States, and their utterance was the exercise of a right which cannot be questioned either in the ordinary courts of law or in a court of impeachment.

The case of Judge Humphreys is not a precedent to sustain this article. He was impeached, to be sure, for a speech made, but the speech was treasonable in character and effect, for it incited to armed resistance against the United States, and gave to the public enemies "aid and comfort." Its utterance was an *act* of treason which, being committed by a civil officer of the United States, rendered him liable to impeachment and removal from office.

THE STEVENS ARTICLE.

The eleventh article is nondescript, and a curiosity in pleading. As an article on which to convict, its strength consists in its weakness—in the obscurity of its charges and the intricacy of its form. As an afterthought of the House of Representatives, or rather as a reluctant concession by the House to the pertinacity of its author, it is not merely supplementary to the other articles in position, but bears upon its face the evidence of its distinct and peculiar origin. Considered in parts it is nothing—the propositions into which it is divisible cannot stand separately as charges of criminal conduct or intention; and considered as a whole it eludes the understanding and baffles conjecture. While we cannot suppose it to have been drawn in scorn of the Senate, before whom it was to be placed as an article of impeachment, it would be true to the paternity of a scornful spirit and a reckless brain if such paternity were assigned to it.

The matter of this article, so far as substance can be detected in it, is drawn mostly from the other articles; but that matter is arranged, manipulated, and combined together in a manner to vex the student and confound the judge; and the new particulars of charge or aggravation (whichever they may be) contained in the article are hinted at rather than expressed, and we vainly explore the context to discover distinctly their antecedents or the conclusions to which they lead.

As no abstract can do justice to this article, it must be given *in extenso*. It is as follows:

ART. 11. That said Andrew Johnson, President of the United States, unmindful of the high duties of his office, and of his oath of office, and in disregard of the Constitution and laws of the United States, did, heretofore, to wit, on the 18th day of August, A. D. 1866, at the city of Washington, and the District of Columbia, by public speech, declare and affirm, in substance, that the 39th Congress of the United States was not a Congress of the United States authorized by the Constitution to exercise legislative power under the same; but, on the contrary, was a Congress of only part of the States, thereby denying, and intending to deny, that the legislation of said Congress was valid or obligatory upon him, the said Andrew Johnson, except in so far as he saw fit to approve the same, and also thereby denying, and intending to deny, the power of the said 39th Congress to propose amendments to the Constitution of the United States; and, in pursuance of said declaration, the said Andrew Johnson, President of the United States, afterwards, to wit, on the 21st day of February, A. D. 1868, at the city of Washington, in the District of Columbia, did, unlawfully, and in disregard of the requirements of the Constitution—that he should take care that the laws be faithfully executed—attempt to prevent the execution of an act entitled "An act regulating the tenure of certain civil offices," passed March 2, 1867, by unlawfully devising and contriving, and attempting to devise and contrive, means by which he should prevent Edwin M. Stanton from forthwith resuming the functions of the office of Secretary for the Department of War, notwithstanding the refusal of the Senate to concur in the suspension theretofore made by said Andrew Johnson of said Edwin M. Stanton from said office of Secretary for the Department of War; and also by further unlawfully devising and contriving, and attempting to devise and contrive, means, then and there, to prevent the execution of an act entitled "An act making appropriations for the support of the army for the fiscal year ending June 30, 1868, and for other purposes," approved March 2, 1867; and also to prevent the execution of an act entitled "An act to provide for the more efficient government of the rebel States," passed March 2, 1867, whereby the said Andrew Johnson, President of the United States, did then, to wit, on the 21st day of February, A. D. 1868, at the city of Washington, commit, and was guilty of, a high misdemeanor in office.

No one having been known to assert that he understood fully this article, it may be thought hazardous to attempt its exposition; but the difficulty of the task will doubtless be taken into due account by all generous persons in judging its performance.

The inducement contained in the first three lines and the conclusion are taken from the formal parts of prior articles.

The clause which sets forth the speech of the 18th of August, 1866, and the intent of that speech, may be considered as constituting the body of the charge, as the ground of the charge, as a part of the charge, or as the introduction to the charge. Whichever it may be, it is borrowed from the tenth article; and, if condemned there, must fall here as a distinct charge or element of accusation.

Next, it is said that the President, "*in pursuance*" of said speech of 18th August, did, on the 21st February, 1868, "attempt to prevent the execution" of the tenure-of-office act by "devising and contriving, and attempting to devise and contrive, means" to prevent Stanton from resuming his office of Secretary of War, &c.

Is this merely a specification under the prior charge, or a continuation of that charge, or a substantive and distinct or separable accusation? If it be the first or second of these, it will share the fate of the prior charge in a vote of guilty or not guilty upon the whole article. And the words *in pursuance*, with which this division begins, may be thought to so connect it with the prior matter as to render this result certain. If, however, this division be a distinct or separable accusation, we are to examine it further. In that view it must aver the substance of a criminal charge. But this it does not do. It avers only certain action of the President's mind—no overt act; no conduct of his, good or bad. He "devised and contrived, and attempted to devise and contrive, means" to keep Mr. Stanton out of office; but he used no means, and he took no steps to create or provide them. It is true, he is charged with an "attempt to prevent the execution of the tenure-of-office act," but only by the "devising and contriving, and attempting to devise and contrive, means" to keep Mr. Stanton out of office.

In brief, this accusation is that the President cogitated the means to keep Mr. Stanton out of office, and thereby violated the tenure-of-office act! It is too plain for question that no criminal act is charged here, nor any fact set forth upon which a judicial investigation can be had or judgment be pronounced. But it has been supposed and asserted that this part of the eleventh article refers to a desire and intention of the President, not on 21st of February, but in January before, to prevent Mr. Stanton from resuming his office. Be it so. If we are to build up a proper charge with a proper date from materials obtained outside of the articles, and proceed to try the President upon it, to what conclusion may we arrive? Why, that the President had an intention to keep Stanton out, and devised a plan or means for that purpose, but did not use those means or put that plan into execution. Here was no breach of the tenure-of-office act, or of any other law. Whether his purpose was good or bad, it did not lead to an actual offence; and if his intention had been carried out in an act, what would that act have been? Why, obviously, *an order for the removal of Stanton* before he had actually resumed his office. But that would have raised precisely the same question which was raised by the order of removal of 21st February, which we are to determine under the first article of impeachment. An order removing

Mr. Stanton would have borne the same legal character whether issued to prevent him from resuming his office or to turn him out after he had resumed it.

The next clauses, and the concluding clauses of accusation in this article, aver a devising and contriving, &c., to prevent the execution of the army appropriation act, (a repetition of the charge in the ninth article, and unproved,) and also to prevent the execution of the reconstruction act of March 2, 1867, (also unproved.) Whether these clauses relate to the same antecedents or not, and whether they are independent of each other or not, we need not inquire. Nor is it necessary to enlarge upon the absurdity of holding that a contriving to prevent the execution of the army appropriation act or the reconstruction act will establish or tend to establish an attempt to prevent the execution of the tenure-of-office act; for, as these averments are not proved, their relations to prior parts of the article and to each other are unimportant.

THE TENURE-OF-OFFICE ACT.

There are several questions relating to the constitutionality and construction of the act of 2d March, 1867, ("to regulate the tenure of certain civil offices,") which remain to be examined. They do not arise upon the consideration of any one article alone, but upon the consideration of nearly all of them, and can be most conveniently presented in this place after the articles have been separately examined.

1. Was the tenure-of-office act constitutional in its application to heads of executive departments who were in office at the time of its passage? This question assumes, for the purposes of argument, that they were brought within the act by its terms and that a new tenure was fixed for them by it. I have no hesitation in answering this question in the negative, and in holding that it was not competent for Congress to assign to Mr. Stanton an office of more extended duration or greater security of tenure than that which he held under his commission by virtue of presidential appointment. This seems to me too clear for doubt or denial when we consider the character of the office and the plain words of the Constitution.

The Secretary of War is the head of an executive department; his office as such head is expressly mentioned in the Constitution, and his appointment must be by the President by and with the advice and consent of the Senate. As he is not an *inferior* officer, within the meaning of the appointment clause of the Constitution, Congress cannot provide another mode of appointing him, much less assume the power of appointing him to themselves. It follows that they cannot give to a Secretary a right to hold his office beyond the term for which he was appointed, or to hold it freed from a condition upon which the appointment was made.

Let this proposition be illustrated by examples, and its truth and soundness will more clearly appear. Take the case of a future Secretary, holding under this tenure-of-office act, for a term of four years and one month by virtue of a presidential appointment to which senatorial advice and consent has been given. Can Congress by law extend his term? Can they by statute authorize him to hold his office for eight or ten years instead of four? If so, the officer will hold under the statute during all the time added to his term in contempt of the constitutional power of appointment. Again, suppose the case of a Secretary appointed and commissioned to hold during the pleasure of the President. Can Congress by statute authorize him to hold during good behavior, thus making his office one for life (unless removed for legal misconduct) instead of one at the pleasure of the appointing power? In this case, also, the new right is conferred in derogation of the power held by the President and Senate under the Constitution. And in the precise case which we have before us, Mr. Stanton holding under his appointment and commission at the pleasure of the President, can

Congress by statute give him a right to hold his office for a term of years against the President's will? If they can do this they can also hereafter, at their pleasure, assign him an additional term of years or give him a life estate in his office. In either case what have we but a new appointment to office by Congress?

By the express words of the Constitution the principal officers of the government (including, I think, the heads of the executive departments) must be appointed by the President by and with the advice and consent of the Senate, and the appointment of inferior officers may be vested by law in the President alone, in the courts of law, or in the heads of departments. Each house of Congress may choose their own officers, but in no case whatever can Congress appoint an officer of the United States. Being clearly incapable of making an appointment, they cannot change one after it is made, giving it a character and duration which were not within the contemplation or intention of the appointing power when the office was conferred.

I conclude, then, that if the tenure-of-office act be construed to place the cases of Mr. Stanton and of the other Lincoln Secretaries within a new tenure-of-office rule, it is so far forth unconstitutional and void, and can afford no support to the first eight and to the eleventh articles of impeachment.

2. It is important to observe that no objection upon constitutional grounds is made, or can be made, to some parts of the tenure-of-office act. The sixth section, for instance, is entirely unexceptionable, and was very properly acted upon by the President in giving notice to the Secretary of the Treasury of Mr. Stanton's suspension in August, 1867. And so the second section of the act, in authorizing the suspension of officers between sessions of the Senate, violates no provision of the Constitution, and denies no just claim of executive power. It was quite competent for the President to suspend Mr. Stanton under that section, notwithstanding his denial of the validity of the first section, and if he had done so in express terms he would not have exposed himself to a charge of inconsistency. It is true he puts his suspension of Mr. Stanton upon the executive power to remove him under the Constitution, holding that the power to remove includes the power to suspend, but still the act of suspension fell within the letter of the law and was in all respects conformed to it. While it was from the President's point of view a good exercise of power under the Constitution, it was also undeniably a good exercise of power within the terms of the law; and if placed upon the latter ground alone it would not be an admission of the constitutionality of the whole law, but only of so much of the second section as authorizes suspension from office. It is only necessary to add here, by way of explanation, that while Mr. Stanton's case is believed not to come within the operation of the first section, the power to suspend him is clearly conferred by the second.

·3. I hold that the violation of law by a President which will constitute an impeachable high crime or misdemeanor must be a wilful and intentional violation, and in its nature calculated to produce serious injury to the public service. Mistake and error of judgment merely are not to be punished by impeachment, but only grievous and wilful crime which endangers the public safety or welfare. Therefore, if there was an honest misconstruction of the tenure-of-office act by the President, in holding that Mr. Stanton's case was not within it, he cannot be convicted. The removal of Mr. Stanton was not an act calculated to injure the public service or shock the moral sense of the people. And the construction of the tenure-of-office act adopted by the President, whether right or wrong, was not an unreasonable or rash one, but was precisely that construction which had been assigned to it in the Senate at the time of its passage, and which appears to be most consistent with its terms.

4. Assuming that the first section of the tenure-of-office act was one of doubtful constitutionality and construction, I hold that the President was fully justified

in challenging its application to his Secretaries, and in taking necessary steps to have its validity and construction determined in the courts of law. But his position as to his right and duty in this respect has been grossly misrepresented and, perhaps, greatly misunderstood. It was stated, however, by Judge Curtis, in his opening for the defence, with a clearness and completeness which leave nothing to be desired, and remove all excuse for misconception or complaint. He said:

I am not intending to advance upon or occupy any extreme ground, because no such ground has been advanced upon or occupied by the President of the United States. He is to take care that the laws be faithfully executed. When a law has been passed through the forms of legislation, either with his assent or without his assent, it is his duty to see that that law is faithfully executed so long as nothing is required of him but ministerial action. He is not to erect himself into a judicial court and decide that the law is unconstitutional, and that therefore he will not execute it. * * * * He asserts no such power. He has no such idea of his duty. His idea of his duty is, that if a law is passed over his veto which he believes to be unconstitutional, and that law affects the interests of third persons, those whose interests are affected must take care of them, vindicate them, raise questions concerning them if they should be so advised. If such a law affects the general and public interests of the people, the people must take care at the polls that it is remedied in a constitutional way.

But when, senators, a question arises whether a particular law has cut off a power confided to him by the people through the Constitution, and he alone can raise the question, and he alone can cause a judicial decision to come between the two branches of the government to say which of them is right, and after due deliberation with the advice of those who are his proper advisers, he settles down firmly upon the opinion that such is the character of the law, it remains to be decided by you whether there is any violation of his duty when he takes the needful steps to raise that question and have it peacefully decided. (Page 382.)

And again he said, (page 391:)

So long as it is a question of administrative duty merely, he, [the President,] holds that he is bound by the law.

It is admitted on all hands that a private citizen may proceed in a peaceful manner to resist any law which violates his personal rights under the constitution, and may bring such law before the courts for judicial condemnation. And even if he should be mistaken as to his right, and as to the invalidity of the law, his error will not be imputed to him as a crime.

And so, where a question arises as to the constitutional right of the President to change his constitutional advisers—the men who constitute his political household, and for whose acts he is responsible to the people and to the law—as against a statute which invades or denies to him such right, can it be doubted that he may challenge the statute and carry it into the courts of law for judgment? And where the statute is plainly in contempt of the past practice of the government, and of the very highest authorities which can be cited upon a question of constitutional law, and no one but the President can bring it to the test of judicial examination and judgment, is not his duty to challenge it as incontestable as his right?

CONCLUSION.

I have now concluded my examination of the several articles of impeachment and of the act of Congress upon which most of them are founded. The general question of presidential power under the Constitution to remove officers of the United States from office at discretion has been but slightly noticed, and no attention has been bestowed upon those topics of declamation and invective which have been intruded into the trial. The constitutional question was discussed by me at length when the tenure-of-office act was passed, and I do not find it necessary to repeat the argument then made by me in order to explain or vindicate my judgment upon these articles of impeachment. As to the extraneous and irrelevant matters introduced into the trial, and particularly into the argument, I put them wholly aside. This case is to be tried upon the laws which apply to it, and upon the facts which are duly proved. The issue joined is not political but judicial, and it is upon specific articles of accusation. They are to be decided honestly and firmly, and nothing beside them is to pass into judgment.

In my opinion the acquittal of the President upon all the charges preferred against him is authorized by law and demanded by justice. He has committed no high crime or misdemeanor. He has trampled upon no man's right; he has violated no public duty. He has kept his oath of office unbroken and has sought in a lawful manner to vindicate and preserve the high constitutional powers confided to him by the people. He cannot and ought not to be punished for his opinions upon public measures and public policy; and, in contemplation of law, his conduct in all the matters brought before us for review has been irreproachable. What he has done indicates not criminal intent but patriotic purpose; and besides, that true courage, sustained and invincible, which grapples with difficulty and defies danger.

OPINION OF MR. SENATOR HARLAN.

In the first article of impeachment the House of Representatives accuse Andrew Johnson, President of the United States, of the commission of "a high misdemeanor in office," in issuing an order, during the session of the Senate, for the removal of Edwin M. Stanton, Secretary of the Department of War, from said office, February 21, 1868, in violation of the Constitution and of an act entitled "An act regulating the tenure of certain civil offices," approved March 2, 1867.

The President in his answer to this article, presented to the Senate March 23, 1868, admits that he did remove said Stanton from said office by suspending him August 12, 1867, and by making it absolute and perpetual, as per order dated February 21, 1868; and justifies the act of removal by asserting—

That the *Constitution* of the United States confers on the President * * * * the *power at any and all times of removing from office all executive officers for cause, to be judged of by the President alone,* and that *the Congress could not deprive him thereof.* (Impeachment Record, p. 23.)

It is proper to observe in the beginning that the President does not justify under any existing statute—that of 1789, creating the Department of War, or any other. He admits the act of removal, and claims that it was not "a high misdemeanor in office." Alleging that the *Constitution* confers on him the absolute and exclusive right to remove all executive officers at discretion, whether the Senate be in session or not, and admitting the existence of an act of Congress prohibiting it, the act of removal was, nevertheless, legal, because, in his opinion, Congress had no right, under the Constitution, to prohibit, to regulate, or in any way to interfere with the exercise of this executive function.

This is the issue joined under the first article, which brings us necessarily to an examination of the provisions of the Constitution which are supposed to clothe the President with this exclusive authority to make *removals* from office.

The Constitution does not anywhere, in terms, confer on the *President* the authority to make *removals;* nor does it anywhere confer on him this right by *necessary implication.* It does confer on him the *qualified right to make appointments.*

The second clause of the second section of article two of the Constitution provides that—

He shall *nominate,* and by and with *the advice and consent of the Senate* shall appoint, ambassadors, other public ministers and consuls, judges of the Supreme Court, and all *other officers of the United States,* whose appointments are not herein otherwise provided for, and which shall be established by law.

It also provides that—

Congress may by law vest the appointment of such inferior officers as they think proper in the President alone, in the courts of law, or in the heads of departments.

And the last clause of this section provides that—

The President shall have power to fill up all vacancies that may happen during the recess of the Senate, by granting commissions which shall expire at the end of their next session.

It is therefore clear the President is clothed by direct grant of the Constitution with the absolute, unrestrained, and exclusive right to make *appointments* to fill *vacancies* temporarily which may *happen* during the *recess* of the Senate, and with the *qualified* right to make permanent *appointments* during the sessions of the Senate; but he is not clothed with the authority by direct grant to make *removals* either in the recess or during the sessions of the Senate.

Nor does the President appear to be vested with the exclusive authority to make removals by *any necessary implication*, or by any necessary construction of any other clause of the Constitution.

It is sometimes argued that the right to remove is a necessary incident or concomitant of the right to appoint. But this is begging the very question at issue. Is it a necessary incident of the power to appoint? If so, why is it so? May not the act of *appointment* be distinct and separate from the act of removal? If not—if they must necessarily go together—if they must necessarily be performed by the same party or parties—if they are necessary concomitants of each other, it will follow irresistibly that the President, having the exclusive and absolute authority to make temporary appointments to fill vacancies during the recess of the Senate, may make removals during the recess; and as he is clothed only with a *qualified* right to make appointments during the session, the right to *remove* during the sessions of the Senate must be *qualified* by the same limitations. To assert the contrary would involve the absurdity of insisting that the *incident* is superior to the *principle*, that the implied power is greater than the *direct grant;* or, to apply the reasoning in physics, it would be to assert that the *reflected* light from another surface may be superior to the direct solar ray—that the momentum of a flying projectile is greater than the original force from which it derived its motion. It is clear, therefore, as it seems to me, if the right of removal is an incident of the right to appoint—if the two acts must go together—if all the authority possessed by the President to *remove* an officer is *derived* from the grant of authority to *appoint*, and if the power to appoint during the sessions of the Senate is qualified, depending on the "advice and consent of the Senate," it must follow that the authority to remove during the sessions is in like manner qualified and dependent on the advice and consent of the Senate.

But if the power of *appointment* and the power of *removal* are separate functions, it would have been possible for the framers of the Constitution to have conferred on the President the authority to perform the one and to have withheld from him the authority to perform the other. Conferring on him the right *to appoint,* they might have left the power *to remove* in abeyance, to be regulated by law, or might have conferred the latter authority on some other officer or department of the government.

And if it should be found on examination that the authority to remove officers of the United States or any of them has been vested by the Constitution in some other organ of the government, it would seem to raise a very strong presumption that it was not the intention of the framers to confer this authority, as them, on the President.

Now, by reference to the fourth section of article two of the Constitution it will be seen that the authority to remove all civil officers is vested in the Senate. It directs that—

The President, Vice-President, and *all* civil officers of the United States shall be *removed from office* on impeachment for and conviction of treason, bribery, or other high crimes and misdemeanors.

The sixth clause of the third section of article one provides that—

The Senate shall have the sole power to try all impeachments.

This, if it were a new question, would seem to make it clear that the President could not make removals of *civil* officers. The Constitution does not confer the right on him by any direct grant, and does confer the power in direct terms on the Senate to remove all civil officers, and, if they should see proper, to disqualify them over afterward from the right to hold office under the United States.

The implied right of the President to make removals at discretion is sometimes claimed under the third section of article three of the Constitution, which provides that the President " shall take care that the laws be faithfully executed." It is insisted that the President must exercise the power of removing unfaithful, incompetent, and corrupt officers in order to secure "the faithful execution of the laws." But if this is a correct construction, if being charged with seeing that the laws are faithfully executed necessarily vests in him the right to remove unfaithful officers at his own discretion, he may remove *judicial* as well as *executive* officers ; the judges of the Supreme Court as well as the heads of executive departments. If not, why not? It may be said that the Constitution provides that "the judges, both of the Supreme and inferior courts, shall hold their offices during good behavior." But who shall judge of their "behavior," whether it be good or bad ? If in the President's opinion the judges do behave badly ; if in his opinion, on account of their malfeasance or misfeasance in office, he could not faithfully execute the laws, why may he not remove them ? It may be said that the Constitution does not in terms confer on the President the right to remove them even for *cause*, however flagrant, and does confer the power on the Senate by impeachment. I answer that it does not confer on the President in express terms the right to remove other officers, even for *cause*, and that it does confer this right on the Senate to remove the latter as well as judges. In this respect the judges are not exceptional.

It may be said, however, that although the Constitution does vest the power to remove all *other* civil officers for impeachable offences in the Senate, it does not provide that they shall not be removed in some other mode or by some other officer or department of the government. I answer, nor does the Constitution provide that judges shall not be removed in any other mode, or by any other officer or department of the government. It simply says that the judges shall hold their offices during good behavior. When they behave badly they may be removed. They may be removed for impeachable offences, like all other civil officers, by the Senate. And if clothing the Senate with power to remove other civil officers does not, by implication, *deprive* the President of the authority to remove them when, in his opinion, the faithful execution of the laws may require it, by what process of reasoning can it be claimed that the judges can be removed by the Senate *only* ? The Constitution does not say so. It does not prohibit the removal of the judges by the President. And if he finds that a judge is corrupt, wilfully misinterprets the laws, or refuses to adjudicate causes, and if Congress should not be in session, or being in session, should refuse or neglect to remove him by impeachment, why may not the President do it ? If it is conceded that he may remove a Secretary of War at discretion, either during the session of the Senate or in the recess, under that clause of the Constitution which makes it his duty "to see that the laws are faithfully executed," why may he not, under the same clause, remove a judge for what he may consider gross misconduct ?

There can be but one answer. The practice of the government has sanctioned the removal of other civil officers by the President at will during the recess of the Senate, and by and with the advice and consent of the Senate during its sessions ; and no President has yet ventured on the exercise of the authority to remove the judges of the courts of the United States. The distinction has no sanction in reason, or in the well-settled rules of legal construction.

But if the President is clothed by the Constitution " with power at any and all *times* (during the session as well as in the recess) of removing from office all executive officers for cause to be judged of by the President alone," and if, as he claims in his answer, "the Congress could not deprive him thereof," may he not also remove at discretion officers of the army and navy? And if not, why not?

The Constitution does not fix their tenure of office. It makes no distinction between them and civil officers (other than judges) in this respect. They are all appointed under that clause of the Constitution, heretofore recited, which provides that the President "shall nominate, and by and with the advice and consent of the Senate shall appoint, * * * * all officers of the United States," and the other provisions which say that Congress shall have power " to raise and support armies" and " to provide and maintain a navy." It does not provide that the officers shall hold for life or good behavior. So far as the Constitution provides, if the President is vested with authority to remove Mr. Stanton, the Secretary of War, he may also remove any officer of the army or navy; and if Congress cannot by law regulate the tenure of office of the former, Congress cannot regulate the tenure of the latter. It is true Congress has from time to time by law regulated the tenure of military officers and provided the mode for their removal.

During nearly the whole period of the existence of the government they have been removable for cause alone, in pursuance of the finding of a court-martial, subject, however, to the approval of the President. During the late war Congress authorized the President to drop any military officer from the rolls at discretion; at the close of the war this act was repealed. But if it should be conceded that Congress cannot by law regulate the tenure of civil officers and the manner of their removal, it must be conceded also that Congress cannot, under the Constitution, regulate the tenure of officers of the army and navy. If the act regulating the tenure of certain civil officers is void by reason of conflict with the Constitution, then all the acts regulating the tenure of military officers are also void. And if the President may innocently violate the former, he may with impunity trample under foot the latter; if he can remove Secretary Stanton, he may dismiss General Grant or Admiral Farragut.

I cannot bring myself to believe that the framers of the Constitution could have intended to vest in the President a purely discretionary power so vast and far-reaching in its consequences, which if exercised by a bad or a weak President would enable him to bring to his feet all the officers of the government, military and civil, judicial and executive, to strike down the republican character of our institutions and establish all the distasteful characteristics of a monarchy. For the participation of the Senate in appointments during its sessions would become nugatory, if the President may legally remove them at discretion, and fill up the vacancies thus made by temporary appointments. And the people would be without remedy if, as he avers in his answer, Congress has not the right to restrain or by law regulate the exercise of this executive function.

This leads me to notice in consecutive order the argument presented by several senators during this consultation, tending to justify this act of removal, drawn from their construction of the statute of August 7, 1789, creating the War Department.

The first section of this act, after creating this department, provides—

That there shall be a principal officer therein, to be called the Secretary for the Department of War.

The second section authorizes the appointment by the Secretary of an inferior officer, to be called the chief clerk—

Who, whenever the said principal officer shall be removed from office by the President of the United States, or in any other case of vacancy, shall, during such vacancy, have the charge and custody of all records, books, and papers appertaining to the said department. (Statutes at Large, vol. 1, p. 50.)

The phrase "whenever the said principal officer shall be removed from office by the President" is in itself, they think, a grant of power to remove the Secretary of War; that this law was not repealed by the act of March 2, 1867, "to regulate the tenure of certain civil offices," but is still in force, and consequently that the removal of Mr. Stanton was legal and innocent.

Before proceeding to examine the law of March 2, 1867, I will express my doubt of the correctness of the construction placed by these senators on the statute of August 7, 1789.

I doubt it because the President, although advised by counsel of the highest professional standing, does not claim protection under this law, but under the Constitution itself; asserting, in his answer to this article, that his authority to make removals is derived from that instrument, and that "the Congress could not deprive him thereof." He does not even so much as name this act of 1789. I doubt it, because a careful examination of the debates of the Congress by whom this law was enacted will show that the members who insisted on placing this phraseology in the text of the act, did not construe it as a grant of authority to make removals. In fact, Marshall, in his Life of Washington, (vol. 2, page 162,) referring to the debate on this subject, says that after words had been incorporated into the bill explicitly authorizing the President to remove the head of the department, they were stricken out and the foregoing words substituted for the express purpose of avoiding the inference that, in the opinion of Mr. Madison and those who agreed with him, Congress could either grant to or withhold this authority from the President. It is perfectly clear that they wished to leave this question of authority to remove where the Constitution left it, with a legislative expression of opinion that the President could make removals. This was doubtless Mr. Madison's opinion and the opinion of a majority of the members of the House, concurred in by one-half of the senators present, as the record shows that the bill passed by the casting vote of the Vice-President. Hence the President's counsel, who doubtless examined this case thoroughly, do not claim authority under this law. They knew its intent was not a grant, but an expression of opinion on a constitutional construction. And as such it is entitled to the weight which may properly attach to the utterances made in congressional debates by members of Congress; which, judging from what I have heard from the President's counsel and senators in this consultation, are not considered infallible—even less authoritative than judicial opinions—and, in my opinion, neither is entitled to any more respect than is required by the weight of the reasoning by which their opinions are supported. In the forum of reason is the tribunal where they and we all are compelled to bring our opinions for arbitrament. As a legislative declaration of opinion injected into the body of a law, granting nothing and denying nothing, commanding nothing and prohibiting nothing, it is no more authoritative than the resolution of the Senate of February 21, 1868, informing the President that, by the removal of Mr. Stanton and the appointment of Mr. Thomas, he violated the Constitution and laws; and, in fact, is not entitled to so much respect as an authority, because in adopting the declaration in the law of 1789, there was in the House a very small majority in the affirmative, and the senators were *equally divided;* while in the adoption of the declaration in the resolution, twenty-eight senators voted in the affirmative, and but six senators voted in the negative; and in the House of Representatives the substantive allegation of the resolution, as set forth in the first and second articles of impeachment, was affirmed by a three-fourths majority.

Nor can the declaration cited by senators from Kent's Commentaries, in which, referring to this debate, he is made to say that this legislative construction of the Constitution "has ever since been acquiesced in and acted upon as of decisive authority in this case," be adopted unquestioned. For he proceeds to say:

It applies to *every other officer of the government* appointed by the President and Senate, whose term of duration is not specially declared. (Kent's Commentaries, vol. 1, p. 310.)

This would include all the officers of the army and navy; and it is known to every reader of the statutes that Congress has from the beginning of the government to the present hour regulated by law the removals of this entire class of officers; and that Congress has, at various times, enacted laws regulating the mode of removal of civilians. Nor has it been held at any time "declaring" by law the tenure of office—that is the term of years during which the commission may run—affects in any way the power of removal. For example, the law creating land officers, postmasters, territorial governors, judges, &c., and many others, authorize appointments for fixed periods, and yet it has been uniformly maintained in practice that the President could at any time during the recess of the Senate remove them at will, and during the sessions with the concurrence of the Senate. It has been thus settled in practice that the limitation of the tenure to a fixed period does not affect the question of removal. Hence, as the commentator's facts prove to be untrue, his conclusions cease to have weight. So far as the uniform legislative action of the government can settle a construction of the Constitution, it has been decided that Congress has the power to fix the tenure of all officers except judges, and also the manner of their removal.

And the executive construction is equally uniform and conclusive. It has been definitely settled in practice that the President may in the recess *remove* all officers at will, except judges and other officers whose tenure and mode of removal is regulated by law, and that during the session removals may be made by the President only with the concurrence of the Senate.

It is extremely doubtful whether the framers of the Constitution intended to confer the power on the President to make removals during the recess. The language used, "*to fill up* vacancies which may *happen*," seems to imply the contrary. And they seem to have carefully provided against the assumption of this power under the plea of necessity, to protect the public interests from unworthy officers during the recess, by authorizing the President to convene the Senate in extra session *whenever* in his judgment the public interests require it, thus enabling him at all times to submit the question of changes to the judgment of that body.

But removals have been made in the civil service during the recess of the Senate by all the Presidents. This power under the Constitution has been during the whole period gravely questioned by the ablest statesmen and jurists. The practice has, nevertheless, obtained. No law existed until recently prohibiting it. It may, therefore, be conceded as settled that the President may, in the absence of law to the contrary, during the recess of the Senate, make removals from office. It is, however, equally well settled by precedent that the President cannot make removals, except in pursuance of law, during the session, otherwise than by appointments of successors, to be made "by and with the advice and consent of the Senate;" and that in making removals in the military service he must follow the mode indicated in the articles of war and army regulations established by law.

This construction has been so uniform as to render it impossible for the learned counsel for the President during this protracted trial to produce even one well-authenticated case to the contrary. The case cited by them of the removal of Timothy Pickering, Secretary of State, by the elder Adams, is the only one which they claim to be an exception. And in that case the letter removing Mr. Pickering and the President's message nominating Mr. Marshall as his successor bear the same date. But if this case were admitted to be an exception to the general rule, it would violate all established principles of correct reasoning to assume that one exceptional case establishes the true construction of the Constitution, it being in direct conflict with the otherwise uniform practice, extending over the entire period of the history of the government.

I therefore conclude that Andrew Johnson, President, violated the Constitution of the United States and his oath of office in issuing his order, February 21, 1868, the Senate being in session, removing Edwin M. Stanton, Secretary of the Department of War, from said office; and that he is guilty of a high misdemeanor in office as charged in this article of impeachment, even if the law "regulating the tenure of certain civil offices," approved March 2, 1867, had never been enacted.

But I am unable to perceive any serious ambiguity in that statute. The authorities all agree that it is legitimate in construing any apparently obscure passage in the text of a new law to ascertain, first, the old law or usage; secondly, the evil or matter of complaint; thirdly, the remedy proposed in the new law. Now let us apply these rules to the statute of March 2, 1867.

First. Under the old law or usage the President had the right, as we have seen, to make removals at will during the recess of the Senate.

Secondly. The evil or subject-matter of complaint was that the President, now arraigned at your bar, had been, during the previous recess of the Senate, removing multitudes of faithful officers from their respective posts of duty, and appointing untrustworthy successors, for purely partisan purposes, to aid him in making war on the measures adopted by Congress to secure the restoration of peace, harmony, and good government in the recently insurrectionary States.

Thirdly. The remedy proposed was to fix by law the tenure of civil offices and regulate the manner of removals, as had been done from the beginning in relation to military officers, so as to prevent the President from making removals at discretion, even during the recess, without the approval of the Senate. Hence the first section enacts—

That every person holding any civil office to which he has been appointed, by and with the advice and consent of the Senate, and every person who shall hereafter be appointed to any such office, and shall become duly qualified to act therein, is, and shall be, entitled to hold such office until a successor shall have been in like manner appointed and duly qualified, except as herein otherwise provided: *Provided*, That the Secretaries of State, of the Treasury, of War, of the Navy, and of the Interior, the Postmaster General, and the Attorney General, shall hold their offices respectively for and during the term of the President by whom they may have been appointed, and for one month thereafter, subject to removal by and with the advice and consent of the Senate.

Does it effect the object proposed? It evidently embraces all existing civil officers appointed by the President, by and with the advice and consent of the Senate, as well as all who may hereafter be appointed. It is evidently not its purpose to *extend* the legal term of service of any of them, for section four provides—

That nothing in this act contained shall be construed to extend the term of any office the duration of which is limited by law.

But its intent is clearly twofold. *First, to prohibit removals; secondly, to limit the terms of service.* The prohibition to remove evidently applies to *all*. The limitation of the term is applied to the Secretaries of State, of the Treasury, of War, of the Navy, of the Interior, the Postmaster General, and the Attorney General, and none others. This analysis removes all ambiguity. The section provides that every civil officer appointed by the President, with the approval of the Senate, shall hold his office until his successor shall be in like manner appointed; that is, no removal shall take place except by the appointment, with the concurrence of the Senate, of a successor; provided, however, that the offices of heads of departments shall terminate by operation of law in one month after the expiration of the presidential term. The assumption that any of the seven officers were intended to be excepted out of the general prohibition of removal at the will of the President alone is clearly inconsistent with the last clause of the proviso, which declares that these seven offices shall be "subject to removal by and with the advice and consent of the Senate." For, if it was in fact, as contended, the intent of this proviso to except any of these officers from the general prohibition to remove by the President alone, why should it confer the authority to remove them with the concurrence of the Senate?

The learned casuistry to which we have listened over the construction of the phrase "term of the President by whom they may have been appointed," has, according to my apprehension, no application to the vital point in this controversy—*the prohibition of removal*. It relates to the *limitation of the term of service*, and nothing else.

I have not been able to perceive anything in the legislative history attending the passage of this act inconsistent with this construction. It is substantially this: the Senate passed the bill prohibiting the removal of all civil officers, except the heads of departments. The House struck out the exception; the Senate declined to concur; the House insisted. The bill was then sent to a joint committee of conference of the two houses. They proposed a compromise, the House yielding something and the Senate yielding something. They finally agreed that the prohibition of removals by the President at discretion should apply to all, including heads of departments, but that the termination of the period of service of the latter should be fixed at one month after the close of each presidential term. They so reported, and their report was adopted by both houses.

I have now only to state that the President has officially construed the law as applicable to Secretary Stanton in his order of August 12, 1867, suspending him from office, as provided in the second section of this act, and in his letter addressed to the Secretary of the Treasury, informing that officer that he had suspended said Stanton, as directed by the eighth section of this act. The letter is in these words:

EXECUTIVE MANSION,
Washington, D. C., August 14, 1867.

SIR: In compliance with the requirements of the eighth section of the act of Congress of March 2, 1867, entitled "An act regulating the tenure of certain civil offices," you are hereby notified that on the 12th instant Hon. Edwin M. Stanton was suspended from office as Secretary of War and General Ulysses S. Grant authorized and empowered to act as Secretary of War *ad interim*.

I am, sir, very respectfully, yours,

ANDREW JOHNSON.

Hon. HUGH MCCULLOCH,
Secretary of the Treasury.

He also admits its application to Stanton by sending to the Senate his message dated December 12, 1867, communicating to that body his reasons for this suspension, as directed by the second section. That he construed this law as applicable to Secretary Stanton, and wilfully violated it, is also established by his answer to the first article of impeachment, as found in the record of the trial. He responds in these words:

This respondent was also aware that this act [of March 2, 1867] was understood and intended to be an expression of the opinion of the Congress by which that act was passed, that the power to remove executive officers for cause might by law be taken from the President and vested in him and the Senate jointly. (Impeachment Trial, p. 24.)

This would seem to settle the question of the President's *purpose*. He admits that he "*was aware* that this act was understood and *intended* to be an expression of the opinion of Congress" that he could not remove executive officers without the concurrence of the Senate. Now, no one will be so hardy as to deny that the *intent* of a law is *the law* in very *essence* and *truth*, for the only object of the analysis of any law by courts or commentators is to ascertain, if possible, the *intent* of the legislature enacting it.

That the President did proceed to inquire, as he asserts in this connection, whether the act was not capable of some other construction, and if in the course of this inquiry he did honestly conclude, as he asserts, that it was susceptible of another construction different from the admitted intent of Congress, so far from being a palliation, was a grave aggravation of his offence; for it is a declaration of a *purpose* to bend the law from its *true intent* to suit his wishes. He thus confesses that he *sought to evade* and did, as he thinks, evade the declared and admitted will of the legislature.

With this admission in his official answer to this article before our eyes, there can be no doubt that he did with *malice prepense* violate the *true, known*, and *admitted intent* of this law. Believing as I do that the President did thus officially place the correct construction on said law, and that said law is in harmony with the Constitution, and that he did wilfully violate its provisions which violation is declared by said law to be "a high misdemeanor," I do not perceive how it is possible for a senator, on his oath, to avoid finding him guilty as charged in the first article of impeachment.

In relation to the second article of impeachment, I may observe, the House of Representatives accuse the President of the committal of a high misdemeanor in office in appointing Lorenzo Thomas, Adjutant General United States army, Secretary of War *ad interim* on the 21st day of February, 1868, there being no vacancy in said office, without the advice and consent of the Senate, the Senate being in session.

The President in his answer admits that he did issue the order of appointment, as charged, without the advice and consent of the Senate, the Senate being in session, (Impeachment trial, p. 27,) and justifies by declaring that there was at the time a vacancy in said office, and that—

It was lawful according to a long and well-established usage to empower and authorize the said Thomas to act as Secretary of War *ad interim*.

To support this justification, his counsel in the argument of this cause, and several senators during this consultation, have cited two statutes which authorize temporary appointments. The first one was enacted May 8, 1792, and the second February 13, 1795. The first one is marked "obsolete" on the statute-book, and is admitted to have been repealed (if not before) by the act of February 20, 1863, which covers all the matter contained in the act of 1792, and is also inconsistent with it. This brings us to the consideration of the plea of authority to appoint Mr. Thomas to the office of Secretary of War *ad interim* during the session and without the consent of the Senate, under the statute of 1795, even if a vacancy did legally exist. These are the exact words of the law:

That in case of vacancy in the office of Secretary of State, Secretary of the Treasury, or of the Secretary of the Department of War, or of any officer of either of the said departments, whose appointment is not in the head thereof, whereby they cannot perform the duties of their said respective offices, it shall be lawful for the President of the United States, in case he shall think it necessary, to authorize any person or persons, at his discretion, to perform the duties of the said respective offices until a successor be appointed or such vacancies be filled: *Provided*, That no one vacancy shall be supplied, in manner aforesaid, for a longer term than six months. Approved February 13, 1795. (Statutes at Large, vol. I, p. 415.)

I notice that the senator from Maine, [Mr. Fessenden,] in the observations submitted by him, has, as I think, misconstrued this law by omitting in the text, as cited by him, an entire clause, necessary to be considered in arriving at a correct construction. It is in these words: "Whereby they cannot perform the duties of their said respective offices." These are words of limitation which the judge or commentator has no right to ignore or erase. Had they been omitted by Congress in enacting the law—did they not stand as a part of it—the senator's rendering would be less vulnerable. But, giving these words their usual meaning and force, his rendering is manifestly erroneous. Applying this law to the actual case at bar, and omitting unnecessary descriptive phrases, it will read:

That in case of *vacancy* in the office of the Secretary of War, *whereby he cannot perform the duties* of his said office, it shall be lawful for the President of the United States, *in case he shall think it necessary*, to authorize any person, at his discretion, to perform the duties of the said office, &c.: *Provided*, That no one vacancy shall be supplied, in manner aforesaid, for a longer term than six months.

Now, it may be observed that there are two classes of vacancies known to the statutes, and which may occur in the administration of the departments: *absolute legal vacancies* in office by death, resignation, or expiration of term of service, whereby there are no officers in existence for the respective offices; and *vacancies* occasioned by the *absence of officers* from their respective offices, on account of sickness, or absence from the seat of government. The question therefore arises *whether* the *vacancies* contemplated and provided for by this statute are of the first or of the second class, or whether both are included.

It appears to my mind perfectly clear that the first class are not intended to be included, and that the law is applicable only to cases of vacancy by the absence of officers from their offices, the said offices being legally filled, but the incumbents being incapable, for any sufficient reason, to perform their official duties.

To construe this statute so as to apply to absolute vacancies in office would, as it appears to me, make it both useless and unconstitutional. For, in case of an absolute legal vacancy in the recess of the Senate, the Constitution itself, in direct terms, authorizes the President to fill it temporarily, to continue for as long or as short a period as he may desire, not extending beyond the end of the next session of the Senate. Hence, if this law was intended to confer on the President the power to fill *legal* vacancies in office, occurring in the recess, it is nugatory—it is perfectly useless—for the President was previously vested by the Constitution with this authority.

And to assume that the intent of this law was to provide for absolute legal vacancies in office occurring during the sessions of the Senate would make it clearly unconstitutional; for the Constitution provides, as we have seen, that the President "shall nominate, and by *and with the advice and consent of the Senate* shall appoint, all officers" whose appointments are not otherwise provided for in the Constitution itself, whether created by the Constitution or by law. The President must, therefore, obtain the consent of the Senate when in session before he can make an appointment to fill an absolute legal vacancy, with the exception of one class of officers only, *inferior* officers, who may be appointed by the President alone when Congress shall so provide by law. But the office of Secretary of War is not of this class. It is not an inferior office, and is declared by the law of 1789 to be a superior office, and the Secretary is styled "a principal officer." Congress could not, therefore, by law vest the appointment of this and similar officers exclusively in the President, either for a short or a long period. To maintain that Congress could by law dispense with the advisory power of the Senate would be equivalent to a declaration that Congress could by law amend the Constitution or abolish it entirely; for if Congress could suspend one of its provisions, they may suspend any or all of them. This would be reducing the authority of that great charter to the grade of a statute only.

The limitation of such appointments to a period not exceeding six months could not change the constitutionality of the provision. For, if Congress could by a statute dispense with the advisory power over appointments during the sessions of the Senate for a single day, they could for a year or ten years or forever. It is not a question of *time* during which such appointment may run, but of constitutional power to deprive the Senate of an opportunity to exercise a judgment in the case. The Constitution vests this authority in the Senate, without regard to the length of *time* of the service of the appointee; and it does not confer the authority on the President to disregard it, nor on Congress the power to set it aside either for a long or a short period.

Congress could, of course, abolish the War or any other department created by law. They could also abolish the office of Secretary of War, or unite the War Department with some other department, temporarily or permanently, and require the head of that other department to perform the duties of both, or might reduce it to the grade of a bureau in another department, and authorize an inferior officer to perform the duties now devolving on the Secretary; and probably might, by law, authorize the President to do this at his discretion; but this is not what is claimed by the President under the law of 1795. He does not claim that this authorizes him to abolish the War Department or the office of Secretary of War, or to unite it with any other department temporarily, or to devolve the duties of Secretary of War on the head of another department, or to reduce it in grade and devolve its duties on an inferior officer. He claims that Congress has by this law, approved February 13, 1795, vested in him the right "to authorize *any person*" (adopting the words of the statute) "*at his discretion* to perform the duties of" Secretary of War during the session of the Senate, there being an actual legal vacancy in said office, for a period not exceeding six months.

Now, if this is the true meaning of this law, it authorizes the President, as we have seen, to dispense with the advisory power of the Senate, when in session, in the appointment of a *great* officer to fill "a principal" office for a period of six months; and, as this would be in direct conflict with the Constitution, the law as thus construed must be void.

To give this law force, we are therefore compelled to construe the word "vacancy," mentioned in the act as meaning a *corporeal* vacancy—the *absence* of the *officer* from his office—the legal tenure still continuing in him as when the officer is out of the city; is disabled by insanity or sickness; is in custody or in prison, or is necessarily occupied with other duties. This interpretation is in perfect harmony with the literal and usual meaning of the words of the statute itself, "in case of vacancy in the office of Secretary *   *   * of the Department of War *   *   *   *whereby 'he cannot perform the duties of*' his 'said office, it shall be lawful for the President of the United States, in case he shall think it necessary, to authorize any person, at his discretion, to perform the duties of the said office,'" &c. And any other construction would render the qualifying phrase, "whereby they cannot perform the duties of their said respective offices," meaningless. It is a settled rule of construction that you must, if possible, give every word of a statute meaning and force.

But what meaning can be attached to this clause if applied to an actual legal vacancy, as by death, resignation, removal, or expiration of legal term of service? In such cases the officer, and his legal functions as such, have ceased to exist. There is no *officer* in existence. To apply these qualifying words in such cases, "whereby they cannot perform the duties of their said respective offices," is sheer nonsense. The law does not provide that "in case of *any* vacancy," or *all* vacancies, but in case of vacancies of this description, "whereby the officers cannot perform the duties of their offices."

The same reasoning would apply to another qualifying phrase in this act, authorizing the President to make temporary appointments. It is in these words: "In case he shall think it necessary." How is it possible to apply this language to an actual legal vacancy in a superior office, such as Secretary of State, Secretary of War, &c.? The necessity of having an officer to fill these great offices was settled by Congress when the law was enacted creating them. If an actual vacancy occurred, the necessity of filling it could not be a question. But if the officer was sick or absent from the city, "whereby he could not perform the duties of his said office," the question of *necessity* for the appointment of some one, by detail or otherwise, to perform these duties, until he recovered or returned to his post, would arise. And no one would be a more fit person to judge of that necessity than the President.

I may observe here, in passing, that the allegation so frequently made during this trial by the President's counsel, and by senators in this consultation, that "the practice" of making temporary appointments, the Senate being in session, to fill absolute legal vacancies in office, "has been frequent and unbroken, *   *

almost from the formation of the government," is not supported by facts. I have examined, as carefully as my time would permit, all that long list of cases of temporary appointments, supposed by the President's counsel to bear on this case, as they stand recorded in the printed record of this trial, beginning on page 575 and ending on page 582, and find that nearly all of them were made, as the list itself shows, on account of the absence or sickness of the regularly appointed officer. And nearly all of the residue were made to fill vacancies occurring during the recess of the Senate, and I do not find a single case of temporary appointment to fill a vacancy occasioned by a *removal* made during the session of the Senate. I therefore conclude that no such case exists, or it would have been produced, as the learned and numerous counsel had full access to the records of the departments and of the chief executive office.

Should it appear, however, that a case or two of temporary appointments had been made by previous Presidents, in a period of nearly eighty years, on account of an actual vacancy occurring by death or resignation, during the session of the Senate, it would not justify the unaccountable allegation of counsel and of senators that the precedents were almost numberless, and that the chain was unbroken. Nor would one case or many of violated law, by others, if they really existed, justify the President in the performance of an illegal act. But when his act is unsupported by a single case, this attempt at justification is most remarkable and startling.

After giving this subject the most careful examination of which I am capable, I am compelled to come to the conclusion that if there had been an existing legal vacancy in the office of Secretary of War, the President had no authority under the statute of 1795, or any other law, the Senate being in session. to fill it in the mode charged in the second article of impeachment, and admitted in the President's answer. Much less had he the right to both create and fill a vacancy, as charged in the first and second articles.

These acts, whether taken jointly or separately, seem to me to be a clear violation both of the Constitution and the law. That they were performed by the President deliberately and wilfully for the purpose of defeating the execution of the latter, according to its true intent and meaning, is, according to my judgment, fully established. I do not, therefore, see my way clear, under the solemnities of my oath, to find him innocent.

Several of the succeeding articles merely recite the offence set forth in article one and article two in different forms, and do not therefore require specific notice, and I do not deem it important to present a formal analysis of the remaining articles which allege other offences, nor of the testimony by which they are supported. On these I will be content to express my opinion by my vote.

OPINION OF MR. SENATOR DOOLITTLE.

I.—OF THE REMOVAL OF STANTON.

Mr. CHIEF JUSTICE AND SENATORS: I concur in so much of the opinions of Senators Hendricks, Grimes, Johnson, Fessenden, Trumbull, and Buckalew, that I shall not go over the grounds so ably stated by them to give a general opinion in this cause. They all concur with the senator from Ohio (Mr. Sherman) and my colleague (Mr. Howe) that the tenure-of-office act left the President at liberty to remove the Secretary of War at pleasure. In this opinion I agree. I think that opinion will command the assent of nine-tenths of the legal profession of the whole country. It is too clear, in my opinion, to admit of serious argument, and I shall spend no time upon that.

II.—OF THE APPOINTMENT OF THOMAS AD INTERIM.

Upon the question whether the act of 1863 in relation to *ad interim* appointments repealed the act of 1795, I wish to say a word. There is no express repeal. If repealed at all it must be by implication.

The act of 1795 covers all vacancies—vacancies by death, by resignation, by removal, and by expiration of term—four in all. Its language is, "That in case of vacancy" (including all vacancies) "it shall be lawful for the President to authorize *any person* to perform the duties," &c., for a term not longer than six months.

The act of 1863 says that in case of two vacancies, namely, by death or by resignation, the President may authorize *some other officer* to perform those duties not longer than six months.

While the act of 1795 covers all vacancies, including vacancies by removal and vacancies by expiration of term, as well as by death and by resignation, the act of 1863 does not provide for the two vacancies first named at all. Of necessity, therefore, it does not repeal or modify that act as to those two vacancies.

My colleague (Mr. Howe) is entirely mistaken in saying that the act of 1795 was made obsolete by the act of 1863. It is true, in the margin of the volume, (first vol., 415,) the word "*obsolete*" is found. But immediately over it are found the words, also, "act of May 8, 1792, ch. 37." It is the act of 1792 which is marked obsolete, not the act of 1795. What makes this certain is, the volume itself was published in 1825, nearly forty years before the act of 1863.

Besides, President Buchanan, in 1860, under the act of 1795, appointed Mr. Holt Secretary of War *ad interim* in place of Floyd. The Senate, by resolution, asked him by what authority he acted, the Senate being in session. His answer was conclusive, overwhelming, giving more than a hundred cases of similar appointments *ad interim*. It is impossible for my colleague to maintain that the statute of 1795 is obsolete.

Neither is the statute of 1795 repealed by the act of March 2, 1867, so far as the case of Stanton is concerned; for unless his case is covered by that act, and my colleague demonstrates that it is not, his removal and the authority issued to General Thomas to perform the duties *ad interim* is no violation of that act. It is clearly within the act of 1795. I shall dwell no longer upon that.

Mr. HARLAN. I desire to call the attention of the Senator from Wisconsin to certain words in the act of 1795 which I have not heard commented upon, and which may be words of limitation, namely, "whereby they cannot perform the duties of their respective offices." Do not these words limit the act to certain vacancies?

Mr. DOOLITTLE. Let me remind my honorable friend from Iowa (Mr. Harlan) that he will find the same words in the act of 1863 applying to vacancies caused by death and resignation, "whereby they cannot perform the duties of their respective offices."

Mr. BUCKALEW. The same words are in the act of 1792. In the acts of 1795 and 1863 these words were borrowed from the act of 1792.

Mr. DOOLITTLE. That is true; I thank the senator from Pennsylvania. I think it clear that, under the act of 1795, the President can authorize a person to do the duties of the head of the War Department in case of vacancy by removal, and the power to remove Mr. Stanton is clear under the act. The senator from Ohio, (Mr. Sherman,) upon the passage of the act, maintained that, and, in his opinion just delivered, makes that point too clear to be questioned.

As to the other charges I concur entirely with the opinions of Senators Hendricks, Grimes, and others, and shall not repeat what they have so well said.

But, Mr. Chief Justice and Senators, there is another point upon which I wish to submit my views very briefly. The senator from Ohio said however conscientiously the President may have believed that he had a right to appoint Mr. Thomas *ad interim,* if two-thirds of the Senate differ with him in opinion in the construction of the law he must be found guilty of a high crime or high misdemeanor, for which he should be removed from his high office. From this doctrine I dissent. The President, as the chief executive, is compelled officially to construe the laws of Congress. He must execute them; and to do that he must know their meaning. If he mistake the meaning of a doubtful statute, upon which the ablest senators and lawyers disagree, to say he can be found guilty of a high crime or high misdemeanor because he mistakes its true meaning while honestly seeking to find it, shocks the moral sense of the civilized world. It is a monstrous proposition. Intention, criminal intention, is of the very essence of crime. A public officer may commit a trespass and become liable to respond, in damages, in a civil suit, when, mistaking the law, he violates the rights of person or property of another. But to say that a high public officer, with good motives and with an honest intent to obey, though he mistake the meaning of a statute, can be found guilty of a high crime and misdemeanor which shall subject him to the heaviest punishment which can fall upon a public man in high office, is to assert a doctrine never before heard in any court of justice. There is no evidence to show on his part an intention to violate the Constitution or the law. From a criminal act a criminal intent, in the absence of proof to the contrary, may be inferred. But in this case all criminal intent is positively disproved by the managers themselves.

The message of the President, which the managers have put in evidence against him—and there is no evidence to contradict it—distinctly avers his entire good faith; and further, that he was advised by all the members of his cabinet, including Mr. Stanton—

First, that the tenure-of-office act was unconstitutional, and therefore no law at all.

Every student at law knows that every enactment of Congress is just as much subject to the higher law of the Constitution as if it contained an express proviso in these words : " Provided that nothing herein contained shall have any force or validity whatever unless it is authorized by the Constitution of the United States." In a word, an unconstitutional enactment is not a law; it is void; and void things are no things at all.

And secondly, the message proves, also, that every member of his cabinet advised him that if the law were constitutional his power to remove Stanton was not limited by the very terms of the act.

It will be remembered, also, the President's counsel offered to prove the fact that the President was so advised by every member of his cabinet, including, of course, the Attorney General.

Now, Mr. Chief Justice and Senators, whatever effect may be given to the opinions of other members of the cabinet, the opinion of the Attorney General, given to the President, must be regarded as judicial so far at least, in the absence of bad faith in him, or in the President when acting upon that opinion, as to protect the President from all charge of crime or high misdemeanor.

The statute providing for an Attorney General enacts—

And there shall also be appointed a meet person, learned in the law, to act as Attorney General of the United States, who shall be sworn or affirmed to a faithful execution of his office, whose duty it shall be to prosecute and conduct all suits in the Supreme Court in which the United States shall be concerned, and to give his advice and opinion upon questions of law, when required by the President of the United States, &c.

This opinion of the Attorney General, if given and acted upon in good faith by the President, is a protection against any charge of high crime or high misdemeanor. The Attorney General is chosen because he is *learned in the law,* to advise a President who may not be a lawyer at all. He is confirmed by the Senate as a judge is confirmed, for high character and legal learning.

Take the case of General Grant, who is a candidate for the presidency. He is no lawyer. Suppose he should be elected, and the senator from New Jersey, who is learned in the law, should be nominated and confirmed by the Senate as his Attorney General, and that some of the many doubtful, hasty, and almost unintelligible acts of Congress came before him, for construction; if General Grant should, in good faith, act upon the opinion of Senator Frelinghuysen as his Attorney General, no matter how erroneous that opinion might be, can any man be so lost to all sense of common justice and fair dealing as to assert that General Grant could be guilty of a high crime or high misdemeanor when acting in accordance with it? And learned in the law as that honorable senator is, high as he deservedly stands in the profession in his State, it is certainly no disparagement to him to say that Mr. Stanbery stands as high as he or any other senator upon this floor in personal character and legal ability.

Sir, much may be forgiven, much must be forgiven in times of high party excitement for the judicial blindness which it begets. But when this temporary and frenzied excitement shall have passed away, as pass it will, and when men shall carefully review this case and all the evidence given on this trial, their surprise will be not that a few republican senators can rise above party prejudice and refuse to be driven from their clear convictions by party furor, but their utter astonishment will be, that any respectable senator should ever for one moment have entertained the thought of convicting the President of the United States of a high crime or a high misdemeanor upon the charges and evidence produced upon this trial.

OPINION OF MR. SENATOR SUMNER.

I voted against the rule of the Senate allowing Opinions to be filed in this proceeding, and regretted its adoption. With some hesitation I now take advantage of the opportunity, if not the invitation, which it affords. Voting "guilty" on all the articles, I feel that there is no need of explanation or apology. Such a vote is its own best defender. But I follow the example of others.

BATTLE WITH SLAVERY.

This is one of the last great battles with slavery. Driven from these legislative chambers, driven from the field of war, this monstrous power has found a refuge in the Executive Mansion, where, in utter disregard of the Constitution and laws, it seeks to exercise its ancient far-reaching sway. All this is very plain. Nobody can question it. Andrew Johnson is the impersonation of the tyrannical slave power. In him it lives again. He is the lineal successor of John C. Calhoun and Jefferson Davis; and he gathers about him the same supporters. Original partisans of slavery north and south; habitual compromisers of great principles; maligners of the Declaration of Independence; politicians without heart; lawyers, for whom a technicality is everything, and a promiscuous company who at every stage of the battle have set their faces against equal rights; these are his allies. It is the old troop of slavery, with a few recruits, ready as of old for violence—cunning in device, and heartless in quibble. With the President at their head, they are now entrenched in the Executive Mansion.

Not to dislodge them is to leave the country a prey to one of the most hateful tyrannies of history. Especially is it to surrender the Unionists of the rebel States to violence and bloodshed. Not a month, not a week, not a day should be lost. *The safety of the Republic requires action at once.* The lives of innocent men must be rescued from sacrifice.

I would not in this judgment depart from that moderation which belongs to the occasion; but God forbid that, when called to deal with so great an offender, I should affect a coldness which I cannot feel. Slavery has been our worst enemy, assailing all, murdering our children, filling our homes with mourning, and darkening the land with tragedy; and now it rears its crest anew, with Andrew Johnson as its representative. Through him it assumes once more to rule the Republic and to impose its cruel law. The enormity of his conduct is aggravated by his barefaced treachery. He once declared himself the Moses of the colored race. Behold him now the Pharaoh. With such treachery in such a cause there can be no parley Every sentiment, every conviction, every vow against slavery must now be directed against him. Pharaoh is at the bar of the Senate for judgment.

The formal accusation is founded on certain recent transgressions, enumerated in articles of impeachment, but it is wrong to suppose that this is the whole case. It is very wrong to try this impeachment merely on these articles. It is unpardonable to higgle over words and phrases when, for more than two years the tyrannical pretensions of this offender, now in evidence before the Senate, as I shall show, have been manifest in their terrible, heart-rending consequences.

IMPEACHMENT A POLITICAL AND NOT A JUDICIAL PROCEEDING.

Before entering upon the consideration of the formal accusation, instituted by the House of Representatives of the United States in their own name and in the name of all of the people thereof, it is important to understand the nature of the proceeding; and here on the threshold we encounter the effort of the apologists who have sought in every way to confound this great constitutional trial with an ordinary case at Nisi Prius and to win for the criminal President an Old Bailey acquittal, where on some quibble the prisoner is allowed to go without day. From beginning to end this has been painfully apparent, thus degrading the trial and baffling justice. Point by point has been pressed, sometimes by counsel and sometimes even by senators, leaving the substantial merits untouched, as if on a solemn occasion like this, involving the safety of the Republic, there could be any other question.

The first effort was to call the Senate, sitting for the trial of impeachment, a court, and not a Senate. Ordinarily names are of little consequence, but it cannot be doubted that this appellation has been made the starting-point for those technicalities which are so proverbial in courts. Constantly we have been reminded of what is called our judicial character and of the supplementary oath we have taken, as if a senator were not always under oath, and as if other things within the sphere of his duties were not equally judicial in character. Out of this plausible assumption has come that fine-spun thread which lawyers know so well how to weave.

The whole mystification disappears when we look at our Constitution, which in no way speaks of impeachment as judicial in character, and in no way speaks of the Senate as a court. On the contrary it uses positive language, inconsistent with this assumption and all its pretended consequences. On this head there can be no doubt.

By the Constitution it is expressly provided that " the *judicial power* shall be vested in one Supreme Court and in such inferior courts as the Congress may from time to time ordain and establish," thus positively excluding the Senate from any exercise of "the judicial power." And yet this same Constitution provides that "the Senate shall have the sole power to try all impeachments." In the face of these plain texts it is impossible not to conclude that in trying impeachments senators exercise a function which is not regarded by the Constitution as "judicial," or, in other words, as subject to the ordinary conditions of judicial power. Call it senatorial or political, it is a power by itself and subject to its own conditions.

Nor can any adverse conclusion be drawn from the unauthorized designation of court, which has been foisted into our proceedings. This term is very expansive and sometimes very insignificant. In Europe it means the household of a prince. In Massachusetts it is still applied to the legislature of the State, which is known as the General Court. If applied to the Senate it must be interpreted by the Constitution, and cannot be made in any respect a source of power or a constraint.

It is difficult to understand how this term, which plays such a part in present pretensions, obtained its vogue. It does not appear in English impeachments, although there is reason for it there, which is not found here. From ancient times Parliament, including both houses, has been called a court, and the House of Lords is known as a court of appeal. The judgment on English impeachments embraces not merely removal from office, as under our Constitution, but also punishment. And yet it does not appear that the lords sitting on impeachments are called a court. They are not so called in any of the cases, from the first in 1330, entitled simply, "Impeachment of Roger Mortimer, Earl of March, for Treason," down to the last in 1806, entitled, "Trial of Right Honorable Henry Lord Viscount Melville before the Lords House of Parliament in Westminster for High Crimes and Misdemeanors whereof he was accused in certain articles of Impeachment." In the historic case of Lord Bacon, we find, at the first stage, this title, "Proceedings in Parliament against Francis Bacon Lord Verulam;" and after the impeachment was presented, the simple title, "Proceedings in the House of Lords." Had this simplicity been followed in our proceedings, one source of misunderstanding would have been removed.

There is another provision of the Constitution which testifies still further, and, if possible, more completely. It is the limitation of the judgment in cases of impeachment, making it political and nothing else. It is not in the nature of *punishment*, but in the nature of *protection to the Republic*. It is confined to removal from office and disqualification; but, as if aware that this was no punishment, the Constitution further provides that this judgment shall be no impediment to indictment, trial, judgment, and punishment "according to law." Thus again is the distinction declared between an impeachment and a proceeding "according to law." The first, which is political, belongs to the Senate, which is a political body; the latter, which is judicial, belongs to the courts, which are judicial bodies. The Senate removes from office; the courts punish. I am not alone in drawing this distinction. It is well known to all who have studied the subject. Early in our history it was put forth by the distinguished Mr. Bayard, of Delaware, the father of senators, in the case of Blount, and it is adopted by no less an authority than our highest commentator, Judge Story, who was as much disposed as anybody to amplify the judicial power. In speaking of this text, he says that impeachment "is not so much designed to punish the offender as *to secure the State against gross official misdemeanors;* that it touches neither his person nor his property, *but simply directs him of his political capacity.* (*Story, Commentaries, vol.* 1, *sec.* 803.) All this seems to have been forgotten by certain apologists on the present trial, who, assuming that impeachment was a proceeding "according to law," have treated the Senate to the technicalities of the law, to say nothing of the law's delay.

As we discern the true character of impeachment under our Constitution we shall be constrained to confess that it is a political proceeding before a political body, with political purposes; that it is founded on political offences, proper for the consideration of a political body and subject to a political judgment only. Even in cases of treason and bribery the judgment is political, and nothing more. If I were to sum up in one word the object of impeachment under our Constitution, meaning that which it has especially in view, and to which it is practically limited, I should say *Expulsion from Office.* The present question is, shall Andrew Johnson, on the case before the Senate, be expelled from office.

Expulsion from office is not unknown to our proceedings. By the Constitution a senator may be expelled with "the concurrence of two-thirds;" precisely as a President may be expelled with "the concurrence of two-thirds." In each of these cases the same exceptional vote of two-thirds is required. Do not the two illustrate each other? From the nature of things they are essentially similar in character, except that on the expulsion of the President the motion is made by the House of Representatives at the bar of the Senate, while on the expulsion of a senator the motion is made by a senator. And how can we require a technicality of proceeding in the one which is rejected in the other? If the Senate is a court, bound to judicial forms on the expulsion of the President, must it not be the same on the expulsion of a senator? But nobody attributes to it any such strictness in the latter case. Numerous precedents attest how, in dealing with its own members, the Senate has sought to do substantial justice without reference to forms. In the case of Blount, which is the first in our history, the expulsion was on the report of a committee, declaring him "guilty of a high misdemeanor, entirely inconsistent with his public trust and duty as a senator." (*Annals of Congress*, 15*th* Congress, 1797, *p.* 44.) At least one senator has been expelled on simple motion, even without reference to a committee. Others have been expelled without any formal allegations or formal proofs.

There is another provision of the Constitution which overrides both cases. It is this: "Each house may determine its rules of proceeding." The Senate on the expulsion of its own members has already done this practically and set an example of simplicity. But it has the same power over its "rules of proceeding" on the expulsion of the President; and there can be no reason for simplicity in the one case not equally applicable in the other. Technicality is as little consonant with the one as with the other. Each has for its object the *Public Safety*. For this the senator is expelled; for this, also, the President is expelled. *Salus populi suprema lex.* The proceedings in each case must be in subordination to this rule.

There is one formal difference, under the Constitution, between the power to expel a senator and the power to expel the President. The power to expel a senator is unlimited in its terms. The Senate may, "with the concurrence of two-thirds, expel a member," nothing being said of the offence; whereas the President can be expelled only "for treason, bribery, or *other high crimes and misdemeanors.*" A careful inquiry will show that, under the latter words, there is such a latitude as to leave little difference between the two cases. This brings us to the question of impeachable offences.

POLITICAL OFFENCES ARE IMPEACHABLE OFFENCES.

So much depends on the right understanding of the character of this proceeding, that even at the risk of protracting this discussion, I cannot hesitate to consider this branch of the subject, although what I have already said may render it superfluous. *What are impeachable offences* has been much considered in this trial, and sometimes with very little appreciation of the question. Next to the mystification from calling the Senate a court has been that other mystification from not calling the transgressions of Andrew Johnson impeachable offences.

It is sometimes boldly argued that there can be no impeachment under the Constitution of the United States, unless for an offence defined and made indictable by an act of Congress; and, therefore, Andrew Johnson must go free, unless it can be shown that he is such an offender. But this argument mistakes the Constitution, and also mistakes the whole theory of impeachment.

It mistakes the Constitution in attributing to it any such absurd limitation. The argument is this: Because in the Constitution of the United States there are no common-law crimes, therefore there are no such crimes on which an impeachment can be maintained. To this there are two answers on the present occasion; first, that the District of Columbia, where the President resides and exercises his functions, was once a part of Maryland, where the common law prevailed; that when it came under the jurisdiction of the United States it brought with it the whole body of the law of Maryland, including the common law, and that at this day the common law of crimes is still recognized here. But the second answer is stronger still. By the Constitution *Expulsion from Office* is "on impeachment for and conviction of treason, bribery, *or other high crimes and misdemeanors;*" and this, according to another clause of the Constitution, is "the supreme law of the land." Now, when a constitutional provision can be executed without superadded legislation, it is absurd to suppose that such superadded legislation is necessary. Here the provision executes itself without any re-enactment; and, as for the definition of "treason" and "bribery" we resort to the common law, so for the definition of "high crimes and misdemeanors" we resort to the parliamentary law and the instances of impeachment by which it is illustrated. And thus clearly the whole testimony of English history enters into this case with its authoritative law. From the earliest text-writer on this subject (*Woodeson, Lectures, vol.* II, *p.* 601) we learn the undefined and expansive character of these offences; and these instances are in point now. Thus, where a lord chancellor has been thought to put the great seal to an ignominious treaty; a lord admiral to neglect the safeguard of the seas; an ambassador to betray his trust; a privy councillor to propound dishonorable measures; a confidential adviser to obtain exorbitant grants or incompatible employments, or *where any magistrate has attempted to subvert the fundamental law or introduce arbitary power;* all these are high crimes and misdemeanors, according to these precedents by which our Constitution must be interpreted. How completely they cover the charges against Andrew Johnson, whether in the formal accusation or in the long antecedent transgressions to which I shall soon call attention as an essential part of the case nobody can question.

Broad as this definition may seem, it is in harmony with the declared opinions of the best minds that have been turned in this direction. Of these none so great as Edmund Burke, who, as manager on the impeachment of Warren Hastings, excited the admiration of all by the varied stores of knowledge and philosophy, illumined by the rarest eloquence, with which he elucidated his cause. These are his words:

It is by this tribunal that statesmen who abuse their power are tried before statesmen and by statesmen, *upon solid principles of state morality. It is here that those who by an abuse of power have polluted the spirit of all laws can never hope for the least protection from any of its forms.* It is here that those who have refused to conform themselves to the protection of law can never hope to escape through any of its defects. (*Bond, Speeches on Trial of Hastings, vol.* 1 *p.* 4.)

The value of this testimony is not diminished, because the orator spoke as a manager. By a professional license an advocate may state opinions which are not his own; but a manager cannot. Representing the House of Representatives and all the people, he speaks with the responsibility of a judge, so that his words may be cited hereafter. In saying this I but follow the claim of Mr. Fox. Therefore, the words of Burke are as authoritative as beautiful.

In different but most sententious terms, Mr. Hallam, who is so great a light in constitutional history, thus exhibits the latitude of impeachment and its comprehensive grasp:

A minister is answerable for *the justice, the honesty, the utility of all measures* emanating from the Crown, *as well as their legality;* and thus the executive administration is or *ought to be subordinate in all great matters of policy* to the superintendence and virtual control of the two houses of Parliament. (*Hallam, Constitutional History,* vol. 2, chap. 12.)

Thus, according to Hallam, even a failure in justice, honesty, and utility, as well as in legality, may be the ground of impeachment; and the administration should in all great matters of policy be subject to the two houses of Parliament—the House of Commons to impeach and the House of Lords to try. Here again the case of Andrew Johnson is provided for.

Our best American lights are similar in character, beginning with the Federalist itself. According to this authority impeachment is for "those offences which proceed from the *misconduct of public men,* or, in other words, from the abuse or violation of some public trust; and they may with peculiar propriety be deemed *political*, as they relate to injuries done immediately to society itself." (No. 65.) If ever injuries were done immediately to society itself; if ever there was an abuse or violation of public trust; if ever there was misconduct of a public man; all these are now before us in the case of Andrew Johnson. The Federalist has been echoed ever since by all who have spoken with knowledge and without prejudice. First came the respected commentator, Rawle, who specifies among causes of impeachment "the fondness for the individual extension of power;" "the influence of party and prejudice;" "the seductions of foreign states;" "the baser appetite for illegitimate emolument;" and "the involutions and varieties of vice too many and too artful to be anticipated by positive law;" all resulting in what the commentator says are "not inaptly termed *political offences*." (Page 19.) And thus Rawle unites with the Federalist in stamping upon impeachable offences the epithet "political." If in the present case there has been on the part of Andrew Johnson no base appetite for illegitimate emolument and no yielding to foreign seductions, there has been most notoriously the influence of party and prejudice, also to an unprecedent degree an individual extension of power, and an involution and variety of vice impossible to be anticipated by positive law, all of which, in gross or in detail, is impeachable. Here it is in gross. Then comes Story, who, writing with the combined testimony of English and American history before him, and moved only by a desire of truth, records his opinion with all the original emphasis of the Federalist. His words are like a judgment. According to him the process of impeachment is intended to reach "personal misconduct, or gross neglect, or usurpation or habitual disregard of the public interests in the discharge of the duties of *political office*;" and the commentator adds that it is "to be exercised over offences committed by public men in violation of their public trust and duties;" that "the offences to which it is ordinarily applied are of a *political* character;" and that strictly speaking "the power partakes of a *political* character." (*Story's Commentaries, vol.* 2, § 746, 764.) Every word here is like an ægis for the present case. The later commentator, Curtis, is, if possible, more explicit even than Story. According to him an "impeachment is not necessarily a trial for crime;" "its purposes lie wholly beyond the penalties of the statute or customary law;" and this commentator does not hesitate to say that it is a "proceeding to ascertain *whether cause exists for removing a public officer from office;*" and he adds that "such cause of removal may exist where no offence against public law has been committed, as, where the individual has, from immorality or imbecility, *or maladministration, become unfit to exercise the office.*" (*Curtis on the Constitution, p.* 360.) Here again the power of the Senate over Andrew Johnson is vindicated, so as to make all doubt or question absurd.

I close this question of impeachable offences by asking you to consider that all the cases which have occurred in our history are in conformity with the rule which so many commentators have announced. The several trials of Pickering, Chase, Peck, and Humphreys exhibit its latitude in different forms. Official misconduct, including in the cases of Chase and Humphreys offensive utterances, constituted the high crimes and misdemeanors for which they were respectively arraigned. These are precedents. Add still further, that Madison, in debate on the appointing power, at the very beginning of our government, said : " I contend that the *wanton removal of meritorious officers* would subject the President to impeachment and removal from his own high trust." (*Elliot's Debates, vol.* 4, *p.* 141.) But Andrew Johnson, standing before a crowd, said of meritorious officers that "he would kick them out," and forthwith proceeded to execute his foul-mouthed menace. How small was all that Madison imagined; how small was all that was spread out in the successive impeachments of our history, if gathered into one case, compared with the terrible mass now before us.

From all these concurring authorities, English and American, it is plain that impeachment is a power broad as the Constitution itself, and applicable to the President, Vice President, and all civil officers through whom the republic suffers or is in any way imperilled. Show me an act of evil example or influence committed by a President, and I show you an impeachable offence, which becomes great in proportion to the scale on which it is done, and the consequences which are menaced. The Republic must receive no detriment; and impeachment is one of the powers of the Constitution by which this sovereign rule is maintained.

UNTECHNICAL FORM OF PROCEDURE.

The *Form of Procedure* is a topic germane to the last head, and helping to illustrate it. Already it has been noticed in considering the political character of impeachment; but it deserves further treatment by itself. Here we meet the same latitude. It is natural that the trial of political offences, before a political body, with a political judgment only, should have less of form than a trial at common law; and yet this obvious distinction is constantly disregarded. The authorities, whether English or American, do not leave this question open to doubt.

An impeachment is not a technical proceeding, as at *nisi prius* or in a county court, where the rigid rules of the common law prevail. On the contrary, it is a proceeding according to parliamentary law, with rules of its own, unknown in ordinary courts. The formal statement and reduplication of words, which constitute the stock-in-trade of so many lawyers, are exchanged for a broader manner more consistent with the transactions of actual life. The precision of history is enough without the technical precision of an indictment. In declaring this rule I but follow a memorable judgment in a case which occupied the attention of England at the beginning of the last century. I refer to the case of the preacher Sacheverell, impeached of high crimes and misdemeanors on account of two sermons, in which he put forth the doctrine of non-resistance, and denounced the revolution of 1688, by which English liberty was saved. After the arguments on both sides, the judges on questions from the Lords answered that by the law of England and constant practice "the particular words supposed to be criminal ought to be specified in indictments." And yet, in face of this declaration by the judges of England of a familiar and indisputable rule of the common law, we have the rule of parliamentary law, which was thus set forth:

It is resolved by the lords spiritual and temporal in Parliament assembled, That by the law and usage of Parliament in prosecutions by impeachments for high crimes and misdemeanors by writing or speaking, *the particular words supposed to be criminal are not necessary to be expressly specified in such impeachments.* (Howell's *State Trials*, vol. 15, p. 467.)

The judgment here does not extend in terms beyond the case in hand; but plainly the principle announced is that in impeachments the technicalities of the common law are out of place, and the proceedings are substantially according to the rule of reason. A mere technicality, much more a quibble, such as is often so efficacious on a demurrer, is a wretched anachronism when we are considering a question of history or political duty. Even if tolerated on the impeachment of an inferior functionary, such a resort must be disclaimed on the trial of a Chief Magistrate, involving the Public Safety.

The technicalities of the law were made for protection against power, not for the immunity of a usurper or a tyrant. They are respectable when set up for the safeguard of the weak, but they are out of place on impeachments. Here again I cite Edmund Burke:

God forbid that those who cannot defend themselves upon their merits and their actions may defend themselves behind those fences and intrenchments that are made to secure the liberty of the people; that power and the abuses of power should cover themselves by those things which were made to secure liberty. (*Bond's Trial of Hastings*, vol. 1, p. 10.)

Never was there a case where this principle, belonging to the law of impeachment, was more applicable than now.

The origin of impeachment in our own Constitution and contemporary authority vindicate this very latitude. One of the apologists sought to sustain himself in an argument against this latitude, by insisting that it was with much hesitation, and only at the last moment, that this jurisdiction over impeachment was originally conferred on the Senate. This is a mistake, as will appear from a simple statement. The proposition to confer this jurisdiction on the Supreme Court was made before it had been determined that the judges should be appointed by the President with the advice and consent of the Senate. The latter conclusion was reached by a unanimous vote of the convention 7th September, 1787. On the next day, 8th September, Roger Sherman raised the objection, that the Supreme Court was "improper to try the President because the judges would be appointed by him." This objection prevailed, and the trial was at once intrusted to the Senate, by the vote of all the States with one exception; and then immediately thereafter, on the same day, the scope of impeachment was extended from "treason to bribery," so as to embrace "other high crimes and misdemeanors," and, thus intrusted and thus enlarged, it was made to embrace "the Vice-President and other civil officers of the United States."

From this simple narrative it appears, that, while the Supreme Court, *a judicial body*, was contemplated for the trial of impeachments, the jurisdiction was restrained to two well-known crimes at common law, which have since been defined by statutes of the United States; but this jurisdiction, when confided to the Senate, *a political body*, was extended to political offences, in the trial of which a commensurate discretion followed from the nature of the case. It was in this light that the proceeding was explained by the Federalist, in words which should be a guide to us now:

The nature of the proceeding can *never be tied down by such strict rules*, either in the delineation of the offence by the prosecutors or in the construction of it by the judges, as in common cases serve to limit the discretion of courts in favor of personal security. (Federalist, No. 65.)

This article was by Alexander Hamilton, writing in concert with James Madison and John Jay. Thus by the highest authority at the adoption of the Constitution we find that impeachment "can never be tied down by strict rules," and that this latitude is applicable to "the delineation of the offence," meaning thereby the procedure or pleading, and also to the "construction of the offence," in both of which cases the "discretion" of the Senate is enlarged beyond that of ordinary courts.

RULES OF EVIDENCE.

From the form of procedure I pass to the *Rules of Evidence;* and here again the Senate must avoid all technicalities and not allow any artificial rule to shut out the truth. It would allow no such thing on the expulsion of a senator. How can it allow any such thing on the expulsion of a President? On this account I voted to admit all evidence that was offered during the trial, believing, in the first place, that it ought to be heard and considered; and, in the second place, that, even if it were shut out from these proceedings, it could not be shut out from the public or be shut out from history, both of which must be the ultimate judges. On the impeachment of Prince Polignac and his colleagues of the cabinet, in 1830, for signing the ordinances which cost Charles X his throne, some forty witnesses were sworn without objection, in a brief space of time, and no testimony was excluded. An examination of the two volumes, entitled *Procès des Derniers Ministres de Charles X* will confirm what I say. This example was to my mind not unworthy of imitation on the present occasion.

There are other rules, which it is not too late to profit by. One of these relates to the burden of proof and is calculated to have a practical bearing. The other relates to matters of which the Senate will take cognizance without any special proof, thus importing into the case unquestionable evidence, which explains and aggravates the transgressions charged.

(1.) Look carefully at the object of this trial. Primarily it is for the expulsion of the President from office. Its motive is not punishment, not vengeance, but the *Public Safety*. Nothing less than this could justify the ponderous proceeding. It will be for the criminal courts to award the punishment due to his offences. The Senate considers only how the safety of the people, which is the supreme law, can be best preserved; and to this end the ordinary rule of evidence is reversed. If on any point you entertain doubts, the benefit of those doubts must be given to your country; and this is the supreme law. When tried on an indictment in the criminal courts Andrew Johnson may justly claim the benefit of your doubts; but at the bar of the Senate on the question of his expulsion from office, his vindication must be in every respect and on each charge beyond a doubt. He must show that his longer continuance in office is not inconsistent with the *Public Safety:*

<blockquote>
Or, at least so prove it,
That the probation bear no hinge or loop
To hang a doubt on.
</blockquote>

Anything short of this is to trifle with the Republic and its transcendent fortunes.

It is by insisting upon doubts that the apologists of the President, at the bar and in the Senate, seek to save him. For myself, I can see none such, but assuming that they exist, then should they be marshalled for our country. This is not a criminal trial, where the rule prevails: better that many guilty men should escape than one innocent man should suffer. This rule, which is so proper in its place, is not applicable to a proceeding for expulsion from office; and who will undertake to say that any claim of office can be set against the Public Safety?

In thus stating the just rule of evidence, I do little more than apply those time-honored maxims of jurisprudence, which require that every interpretation shall be always in favor of liberty. Early in the common law we were told that he is to be adjudged impious and cruel who does not favor liberty: *impius et crudelis judicandus est qui libertati non favet.* Blackstone, whose personal sympathies were with power, is constrained to confess that "the law is always ready to catch at anything in favor of liberty." (*Blackstone's Commentaries*, vol. 2, p. 94.) But liberty and all else are contained in the Public Safety; they depend on the rescue of the country from a presidential usurper. Therefore should we now, in the name of the law, "catch at anything" to save the Republic.

2. There is another rule of evidence which, though of common acceptance in the courts, has peculiar value in this case, where it must exercise a decisive influence. It is this: *Courts will take judicial cognizance of certain matters, without any special proof on the trial.* Some of these are of general knowledge, and others are within the special knowledge of the court. Among these, according to express decision, are the frame of government and the public officers administering it; the accession of the Chief Executive; the sitting of Congress and its usual course of proceeding; the usual course of travel; the ebbs and flows of the tide; *also whatever ought to be generally known within the limits of the jurisdiction, including the history of the country.* Besides these matters of general knowledge a court will take notice of its own records, the conduct of its own officers, and whatever passes in its own presence or under its own eyes. For all this I cite no authority; it is superfluous. I add a single illustration from the great English commentator: "If a contempt be committed in the face of the court, the offender may be instantly apprehended and imprisoned at the discretion of the judges, without any further proof or examination." (*Blackstone's Commentaries*, vol. 4, p. 286.)

If this be the rule of courts, *a fortiori* it must be the rule of the Senate on impeachments; for we have seen that, when sitting for this purpose, the Senate enjoys a latitude of its own. Its object is the Public Safety, and, therefore, no aid for the arrival at truth can be rejected. No gate can be closed. But here is a gate opened by the sages of the law and standing open always, to the end that justice may not fail.

Applying this rule to the present proceeding, it will be seen at once how it brings before the Senate, without any further evidence, a long catalogue of crime, affecting the character of the President beyond all possibility of defence, and serving to explain the latter acts on which the impeachment is founded. It was in this chamber, in the face of the Senate and the ministers of foreign powers, and surrounded by the gaze of thronged galleries, that Andrew Johnson exhibited himself in beastly intoxication while he took his oath of office as Vice-President; and all that he has done since is of record here. Much of it appears on our journals. The rest is in authentic documents published by the order of the Senate. Never was a record more complete.

Here in the Senate we know officially how he has made himself the attorney of slavery—the usurper of legislative power—the violator of law—the patron of rebels—the helping hand of rebellion—the kicker from office of good citizens—the open bung-hole of the treasury—the architect of the "whiskey ring"—the stumbling block to all good laws by wanton vetoes and then by criminal hindrances; all these things are known here beyond question. To the apologists of the President, who set up the quibbling objection that they are not alleged in the articles of impeachment, I reply that, even if excluded on this account from judgment, they may be treated as evidence. They are the reservoir from which to draw in determining the true character of the latter acts for which the President is arraigned, and especially the *intent* by which he was animated. If these latter were alone, without connection with the transgressions of the past, they would have remained unnoticed. Impeachment would not have been ordered. It is because they are a prolongation of that wickedness, under which the country has so long suffered, and spring from the same bloody fountain, that they are now presented for judgment. They are not alone; nor can they be faithfully considered without drawing upon the past. The story of the God Thor in Scandinavian mythology is revived, whose drinking-horn could not be drained by the strongest quaffer, for it communicated with the vast and inexhaustible ocean. Andrew Johnson is our God Thor, and these latter acts for which he stands impeached are the drinking-horn whose depths are unfathomable.

OUTLINE OF TRANSGRESSIONS OF ANDREW JOHNSON.

From this review of the character of this proceeding, showing how it is political in character—before a political body—and with a political judgment, being expulsion from office and nothing more; then how the transgressions of the President, in their protracted line, are embraced under "impeachable offences;" then how the form of procedure is liberated from the ordinary technicalities of the law; and lastly how unquestionable rules of evidence open the gates to overwhelming testimony, I pass now to the consideration of this overwhelming testimony and how the present impeachment became a necessity. I have already called it one of the last great battles with slavery. See now how the battle began.

Slavery in all its pretensions is a defiance of law; for it can have no law in its support. Whoso becomes its representative must act accordingly; and this is the transcendent crime of Andrew Johnson. For the sake of slavery and to uphold its original supporters in their endeavors to continue this wrong under another name, he has set at defiance the Constitution and laws of the land, and he has accompanied this unquestionable usurpation by brutalities and indecencies in office without precedent, unless we go back to the Roman emperor fiddling, or the French monarch dancing among his minions. This usurpation, with its brutalities and indecencies, became manifest as long ago as the winter of 1866, when, being President, and bound by his oath of office to preserve, protect, and defend the Constitution, and to take care that the laws are faithfully executed, he took to himself legislative powers in the reconstruction of the rebel States, and, in carrying forward this usurpation, nullified an act of Congress, intended as the corner-stone of reconstruction, by virtue of which rebels are excluded from office under the government of the United States, and thereafter, in vindication of this misconduct, uttered a scandalous speech in which he openly charged members of Congress with being assassins, and mentioned some by name. Plainly he should have been impeached and expelled at that early day. The case against him was complete. That great patriot of English history, Lord Somers, has likened impeachment to Goliath's sword hanging in the temple to be taken down only when occasion required; but if ever there was an occasion for its promptest vengeance it was then. . Had there been no failure at that time we should be now nearer by two years to restoration of all kinds, whether political or financial. So strong is my conviction of the fatal remissness of the House, that I think the Senate would do a duty in strict harmony with its constitutional place in the government, and the analogies of judicial tribunals so often adduced, if it reprimanded the House of Representatives for this delay. Of course the Senate could not originate an impeachment: It could not take down the sword of Goliath. It must wait on the House, as the court waits on the grand jury. But this waiting has cost the country more than can be told.

Meanwhile the President proceeded in his transgressions. There is nothing of usurpation which he has not attempted. Beginning with an assumption of all power in the rebel States, he has shrunk from nothing in the maintenance of this unparalleled assumption. This is a plain statement of fact. Timid at first, he grew bolder and bolder. He saw too well that his attempt to substitute himself for Congress in the work of reconstruction was sheer usurpation, and, therefore, by his Secretary of State, did not hesitate to announce that "it must be distinctly understood that the restoration will be *subject to the decision of Congress.*" On two separate occasions, in July and September, 1865, he confessed the power of Congress over the subject; but when Congress came together in December, this confessor of congressional power found that he alone had this great prerogative. According to his new-fangled theory, Congress had nothing to do but admit the States with the governments which had been instituted through his will alone. It is difficult to measure the vastness of this usurpation, involving as it did a general nullification. Strafford was not bolder, when, speaking for Charles I, he boasted that "the little finger of prerogative was heavier than the loins of the law;" but these words helped the proud minister to the scaffold. No monarch, no despot, no Sultan, could claim more than an American President; for he claimed all. By his edict alone governments were organized, taxes were levied, and even the franchises of the citizen were determined.

Had this assumption of power been incidental, for the exigency of the moment, as under the pressure of war, and especially to serve the cause of human rights, to which before his elevation the President had professed such vociferous devotion, it might have been pardoned. It would have passed into the chapter of unauthorized acts which a patriot people had condoned. But it was the opposite in every particular. Beginning and continuing in usurpation, it was hateful beyond pardon, because it sacrificed the rights of Unionists, white and black, and was in the interest of the rebellion and of those very rebels who had been in arms against their country.

More than one person was appointed provisional governor who could not take the oath of office required by act of Congress. Other persons in the same predicament were appointed in the revenue service. The effect of these appointments was disastrous. They were in the nature of notice to rebels everywhere, that participation in the rebellion was no bar to office. If one of their number could be appointed governor, if another could be appointed to a confidential position in the Treasury Department, then there was nobody on the long list of blood who might not look for preferment. And thus all offices from governor to constable were handed over to a disloyal scramble. Rebels crawled forth from their retreats. Men who had hardly ventured to expect their lives were now candidates for office, and the rebellion became strong again. The change was felt in all the gradations of government, whether in States, counties, towns, or villages. Rebels found themselves in places of trust, while the true-hearted Unionists, who had watched for the coming of our flag and ought to have enjoyed its protecting power, were driven into hiding-places. All this was under the auspices of Andrew Johnson. It was he who animated the wicked crew. He was at the head of the work. Loyalty everywhere was persecuted. White and black, whose only offence was that they had been true to their country, were insulted, abused, murdered. There was no safety for the loyal man except within the flash of our bayonets. The story is as authentic as hideous. More than two thousand murders have been reported in Texas alone since the surrender of Kirby Smith. In other States there was a similar carnival. Property, person, life, were all in jeopardy. Acts were done "to make a holiday in hell." At New Orleans there was a fearful massacre, which, considering the age and the place, was worse than that of St. Bartholomew, which darkens a century of France, or that of Glencoe, which has printed an ineffaceable stain upon one of the greatest reigns of English history. All this is directly traced to Andrew Johnson. The words of bitterness uttered at another time are justified, while Fire, Famine, and Slaughter shriek forth—

He let me loose, and cried Halloo!
To him alone the praise is due.

ACCUMULATION OF IMPEACHABLE OFFENCES.

This is nothing but the outline, derived from historic sources *which the Senate on this occasion is bound to recognize.* Other acts fall within the picture. The officers he had appointed in defiance of law were paid also in the same defiance. Millions of property were turned over without consideration to railroad companies, whose special recommendation was their participation in the rebellion. The Freedman's Bureau, that sacred charity of the Republic, was despoiled of its possessions for the sake of rebels, to whom their forfeited estates were given back after they had been vested by law in the United States. The proceeds of captured and abandoned property, lodged under the law in the national treasury, were ravished from their place of deposit and sacrificed. Rebels were allowed to fill the ante-chambers of the Executive Mansion and to enter into his counsels. The pardoning power was prostituted, and pardons were issued in lots to suit rebels, thus grossly abusing that trust whose discreet exercise is so essential to the administration of justice. The powers of the Senate over appointments were trifled with and disregarded by reappointing persons who had been already rejected, and by refusing to communicate the names of others appointed by him during the recess. The veto power conferred by the Constitution as a remedy for ill-considered legislation, was turned by him into a weapon of offence against Congress and into an instrument to beat down the just opposition which his usurpation had aroused. The power of removal, which patriot Presidents had exercised so sparingly, was seized as an engine of tyranny and openly employed to maintain his wicked purposes by the sacrifice of good citizens who would not consent to be his tools. Incompetent and dishonest creatures, whose only recommendation was that they echoed his voice, were appointed to office, especially in the collection of the internal revenue, through whom a new organization, known as the "Whisky Ring," has been able to prevail over the government and to rob the treasury of millions at the cost of tax-paying citizens, whose burdens are thus increased. Laws enacted by Congress for the benefit of the colored race, including that great statute for the establishment of the Freedmen's Bureau, and that other great statute for the establishment of Civil Rights, were first attacked by his veto, and, when finally passed by the requisite majority over his veto, were treated by him as little better than dead letters, while he boldly attempted to prevent the adoption of a constitutional amendment, by which the right of citizens and the national debt were placed under the guarantee of irrepealable law. During these successive assumptions, usurpations, and tyrannies, utterly without precedent in our history, this deeply guilty man ventured upon public speeches, each an offence to good morals, where, lost to all shame, he appealed in coarse words to the coarse passions of the coarsest people, scattering firebrands of sedition, inflaming anew the rebel spirit, insulting good citizens, and, with regard to office-holders, announcing in his own characteristic phrase that he would "kick them out"—the whole succession of speeches being from their brutalities and indecencies in the nature of a "criminal exposure of his person," indictable at common law, for which no judgment can be too severe. But even this revolting transgression is aggravated, when it is considered that through these utterances the cause of justice was imperiled and the accursed demon of civil feud was lashed again into vengeful fury. All these things from beginning to end are plain facts, already recorded in history and known to all. And it is further recorded in history and known to all, that, through these enormities, any one of which is enough for condemnation, while all together present an aggregation of crime, untold calamities have been brought upon our country; disturbing business and finance; diminishing the national revenues; postponing specie payments; dishonoring the Declaration of Independence in its grandest truths; arresting the restoration of the rebel States; reviving the dying rebellion, and instead of that peace and reconciliation so much longed for, sowing strife and wrong, whose natural fruit is violence and blood.

OPEN DEFIANCE OF CONGRESS.

For all these, or any one of them, Andrew Johnson should have been impeached and expelled from office. The case required a statement only; not an argument. Unhappily this was not done. As a petty substitute for the judgment which should have been pronounced, and as a bridle on presidential tyranny in "kicking out of office," Congress enacted a law known as the tenure-of-office act, passed March 2, 1867, over his veto by the vote of two-thirds of both houses. And in order to prepare the way for impeachment, by removing certain scruples of technicality, its violation was expressly declared to be a high misdemeanor.

The President began at once to chafe under its restraint. Recognizing the act and following its terms, he first suspended Mr. Stanton from office, and then, on his restoration by the Senate, made an attempt to win General Grant into a surrender of the department, so as to oust Mr. Stanton and to render the restoration by the Senate ineffectual. Meanwhile Sheridan in Louisiana, Pope in Alabama, and Sickles in South Carolina, who, as military commanders, were carrying into the pacification of these States all the energies which had been so brilliantly displayed in the war, were pursued by the same vindictive spirit. They were removed by the President, and rebellion throughout that whole region clapped its hands. This was done in the exercise of his power as Commander-in-chief. At last, in his unappeased rage, he openly violated the tenure-of-office act, so as to bring himself under its judgment, by the defiant attempt to remove Mr. Stanton from the War Department, without the consent of the Senate, and the appointment of Lorenzo Thomas, Adjutant General of the United States, as Secretary of War *ad interim*.

IMPEACHMENT AT LAST.

The Grand Inquest of the nation, which had slept on so many enormities, was awakened by this open defiance. The gauntlet was flung into its very chamber, and there it lay on the floor. The President, who had already claimed everything for the Executive with impunity, now rushed into conflict with Congress on the very ground selected in advance by the latter. The field was narrow, but sufficient. There was but one thing for the House of Representatives to do. Andrew Johnson must be impeached, or the tenure-of-office act would become a dead letter, while his tyranny would receive a letter of license, and impeachment as a remedy for wrong-doing would be blotted from the Constitution.

Accordingly it was resolved that the offender, whose crimes had so long escaped judgment, should be impeached. Once entered upon this work, the House of Representatives, after setting forth the removal of Mr. Stanton and the appointment of General Thomas in violation of the law and Constitution, proceeded further to charge him in different forms with conspiracy wrongfully to get possession of the War Department; also with an attempt to corrupt General Emory and induce him to violate an act of Congress; also with scandalous speeches, such as no President could be justified in making; concluding with a general article setting forth attempts on his part to prevent the execution of certain acts of Congress.

Such is a simple narrative, which brings us to the articles of impeachment. Nothing that I have said thus far is superfluous; for it shows the origin of this proceeding, and illustrates its moving cause. The articles themselves are narrow, if not technical. But they are filled and broadened by the transgressions of the past, all of which enter into the present offences. The whole is an unbroken series with a common life. As well separate the Siamese twins as separate the offences now charged from that succession of antecedent crimes with which they are linked, any one of which is enough for judgment. The present springs from the past and can be truly seen only in its light, which, in this case, is nothing less than "darkness visible."

ARTICLES OF IMPEACHMENT.

In entering upon the discussion of the articles of impeachment, I confess my regret that so great a cause, on which so much depends, should be presented on such narrow ground, although I cannot doubt that the whole past must be taken into consideration in determining the character of the acts alleged. If there has been a violation of the Constitution and laws, the apologists of the President then insist that all was done with good intentions. In reply to this it is enough if we point to the past, which thus becomes a part of the case. But of this hereafter. It is unnecessary for me to take time in setting forth the articles. The abstract already presented is enough. They will naturally come under review before the close of the inquiry.

Of the transactions embraced by the articles, the removal of Mr. Stanton has unquestionably attracted the most attention, although I cannot doubt that the scandalous harangues are as justly worthy of condemnation. But the former has been made the pivot of this impeachment; so much so that the whole case seems to revolve on this transaction. Therefore I shall not err, if, following the articles, I put this foremost in the present inquiry.

This transaction may be brought to the touchstone of the Constitution, and also of the tenure-of-office act. But since the allegation of a violation of this act has been so conspicuous, and this act may be regarded as a congressional interpretation of the power of removals under the Constitution, I begin with the consideration of the questions arising under it.

TENURE-OF-OFFICE ACT.

The general object of the tenure-of-office act was to protect civil officers from removal without the advice and consent of the Senate; and it was made in express terms applicable to "every person holding any civil office to which he has been appointed by and with the advice and consent of the Senate." To this provision, so broad in its character, was appended a proviso as follows:

Provided, That the Secretaries of State, of the Treasury, of War, of the Navy, and of the Interior, the Postmaster General, and the Attorney General shall hold their offices respectively for and during the term of the President by whom they may have been appointed and for one month thereafter, subject to removal by and with the advice and consent of the Senate.

As this general protection from removal without the advice and consent of the Senate might be productive of embarrassment during the recess of the Senate, it was further provided, in a second section, that during such recess any person may be suspended from office by the President on reasons assigned, which it is made his duty to report to the Senate within twenty days after its next meeting, and if the Senate concurs, then the President may remove the officer and appoint a successor; but if the Senate does not concur, then the suspended officer shall forthwith resume his functions.

On this statute two questions arise: first as to its constitutionality, and secondly as to its application to Mr. Stanton, so as to protect him from removal without the advice and consent of the Senate. It is impossible not to confess in advance that both have been already practically settled. The statute was passed over the veto of the President by a vote of two-thirds, who thus solemnly united in declaring its constitutionality. Then came the suspension of Mr. Stanton, and his restoration to office by a triumphant vote of the Senate, being no less than 35 to 6, thus establishing not only the constitutionality of the statute, but also its protecting application to Mr. Stanton. And then came the resolution of the Senate, adopted after protracted debate on the 21st February, by a vote of 27 to 6, declaring, that, under the Constitution and laws of the United States, the President has no power to remove the Secretary of War and to designate any other officer to perform the duties of that office *ad interim ;* thus for the third time affirming the constitutionality of the statute, and for the second time its protecting application to Mr. Stanton. There is no instance in our history where there has been such a succession of votes, with such large majorities, declaring the conclusions of the Senate and fixing them beyond recall. "Thrice is he armed who hath his quarrel just;" but the tenure-of-office act is armed *thrice* by the votes of the Senate. The apologists of the President seem to say of these solemn votes, "Thrice the brinded cat hath mewed;" but such a three-fold record of the Senate cannot be treated with levity.

The question of the constitutionality of this statute complicates itself with the power of removal under the Constitution; but I shall not consider the latter question at this stage. It will naturally present itself when we consider the power of removal under the Constitution which has been claimed by the President. For the present I assume the constitutionality of the statute.

ITS APPLICATION TO MR. STANTON.

I come at once to the question of the application of the statute to Mr. Stanton, so as to protect him against removal without the consent of the Senate. And here I doubt if any question would have arisen but for the hasty words of the senator from Ohio, [Mr. Sherman,] so often quoted in this proceeding.

Unquestionably the senator from Ohio, when the report of the conference committee of the two houses was under discussion, stated that the statute did not protect Mr. Stanton in his office; but this was the individual opinion of this senator, and nothing more. On hearing it I cried from my seat, "The senator must speak for himself;" for I held the opposite opinion. It was clear to my mind that the statute was intended to protect Mr. Stanton, and that it did protect him. The senator from Oregon, [Mr. Williams,] who was the chairman of the conference committee and conducted its deliberations, informs us that there was no suggestion in the committee that the statute did not protect all of the President's cabinet, including, of course, Mr. Stanton. The debates in the House of Representatives are the same way. Without undertaking to hold the scales in which to weigh any such conflicting opinions, I rest on the received rule of law that they cannot be taken into account in determining the meaning of the statute. And here I quote the judgment of the Supreme Court of the United States, pronounced by Chief Justice Taney:

In expounding this law, the judgment of *the court cannot in any degree be influenced by the construction placed upon it by individual members of Congress in the debate which took place on its passage,* nor by the motives or reasons assigned by them for supporting or opposing amendments that were offered. The law that passed is the will of the majority of both houses, and the only mode in which that will is spoken is in the act itself: and we must gather their intention from the language there used, comparing it, when any ambiguity exists, with the laws upon the same subject, and *looking, if necessary, to the public history of the times in which it was passed.* (*Aldridge* vs. *Williams*, 3 Howard's Rep., 24.)

It is obvious to all acquainted with a legislative body that the rule thus authoritatively declared is the only one that could be safely applied. The Senate in construing the present statute must follow this rule. Therefore, I repair to the statute, stopping for a moment to glance at the public history of the times, in order to understand its object.

Already, we have seen how the President, in carrying forward his usurpation in the interest of the rebellion, has trifled with the Senate in regard to appointments, and abused the traditional power of removal, openly threatening good citizens in office that he would "kick them out," and filling all vacancies, from high to low, with creatures whose first promise was to sustain his barbarous policy. I do not stop to portray the extent of this outrage, constituting an impeachable offence, according to the declared opinion of Mr. Madison, one of the strongest advocates of the presidential power of removal. Congress, instead of adopting the remedy, suggested by this father of the Constitution, and expelling the President by process of impeachment, attempted to wrest from him the power he was abusing. For this purpose the tenure-of-office act was passed. It was deemed advisable to include the cabinet officers within its protection; but, considering the intimate relations between them and the President, a proviso was appended securing to the latter the right of choosing them in the first instance. Its object was, where the President finds himself, on accession to office, confronted by a hostile Senate to secure to him this right of choice, without obliging him to keep the cabinet of his predecessor; and accordingly it says to him, "Choose your own cabinet, but expect to abide by your choice, unless you can obtain the consent of the Senate to a change."

Any other conclusion is flat absurdity. It begins by misconstruing the operative words of the proviso, that the cabinet officers "shall hold their offices respectively for and during the term of the President by whom they are appointed." On its face there is no ambiguity here. It is only by going outside that any can be found, and this disappears on a brief inquiry. At the date of the statute Andrew Johnson had been in office two years. Some of his cabinet were originally appointed by President Lincoln; others had been formally appointed by himself. *But all were there equally by his approval and consent.* One may do an act himself, or make it his own by ratifying it when done by another. In law it is equally his act. Andrew Johnson did not originally appoint Mr. Stanton, Mr. Seward, or Mr. Welles, but he adopted their appointments, so that at the passage of the statute they stood on the same footing as if originally appointed by him. *Practically and in the sense of the statute, they were appointed by him.* They were a cabinet of his own choice, just as much as the cabinet of his successor, duly appointed, will be of his own choice. If the statute compels the latter, as it clearly does, to abide by his choice, it is unreasonable to suppose that it is not equally obligatory on Andrew Johnson. Otherwise we find a special immunity for that President whose misconduct rendered it necessary, and Congress is exhibited as legislating for some future unknown President, and not for Andrew Johnson, already too well known.

Even the presidential apologists do not question that the members of the cabinet commissioned by Andrew Johnson are protected by the statute. How grossly unreasonable to suppose that Congress intended to make such a distinction among his cabinet as to protect those whose support of his usurpation had gained them seats which they enjoyed, while it exposed to his caprice a great citizen, whose faithful services during the war had won the gratitude of his country, whose continuance in office was regarded as an assurance of public safety, and whose attempted removal has been felt as a national calamity. Clearly, then, it was the intention of the statute to protect the whole cabinet, whether originally appointed by Andrew Johnson or originally appointed by his predecessor and continued by him.

I have no hesitation in saying that no other conclusion is possible without doing violence to the statute. I cannot forget that, while we are permitted "to open the law on doubts," we are solemnly warned "not to open doubts on the law." It is Lord Bacon who gives us this rule, whose obvious meaning is, that where doubts do not exist they should not be invented. It is only by this forbidden course that any question can be raised. If we look at the statute in its simplicity, its twofold object is apparent: first, to prohibit removals; and secondly, to limit certain terms of service. *The prohibition to remove plainly applies to all. The limitation of service applies only to members of the cabinet.* I agree with the excellent senator from Iowa [Mr. Harlan] that this analysis removes all ambiguity. The pretension that any one of the cabinet was left to the unchecked power of the President is irreconcilable with the concluding words of the proviso, which declares that they shall "be subject to removal by and with the advice and consent of the Senate;" thus expressly excluding the prerogative of the President.

Let us push this inquiry still further by looking more particularly at the statute, reduced to a skeleton, so that we may see its bones. It is as follows:

(1.) *Every person holding any civil office*, by and with the advice and consent of the Senate, shall be entitled to hold such office until a successor is appointed.

(2.) If members of the cabinet, *then during the term of the President by whom they may have been appointed* and one month thereafter, unless sooner removed by consent of the Senate.

Mr. Stanton obviously falls within the general class, "every person holding any civil office;" and he is entitled to the full benefit of the provision for their benefit.

As obviously he falls within the sub-class, "members of the cabinet."

In this latter class his rights are equally clear. It is in the discussions under this head that the ingenuity of lawyers has found the amplest play, mainly turning upon what is meant by "term" in the statute. I glance for a moment at some of these theories.

(1.) One pretension is that the "term," having expired with the life of President Lincoln, Mr. Stanton is retroactively legislated out of office on the 15th May, 1865. As this is a penal statute, this construction makes it *ex post facto*, and therefore unconstitutional. It also makes Congress enact this absurdity that Mr. Stanton had for two years been holding office illegally, whereas he had been holding under the clearest legal title, which could no more be altered by legislation than black could be made white. A construction which makes the statute at once unconstitutional and absurd must be rejected.

(2.) The quibble that would exclude Mr. Stanton from the protection of the statute, because he was appointed during the first "term" of President Lincoln, and the statute does not speak of "terms," is hardly worthy of notice. It leads to the same absurd results as follow from the first supposition, enhanced by increasing the retroactive effect.

(3.) Assuming that the statute does not terminate Mr. Stanton's right a month after President Lincoln's death, it is insisted that it must take effect at the earliest possible moment, and therefore on its passage. From this it follows that Mr. Stanton has been illegally in office since the 2d March, 1867, and that both he and the President have been guilty of a violation of law, the former in exercising the duties of an office to which he had no right, and the latter for appointing him, or continuing him, in office, without the consent of the Senate, in violation of the Constitution and the statute in question. Here is another absurdity to be rejected.

(4.) Assuming, as it is easy to do, that it is President Lincoln's "term," we have the better theory, that it did not expire with his life, but continues until the 4th of March, 1869, in which event Mr. Stanton is clearly entitled to hold until a month thereafter. This construction is entirely reasonable and in harmony with the Constitution and legislation under it. I confess that it is one to which I have often inclined.

This brings me back to the construction with which I began, and I find Andrew Johnson is the President who appointed Mr. Stanton. To make this simple, it is only necessary to read "chosen" for "appointed" in the statute, or, if you please, consider the continuance of Mr. Stanton in office, with the concurrence of the President, as a practical appointment or equivalent thereto. Clearly Mr. Stanton was in office, when the statute passed, from the "choice" of the President. Otherwise he would have been removed. His continuance was like another commission. This carries out the intention of the framers of the statute, violates no sound canon of construction, and is entirely reasonable in every respect. Or, if preferred, we may consider the "term" to be that of President Lincoln, and then Mr. Stanton would be protected in office until one month after the 4th of March next. But whether the "term" be of Andrew Johnson or of President Lincoln, he is equally protected.

Great efforts have been made to show that Mr. Stanton does not come within the special protection of the proviso, without considering the irresistible consequence that he is then within the general protection of the statute, being "a person holding a civil office." Turn him out of the proviso and he falls into the statute, unless you are as imaginative as one of the apologists, who placed him in a sort of intermediate limbo, like a lost spirit floating in space, as in one of Flaxman's Illustrations of Dante. But the imagination of this conception cannot make us insensible to its surpassing absurdity. It is utterly unreasonable, and every construction must be rejected which cannot stand the touchstone of common sense.

THE SUSPENSION OF MR. STANTON RECOGNIZED HIM AS PROTECTED BY THE STATUTE.

Here I might close this part of the case; but there is still another illustration. In suspending Mr. Stanton from office, as long ago as August, the President himself recognized that he was protected by the statute. The facts are familiar. The President, in formal words, undertook to say that the suspension was by virtue of the Constitution; but this was a dishonest pretext in harmony with so much in his career. Whatever he may say, his acts speak louder than his words. In sending notice of the suspension to the Secretary of the Treasury, and then again in sending a message to the Senate assigning his reasons for the suspension, both being according to the requirements of the statute, he testified that, in his judgment at that time, Mr. Stanton came within its protection. If not, why thus elaborately comply with its requirements? Why the notice to the Secretary of the Treasury? Why the reasons to the Senate? All this was novel and without example. Why write to General Grant of "being sustained" by the Senate? The approval or disapproval of the Senate could make no difference in the exercise of the power which he now sets up. The approval could not confirm the suspension; the disapproval could not restore the suspended Secretary of War. In fine, why suspend at all? Why exercise the power of suspension when the President sets up the power of removal? If Mr. Stanton was unfit for office and a thorn in his side, why not remove him at once? Why resort to this long and untried experiment merely to remove at last? There is but one answer. Beyond all question the President thought Mr. Stanton protected by the statute, and sought to remove him according to its provisions, beginning, therefore, with his suspension. Failing in this, he undertook to remove him in contravention of the statute, relying in justification on his pretension to judge of its constitutionality, or the pusillanimity of Congress, or something else "to turn up," which should render justification unnecessary.

Clearly the suspension was made under the tenure-of-office act and can be justified in no other way. From this conclusion the following dilemma results: If Mr. Stanton was within the statute, by what right was he removed? If he was not, by what right was he suspended? The President may choose his horn. Either will be sufficient to convict.

I should not proceed further under this head but for the new device, which makes its appearance under the auspices of the senator from Maine, [Mr. Fessenden,] who tells us that "whether Mr. Stanton came under the first section of the statute or not, the President had a clear right to suspend him under the second." Thus, a statute, intended as a bridle on the President, gives to the President the power to suspend Mr. Stanton, but fails to give to Mr. Stanton any protection against the President. This statement would seem to be enough. The invention of the senator is not less fallacious than the pretext of the President. It is a device well calculated to help the President and to hurt Mr. Stanton, with those who regard devices more than the reason of the statute and its spirit.

Study the statute in its reason and its spirit, and you cannot fail to see that the second section was intended merely as a pendant to the first, and was meant to apply to the cases included in the first, and none other. It was a sort of safety-valve or contrivance to guard against the possible evils from bad men, who could not be removed during the recess of the Senate. There was no reason to suspend a person who could be removed. It is absurd to suppose that a President would resort to a dilatory and roundabout suspension, when the short cut of removal was open to him. Construing the statute by this plain reason, its second section must have precisely the same sphere of operation as the first. By the letter, Mr. Stanton falls within both; by the intention, it is the same. It is only by applying to the first section his own idea of the intention, and by availing himself of the letter of the second, that the senator is able to limit the one and to enlarge the other, so as to exclude Mr. Stanton from the protection of the statute, and to include him in the part allowing suspensions. Applying either letter or spirit consistently, the case is plain.

I turn for the present from the tenure-of-office act, insisting that Mr. Stanton is within its protection, and being so, that his removal was, under the circumstances, a high misdemeanor, aggravated by its defiant purpose and the long series of transgressions which preceded it, all showing a criminal intent. The apologies of the President will be considered hereafter.

THE SUBSTITUTION OF THOMAS AD INTERIM

The case of Mr. Stanton has two branches: first, his removal, and, secondly, the substitution of General Thomas as Secretary of War *ad interim*. As the first was contrary to positive statute, so also was the latter without support in the acts of Congress. For the present I content myself with this latter proposition, without opening the question of the powers of the President under the Constitution.

The offender rests his case on the act of Congress of February 13, 1795, (1 *Statutes at Large*, 415,) which authorizes the President, "in case of *vacancy* in the office of Secretary of War, whereby he cannot perform the duties of said office," to appoint "any person" until a successor be appointed or such vacancy be filled; and the supply of the vacancy is limited to six months. Under this early statute the President defends himself by insisting that there was a "vacancy," when, in fact, there was none. All this is in that unfailing spirit of prerogative which is his guide. Here is an assumption of power. In point of fact, Mr. Stanton was at his office quietly discharging its duties when the President assumed that there was a "vacancy," and forthwith sent the valiant Adjutant General to enter upon possession. The assumption and the commission were on a par. There is nothing in any law of the land to sanction either. Each testifies against the offender.

The hardihood of this proceeding becomes more apparent, when it is understood that this very statute of 1795, on which the offender relies, was repealed by the statute of February 20, 1863, passed in our own day, and freshly remembered by many of us. The latter statute, by necessary implication, obliterated the former. Such is the obvious intention, and I do not hesitate to say that any other construction leads into those absurdities which constitute the staple of the presidential apologists. The object of Congress was to provide a substitute for previous statutes, restricting at once the number of vacancies which might be filled and the persons who might fill them. And this was done.

As by the Constitution all appointments must receive the consent of the Senate, therefore any legislation in derogation thereof must be construed strictly; but the President insists that it shall be extended even in face of the constitutional requirement. To such pretensions is he driven. The exception recognized by the Constitution is only where a vacancy occurs during the recess of the Senate, when the President is authorized to appoint until he can obtain the consent of the Senate and no longer. It is obvious, however, that cases may arise where a sudden accident vacates the office or where the incumbent is temporarily disabled. Here was the occasion for an *ad interim* appointment, and the repealing statute embodying the whole law of the subject, was intended to provide for such cases; securing to the President time to select a successor, and also power to provide for a temporary disability. Such is the underlying principle of this statute, which it is for us to apply on the present occasion. The expiration of a commission, which ordinary care can foresee, is not one of these sudden emergencies for which provision must be made; and, assuming that vacancies by removal were contemplated, which must be denied, it is plain that the delay required for the examination of the case would give time to select a successor, while a removal without cause would never be made until a successor was ready.

Look now at the actual facts and you will see how little they come within the reason of an *ad interim* appointment. Evidently the President had resolved to remove Mr. Stanton last summer. Months passed, and he did not consummate his purpose till February. All the intervening time was his to select a successor, being a period longer than the longest fixed for the duration of an *ad interim* appointment by the very statutes under which he professed to act. In conversation with General Sherman, a month before the removal, he showed that he was then looking for a successor *ad interim*. Why not a *permanent* successor?

It took him only a day to find Mr. Ewing. If, as there is reason to suppose, Mr. Ewing was already selected, when General Thomas was pushed forward, *why appoint General Thomas at all?* Why not, in the usual way, transmit Mr. Ewing's name as the successor? For the excellent reason, that the offender knew the Senate would not confirm him, and that, therefore, Mr. Stanton would remain in office; whereas through an *ad interim* appointment he might obtain possession of the War Department, which was his end and aim. The *ad interim* appointment of General Thomas was, therefore, an attempt to obtain possession of an office without the consent of the Senate, precisely *because the offender knew that he could not obtain that consent.* And all this was under the pretext of an act of Congress, which, alike in letter and spirit, was inapplicable to the case.

Thus does it appear, that, while Mr. Stanton was removed in violation of the tenure-of-office act, General Thomas was appointed Secretary of War *ad interim* in equal derogation of the acts of Congress regulating the subject.

REMOVAL AND SUBSTITUTION AD INTERIM A VIOLATION OF THE CONSTITUTION.

It remains to consider if the removal and substitution were not each in violation of the Constitution. The case is new, for never until now could it arise. Assuming that the tenure-of-office act does not protect Mr. Stanton, who is thus left afloat in the limbo between the body of the act and the proviso, then the President is remitted to his prerogative under the Constitution, and he must be judged accordingly, independent of statute. Finding the power of removal there, he may be justified; but not finding it there, he must bear the consequences. And here *the tenure-of-office act furnishes a living and practical construction of the Constitution from which there is no appeal.*

From the Constitution it appears that the power of appointment is vested in the President and Senate conjointly, and that nothing is said of the power of removal, except in case of impeachment, when it is made by the Senate. Therefore, the power of removal is not express, but implied only, and must exist, if at all, as a necessary consequence of the power to appoint. In whom must it exist? It is a familiar rule that the power which makes can unmake. Unless this rule be rejected, the power of removal must exist in the President and Senate conjointly; nor is there anything unreasonable in this conclusion. Removal can always be effected during the session of the Senate by the nomination and confirmation of a successor, while provision can be made for the recess by an act of Congress. This conclusion would be irresistible, were the Senate always in session, but since it is not, and since cases may arise during the recess requiring the immediate exercise of this power of removal, it has been argued that at least during the recess it must be in the President alone. From this position there has been a jump to the next, and it has been insisted that since, for the sake of public convenience, the power of removal exists in the President, he is at liberty to exercise it, either during the recess or the session itself. Here is an obvious extension of the conclusion which the premises do not warrant. The reason failing the conclusion must fail. *Cessante ratione cessat etiam ipsa lex.* Especially must this be the case under the Constitution. A power founded on implied necessity must fail when that necessity does not exist. The implication cannot be carried beyond the reason. Therefore, the power of removal during the recess, doubtful at best unless sanctioned by act of Congress, cannot be extended to justify the exercise of that power while the Senate is in session, ready to act conjointly with the President.

Against this natural conclusion we have the assumption that a contrary construction of the Constitution was established after debate in 1789. I avoid all details with regard to this debate which has been considered and cited so often. I content myself by asking if at best it was anything but a congressional construction of the Constitution, and, as such, subject to be set aside by another voice from the same quarter. It was, moreover, a congressional construction adopted during the administration of Washington, whose personal character must have influenced opinion largely; and it prevailed in the House of Representatives only after earnest debate, by a bare majority, and in the Senate only by the casting vote of the Vice-President, John Adams, who, from position as well as principle, was not inclined to shear the President of any prerogative. Once adopted, and no strong necessity for a change occurring, it was allowed to go unaltered, but not unquestioned. Jurists like Kent and Story, statesmen like Webster, Clay, Calhoun, and Benton, recorded themselves adversely, and it was once reversed by the vote of the Senate. This was in 1835, when a bill passed the Senate, reported by Mr. Calhoun and sustained by the ablest statesmen of the time, practically denying the power of the President. The tenure-of-office act was heralded in 1863 by a statute making the Comptroller of the Currency removable "by and with the advice and consent of the Senate," thus, in this individual case, asserting for the Senate a check on the President; and then in 1866, by a more important measure, being the provision in the army appropriation act, that "no military or naval officer shall be dismissed except upon the sentence of a court-martial;" thus putting another check on the President. Finally, this congressional construction, born of a casting vote, and questioned ever since, has been overruled by another congressional construction, which has been twice adopted in both houses, first by large majorities on the original passage of the tenure-of-office act, and then by a vote of two-thirds on the final passage of the same act over the veto of the President; and then again adopted by a vote of more than two-thirds of the Senate, when the latter condemned the removal of Mr. Stanton; and all this in the light of experience, after ample debate, and with all the consequences before them. Such a congressional construction must have a controlling influence, and the fact that it reversed the practice of eighty years and overcame the disposition to stand on the ancient ways, would seem to increase rather than diminish its weight.

Now, mark the consequences. Originally, in 1789, there was a congressional construction, which, in effect, made the Constitution read:

The President *shall have* the power of removal.

For the next eighty years all removals were made under this construction. The tenure-of-office act was a new congressional construction, overruling the first and entitled to equal if not superior weight. By virtue of this congressional construction, the Constitution now reads:

The President *shall not have* the power of removal.

It follows, then, that in removing Mr. Stanton the President violated the Constitution as now construed.

The dilemma is this: If the President can remove Mr. Stanton during the session of the Senate, without any power by statute, it is only by virtue of a prerogative vested in him by the Constitution, which must necessarily override the tenure-of-office act, as an unconstitutional effort to abridge it. If, on the other hand, this act is constitutional, the prerogative of removal is not in the President, and he violated the Constitution when he assumed to exercise it.

The tenure-of-office act cannot be treated otherwise than constitutional. Certainly not in the Senate, where some among the apologists of the President voted for it. Therefore the prerogative of removal is not in the President. The long practice which grew up under a mere reading of the Constitution, has been declared erroneous. To this extent the Constitution has been amended, and it is as absurd to plead the practice under the first reading in order to justify an offence under the second, as to plead the existence of slavery before the constitutional amendment in order to justify this monstrosity now.

Thus must we conclude that the offender has not only violated the tenure-of-office act, but also the Constitution; that, even assuming that Mr. Stanton is not protected by the statute, the case is not ended; that this statute, if coustrued so as to exclude him, cannot be rejected as a congressional construction of the Constitution; and that, under this congressional construction, which in value is second only to a constitutional amendment, the prerogative of removal without the consent of the Senate does not belong to the President. Of course the power of suspension under the Constitution, which is only an incident of the larger pretension, must fall also. Therefore, in the defiant removal of Mr. Stanton, and also in the pretended suspension under the Constitution with which the transaction began, the President violated the Constitution, and was guilty of an impeachable offence.

And so, also, we must conclude that, in the substitution of Lorenzo Thomas as Secretary of War *ad interim*, the offender violated not only the acts of Congress for the supply of vacancies, but also the Constitution. Knowing that he could not obtain possession of the office with the consent of the Senate, he sought to accomplish this purpose without that consent. Thus, under color of a statute, he practically set the Constitution at defiance. Mark here his inconsistency. He violates the tenure-of-office act, alleging that it is against the Constitution, whose champion he professes to be, and then takes advantage of the acts of Congress for the supply of vacancies to set aside the Constitution in one of its most important requirements; for all which he is justly charged with an impeachable offence.

All this seems clear. Any other conclusion gives to the President the power under the Constitution to vacate all national offices and leaves the republic the wretched victim of tyranny, with a ruler who is not even a constitutional monarch, but a king above all laws. It was solemnly alleged in the articles against Charles I of England, that "being admitted king of England, and therein trusted with a limited power *to govern by and according to the laws of the land and* NOT OTHERWISE," he nevertheless undertook "*to rule according to his will* and to overthrow the rights and liberties of the people." These very words might be adopted now to declare the crime of Andrew Johnson.

THE APOLOGIES.

Here I might close; but the offender has found apologists, who plead his cause at the bar and in the Senate. The apologies are a strange compound, enlarging rather than diminishing the offences proved. There is, first, the Apology of Good Intentions; next, the Apology of making a case for the Supreme Court, being the Moot Court Apology; and, then, the Apology that the President may sit in judgment on the laws, and determine whether they shall be executed, which I call the Apology of Prerogative. Following these is a swarm of technicalities, devices, and quibbles, utterly unworthy of the Senate, and to be reprobated by all who love justice.

THE APOLOGY OF GOOD INTENTIONS.

I begin with the Apology of *Good Intentions*. In the light of all that has occurred, with the volume of history open before us, with the records of the Senate in our hands, and with the evidence at the bar not utterly forgotten, it is inconceivable that such an apology can be put forward. While making it the apologists should be veiled, so that the derisive smile on their faces may not be observed by the Senate, to whose simplicity it is addressed. It is hard to treat this apology; but it belongs to the case, and therefore I deal with it.

Of course a mere technical violation of law, with no evil consequences and without any claim of title, is followed by nominal damages only. If a person steps on a field of grass belonging to another, without permission, he is a trespasser, and the law furnishes a familiar proceeding against him; but if he has done this accidentally, and without any real damage, it would be hard to pursue him, unless the assertion of the title were thought important. But if this trespasser is an old offender, who from the beginning has broken fences, ruined trees, and trampled down the garden, and who now defiantly comes upon the field of grass, insisting upon absolute ownership, then it is vain to set up the apology that very little damage is done. The antecedent transgressions, ending in a claim of title, enter into the present trespass and make it a question whether the rightful owner or the trespasser shall hold possession. Here the rightful owner is the people of the United States, and the trespasser is Andrew Johnson. Therefore in the name of the people is he impeached.

This simple illustration opens the whole case. The mere technical violation of a statute or of the Constitution, without antecedents and without consequents, would not justify an impeachment. All of us can recall such, even in the administration of Abraham Lincoln, and I cannot doubt that, since this proceeding began, the Chief Justice violated the Constitution when he undertook to give a casting vote, not being a member of the Senate. But these were accidents, besides being innocuous. From a violation of the Constitution or of a statute, the law ordinarily infers evil intent, and where such a case is submitted to judgment, it throws upon the violator the burden of exculpation. He must show that his conduct was innocent; in other words, that it was without evil intent or claim of title. In the present cause we have a denial of evil intent, with a claim of title.

The question of intent thus raised by this offender cannot be considered narrowly. This is a trial of impeachment, and not a criminal case in a county court. It is a proceeding for expulsion from office on account of political offences, and not a suit at law. When the offender sets up good intentions, he challenges inquisition, according to the latitude of such a proceeding. The whole past is unrolled by himself, and he cannot prevent the Senate from seeing it. By a commanding rule of evidence it is all before us without any further proof. You cannot shut it out; you cannot refuse to look at it. And yet we have been seriously told that we must shut out from sight everything but the technical trespass. It only remains that, imitating the ostrich, we should thrust our heads in the sand, and, not seeing danger, foolishly imagine it does not exist. This may do at Nisi Prius; it will not do in the Senate.

To such extent has this ostrich pretension been carried, that we have been solemnly admonished at the bar, and the paradox has found voice in the Senate, that we must judge the acts of Andrew Johnson "as if committed by George Washington." Here is the paradox in its length and breadth. I deny it. I scout it. On the contrary, I say that we must judge all these acts as if committed by Andrew Johnson, and nobody else. In other words, we must see things as they are. As well insist that an act of guilt should be judged as the mistake of innocence. As well argue that the stab of the assassin should be treated as the cut of the surgeon.

To the Apology of Good Intentions, I oppose all that long unbroken series of transgressions, each with a voice to drown every pretext of innocence. I would not repeat what I have already said, but, in the presence of this apology, it is my duty to remind the Senate how the career of this offender is compounded of falsehood and usurpation; how, beginning with promises to make treason odious, he soon installed it in authority; how, from declared sympathy with Unionists, white and black, he changed to be their persecutor; how in him are continued the worst elements of slavery, an insensibility to right and a passion for power; how in this spirit he usurped great prerogatives which did not belong to him; how in the maintenance of this usurpation he stuck at nothing; how he violated law; how he abused the pardoning power; how he prostituted the appointing power; how he wielded the power of removal to maintain his tyranny; how he sacrificed the Freedmen's Bureau and lifted up the Whiskey Ring; how he patronized massacre and bloodshed, and gave a license to the Ku-Klux-Klan; how, in madness, he entered into conflict with Congress, contesting its rightful power over the reconstruction of the rebel States, and, when Congress would not succumb to his usurpation, how he thwarted and villified it, expectorating foul-mouthed utterances, which are a disgrace to human nature; how he so far triumphed in his wickedness that in nine States no Union man is safe and no murderer of a Union man can be punished; and, lastly, for time fails, though not the long list of transgressions, how he conspired against the patriot Secretary of War, because he found in that adamantine character an obstacle to his revolutionary career. And now, in the face of this terrible and indisputable record, entering into and filling this impeachment, I hear a voice saying that we must judge the acts in question "as if committed by George Washington." The statement of this pretension is enough. I hand it over to the contempt it deserves.

THE MOOT-COURT APOLOGY.

Kindred to the Apology of Good Intentions, or, perhaps, a rib out of its side, is the Moot Court Apology, which pretends that the President, in removing Mr. Stanton, only wished to make a case for the Supreme Court, and thus submit to this tribunal the constitutionality of the tenure-of-office act.

By this pretension the Supreme Court is converted into a moot-court to sit in judgment on acts of Congress, and the President becomes what, in the time of Charles II, Roger North said good lawyers must be, a "put case." Even assuming *against the evidence* that such was his purpose, it is hard to treat it without reprobation. The Supreme Court is not the arbiter of acts of Congress. If this pretension ever found favor, it was from the partisans of slavery and State rights, who, assured of the sympathy of the court, sought in this way to complete an unjust triumph. The power claimed is tribunitial in character, being nothing less than a veto. Its nearest parallel in history is in the ancient Justitia of Arragon, which could set aside laws as unconstitutional. Our Constitution leaves no doubt as to the proper functions of the Supreme Court. It may hear and determine "all cases in law and equity arising under the Constitution, the laws of the United States, and the treaties made under their authority;" but this is all. Its business is to decide "cases;" not to sit in judgment on acts of Congress and issue its tribunitial veto. If a "case" arises where a statute is said to clash with the Constitution, it must be decided as any other case of conflict of laws. But nothing within the just powers of the court can touch an act of Congress, *except incidentally*, and then its judgment is binding only on the parties. The incidental reason assigned, as, for instance, that a statute is unconstitutional, does not bind anybody, not even the parties or the court itself. Of course, this incidental reason cannot bind Congress.

On the evidence it is clear enough that the President had no honest purpose to make a case for the Supreme Court. He may have talked about it, but he was never in earnest. When asked by General Sherman "why the lawyers could not make a case," he said in reply that "it was found impossible, or that a case could not be made up." And so at each stage we find him practically discarding the idea. He issues the order of removal. Mr. Stanton disobeys. Here was exactly his opportunity. Instead of making the case by commencing the proper process, he tells General Thomas to "go on and take possession of the office;" and then, putting an end to this whole pretension of a case for the court, he proceeds to treat the latter in every respect, whether of law or fact, as Secretary, welcomes him to his cabinet, invites him to present the business of his department, and, so far from taking advantage of the opportunity he had professed to desire, denies its existence. How could he inquire by what authority Mr. Stanton assumed to hold the office of Secretary of War, when he denied, in fact, that he was holding it?

Look a little further and you cannot fail to see the reason of this indifference. The old writ of *quo warranto* was the only process by which a case could be made; and this could be issued only at the suit of the Attorney General. Had the President made an order of removal, the Secretary would have been compelled to hold only by virtue of the law and the Constitution. In answer to the writ he would have pleaded this protection, and the court must have decided the validity of the plea Meanwhile he would have remained in office. Had he left, the process would have failed, and there was no other process by which he could raise the question. The decision of the Supreme Court in *Wallace* vs. *Anderson* would prevent a resort to a *quo warranto* on his part, while the earlier case of *Marbury* vs. *Madison* would shut him out from a *mandamus*. The apologists have not suggested any other remedy. It is clear, therefore, that Mr. Stanton's possession of the office was a *sine qua non* to a case in the Supreme Court; and that this could be only by *quo warranto*. The local attorney employed by the President testifies that a judgment in such a case could not be reached within a year. This was enough to make it impracticable; for, if commenced, it would leave the hated Secretary at his post for the remainder of the presidential term. During the pendency of the proceeding Mr. Stanton would continue the legitimate possessor of the office. Therefore the commencement of a case would defeat the presidential passion for his instant removal. True to his passion, he removed the Secretary, well knowing that in this way he prevented a case for the court.

Against this conclusion, where all the testimony is harmonized, we have certain fruitless conversations with his cabinet, and an attempt to raise the question on a *habeas corpus* after the arrest of General Thomas. The conversations, whose exclusion has given a handle to the apologists, which they do not fail to use, only show that the President had made this question a subject of talk, and that, in the end, it was apparent that he could not make a case for the court so as to remove Mr. Stanton during his term, and as this was his darling object the whole idea was abandoned. The arrest of General Thomas seemed for a moment to furnish another chance; but it is enough to say of the futile attempt at that time, that it was not only after the removal of Mr. Stanton but after the impeachment had been voted by the House.

Had the President been in earnest, it was very easy for him to make a case by proceeding against a simple postmaster; but this did not suit him. He was in earnest only to remove Mr. Stanton.

Nothing is clearer than that this Moot Court Apology is a wretched pretension and after-thought. It is the subterfuge of a criminal to cover up his crime—as if a surgeon had committed murder and then set up the apology that it was an experiment in science.

THE APOLOGY OF PREROGATIVE.

Then comes the Apology of Prerogative, being nothing less than the intolerable pretension that the President can sit in judgment on acts of Congress, and, in his discretion, refuse to execute them. This apology is in the nature of a claim of right. Let this be established, and instead of a government of laws, which is the glory of a republic, we have only the government of a single man. Here is the one-man power with a vengeance.

Of course, if the President can sit in judgment on the tenure-of-office act, and set it aside as unconstitutional, there is no act of Congress which he may not treat in the same way. He may set aside the whole succession of statutes for the government of the army; and his interview with General Emory attests his willingness to venture in that direction. In that spirit of oppression which seems to govern him, he may set aside the great statute for the establishment of civil rights without distinction of color. But why confine myself to instances? The whole statute-book will be subject to his prerogative. Vain is the requirement of the Constitution that "the President shall take care that the laws be faithfully executed." Vain is that other requirement, that a bill, approved by two-thirds of both houses over his veto, "shall become a law." His veto is perpetual; nor is it limited to any special enactment. It is as broad as the whole recorded legislation of the Republic. There is nothing which it cannot hurry into that maelstrom engulfing all.

The President considers the statute unconstitutional, say the apologists. A mistake in judgment on such a question is not an impeachable offence, add the apologists. To which I reply, that it is not for a mistake in judgment but for usurpation in undertaking to exercise his judgment at all on such a question that he is impeached; in other words, he is impeached for undertaking to set aside a statute. Whether the statute is constitutional or not is immaterial in this view. The President, after the statute has become a law, is not the person to decide.

Ingenuity seeks to perplex the question by putting impossible cases. For instance, suppose Congress should have lost its wits, so far as to enact, in direct terms, that the President should not be Commander-in-chief of the army and navy, or that he should not have the power to grant pardons ; and suppose still further, that Congress, in defiance of the positive text of the Constitution, should undertake to create "titles of nobility," must not the President treat such enactments as unconstitutional? Of course he must; but such instances do not help the prerogative now claimed. Every such enactment would be *on its face unconstitutional*. It would be an act of unreasoning madness, which the President, as well as the courts, must disregard as if it were plain nonsense. Its unconstitutionality would be like an axiom, not to be questioned. No argument or authority would be needed. It proves itself. Nor would the duty of disobedience be less obligatory, even if the enactment had been sanctioned by the Supreme Court; and it is not more violent for me to suppose it sanctioned by the Supreme Court, than for the apologists to suppose it sanctioned by Congress. The enactment would be a self-evident monstrosity, and therefore must be disobeyed as much as if one of the ten commandments were reversed, so that it should read, "Thou shalt kill." Such extreme cases serve no good purpose. The Constitution is the supreme law of the land, and the people will not allow its axiomatic requirements to be set aside. An illustration outside the limits of reason is of no value.

In the cases supposed, the unconstitutionality of the enactment is axiomatic, excluding opinion or argument. It is a matter of fact and not a matter of opinion. When the case is one on which there are two sides or two different views, it is then within the domain of argument. It is in no sense axiomatic. It is no longer a matter of fact but a matter of opinion. When submitted to the Supreme Court it is for their "opinion." Without occupying time with refinements on this head, I content myself with asserting that the judgment of the court must be a matter of opinion. One of the apologists has asserted that such a judgment is a matter of fact, and, generally, that the constitutionality of a statute is a matter of fact. I assert the contrary. When a bench of judges stands five to four, shall we say that the majority declare a fact and the minority declare an opinion?

Assuming, then, what I think cannot be denied, that the constitutionality of a statute is a matter of opinion, the question occurs, what opinion shall be regarded for the time as decisive. Clearly the opinion of Congress must control all executive officers, from the lowest to the President. According to a venerable maxim of jurisprudence, all public acts are presumed to be correct ; *omnia rite presumuntur*. A statute must be presumed constitutional, unless on its face the contrary; and no decision of any court is required in its favor. It is the law of the land, and must be obeyed as such. The maxim which presumes constitutionality is just as binding as the analogous maxim of the criminal law, which presumes innocence. The President reversing all this has presumed the statute unconstitutional, and acted accordingly. In the name of prerogative he has set it aside.

The apologists have been driven to invoke the authority of President Jackson, who asserted for himself the power to judge the constitutionality of an act of Congress, which in the course of legislation required his approval, although the question involved had been already adjudged by the Supreme Court. And he was clearly right. The court itself would not be bound by its adjudication. How could it constrain another branch of the government? But Andrew Jackson never put forth the pretension that it was within his prerogative to nullify a statute which had been passed over his veto in the way prescribed by the Constitution. He was courageous, but there was no such unconstitutional audacity in his life.

The apologists have also summoned to their aid those great instances where conscientious citizens have refused obedience to unjust laws. Such was the case of Hampden, who set an example for all time in refusing to pay ship money. Such also was the case of many in our own country who spurned the fugitive slave bill. These exalted characters, on their conscience, refused to obey the law and suffered accordingly. The early Christians were required by imperial mandate to strew grain on the altar of Jove. Though good citizens, they preferred to be martyrs. Such a refusal can be no apology for a President, who, in the name of prerogative breaks the great oath which he has sworn to see that the laws are faithfully executed. Rather do these instances, in their moral grandeur, rebuke the offender.

Here I turn from this Apology of Prerogative, regretting that I cannot say more to unfold its destructive character. If anything could aggravate the transgressions of Andrew Johnson, stretching in long line from the beginning of his administration, it would be the claim of right which he sets up. Under such a claim the slenderest violation of law becomes a high crime and misdemeanor, to be pursued and judged by an indignant people. The supremacy of the laws must be preserved or the liberties of all will suffer.

SWARM OF TECHNICALITIES AND QUIBBLES.

I now come upon that swarm of technicalities, devices, quirks, and quibbles, which, from the beginning, have infested this great proceeding. It is hard to speak of such things without giving utterance to a contempt not entirely parliamentary. To say that they are petty and miserable is not enough. To say that they are utterly unworthy of this historic occasion is to treat them politely. They are nothing but parasitic insects, like "vermin gendered in a lion's mane;" and they are so nimble and numerous that to deal with them as they skip about, one must have the patience of the Italian peasant, who catches and kills, one by one, the diminutive animals that infest his person. The public has not forgotten the exhibition of "industrious fleas." The Senate has witnessed the kindred exhibition of "industrious quibbles."

I can give specimens only, and out of many I take one which can never be forgotten. It will be found in the Opinion of the senator from West Virginia, (Mr. Van Winkle,) which, from beginning to end, treats this impeachment as if it were a prosecution for sheep-stealing in the police court of Wheeling, and brings to the defence all the unhesitating resources of a well-trained criminal lawyer. This famous Opinion, which is without a parallel in the annals of jurisprudence, must always be admired as the marvel of technicality in a proceeding where technicality should not intrude. It stands by itself, solitary in its originality. Others have been technical also, but the senator from West Virginia is nothing else. Travelling from law point to law point, or rather seeing law point after law point skip before him, at last he lights upon one of the largest dimensions, and this he boldly seizes and presents to the Senate.

According to him there is no allegation in the articles, that the order for the removal of Mr. Stanton was actually delivered to him, and, this being so, the senator declares that "if there is evidence of a delivery to be found in the proceedings it cannot be applied to this article, in which there is no charge or averment." And this is gravely uttered on this transcendent occasion, when an indignant people has risen to demand judgment of a criminal ruler. The article alleges that the order was "unlawfully issued," and nobody doubts that its delivery was proved; but this is not enough, according to this senator. I challenge history for another instance of equal absurdity in legal pretension. The case which approaches it the closest is the famous extravagance of the Crown lawyer in the British Parliament, who, in reply to the argument of our fathers, that they could not be taxed without representation, bravely insisted that they were represented, and sustained himself by saying that, under the colonial charters, the lands were held "in common socage as of the borough of Greenwich in Kent," and, as Greenwich was represented in Parliament, therefore the colonies were represented there. The pretension was perfect in form, but essentially absurd. The senator from West Virginia has outdone even this climax of technicality. Other generations, as they read this great trial, with its accumulation of transgressions ending in the removal of Mr. Stanton, will note with wonder that a principal reason assigned for the verdict of not guilty was that there was no allegation in the articles, that the order for the removal was actually received by Mr. Stanton, although there was a distinct allegation that it was "unlawfully issued," and, in point of fact, it was in evidence that the order was received by him, and no human being, not even the technical senator, imagined that it was not.

There is another invention, which has in its support some of the ablest of the apologists, like the senator from Iowa, (Mr. Grimes,) the senator from Maine, (Mr. Fessenden,) and the senator from Illinois, (Mr. Trumbull.) It is said that "as Mr. Stanton did not go out, therefore there was no removal;" and therefore Andrew Johnson is not guilty. If, on an occasion like the present, the authority of names could change the unreal into the real, then this pretension might have weight. But it is impossible that anything so essentially frivolous should be recognized in this proceeding. Such are the shifts of a cause to be defended only by shifts. Clearly the offence of the President was in the order "unlawfully issued," and this was complete the moment it was delivered. So far as depended upon him, Mr. Stanton was removed. This was the way in which the country saw the transaction; and this is the way in which it will be recorded by history.

But these same apologists, with curious inconsistency, when they come to consider the appointment of General Thomas, insist that there was a vacancy in point of law, called by the senator from Maine a *legal vacancy*. If there was such a vacancy, it was because there had been a removal in point of law. There is no escape from this consequence. If there was a removal in point of law, and there was no right to make it, the President was guilty of a misdemeanor in point of law and must take the consequences.

It would be unprofitable to follow these inventions further. From these know all. In the face of presidential pretensions, inconsistent with constitutional liberty, the apologists have contributed their efforts to save the criminal by subtleties, which can secure his acquittal in form only, as by a flaw in an indictment, and they have done this, knowing that he will be left in power to assert his prerogative, and that his acquittal will be a new letter of license. Nothing which the skill of the lawyer could supply has been wanting. This learned profession has lent to the criminal all the arts in which it excels, giving all to him and forgetting the Republic. Every doubt, every scruple, every technicality, every subtlety, every quibble has been arrayed on his side, when, by every rule of reason and patriotism, all should have been arrayed on the side of our country. The Public Safety, which is the supreme law, is now imperilled. Are we not told by Blackstone that the law is always ready to catch at anything in favor of liberty? But these apologists "catch at anything" to save a usurper. In the early days of the common law there were technicalities in abundance, but these were for the maintenance of justice. On such was founded that extensive *ac etiam* jurisdiction of the King's Bench, which gives occasion for the elegant commentator to remark that, however startling these may be at first to the student, "he will find them, upon further consideration, to be highly beneficent and useful." (*Blackstone's Com.*, vol. III, p. 43.) But these generous fictions for the sake of justice must not be confounded with the devices by which justice is defeated.

The trick of the apologists has been this: by the stringent application of technical rules to shut out all except the offences charged in the articles, and then, when stress was laid upon these offences, to cry out that at most they were only technical, and too trifling for impeachment. To satisfy lawyers the House weakly declined to act on the bloody transgressions of two years; but they sought to provide against the future. Like the Roman ambassadors, they traced a line about the offender, which he was not to pass except at his peril. This was the line of law. At last he passed this line, openly, knowingly, defiantly, and now, that he is arraigned for this plain offence, we are told that it is nothing, only a little technicality. One of the counsel at the bar, Mr. Groesbeck, in a speech which showed how much feeling and talent could be given to a wrong side, exclaimed:

It almost shocks me to think that the President of the United States is to be dragged out of office on these miserable little questions whether he could make an *ad interim* appointment for a single day.

Only by excluding the whole context and all its antecedents could the question be reduced to this trivial form; and yet, even thus reduced, it involved nothing less than the supremacy of the laws.

I know not how such a question can be called "trifling." Often a great cause is presented on a narrow issue. Thus it was when English liberty was argued on the claim of ship-money, which was a tax of a few shillings only. Behind this question, called trifling by the kingly apologists of that day, loftily stood the great cause of the People against Prerogative, being the same which is now pending before the Senate. That other cause, on which at a later day hung the destinies of this continent, was presented on a narrower issue still. There was a tax of threepence a pound on tea, which our fathers refused to pay. But behind this question, so trifling to the apologists of prerogative, as behind that of ship-money, stood loftily the same great cause. The first cost Charles I his head. The second cost George III his colonies. If such a question can be disparaged as of small moment, then have the martyred dead in all times suffered in vain; then was the costly blood lavished for the suppression of our rebellion an empty sacrifice.

Constantly we are admonished that we must confine ourselves to the articles. Senators express a pious horror at looking outside the articles, and insist upon directing attention to these only. Here the senator from Maine is very strong. It is the "specific offences charged" and these only that he can see. He will not look at anything else, although spread upon the record of the Senate, and filling the land with its accumulated horrors. Of course such a system of exclusion sacrifices justice, belittles this trial, and forgets that essential latitude of inquiry which belongs to a political proceeding, having for its object Expulsion from Office only and not punishment. It is easy by looking at an object through the wrong end of an opera glass to find it dwarfed, contracted, and solitary. This is not the way to look at nature; nor is it the way to look at Andrew Johnson. This great offender should be seen in the light of day; precisely as he is; nor more, nor less; with nothing dwarfed; with no limits to the vision, and with all the immense background of accumulated transgressions filling the horizon as far as the eye can reach. The sight might ache; but how else can justice be done? A senator who begins by turning these articles into an inverted opera glass, takes the first step towards a judgment of acquittal.

Alas! that the words of Burke are not true, when, asserting the comprehensive character of impeachment, he denied that, under it, "they who have no hope in the justice of their cause can have any hope that by some subtleties of form, some mode of pleading, by something, in short, different from the merits of the case, they may prevail." (*Bond's Trial of Hastings, vol.* 1, *p.* 11.) The orator was right in thus indignantly dismissing all questions of pleading and all subtleties of form. This proceeding is of substance and not of form. It is on the merits only that it can be judged. Anything short of this is the sacrifice of justice.

Such is the case of this enormous criminal. Events belonging to history, enrolled in the records of the Senate, and familiar to the country, are deliberately shut out from view, while we are treated to legal niceties without end. The lawyers have made a painful record. Nothing ever occurred so much calculated to bring the profession into disrepute; for never before has been such a theatre where lawyers were the actors. Their peculiarities have been exhibited to the world. Here was a great question of justice appealing to the highest sentiments and involving the best interests of the country—one of the greatest questions of all time; but the lawyers, in their instincts for the dialectics of the profession, forgot that everlasting truth which cannot be forgotten with impunity. They started at once in full cry. A quibble is to a lawyer what Dr. Johnson says it was to Shakspeare: "He follows it at all adventures; it is sure to lead him out of the way; it has some malignant power over his mind, and its fascinations are irresistible. A quibble is the golden apple for which he will always turn aside from his career; a quibble, poor and barren as it is, gives him such delight that he is content to purchase it by the sacrifice of reason, propriety, and truth." In this Shakspearian spirit our lawyers have acted. They have pursued their quibbles with the ardor of the great dramatist; and even now are chasing them through the Senate chamber.

Unhappily this is according to history, and our lawyers are not among the splendid exceptions. But there is a reward for those who stand firm. Who does not honor the exalted magistrate of France, the Chancellor L'Hospital, who set such an example of rectitude and perfect justice? Who does not honor those lawyers of English history, through whose toils liberty was upheld? There was Selden, so wise and learned; Pym, so grand in statesmanship; Somers, who did so much to establish the best securities of the constitution. Nor can I forget, at a later day, that greatest advocate, Erskine, who lent to the oppressed his wonderful eloquence; nor Mackintosh and Brougham, who carried into the courts that enlarged intelligence and sympathetic nature which the profession of the law could not constrain. These are among the names that have already had their reward, above the artful crowd which in all times has come to the defence of prerogative. It is no new thing that we witness now. The lawyer in other days has been, as we know him, prone to the support of power and ready with his technical reasons. Whichever side he takes he finds reasons, plenty as pins. When free to choose and not hired, his argument is the reflection of himself. All that he says is his own image. He takes sides on a law point according to his sentiments. Cultured in the law, and with that aptitude which is sharpened by its contests, too easily he finds a legal reason for an illegal judgment. Next to an outright mercenary, give me a lawyer to betray a great cause. The forms of law lend themselves to the betrayal. It is impossible to forget that the worst pretensions of prerogative, no matter how colossal, have been shouldered by the lawyers. It was they who carried ship-money against the patriot exertions of Hampden; and in our country it was they who held up slavery in all its terrible pretensions from beginning to end. What is sometimes called the legal mind of Massachusetts, my own honored State, bent before the technical reasoning which justified the unutterable atrocities of the fugitive slave bill, while the supreme court of the State adopted this crime from the bench. Alas! that it should be so. When will lawyers and judges see that nothing short of justice can stand?

GUILTY ON ALL THE ARTICLES.

After this survey it is easy for me to declare how I shall vote. My duty will be to vote guilty on all the articles. If consistent with the rules of the Senate I should vote, "Guilty of all and infinitely more."

Not doubting that Mr. Stanton was protected by the tenure-of-office act, and that he was believed to be so by the President, it is clear to me that the charges in the first and second articles are sustained. These two articles go together. I have already said in the course of this Opinion that the appointment of General Thomas as Secretary of War *ad interim* was without authority of law, and under the circumstances a violation of the Constitution. Accordingly the third article is sustained.

Then come what are called the conspiracy articles. Here also I am clear. Plainly there was an agreement between the President and General Thomas to get possession of the War Department, and to prevent Mr. Stanton from continuing in office, and this embraced the control of the mails and property belonging to the department, all of which was contrary to the tenure-of-office act. Intimidation and threats were certainly used by one of the conspirators, and in the case of conspiracy the acts of one are the acts of all. The evidence that force was intended is considerable, and all this must be interpreted by the general character of the offender, his menacing speeches, and the long series of transgressions which preceded this conspiracy. I cannot doubt that the conspiracy was to obtain possession of the War Department, peaceably if possible, forcibly if necessary. As such it was a violation of law, worthy of the judgment of the Senate. This disposes of the fourth, fifth, sixth, and seventh articles.

The eighth article charges that General Thomas was appointed to get the control of the moneys appropriated for the military service and the Department of War. All this would be an incident to the control of the War Department. In getting the control of the latter he would be able to wield the former. The evidence applicable to the one is also applicable to the other.

The ninth article opens a different question. This charges a wicked purpose to corrupt General Emory and draw him from his military duty. Not much passed between the President and the General; but it was enough to show that the President was playing the part of Iago. There was a hypocritical profession of regard for the Constitution, while he was betraying it. Here again his past character explains his purpose, so as not to leave any reasonable doubt with regard to it.

Then come the scandalous speeches, proved as set forth in the articles, so that even the senator from Virginia [Mr. Van Winkle] must admit that the evidence and the pleading concur. Here is no question of form. To my mind this is one of the strongest articles. On this alone, without anything else, I should deem it my duty to vote for expulsion from office. A young lieutenant, at the bottom of the ladder, if guilty of such things, would be "cashiered" at once. A President, at the top of the ladder, with less excuse from the inexperience of early life, and with greater responsibility from the elevation he had reached, should be "cashiered" also; and this is the object of impeachment. No person capable of such speeches should be allowed to govern this country. It is absurd to tolerate the idea. Besides being degraded, the country cannot be safe in such hands. The speeches are a revelation of himself, not materially different from well-known incidents; but they serve to exhibit him in his true character. They show him to be unfit for the official trust he enjoys. They were the utterances of a drunken man; and yet it does not appear that he was drunk. Now it is according to the precedents of our history that a person disqualified by drunkenness shall be removed from office. This was the case of Pickering in 1804. But a sober man, whose conduct suggests drunkenness, is as bad at least as if he were drunk. Is he not worse? If without the explanation of drunkenness he made such harangues, it seems to me that his unfitness for office becomes more evident, inasmuch as his deplorable condition is natural and not abnormal. The drunken man has lucid intervals; but where is the assurance of a lucid interval for this perpetual offender? Derangement is with him the normal condition.

It is astonishing to find that these infamous utterances, where ribaldry vies with blasphemy, have received a coat of varnish from the senator from Maine, [Mr. Fessenden,] who pleads that they were not "official;" nor did they "violate the Constitution, or any provision of the common or statute law, either in letter or spirit." In presence of such apologies for revolting indecencies, it is hard to preserve a proper calmness. Were they not uttered? This is enough. The drunkenness of Andrew Johnson, when he took his oath as Vice-President, was not "official;" but who will say that it was not an impeachable offence? And who will say that these expectorations differ in vileness from that drunkenness? If they did not violate the Constitution or any provision of the common or statute law, as is apologetically alleged, I cannot doubt that they violated the spirit of all laws. And then we are further reminded by the apologist of that "freedom of speech" which is a constitutional right; and thus, in the name of a great right, we are to give a license to utterances that shock the moral sense, and are a scandal to human nature. Spirit of John Milton! who pleaded so grandly for this great liberty, but would not allow it to be confounded with license, speak now to save this republic from the shame of surrender to an insufferable pretension!

The eleventh article is the most comprehensive of all. In some respects it is an *omnium gatherum*. Here in one mass is what is contained in other articles, and something else beside. Here is an allegation of a speech by the President in which he denied that Congress was a Congress; and then, in pursuance of this denial, it is alleged that he attempted to prevent the execution of the tenure-of-office act; also of an important clause in the army appropriation act; and also of the reconstruction act; and then the evidence followed, sustaining completely the allegation. The speech was made as set forth. The attempt to prevent the execution of the tenure-of-office act, who can question? The attempt to corrupt General Emory is in evidence. The whole history of the country shows how earnest the President has been to arrest the reconstruction act, and generally the congressional scheme of reconstruction. The removal of Mr. Stanton was in order to be relieved of an impediment to his purpose. I accept this article in gross and in detail. It has been proved in all its parts.

CONCLUSION.

In the judgment which I now deliver I cannot hesitate. To my vision the path is clear as day. Never in history was there a great case more free from all just doubt. If Andrew Johnson is not guilty, then never was a political offender guilty before; and, if his acquittal is taken as a precedent, never can a political offender be found guilty again. The proofs are mountainous. Therefore, you are now determining whether impeachment shall continue a beneficent remedy in the Constitution, or be blotted out forever, and the country handed over to the terrible process of revolution as its sole protection. If the milder process cannot be made effective now, when will it ever be? Under what influences? On what proofs? You wait for something. What? Is it usurpation? You have it before you, open, plain, insolent. Is it the abuse of delegated power? That, too, you have in this offender, hardly less broad than the powers he has exercised. Is it the violation of law? For more than two years he has set your laws at defiance; and when Congress, by a special enactment, strove to constrain him, he broke forth in rebellion against this constitutional authority. Perhaps you ask still for something more. Is it a long catalogue of crime, where violence and corruption alternate, while loyal men are sacrificed and the rebellion is lifted to its feet? That also is here.

The apologists are prone to remind the Senate that they are acting under the obligation of an oath. So are the rest of us, even if we do not ostentatiously declare it. By this oath, which is the same for all, we are sworn to do "impartial justice." It is justice, and this justice must be impartial. There must be no false weights and no exclusion of proper weights. Therefore, I cannot allow the jargon of lawyers on mere questions of form to sway this judgment against justice. Nor can I consent to shut out from view that long list of transgressions explaining and coloring the final act of defiance. To do so is not to render impartial justice, but to depart from this golden rule. The oath we have taken is poorly kept if we forget the Public Safety in devices for the criminal. Above all else, now and forever, is that justice which "holds the scales of right with even hand." In this sacred name, and in the name also of country, that great charity embracing so many other charities, I now make this final protest against all questions of form at the expense of the Republic.

Something also has been said of the people, now watching our proceedings with patriotic solicitude, and it has been proclaimed that they are wrong to intrude their judgment. I do not think so. This is a political proceeding, which the people at this moment are as competent to decide as the Senate. They are the multitudinous jury, coming from no small vicinage, but from the whole country; for, on this impeachment, involving the Public Safety, the vicinage is the whole country. It is they who have sent us here, as their representatives, and in their name to consult for the common weal. In nothing can we escape their judgment, least of all on a question like that now before us. It is a mistake to suppose that the Senate only has heard the evidence. *The people have heard it also, day by day, as it was delivered, and have carefully considered the case on its merits, properly dismissing all apologetic subtleties.* It will be for them to review what has been done. They are above the Senate, and will "rejudge its justice." Thus it has been in other cases. The popular superstition, which long surrounded the Supreme Court, could not save this tribunal from condemnation, amounting sometimes to execration, when, by an odious judgment, it undertook to uphold slavery; and down to this day Congress has justly refused to place the bust of the Chief Justice, who pronounced this judgment, in the hall of that tribunal where he presided so long. His predecessors are all there in marble; no marble of Taney is there. The present trial, like that in the Supreme Court, is a battle with slavery. *Acquittal is another Dred Scott decision,* and another chapter in the Barbarism of Slavery. How can senators, who are discharging a political function only, expect that the voice of the people will be more tender for them than it was for a Chief Justice pronouncing judgment from the bench of the Supreme Court, in the exercise of judicial power? His fate we know. Nor learning, nor private virtues, nor venerable years, could save him from justice. In the great pillory of history he stands, and there he must stand forever.

The people cannot witness with indifference the abandonment of the great Secretary, who organized their armies against the rebellion and then organized victory. Following him gratefully through the trials of the war, they found new occasion for gratitude when he stood out alone against that wickedness which was lifted to power on the pistol of an assassin. During these latter days, while tyrannical prerogative invaded all, he has kept the bridge. When at a similar crisis of English history Hampden stood out against the power of the Crown, it is recorded by the contemporary historian, Clarendon, that "he became the argument of all tongues; every man inquiring who and what he was, that durst at his own charge support the liberty and property of the kingdom and rescue his country from being made a prey to the Court." Such things are also said with equal force of our Secretary. Nor is it forgotten that the Senate, by two solemn votes of more than two-thirds, has twice instructed him to stay at the War Department, the President to the contrary notwithstanding. The people will not easily understand on what principle of Constitution, law, or morals, the Senate can twice instruct the Secretary to stay, and then, by another vote, deliberately surrender him a prey to presidential tyranny. Talk of a somersault; talk of self-stultification; are not both here? God save me from participation in this disastrous wrong, and may He temper it kindly to our afflicted country.

For myself, I cannot despair of the Republic. It is a life-boat, which wind and wave cannot sink; but it may suffer much and be beaten by storms. All this I clearly see before us, if you fail to displace an unfit commander, whose power is a peril and a shame.

Alas! for all the evil that must break upon the country, especially in the suffering south, as it goes forth that this bad man is confirmed in the prerogatives he has usurped.

Alas! for that peace and reconciliation, the longing of good men, now postponed.

Alas! for that security, so important to all, as the only foundation on which to build, politically or financially. This, too, is postponed. How can people found a government or plant or buy, unless they are first secure?

Alas! for the Republic, degraded as never before, while the Whiskey Ring holds its orgy of corruption, and the Ku-Klux-Klan holds its orgy of blood!

Alas! for the hearts of the people, bruised to unutterable sadness, as they witness a cruel tyranny installed once more!

Alas! for that race so long oppressed, but at last redeemed from bondage, now plunged back into another hell of torment.

Alas! for the fresh graves, which already begin to yawn, while violence, armed with your verdict, goes forth, like another Fury, and murder is quickened anew.

Alas! for the Unionists, white and black alike, who have trusted to our flag. You now offer them a sacrifice to those persecutors whose representative is before you for judgment. They are the last in my thoughts, as I pronounce that vote which is too feeble to save them from intolerable wrong and outrage. They are fellow-citizens of a common country, brethren of a common humanity, two commanding titles, both strong against the deed. I send them at this terrible moment the sympathy and fellowship of a heart that suffers with them. So just a cause cannot be lost. Meanwhile may they find in themselves, and in the goodness of an overruling Providence, that rescue and protection which the Senate refuses to give.

APPENDIX TO MR. SUMNER'S OPINION.

[In the course of this trial there was an important claim of power by the Chief Justice, as presiding officer of the Senate, on which at the time Mr. Sumner expressed his opinion to the Senate, when it withdrew for consultation. As this claim was calculated in certain contingencies to affect the course of proceedings, possibly the final judgment, and as it may hereafter be drawn into a precedent, Mr. Sumner has been unwilling to lose this opportunity of recording his reasons against it. Therefore, to his Opinion on the merits, he annexes this further Opinion on an incidental question in the proceedings.]

Opinion of Hon. Charles Sumner, of Massachusetts, on the question Can the Chief Justice, presiding in the Senate, rule or vote?

In determining the relations of the Chief Justice to the trial of the President, we must look, first, to the Constitution; for it is solely by virtue of the Constitution that this eminent magistrate is transported from his own natural field to another, where he is for the time an exotic. Of course, the Chief Justice in his own court is at home; but it is equally clear that when he comes into the Senate he is a stranger. Though justly received with welcome and honor, he cannot expect membership or anything beyond those powers which are derived directly from the Constitution, by virtue of which he temporarily occupies the chair.

Repairing to our authoritative text we find the only applicable words to be these:

> The Senate shall have the sole power to try all impeachments. When the President of the United States is tried, the Chief Justice shall *preside;* and no person shall be convicted without the concurrence of two-thirds of the members present.

This is all. The Chief Justice shall *preside* but this is subject to two limitations specifically declared. First, the trial is to be by the Senate *solely*, and nobody else; thus carefully excluding the presiding officer from all participation, except so far as is implied in the power to *preside;* and secondly, judgment of conviction can be only by a vote of "two-thirds of the *members present*," thus again excluding the presiding officer, unless it is assumed that he is a member of the Senate.

On the face of this text it is difficult to find any ambiguity. Nobody questions that the Chief Justice must preside. Can anybody question that the trial must be by the Senate *solely*, and nobody else? To change this requirement is to fly in the face of the Constitution. Can anybody question that the judgment of conviction must be by the votes of "*members* present," and nobody else? Now, since the Chief Justice is not a "member" of the Senate, it is plain that he is positively excluded from any vote on the final question. It only remains that he should "preside." And here the question recurs as to the meaning of this familiar term.

The person who presides is simply, according to the language of our rules, "presiding officer," and this designation is the equivalent or synonym of speaker, and also of prolocutor, each of which signifies somebody who speaks for the house. It is not implied that he votes with the house, much less that he decides for the house, but only that he is the voice of the house—its *speaker*. What the house has to say it says through him; but, except as the organ of the house, he is silent, unless he be also a member, when he superadds to his powers as presiding officer the powers of a member also. From this brief statement it appears at once how limited his functions must be.

Here I might stop; but, since this question has assumed an unexpected importance, I am induced to go further. It will be easy to show that the language of the Constitution, if seen in the light of English parliamentary history, must have an interpretation identical with its natural import.

Nothing is clearer than this. If language employed in the Constitution had already, at the time of its formation, received a definite meaning, it must be interpreted accordingly. Thus, when the Constitution secures the "trial by jury," it secures that institution as defined by antecedent English law. So, also, when it declares that the judicial power shall extend to "all cases in law and equity" arising under the Constitution, it recognizes the distinction between law and equity peculiar to English law. Courts of common law and courts of equity are all implied in this language; and, since there is no further definition of their powers, we must ascertain them in England. Cushing, in determining the rules of proceeding in our American legislatures, says:

> Such was the practice of the two houses of the British Parliament when our ancestors emigrated; and such has continued to be and now is the practice in that body. (Cushing, *Lex Parliamentaria*, sec. 302.)

This resource has been most persuasively presented by Mr. Wirt, in his remarkable argument on the impeachment of Judge Peck, where he has vindicated and expounded the true rule of interpretation.

According to this eminent authority, what he calls "the English archetypes" were the models for the framers of our Constitution. The courts were fashioned after these "archetypes." They were instituted according to "English *originals*, to which they were manifestly referred by the Constitution itself." (Trial of Peck, p. 499.) Here again I quote the words of Mr. Wirt.

All this is precisely applicable to that part of the Constitution now under consideration. In its essential features it was borrowed from England. There is its original, its model, its archetype. Therefore, to England we go.

Not only to England must we go, but also to parliamentary law, as recognized in England at the adoption of our Constitution. The powers of a presiding officer, where not specifically declared, must be found in parliamentary law. The very term *preside* is parliamentary. It belongs to the technicalities of this branch of law as much as *indict* belongs to the technicalities of the common law. In determining the signification of this term it will be of little avail to show some local usage, or, perhaps, some decision of a court. The usage or decision of a Parliament must be shown. Against this all vague speculation or divination of reason is futile. I will not encumber this discussion by superfluous authorities. In now insisting that this question must be determined by parliamentary law, I content myself with citing the often-cited words of Lord Coke in his Fourth Institute :

And as every court of justice hath laws and customs for its direction, some by the common law, some by the civil and canon laws and customs, so the high court of Parliament *suis propriis legibus et consuetudinibus subsistit;* all weighty matters in any Parliament, moved concerning the peers of the realm or commons in Parliament assembled, *ought to be determined, adjudged, and discussed by the court of Parliament,* and not by the civil law, nor yet by the common laws of this realm, used in more inferior courts. (Coke, 4th Institute, p. 15.)

Here is the true rule. It is to "the course of Parliament" that we must resort. It is in "the course of Parliament" that we must find all the powers of a presiding officer, and all that is implied in the authority *to preside*. "The Chief Justice shall *preside*." Such is the Constitution. Nothing is specified with regard to his powers. Nothing is said. What was intended was left to inference from the language employed, which must be interpreted according to "the course of Parliament;" precisely as what was intended by *trial by jury* is ascertained from the "common law." In the latter case we go to the "common law," in the former case we go to the "course of Parliament." You may as well turn away from the common law in the one as from the "course of Parliament" in the other. In determining the "course of Parliament" we may resort to the summary of text-writers, and, better still, to the authentic instances of history.

Something has been said in this discussion with regard to the example of Lord Erskine, who presided at the impeachment of Lord Melville. This was in 1806, during the short-lived ministry of Fox, when Erskine was chancellor. It is by a misapprehension that this instance is supposed to sustain the present assumption. When seen in its true light it will be found to be in harmony with what appears to be the general rule. Erskine had at the time two characters. He was lord chancellor, and in this capacity was presiding officer of the House of Lords, without the right to rule or vote or even to speak. Besides being chancellor he was also a member of the House of Lords, with all the rights of other members. It will be seen, as we advance in this inquiry, that, again and again, it has been practically decided, that, whatever may be the powers of a presiding officer, who is actually a member of the body, a presiding officer who is not a member cannot rule or vote or even speak. In making this statement now I anticipate the argument. I do it at this stage only to put aside the suggestion founded on the instance of Lord Chancellor Erskine.

I begin with the most familiar authority—I mean the eminent writer and judge, Sir William Blackstone. In his Commentaries, where will be found, in elegant form, the complete body of English law, you have this whole matter stated in a few suggestive words:

> The speaker of the House of Lords, *if a lord of Parliament*, may give his opinion or argue any question in the House.

Of course, if not a lord of Parliament, he could not give his opinion or argue any question. This is in accordance with all the authorities and unbroken usage; but it has peculiar value at this moment, because it is the text of Blackstone. This work was the guide-book of our fathers. It first appeared in 1765–'69, the very period when the controversy with the mother country was fervid; and it is an unquestionable fact of history that it was read in the colonies with peculiar interest. Burke, in one of his masterly orations, portraying the character of our fathers, says that more than one-half of the first edition of Blackstone's Commentaries was bought by them. Nothing can be clearer than that they knew it well.

The framers of the Constitution had it before them constantly. It was their most familiar work. It was to them as Bowditch's Navigator is to the mariner in our day. They looked to it for guidance on the sea they were traversing. When they undertook to provide that the Chief Justice, who was not a member of the Senate, should preside at the impeachment of the President, they knew well that he could have no power "to give an opinion or argue any question in the House;" for Blackstone had instructed them explicitly on this head. They knew that he was simply a presiding officer according to the immemorial usage of the upper House in England, *with such powers as belong to a presiding officer who is not a member of the house, and none other.*

The powers of the presiding officer of the House of Lords are illustrated by authority and precedents, all in harmony with the statement of Blackstone. Ordinarily the keeper of the great seal is the presiding officer; but he can do little more than put the question, unless he is a member of the body. Any other person, as a chief justice, may be delegated by royal commission. According to the rules of the house, even if he is a peer, he cannot speak without quitting the woolsack, which is the chair, and going "to his own place as a peer." The right of speech belongs to him as a member, but he cannot exercise it without leaving his place as presiding officer. To this extent is he circumscribed.

A late writer on parliamentary law, whose work is a satisfactory guide, thus sententiously sums up the law and usage:

> The position of the speaker of the House of Lords is somewhat anomalous, for though he is the president of a deliberative assembly, he is invested with no more authority than any other member; and *if not himself a member, his office is limited to the putting of questions and other formal proceedings.* (May, Parliamentary Practice, p. 220, chap. 7.)

This statement is in obvious harmony with that of Blackstone, so that there is no difference between the writer who is our guide to-day, and the learned commentator who was the guide of our fathers.

Mr. May goes still further, and lets us know that it is only as a member of the house that the presiding officer can address it, *even on points of order.*

> Upon points of order the speaker, *if a peer*, may address the house, but as his opinion is liable to be questioned, *like that of any other peer*, he does not often exercise the right. (P. 220.)

Thus, even if a peer—even if a member of the upper house—the presiding officer cannot rule a point of order nor address the house upon it, except as any other member; and what he says is open to question, like the utterance of any other member. Such is the conclusion of the most approved English authority.

American writers on parliamentary law concur with the English. Cushing, who has done so much to illustrate this whole subject, says of the presiding officer of the lords that "he is invested with no more authority for the preservation of order than any other member, and if not a member, his office is limited to the putting of questions and other formal proceedings; if he is a peer, he may address the house and participate in the debate as a member." He then says again, "if a peer he votes with the other members; if not, *he does not vote at all;*" and he adds, "*there is no casting vote in the lords.*" (§ 288.) This statement was made long after the adoption of the national Constitution, and anterior to the present controversy.

There are occasions when the lords have a presiding officer, called a lord high steward.* This is on the trial of a peer, whether upon impeachment or indictment. Here again we find the same rule stated by Edmund Burke, in his masterly report to the House of Commons on the impeachment of Warren Hastings. These are his words:

Every peer present at the trial and every temporal peer hath a right to be present in every part of the proceeding, *voteth upon every question of law and fact;* and the question is carried by the major vote, *the lord high steward himself voting merely as a peer and member of that court, in common with the rest of the peers, and in no other right.* (Burke's Works, vol. 6, p. 512, Bohn's Edition.)

In another place the report, quoting the Commons' journal, says:

That the lord high steward was but as a speaker or *chairman* for the more orderly proceeding at the trial. (Ibid., p. 515.)

In our day there have been instances where the lord chancellor sat as presiding officer without being a peer. Brougham took his seat on the 22d November, 1830, before his patent as a peer had been made out, and during this interval his energies were suppressed while he was simply presiding officer and nothing else. The same was the case with that eminent lawyer, Sir Edward Sugden, who sat as presiding officer on the 4th of March, 1852, although he was still a commoner; and it was also the case with Sir Frederick Thesiger, who sat as presiding officer on the 1st March, 1858, although he was still a commoner. These instances attest practically the prevalence of the early rule down to our day. Even Brougham, who never shrank from speech or from the exercise of power, was constrained to bend to its exigency. He sat as lord chancellor, and in that character put the question; but this was all until he became a member of the house. Lord Campbell expressly records that, while his name appears in the entry of those present on the 22d November, 1830, as *Henricus Brougham, Cancellarius,* "he had no right to debate and vote till the following day," when the entry of his name and office appears as *Dominus Brougham et Vaux, Cancellarius.*

I pass from these examples of recent history and go back to the rule as known to our fathers at the adoption of the Constitution. On this head the evidence is complete. It will be found in the State Trials of England, in parliamentary history, and in the books of law, but it is nowhere better exhibited than in the Lives of the Chancellors, by Lord Campbell, himself a member of the House of Lords and a chancellor, familliar with it historically and practically. He has stated the original rule, and in his work, which is as interesting as voluminous, has furnished constantly recurring illustrations of it. In the introduction to his Lives, where he describes the office of chancellor, Lord Campbell enunciates the rule, which I give in his own words:

Whether peer or commoner, the Chancellor is not, like the Speaker of the Commons, *moderator* of the proceedings of the house in which he seems to preside. He is not addressed in debate; he does not name the peer who is to be heard. *He is not appealed to as an authority on points of order,* and he may cheer the sentiments expressed by his colleagues in the ministry. (Campbell's Lives of Chancellors, vol. 1, p. 17.)

The existing rules of the Senate have added to these powers; but such is the rule with regard to the presiding officer of the House of Lords, *even when a peer.* He is not appealed to on points of order. If a commoner, his power is still less.

If he be a commoner, notwithstanding a resolution of the House that he is to be proceeded against for any misconduct as if he were a peer, *he has neither vote nor deliberative voice, and he can only put the question, and communicate the resolutions of the House according to the directions he receives.* (Ibid.)

In the early period of English history the chancellors were often ecclesiastics, though generally commoners. Fortescue, Wolsey, and More were never peers. This also was the case with Sir Nicholas Bacon, the father of Lord Bacon, who held the seals under Queen Elizabeth for twenty years, and was the colleague in the cabinet of Burleigh. Lord Campbell thus remarks on his position as presiding officer of the House of Lords :

Not being a peer, he could not take a share in the Lords debates, but presiding as Speaker on the woolsack he exercised a considerable influence over their deliberations. (Ibid., vol. 2, p. 104.)

Then again we are told :

Being a commoner, he could neither act as Lord Steward nor sit upon the trial of the Duke of Norfolk, who was the first who suffered for favoring Mary's cause. (Ibid., p. 105.)

Thus early do we find an illustration of this rule, which constantly reappears as we travel down the annals of Parliament.

The successor of Sir Nicholas Bacon was Lord Chancellor Bromley; and here we find a record interesting to us at this moment. After presiding at the trial of Mary, Queen of Scots, the lord chancellor became ill and took to his bed. Under the circumstances Sir Edmund Anderson, *chief justice of the common pleas, was authorized by the Queen to act as a substitute for the chancellor,* and thus the chief justice became the presiding officer of the House of Lords to the close of the session without being a peer.

Then came Sir Christopher Hatton, the favorite of Queen Elizabeth, and so famous as the dancing chancellor, who presided in the House of Lords by virtue of his office, but never as a peer. He was followed by the exemplary Ellesmere, who was for many years chancellor without being a peer, but finished his career by adding to his title as presiding officer the functions of a member. The greatest of all in the list now followed. After much effort and solicitation Bacon becomes chancellor with a peerage; but it is recorded in the Lords' journals that when he spoke he removed "from the woolsack to his seat as a peer," thus attesting that he had no voice as presiding officer. At last, when the corruptions of this remarkable character began to overshadow the land, *the chief justice of the King's Bench,* Sir James Ley, was designated by the King to act as Speaker of the House of Lords. Soon afterward Bacon fell. Meanwhile it is said that the chief justice had very creditably performed "the duties of Speaker of the House of Lords." (Campbell's Lives of Chancellors, vol. 2, p. 443.) In other words, according to the language of our Constitution, he had *presided* well.

Then came Coventry and Finch as lord keepers. As the latter absconded to avoid impeachment by the House of Commons Littleton, *chief justice of the common pleas,* "was placed on the woolsack as Speaker." At a later time he received the great seal as lord keeper. This promotion was followed by a peerage, at the prompting of no less a person than the Earl of Strafford, "who thought he might be more useful if permitted to take part in the proceedings of the House as a peer than if he could *only put the question as Speaker.*" (Ibid., vol. 2, p. 585.) Clarendon in his history says that, as a peer, he could have done Strafford "notable service." (History of the Rebellion, book 3, p. 104.). But the timid peer did not render the expected service.

Then came the period of civil war, when one great seal was with the King and another was with Parliament. Meanwhile the Earl of Manchester was appointed Speaker of the upper house, and as such took his place on the woolsack. As a peer he had all the privileges of a member of the house over which he presided. Charles II, during his exile, had appointed Hyde, afterward Earl of Clarendon, as chancellor; but the monarch was for the time without a court and without a Parliament. On the restoration in 1660 the chancellor at once entered upon all his duties, judicial and parliamentary; and it is recorded that, "though still a commoner, he took his place on the woolsack as Speaker by prescription." (Campbell's Lives, vol. 3, p. 187.) A year later the commoner was raised to the peerage, thus becoming more than presiding officer. During illness from the gout the place of the chancellor as presiding officer was sometimes supplied by Sir Orlando Bridgman, *chief justice of the common pleas*, who, on these occasions, was presiding officer, and nothing more. Lord Campbell says "he frequently sat as Speaker in the House of Lords"—(Ibid., 279)—which means that he *presided*.

On the disgrace of Lord Clarendon, the disposal of the great seal was the occasion of perplexity. The historian informs us that "after many doubts and conflicting plans among the King's male and female advisers it was put into the hands of a grave common-law judge," (ibid., p. 272,) being none other than *the chief justice of the common pleas*, who had already presided in the absence of Lord Clarendon; but he was never raised to the peerage. Here we have another explanation of the precise relation of such an official to the House. Lord Campbell expressly remarks that "never being created a peer, *his only duty in the House of Lords was to put the question*, and to address the two houses in explanation of the royal will on the assembling of Parliament." (Ibid., p. 281.) Here is the same recurring definition of the term *preside*.

For some time afterward there seems to have been little embarrassment. Nottingham, who did so much for equity; Shaftsbury, who did so little; Guilford, so famous through contemporary biography, and Jeffries, so justly infamous—successively heads of the law—were all peers. But at the revolution of 1688 there was an interregnum, which brought into relief the relations between the upper house and its presiding officer. Jeffries, on his flight, dropped the great seal in the Thames. King James had gone. There was, therefore, no presiding officer for the Lords. In order to supply this want, the Lords, at the meeting of the Convention Parliament, chose one of their own number, the Marquis of Halifax, as their Speaker, and, in the exercise of the power inherent in them, they continued to re-elect him day by day. During this period he was strictly President *pro tempore*. At last, Sir Robert Atkyns, chief baron of the exchequer, a commoner, took his seat upon the woolsack as Speaker, appointed by the Crown. Here, again, we learn that "serious inconvenience was experienced from the occupier of the woolsack *not being a member of the House*." (Ibid., vol. 4, p. 53.) At last, in 1693, the great seal was handed to Sir John Somers, lord keeper; and here we have another authentic illustration of the rule. Although the official head of the English law, and already exalted for his ability and varied knowledge, this great man, one of the saviors of constitutional liberty in England, was for some time merely presiding officer. The historian records that "while he remained a commoner he *presided* on the woolsack only as Speaker," (ibid., p. 118;) that he "had only to put the question, and took no part in debate." (Ibid., p. 122.) This is the more worthy of notice because Somers was recognized as a consummate orator. At last, according to the historian, "there was a strong desire that he should take part in the debates;" and the King, to enable him to do this, pressed his acceptance of a peerage, which, after some further delay, he did, and he was afterward known as Lord Somers. (Ibid., p. 125.)

In the vicissitudes of public life this great character was dismissed from office, and a successor was found in an inferior person, Sir Matthew Wright, who was created lord keeper without a peerage. For the five years of his official life it is recorded that he occupied the woolsack, "*merely putting the question, and having no influence over the proceedings*." (Ibid., p. 245.) Thus he *presided*.

Then came the polished Cowper, at first without a peerage, but after a short time created a member of the House. Here again the historian records that while he remained a com·noner "*he took his place on the woolsack as Speaker, without a right to debate or vote*." It appears that "not being permitted to share in the debates of the House of Lords, he amused himself by taking notes of the speeches on the opposite sides." (Ibid., pp. 304, 305.) Afterward, even when a peer, and as chancellor, *presiding* at the impeachment of Sacheverell, Lord Cowper did not interfere further than by saying, "Gentlemen of the House of Commons," or "Gentlemen, you that are counsel for the prisoner may proceed." (Ibid., p. 318.)

Harcourt followed Cowper as keeper of the great seal, but he was not immediately raised to the peerage. It is recorded that during one year he had "only to sit as Speaker." (Ibid., p. 456.) That is, he had only to *preside*. Afterwards, as a peer, he became a member of the body. He was succeeded as chancellor by the Earl of Macclesfield, with all the rights of membership.

Lord Macclesfield, being impeached of high crimes and misdemeanors as chancellor, Sir Peter King, *at the time chief justice of the common pleas, was made presiding officer of the upper house*, with only the limited powers belonging to a presiding officer, who is not a member of the body. Here the record is complete. Turn to the trial and you will see it all. It was he who gave directions to the managers, and also to the counsel; who put the question, and afterward pronounced the sentence; but he acted always as presiding officer, and nothing else. I do not perceive that he made any rulings during the progress of the trial. He was chief justice of the common pleas, acting as president *pro tempore*. The report describing the opening of the proceedings says that the articles of impeachment, with the answer and replication, were read "by direction of Lord Chief Justice King, speaker of the House of Lords." (Howell, State Trials, vol. 16, p. 768.) This instance furnishes another definition of the term *preside*.

All this is compendiously described by Lord Campbell, as follows :

Sir Peter, *not being a peer, of course had no deliberative voice*, but, during the trial, as the organ of the house of peers, he regulated the procedure without any special vote, intimating to the managers and to the counsel for the defendant when they were to speak and to adduce their evidence. After the verdict of guilty, he ordered the Black Rod to produce his prisoner at the bar; and the speaker of the House of Commons having demanded judgment, he, in good taste, abstaining from making any comment, dryly, but solemnly and impressively pronounced the sentence which the house had agreed upon. (Campbell's Lives, vol. 4, p. 609.)

This proceeding was in 1725. At this time, Benjamin Franklin, the printer-boy, was actually in London. It is difficult to imagine that this precocious character, whose observation in public affairs was as remarkable as in philosophy, should have passed 18 months in London at this very period without noting this remarkable trial and the manner in which it was conducted. Thus, early in life he saw that a chief justice might *preside* at an impeachment without being a member of the House of Lords or exercising any of the powers which belong to membership.

Besides his eminence as a chief justice, King was the nephew of the great thinker who has exercised such influence on English and American opinion, John Locke. Shortly after *presiding* at the impeachment as chief justice he became chancellor, with a peerage.

He was followed in his high post by Talbot and Hardwicke, each with a peerage. Jumping the long period of their successful administrations, when the presiding officer was also a member of the upper house, I come to another instance where the position of the presiding officer became peculiarly apparent; and this, too, occurred when Benjamin Franklin was on his protracted visit to London as agent for the colonies. I refer to Sir Robert Henley, who became lord keeper in 1757, without a peerage. The King, George II, did not like him, and therefore, while placing him at the head of the law, declined to make him a member of the house over which he was to preside. At last, in 1760, the necessities of the public service constrained his elevation to the peerage, and soon afterward George III. who succeeded to the throne without the animosities of his grandfather, created him chancellor and Earl of Northington.

For four years Henley, while still a commoner, was presiding officer of the

IMPEACHMENT OF THE PRESIDENT. 289

House of Lords. During this considerable period he was without a voice or vote. The historian remarks that "if there had been any debates he was precluded from taking part in them." (Campbell's Lives, vol. 4, p. 188.) And then, again, in another place, he pictures the defenceless condition of the unhappy magistrate with regard to his own decisions in the court below, when heard on appeal, as follows:

> Lord Keeper Henley, till raised to the peerage, used to complain bitterly of being obliged to put the question for the reversal of his own decrees, without being permitted to say a word in support of them. (Ibid., vol. 1, p. 17, note.)

Lord Eldon, in his Anecdote Book, furnishes another statement of this case, as follows:

> When Sir Robert Henley *presided* in the House of Lords as lord keeper, he could not enter into debate as a chancellor being a peer, does; and, therefore, when there was an appeal from his judgment to the court of chancery, and the law lords then in the house moved to reverse his judgments, he could not state the grounds of his opinions and support his decisions. (Twiss's Life of Eldon, vol. 1, p. 319.)

And thus for four years this commoner *presided* over the House of Lords.

A few months before Henley first took his place as presiding officer, Franklin arrived in London for the second time, and continued there, a busy observer, until after the judge was created a peer. Even if he had been ignorant of parliamentary usage, or had forgotten what passed at the trial of Lord Macclesfield, he could not have failed to note that the House of Lords had for its presiding officer an eminent judge, who, not being a member, could take no part in its proceedings beyond putting the question.

Afterward, in 1790, there was a different arrangement. Owing to a difficulty in finding a proper person as chancellor, the great seal was put in commission, and Lord Mansfield, chief justice of England, was persuaded to act as presiding officer of the upper house. Curiously enough, Franklin was again in England, on his third visit, and remained through the service of Lord Mansfield in this capacity. Thus this illustrous American, afterward a member of the convention that framed the National Constitution, had, at two different times, seen the House of Lords with a presiding officer who, not being a member of the body, could only put the question, and then again with another presiding officer, who, being a member of the body, could vote and speak, as well as put the question.

But Franklin was not the only member of the national convention to whom these precedents were known. One or more had been educated at the Temple in London. Others were accomplished lawyers, familiar with the courts of the mother country. I have already mentioned that Blackstone's Commentaries, where the general rule is clearly stated, was as well known in the colonies as in the mother country. Besides, our fathers were not ignorant of the history of England, which, down to the Declaration of Independence, had been their history. The English law was also theirs. Not a case in its books which did not belong to them as well as to the frequenters of Westminster Hall. The State Trials, involving principles of constitutional law, and embodying these very precedents, were all known. Hargrave's collection, in several folios, had already passed through at least four editions some time before the adoption of our National Constitution. I cannot err in supposing that all these were authoritative guides in our country at that time, and that the National Constitution was fashioned in all the various lights, historical and judicial, which they furnished.

The conclusion is irresistible, that when our fathers provided that on the trial of the President of the United States "the Chief Justice shall *preside*," they used the term "preside" in the sense it had already acquired in parliamentary law, and did not intend to attach to it any different signification; that they knew perfectly well the parliamentary distinction between a presiding officer a member of the house and a presiding officer not a member; that in constituting the Chief Justic presiding officer for a special temporary purpose they had in view similar instances in the mother country, when the lord keeper, chief justice, or other judicial personage had been appointed to "preside" over the House of Lords, of which he was not a member, as our Chief Justice is appointed to preside over the Senate, of which he is not a member; that they found in this constantly recurring example an apt precedent for their guidance; that they followed this precedent to all intents and purposes, using, with regard to the Chief Justice, the received parliamentary language, that he shall "preside," and nothing more; that, according to this precedent, they never intended to impart to the Chief Justice, president *pro tempore* of the Senate, any other powers than those of a presiding officer, not a member of the body; and that these powers, as exemplified in an unbroken series of instances extending over centuries, under different kings and through various administrations, were simply to put the question and to direct generally the conduct of business, without undertaking in any way, by voice or vote, to determine any question preliminary, interlocutory, or final.

In stating this conclusion I present simply the result of the authorities. It is not I who speak; it is the authorities. My own judgment may be imperfect; but here is a mass of testimony, concurring and cumulative, without a single exception, which cannot err.

Plainly and unmistakably the provision in our Constitution authorizing the Chief Justice to *preside* in the Senate, of which he is not a member, was modelled on the English original. This English original was, according to the language of Mr. Wirt, the "archetype" which our fathers followed. As such it was embodied in our Constitution as much as if the Constitution in its text expressly provided that the Chief Justice, when *presiding* in the Senate, had all the powers accorded by parliamentary usage to such a functionary when *presiding* in the upper house of Parliament, without being a member thereof. In saying that he shall "preside" the Constitution confers on the Chief Justice no powers of membership in the Senate, and by the well-defined term employed, limits him to those precise functions sanctioned at the time by immemorial usage.

Thus far I have considered this provision in the light of authorities already known and recognized at the adoption of the national Constitution. This is enough; for it is by these authorities that its meaning must be determined. You cannot reject these without setting at defiance a fixed rule of interpretation, and resorting instead to vague inference or mere imagination, quickened, perhaps, by your desires. Mere imagination and vague inference—quickened, perhaps, by your desires—are out of place when parliamentary law is beyond all question.

Pardon me if I protract this argument by an additional illustration derived from our own congressional history. This will be found under the parallel provision of the Constitution relating to the Vice-President, which, after much debate in another generation, received an authoritative interpretation. It is as follows: "The Vice-President of the United States shall be *President of the Senate*, but shall have no vote unless they be equally divided." In other words, the Vice-President, like the Chief Justice, shall *preside in the Senate*, but, unlike the Chief Justice, with a casting vote. His general powers are all implied in the provision that he shall *preside.*

No question has occurred with regard to the vote of the Vice-President, for this is expressly regulated by the Constitution. But the other powers of the Vice-President, when *presiding* in the Senate, are left to parliamentary law and express rules of the body. Some of the latter were settled at an early day. On looking at the rules of the Senate adopted at the beginning it will be found that, independent of his casting vote, nothing was originally recognized as belonging to a *presiding* Vice-President beyond his power to occupy the chair. All else was determined by the rules. For instance, senators, when speaking, are to address the Chair. This rule, which seems to us so superfluous, was adopted 16th April, 1789, early in the session of the first Congress, in order to change the existing parliamentary law, under which a member of the upper house of Parliament habitually addresses his associates, and never the Chair. Down to this day, in England, a peer, rising to speak, says, "My Lords," and never "My Lord Chancellor," although the latter *presides*. Another rule, adopted at the same date, has a similar origin. By parliamentary law, in the upper house of Parliament, when two members rise at the same time, the House, by their cry, indicate who shall speak. This was set aside by a positive rule of the Senate that in such a case "the president shall name the person to speak." The parliamentary law, that the presiding officer, whether a member or not a member, shall put the question, was re-enforced by an express rule that "all questions shall be put by the president of the Senate."

Although the rules originally provided that when a member is called to order "the president shall determine whether he is in order or not," they failed to declare by whom the call to order should be made. There was nothing conferring this power upon the presiding officer, while, by parliamentary law in the upper house of Parliament, no presiding officer, *as such*, could call to order, whatever he might do as a member. The powers of the presiding officer in the Senate were left in this uncertainty; but the small numbers of senators and the prevailing courtesy prevented trouble. At last, in the lapse of time, the numbers increased and the debates assumed a more animated character. Meanwhile, in 1825, Mr. Calhoun became Vice-President. This ingenious person, severely logical, and at the same time enjoying the confidence of the country to a rare degree, insisted that, as a presiding officer, he had no power but to carry into effect the rules adopted by the body, and that, therefore, in the absence of any rule on the subject, he was not empowered to call a senator to order for words spoken in debate. His conclusion was given as follows:

> The chair had no power beyond the rules of the Senate. *It would stand in the light of a usurper were it to attempt to exercise such a power. It was too high a power for the Chair.* * * * * The Chair would never assume any power not vested in it; but would ever show firmness in exercising those powers that were vested in the Chair. (Congressional Debates, 1825-'26, p. 759.)

The question with regard to the powers of the Chair was transferred from the Senate chamber to the public press, where it was discussed with memorable ability. An article in the National Intelligencer, under the signature of Patrick Henry, attributed to John Quincy Adams, at the time President, assumed that the powers of the Vice-President, in calling to order, were not derived from the Senate, but that they came strictly from the Constitution itself, which authorizes him *to preside*, and that in their exercise the Vice-President was wholly independent of the Senate. To this assumption Mr. Calhoun replied in two articles, under the signature of Onslow, where he shows an ability not unworthy of the eminent parliamentarian whose name he for the time adopted. The point in issue was not unlike that now before us. It was insisted, on the one side, that certain powers were *inherent* in the Vice-President as presiding officer of the Senate, precisely as it is now insisted that certain powers are *inherent* in the Chief Justice when he becomes presiding officer of the Senate. Mr. Calhoun thus replied, in words applicable to the present occasion:

> I affirm that, as a presiding officer, the Vice-President has no *inherent* power whatever, *unless that of doing what the Senate may prescribe by its rules be such a power*. There are, indeed, inherent powers, but they are in the *body* and not in the *officer*. He is a mere agent to exercise the will of the former. He can exercise no power which he does not hold by delegation, express or implied. (Calhoun's Life and Speeches, p. 17.)

Then again he says, in reply to an illustration that had been employed:

> *There is not the least analogy between the rights and duties of a judge and those of a presiding officer in a deliberative assembly.* The analogy is altogether the other way. It is between the court and the House. (Ibid., p. 20.)

It would be difficult to answer the reasoning of Mr. Calhoun. Unless all the precedents, in unbroken series, are set aside, a presiding officer not a member of the Senate has no *inherent* powers except to occupy the chair and to put the question. All else must be derived from grant in the Constitution or in the rules of the body. In the absence of any such grant we must be contented to observe the mandates of the "*Lex Parliamentaria.*" The objections of Mr. Calhoun brought to light the feeble powers of our presiding officer, and a remedy was forthwith applied by an amendment of the rules, making it his duty to call to order. Thus to his general power as presiding officer was superadded, by express rule, a further power not existing by parliamentary law; and such is the rule of the Senate at this day.

I turn away from this Vice-Presidential episode, contenting myself with reminding you how clearly it shows that, independent of the rules of the Senate, the presiding officer *as such* had small powers; that he could do very little more than put the question and direct the Secretary; and, in short, that our fathers, in the interpretation of his powers, had tacitly recognized the time-honored and prevailing usage of Parliament, which in itself is a commanding law. But a Chief Justice, when presiding in the Senate, is not less under this commanding law than the Vice-President.

Thus far I have confined myself to the parliamentary law governing the Upper House of Parliament and of Congress. Further illustration may be found in the position of the Speaker, whether in the House of Commons or the House of Representatives. Here there is one cardinal distinction to be noted at the outset. *The Speaker is always a member of the House*, in which respect he differs from the presiding officer of the upper house in either country. As a member he has a constituency which is represented through him; and here is another difference. The presiding officer of the upper house has no constituency. Therefore his only duty is *to preside*, unless some other function be superadded by the constitution or the rules of the body.

All the authorities make the Speaker merely the organ of the House, except so far as his representative capacity is recognized. In the Commons he can vote only when the house is equally divided. In our House of Representatives his name is sometimes called, although there is no tie; but in each case he votes in his representative capacity, and not as Speaker. In the time of Queen Elizabeth it was insisted that "because he was one out of our own number and *not a stranger*, therefore he hath a voice." But Sir Walter Raleigh replied that "the speaker was foreclosed of his voice *by taking that place*." (D'Ewes's Journals, 683, 684.) The latter opinion, which has been since overruled, attests the disposition at that early day to limit his powers.

Cushing, in his elaborate work, brings together numerous illustrations under this head. Here is his own language containing the essence of all:

The presiding officer, though entitled on all occasions to be treated with the greatest attention and respect by the individual members, because the power and dignity and honor of the assembly are officially embodied in his person, *is yet but the servant of the House, to declare its will and to obey implicitly all its commands.* (Cushing's *Lex Parliamentaria*, sec. 294.)

The duties of a presiding officer are of such a nature, and require him to possess so entirely and exclusively the confidence of the assembly, that, with certain exceptions, which will presently be mentioned, he is not allowed to exercise any other functions than those which properly belong to his office; *that is to say, he is excluded from submitting propositions to the assembly, from participating in its deliberations, and from voting.* (Ibid., section 300.)

At an early day an English Speaker vividly characterized his relations to the House when he describes himself, as "one of themselves to be the mouth, and, indeed, the servant of all the rest." (Hansard's Parliamentary History, vol. 2, p. 535.) This character appears in the memorable incident when King Charles in his madness entered the Commons, and going directly to the Speaker asked for the five members he wished to arrest. Speaker Lenthall replied in ready words, which reveal the function of the presiding officer: "May it please your

Majesty, I have neither eyes to see, nor tongue to speak, *in this place*, but as the House is pleased to direct me, whose servant I am *here*." (Hatsell, vol. 2, p. 242.) This reply was as good in law as in patriotism. Different words were employed by Sir William Scott, afterward Lord Stowell, when, in 1802, on moving the election of Mr. Speaker Abbott, he declared that a Speaker must add "to a jealous affection for the privileges of the House an awful sense of its duties." (Hansard's Parliamentary History, vol. 36, p. 915.) But the early Speaker and the great judge did not differ in substance. They both attest that the Speaker, when in the chair, is only the organ of the House and nothing more.

Passing from the Speaker to the Clerk, we shall find still another illustration showing that the word *preside*, under which the Chief Justice derives all his powers, has received an authoritative interpretation in the Rules of the House of Representatives, and the commentaries thereon. I cite from Barclay's Digest the following summary:

> Under the authority contained in the manner and the usage of the House, the Clerk presided over its deliberations while there was no Speaker, but *simply put questions and where specially authorized preserved order, not, however, undertaking to decide questions of order*. (Barclay's Digest, p. 44.)

In another place, after stating that in several Congresses there was a failure to elect a Speaker for several days; that in the twenty-sixth Congress there was a failure for eleven days; that in the thirty-first Congress there was a failure for nearly a month; that in the thirty-fourth and thirty-sixth Congresses, respectively, there was a failure for not less than two months, the author says:

> During the three last-named periods, while the House was without a Speaker, the Clerk *presided* over its deliberations; *not, however, exercising the functions of Speaker to the extent of deciding questions of order*, but, as in the case of other questions, putting them to the House for its decision. (Page 114.)

This limited power of the Clerk is thus described in a marginal note of the author—"Clerk *presides*." The author then proceeds to say:

> To relieve future houses of some of the difficulties which grew out of the very limited power of the Clerk as a *presiding officer*, the House of the thirty-sixth Congress adopted the present 146th and 147th rules, which provide that, pending the election of a Speaker, the Clerk shall preserve order and decorum, and shall decide all questions of order that may arise, subject to appeal to the House. (Page 114.)

From this impartial statement we have a *practical definition* of the word *preside*. It is difficult to see how it can have a different signification when it is said in the Constitution " the Chief Justice shall *preside*." The word is the same in the two cases, and it must have substantially the same meaning, whether it concern a Clerk or a Chief Justice. Nobody ever supposed that a *presiding* Clerk could rule or vote. Can a *presiding* Chief Justice?

The claim of a *presiding* Chief Justice becomes still more questionable when it is considered how positively the Constitution declares that the Senate "shall have the *sole* power to try all impeachments," and, still further, that conviction can be only by " the concurrence of two-thirds of the *members present*." These two provisions accord powers to *the Senate solely*. If a *presiding* Chief Justice can rule or vote, the Senate has not " the sole power to try;" for ruling and voting, even on interlocutory questions, may determine the *trial*. A vote to postpone, to withdraw, even to adjourn, might, under peculiar circumstances, exercise a decisive influence. *A vote for a protracted adjournment might defeat the trial.* Notoriously such votes are among the devices of parliamentary opposition. In doing anything like this a *presiding* Chief Justice makes himself a *trier*, and, if he votes on the final judgment, he makes himself *a member of the Senate;* but he cannot be either.

It is only a casting vote that thus far the *presiding* Chief Justice has assumed to give. But he has the same power to vote always as to vote when the Senate are equally divided. No such power in either case can be found in the Constitution or in parliamentary law. By the Constitution he *presides* and nothing more, while by parliamentary law there is no casting vote where the presiding officer is not a member of the body. Nor does there seem to be any difference between a casting vote on an interlocutory question and a casting vote on the final question. The first is determined by a majority, and the latter by two-thirds; but it has been decided in our country that "if the assembly on a division stands exactly one-third to two-thirds there is the occasion for the giving of a casting vote, because the presiding officer can then, by giving his vote, decide the question either way." (Cushing, Lex Parliamentaria, section 306.) This statement reveals still further how inconsistent is the claim of the *presiding* Chief Justice with the positive requirement of the Constitution.

I would not keep out of sight any consideration which seems in any quarter to throw light on this claim; and therefore I take time to mention an analogy which has been invoked. The exceptional provision in the Constitution, under which the Vice-President has a casting vote on ordinary occasions, is taken from its place in another clause and applied to the Chief Justice. It is gravely argued that the Chief Justice is a substitute for the Vice-President, and, as the latter, by express grant, has a casting vote on ordinary occasions, therefore the Chief Justice has such when presiding on an impeachment. To this argument there are two obvious objections: first, there is no language giving any casting vote to the Chief Justice, and in the absence of express grant, it is impossible to imply it in opposition to the prevailing rule of parliamentary law; and, secondly, it is by no means clear that the Vice-President has a casting vote when called to preside on an impeachment. On ordinary occasions, in the business of the Senate, the grant is explicit; but it does not follow that this grant can be extended to embrace an impeachment, in face of the positive provisions of the Constitution, by which the power to *try* and *vote* are confined to *senators*. According to the undoubted rule of interpretation, *ut res magis valeat quam pereat*, the casting vote of the Vice-President must be subject to this curtailment. Therefore, if the Chief Justice is regarded as a substitute for the Vice-President, it will be only to find himself again within the limitations of the Constitution.

I cannot bring this survey to an end without an expression of deep regret that I find myself constrained to differ from the Chief Justice. In faithful fellowship for long years we have striven together for the establishment of liberty and equality as a fundamental law of this republic. I know his fidelity and revere his services, but not on this account can I hesitate the less when I find him claiming for himself in this chamber an important power which, in my judgment, is three times denied in the Constitution: first, when it is declared that the Senate alone shall *try* impeachments; secondly, when it is declared that members only shall convict; and, thirdly, when it is declared that the Chief Justice shall *preside*, and nothing more, thus conferring upon him those powers only which by parliamentary law belong to a presiding officer not a member of the body. In the face of such a claim, so entirely without example, and of such possible consequences, I cannot be silent. Reluctantly and painfully I offer this respectful protest.

There is a familiar saying of jurisprudence, that it is the part of a good judge to amplify his jurisdiction; *Boni judicis est ampliare jurisdictionem*. This maxim, borrowed from the horn-books, was originally established for the sake of justice and humanity, that they might not fail; but it has never been extended to other exercises of authority. On the contrary, all accepted maxims are against such assumption in other cases. Never has it been said that it is the part of a good presiding officer to amplify his power; and there is at least one obvious reason—a presiding officer is only an *agent*, acting always in the presence of his *principal*. Whatever may be the promptings of the present moment, such an amplification can find no sanction in the Constitution or in that parliamentary law from which there is no appeal.

Thus, which way soever we turn, whether to the Constitution or to parliamentary law, as illustrated in England or the United States, we are brought to conclude that the Chief Justice in the Senate chamber is not in any respect Chief Justice, but only presiding officer; that he has no judicial powers, or, in other words, powers *to try,* but only the powers of a presiding officer, not a member of the body. According to the injunction of the Constitution, he can *preside*—"the Chief Justice shall *preside;*" but this is all, unless other powers are superadded by the concession of the Senate, subject always to the constitutional limitation that the Senate alone can *try,* and, therefore, alone can rule or vote on questions which enter into the trial. The function of a presiding officer may be limited, but it must not be disparaged. For a succession of generations great men in the law, chancellors and chief justices, have not disdained to discharge it. Out of the long and famous list I mention one name of surpassing authority. Somers, the illustrious defender of constitutional liberty, unequalled in debate as in judgment, exercised this limited function without claiming other power. He was satisfied to *preside.* Such an example is not unworthy of us. If the present question could be determined by sentiments of personal regard, I should gladly say that our Chief Justice is needed to the Senate more than the Senate is needed to him. But the Constitution, which has regulated the duties of all, leaves to us no alternative. We are the Senate; he is the presiding officer; although, whether in the court-room or the Senate chamber, he is always the most exalted servant of the law. This character he cannot lose by any change of seat. As such he lends to this historic occasion the dignity of his presence and the authority of his example. Sitting in that chair, he can do much to smooth the course of business, and to fill the chamber with the spirit of justice. Under the rules of the Senate he can become its organ, but nothing more.

OPINION OF MR. SENATOR HENDERSON.

On the 21st day of February last the President of the United States issued an order directed to Edwin M. Stanton, Secretary of War, declaring that Stanton thereby was removed from his said office, and his functions as Secretary would cease on receipt of the order.

On the same day he issued and delivered to Lorenzo Thomas, Adjutant General of the army, a letter of authority to act as Secretary of War *ad interim,* in place of Stanton removed; Stanton being directed to transfer to Thomas all the records, books, papers, and other property of the department.

These two acts of the President, varied only in the form of the charges, constitute the chief offences contained in the first eight articles of impeachment. It is true that the fourth, fifth, sixth, and seventh articles charge an unlawful conspiracy between the President and Thomas to put Stanton out and get Thomas in, and some of these articles charge that the President designed to carry out this conspiracy by force and violence.

Waiving for the present all questions touching the technical sufficiency of the charges, as well as the weight and sufficiency of the evidence adduced to support them, I will first inquire whether the President could legally do what he intended to do by issuing the orders.

In my view of the law, the first and only really important question to be settled is this: could the President lawfully remove Mr. Stanton as Secretary of War on the 21st day of February last? I am aware that the other question has been discussed at great length, and not without much learning, to wit: could the President, even admitting his power to remove Stanton, make an *ad interim* designation to fill the vacancy thus created, until an appointment could be regularly made?

I think that to answer the former proposition furnishes a full answer to the latter. If the President could not remove Stanton, then there was no vacancy to be filled by the designation of Thomas. If he could legally remove Stanton, a vacancy was created which, under the laws as they existed on that day, could be filled by this *ad interim* appointment.

As the two questions are so intimately connected, I may examine them together, and I proceed to show that the President possessed the undoubted power, under the laws of Congress, to remove Mr. Stanton on the day he attempted to do so by issuing the order. This is the opinion that I have entertained at all times, and which I repeatedly avowed, both before and after the passage of the tenure-of-office bill.

The Constitution "vests the executive power" in the President. He is sworn faithfully to "execute the office of President," and that he will "preserve, protect, and defend the Constitution of the United States." A part of the executive power expressly placed in his hands is that "he shall take care that the laws be faithfully executed." The Constitution is silent as to the power of removing officers. It provides for their appointment by nomination by the President with the advice and consent of the Senate. But if the Senate should not be in session when a vacancy shall "happen," it is provided that the President may "fill up" such vacancy—

By granting a commission, which shall expire at the end of their next session; but the Congress may by law vest the appointment of such inferior officers as they think proper in the President alone, in the courts of law, or in the heads of departments.

It will be observed that ample provision is made for the *filling* of offices, but no express provision is made for *vacating* them. It is made the duty of the President to "execute" the laws, and he can only do it through the officers provided by law for that purpose. If they become corrupt or incompetent or refuse to execute the law, there is no express remedy named in the Constitution except the impeachment process. The impeachment clause, it was at once seen, was wholly inefficient as a remedy. The offices of government would, in the natural course of things, become so numerous as to occupy the entire time of Congress in trying the delinquencies of incumbents. And unless the offending officer could be removed by some other means, the government might be brought into the greatest possible danger, if not entirely overthrown, by the treason and corruption of high officials, during the recess of Congress, or even during its session, but before an effective remedy could be applied.

Therefore it is that this question of removals from office challenged such early attention and was so ably and so exhaustively examined by the first Congress which met under the Constitution. Many of the men who assisted in framing the Constitution were in this Congress and participated in the debate. The first offices created by this Congress were the Secretaryships of Foreign Affairs, of War, and the Treasury; and the questions debated were the power of the President, under the Constitution, to remove these officers at his will and pleasure, and the necessity and propriety of so declaring by law. The House of Representatives, under the lead of Mr. Madison, by a large majority, and the Senate, by the casting vote of John Adams, decided that the power of removal existed in the President by virtue of the Constitution itself. All agreed that officers must and should be removable in some way other than by impeachment. Some of the members said the power was in the President alone; others contended it rested in the President and Senate, precisely as did the power of appointment.

I am aware that some persons now insist that the result of the votes establishing these departments, in the first Congress, was not such as to indicate a constitutional construction in favor of the presidential power of removal. I think otherwise. I am satisfied that a careful examination of the debate and the conclusion arrived at by the votes, will convince any unprejudiced mind that the first Congress clearly and explicitly conceded this power to the President as a constitutional prerogative which could not be limited or controlled by law. Whatever we may urge against this conclusion as a correct exposition of the Constitution, we cannot well doubt that such was the conclusion arrived at.

Judge Story, in his Commentaries on the Constitution, Chancellor Kent, in his work on American Law, the Supreme Court of the United States, and the most distinguished of our statesmen, at all periods from that day to this, admit that the decision of the first Congress was such as I have stated it. Many of them think the conclusion was wrong, but the fact itself is a part of the history of the country. But whether this first Congress was right or wrong in its construction of the Constitution amounts to but little, as I view this subject, except as it may tend to interpret and explain its legislation. Let it be kept in mind, while we refer to these laws, that they were passed by men who believed that the power of removing all appointed officers, except judges of the Supreme Court, who held by fixed tenure, was vested in the President by the Constitution, and could not be withdrawn by law. The power of appointing their successors was in the President and Senate, and the exercise of this power, they thought, could be regulated by law.. Believing that they could not take away the power of removal, if they desired, they were yet further clearly of the opinion, and so expressed themselves, that cabinet officers should, and must necessarily, be removable at the will of the President, he being responsible for their acts.

On the 9th of August, 1789, the act was passed creating the War Department. The first section of the act declares that the Secretary—

Shall perform and execute such duties as shall from time to time be enjoined on or intrusted to him by the President of the United States, agreeably to the Constitution, relative to military commissions or to the land and naval forces, ships, or warlike stores of the United States, or to such other matters respecting military or naval affairs as the President of the United States shall assign to said department, &c.

And further, that the Secretary—

Shall conduct the business of the said department in such manner as the President of the United States shall from time to time order and instruct.

The second section provides for a chief clerk to the Secretary, who—

Whenever the said principal officer shall be removed from office by the President of the United States, or in any other case of vacancy, shall, during such vacancy, have the charge and custody of all records, books, and papers of the department.

On the 27th of July preceding, the Department of Foreign Affairs had been established with precisely similar provisions, and on the 2d of September following the Treasury Department was established with the same provisions, except that if the Secretary should be removed by the President, or a vacancy otherwise occur, the Assistant Secretary, who was really clerk, should have charge during the vacancy. Now, whether I look to the words of these acts, to the contemporaneous history of their passage, to the subsequent construction given them by our statesmen and jurists, or to the action of the government under them, I am forced to the conclusion that, whatever may be the President's constitutional power in the premises, the power to remove these officers absolutely is given to the President by the laws themselves, and was so intended at the time. The departments are called executive departments. They are required to conduct their affairs as the "President shall order or instruct," and he is authorized to assign them duties not specified in the acts, which duties shall be discharged "in the manner directed by him." He is clearly responsible for their conduct, and each one of the acts provides in terms that he may remove the officer at any time, and the acts designate who shall succeed them in case of removal or other vacancy.

In this state of the law it will be observed that no possible difference can exist in the succession whether the removal or other vacancy should occur during the recess or session of Congress. In the cases of the State and War Departments, the chief clerk, and in that of the Treasury Department the Assistant Secretary, must succeed by virtue of the law.

And under such circumstances why should the power of removal be confined to the recess of the Senate and be dormant during the session? No matter when the removal is made the same person takes the office. If made in recess he will hold on during the succeeding session, unless the President should see fit to make a new nomination, and the Senate should confirm. If made during the session, the successor fixed by law holds during that session and through the coming recess, if the President so wills. Hence it seems clear that so far, at least, as these cabinet officers are concerned, there is no foundation for the pretense that the President may remove, as General Jackson did in the case of Duane, and as other Presidents have done without question, during the recess, but cannot remove during the session. There is no possible reason for the distinction, and in the absence of any such reason I take it the distinction itself does not exist. Let it be remembered that the law was made by men who admitted that the President could remove by virtue of the Constitution and independently of the law. They so worded the law as merely to conform it to the Constitution, as they understood it. If the power was a constitutional power, it was surely as vigorous and effective during the session as in the recess of the Senate, and the law being designed, no doubt, to be as broad as they held the Constitution itself to be, I cannot suppose it was intended to confine removals to time or limit them by circumstances. To the President is given the unlimited power to remove. If he does remove, whenever it occurs the law has fixed the successor.

In this state of the law I will admit that if the President had removed one of these Secretaries during the session of the Senate, and had nominated a successor to the Senate, this successor could not have entered on his duties until he had been confirmed. The chief clerk or Assistant Secretary, as the case might be, would have held the office till confirmation.

Thus stood the law on the subject of these three departments until May 8, 1792. The eighth section of the act of that date changed the rule for these temporary successions in certain cases, and extended the same rule to other officers in the departments beside the heads thereof. Under the former acts, however the vacancy might be occasioned, whether by removal or otherwise, the person to take the office temporarily was fixed, and must be the clerk or Assistant Secretary. But it was now provided—

That in case of death, absence from the seat of government, or sickness of these Secretaries, it shall be lawful for the President of the United States, in case he shall think it necessary, to authorize any person or persons, at his discretion, to perform the duties of the said respective offices until a successor be appointed, or until such absence or inability by sickness shall cease.

After the passage of this act, if a vacancy should have been created by removal in the head of a department, the President could not have "authorized any person or persons," at his discretion, to take charge of the office. For instance, he could remove the Secretary of War, but the chief clerk still would become the acting Secretary. He could only designate another person in case the vacancy occurred from death or from temporary absence or sickness. It will be observed that this act fixes no limitation of service for the temporary successor.

The next change made was by the act of July 13, 1795. This act provides "that in case of vacancy in the office of Secretary of State, Secretary of the Treasury, or of Secretary for the Department of War," (being the only executive departments yet established,) "it shall be lawful for the President of the United States, in case he shall think it necessary, to authorize any person or persons, at his discretion, to perform the duties of the said respective offices until a successor be appointed or such vacancy be filled." The effect of this act is simply to extend the discretionary power of the President, in making temporary appointments, to cases of removal and expiration of term, which were not provided for in the act of 1792. But inasmuch as the President could now remove any of the Secretaries and all subordinates in their departments not appointed by the heads thereof and appoint others at his own will, Congress thought it wise to limit the term of the succeeding temporary incumbent by adding the following proviso, to wit: "That no one vacancy shall be supplied in the manner aforesaid for a longer term than six months." The President's power of removal was not interfered with. He could still remove in session or vacation, and now he could designate at discretion the temporary successor, but at the expiration of six months the office became vacant, and thus the Senate retained its advisory power, so far as it chose to retain it, over appointments. It was under this state of the law that Mr. Adams peremptorily removed Mr. Pickering, on the 12th of May, 1800.

And we can readily discover a good reason—whether the true one or not I cannot say—for Mr. Adams's desire that Mr. Marshall's nomination should be confirmed before the adjournment of the Senate. Under his own appointment, without the action of the Senate, the office of Secretary of State would become hopelessly vacant before the next meeting of Congress, and would remain so till action could be had by the Senate.

But whatever may have been Mr. Adams's reasons for wanting Marshall's confirmation before the Senate adjourned, it is quite clear that he entertained no doubt of his power to remove Mr. Pickering during the session of that body He had asked Pickering to resign in language very similar to that employed by Mr. Johnson in asking Stanton to resign. Pickering refused, and Mr. Adams issued an order of positive and absolute removal. It is true that Mr. Marshall's name was sent in for confirmation the same day, but it was declared to be "in place of Timothy Pickering, esq., removed." The President acted strictly in accordance with his previous opinions, as indicated by his vote when presiding over the Senate in 1789, when the laws creating the departments were passed. It is not reasonable that he should have doubted, and surely the history of that time discloses no expression of doubt or censure by the most virulent of his political opponents.

The law on this subject remained unchanged up to February 20, 1863. At this time the other departments of the government had been established; but the provisions of law for temporary appointments made applicable to the first three by the acts of 1792 and 1795 had not, in words, been applied to those subsequently created. Mr. Lincoln having this difficulty sharply presented to his mind by an exigency arising in the Post Office Department, took the responsibility of acting outside the letter of the law, and made an *ad interim* appointment. He, however, sent a communication to Congress, dated January 2, 1863, in the following words:

WASHINGTON, *January* 2, 1863.

To the Senate and House of Representatives:

I submit to Congress the expediency of extending to other departments of the government the authority conferred on the President by the eighth section of the act of 8th May, 1792, to appoint a person to temporarily discharge the duties of Secretary of State, and Secretary of the Treasury, and Secretary of War, in case of death, absence from the seat of government, or sickness of either of those officers.

ABRAHAM LINCOLN.

(See Congressional Globe, 1862-63, part 1, p. 185.)

Congress took action in the premises, as requested, but seems to have directed its attention rather to amending the legislation of 1792 than that of 1795. Instead of putting the more recently established departments by name on the same footing with those established prior to 1792, the act of 1863 extends the cases for temporary appointments from "death, absence from the seat of government, or sickness," as fixed by the act of 1792, so as to include also cases of resignation, and then makes its provisions applicable to all the executive departments. It provides:

> That in case of death, resignation, absence from the seat of government, or sickness of the head of any executive department, &c., the President may authorize the head of another department, or other officer in either of said departments, to perform the duties, &c., but no vacancy shall be thus supplied for a longer term than six months.

If this act had taken away the power of removal, as fixed by the act of 1789, then it could be possibly said that so far as this case is concerned it renders imperative the act of 1795. But if the power to remove still remains after this legislation, then a vacancy may be created which is not provided for in the act of 1863. Death, resignation, absence, and sickness constitute the only cases of vacancy for which provision is made in this latter act. Beside the vacancy arising from removal, if the power yet exists, (and I can find no statute, up to the year 1863, taking it away,) vacancies may occur from expiration of term; and this class of vacancies, too, is wholly unprovided for. Upon the passage of the act of 1863, it follows that if a vacancy should have occurred in the War, Treasury, or State Departments from removal or expiration of term, the President could still have designated "any person or persons" whatever, under the act of 1795, to perform the duties for six months. But no such vacancy in the heads of other departments could be supplied at all. In the Navy, Interior, and Post Office Departments the only vacancies that could be temporarily filled are those occurring from death, resignation, absence, and sickness. And for all the vacancies last named, in any of the departments provided for by the act of 1863, the President is confined in selecting the temporary successor to the head of some other department or to some other officer in one of said departments. And now it may be said that the act of 1863, with this construction, partly failed of its object. Even if this be so it is only what frequently occurs in legislation. The law-maker often comes short of the purposes designed by the law. But it does secure all that was asked by Mr. Lincoln, and even more. He asked for power to fill vacancies *ad interim* occurring by death, absence, and sickness, and Congress gave him power to fill not only these, but also vacancies occurring by resignation. It did not give him authority thus to fill a vacancy in the Post Office, Navy, and Interior Departments arising from removal or expiration of term, but to fill such vacancies in the War, State, and Treasury Departments, he had ample power under the act of 1795, which yet remains unrepealed.

Having now examined all the legislation up to the tenure-of-civil-office act of March 2, 1867, I come to the conclusion that—previous to that act, at least—it was quite clear that the President possessed the undoubted power to remove a cabinet officer commissioned, as he must have been, to hold during the pleasure of the President, either in the recess or during the session of the Senate. I also conclude that if a vacancy could be thus created, that vacancy, under the law, could be filled by a temporary *ad interim* appointment, to continue for six months. Of the latter proposition I have no doubt at all. Whatever of offence exists in these articles must be found in the first one. If the President could remove, he could unquestionably fill the place for the limited period named. When Mr. Buchanan was called on by the Senate in January, 1861, to show under what authority during its session he had appointed Joseph Holt, a loyal man, Secretary of War *ad interim* to fill the vacancy created by the resignation of Mr. Floyd, a rebel, he presented the law so forcibly as, in my judgment, to silence all cavil, and settle the question forever. In his communication to the Senate he truly refers to the practice of the government, and shows that 179 such appointments in the chief departments of the government alone had been made from 1829 to 1856, a large number of them made, too, during the session of the Senate. It will be observed too, from the evidence in this case, that in the bureaus and inferior offices of the government, many *ad interim* or acting appointments have been made to fill vacancies of every character, including those made by removal. If it be said that no vacancy by removal in the head of a department was ever thus filled, it may be answered that but one Secretary, up to the date of which we speak, ever refused, during the session of the Senate, to resign when asked, and *he* was promptly removed by the sole act of the President without consultation with the Senate. The vacancy being once created can be filled as any other vacancy by an *ad interim* appointment.

I come now to the act of March 2, 1867—the civil-tenure act. Does it change the law, as I state it to have been before its passage? The act I will admit to be clearly constitutional in all its parts. The only difficulty, in my mind, grows out of its construction; and this difficulty of construction is the result of the effort made on the passage of the bill to reconcile a radical difference between the two houses of Congress on this very question of cabinet officers. It has sprung out of a most reprehensible and vicious practice—that to save important measures from defeat these differences between the two houses are to be healed and covered up in conference committees with ambiguous or unmeaning phrases. The truth is, that, instead of clearing up doubts, and making that plain which, above all things, should be plain, we often purposely obscure the controverted point, and devolve its solution upon the courts, or the President, if you please, each of us hoping, no doubt, that the solution will accord with his own wishes, and ready to cavil if it does not. And so it was with this act. The Senate repeatedly demanded that cabinet officers should be entirely excepted from the general provisions of the act, thereby leaving them subject to removal as under previous laws. The House insisted that they should be put upon the same footing with other officers; that they should not be removed except by consent of the Senate.

The compromise in the conference committee is contained in the proviso which declares that cabinet officers "shall hold their offices respectively for and during the term of the President by whom they may have been appointed, and for one month thereafter, subject to removal by and with the advice and consent of the Senate." To construe this law according to its letter two things must be kept in mind—first, the President who appoints; and second, the term during which he appoints. In this case Mr. Lincoln is the President who appointed. Mr. Stanton was appointed in January, 1862, and hence "the term of the President" by whom Stanton was appointed terminated under the Constitution and laws on the 4th March, 1865. If the act had used the word "terms" instead of "term," I would readily assent that Mr. Stanton's case was intended to be covered and protected by the act. But I cannot separate the act of appointment from the one identical and single current term of the President who made it. For instance, if Mr. Lincoln had been living when the tenure-of-office act passed, I cannot doubt his power to have removed any officer appointed by him during his previous term. This law surely was not intended to prevent a President, should he be elected to the presidency a dozen times, from changing his cabinet without the consent of the Senate at the commencement or in the middle of each administration; and if this position be conceded, it disposes of this case. If Mr. Lincoln could have removed, Mr. Johnson can also remove the same officers; and if Mr. Johnson cannot remove the officer succeeding him in case of Johnson's impeachment and removal cannot rid himself of the existing cabinet, because it is still said to be Mr. Lincoln's term.

If the term which Johnson is now serving out is Johnson's term, and not Lincoln's, then everybody admits that Stanton may be legally removed, because he can only hold "for and during the term of the President by whom he may have been appointed." It is only by insisting that Lincoln's term does not cease till March 4, 1869, that Stanton is supposed for a moment to be protected. This position leaves no term at all for Johnson, and if Johnson shall be removed by impeachment and Wade shall take his place and serve as President till the 4th of March next, he too will have no term, because Lincoln's term covers the full period of his service. Now, there are members of the present cabinet serving who were appointed by Mr. Johnson, to wit, Mr. Browning and Mr. Randall. If these gentlemen can serve as cabinet ministers during the term of the President appointing them and for one month thereafter, will some senator indicate to me when Browning's and Randall's terms expire? The law does not seem to contemplate a case of President without a term. If Johnson has no term, then Browning and Randall either have no terms or their terms last forever.

When Mr. Wade becomes President he will surely change his cabinet. But Wade having no presidential term, he being simply an *ad interim* President, filling out a part of Mr. Lincoln's term, when will his cabinet appointments go out of office? The law declares that they shall "hold during the term of the President by whom" they were appointed. They were not appointed by Mr. Lincoln for Lincoln was dead when they came into the cabinet, and the dead have no terms. Hence, under this construction, they would not have to retire at the end of a month from March 4, 1869.

I need not elaborate. This mere statement will show the absurdity of the pretensions now set up in reference to this law. We ourselves never gave it such a construction until that unfounded and extraordinary excitement sprang up on the attempted removal of Mr. Stanton. The Senate gave construction to this law when it passed. I accepted that construction at the time. It is according to the letter and the spirit of the act. The Senate at all times protested against forcing on any President an obnoxious or disagreeable cabinet minister. The House insisted on doing so. The bill then went to a conference committee, and on that committee, in behalf of the Senate, were two of our ablest lawyers, Messrs. Sherman and Williams. When the bill was reported from this conference committee, Mr. Howard and Mr. Doolittle called for an explanation of this provision. Mr. Sherman gave it. He said:

That this provision does not apply to the present case is shown by the fact that its language is so framed as not to apply to the present President. The senator shows that himself, and argues truly that it could not prevent the present President from removing the Secretary of War, the Secretary of the Navy, and the Secretary of State.

And again he said:

If the President dies the cabinet goes out. If the President is removed for cause by impeachment the cabinet goes out. At the expiration of the term of the President's office the cabinet goes out.

Mr. Howard expressed himself satisfied; the Senate was satisfied. Mr. Williams did not take issue on construction, but acquiesced by saying that—

The effect of this proviso will amount to very little one way or the other, for I presume that whenever the President sees proper to rid himself of an offensive or disagreeable cabinet minister he will only have to specify that desire, and the minister will retire and a new appointment be made.

Mr. Howe, the senator from Wisconsin, who had offered in the Senate the amendment to include cabinet officers, declared that he was not satisfied with the bill, and clearly intimated that the House amendment had been abandoned; and such is yet the opinion of that distinguished senator, and hence he cannot convict for the removal of Stanton. It will be rather a bad record now to convict the President of crime for taking the same view that we ourselves took on the passage of the act. I took that view of the law then, and have entertained it ever since.

But we are told that the President claims in his answer the power to have removed Stanton under the Constitutoin and in defiance of law. I am not trying him for his opinions. I am called to pass judgment on what he *has* done, not on what he claims a *right* to do. We must not convict men in this country for entertaining false notions of politics, morals, or religion. It is often difficult to determine who is right and who is wrong. In moments of temporary excitement and unfounded alarm whole masses of people have rushed wildly to incorrect conclusions. The late rebellion shows how unreasonable, how insane and foolish, large and overwhelming majorities may become. And in this condition they are intolerant of moderation, and even of common sense. From this spring mobs, derision, jeers, insults, and personal violence. He who cannot resist these things and proclaim the right at the risk of personal sacrifice, cannot expect to promote the great cause of truth, and such a man has no business whatever in this body.

When the President attempts to exercise an alleged constitutional power against the law, I will then judge of his crime. "Sufficient unto the day is the evil thereof." For the removal of Stanton and the appointment of Thomas he has undoubted authority under the laws of Congress. I cannot convict him of crime, either for doing something under the law which I may not approve, or for simply entertaining an opinion about the Constitution which was entertained and acted on by Madison, Jefferson, Adams, Jackson, and others as patriotic and as wise and conscientious as ourselves.

But suppose I am wrong in my construction of the law; must I necessarily convict the President of a wicked and corrupt intent in doing just what nearly all our Presidents have done under a claim of authority from the Constitution itself? The President is a co-ordinate department of the government. He is elected by the people and responsible to them, as we are. He is to execute the law. But an unconstitutional law is no law at all. It never has binding force. It is void from its inception. Jefferson and Jackson, as Presidents, expressly claimed the right to judge in the first instance of the constitutionality of laws, and even so to judge in the face of a decision of the Supreme Court. If a President is bound to execute one void act he is equally bound to execute others. Suppose that Congress should pass an act depriving the citizen of the right of trial by jury, shall the President execute it? Suppose Congress shall declare that the President shall grant no certificate of pardon without consent of the Senate? The Constitution gives him full and exclusive power "to grant pardons." If he, then, does what he and everybody else knows he has a right to do, he may under the law fall guilty of a high crime or misdemeanor, but unless he violates the law, and at some time issues a pardon, this outrage on the Constitution must stand forever as a valid law. Must the President, elected by the people and for a shorter term than ourselves, thus abdicate his authority as a part of the government and suffer this congressional usurpation? If he does not violate such a law he is himself perjured, for he is sworn to "preserve, protect and defend" not an invalid law, but "the Constitution." I do not claim that he may violate every law passed even for the purpose of procuring a judicial construction. I do not say that he may in mere wantonness violate or disregard any law. I only insist that each case shall stand on its own merits. If the President's purpose be criminal and corrupt, he should be removed. If he honestly intended only to procure what he says in this case, to wit, a judicial construction of a doubtful law, doubtful not only in its terms, but doubtful in its constitutionality, what right have we to pronounce him guilty of high crime? Mr. Lincoln, without law and against law, increased the regular army and the navy. Instead of impeaching, we applauded him and passed laws to justify and protect him. Why did we do this? Because we looked beyond the act to the motive. We then declared it proper to inquire into the *animus*, the intention of the President. I have thought it proper, also, in this case to examine into the President's intentions. I am satisfied that all evidence tending to explain his intention should have gone before the court. We sit in the capacity of a court and also a jury. As a court we must hear all evidence; as a jury we must consider that only which is competent and relevant.

The constitution, in making us the "sole" judges of the law and the fact, presumes that we are sufficiently intelligent to hear all testimony offered, whether competent or incompetent, and to exclude from our minds that which is improper. When the court and jury are different persons it may be well to confine the testimony going before the jury to that which is clearly competent and relevant; but no such rule applies to the court. It is the duty of the judge to be informed of the nature and the precise character of the testimony proposed before he can determine the propriety of its introduction. So in this case. An essential element of guilt charged in these articles against the President is a wicked intent to violate the Constitution and the laws. He offered to show that his constitutional advisers, his cabinet ministers, counselled him to the course pursued, and that the whole object, end, and aim of his action in the premises was to subject the law to the test of judicial examination. This advice, he alleges, was a part of the *res gestæ* and the foundation on which his conduct was based. Even Mr. Stanton had concurred with the other members of the cabinet that this very law, the tenure-of-office act, was unconstitutional and invalid. If so, it was an infringement of the President's constitutional powers, and the least he could do, it seems, was to submit the differences between himself and Congress to that tribunal which was erected to settle such differences, and to the judgments of which we must all submit if we would avoid anarchy and civil war.

Whether the President's intentions were as pacific and innocent as he alleges them to have been, I do not pretend to say. I only insist that competent evidence, such as this, going to explain the character of his intentions, should not have been rejected by the court. It should have been received and properly weighed. Even in a civil suit for damages in a case of false imprisonment the advice of hired attorneys is competent to show a want of malice or corrupt intention in instigating the prosecution. Why should the President, however wicked or corrupt he may be, in a greater criminal proceeding, where the presumptions of law must favor his innocence, be deprived of this just and reasonable rule? If he cannot change his cabinet without our consent, then we are more or less responsible for the advice given him by the cabinet. We propose to force a cabinet on him against his will and compel him to be governed by their advice or take the responsibility of rejecting it. If he disregards this advice he should be punished, I presume, for obstinacy and dangerous purposes of usurpation. If he take their advice he is not permitted to show this fact in order to negative the inference of wilful, wicked, and corrupt intentions.

A verdict of guilty on these articles, after the exclusion of this testimony, would fail to command the respect and approval of any enlightened public judgment.

In addition to what I have said, permit me to add one other reason why no conviction can be had on the articles connected with the removal of Stanton and the appointment of Thomas. It is not alleged in any of them that Stanton is actually removed, nor that Thomas is actually assigned to duty. And if it were so charged, the evidence is wholly insufficient to support it. The evidence shows that Stanton is yet in the office discharging its duties, and that Thomas is yet a private citizen. He asked for the office, but Stanton refused to yield it; Stanton remained in and Thomas has remained out. This is the theory of the prosecution. Then what is the offence? Not that a removal has been made, nor that an appointment *ad interim* has been effected. The worst phase of the matter is that the President has attempted to do these things and failed. This is not a high crime or misdemeanor for two reasons: first, he had full power under the laws of Congress to remove and appoint as he tried to do; and second, if he had no such power, the *attempt* thus to exercise it is not by statute law nor by common law nor by common sense a high crime or misdemeanor.

This, in my judgment, disposes of the first eight articles. I know that in the fourth, fifth, sixth, and seventh articles there is an allegation of conspiracy by the President with General Thomas to seize and possess the War Department.

In the first place, there is not a particle of testimony proving a prior agreement, much less a conspiracy between these parties.

Second, a conspiracy to be unlawful must contemplate an unlawful act, or a lawful act by unlawful means. The objects designed by the President—the removal of Stanton and the appointment of Thomas *ad interim*—were lawful acts, and hence any conspiracy based on these facts must fail. And no unprejudiced man can say that the proof shows any purpose on the part of the President to use force in the removal of Mr. Stanton. The evidence throughout disproves any such charge. The ninth article fails to charge any offence whatever. It alleges that the President declared to General Emory that in his opinion a certain law, passed in 1867, taking away some of his prerogatives as commander-in-chief, is an unconstitutional law. A great many people besides the President entertain the same opinion. The right of private judgment has been punished in some countries, and some even have suffered in the United States for this alleged offence, but the precedents are very bad, and should not be followed. He who follows them far in this country will follow them to his own destruction.

It is not charged that the President violated this law, although he thought it unconstitutional. But it is said that he expressed this simple opinion to Emory " to induce said Emory, in his official capacity as commander of the department of Washington, to violate the provisions of said act," &c. It is not pretended that Emory was influenced by the President's opinions. The President gave him no order to violate it, nor did he insinuate that he would like to have him do so.

And had he so ordered, I presume that Emory would not have gratified him by obedience, for he seems to have had a different opinion, and maintained it with great zeal and confidence against his commander-in-chief.

The truth is that after the unfortunate misunderstanding between the President and General Grant, and after the proceeding in reference to the removal of Stanton, the President learned through the Secretary of the Navy that some extraordinary movements of military officers in the district were being made, to be followed in all probability by some unauthorized and dangerous disposition of troops. To show that the President contemplated no violence in the premises, it is sufficient to say that when he removed Stanton he had not seen Emory, and knew that General Grant was inimical to him. He seems not to have known a word about troops in the district. He did not know how many were here or what troops they were. He had not consulted a single officer, and seems not to have known but that all the troops had been sent away or others brought in. Being informed of these movements, and no doubt fearing that he himself might be violently seized by military power and dragged from the Executive Mansion, he sent for the commander of the district to ascertain what was going on. The interview resulted in a conversation clearly indicating the fears of the President, and on these fears is based this article of impeachment. It will not likely receive a respectable vote, and I dismiss it for the consideration of those who find in it more than I have found.

The tenth article arraigns the President for making grossly abusive and indecent speeches for the purposes " of setting aside the rightful authority and powers of Congress," and to bring Congress into " disgrace, ridicule, hatred, contempt, and reproach." After setting out the language of some of the speeches in the form of specifications, the article concludes as follows, to wit :

Which said utterances, declarations, threats, and harangues, highly censurable in any, are peculiarly indecent and unbecoming in the Chief Magistrate of the United States, by means whereof said Andrew Johnson has brought the high office of the President of the United States into contempt, ridicule, and disgrace, to the great scandal of all good citizens, whereby said Andrew Johnson, President of the United States, did commit, and was then and there guilty of a high misdemeanor in office.

In my judgment these speeches are highly censurable. They were, perhaps, made to bring contempt and ridicule on Congress as charged, but if so made they failed of their object. Indeed it is specially charged that they failed. It is alleged that the President intended to disgrace Congress, but succeeded only in disgracing "the office of President." Whatever else may be said of the President's intentions, or the result of his conduct on the occasions alluded to, it may be perhaps safely assumed that he succeeded in bringing ridicule and contempt, if not disgrace, upon himself. Congress survived the attack. Indeed, the speeches greatly assisted the friends of Congress in carrying the election which immediately followed. If this be a political or partisan trial we should thank the President for these disgraceful harangues, for in a party point of view he and his policy were greatly damaged by them. I am inclined to think that the office of President suffered more than Congress. But that office will survive the humiliation of these speeches.

They are not official papers. They did not emanate from Mr. Johnson as President, but from Mr. Johnson as a stump speaker. In his latter capacity he forgot the dignity of his office. In fact, he seems to have left the office behind him and turned himself loose as a private citizen, to bandy epithets with that great people from whom he had sprung and with whom he longed for a short revel even before the expiration of his term.

I perceive much for criticism, and, indeed, for censure, in these speeches, but I cannot for a moment think they contain the elements of crime for which the President may rightfully be impeached.

The Constitution provides that Congress "shall make no law abridging the freedom of speech or of the press." The President, like other persons, is protected under this clause. He, too, has the right to make foolish speeches. I do not now say that there is no limit to the enjoyment of this right, or that it might not be so much abused by a President as to demand his impeachment and removal from office. But in this case the offence is certainly not of so heinous a character as to demand punishment in the absence of a law defining the right and providing specific penalties, and also in the face of a constitutional provision declaring that the freedom of speech cannot be abridged by law.

I have examined these ten articles as though the offences were formally and sufficiently charged. I have taken no technical exception, but have considered the indictment as good on its face. I look more to substance than to form in this proceeding. No rules of pleading are prescribed for our government, and if I could find an offence charged, however inartificially presented, I should deem it my duty to disregard the mere defects of form. But we cannot go outside of the charges presented. If one offence is charged we cannot convict of another. If the President corruptly pardoned a convicted criminal, we cannot pronounce him guilty of that act on an indictment for removing Stanton. If he usurped power in appointing military governors in the southern States, and violated all law in ordering them paid for their services from the public funds, we cannot pronounce him guilty thereof on a presentment charging that he made a maudlin or disgraceful speech at St. Louis.

If I were disposed to criticise severely the emptiness and insufficiency of these articles, I might refer to the language of honorable Thaddeus Stevens, in the House of Representatives, on the 3d day of March last, after they had been adopted, and at the time when he offered for the consideration of that body the eleventh article. Referring to these ten articles, he said, (advocating the eleventh article:)

I will, therefore, read it and call it one and a half, as, in my judgment, it is the gist and vital portion of this whole prosecution. I wish this to be particularly noticed, for I intend to offer it as an amendment. I wish gentlemen to examine and see that this charge is nowhere contained in any of the articles reported, and unless it be inserted there can be no trial upon it; and if there be shrewd lawyers, as I know there will be, and cavilling judges, and, without this article, they do not acquit him, they are greener than I was in any case I ever undertook before the court of quarter sessions.

I now come to the eleventh article. It is the only one upon which I have ever entertained serious doubts, and I will therefore set it out in full. It is as follows:

ART. 11. That said Andrew Johnson, President of the United States, unmindful of the high duties of his office, and of his oath of office, and in disregard of the Constitution and laws of the United States, did heretofore, to wit, on the 18th day of August, A. D. 1866, at the city of Washington, and the District of Columbia, by public speech, declare and affirm, in substance, that the thirty-ninth Congress of the United States was not a Congress of the United States authorized by the Constitution to exercise legislative power under the same, but, on the contrary was a Congress of only part of the States, thereby denying, and intending to deny, that the legislation of said Congress was valid or obligatory upon him, the said Andrew Johnson, except in so far as he saw fit to approve the same, and also thereby denying, and intending to deny, the power of the said thirty-ninth Congress to propose amendments to the Constitution of the United States; and, in pursuance of said declaration, the said Andrew Johnson, President of the United States, afterward, to wit, on the 21st day of February, A. D. 1868, at the city of Washington, in the District of Columbia, did, unlawfully, and in disregard of the requirements of the Constitution, that he should take care that the laws be faithfully executed, attempt to prevent the execution of an act entitled "An act regulating the tenure of certain civil offices," passed March 2, 1867, by unlawfully devising and contriving, and attempting to devise and contrive means by which he should prevent Edwin M. Stanton from forthwith resuming the functions of the office of Secretary for the Department of War, notwithstanding the refusal of the Senate to concur in the suspension theretofore made by said Andrew Johnson of said Edwin M. Stanton from said office of Secretary for the Department of War; and also by further unlawfully devising and contriving, and attempting to devise and contrive, means, then and there, to prevent the execution of an act entitled "An act making appropriations for the support of the army for the fiscal year ending June 30, 1868, and for other purposes," approved March 2, 1867; and also to prevent the execution of an act entitled "An act to provide for the more efficient government of the rebel States," passed March 2, 1867, whereby the said Andrew Johnson, President of the United States, did then, to wit, on the 21st day of February, A. D. 1868, at the city of Washington, commit, and was guilty of, a high misdemeanor in office.

The great difficulty presented to my mind in connection with this article is to ascertain what it really charges. It will be observed that one thing is distinctly charged, and that is, that the President, in August, 1866, declared and affirmed, not in words, but "in substance," that "the thirty-ninth Congress was not a Congress of the United States, authorized by the Constitution to exercise legislative power under the same, but, on the contrary, was a Congress of only part of the States, thereby denying and intending to deny that the legislation of said Congress was valid or obligatory on him," &c. The article then proceeds to declare that "in pursuance of said declaration" the President did three certain things, to wit:

1. He attempted to prevent the execution of the tenure-of-office act "by unlawfully devising and contriving, and attempting to devise and contrive means by which he should prevent Edwin M. Stanton from forthwith resuming the functions of the office of Secretary for the Department of War, notwithstanding the refusal of the Senate to concur in the suspension," &c.

2. And, also, "by further unlawfully devising and contriving, and attempting to devise and contrive, means, then and there, to prevent the execution" of the army appropriation act, of 1867, requiring that all military orders by the President to inferior officers be countersigned by General Grant. And, also,

3. "To prevent the execution" of the act of March 2, 1867, for the government and reconstruction of the rebel States; whereby it is charged that the President "did then, to wit, on the 21st day of February, A. D. 1868, at the city of Washington, commit, and was guilty of, a high misdemeanor in office."

It will be seen the article winds up with charging one single offence, and that offence is said to have been committed on the 21st day of February, 1868.

This produces confusion. One would suppose on first reading the indictment, that the body of the offence consisted in the declaration of the President that the thirty-ninth Congress was not a lawful Congress. But that hypothesis is shaken when we reflect that this declaration appears to have been made on the

18th of August, 1866. And again, if this declaration of the President be the real offence, and the enumerated instances of resistance to the laws passed by Congress be merely the proofs or evidences showing the President's disregard or contempt of its legislation, the article must fail, for two reasons: first, the criminal words charged are not supported by the evidence; and second, if the words were proved as laid, no mere words, declaration, or opinion, in reference to the constitutional character of Congress or the validity of its laws can be tortured into a high crime or misdemeanor. Such an expression is not now known as a crime under any statute, and no statute can make it a crime, for the reason, as already stated, that the Constitution forbids it.

If, then, there be an offence charged in the article, it must consist in the allegation that the President devised ways and means to prevent the execution of certain acts of Congress.

By carefully examining the evidence, it will be found that no testimony was offered to show that the President attempted to prevent the execution of the reconstruction act, except a telegram to Governor Jenkins, which telegram was sent long before the passage of the reconstruction act, and could have had no reference to it whatever. It will also be seen that the only evidence adduced to show resistance to the army appropriation bill is that of General Emory. It is the same offered in support of the ninth article. Instead of proving the charge it actually disproves it. Hence, nothing is now left in the eleventh article except the allegation that the President attempted to prevent Mr. Stanton from resuming his duties as Secretary of War after the Senate had refused to concur in his suspension. It is true that the President, in a letter addressed to General Grant, on the 10th of February, 1868, admits that he had expressed to Grant a wish that he would either hold the office and contest Stanton's right to it in the courts, or that he (Grant) would surrender it to the President in time to fill it with another name. On first impression it appeared to me that this charge was established by the President's own admission, and that, being established, it was an offence under the civil-tenure act; and so believing, I had at one time partially come to the conclusion to vote for this one single charge in all the 11 articles; but, upon a more careful examination and comparison of views with fellow-senators, I became satisfied that the article failed to charge any offence.

In the first place, admitting the charge alleged to be fully proved, neither the civil-tenure act nor any other law declared it a crime or misdemeanor. The civil-tenure act declares a removal or an appointment made contrary to its provisions a misdemeanor, but it does not make penal an effort to keep out of office one who, for the time being, stands legally suspended.

2. The charge itself is wholly unproved. By examining the President's letter, in which appears the admission, it will be seen that no attempt, nor even a declaration of intention, was made by the President to prevent Stanton from resuming the War Office after the Senate had passed on the suspension. Indeed, if senators will reflect, they will remember that the Senate acted on this question late at night, and Stanton entered the War Department early the next morning, and that in the mean time there was no interview between the President and General Grant. The only offence, therefore, consists in a mere declaration, or the expression of a wish, by the President made long before the Senate acted on Stanton's suspension, and while it is admitted that he was legally out of the office. Grant, it seems, partially consented to this request of the President, but no act was done either by the President or by General Grant to carry out this expressed wish.

3. It will be observed that the President's request to Grant was in the alternative, and it was a mere request. The President did not ask him to keep Stanton out. He asked him either to contest Stanton's right in the courts or to surrender the office back to him. Grant at first promised to do so. If, then,

the President devised ways and means to do an unlawful act, Grant must be implicated with him, and nobody pretends that such is the case.

4. Even if it appear that the President did all that can be charged on the subject, that is, if he had resolved, and even endeavored by act, to keep Stanton out of the War Office, after the action of the Senate, it does not follow that he committed even an improper, much less an unlawful act. In my view of the subject, he had a perfect right to suspend Mr. Stanton under the second section of the tenure-of-office act, and if the Senate found against the suspension, he had an equal right under the act of 1789 to remove him from office absolutely. Having, therefore, full and complete authority to do all that the charge can possibly include, I cannot, on further reflection, consent that this article contains matter upon which an impeachment may be properly predicated.

If any further reason were needed for voting against this article, it might be found in the fact that there is absent from the proof all pretence of a corrupt or wicked design in this request of the President. The only evidence adduced is his own admission, and when the whole letter is taken together it appears that the President was of the opinion that Stanton was already permanently removed, and he designed only to test that question before the courts.

I might extend this examination to much greater length. But the intelligent reader of this trial will look to the charges and the evidence for himself. I have not attempted to elaborate any point. I have simply endeavored to present some of the leading points which influence my judgment in voting against this prosecution. I do not say that the President is void of offence. I have not said even that he ought not to be impeached and removed from office. But I have said, and I now repeat it with emphasis, that in my judgment a cool and deliberate future will not fail to look with amazement on this extraordinary proceeding as it is now presented to us, and the legal and discriminating minds of the world would visit with deserved condemnation a judgment of conviction on any one of the articles now pending. I have taken up too much time already, and hence I forbear to allude to the political aspects of the question. We are told that the people clamor for the President's conviction. It may be so. But I cannot believe that one-third of the people of this country would, as jurors, convict the President on these articles. If they clamor for conviction it is on account of other matters and for other offences than these. Suppose, however, I am mistaken, and that nine-tenths of the people desire his removal, is that a reason why we should surrender our convictions of duty? We have been sworn to examine this case from a legal and not a party point of view. If this were a vote whether Johnson should be elected President, or whether, being in, he is a fit person for the exalted office, our position might be relieved of much embarrassment. The question is simply one of guilt under the charges as presented by the House, and I cannot, in justice to the laws of the land, in justice to the country or to my own sense of right, render any other response to the several articles than a verdict of "not guilty."

OPINION OF MR. SENATOR PATTERSON, *of New Hampshire.*

We have been brought to a new illustration and test of our institutions. The responsibility of the Chief Magistrate to the people and their power to remove him from his place, if faithless and treacherous to his high trusts, are on trial in the Senate. If before civil order is restored and the animosities of war allayed the temper of forty millions of people shall be self-controlled; if the currents of business are uninterrupted and society discharges its ordinary functions without disorder, as the case passes to its final issue of conviction or acquittal, it will not only prove the capacity of the people for self-government but will reassure the strength and stability of the republic. It will be a triumph of popular institutions which must unsettle the foundations of arbitrary power and hasten the establishment of free governments.

The first of the articles exhibited by the House of Representatives against the President of the United States charges a violation of the Constitution of the United States and of an act regulating the tenure of certain civil offices, passed March 2, 1867, in the issuance of "an order, in writing, for the removal of Edwin M. Stanton from the office of Secretary for the Department of War."

It is alleged that this was done contrary to the provisions of the Constitution and with the intent to violate the act above named, and was, therefore, a high misdemeanor, for which he should be removed from office.

First, was it a violation of the Constitution?

An unlimited power of removal from office cannot, I think, belong to the President by force of the Constitution. There certainly is no word in that instrument which confers any such authority directly. It says "the executive power shall be vested in a President of the United States of America," but that power is limited by the letter of the Constitution and by direct grants of power to other departments of the government. If the Executive possesses the right of removal in the case of officers appointed by the co-ordinate action of himself and the Senate it must be by implication.

The Constitutution says the President "shall nominate, and, by and with the advice and consent of the Senate, appoint," &c. Now, the right to remove cannot be drawn from the right to nominate, and, if it comes from the right to appoint, then it exists conjointly in the President and Senate.

There is an objection to this doctrine, however, more fundamental. We cannot by inference lodge in the President a power which would enable him to destroy another power vested expressly in the legislative branch of the government. The Constitution co-ordinates the Senate with the President in the appointment of the higher officials. Hamilton, in speaking of this, says:

It would be an excellent check upon a spirit of favoritism in the President, and would tend greatly to prevent the appointment of unfit characters from State prejudice, from family connection, from personal attachment, or from a view to popularity. In addition to this, it would be an efficacious source of stability in the administration.

But it will be readily seen that if the President has the right to remove and make *ad interim* appointments at pleasure, the co-ordinate function of the Senate in appointments may become a nullity and the purpose of the Constitution be defeated. It destroys at one blow this great safeguard against usurpation and maladministration in the Executive.

Without delaying to discuss this subject further, I simply say that, to my mind, a natural interpretation of the Constitution would give the appointing and removing power to the same parties.

But the acts of 1789 and 1795 gave a legislative construction adverse to this view, and, whether these acts are repealed or not, if it can be shown that the President violated no *law* in the removal of Mr. Stanton, it would be clearly unjust to impeach him for having conformed to a legislative construction of the Constitution, unquestioned for fifty years, against the views and wishes of the majority of Congress. So heavy a judgment should not fall upon the Chief Magistrate for having followed an exposition of the fudamental law, authorized by solemn enactment and supported by some of the ablest among the earliest statesmen of the republic.

The second allegation in the article is a violation of *law* in the removal of Mr. Stanton.

The respondent urges a threefold defence against this charge:

1st. That the non-execution of the act of March 2, 1867, "regulating the tenure of certain civil offices," was not a breach of executive trusts, as the law was unconstitutional and void.

2d. That a denial of the validity of the act and an intentional disregard of its provisions in order to bring the statute into court and test its constitutionality is not an impeachable offence.

3d. That the language of the statute does not include Mr. Stanton, and hence his removal was no violation of law.

Whether the President had or had not a constitutional right to remove at pleasure officers confirmed by the Senate was the theme of the great debate in 1789 upon the establishment of the State Department. It was purely a question of interpretation, and was argued upon both sides by lawyers of unsurpassed ability. Even the great statesmen who had been master spirits in the constitutional convention, and whose genius had passed largely into the framework of the government, entered the lists and battled earnestly on either side. When the Constitution was before the State conventions for adoption the Federalist expressly denied this right to the Executive, but the Congress of 1789 reversed that interpretation which had received the popular approval by a close vote of 34 to 20 in the House and by the casting vote of the Vice President in the Senate. It is believed that the character of Washington, then Chief Magistrate, largely influenced the result, and statesmen as patriotic and enlightened as any who took part in the deliberations of the first Congress have since deprecated a construction which they believe a hazardous and unwarranted change of the Constitution.

In 1835, a committee of Congress, composed of such men as Calhoun, Webster, and Benton, reported a bill designed to limit the abuse of executive patronage, and requiring the President in all cases of removal to state the reasons thereof. In the debate, Mr. Clay spoke as follows :

> It is legislative authority which creates the office, defines its duties, and may prescribe its duration. I speak, of course, of offices not created by the Constitution, but the law. The office coming into existence by the will of Congress, the same will may provide how and in what manner the office and officer shall cease to exist. It may direct the conditions on which he shall hold the office, and when and how he shall be dismissed.
> It would be unreasonable to contend that, although Congress, in pursuance of the public good, brings the office and the officer into being, and assigns their purposes, yet the President has a control over the officer which Congress cannot reach and regulate. * * * The precedent of 1789 was established in the House of Representatives against the opinion of a large and able minority, and in the Senate by the casting vote of the Vice-President, John Adams. It is impossible to read the debate which it occasioned without being impressed with the conviction that the just confidence reposed in the Father of his Country, then at the head of the government, had great, if not decisive influence in establishing it. It has never, prior to the commencement of the present administration, been submitted to the process of review. * * * * No one can carefully examine the debate in the House of Representatives in 1789 without being struck with the superiority of the argument on the side of the minority, and the unsatisfactory nature of that of the majority.

The language of Mr. Webster was not less explicit or emphatic :

> I think, then, sir, that the power of appointment naturally and necessarily includes the power of removal, where no limitation is expressed, nor any tenure but that at will declared. The power of appointment being conferred on the President and Senate, I think the power of removal went along with it, and should have been regarded as a part of it and exercised by the same hands. I think the legislature possesses the power of regulating the condition, duration, qualification, and tenure of office in all cases where the Constitution has made no express provision on the subject. I am, therefore, of opinion that it is competent for Congress to decide by law, as one qualification of the tenure of office, that the incumbent shall remain in place till the President shall remove him, for reasons to be stated to the Senate. And I am of opinion that this qualification, mild and gentle as it is, will have some effect in arresting the evils which beset the progress of the government and seriously threaten its future prosperity. * * * * * *
> After considering the question again and again within the last six years, I am willing to say that, in my deliberate judgment, the original decision was wrong. I cannot but think that those who denied the power of 1789 had the best of the argument. It appears to me, after thorough and repeated and conscientious examination, that an erroneous interpretation was given to the Constitution in this respect by the decision of the first Congress. * *
> I have the clearest conviction that they (the convention) looked to no other mode of dis-

placing an officer than by impeachment or the regular appointment of another person to the same place.

* * * * *

I believe it to be within the just power of Congress to reverse the decision of 1789, and I mean to hold myself at liberty to act hereafter upon that question as the safety of the government and of the Constitution may require.

Mr. Calhoun and Mr. Ewing were equally positive in their advocacy of the bill, and Marshall, Kent, and Story seem to have entertained similar views in respect to the original intent of the Constitution.

But there has been a conflict of legislative constructions as well as of individual opinions upon this subject. Subsequent Congresses have claimed and exercised, without the obstruction of an executive veto, the power to regulate the tenure of office, both civil and military.

A law of February 25, 1863, provides that the Comptroller of the Currency "shall hold his office for the term of five years unless sooner removed by the President *by and with the advice and consent of the Senate.*"

By section five of an act of July 13, 1866, it is provided that—

No officer in the military or naval service shall, in time of peace, *be dismissed from service except upon and in pursuance of the sentence of a court-martial,* to that effect or in commutation thereof.

These are late acts, but they are only instances of other similar acts scattered through our statutes, whose validity has never been questioned. There is, therefore, no decision of the Supreme Court or settled precedent of legislation which can bar the right of Congress to regulate by law both appointments to and removals from office. Never until now, so far as I know, has the right been questioned. Whatever differences of opinion legislators may have entertained in respect to the original grant of power, all have acquiesced in the exercise of legislative authority over the tenure of office.

Hence the claim of the President of a judicial right to settle *ex cathedra* the constitutionality of a law upon this subject is inadmissible and subversive of the powers and independence of a co-ordinate branch of the government. In a clear case of a legislative usurpation of his constitutional prerogatives, such as would occur in an effort to destroy his veto or pardoning power, he might be justified in treating the act as a nullity, but not when Congress moves in the path of authoritative precedents, and where, at most, only a doubt can be raised against its original right of jurisdiction.

At an earlier period I apprehend such a claim would not have been advanced. Civil war naturally tends to concentrate power in the chief who administers it. Forces and resources must be at his disposal. Defeat waits upon the commander who is hampered by the forms and delays of law. His authority is nothing if not supreme. The laws of war are swift and absolute, and can recognize no personal rights, no claims of Magna Charta. Active warfare necessarily encroaches upon the domain of legislation, and familiarizes the Executive with a use of authority hazardous in a time of peace.

Power once possessed is soon felt to be a right, and is yielded with reluctance. Our experience has added another example to the long record of history. The President's defence denies the supremacy of law, and is more dangerous to the government than the alleged crime which has brought him to the bar of the Senate. If he can determine the validity of law, the Supreme Court is an empty mockery. No act can pass his veto, and all legislation may be subverted at pleasure. The right to substitute the judgment of the ruler for the judgment of the people, and to override their laws by his will, is absolutism. If the plea is good, it is a valid defence for unlimited usurpation.

The plea of the President that he removed Mr. Stanton for the purpose of securing a decision of the court upon the constitutionality of the law is equally untenable as a ground of defence. It is inconsistent with the answer which he made by his counsel, that he effected the removal in the exercise of an executive power of which Congress could not deprive him, "because satisfied that he could not allow the said Stanton to continue to hold the office of Secretary of the Department of War without hazard of the public interests." It is irreconcilable with the further answer that, "in his capacity of President of the United States," he "did form the opinion that the case of the said Stanton and his tenure of office were not affected by the first section of the last-named act," referring thereby to the tenure-of-office act.

But, passing over the contradictory nature of this defence, we submit that the evidence shows an anxious and persistent effort to get possession of the War Office, and not a purpose to have the law adjudicated. If to test the law had been his desire, he should have sued out a writ of "*quo warranto*" on the refusal of Stanton to obey his order of removal. Instead of that, he not only endeavored to keep him out of office by an unworthy trick when we had annulled his suspension, but issued a letter of absolute removal in the face of Congress after it had rejected his judicial opinion of the constitutionality of the law, and had passed it by a two-thirds vote over his veto. After it had reaffirmed the validity of its action and the invalidity of his on this very subject, and assuming that the removal had been effected, he issued a letter of authority to fill the *vacancy*. To crown the effrontery he nominates General Schofield to the vacant Secretaryship, while urging upon the Senate his acquittal on the ground that the removal was not effected, but only attempted. Thus duplicity is made the proof of innocence. Having put the case into a condition in which he could not sue out a writ of *quo warranto*, I deny that he can honestly plead a desire to test the law. He knew full well if Stanton was not in the law he could not test it by his removal.

This defence is clearly an afterthought. Having recognized the validity of the law by conforming all commissions to its provisions; having suspended Mr. Stanton and appointed General Grant under it; having notified the Secretary of the Treasury of the change, to wit, as follows:

SIR: In compliance with the requirements of the act entitled "An act to regulate the tenure of certain civil offices," you are hereby notified that on the 12th instant Hon. Edwin M. Stanton was suspended from his office as Secretary of War, and General U. S. Grant authorized and empowered to act as Secretary of War *ad interim*—

and having afterward transmitted a message to the Senate giving the reasons for the suspension, as required by the act, he cannot, without criminality, under the pretext of seeking a judicial decision, set aside or trample upon the law at the point where it baffled his cherished political policy and curbed a career which the law-makers believed dangerous to the peace and liberties of the country. If regard for the Constitution, and not a desire to get control of the army, had been his purpose, why did he not test the law in the first instance when called upon to execute it, and when his motive would have been simple and unquestioned? Facts show that it was not the nature but the effect of the law which troubled the President.

The enactment was designed to circumscribe and limit his power, lest he should abuse it to the injury of the country. It was effective; and when it arrested the execution of his policy, regardless alike of his oath and the wishes of the nation, he defiantly violated the law to remove the man who was a trammel upon his will.

The evidence demonstrates a purpose to get possession of the Department of War, and disproves the pretence that he was seeking a judicial decision upon the constitutionality of the law.

Finally, was Mr. Stanton's removal a violation of the act entitled "An act regulating the tenure of certain civil offices?"

The purpose of the law was to hold in office men whom the policy of Mr. Johnson threatened to remove. It is both claimed and denied that the Secretary of War who held a commission under President Lincoln is protected by the law.

The true construction must be drawn from the letter of the statute itself, and not from any conflicting opinions expressed in debate at the time of its passage.

The first section of the act reads as follows:

That every person holding any civil office to which he has been appointed by and with the advice and consent of the Senate, and every person who shall hereafter be appointed to any such office, and shall become duly qualified to act therein, is, and shall be, entitled to hold such office until a successor shall have been in like manner appointed and duly qualified, except as herein otherwise provided: *Provided,* That the Secretaries of State, of the Treasury, of War, of the Navy, and of the Interior, the Postmaster General, and the Attorney General, shall hold their offices respectively for and during the term of the President by whom they may have been appointed, and for one month thereafter, subject to removal by and with the advice and consent of the Senate.

It will be observed that the body of the section includes *all persons* who have been or who shall be appointed to civil office by and with the advice and consent of the Senate, "except as herein otherwise provided."

This last clause which I have quoted was in the bill before the committee of conference, who added the proviso, was appointed, and undoubtedly refers to officers mentioned in the fourth section whose term is limited by law. The Secretaries were not of this number, and the effect of the proviso which was added by the conferees was simply to limit their time to the term of the President under whom they served and one month thereafter.

The meaning of the section clearly is that *every* civil officer who has been confirmed by the Senate shall hold his office until the Senate shall confirm a successor, but provides that such officers as hold a term limited by law shall lose their office by the expiration of their term without the action of the Senate. The only effect of the proviso is to bring the heads of departments into this last class of officers whose terms are limited by law. The intent and effect of the law is to take the removal of every officer confirmed by the Senate out of the pleasure of the President; and it is a perversion of language to say that the proviso places the tenure of the Secretary of War, or of any other Secretary, at the option of the President. They are all removable by the confirmation of a successor or by the expiration of their term.

It has been said that the proviso brings the office of Secretary of War out of the body of the section into itself, but that the clause which provides that the Secretaries " shall hold their offices respectively for and during the term of the President by whom they may have been appointed, and for one month thereafter," excludes Mr. Stanton from it because he was not appointed by Mr. Johnson.

The office could not be taken out of the body of the section unless it was first in it, and if there, the Secretary was there also. If, now, the office of Secretary of War is brought into the proviso, and Mr. Stanton excluded, he is left in the section and covered by its provisions. If not there, to what limbo have the gods assigned him?

The conception of a Secretary of War without an office is worthy of a lawyer without a brief. The argument is a pure creation, and a miserable fallacy at that. The language of the section is in relation to persons, not offices. It says, "every person holding any civil office shall be entitled to hold," &c.; "the Secretaries, &c., shall hold their offices," &c. The construction of the section is simple and unmistakable. There are certain officers referred to in the fourth section whose terms are limited by law, and the proviso adds the heads of departments to this number, but the terms of the law allow no officer to be *removed* who has been appointed by and with the advice and consent of the Senate, except by the appointment of a successor in the same way.

The language of the proviso itself is, that the Secretaries are "subject to removal by and with the advice and consent of the Senate." If, therefore, Mr. Stanton is not in the proviso, he is in the body of the section, and the law was violated by his removal. I will not stay to inquire in whose term he was holding, for the argument is perfect without it.

This is not all. The President violated the second as well as the first section of the law. It reads as follows:

That when any officer appointed as aforesaid, excepting judges of the United States courts, shall, during a recess of the Senate, be shown, by evidence satisfactory to the President, to be guilty *of misconduct in office, or crime, or for any reason shall become incapable or legally disqualified to perform its duties, in such case, and in no other, the President may suspend such officer*, &c.

If, now, the President can suspend an officer during the *recess only*, and that, for the reasons specified in the law and *no other*, can he remove him outright during the *session* of the Senate, and when he is free from all the legal disqualifications enumerated in the act?

The act further provides, in respect to a suspension, that—

If the Senate shall concur in such suspension, and advise and consent to the removal of such officer, they shall so certify to the President, who may thereupon remove such officer. But if the Senate shall refuse to concur in such suspension, such officer so suspended shall forthwith resume the functions of his office, &c.

The Senate refused to concur in the suspension of Mr. Stanton, refused to advise and consent to his removal, but the President removed him in defiance of the letter of the act and of the will of the Senate. No amount of genius for legal sophistries can torture that act of the President into anything less than a wilful violation of law. This simple statement of the case, without argument, is sufficient to command the approval of every mind.

Counsel must have forgotten that the Senate, acting under the solemnity of an oath, had repeatedly decided that the law applied to Mr. Stanton. On the 12th of December the Senate, remembering that the "tenure-of-office act" was passed expressly to protect officers whose retention was thought indispensable to the public service against an abuse of executive power, and moved by the eloquent and powerful appeal of the senator from Maine, refused their assent to the removal of Mr. Stanton, which they had no right to do, or even act upon at all, unless he was covered by the law of March 2, 1867.

Again, on the 21st of February, when the President, failing in his attempt to prevent the return of the Secretary by the use of General Grant, informed this body of his absolute dismissal, it was resolved by the Senate—

That under the Constitution and laws of the United States the President has no power to remove the Secretary of War and to designate any other officer to perform the duties of that office *ad interim*.

With such action upon our records we have a right to assume that argument upon this is foreclosed, and that senators who took part with the majority in those transactions will sustain the construction which they helped to establish, and upon which the conduct of the Secretary is based.

We are brought next to consider the charges as stated in the second and third articles. It is alleged that the appointment of Lorenzo Thomas as Secretary of War "*ad interim*" was a high misdemeanor, being made without law, and in violation of both law and the Constitution. The provision of the Constitution is, that—

The President shall have power to fill up all vacancies that may *happen* [not such as he may make] *during the recess* of the Senate, by granting commissions which shall expire at the end of their next session.

This certainly does not confer the right to make "*ad interim*" appointments during the *session* of the Senate, but, by necessary inference, denies it, by expressly granting the power for the recess only. Hence, to fill a *vacancy* in this way, while the Senate is in session and ready to provide for any emergency, is, in the absence of positive law authorizing it, a clear violation of the Constitution. The guilt was in this case enhanced by an attempt to fill an office which the respondent himself claims has never been vacated.

But the President is equally unfortunate in his appeal to *law*. The act of 1789 makes no provision for "*ad interim*" appointments. That of May 2, 1792, authorizes temporary appointments in case of death, absence, or sickness, but not for vacancies created by removal. That of February 13, 1795, allows the President to appoint for six months, " in case of vacancy, whereby the Secretaries or any officer in any of the departments *cannot perform the duties of his office.*"

The construction of this act is somewhat obscure and doubtful. It applies to such vacancies of office as are occasioned by the inability of the officer to "perform the duties of his office." An officer removed cannot perform the duties of his office, it is true, but the natural implication of the language runs *pari passu* with that of 1792, confining it to such vacancies as occur from death, absence, or sickness. But if we give it the broadest application, and cover all vacancies, the limitation of six months placed upon the temporary appointments which it authorizes is designed clearly to cover the interim between the sessions of Congress, and recognizes the hitherto unbroken practice of the Executive to create and fill vacancies only during the recess of the Senate. I conclude, therefore, it was not designed to authorize by this act an appointment like that of General Thomas.

The act of February 20, 1863, fails equally to provide for this case.

But even if these statutes by a proper construction covered the action of the President, he cannot use them, for they have been swept away by the tenure-of-office act, and he is remitted to its provisions alone, which explicitly prohibited any such appointment.

If the 1st and 2d sections take from him, as I have argued, the right to remove Stanton, then there was no vacancy, and the appointment of Thomas was made "contrary to the provisions of this act," and was by the 6th section of the same a high misdemeanor.

It has been urged that the last clause of the 3d section empowers the President to make such an appointment, but an examination of the section shows this to be a perversion. It simply provides that in case the Senate shall fail to fill a vacancy which has occurred by *death* or *resignation* during the recess of the same, such officers as may *by law exercise such powers and duties* shall exercise all the powers and duties belonging to such office *so vacant*, but that "such office shall remain in abeyance without any salary, fees, or emoluments attached thereto, until the same shall be filled by appointment thereto *by and with the advice and consent of the Senate.*"

General Thomas was not so appointed. The law cannot possibly be stretched to cover and justify his case.

Equally fallacious is the interpretation which has been given to the eighth section. This simply makes it the duty of the President to notify the Secretary of the Treasury whenever he shall have "designated, authorized, or employed any person to perform the duties of any office" temporarily vacated, as designated in the third article.

This is the whole extent of its meaning, and it cannot be so tortured as to authorize an "*ad interim*" appointment, made during the session of the Senate.

I conclude, therefore, that the President, having violated the act of March 2, 1867, as alleged in the first, second, and third articles, is guilty of a high misdemeanor.

Of the fourth, sixth, seventh, and ninth articles, I need not speak, as the trial failed entirely, to my apprehension, in establishing the allegations therein set forth by any substantial proof. No satisfactory evidence was presented to my mind of a conspiracy, as alleged in either of the articles. In this I think the House entirely failed to make good their charges.

The fifth article charges that the President conspired with Lorenzo Thomas and others to " prevent and hinder the execution of an act entitled 'An act regulating the tenure of certain civil offices,' and in pursuance of said conspiracy did unlawfully attempt to prevent Edwin M Stanton" from holding the office of Secretary of War. That there was an understanding between the President and Thomas that the latter was to be substituted for Stanton in the office of Secretary of War, in disregard of the act of March 2, 1867, is clear, but that there was any concert to use force to bring it about does not appear from the evidence.

The eighth article charges upon Andrew Johnson a high misdemeanor, in that he issued a letter of authority to Lorenzo Thomas, transferring to him the office of Secretary for the Department of War, in violation of law, when there was no vacancy in said office, and when the Senate was in session, with intent unlawfully to control the disbursements of the moneys appropriated for the military service and for the Department of War.

I have already given my opinion upon the issuance of the letter to Thomas in what I have said in respect to the second and third articles. That a control of the money appropriated for the military service and the Department of War was a principal motive for securing the place of Mr. Stanton is self-evident; for without it the office could not be administered, and would be a vain and useless shadow of power. I do not see that this article adds anything new; for the gravamen of the charge is involved in the third article. The final judgment upon this must be the same as upon that.

The facts alleged in the tenth article are known and read of all men, and are not denied by the respondent. That the speeches referred to in this article were "slanderous harangues," showing not only a want of culture, but the entire absence of good sense, good taste, or good temper, nobody can deny. But in view of the liberty of speech which our laws authorize, in view of the culpable license of speech which is practiced and allowed in other branches of the government, I doubt if we can at present make low and scurrilous speeches a ground of impeachment. I say this in sorrow, and not in any spirit of palliation; for the speeches referred to in the charges were infamous and blasphemous, and could not have been uttered by any man worthy to hold the exalted position of Chief Magistrate of an intelligent and virtuous people. Personal decency should be deemed essential to high official responsibility in this republic, but it must be secured by a public sentiment which shall exact virtue rather than availability in those whom it advances to the great trusts of society. When we reflect how essential to national welfare and human progress is that liberty of speech which we have inherited, and how readily a restriction upon its abuse may turn to an abuse upon its restriction, we hesitate to inflict a merited penalty upon this prominent offender. We deem it safer to—

> Bear those ills we have
> Than fly to others that we know not of.

There are four distinct allegations in the eleventh article. The first relates to the President's misrepresentations of Congress in public speech, and has already been reviewed in considering the tenth article.

The second charges a violation of "an act regulating the tenure of certain civil offices," by unlawfully devising and contriving, and attempting to devise and contrive, means to prevent Mr. Stanton from resuming his office of Secretary of War after the Senate had refused to concur in his suspension. This is a charge not mentioned in any preceding article and its proof is unequivocal and satisfactory.

The attempt was made through General Grant, and the President's letter of reproof to that distinguished citizen for defeating his wicked purpose by refusing to participate with him in a premeditated breach of law and contempt of the Senate, is the impregnable demonstration of the allegation. The following is the language of his letter:

You had found in our first conference "that the President was desirous of keeping Mr. Stanton out of office, *whether sustained in the suspension or not.*" You knew what reasons had induced the President to ask from you a promise; you also knew that in case your views of duty did not accord with his own convictions it was his purpose to fill your place by another appointment. Even ignoring the existence of a positive understanding between us, these conclusions were plainly deducible from our various conversations. It is certain, however, that even under these circumstances you did not offer to return the place to my possession, but, according to your own statement, placed yourself in a position where, could I have anticipated your action, I would have been compelled to ask of you, as I was compelled to ask of your predecessor in the War Department, a letter of resignation, or else to resort to the more disagreeable expedient of suspending you by a successor.

The third and fourth allegations of this article do not seem to have received that attention which their importance would justify. The evidence upon the records by which they are supported is very slight. I have been the more surprised at this inasmuch as the last sets forth that the President attempted to prevent the execution of the act entitled "An act to provide for the more efficient government of the rebel States." This I have deemed the *primum mobile* which has impelled the entire policy of the Executive.

This has been the motive of all our exceptional legislation; this has prolonged and multiplied our sessions; this has distracted business, and protracted the unrest of society, and this will be the crowning infamy of an administration inaugurated by assassination. All these wilful violations of law have drawn their inspiration from this fell intent. If they had been only technical and inadvertent lapses, or had resulted from misapprehension, they might be pardoned, but being specimens from a flagrant catalogue of persistent law-breaking, public safety demands a resort to constitutional remedies.

There may be wise and patriotic men who fear lest conviction should impress a habit of instability upon our institutions and unsettle the foundations of society. No statesman should be censured for a prudent forecast, but he should not hesitate to use the means which the experience of ages has shown to be essential safeguards of popular rights. The English ministry retire with every defeat, and these frequent changes of administration strengthen rather than weaken the government. A people careless and not over-jealous of their rights are in danger of overthrow. History teaches that great wars enhance the powers of the Executive at the expense of popular rights, and that powers once exercised are likely to be held as an inalienable prerogative. We are no exception to the rule. With us, the temptation of the Chief Magistrate to overstep his authority is even greater than in governments where executive power is less limited. It is difficult for a ruler who has used for years without wrong the unlimited powers of war to restrict himself at once, on the return of peace, to the narrow limits then essential to the security of popular rights.

Abraham Lincoln in a few instances transcended the ordinary exercise of executive authority and we legalized it as a military necessity. Four years of laborious, patriotic, suffering life, devoted to a rescue of the liberties and integrity of the republic, were the pledges he gave that he would not usurp or abuse his power for the gratification of either revenge or ambition. Andrew Johnson has no such excuse and can give no such security when he oversteps his constitutional limits and sets aside law.

There have been no "public considerations of a high character" to justify his high-handed usurpation of power. There was nothing in the personal character and nothing in the official conduct of this distinguished minister of war, who, more than the great French minister, may be said to have "organized victory," which could give the shadow of a pretext for his suspension or removal. His offence was that at the expense of personal comfort he fulfilled the purpose of Congress and checked, if he did not baffle, the effort of the Executive to arrest the legal and peaceful reorganization of the South. His obedience to the spirit and letter of our laws "constrained" the President to "cause him to surrender the office."

If the President is convicted he suffers for a violation of law: if acquitted, Mr. Stanton suffers for obedience to the law. Back of the acts for which the former is on trial lie the three years of malignant obstruction of law and public order pouring a wicked intent into the allegations of this indictment. Back of this attempted removal of Mr. Stanton lies the splendid record of the great Secretary, which will hereafter thread your history like a path of gold. Who shall fall in the final issue, he who obeys or he who defies your legislation?

If conviction may impress instability upon our institutions, acquittal may destroy the original adjustment and balance of their powers and hasten their overthrow. The lessons of history warn us rather against the indulgence than the arrest of arbitrary power.

When power flows back into the hands of the people it only returns to its original and rightful source; but when it passes up into the hands of a usurper, the reign of despotism is inaugurated. History has been a perpetual struggle between popular rights and personal ambition, and experience shows that we do not utter empty words when we say that "vigilance is the price of liberty."

As a member of the House of Representatives, I voted under the obligations of an oath for the act of March 2, 1867, with a clear understanding that it protected Mr. Stanton as Secretary of War against removal at pleasure by the President; and now, when he is brought to our bar, to be tried for the consummation of that act, I but discharge a solemn duty, from which I cannot escape, when, as a senator, I pronounce Andrew Johnson guilty of a violation of that law.

OPINION OF MR. SENATOR TRUMBULL.

To do impartial justice in all things appertaining to the present trial, according to the Constitution and laws, is the duty imposed on each senator by the position he holds and the oath he has taken, and he who falters in the discharge of that duty, either from personal or party considerations, is unworthy his position, and merits the scorn and contempt of all just men.

The question to be decided is not whether Andrew Johnson is a proper person to fill the presidential office, nor whether it is fit that he should remain in it, nor, indeed, whether he has violated the Constitution and laws in other respects than those alleged against him. As well might any other 54 persons take upon themselves by violence to rid the country of Andrew Johnson, because they believe him a bad man, as to call upon 54 senators, in violation of their sworn duty, to convict and depose him for any other causes than those alleged in the articles of impeachment. As well might any citizen take the law into his own hands, and become its executioner, as to ask the senators to convict outside of the case made. To sanction such a principle would be destructive of all law and all liberty worth the name, since liberty unregulated by law is but another name for anarchy.

Unfit for President as the people may regard Andrew Johnson, and much as they may desire his removal, in a legal and constitutional way, all save the unprincipled and depraved would brand with infamy and contempt the name of any senator who should violate his sworn convictions of duty to accomplish such a result.

Keeping in view the principles by which, as honest men, we are to be guided, let us inquire what the case is.

The first article charges Andrew Johnson, President of the United States, with unlawfully issuing an order, while the Senate was in session, and without its advice and consent, with the intent to remove Edwin M. Stanton from the office of Secretary for the Department of War, contrary to the Constitution and the "act regulating the tenure of certain civil offices," passed March 2, 1867. It will be observed that this article does not charge a removal of the Secretary, but only an intent to remove, which is not made an offence by the tenure-of-office act or any other statute; but, treating it as if the President's order had been obeyed, and an actual removal had taken place, would such removal, had it been consummated, have been a violation of the Constitution irrespective of the tenure-of-office act? The question of the power to remove from office arose in 1789, in the first Congress which assembled under the Constitution, and, except as to offices whose tenure was fixed by that instrument, was then recognized as belonging to the President; but whether as a constitutional right, or one which the Congress might confer, was left an open question. Under this recognition by the Congress of 1789, every President, from that day till 1867, had exercised this power of removal, and its exercise during all that time had been acquiesced in by the other departments of the government, both legislative and judicial. Nor was this power of removal by the President exercised only in the recess of the Senate, as some have supposed, but it was frequently exercised when the Senate was in session, and without its consent.

Indeed, there is not an instance on record prior to the passage of the tenure-of-office act in which the consent of the Senate had been invoked simply for the removal of an officer. It is *appointments to*, and not *removals from*, office that the Constitution requires to be made by and with the advice and consent of the Senate. It is true that an appointment to an office, when the appointee becomes duly qualified, authorizes him to oust the prior incumbent, if there be one, and in that way effects his removal; but this is a different thing from a simple removal. The Constitution makes no distinction between the power of the President to remove during the recess and the sessions of the Senate, nor has there been any in practice. The elder Adams, on the 12th of December, 1800, the Senate having been in session from the 17th of November preceding, in a communication to Timothy Pickering used this language: "You are hereby discharged from any further service as Secretary of State." Here was a positive dismissal of a cabinet officer by the President while the Senate was in session, and without its consent. It is no answer to say that President Adams the same day nominated John Marshall to be Secretary of State in place of "Timothy Pickering, removed."

The nomination of a person for an office does not, and never did, effect the removal of an incumbent. And such incumbent, unless removed by a distinct order, holds on till the nominee is confirmed and qualified. The Senate might never have given its advice and consent to the appointment of John Marshall, and did not in fact do so until the following day. The removal of Pickering was complete before Marshall was nominated to the Senate, as the message nominating him shows. But whether this was so or not, we all know that a person in office is never removed by the mere nomination of a successor.

Thomas Eastin, navy agent at Pensacola, was removed from office by President Van Buren on the 19th of December, 1840, while the Senate was in session, and the office the same day placed temporarily in charge of Dudley Walker, and it was not till the 5th of January following that George Johnson was, by and with the advice and consent of the Senate, appointed navy agent to succeed Eastin.

June 20, 1864, and while the Senate was in session, President Lincoln removed Isaac Henderson, navy agent at New York, an officer appointed by and with the advice and consent of the Senate, and placed the office in charge temporarily of Paymaster John D. Gibson.

Isaac V. Fowler, postmaster at New York, Samuel F. Marks, postmaster at New Orleans, and Mitchell Steever, postmaster at Milwaukee, all of whom had previously been appointed by and with the advice and consent of the Senate, were severally removed by the President during the sessions of the Senate in 1860 and 1861, the offices placed temporarily in charge of special agents, and it was not till some time after the removals that nominations were made to fill the vacancies.

Other cases during other administrations might be referred to, but these are sufficient to show that removals from office by the President during the session of the Senate have been no unusual thing in the history of the government.

Of the power of Congress to define the tenure of the offices it establishes and make them determinable either at the will of the President alone, of the President and Senate together, or at the expiration of a fixed period, I entertain no doubt. The Constitution is silent on the subject of removals except by impeachment, which it must be admitted only applies to removals for crimes and misdemeanors; and if the Constitution admits of removals in no other way, then a person once in office would hold for life unless impeached, a construction which all would admit to be inadmissible under our form of government. The right of removal must, then, exist somewhere. The first Congress, in the creation of the Department of War, in 1789, recognized it as existing in the President, by providing that the chief clerk should perform the duties of the principal officer, called a Secretary, "whenever the said principal officer shall be removed from office by the President of the United States, or in any other case of vacancy." Under this act the power of the President to remove the Secretary of War, either during the recess or session of the Senate, is manifest. The law makes no distinction in that respect, and whether it was an inherent power belonging to the President, under the Constitution as President, or was derived from the statute creating the office, is not material so far as relates to the power of the President to remove that officer.

This continued to be the law until the passage of the tenure-of-office act, March 2, 1867; and had the President issued the order for the removal of the Secretary of War prior to the passage of that act, it would hardly be contended by any one that, in so doing, he violated any law constitutional or statutory. The act of March 2, 1867, was passed to correct the previous practice, and had there been no such practice there would have been no occasion for such a law. Did that act, constitutional and valid as it is believed to be, change the law so far as it related to a Secretary then in office, by virtue of an appointment made by a former President during a presidential term which ended March 4, 1865?

The language of the first section of the act is:

That every person holding any civil office to which he has been appointed by and with the advice and consent of the Senate, and every person who shall hereafter be appointed to any such office, and shall become duly qualified to act therein, is and shall be entitled to hold such office until a successor shall have been in like manner appointed and duly qualified, except as herein otherwise provided: *Provided*, That the Secretaries of State, of the Treasury, of War, of the Navy, and of the Interior, the Postmaster General, and the Attorney General, shall hold their offices respectively for and during the term of the President by whom they may have been appointed, and one month thereafter, subject to removal by and with the advice and consent of the Senate.

Mr. Lincoln, by and with the advice and consent of the Senate, appointed Mr. Stanton Secretary of War on the 15th of January, 1862, and commissioned him to hold the office "during the pleasure of the President of the United States for the time being." He was never reappointed, either by Mr. Lincoln after his re-election, or by Mr. Johnson since Mr. Lincoln's death. The continuance of Mr. Stanton in office by Mr. Lincoln after his second term commenced, and by Mr. Johnson after Mr. Lincoln's death, cannot be construed as a reappointment during that term, because the word "appointed" in the tenure-of-office act must be construed to mean a legal appointment, which could only be made by and with the advice and consent of the Senate. The term of the President by whom Mr. Stanton was appointed, and the one month thereafter, expired nearly two years before the passage of the tenure-of-office act. It will not do to say that because Mr. Lincoln was elected for a second term that therefore the term of the President by whom Mr. Stanton was appointed has not expired. The fact that Mr. Lincoln was his own successor in 1865 did not make the two terms one any more than if any other person had succeeded him, and were he now alive the presidential term during which he appointed Mr. Stanton would long since have expired. But Mr. Lincoln, in fact, deceased soon after his second term commenced, and was succeeded by the Vice President, elected for the same term, on whom the office of President was by the Constitution devolved.

It has been argued that this is Mr. Lincoln's term. If this be so, it is his second term, and not the term during which Mr. Stanton was appointed; but if this be Mr. Lincoln's and not Mr. Johnson's term, when will the "term of the President" by whom Mr. Browning and the other cabinet officers appointed since Mr. Lincoln's death expire? Mr. Lincoln never appointed them, and if they are to hold "during the term of the President by whom they were appointed and for one month thereafter" they hold indefinitely, because, according to this theory, Mr. Johnson, the President by whom they were appointed, never had a term, and we have the anomaly of a person on whom the office of President is devolved, and who is impeached as President, and whom the Senate is asked to convict as President, who has no term of office. The clause of the Constitution which declares that the President "shall hold his office during the term of four years" does not mean that the *person* holding the office shall not die, resign, or be removed during that period, but to fix a term or limit during which he may, but beyond which he cannot, hold the office. If he die, resign, or be removed in the mean time, manifestly the term, so far as he is concerned, has come to an end. The term of the presidential *office* is four years, but the Constitution expressly provides that different persons may fill the office during that period, and in popular language it is called the term of the person who happens for the time being to be in the office. It is just as impossible for Mr. Stanton to now serve as Secretary of War for the term of the President by whom he was appointed as it is for Mr. Lincoln to serve out the second term for which he was elected. Both the presidential term of the President who appointed Mr. Stanton and the person who made the appointment have passed away, never to return; but the presidential office remains, filled, however, by another person, and not Mr. Lincoln.

It being apparent that so much of the proviso to the first section of the tenure-of-civil-office act of March 2, 1867, as authorizes the Secretary of War to hold the office for and during the term of the President by whom he was appointed is inapplicable to the case of Mr. Stanton, by what tenure did he hold the office on the 21st of February last, when the President issued the order for his removal?

Originally appointed *to hold office during the pleasure of the President for the time being*, and, as has already been shown, removable at the will of the President, according to the act of 1789, there would seem to be no escape from the conclusion that the President had the right to issue the order for his removal. It has, however, been insisted that if the proviso which secures to the Secretaries the right to hold their respective offices during the term of the President by whom they may have been appointed and for one month thereafter does not embrace Mr. Stanton, because Mr. Johnson did not appoint him, that then, as a civil officer, he is within the body of the first section of the act and entitled to hold his office until by and with the advice and consent of the Senate a successor shall have been appointed and duly qualified. Not so; for the reason that the body of the first section can have no reference to the tenure of an office expressly excepted from it by the words "except as herein otherwise provided," and the provision which follows, fixing a different tenure for the Secretary of War. Can any one doubt that the law was intended to make, and does make a distinction between the tenure of office given to the Secretaries and that given to other civil officers? How, then, can it be said that the tenures are the same, or the same as to any particular Secretaries?

The meaning of the section is not different from what it would be if instead of the words, "every person holding any civil office," there had been inserted the words *marshal, district attorney, postmaster*, and so on, enumerating and fixing the tenure of all other civil officers except the Secretaries; and then had proceeded to enumerate the different Secretaries and fix for them a different tenure from that given to the other enumerated officers. Had the section been thus written, would any one think, in case a particular Secretary for some personal reason was unable to avail himself of the benefit of the law securing to Secretaries a certain tenure of office, that he would therefore have the right to the benefit of the law in which Secretaries were not mentioned, securing to marshals and others a different tenure of office? The object of an exception or proviso in a statute is to limit or take something out of the body of the act, and is usually resorted to for convenience, as a briefer mode of declaring the object than to enumerate everything embraced in the general terms of the act, and then provide for the excepted matter. The fact that the terms of the proviso which fix the tenure of office of all Secretaries are such that a particular Secretary, for reasons personal to himself, cannot take advantage of them, does not operate to take from the proviso the office of a Secretary, and the tenure attached to it, and transfer them to the body of the section which provides a tenure for holding office from which the office of Secretary is expressly excepted.

The meaning of the first section will be still more apparent by supposing a case involving the same principle but wholly disconnected with the one under consideration. Suppose Congress were to-day, May —, 1868, to pass an act declaring that "two terms of the district court in every judicial district of the United States shall be held during the year 1868, commencing on the first Monday of June and November, except as herein otherwise provided; provided, that two terms of the district court in each of the judicial districts in the State of New York shall be held during the year 1868, commencing on the first Monday of April and September:" manifestly it would at this time be as impossible to comply with so much of the proviso as requires a court to be held in the New York districts in April, 1868, as it now is for Mr. Stanton to serve out the term of the President by whom he was appointed, which ended March 4, 1865.

Would that circumstance take the provision for the New York districts out of the proviso, and because, by the body of the act, two terms are required to be held in every judicial district in the United States on the first Monday of June and November, authorize the holding of courts in the New York districts at those periods? It is believed that no judge would for a moment think of giving such a construction to such an act; and yet this is precisely the construction of an act believed to be analogous in principle which must be resorted to to bring Mr. Stanton within the body of the first section of the tenure-of office act.

Laying out of view what was said at the passage of the tenure-of-office act, as to its not interfering with Mr. Johnson's right to remove the Secretaries appointed by his predecessor, and the unreasonableness of a construction of the act which would secure them in office longer than the Secretaries he had himself appointed, and fasten them for life on all future Presidents, unless the Senate consented to the appointment of successors, the conclusion seems inevitable, from the terms of the tenure-of-office act itself, that the President's right to remove Mr. Stanton, the Secretary of War appointed by his predecessor, is not affected by it, and that, having the authority to remove that officer under the act of 1789, he did not violate either the Constitution or any statute in issuing the order for that purpose. But even if a different construction could be put upon the law, I could never consent to convict the Chief Magistrate of a great people of a high misdemeanor and remove him from office for a misconstruction of what must be admitted to be a doubtful statute, and particularly when the misconstruction was the same put upon it by the authors of the law at the time of its passage.

The second article charges that the President, in violation of the Constitution, and contrary to the tenure-of-office act, and with intent to violate the same, issued to Lorenzo Thomas a letter of authority empowering him to act as Secretary of

War *ad interim*, there being no vacancy in the office of Secretary of War. There is nothing in the tenure-of-office act, or any other statute, prohibiting the issuing of such a letter, much less making it a crime or misdemeanor. The most that can be said is that it was issued without authority of law.

The Senate is required to pass judgment upon each article separately, and each must stand or fall by itself. There is no allegation in this article of any design or attempt to use the letter of authority, or that any harm came from it; and any senator might well hesitate to find the President guilty of a high misdemeanor for simply issuing such a letter, although issued without authority of law. The proof, however, shows that the letter was issued by the President in connection with the order for the removal of Mr. Stanton, which, as has already been shown, was a valid order. The question, then, arises whether the President was guilty of a high misdemeanor in issuing to the Adjutant General of the army a letter authorizing him, in view of the contemplated vacancy, temporarily to discharge the duties of Secretary of War.

Several statutes have been passed providing for the temporary discharge of the duties of an office by some other person in case of a vacancy, or when the officer himself is unable to perform them. The first was the eighth section of the act of May 8, 1792, and is as follows:

> That in case of the death, absence from the seat of government, or sickness of the Secretary of State, Secretary of the Treasury, or of the Secretary of the Department of War, or of any other officer of either of the said departments whose appointment is not in the head thereof, whereby they cannot perform the duties of their respective offices, it shall be lawful for the President of the United States, in case he shall think it necessary, to authorize any person or persons, at his discretion, to perform the duties of the said respective offices until a successor be appointed, or until such absence or inability by sickness shall cease.

The second act, passed February 13, 1795, declares:

> That in case of vacancy in the office of Secretary of State, Secretary of the Treasury, or of the Secretary of the Department of War, or of any officer of either of the said departments whose appointment is not in the head thereof, whereby they cannot perform the duties of their said respective offices, it shall be lawful for the President of the United States, in case he shall think it necessary, to authorize any person or persons, at his discretion, to perform the duties of the said respective offices, until a successor be appointed or such vacancy be filled: *Provided*, That no one vacancy shall be supplied in manner aforesaid for a longer term than six months.

Neither of these acts provided for vacancies in the Navy, Interior or Post Office Department. Mr. Lincoln, in 1863, called attention to this defect in a special message, as follows:

To the Senate and House of Representatives:
I submit to Congress the expediency of extending to other departments of the government the authority conferred on the President by the eighth section of the act of the 8th of May, 1792, to appoint a person to temporarily discharge the duties of Secretary of State, of the Treasury, and the Secretary of War, in case of the death, absence from the seat of government, or sickness of either of those officers.

ABRAHAM LINCOLN.

WASHINGTON, *January* 2, 1863.

February 20, 1863, Congress passed a third act on this subject, which declares:

> In the case of the death, resignation, absence from the seat of government, or sickness of the head of any executive department of the government, or of any officer of either of the said departments whose appointment is not in the head thereof, whereby they cannot perform the duties of their respective offices, it shall be lawful for the President of the United States, in case he shall think it necessary, to authorize the head of any other executive department, or other officer in either of said departments whose appointment is vested in the President, at his discretion, to perform the duties of the said respective offices until a successor be appointed, or until such absence or disability by sickness shall cease: *Provided*, That no one vacancy shall be supplied in manner aforesaid for a longer term than six months.

These statutes contain all the legislation of Congress on the subject to which they relate. It has been insisted that, inasmuch as under the act of 1863 the President had no authority to designate any other person to perform the duties of Secretary of War than an officer in that or some of the other executive departments, and then in case of vacancy to supply such only as are occasioned by death or resignation, his designation of the Adjutant General of the army to supply temporarily a vacancy occasioned by *removal* was without authority. If the act of 1863 repealed the act of 1795 this would doubtless be so; but if it did not repeal it, then the President clearly had the right, under that act, which provided for the temporary discharge of the duties of the Secretary of War in *any* vacancy by *any* person, to authorize General Thomas temporarily to discharge those duties. The law of 1863, embracing, as it does, all the departments, and containing provisions from both the previous statutes, may, however, be construed to embrace the whole subject on which it treats, and operate as a repeal of all prior laws on the same subject. It must, however, be admitted that it is by no means clear that the act of 1863 does repeal so much of the act of 1795 as authorizes the President to provide for the temporary discharge of the duties of an office from which an incumbent has been removed, or whose term of office has expired by limitation before the regular appointment of a successor.

It has been argued that the tenure-of-office act of March 2, 1867, repealed both the act of 1795 and that of 1863, authorizing the temporary supplying of vacancies in the departments. This is an entire misapprehension. The eighth section of the tenure-of-office act recognizes that authority by making it the duty of the President, when such designations are made, to notify the Secretary of the Treasury thereof; and if any one of the Secretaries were to die or resign to-morrow the authority of the President to detail an officer in one of the departments to temporarily perform the duties of the vacant office, under the act of 1863, would be unquestioned. This would not be the appointment of an officer while the Senate was in session without its consent, but simply directing a person already in office to discharge temporarily, in no one case exceeding six months, the duties of another office not then filled.

It is the issuing of a letter of authority in respect to a removal, appointment, or employment "*contrary to the provisions*" *of the tenure-of-office act* that is made a high misdemeanor. As the order for the removal of Mr. Stanton has already been shown not to have been "contrary to the provisions of this act," any letter of authority in regard to it is not forbidden by the sixth section thereof.

Admitting, however, that there was no statute in existence expressly authorizing the President to designate the Adjutant General of the army temporarily to discharge the duties of the office of Secretary of War, made vacant by removal, till a successor, whose nomination was proposed the next day, could be confirmed, does it follow that he was guilty of a high misdemeanor in making such temporary designation when there was no law making it a penal offence or prohibiting it? Prior to 1863, as Mr. Lincoln's message shows, there was no law authorizing these temporary designations in any other than the three Departments of State, Treasury, and War; and yet President Lincoln himself, on the 22d of September, 1862, prior to any law authorizing it, issued the following letter of authority, appointing a Postmaster General *ad interim*:

> I hereby appoint St. John B. L. Skinner, now acting First Assistant Postmaster General, to be acting Postmaster General *ad interim*, in place of Hon. Montgomery Blair, now temporarily absent.
>
> ABRAHAM LINCOLN.
>
> WASHINGTON, *September* 22, 1862.

To provide for temporary disabilities or vacancies in the Navy Department, and for which no law at the time existed, President Jackson, during his administration, made ten different designations or appointments of Secretaries of the Navy *ad interim*. Similar *ad interim* designations in the Navy Department were made by Presidents Van Buren, Harrison, Tyler, Polk, Filmore, and others; and these appointments were made indiscriminately during the sessions of the Senate as well as during its recess. As no law authorizing them existed at the time these *ad interim* appointments were made in the Navy and Post Office Departments, it must be admitted that they were made without authority of law; and yet who then thought, or would now think, of impeaching for high crimes and misdemeanors the Presidents who made them? President Buchanan, in a communication to the Senate, made January 15, 1861, on the subject of *ad interim* appointments, used this language:

Vacancies may occur at any time in the most important offices which cannot be immediately and permanently filled in a manner satisfactory to the appointing power. It was wise to make a provision which would enable the President to avoid a total suspension of business in the interval, and equally wise so to limit the executive discretion as to prevent any serious abuse of it. This is what the framers of the act of 1795 did, and neither the policy nor the constitutional validity of their law has been questioned for 65 years.

The practice of making such appointments, whether in a vacation or during the session of Congress, has been constantly followed during every administration from the earliest period of the government, and its perfect lawfulness has never, to my knowledge, been questioned or denied. Without going back further than the year 1829, and without taking into the calculation any but the chief officers of the several departments, it will be found that provisional appointments to fill vacancies were made to the number of 179 from the commencement of General Jackson's administration to the close of General Pierce's. This number would probably be greatly increased if all the cases which occurred in the subordinate offices and bureaus were added to the count. Some of them were made while the Senate was in session; some which were made in vacation were continued in force long after the Senate assembled. Sometimes the temporary officer was the commissioned head of another department, sometimes a subordinate in the same department. Sometimes the affairs of the Navy Department have been directed *ad interim* by a commodore, and those of the War Department by a general.

Importance is sought to be given to the passage by the Senate, before the impeachment articles were found by the House of Representatives, of the following resolution:

Resolved by the Senate of the United States, That under the Constitution and laws of the United States the President has no power to remove the Secretary of War and designate any other officer to perform the duties of that office *ad interim*—

as if senators sitting as a court on the trial of the President for high crimes and misdemeanors would feel bound or influenced in any degree by a resolution introduced and hastily passed before an adjournment on the very day the orders to Stanton and Thomas were issued. Let him who would be governed by such considerations in passing on the guilt or innocence of the accused, and not by the law and the facts as they have been developed on the trial, shelter himself under such a resolution. I am sure no honest man could. It is known, however, that the resolution coupled the two things, the removal of the Secretary of War and the designation of an officer *ad interim*, together, so that those who believed either without authority were compelled to vote for the resolution.

My understanding at the time was, that the act of 1863 repealed that of 1795 authorizing the designation of a Secretary of War *ad interim* in the place of a Secretary *removed;* but I never entertained the opinion that the President had not power to remove the Secretary of War appointed by Mr. Lincoln during his first term. Believing the act of 1795 to have been repealed, I was bound to vote that the President had no power under the law to designate a Secretary of War *ad interim* to fill a vacancy caused by removal, just as I would feel bound to vote for a resolution that neither President Jackson nor any of his successors had the power, under the law, to designate *ad interim* Postmasters General or Secretaries of the Navy and Interior prior to the act of 1863; but it by no means follows that they were guilty of high crimes and misdemeanors in making such temporary designations. They acted without the shadow of statutory authority in making such appointments. Johnson claims, and not without plausibility, that he had authority under the act of 1795 to authorize the Adjutant General of the army to perform temporarily the duties of Secretary of War; but if that act was repealed, even then he simply acted as his predecessors had done with the acquiescence of the nation for forty years before. Considering that the facts charged against the President in the second article are in no respect contrary to any provision of the tenure-of-office act; that they do not constitute a misdemeanor, and are not forbidden by any statute; that it is a matter of grave doubt whether so much of the act of 1795 as would expressly authorize the issuing of the letter of authority to General Thomas is not in force, and if it is not, that President Johnson still had the same authority for issuing it as his predecessors had exercised for many years in the Navy, Interior, and Post Office Departments, it is impossible for me to hold him guilty of a high misdemeanor under that article. To do so would, in my opinion, be to disregard, rather than recognize, that impartial justice I am sworn to administer.

What has been said in regard to the second article applies with equal force to the third and eighth articles: there being no proof of an unlawful intent to control the disbursements of the moneys appropriated for the military service, as charged in the eighth article.

Articles four, five, six, and seven, taken together, charge in substance that the President conspired with Lorenzo Thomas and other persons with intent, by intimidation and threats, to prevent Edwin M. Stanton from holding the office of Secretary of War, and by force to seize and possess the property of the United States in the Department of War; also that he conspired to do the same things contrary to the tenure-of-office act, without any allegation of force or threats. The record contains no sufficient proof of the intimidation, threats, or force charged; and as the President had, in my opinion, the right to remove Mr. Stanton, his order for that purpose, as also that to General Thomas to take possession, both peacefully issued, have, in my judgment, none of the elements of a conspiracy about them.

The ninth article, known as the Emory article, is wholly unsupported by evidence.

The tenth article, relating to the speeches of the President, is substantially proven, but the speeches, although discreditable to the high office he holds, do not, in my opinion, afford just ground for impeachment.

So much of the eleventh article as relates to the speech of the President made August 18, 1866, is disposed of by what has been said on the tenth article.

The only proof to sustain the allegation of unlawfully attempting to devise means to prevent Edwin M. Stanton from resuming the office of Secretary of War is to be found in a letter from the President to General Grant, dated February 10, 1868, written long after Mr. Stanton had been restored. This letter, referring to a controversy between the President and General Grant in regard to certain communications, oral and written, which had passed between them, shows that it was the President's intent, in case the Senate did not concur in Stanton's suspension, to compel him to resort to the courts to regain possession of the War Department, with a view of obtaining a judicial decision on the validity of the tenure-of-office act; but the intention was never carried out, and Stanton took possession by the voluntary surrender of the office by General Grant. Was this intent or purpose of the President to obtain a judicial decision in the only way then practicable a high misdemeanor?

It is unnecessary to inquire whether the President would have been justified in carrying his intention into effect. It was not done, and his entertaining an intention to do it constituted, in my opinion, no offence. There is, however, to my mind another conclusive answer to this charge in the eleventh article. The President, in my view, had authority to remove Mr. Stanton, and this being so, he could by removal at any time have lawfully kept him from again taking possession of the office.

There is no proof to sustain the other charges of this article. In coming to the conclusion that the President is not guilty of any of the high crimes and misdemeanors with which he stands charged, I have endeavored to be governed by the case made without reference to other acts of his not contained in the record, and without giving the least heed to the clamor of intemperate zealots who demand the conviction of Andrew Johnson as a test of party faith, or seek to identify with and make responsible for his acts those who from convictions of duty feel compelled on the case made to vote for his acquittal. His speeches and the general course of his administration have been as distasteful to me as to any one, and I should consider it the great calamity of the age if the disloyal element, so often encouraged by his measures, should gain political ascendency. If the question was, Is Andrew Johnson a fit person for President? I should answer, *no;* but it is not a party question, nor upon Andrew Johnson's deeds and acts, except so far as they are made to appear in the record, that I am to decide.

Painful as it is to disagree with so many political associates and friends whose conscientious convictions have led them to a different result, I must, nevertheless, in the discharge of the high responsibility under which I act, be governed by what my reason and judgment tell me is the truth and the justice and the law of this case. What law does this record show the President to have violated? Is it the tenure-of-office act? I believe in the constitutionality of that act, and stand ready to punish its violators; but neither the removal of that faithful and efficient officer, Edwin M. Stanton, which I deeply regret, nor the *ad interim* designation of Lorenzo Thomas, were, as has been shown, forbidden by it. Is it the reconstruction acts? Whatever the facts may be, this record does not contain a particle of evidence of their violation. Is it the conspiracy act? No facts are shown to sustain such a charge, and the same may be said of the charge of a violation of the appropriation act of March 2, 1867; and these are all the laws alleged to have been violated. It is, however, charged that Andrew Johnson has violated the Constitution. The fact may be so, but where is the evidence of it to be found in this record? Others may, but I cannot find it. To convict and depose the Chief Magistrate of a great nation, when his guilt was not made palpable by the record, and for insufficient cause, would be fraught with far greater danger to the future of the country than can arise from leaving Mr. Johnson in office for the remaining months of his term, with powers curtailed and limited as they have been by recent legislation.

Once set the example of impeaching a President for what, when the excitement of the hour shall have subsided, will be regarded as insufficient causes, as several of those now alleged against the President were decided to be by the House of Representatives only a few months since, and no future President will be safe who happens to differ with a majority of the House and two-thirds of the Senate on any measure deemed by them important, particularly if of a political character. Blinded by partisan zeal, with such an example before them, they will not scruple to remove out of the way any obstacle to the accomplishment of their purposes, and what then becomes of the checks and balances of the Constitution, so carefully devised and so vital to its perpetuity? They are all gone. In view of the consequences likely to flow from this day's proceedings, should they result in conviction on what my judgment tells me are insufficient charges and proofs, I tremble for the future of my country. I cannot be an instrument to produce such a result; and at the hazard of the ties even of friendship and affection, till calmer times shall do justice to my motives, no alternative is left me but the inflexible discharge of duty.

OPINION OF MR. SENATOR GRIMES.

The President of the United States stands at the bar of the Senate charged with the commission of high crimes and misdemeanors. The principal offence charged against him is embodied in various forms in the first eight articles of impeachment. This offence is alleged to consist in a violation of the provisions of the first section of an act of Congress entitled "An act regulating the tenure of certain civil offices," approved March 2, 1867, in this, that on the 21st day of February, 1868, the President removed, or attempted to remove, Edwin M. Stanton from the office of Secretary for the Department of War, and issued a letter of authority to General Lorenzo Thomas as Secretary for the Department of War *ad interim*.

The House of Representatives charge in their three first articles that the President attempted to remove Mr. Stanton, and that he issued his letter of authority to General Thomas with an intent to violate the law of Congress, and with the further "intent to violate the Constitution of the United States." The President, by his answer, admits that he sought to substitute General Thomas for Mr. Stanton at the head of the Department of War; but insists that he had the right to make such substitution under the laws then and now in force, and denies that in anything that he has done or attempted to do, he intended to violate the laws or the Constitution of the United States.

To this answer there is a general traverse by the House of Representatives, and thereon issue is joined; of that issue we are the triers, and have sworn that in that capacity we will do "impartial justice according to the Constitution and the laws."

It will be perceived that there is nothing involved in the first eight articles of impeachment but pure questions of law growing out of the construction of statutes. Mr. Johnson's guilt or innocence upon those articles depends wholly on the fact whether or not he had the power, after the passage of the tenure-of-office act of March 2, 1867, to remove Mr. Stanton and issue the letter of appointment to General Thomas, and upon the further fact, whether, having no such legal authority, he nevertheless attempted to exercise it "with intent to violate the Constitution of the United States."

Mr. Stanton was appointed Secretary for the Department of War by Mr. Lincoln on the 15th day of January, 1862, and has not since been reappointed or recommissioned. His commission was issued to continue "for and during the pleasure of the President." His appointment was made under the act of August 7, 1789, the first two sections of which read as follows:

> There shall be an executive department to be denominated the Department of War; and there shall be a principal officer therein, to be called the Secretary for the Department of War, who shall perform and execute such duties as shall from time to time be enjoined on or intrusted to him by the President of the United States, and the said principal officer shall conduct the business of the said department in such manner as the President of the United States shall from time to time order and instruct.
>
> There shall be in the said department an inferior officer, to be appointed by said principal officer, to be employed therein as he shall deem proper, and to be called the chief clerk of the Department of War; *and whenever the said principal officer shall be removed from office by the President of the United States*, and in any other case of vacancy, shall, during the same, have charge of the records, books, &c.

At the same session of Congress was passed the act of July 27, 1789, creating the Department of Foreign Affairs. The first two sections of the two acts are precisely similar except in the designations of the two departments. Upon the passage of this last act occurred one of the most memorable and one of the ablest debates that ever took place in Congress. The subject under discussion was the tenure of public officers, and especially the tenure by which the Secretaries of the executive departments should hold their offices. Without going into the particulars of that great debate, it is sufficient to say that the reasons assigned by Mr. Madison and his associates in favor of a "tenure during the pleasure of the President" were adopted as the true constitutional theory on this subject. That great man, with almost a prophetic anticipation of this case, declared on the 16th June, 1789, in his speech in the House of Representatives, of which he was a member from Virginia, that—

> It is evidently the intention of the Constitution that the first magistrate should be responsible for the executive department. So far, therefore, as we do not make the officers who are to aid him in the duties of that department responsible to him, he is not responsible to the country. Again, is there no danger that an officer, when he is appointed by the concurrence of the Senate and his friends in that body, may choose rather to risk his establishment on the favor of that branch than rest it upon the discharge of his duties to the satisfaction of the executive branch, which is constitutionally authorized to inspect and control his conduct? And if it should happen that the officers connect themselves with the Senate, they may mutually support each other, and for want of efficacy reduce the power of the President to a mere vapor, in which case his responsibility would be annihilated, and the expectation of it unjust. The high executive officers joined in cabal with the Senate would lay the foundation of discord, and end in an assumption of the executive power, only to be removed by a revolution of the government.

It will be observed that it is here contended that it is the Constitution that establishes the tenure of office. And in order to put this question beyond future cavil, Chief Justice Marshall, in his Life of Washington, volume 2, page 162, says:

> After an ardent discussion, which consumed several days, the committee divided, and the amendment was negatived by a majority of 34 to 20. The opinion thus expressed by the House of Representatives did not explicitly convey their sense of the Constitution. Indeed, the express grant of the power to the President rather implied a right in the legislature to give or withhold it at their discretion. To obviate any misunderstanding of the principle on which the question has been decided, Mr. Benson moved in the House, when the report of the Committee of the Whole was taken up, to amend the second clause in the bill so as clearly to imply the power of removal to be solely in the President. He gave notice that if he should succeed in this he would move to strike out the words which had been the subject of debate. If those words continued, he said, the power of removal by the President might hereafter appear to be exercised by virtue of a legislative grant only, and consequently be subjected to legislative instability, when he was well satisfied in his own mind that it was by fair construction fixed in the Constitution. The motion was seconded by Mr. Madison, and both amendments were adopted.

And Judge Marshall adds:

> As the bill passed into a law it has ever been considered as a full expression of the sense of the legislature on this important part of the American Constitution.

And Chancellor Kent says, when speaking of the action of this Congress, many of the members of which had been members of the Convention that framed the Constitution, the chiefest among them, perhaps, being Madison, who has been called the father of that instrument:

> This amounted to a legislative construction of the Constitution, and it has ever since been acquiesced in and acted upon as of decisive authority in the case. It applies equally to every other officer of the government appointed by the President and Senate whose term of duration is not specially declared. It is supported by the weighty reason that the subordinate officers in the executive department ought to hold at the pleasure of the head of that department, because he is invested generally with the executive authority, and every participation in that authority by the Senate was an exception to a general principle, and ought to be taken strictly. The President is the great responsible officer for the faithful execution of the law, and the power of removal was incidental to that duty, and might often be requisite to fulfil it. (1 Kent. Com., 310.)

Thus the Constitution and the law stood as expounded by the courts, as construed by commentators and publicists, as acted on by all the Presidents, and acquiesced in by all of the Congresses from 1789 until the 2d March, 1867, when the tenure-of-office act was passed. The first section of this act reads as follows:

> That every person holding any civil office to which he has been appointed by and with the advice and consent of the Senate, and every person who shall hereafter be appointed to any such office, and shall become duly qualified to act therein, is and shall be entitled to hold such office until a successor shall have been in a like manner appointed and duly qualified, except as herein otherwise provided.

Then comes what is "otherwise provided:"

Provided, That the Secretaries of State, of the Treasury, of War, of the Navy, and of the Interior, the Postmaster General, and the Attorney General shall hold their offices respectively for and during the term of the President by whom they may have been appointed, and for one month thereafter, subject to removal by and with the advice and consent of the Senate.

The controversy in this case grows out of the construction of this section. How does it affect the act of 1789, and does it change the tenure of office of the Secretary for the Department of War as established by that act? To that inquiry I propose to address myself. I shall not deny the constitutional validity of the act of March 2, 1867. That question is not necessarily in this case.

The first question presented is, is Mr. Stanton's case within the provisions of the tenure-of-office act of March 2, 1867?

Certainly it is not within the body of the first section. The tenure which that provides for is not the tenure of *any* secretary. *All* secretaries whose tenure is regulated by this law at all are to go out of office at the end of the term of the President by whom they shall be appointed, and one month thereafter, unless sooner removed by the President, by and with the advice and consent of the Senate, while all other civil officers are to hold until a successor shall be appointed and duly qualified. The office of Secretary has attached to it one tenure; other civil officers another and different tenure, and no one who holds the office of Secretary can, *by force of this law*, hold by any other tenure than the one which the law specially assigns to that office. The plain intent of the proviso to the first section is to prescribe a tenure for the office of Secretary different from the tenure fixed for other civil officers. This is known to have been done on account of the marked difference between the heads of departments and all other officers, which made it desirable and necessary for the public service that the heads of departments should go out of office with the President by whom they were appointed. It would, indeed, be a strange result of the law if those Secretaries appointed by Mr. Lincoln should hold by the tenure fixed by the act for ordinary civil officers, while all the other Secretaries should hold by a different tenure; that those appointed by the present and all future Presidents should hold only during the term of the President by whom they may have been appointed, while those not appointed by him should hold indefinitely; and this under a law which undertakes to define the tenure of all the Secretaries who are to hold their offices under the law. I cannot come to that conclusion. My opinion is, that if Mr. Stanton's tenure of office is prescribed by this law at all, it is prescribed to him as Secretary of War, under and by force of the proviso to the first section; and if his case is not included in that proviso it is not included in the law at all.

It is clear to my mind that the *proviso* does not include, and was not intended to include, Mr. Stanton's case. It is not possible to apply to his case the language of the proviso unless we suppose it to have been intended to legislate him out of office; a conclusion, I consider, wholly inadmissible. He was appointed by President Lincoln during his first term of office. He cannot hereafter go out of office at the end of the term of the President by whom he was appointed. That term was ended before the law was passed. The proviso, therefore, cannot have been intended to make a rule for his case; and it is shown that it was not intended. This was plainly declared in debate by the conference committee, both in the Senate and in the House of Representatives, when the proviso was introduced and its effect explained. The meaning and effect of the *proviso* were then explained and understood to be that the only tenure of the Secretaries provided for by this law was a tenure to end with the term of service of the President by whom they were appointed, and as this new tenure could not include Mr. Stanton's case, it was here explicitly declared that it did not include it. When this subject was under consideration in the House of Representatives on the report of the conference committee on the disagreeing votes of the two houses, Mr. Schenck, of Ohio, chairman of the conference committee on the part of the House, said:

It will be remembered that by the bill as it passed the Senate it was provided that the concurrence of the Senate should be required in all removals from office, except in the case of the heads of departments. The House amended the bill of the Senate so as to extend this requirement to the heads of departments as well as to their officers.

The committee of conference have agreed that the Senate shall accept the amendment of the House. But inasmuch as this would compel the President to keep around him heads of departments until the end of his term who would hold over to another term, a compromise was made by which a further amendment is added to this portion of the bill, so that the term of office of the heads of departments shall expire with the term of the President who appointed them, allowing these heads of departments one month longer.

When the bill came to the Senate and was considered on the disagreeing votes of the two houses, and Mr. Doolittle, of Wisconsin, charged that although the purpose of the measure was, in his opinion, to force the President against his will to retain the Secretaries appointed by Mr. Lincoln, yet that the phraseology was such that the bill, if passed, would not accomplish that object, Mr. Sherman, of Ohio, who was a member of the conference committee and assisted to frame the proviso, said:

I do not understand the logic of the senator from Wisconsin. He first attributes a purpose to the committee of conference which I say is not true. I say that the Senate have not legislated with a view to any persons or any President, and therefore he commences by asserting what is not true. We do not legislate in order to keep in the Secretary of War, the Secretary of the Navy, or the Secretary of State.

Then a conversation arose between the senator from Ohio and another senator, and the senator from Ohio continued thus:

That the Senate had no such purpose is shown by its vote twice to make this exception. That this provision does not apply to the present case is shown by the fact that its language is so framed as not to apply to the present President. The senator shows that himself, and argues truly that it would not prevent the present President from removing the Secretary of War, the Secretary of the Navy, and the Secretary of State. And if I supposed that either of these gentlemen was so wanting in manhood, in honor, as to hold his place after the politest intimation by the President of the United States that his services were no longer needed, I certainly, as a senator, would consent to his removal at any time, and so would we all.

Did any one here doubt the correctness of Mr. Sherman's interpretation of the act when he declared that it "*would not prevent the present President from removing the Secretary of War, the Secretary of the Navy, and the Secretary of State?*" Was there any dissent from his position? Was there not entire acquiescence in it?

Again said Mr. Sherman:

In this case the committee of conference—I agreed to it, I confess, with some reluctance—came to the conclusion to qualify to some extent the power of removal over a cabinet minister. We provide that a cabinet minister shall hold his office not for a fixed term, not until the Senate shall consent to his removal, *but as long as the power that appoints him holds office.*

But whatever may have been the character of the debates at the time of the passage of the law, or whatever may have been the contemporaneous exposition of it, I am clearly convinced that the three Secretaries holding over from Mr. Lincoln's administration do not fall within its provisions under any fair judicial interpretation of the act; that Mr. Stanton held his office under the act of 1789, and under his only commission, issued in 1862, which was at the pleasure of the President; and I am, consequently, constrained to decide that the order for his removal was a lawful order. Any other construction would involve us in the absurdity of ostensibly attempting to limit the tenure of all cabinet officers to the term of the officer having the power to appoint them, yet giving to three of the present cabinet ministers an unlimited tenure; for, if the construction contended for by the managers be the correct one, while four of the present cabinet officers will go out of office absolutely, and without any action by the Senate, on the 4th of April next, they having been appointed by Mr. Johnson, the three cabinet officers appointed by Mr. Lincoln will hold by another and different tenure, and cannot be removed until the incoming President and the Senate shall mutually agree to their removal.

If I have not erred thus far in my judgment, then it follows that the order for the removal of Mr. Stanton was not a violation of the Constitution of the United States by reason of its having been issued during the session of the Senate. If Mr. Stanton held his office at the pleasure of the President alone under the act of 1789, as I think he did, it necessarily follows that the President alone could remove him. The Senate had no power in reference to his continuance in office. I am wholly unable to perceive, therefore, that the power of the President to remove him was affected or qualified by the fact that the Senate was in session.

It has sometimes been put forward, as it was by Mr. Webster in the debate of 1835, that the usual mode of removal from office by the President during a session of the Senate had been by the nomination of a successor in place of A B, removed. This would naturally be so in all cases except the few in which the officer could not be allowed, consistently with the public safety, to continue in office until his successor should be appointed and qualified and also should refuse to resign. Such cases cannot often have occurred. But when they have occurred I believe the President has exercised that power which was understood to belong to him alone, and which in the statute tenure of most offices is recognized by the acts of Congress creating them to be the pleasure of the President of the United States. A number of cases of this kind have been put in evidence. I do not find, either in the debates which have been had on the power of removal, or in the legislation of Congress on the tenure of offices, any trace of a distinction between the power of the President to remove in recess and his power to remove during a session of the Senate an officer who held solely by his pleasure and I do not see how such a distinction could exist without some positive and distinct provision of law to make and define it. I know of no such provision. If that was the tenure by which Mr. Stanton held the office of Secretary for the Department of War, and I think it was, then I am also of the opinion that it was not a violation of the Constitution to remove him during a session of the Senate.

If Mr. Stanton held under the act of 1789, no permission of the President to continue in office, no adoption of him as Secretary for the Department of War, could change the legal tenure of his office as fixed by law or deprive the President of the power to remove him.

My opinion on the matter of the first article is not affected by the facts contained in it, that the President suspended Mr. Stanton and sent notice of the suspension to the Senate, and the Senate refused to concur in that suspension. In my opinion that action of the President could not and did not change the tenure of Mr. Stanton's office, as it subsisted by law at the pleasure of the President, or deprive the President of that authority to remove him which necessarily arose from that tenure of office.

If the order of the President to Mr. Stanton was a lawful order, as I have already said I thought it was, the first question under the second article is whether the President did anything unlawful in giving the order to General Thomas to perform the duties of Secretary for the Department of War *ad interim*.

This was not an appointment to office. It was a temporary designation of a person to discharge the duties of an office until the office could be filled. The distinction between such a designation and an appointment to office is in itself clear enough, and has been recognized certainly since the act of February 13, 1795. Many cases have occurred in which this authority has been exercised. The necessity of some such provision of law, in cases of vacancy in offices which the Executive cannot instantly fill, must be apparent to every one acquainted with the workings of our government, and I do not suppose that a reasonable question can be made of the constitutional validity of a law providing for such cases.

The law of 1795 did provide for such cases; and the President, in his answer, says he was advised that this was a subsisting law not repealed. It may be a question whether it has been repealed; but from the best examination I have been able to bestow upon the subject I am satisfied it has not been repealed.

I do not propose to enter into the technical rules as to implied repeals. It is a subject of great difficulty, and I do not profess to be able to apply those rules; I take only this practical view of the subject: when the act of February 20, 1863, was passed, which it is supposed may have repealed the act of 1795, it is beyond all dispute that vacancies in office might be created by the President; and there might be the same necessity for making temporary provision for discharging the duties of such vacant offices as was provided for by the act of 1795. The act of 1863 is wholly silent on this subject. Why should I say that a public necessity provided for in 1795 and not negatived in 1863, was not then recognized; or why should I say that, if recognized, it was intended by the act of 1863 that it should not thereafter have any provision made for it? Comparing the act of 1863 and the cases it provided for, I see no sufficient reason to say that it was the intention of Congress in 1863 to deprive the President of the power given by the act of 1795 to supply the temporary necessities of the public service in case of vacancy caused by removal.

But if I thought otherwise I should be unable to convict the President of a crime because he had acted under the law of 1795. Many cases of *ad interim* appointments have been brought before us in evidence. It appears to have been a constant and frequent practice of the government, in all cases when the President was not prepared to fill an office at the moment when the vacancy occurred, to make an *ad interim* appointment. There were 179 such appointments specified in the schedule annexed to the message of President Buchanan, found on page 584 of the printed record, as having occurred in little more than the space of 30 years. I have not minutely examined the evidence to follow the practice further, because it seems to me that if, as I think, the President had the power to remove Mr. Stanton, he might well conclude, and that it cannot be attributed to him as a high crime and misdemeanor that he did conclude, that he might designate some proper officer to take charge of the War Department until he could send a nomination of a suitable person to be Secretary; and when I add that on the next day after this designation the President did nominate for that office an eminent citizen in whose loyalty to our country and in whose fitness for any duties he might be willing to undertake the people would be willing to confide, I can find no sufficient reason to doubt that the President acted in good faith and believed that he was acting within the laws of the United States. Surely the mere signing of that letter of appointment, "neither attended or followed by the possession of the office named in it or by any act of force, of violence, of fraud, of corruption, of injury, or of evil, will not justify us in depriving the President of his office."

I have omitted to notice one fact stated in the second article. It is that the designation of General Thomas to act *ad interim* as Secretary of War was made during a session of the Senate. This requires but few words. The acts of Congress, and the nature of the cases to which they apply, admit of no distinction between *ad interim* appointments in the sessions or the recess of the Senate. A designation is to be made when necessary, and the necessity may occur either in session or in recess.

I do not deem it necessary to state any additional views concerning the third article, for I find in it no allegations upon which I have not already sufficiently indicated my opinion.

The fourth, fifth, sixth and seventh articles charge a conspiracy. I deem it sufficient to say that, in my judgment, the evidence adduced by the House of

Representatives not only fails to prove a conspiracy between the President and General Thomas to remove Mr. Stanton from office by force or threats, but it fails to prove any conspiracy in any sense I can attach to that word.

The President, by a written order committed to General Thomas, required Mr. Stanton to cease to act as Secretary for the Department of War, and informed him that he had empowered General Thomas to act as Secretary *ad interim*. The order to General Thomas empowered him to enter on the duties of the office, and receive from Mr. Stanton the public property in his charge. There is no evidence that the President contemplated the use of force, threats, or intimidation; still less that he authorized General Thomas to use any. I do not regard the declarations of General Thomas, as explained by himself, as having any *tendency* even to fix on the President any purpose beyond what the orders on their face import.

Believing, as I do, that the orders of the President for the removal of Mr. Stanton, and the designation of General Thomas, to act *ad interim*, were legal orders, it is manifestly impossible for me to attach to them any idea of criminal conspiracy. If those orders had not been, in my judgment, lawful, I should not have come to the conclusion, upon the evidence, that any actual intent to do an unlawful act was proved.

The eighth article does not require any particular notice after what I have said of the first, second, and third articles, because the only additional matter contained in it is the allegation of an intent to unlawfully control the appropriations made by Congress for the military service by unlawfully removing Mr. Stanton from the office of Secretary for the Department of War.

In my opinion, no evidence whatever, tending to prove this intent, has been given. The managers offered some evidence which they supposed might have some tendency to prove this allegation, but it appeared to the Senate that the supposed means could not, under any circumstances, be adequate to the supposed end, and the evidence was rejected. Holding that the order for the removal of Mr. Stanton was not an infraction of the law, of course this article is, in my opinion, wholly unsupported.

I find no evidence sufficient to support the *ninth* article.

The President, as Commander-in-chief of the army, had a right to be informed of any details of the military service concerning which he thought proper to inquire. His attention was called by one of his Secretaries to some unusual orders. He sent to General Emory to make inquiry concerning them. In the course of the conversation General Emory himself introduced the subject which is the gist of the ninth article, and I find in what the President said to him nothing which he might not naturally say in response to General Emory's inquiries and remarks without the criminal intent charged in this ninth article.

I come now to the question of intent. Admitting that the President had no power under the law to issue the order to remove Mr. Stanton and appoint General Thomas Secretary for the Department of War *ad interim*, did he issue those orders with a manifest *intent* to violate the laws and "the Constitution of the United States," as charged in the articles, or did he issue them, as he says he did, with a view to have the constitutionality of the tenure-of-office act judicially decided?

It is apparent to my mind that the President thoroughly believed the tenure-of-office act to be unconstitutional and void. He was so advised by every member of his cabinet when the bill was presented to him for his approval in February, 1867. The managers on the part of the House of Representatives have put before us and made legal evidence in this case the message of the President to the Senate, dated December 12, 1867. In that message the President declared—

That tenure-of-office law did not pass without notice. Like other acts it was sent to the President for approval. As is my custom, I submitted its consideration to my cabinet for their advice upon the question, whether I should approve it or not. It was a grave question of constitutional law, in which I would of course rely most upon the opinion of the Attorney General and of Mr. Stanton, who had once been Attorney General. Every member of my cabinet advised me that the proposed law was unconstitutional. All spoke without doubt or reservation, but Mr. Stanton's condemnation of the law was the most elaborate and emphatic. He referred to the constitutional provisions, the debates in Congress—especially to the speech of Mr. Buchanan when a senator—to the decisions of the Supreme Court, and to the usage from the beginning of the government through every successive administration, all concurring to establish the right of removal as vested by the Constitution in the President. To all these he added the weight of his own deliberate judgment, and advised me that it was my duty to defend the power of the President from usurpation and to veto the law.

The counsel for the respondent not only offered to prove the truth of this statement of the President by members of the cabinet; but they tendered in addition thereto the proof "that the duty of preparing a message, setting forth the objections to the constitutionality of the bill, was devolved on Mr. Seward and Mr. Stanton." They also offered to prove:

That at the meetings of the cabinet, at which Mr. Stanton was present, held while the tenure-of-office bill was before the President for approval, the advice of the cabinet in regard to the same was asked by the President and given by the cabinet; and thereupon the question whether Mr. Stanton and the other Secretaries who had received their appointment from Mr. Lincoln were within the restrictions upon the President's power of removal from office created by said act was considered, and the opinion expressed that the Secretaries appointed by Mr. Lincoln were not within such restrictions.

And,

That at the cabinet meetings between the passage of the tenure-of-civil-office bill and the order of the 21st of February, 1868, for the removal of Mr. Stanton, upon occasions when the condition of the public service as affected by the operation of that bill came up for the consideration and advice of the cabinet, it was considered by the President and cabinet that a proper regard to the public service made it desirable that upon some proper case a judicial determination on the constitutionality of the law should be obtained.

This evidence was, in my opinion, clearly admissible as cumulative of, or to explain or disprove, the message of the President, which narrates substantially the same facts, and which the managers have introduced and made a part of their case; but it was rejected as incompetent testimony by a vote of the Senate. I believe that decision was erroneous; and inasmuch as there is no tribunal to revise the errors of this, and it is impossible to order a new trial of this case, I deem it proper to regard these offers to prove as having been proved.

We have in addition to this testimony, as to the intent of the President, the evidence of General Sherman. The President desired to appoint General Sherman Secretary *ad interim* for the Department of War, and tendered to him the office. The complications in which the office was then involved were talked over between them. General Sherman says that the subject of using force to eject Mr. Stanton from the office was only mentioned by the President to repel the idea. When General Sherman asked him why the lawyers could not make up a case and have the conflicting questions decided by the courts, his reply was "that it was found impossible, or a case could not be made up; but," said he, "if we can bring the case to the courts it would not stand half an hour."

Here, then, we have the President advised by all of the members of his cabinet, including the Attorney General, whose duty it is made by law to give legal advice to him, including the Secretary for the Department of War, also an eminent lawyer and an Attorney General of the United States under a former administration, that the act of March 2, 1867, was unconstitutional and void, that the three members of the cabinet holding over from Mr. Lincoln's administration were not included within its provisions, and that it was desirable that upon some proper case a judicial determination on the constitutionality of the law should be obtained.

Now, when it is remembered that, according to Chief Justice Marshall, the act of 1789, creating the Department of War, was intentionally framed "so as to clearly imply the power of removal to be solely in the President," and that "as the bill passed into a law, it has ever been considered as a full expression of the sense of the legislature on this important part of the American Constitution;" when it is remembered that this construction has been acquiesced in and acted on by every President from Washington to Johnson, by the Supreme Court, by every Congress of the United States from the first that ever assembled under the Constitution down to the 39th; and when it is remembered that all of the President's cabinet and the most eminent counsellors within his reach advised him that the preceding Congresses, the past Presidents and statesmen, and Story and Kent and Thompson and Marshall were right in their construction of the Constitution, and the 39th Congress wrong, is it strange that he should doubt or dispute the constitutionality of the tenure-of-office act?

But all this is aside from the question whether Mr. Stanton's case is included in the provisions of that act. If it was not, as I think it clearly was not, then the question of intent is not in issue, for he did no unlawful act. If it was included, then I ask whether, in view of those facts, the President's *guilty intent* to do an unlawful act "shines with such a clear and certain light" as to justify, to require us to pronounce him guilty of a high constitutional crime or misdemeanor? The manager, Mr. Boutwell, admits that—

> If a law passed by Congress be equivocal or ambiguous in its terms, the Executive, being called upon to administer it, may apply his own best judgment to the difficulties before him, or he may seek counsel of his advisers or other persons; and acting thereupon without evil intent or purpose, he would be fully justified, and upon no principle of right could he be held to answer, as for a misdemeanor in office.

Does not this admission cover this case? Is there not doubt about the legal construction of the tenure-of-office act? Shall we condemn the President for following the counsel of his advisers and for putting precisely the same construction upon the first section of the act that we put upon it when we enacted it into a law?

It is not necessary for me to refer to another statement made by a manager in order to sustain my view of this case; but I allude to it only to put on record my reprobation of the doctrine announced. It was said that—

> The Senate, for the purpose of deciding whether the respondent is innocent or guilty, can enter into no inquiry as to the constitutionality of the act, which it was the President's duty to execute, and which, upon his own answer, and by repeated official confessions and admissions, he intentionally, wilfully, deliberately set aside and violated.

I cannot believe it to be our duty to convict the President of an infraction of a law when, in our consciences, we believe the law itself to be invalid, and therefore having no binding effect. If the law is unconstitutional it is null and void, and the President has committed no offence and done no act deserving of impeachment.

Again, the manager said:

> The constitutional duty of the President is to obey and execute the laws. He has no authority under the Constitution or by any law to enter into any schemes or plans for the purpose of testing the validity of the laws of the country, either judicially or otherwise. Every law of Congress may be tested in the courts, but it is not made the duty of any person to so test the laws.

Is this so? It is not denied, I think, that the constitutional validity of this law could not be tested before the courts unless a case was made and presented to them. No such case could be made unless the President made a removal. That act of his would necessarily be the basis on which the case would rest. He is sworn to "preserve, protect, and defend the Constitution of the United States." He must *defend* it against all encroachments from whatever quarter. A question arose between the legislative and executive departments as to their relative powers in the matter of removals and appointments to office. That question was, Does the Constitution confer on the President the power which the tenure-of-office act seeks to take away? It was a question manifestly of construction and interpretation. The Constitution has provided a common arbiter in such cases of controversy—the Supreme Court of the United States. Before that tribunal can take jurisdiction a removal must be made. The President attempted to give the court jurisdiction in that way. For doing so he is impeached, and for the reason, as the managers say, that—

He has no authority under the Constitution, or by any law, to enter into any schemes or plans for the purpose of testing the validity of the laws of the country, either judicially or otherwise.

If this be true, then if the two houses of Congress should pass by a two-thirds vote over the President's veto an act depriving the President of the right to exercise the pardoning power, and he should exercise that power nevertheless, or if he should exercise it only in a single case for the purpose of testing the constitutionality of the law, he would be guilty of a high crime and misdemeanor and impeachable accordingly. The managers' theory establishes at once the complete supremacy of Congress over the other branches of government. I can give my assent to no such doctrine.

This was a *punitive* statute. It was directed against the President alone. It interfered with the prerogatives of his department as recognized from the foundation of the government. It wrested from him powers which, according to the legislative and judicial construction of 80 years, had been bestowed upon him by the Constitution itself. In my opinion it was not only proper, but it was his duty to cause the disputed question to be determined in the manner and by the tribunal established for such purposes. This government can only be preserved and the liberty of the people maintained by preserving intact the co-ordinate branches of it—legislative, executive, judicial—alike. I am no convert to any doctrine of the omnipotence of Congress.

But it is said that in our legislative capacity we have several times decided this question and that our judgments on this trial are therefore foreclosed. As for myself, I have done no act, given no vote, uttered no word inconsistent with my present position. I never believed Mr. Stanton came within the provisions of the tenure of-office act, and I never did any act or gave any vote indicating such a belief. If I had done so, I should not consider myself precluded from revising any judgment then expressed, for I am now acting in another capacity, under the sanction of a new oath, after a full examination of the facts, and with the aid of a thorough discussion of the law as applicable to them. The hasty and inconsiderate action of the Senate on the 21st February may have been, and probably was, a sufficient justification for the action of the House of Representatives, as the grand inquest of the nation, in presenting their articles of impeachment, but it furnishes no reason or apology to us for acting otherwise than under the responsibilities of our judicial oath, since assumed.

The *tenth* article charges that, in order to

Bring into disgrace, ridicule, hatred, contempt, and reproach, the Congress of the United States, and the several branches thereof, to impair and destroy the regard and respect of all the good people of the United States for the Congress and legislative power thereof, (which all officers of the government ought inviolably to preserve and maintain,) and to excite the odium and resentment of all the good people of the United States against Congress, and the laws by it duly and constitutionally enacted; and in pursuance of his said design and intent, openly and publicly, and before divers assemblages of the citizens of the United States convened, in divers parts thereof to meet and receive said Andrew Johnson as the Chief Magistrate of the United States, did, on the 18th day of August, in the year of our Lord 1866, and on divers other days and times, as well before as afterward, make and deliver with a loud voice certain intemperate, inflammatory, and scandalous harangues, and did therein utter loud threats and bitter menaces.

These speeches were made in 1866. They were addressed to promiscuous popular assemblies, and were unattended by any official act. They were made by the President in his character of a citizen. They were uttered against the 39th Congress, which ceased to exist more than a year ago. That body deemed them to be unworthy of their attention, and the present House of Representatives decided by an overwhelming majority that they, too, did not consider them worthy to be made the ground of impeachment.

IMPEACHMENT OF THE PRESIDENT.   339

The first amendment to the Constitution of the United States declares that "Congress shall make no law" "abridging the freedom of speech." Congress, therefore, could pass no law to punish the utterance of those speeches before their delivery; but according to the theory of this prosecution, we, sitting as a court *after* their delivery, can make a law, each for himself, to govern this case and to punish the President.

I have no apology to make for the President's speeches. Grant that they were indiscreet, indecorous, improper, vulgar, shall we not, by his conviction on this article, violate the spirit of the Constitution which guarantees to him the freedom of speech? And would we not also violate the spirit of that other clause of the Constitution which forbids the passage of *ex post facto* laws? We are sworn to render impartial justice in this case according to the Constitution and the laws. According to what laws? Is it to be, in the absence of any written law on the subject, according to the law of each senator's judgment, enacted in his own bosom, after the alleged commission of the offence? To what absurd violations of the rights of the citizen would this theory lead us? For my own part I cannot consent to go beyond the worst British Parliaments in the time of the Plantagenets in attempts to repress the freedom of speech.

The *eleventh* article contains no matter not already included in one or more of the preceding articles, except the allegation of an intent to prevent the execution of the act of March 2, 1867, for the more efficient government of the rebel States.

Concerning this a telegraphic despatch from Governor Parsons, of Alabama, and the reply of the President thereto, each dated in January preceding the passage of the law, appears to be the only evidence adduced. These despatches are as follows:

MONTGOMERY, ALABAMA, *January* 17, 1867.

Legislature in session. Efforts making to reconsider vote on constitutional amendment. Report from Washington says it is probable an enabling act will pass. We do not know what to believe. I find nothing here.
LEWIS E. PARSONS,
Exchange Hotel.

His Excellency ANDREW JOHNSON, *President.*

The response is:

UNITED STATES MILITARY TELEGRAPH, EXECUTIVE OFFICE,
Washington, D. C., January 17, 1867.

What possible good can be obtained by reconsidering the constitutional amendment? I know of none in the present posture of affairs; and I do not believe the people of the whole country will sustain any set of individuals in attempts to change the whole character of our government by enabling acts or otherwise. I believe, on the contrary, that they will eventually uphold all who have patriotism and courage to stand by the Constitution, and who place their confidence in the people. There should be no faltering on the part of those who are honest in their determination to sustain the several co-ordinate departments of the government in accordance with its original design.
ANDREW JOHNSON.

Hon. LEWIS E. PARSONS, *Montgomery, Alabama.*

I am wholly unable, from these despatches, to deduce any criminal intent. They manifest a diversity of political views between the President and Congress. The case contains ample evidence outside of these despatches of that diversity of opinion. I do not perceive that these despatches change the nature of that well-known and, in my opinion, much to be deplored diversity.

I have thus, as briefly as possible, stated my views of this case I have expressed no views upon any of the questions upon which the President has been arraigned at the bar of public opinion outside of the charges. I have no right to travel out of the record.

Mr. Johnson's character as a statesman, his relations to political parties, his conduct as a citizen, his efforts at reconstruction, the exercise of his pardoning power, the character of his appointments, and the influences under which they were made, are not before us on any charges, and are not impugned by any testimony.

Nor can I suffer my judgment of the law governing this case to be influenced by political considerations. I cannot agree to destroy the harmonious working of the Constitution for the sake of getting rid of an unacceptable President. Whatever may be my opinion of the incumbent, I cannot consent to trifle with the high office he holds. I can do nothing which, by implication, may be construed into an approval of impeachments as a part of future political machinery.

However widely, therefore, I may and do differ with the President respecting his political views and measures, and however deeply I have regretted, and do regret, the differences between himself and the Congress of the United States, I am not able to record my vote that he is guilty of high crimes and misdemeanors by reason of those differences. I am acting in a judicial capacity, under conditions whose binding obligation can hardly be exceeded, and I must act according to the best of my ability and judgment, and as they require. If, according to their dictates, the President is guilty, I *must* say so; if, according to their dictates, the President is not guilty, I *must* say so.

In my opinion the President has not been guilty of an impeachable offence by reason of anything alleged in either of the articles preferred against him at the bar of the Senate by the House of Representatives.

OPINION OF MR. SENATOR POMEROY.

As no man can see with the eyes of another, so no one can control his judgment upon the precise views and opinions of others. And although other senators may and have given better and perhaps more logical reasons for their votes upon questions involved in this *great trial* of *impeachment* of the *President*, still, as my own judgment must be controlled by my own *views* and *opinions*, I propose to set them forth, as briefly as possible, in the opinion and views I now submit.

The people of the United States, through the House of Representatives in Congress assembled, have, in constitutional form, presented at the bar of the Senate 11 articles of impeachment against Andrew Johnson, President of the United States, for high *crimes* and *misdemeanors* in office. The charges have been answered by him; and after over 40 days of patient trial, the time has come when senators are required or allowed to state their conclusions upon the pleadings and proofs. This brief statement will explain the reasons of the judgment I am prepared to give by my response to each article.

In considering the questions to be decided, it is to be borne in mind that this proceeding is not a suit between Andrew Johnson and Edwin M. Stanton, or between the persons appearing here as managers and Andrew Johnson. The Senate of the United States has no jurisdiction of such controversies, nor should they be influenced by considerations relating to individual persons.

The proceeding is national; the people of the United States impeaching, through their constitutional agents, a public officer, high in place and power, for his public acts, and demanding judgment against him, not for a private injury, but for public wrongs, violations of the Constitution, which they formed and adopted for the *general welfare*, and transgressing laws enacted by them through their constitutional representatives in Congress assembled. If these violations are set forth in the articles of impeachment, and admitted in the answer, or proven on the trial, then the verdict of conviction must not be withheld. To this point I now address myself.

The first, second, and third articles of impeachment relate to the removal of

Mr. Stanton from the office of Secretary of War and the appointment of Lorenzo Thomas as Secretary of War *ad interim* on the 21st day of February, 1868, without the advice and consent of the Senate, then in session, there being no vacancy in the office of Secretary, and having been none during the recess of the Senate.

These official acts of Mr. Johnson are averred to be in violation of the tenure-of-office act, and of the Constitution of the United States.

It is set up in defence or excuse—

1. That Mr. Stanton was not removed on the 21st day of February, and is still Secretary of War.
2. That Mr Stanton is not Secretary of War, because his term expired at the death of Mr. Lincoln.
3. That Lorenzo Thomas was not appointed Secretary of War *ad interim* on the 21st day of February.
4. That Lorenzo Thomas was lawfully appointed Secretary of War *ad interim*, Mr. Johnson having the constitutional power to appoint him without the advice and consent of the Senate.
5. That the act regulating the tenure of office is unconstitutional.
6. That Mr. Johnson has the "*power at any and all times of removing from office all executive officers, for cause to be judged of by the President alone.*"
7. That the removal and appointment were made only to test the validity of the tenure-of-office act before the judicial tribunals.

It needs but a glance to see that the grounds of defence are absolutely inconsistent with each other, conflict with the Constitution and act of Congress, and tend to overthrow the form and spirit of republican government.

No question has been discussed so fully since the foundation of the government as the constitutionality of the tenure-of-office act, and four successive times the Senate's judgment pronounced the act to be in conformity with the Constitution, and that judgment of the Senate was pronounced deliberately by senators upon their official oaths; no less solemnly than the oath under which they have conducted this trial. No new view or argument has been presented on this trial to shake the validity of *that* act.

The effort, on the ground of former precedents, to excuse the removal of Stanton and the *ad interim* appointment of Thomas without the advice and consent of the Senate in session, and no vacancy existing in the office, *fails*, because no similar instance can be found, but in every case save one there was an existing vacancy; and in that one the removal was accomplished by the submission of an appointment to the Senate, and a distinct recognition of its constitutional authority. The President on the 21st of February, by an order of that date, declared that Mr. Stanton was thereby removed from the office of Secretary of War; and by another order of the same date, "on that day Mr. Stanton was removed from the office of Secretary of War, and Lorenzo Thomas appointed Secretary of War *ad interim*." And also, on the same day, by an official message to the Senate, announced the removal and the appointment.

If in the face of his own official acts and records he can send lawyers to the bar of the Senate to plead and pretend there was no removal, and that his message to the Senate was false, it would be an example of official prevarication without a parallel in the history of mankind!

Finally, the claim set up in Mr. Johnson's answer of power at any and all times to remove executive officers, for cause to be judged of by him alone, effectually abrogates the constitutional authority of the Senate in respect to official appointments, subverts the principles of republican government, and usurps the unlimited authority of an autocrat. It moreover puts to flight the ridiculous pretense that the President designed only to submit the tenure-of-office act to the test of judicial decision.

In my deliberate judgment, therefore, I must believe the people of the United

States have clearly maintained and substantiated the allegations contained in the first, second, and third articles of impeachment.

But to be more particular, I will for a few moments consider these first three articles separately and in detail, as we must answer, in our judgment, of guilty or not guilty upon each one separately.

The *first article* charges a violation of the act of Congress regulating the tenure of civil offices by the unlawful removing of Edwin M. Stanton from the office of Secretary of War.

The *fact of removal*, as I have said, is fully established by official acts and records, namely:

1. The President's order of removal on the 21st day of February, 1868, which states that Mr. Stanton is "*hereby removed from the office as Secretary for the Department of War*," and that his functions as such would terminate upon the receipt of said communication, and directs him to transfer to Lorenzo Thomas, as Secretary of War *ad interim*, "all records, books, papers," &c.

2. The order of the same date to said Lorenzo Thomas, declaring that Edwin M. Stanton "*having been this day removed* from the office as Secretary for the Department of War," he, the said Thomas, was authorized and empowered to act as Secretary of War *ad interim*, and directed immediately to enter upon the discharge of the duties pertaining to that office.

3. By the message of the same date to the President of the Senate announcing that he had removed Mr. Stanton.

4. By the continual recognition of Mr. Thomas as Secretary of War *ad interim* from that until the present day.

The fact of removal being thus established, it is sought to justify it on two grounds: first, that the tenure-of-office act is unconstitutional; and second, that if valid, its provisions do not restrict the President from removing Mr. Stanton. Without entering into a protracted discussion, it is sufficient to say that the constitutionality of the "tenure act" was fully discussed in the Senate before its original passage, and by a large and solemn vote it was held to be constitutional.

The objection was again specifically made by the President in his veto message, and the act was again held to be constitutional by a vote exceeding two-thirds of the senators present. The question was a third time made in the Senate by the President in his message relating to Mr. Stanton's suspension; and was a fourth time decided upon the consideration of the message of the 21st of February announcing Mr. Stanton's removal. No question, I repeat, has been so fully and thoroughly considered or so often deliberately decided as the constitutionality of the tenure-of-office act. And in the discussion during this trial the counsel for the President have advanced no new views or arguments which had not been several times considered in the Senate. So that if any question can be settled by this Senate and put by us at least forever at rest, so that there is no room for further dispute, *it is the constitutionality of the tenure-of-office act.* That Mr. Stanton's tenure of office as Secretary of War was at the time of his removal within the provisions of that act, and hence his removal was a violation of the act, is also equally plain.

The first clause of the first section of the act applies to all civil officers, and prohibits their removal without the advice and consent of the Senate. The proviso makes an exception and limitation in respect to cabinet officers. It was admitted that Mr. Stanton had been duly appointed Secretary of War by Mr. Lincoln, and was serving out, as was Mr. Johnson, the residue of Mr. Lincoln's term. If the cabinet were not within the proviso, then by the first clause of the first section of the act they were not subject to *removal or suspension* without the sanction of the Senate. If within the proviso, they could not be removed without such sanction until the expiration of thirty days after the *term of appointment*. So that it makes no difference which horn of the dilemma Mr. Johnson selects, for in either case he transgressed the law. Mr. Johnson is, moreover, concluded absolutely on this point by his own official acts and records. During his administration treaties with foreign nations have been made, foreign territory has been purchased. Every civilized nation of the globe has been dealt and negotiated with by Mr. Seward as Secretary of State. Loans have been contracted, revenues collected, taxes imposed, thousands of millions of dollars in money or public credit have been expended or invested by Mr. McCulloch as Secretary of the Treasury. Fleets have been dismantled, naval vessels and armaments sold by Mr. Welles as Secretary of the Navy. Armies have been disbanded, a new army raised and organized, and millions of dollars of military disbursements expended every month under the direction of Mr. Stanton as Secretary of War. The Departments of State, Treasury, War, and Navy for three years have been held under the same tenure. How, then, can it now be pretended by Mr. Johnson that the term of these officers expired at the death of Mr. Lincoln, or that a new appointment was necessary, when none was made? What, in such a view, would be the condition of our foreign relations or national credit? But the objection now raised by or in behalf of Mr. Johnson is not only answered by these acts done under his authority, but it is also repelled by the most solemn records under his own hand. The order suspending Mr. Stanton was addressed to him as "Secretary of War," and professed to suspend him from *that office*. The veto message of the *tenure act* insisted that its operations extended to cabinet officers. The annual message urged that specific objection. The message to the Senate relating to the suspension of Mr. Stanton again *pressed* that point. And the order of removal specially stated that he *was on that day* (February 21, 1868) *removed* from office as Secretary for the Department of War. The *ad interim* appointment of Thomas, the appointments of Ewing and Schofield, declare Mr. Stanton "removed," not pretending that his office had expired by the death of Mr. Lincoln.

Without pursuing the subject further, the terms of the Constitution, the plain words of the act of Congress, the acts and the official records of the President, and the solemn judgment of the Senate, determine clearly as human understanding can comprehend that the tenure-of-office act is constitutional, and that Mr. Stanton did lawfully hold the office of Secretary of War on the 21st day of February last by the tenure-of-office act beyond removal without the advice and consent of the Senate; and that his removal "on that day" by Andrew Johnson was in contemptuous disobedience and flagrant violation of the law, constituting a high misdemeanor; and, consequently, that Andrew Johnson is guilty in manner and form as charged in the first article of impeachment.

The *second article* charges that on the 21st day of February, 1868, the Senate being in session, and there being no vacancy in the office of Secretary of War, with intent to violate the Constitution of the United States and the act of Congress regulating the tenure of certain civil offices, Andrew Johnson, President, &c., did issue and deliver to Lorenzo Thomas a letter of authority, set forth in the article of impeachment, whereby Thomas was authorized and empowered to act as Secretary of War *ad interim*, and directed immediately to enter upon the discharge of the duties pertaining to that office; that the Senate was in session on the 21st day of February last; that there was no vacancy in the office of Secretary of War, and that the President on that day did issue the letter of authority as charged, are fully proved; first, by the letter of authority having the genuine signature of Andrew Johnson; second, by the statement in the said letter of authority that Edwin M. Stanton had "been this day removed from office as Secretary of War;" and, third, by the President's message of the same date to the Senate.

Issuing this letter of authority to Lorenzo Thomas, was a direct violation of the tenure-of-office act. Now, if that act be constitutional—as I have shown—

then the President's guilt under the *second*, as well as the first, article stands without defence; and hence I am forced to the conclusion that the President is guilty *as he stands charged in the second article of impeachment*.

The *third article* charges that on the 21st of February last, while the Senate was in session, Andrew Johnson, President, &c., without authority of law, did appoint one Lorenzo Thomas Secretary of War *ad interim*, without the advice and consent of the Senate, with the intent to violate the Constitution of the United States, no vacancy in said office having happened during the recess of the Senate, and no vacancy existing at the time of the appointment of the said Thomas. That the President did make the appointment, that the Senate was in session, that no vacancy existed at the time of the appointment, are all *facts* undenied and fully proved by the evidence referred to in the preceding article.

But the President sets up in defence that similar appointments were made by his predecessors, and that he is vested, as President, with "the power at any and all times of removing from office all executive officers for cause to be judged of by the President alone." This ground of defence fails, because no tenure-of-office law prohibited his predecessors from making such appointments; and because no case has been found in which a President assumed the right to create a vacancy by removal, and then make an appointment without the advice and consent of the Senate, when this body was in session.

Before Mr. Johnson usurped authority independent of the Senate, removals during the session recognized in every instance the constitutional authority of the Senate over the proposed appointment. Its denial would deprive the Senate of that constitutional check which constitutes one of its most important functions, and would establish the distinctive claim of independent, exclusive executive power, now, for the first time in our national history, boldly and defiantly avowed.

The act of President Johnson is not only unsanctioned by precedent, but on principle the claim of power set up is contrary to the Constitution, which says "the President may nominate, and by and with the advice and consent of the Senate appoint," &c., *but it is also incompatible with the honor, safety, and existence of our form of government.*

Regarding the act of the President, in appointing Lorenzo Thomas Secretary of War *ad interim*, as an unlawful usurpation of power, violating the Constitution and an act of Congress, the President is *guilty*, in my judgment, in manner and form as charged in the third article of impeachment.

The *fourth, fifth, sixth*, and *seventh* articles of impeachment charge an unlawful conspiracy by Mr. Johnson with Lorenzo Thomas, to accomplish the unlawful object specially set forth in *each* of the before-named articles. Whatever conclusion might be formed on these articles, if they stood alone, unaccompanied by any *overt acts*, in furtherance of the objects stated, the evidence in this case, taken in connection with the several acts named, compels the belief that there was a *clear*, distinct understanding, combination, and conspiracy between Johnson and Thomas, with the intent and purpose set forth in the several articles. His efforts to have orders issued and obeyed without (as provided by law) their going through the office of the general of the army; his finding a man who "would obey his orders without regard to the law," and appointing him for the time being; his reappointment of Colonel Cooper as Assistant Secretary of the Treasury after he had been rejected by the Senate at this very session; all these acts taken together, and others of the same character, compel in me the belief that the President did unlawfully conspire with others to violate the law, and hence is guilty in manner and form as charged in the fourth, fifth, sixth, and seventh articles of impeachment.

The eighth article charges that the letter of authority of February 21, 1868, was issued by President Johnson to Lorenzo Thomas with intent to control the moneys appropriated to be disbursed for the military service in violation of the Constitution and of the civil-tenure act.

It is not denied that the appointment of Lorenzo Thomas Secretary of War *ad interim* would give him, while he acted under such appointment, the same control exercised by a Secretary of War duly nominated and confirmed by the Senate. The military disbursements, amounting to many millions of dollars, were placed in the hands and at the power of a mere appointee of the President and the creature of his will, made and unmade by the breath of his power alone.

It is an invariable maxim that every man—and especially every high official—intends the consequences of his own acts; and hence that Mr. Johnson designed to invest Lorenzo Thomas with power over the military disbursements—especially when aided by Cooper, unlawfully in the door of the treasury—thus putting the treasury within reach of the arm of the President alone. This is both a crime and a misdemeanor; and, therefore, he is guilty in manner and form as charged in the eighth article of impeachment.

The ninth article charges that the President instructed General Emory, commander of the military department of the District of Columbia, that the law which required all orders and instructions relating to military operations be issued through the General of the army, was unconstitutional and in contravention with General Emory's commission, and this was done with intent to induce General Emory, in his official capacity as commander of the department, to violate the provisions of the act of Congress aforesaid, and with further intent to prevent the execution of the *tenure of office act*, and to prevent Mr. Stanton from holding and executing the duties of the office of Secretary of War.

The fact that the President did instruct the military commander of this department that the law requiring military orders to be issued by the President through the General of the army was unconstitutional, is distinctly proved by General Emory. Why was such instruction given *at that time*, and why were there such suspicions aroused because officers were called at General Emory's headquarters? It was only on account of what the President had decided *to do*—to control the Department of War! It was in furtherance of what he had said to General Grant—"that as early as last August he had determined to dispossess Mr. Stanton of the War Office at all hazards." These whisperings to General Emory have a peculiar significance to my mind, when I remember what was at that moment in the mind of the President relating to getting possession of the Department of War and dispossessing Mr. Stanton and getting around General Grant by issuing orders *direct* to his subordinate officers.

It, to my mind, admits of no other motive or intention than that which is charged, and, taken with all attendant circumstances, forces the conclusion that the President is guilty in manner and form as charged in the ninth article of impeachment.

The tenth article charges that at sundry times and places therein set forth, Andrew Johnson, President, &c., made certain intemperate, inflammatory, and scandalous harangues, and uttered loud threats and bitter menaces as well against Congress as the laws of the United States, with intent and design to set aside the powers of Congress, and to bring the legislature and the several branches thereof into disgrace, ridicule, hatred, and reproach, and to impair and destroy the regard and respect of the good people of the United States for Congress and the legislative powers thereof, and to excite odium and resentment against Congress and the *laws* duly and constitutionally enacted. And all this while the President was under his oath to see that the laws were faithfully executed. It has been established beyond dispute that the scandalous harangues set forth in this article were made by the President at the times and places stated. Their intent is manifest as plainly as human speech can exhibit the motive and impulse of man's heart. And these denunciations, threatening to "veto their bills," were spoken out of the "abundance of the heart" which led him thus to "impromptu speak," and to defy the very laws he was sworn to execute.

Our government was framed to rest upon opinion and reason, and not upon *force*. The good will of the nation toward the laws and the law-makers is of the highest importance to secure obedience, and the man or the public officer who, by act or speech, strikes at this foundation does an irreparable injury.

The history of republican governments shows that the first efforts of tyrants and usurpers has been directed to undermining and destroying the faith of the people in their representative and legislative bodies.

In his harangues, Andrew Johnson followed with more than usual directness the beaten path towards the overthrow of constitutional government; a government which encourages and secures the largest freedom of speech consistent with its own perpetuity; a government, too, that has provided for striking down the sappers and miners who work at its own foundations. Under this charge and by the proofs the President must stand guilty of the high misdemeanor charged in this tenth article of impeachment.

The eleventh and last article charges that, on the 18th day of August, 1866, Andrew Johnson, President, &c., did, by a public speech, declare and affirm that the thirty-ninth Congress was not a Congress authorized by the Constitution to exercise legislative powers; that its legislation was not valid or obligatory upon him, except so far as he might approve the same; and also denied its power to propose amendments to the Constitution This article further specifies certain of his official acts, done in pursuance of that declaration, devising and contriving, among other things, to prevent the execution of the tenure-of-office act, and to prevent the execution of other laws, especially the "acts to provide for the more efficient government of the rebel States."

The public speech referred to in this article was made before a large assemblage at the Executive Mansion, and clearly proved as well as substantially admitted. It imports nothing less than a total denial of the constitutional power of Congress to pass any laws but such as he approves. It usurps the whole law-making power, and vests its validity absolutely in his approval The powers of Congress are thus abrogated, and the government of the United States is practically vested in Andrew Johnson!

It is vain to treat this and the preceding article with levity or to affect to pass them over with contemptuous indifference or frivolous excuse. They are public declarations by the Chief Executive, preceded, accompanied, and followed by *acts* in strict accordance with the same. They have thus become significant facts, full of enormity in themselves, and boldly threatening the peace, welfare, and existence of constitutional government.

While some of the articles which would seem to operate in the first instance only on an individual, the offences charged in the tenth and eleventh articles embrace in their range all the powers of the government, and the validity of all the legislation of Congress since the rebellion began. The national debt, the taxes imposed and collected by acts of Congress, the collection of the revenue—in short, every operation of the government depending upon the action of Congress during and since the rebellion, are struck at by the hand of the President. And if I was to declare, on my oath, for the acquittal of the President under these articles, charged and proved, then indeed would I feel myself to be guilty of perverting the trust imposed upon me under the Constitution of the United States as a member of this high court of impeachment.

If I am to vote for acquittal I shall sanction these new violations of law and of the Constitution; I shall consent that the President may possess himself of each and all departments of this government, and merge into one head all the independent prerogatives of each of the departments, as were wisely provided by the early framers of our representative government.

I cannot be thus false to my convictions of duty, false to the trusts imposed by my position as a senator sitting upon this great trial, nor false to my loyal, earnest, and devoted constituency, whose every impulse I feel, nor false to my anxious countrymen, whose eyes are upon me. Conviction to my mind is a duty, ay, a necessity under my oath as a senator trying this cause. I cannot escape, if I would, the conviction which the evidence in this case forces upon me. And conviction is, to my vision, *peace.* It is quiet to our long-distracted country. It means *restoration* upon the basis of loyalty, liberty, and equal suffrage, which secures and perpetuates equal rights to all American freemen—now, thank God, American citizens!

Charged by the Constitution with a share in this trial, I cannot shut my eyes to the crimes and misdemeanors charged, and proved also, in this the eleventh article of impeachment; and with uplifted hand and heart I declare my belief to be *that the President is guilty!*

OPINION OF MR. SENATOR WILLIAMS.

Mr. PRESIDENT: Deeply impressed with a sense of my responsibility and duty in the case now before the Senate. I shall vote for the conviction of the President upon the first three articles of impeachment, upon the ground that the removal of Secretary Stanton, and the appointment of Adjutant General Thomas, as charged in said articles, were in violation of the Constitution of the United States.

To decide otherwise would be to say that the President has the absolute and unlimited power at all times and under all circumstances to remove from and appoint to office and, that so much of the Constitution as provides that the President "shall nominate, and by and with the advice and consent of the Senate, appoint," is of no effect. Nothing would be necessary to annihilate all participation by the Senate in appointments, except to call the appointee in case of removal; an officer *ad interim*—that, is an officer to hold until it suits the purposes of the President to send a nomination to the Senate to which it is willing to agree.

Untiring and exhaustive researches, on behalf of the President, do not show, and I venture to assert that not one single instance can be found in the history of the government, where the head of a department has been removed and a successor appointed while the Senate was in session, without the advice and consent of that body. Nothing is clearer to my mind than that the power of the President over the offices of the country, during the session of the Senate, is one thing, and his power during the recess of the Senate is another and a different thing.

When the Constitution says that the President may fill up all vacancies that may happen during the recess of the Senate, it certainly confers upon him a power which he does not possess and cannot exercise while the Senate is in session.

When removals have been made during the recess of the Senate, it has been argued that vacancies made in this way have happened; therefore they could be filled temporarily by the President; but now it is proposed, by building one inference upon another, to include a session as well as a recess, and so abrogate the authority of the Senate and invest the executive with absolute and despotic power. I am very certain that the practice of removals and temporary appointments stands upon that clause of the Constitution which refers to the recess of the Senate, and in my judgment it is not only a total departure from the precedents, but a plain violation of the Constitution, to make one of its sections which applies exclusively to a recess apply also and equally to a session of the Senate.

Congress, if it should try, could not delegate any such power to the President.

Congress may vest the appointment of certain inferior officers in the President alone, in the courts of law, or in the heads of departments; but Congress can no more vest the power in the President of removing and appointing the head of a department, without the advice of the Senate, than it can vest the power in the President to make a treaty without the concurrence of the Senate.

The practice of the government has not been inconsistent with this view of the Constitution. Pickering's case, in 1800, is cited, but there the removal and nomination to the Senate were simultaneous acts. President Adams did not attempt to make any appointment.

Some cases of *ad interim* appointments, to provide for casualties, have been produced, but no case can be found where the President, *uno flatu*, removed and appointed the head of a department while the Senate was in session without its consent.

President Johnson cannot say that he was mistaken as to this point, for, in addition to what he must have learned from many years of public service, he declared in a speech which he delivered in the Senate on the 10th day of January, 1861, in the most emphatic manner, that the President had no such power as he has exercised in the removal of Stanton and the appointment of Thomas.

I do not find that the act of 1789, or subsequent acts upon this subject, have ever been so construed as to warrant the executive acts in question, and they could not be so construed without ignoring the clear distinction which the Constitution makes between a recess and a session of the Senate. Concerning the decision of 1789, which is made the head and front of the defence in this case, it may be said that it was brought about by the arguments of James Madison in the House and the casting vote of Vice-President Adams in the Senate, both of whom at the time expected to fill the executive office, and both of whom, it has been said, looked upon a contrary decision as expressing a want of confidence in the then administration of Washington. Most if not all of the distinguished legislators and judges of the nation, such as Webster, Clay, Calhoun, Kent, Story, and the Supreme Court of the United States, with Marshall at its head, have affirmed the incorrectness of that decision, and experience has demonstrated its mischievous and corrupting tendencies and effects. Webster, commenting upon this decision, and speaking of the framers of the Constitution, in 1835, said: "I have the clearest conviction that they looked to no other mode of displacing an officer than by impeachment, or by the regular appointment of another person to the same place."

I think it wholly unnecessary to discuss the acts of 1792, 1795, and 1863, because they have been swept out of existence by the tenure-of-office act of March 2, 1867. This is established by the application of two familiar rules of law. One is, that the act of March 2, 1867, embraced and provided for the temporary and permanent appointment and removal of every officer whose appointment is vested in the President and the Senate; and the other is, its clear repugnancy to all preceding legislation on the subject.

Great effort has been made to show that the removal of Stanton and the appointment of Thomas were unimportant infractions of the statute, and therefore the President ought to be acquitted.

Adopting the views of the President that this Senate is a court, and finding that the accused has committed an act which the law declares to be a high misdemeanor, then it follows, according to all rules governing judicial tribunals, that a judgment for conviction must be given, no matter what senators may think of the wisdom of the law, or the nature of the offence. Much of the argument for the defence proceeds upon the ground that the President has a right to decide for himself as to the constitutionality of an act of Congress. Whatever may be the correct view of this question, it must be admitted that if the President violates a penal law of Congress he does so at his peril. When impeached for such an act, if the Senate upon the trial holds the law to be unconstitutional and void, he must, of course, be acquitted; but if the Senate holds the law to be constitutional and valid, it must necessarily convict. Any public officer or private citizen may test the validity of a criminal statute by its violation, but in so doing he undertakes to suffer its penalties, if, upon his trial, it is upheld and enforced by judicial authority.

To allow any person not acting judicially when arraigned for crime to plead, in bar of the prosecution, his mistaken opinion of the justice or validity of the law, would be to deliver over the land to anarchy and crime.

Two questions only as to this law are before the Senate. One is, Is it constitutional? and the other is, Has it been violated by the President? Webster said, in one of his great speeches, that "the regulation of the tenure of office is a common exercise of legislative authority, and the power of Congress in this particular is not at all restrained or limited by anything contained in the Constitution, except as to judicial officers;" and I am very sure that the Senate, after having three times decided by more than a two-thirds vote of the members present each time that the tenure-of-office act is constitutional, will now regard that question as *res adjudicata*.

Has the President broken any of the provisions of the act? Nobody denies that the body of the first section, which provides that every person appointed to office by and with the advice and consent of the Senate, shall hold until his successor is in like manner appointed and qualified, embraces the Secretary of War; but an attempt is made to construe the proviso to the section, so as to exclude that officer from the protection of the act. To maintain this construction reliance is chiefly placed upon some remarks of Senator Sherman, in connection with the bill. I presume, on this account it may be proper for me to say that I introduced the original bill, and had the honor to be chairman of the committee of conference by whom this proviso was reported. When the bill passed the Senate the heads of departments were expressly excepted, but the House of Representatives amended it by striking out that exception, and the conference committee agreed to the House amendment, with a modification as to the time during which such officers should be under the protection of the law. There was no suggestion or intimation in the committee that the act did not apply to Mr. Johnson's cabinet, and the only purpose of the proviso was to put a limitation upon the holding of cabinet officers, and that is its fair construction.

Great stress has been put upon the words "except as herein otherwise provided" just preceding the proviso, but the fact is that these words were in the bill before the proviso was attached and refer to the fourth section, and therefore, instead of being an exception, the proviso is a mere qualification of the general words of the section. I do not see how it is possible to conclude that Mr. Stanton is not protected by the body of the section or the proviso. If he is within the proviso, then he has a right to hold for one month after the end of some presidential term, and cannot in the mean time be removed without the consent of the Senate. That is the time expressly fixed by the proviso when a Secretary ceases to be under the protection of the Senate, and it makes no difference whether the present is Lincoln's or Johnson's presidential term. If Mr. Stanton is not affected by the proviso, then he is necessarily within the body of the section, for that includes every officer in the United States appointed by and with the advice and consent of the Senate, which is exactly Stanton's case.

The idea that this act took effect two years before it was enacted, so as to remove anybody from office at that time, is a simple absurdity. Considerable discussion has taken place as to whether or not the present is Mr. Lincoln's or Mr. Johnson's presidential term. This, as it seems to me, is an unimportant but not doubtful question. When the Constitution speaks of the term of the President it means a definite period of four years, not an uncertain time dependant upon the death, resignation or removal of the person who takes possession of the office; and therefore the present is Mr. Lincoln's term, unless there can be two presidential terms between the 4th of March, 1865, and the 4th of March, 1869.

Let us look at the 2d section of the tenure-of-office act. That provides that when any officer appointed as aforesaid, that is, by and with the advice and consent of the Senate, is suspended, and the Senate do not concur in the suspension, such officer shall forthwith resume the functions of his office.

E. M. Stanton was appointed by and with the advice and consent of the Senate. He was suspended. The Senate did not concur in his suspension. It was then his right and duty forthwith to resume the functions of his office; but the President would not allow him so to do, for he not only cut off all official relations with Mr. Stanton, but appointed, received, and recognized another person as Secretary of War. What quibble can be found to excuse this plain violation of the law? Admitting, for the sake of argument, that the President could legally remove Mr. Stanton, then I deny that he could legally appoint Thomas *ad interim*, for the reason that the 2d section of the tenure-of-office act declares that upon the suspension of an officer an *ad interim* appointment may be made, "and in no other case." When Stanton was suspended, the *ad interim* appointment of General Grant was legal; but any *ad interim* appointment upon a removal is absolutely prohibited. Vacancies in office can only be filled in two ways under the tenure-of-office act. One is by temporary appointment, as provided in the Constitution, during the recess of the Senate, and the other is by an appointment by and with the advice and consent of the Senate during the session.

One might reasonably suppose that the construction of this act was settled so far as the Senate was concerned.

On the 12th of December the President communicated to the Senate the fact that, on the 12th of the preceding August, he had suspended Mr. Stanton, and gave his reasons therefor; and the Senate, assuming that Mr. Stanton was within the protection of the tenure of office act, proceeded to consider the President's reasons, and, under the leadership of the distinguished senator from Maine, [Mr. Fessenden,] refused, by an overwhelming vote of thirty-five to six, to concur in the suspension. Every one of the majority then understood that the effect of that vote was to re-establish Mr. Stanton in his office, under the provisions of the tenure-of-office act.

On the 21st of February, 1868, the President informed the Senate that he had removed Mr. Stanton and appointed Adjutant General Thomas Secretary of War *ad interim*, and the Senate proceeded to consider that communication, and, after protracted argument, decided, by a vote of twenty-seven to six, "that, under the Constitution and laws of the United States, the President has no power to remove the Secretary of War and to designate any other officer to perform the duties of that office *ad interim*."

Among those who voted to affirm this doctrine was the distinguished senator from Illinois, [Mr. Trumbull.]

Now, after these proceedings, which go upon the express ground that Mr. Stanton is within the provisions of the tenure-of-office act, we are asked to eat up our own words and resolutions and stultify ourselves by holding that the act did not apply to Mr. Stanton.

President Johnson is also fully committed to the same construction of the act. On the 12th of August he suspended Mr. Stanton, a proceeding provided for by said act, but otherwise unwarranted by law and unknown to the practice of the government.

On the 14th day of August, 1867, he notified the Secretary of the Treasury as follows:

SIR: In compliance with the requirements of the act entitled "An act to regulate the tenure of certain civil offices," you are hereby notified that, on the 12th instant, Hon. Edwin M. Stanton was suspended from his office as Secretary of War and General U. S. Grant authorized and empowered to act as Secretary *ad interim*.

He also reported his reasons to the Senate for the suspension of Mr. Stanton within 20 days from its meeting, as required by said act. Having vainly tried to oust Mr. Stanton by an observance of the act, he boldly determined upon its violation by Stanton's removal. This he admits, but says it was with a view to test the constitutionality of the act, forgetting, as it seems, that such a question could not possibly arise if the act did not apply to Mr. Stanton. To argue, in view of these facts, that the President removed Stanton through a mistaken idea that the law did not apply to him, is trifling with common sense.

Taking the ground of the President that the present is his presidential term, then, I say, to all intents and purposes, he has appointed Stanton Secretary of War. Time and again, in official communications to the Senate, he has declared Mr. Stanton to be Secretary of War, and in his message of December 12, 1867, he submitted to the Senate the question as to whether or not Mr. Stanton should continue to be Secretary of War, and the Senate confirmed him in that position; so that, without the usual forms, there has been that concurrence between the Executive and the Senate as to the secretaryship of Mr. Stanton which the Constitution contemplates. The commission is no part of the appointment. The President cannot hold and treat Mr. Stanton as his Secretary of War for two or three years, and then, when questioned for an illegal act upon or through such Secretary, deny his official character and relations. If he was the President's Secretary of War for executive purposes, he was such Secretary of War for the purposes of Congress.

Much discussion has taken place in this case as to the intent of the President. There is nothing of this question. His intent was to transfer the War Department from E. M. Stanton to some other person of his choice without the consent and in defiance of the will of the Senate. This is obvious and undeniable, and every senator must believe it. The pretext that all his proceedings for the removal of Stanton and the appointment of Thomas were to get up a law-suit, is a shallow and miserable subterfuge.

One question made is that the President has not removed Mr. Stanton. Stanton was either removed or he was not. If he was not removed, then the appointment of Thomas was a clear violation of the sixth section of the tenure-of-office act, for it was an appointment to fill a vacancy where no vacancy existed.

Assuming that the tenure-of-office act is valid and applicable to Mr. Stanton, then the President could not remove him.

Suppose Stanton, to avoid conflict under the orders of the 21st of February, had given possession of the War Office to Thomas. He would still have been Secretary of War, because those orders were illegal and void. What the tenure-of-office law intended to prohibit and punish was the action of the President as to removals and appointments without the consent of the Senate, though of course such action, being in contravention of law, would have no force. Great effort has been made to show that the removal of Stanton and the appointment of Thomas were insignificant acts. They might possibly be so regarded if there was harmony and peace in the country.

Congress has passed laws for the reconstruction of the States lately in rebellion, and the execution of these falls within the jurisdiction of the War Department. The President holds them to be unconstitutional, and is bitterly opposed to their existence. Stanton is understood to be friendly to this legislation. He stands, therefore, in the way of the President, and his removal and the appointment of an executive puppet in his place may involve the lives and liberties of thousands of citizens, and perchance the peace and integrity of the nation.

During this trial we have been treated to much from the writings of James Madison. Arguing about executive power in the Congress of 1789, he said:

If an unworthy officer be continued in office by an unworthy President, the House of Representatives can at any time impeach him, and the Senate can remove him whether the President chooses or not.

Speaking again of the President, he says:

I contend that the wanton removal of meritorious officers would subject him to impeachment and removal from his high trust."

No man can deny that E. M. Stanton, by his ability and experience, his patriotism and personal integrity, is eminently fitted for the head of the War Department.

Andrew Johnson has removed him because his unbending loyalty made him an obstacle to the President's ambitious and partisan purposes, and appointed to his place a man wholly incompetent, whose only mer t is abject servility to the will of his master. If James Madison was a judge here to-day he would vote for impeachment upon that ground alone.

We have been earnestly warned by the President's counsel not to encroach upon the execu ive department of the government. Considering that the President usurped the legislative control and reconstruction of the States lately in rebellion; that he has vetoed fifteen acts of Congress, to say nothing of those he has pocketed; that he comes now by h.s confidential counsel to say what he has before said, that there is no Congress, and we are no Senate; that without acknowledging our authority, he appears simply to avoid civil commotion, and we are prepared to appreciate the modesty and grace of this admonition.

I am surprised to find so many holding the opinion that the President is not impeachable for anything that the law does not declare a crime or a misdemeanor. Cannot he be impeached for a violation of the Constitution? Suppose he should declare war, or borrow money, or levy taxes without authority of law? Is there no remedy? Suppose, for partisan purposes, he should veto all the acts of Congress, or in some mad freak pardon all the criminals of the United States. Suppose by drunkenness and debauchery he should become incompetent to perform the duties of the office. Is Congress bound to tolerate wickedness, corruption, and treachery in the executive office, so long as there is no violation of a penal statute?

I shall vote for conviction on the tenth article. Whenever the Chief Magistrate of this country, whose wisdom and virtue ought to exalt the nation, makes a public blasphemer of himself, and going about the country in speeches excites resistance to law, and defends mob violence and murder, I think he ought to be removed from office.

This is no question of taste or good manners, or of unfriendly criticism upon Congress. Those speeches were crimes. When they were delivered they took the wings of the wind They were published and read throughout the turbulant south. They imparted boldness to violence and revenge, and I have little doubt that many a poor man is sleeping in a bloody grave in consequence of those speeches. Official duties and relations impose restraint upon freedom of speech as well as upon freedom of action.

Suppose a judge of the Supreme Court should go about making speeches and telling the people that the reconstruction or other acts of Congress were void, and that he would so decide when opportunity should arise. Is there any doubt that he could be impeached for conduct so indecent and so disastrous to the peace and good order of society?

West H. Humphreys, United States district judge for Tennessee, was convicted by the unanimous vote of this Senate of high crimes and misdemeanors for what he said in a public speech in the city of Nashville, on the 29th December, 1860.

Whether Andrew Johnson shall be removed from office or not is the least

To acquit is to hold that the laws of the land are not what they are written down in the statute-books of the country to be, but are the unwritten and, it may be, unknown will of one man who happens to fill the executive office of the nation.

All courts may take judicial notice of history, and by what I have a right to know in this case I have been sorrowfully and reluctantly brought to the conclusion that Andrew Johnson is a bad man; that the policy of his administration has been to rule or ruin; that he has endeavored by usurpation and the abuse of his veto to subordinate the legislative power to his personal views and purposes, and that his official career and example have been to injure, degrade, and demoralize the country; and I believe that his removal from office will invigorate the laws, vindicate the Constitution, and tend greatly to restore unity and peace to the nation.

APPENDIX.

ADDITIONAL NOTES TO THE BRIEF OF THE AUTHORITIES ON THE LAW OF IMPEACHABLE CRIMES AND MISDEMEANORS.

Judge Lawrence, who prepared the "Brief of the Authorities upon the Law of Impeachable Crimes and Misdemeanors," found in the body of this work, (p. 82,) has furnished the following additional notes to the brief:

Addition to first note, on page 1, 125, ante.

Cicero, prosecuting the Prætor Verres before the Roman Senate for acts done during his prætorship in Sicily, said:

The mischiefs done by him in that unhappy country during the three years of his iniquitous administration are such that many years under the wisest and best of prætors will not be sufficient to restore things to the condition in which he found them; for it is notorious that during the time of his tyranny the Sicilians enjoyed neither the protection of their own original laws, of the regulations made for their benefit by the Roman Senate upon their coming under the protection of the Commonwealth, nor of the natural or inalienable rights of men.

The following is the substance of the charges upon which Charles I of England was arraigned:

That he, the said Charles Stuart, being admitted king of England, and therein trusted with a *limited power to govern by and according to the laws of the land*, and NOT OTHERWISE; and by his trust, oath, and office being obliged (that is, under obligation) to use the power committed to him for the good and benefit of the people, and for the preservation of their rights and liberties; yet, nevertheless, out of a wicked design to erect and uphold in himself an unlimited and tyrannical power, *to rule according to his* WILL, and to overthrow the rights and liberties of the people; yea, to take away and make void the foundations thereof, and of all redress and remedy of misgovernment, which, by the fundamental constitutions of this kingdom, were reserved on the people's behalf, in the right and power of frequent and successive Parliaments, or national meetings in council; he, the said Charles Stuart, for the accomplishment of such, his designs, and for the protecting of himself and his adherents, in his and their wicked practices, to the same end, hath traitorously and maliciously levied war against the Parliament and the people therein represented.

In his reply Charles persistently asserted the rightfulness and constitutionality of all that he had done, and denied the authority and jurisdiction of the court or commission that tried him, as well as of the House of Commons that created said court and designated its members. He said:

I am most confident this day's proceeding cannot be warranted by God's law; for, on the contrary, the authority and *obedience unto kings* is clearly warranted and *strictly commanded*, both in the *Old* and *New Testament;* which, if denied, I am ready instantly to prove. And for the question now in hand, there it is said: that *where the word of a king is, there is power; and who may say unto him, What doest thou?* (Eccles. viii, 4.) Then for the law of this land, I am no less confident that no learned lawyer will affirm that an impeachment can lie against the king, they all going in his name. Besides, the law upon which you ground your proceedings must either be old or new; if old, show it; if new, tell what authority warranted by the fundamental laws of the land hath made it, and when.

During the trial, when the solicitor for the Commons arraigned him "in the name of the people of England," Lady Fairfax, who was among the spectators, cried out, "Not one half of them!" and some said she exclaimed, "Not one-tenth of them!"

Charles's trial lasted but eight days—having been commenced January 20, 1648, (old reckoning, properly 1649,) and finished January 28; and the 29th being Sunday, his head was cut off on Monday, the 30th.

Addition to first note on page I, 130, ante.

In the Convention the plan of the Committee of the Whole referred the trial of impeachments to the Supreme Court. This was changed so as to give the jurisdiction to the Senate. Curtis, in referring to this, says:

> The cognizance of impeachments of national officers was taken from their [the Supreme Court] jurisdiction, and the principle was adopted which extended that jurisdiction to "all cases arising under the national laws, and to such other questions as may involve the national peace and harmony."—2 *Curtis Hist. Const.*, p. 176.

Hon. John C. Hamilton, in an able article, says:

> It is urged on behalf of the President that it was with much doubt and hesitation that the jurisdiction to try impeachment at all was intrusted to the Senate of the United States. The grant of jurisdiction to the Senate was deferred to the last moment.
>
> The intrustment of this power to the Senate was *not* delayed because of any doubt or hesitation; nor was it deferred. The proposed intrusting this power to the Supreme Court was before it was determined that the appointment of the judges should be made by the President with the consent of the Senate. This mode of appointment was agreed to unanimously in the Convention on the 7th of September, 1787; and the next day, the 8th of September, Roger Sherman raised the objection that the Supreme Court was "improper to try the President, because the judges would be appointed by him." This objection prevailed, and the trial was intrusted to the Senate by the vote of all the States with one exception; and thus, on the same day, immediately after, the subjects of impeachment were extended from treason and bribery to "*other high crimes and misdemeanors*," and thus intrusted and thus enlarged, it was on the same day made to embrace "the Vice-President and other civil officers of the United States."
>
> Thus it is seen that while the Supreme Court—a judicial body—was contemplated as the court for the trial of impeachments, its jurisdiction was proposed to be limited to two crimes—statutory offences—and therefore to be governed by "strict rules" of law; but when confided to the Senate—a political body—the jurisdiction was extended to political offences, in the trial of which, from "the nature of the proceeding a national inquest," a commensurate discretion necessarily followed. Thus it is a strange venture for any man to declare in the presence of this whole country "that it is impossible to observe the progress of the deliberations of that Convention upon this single question, beginning with the briefest and most open jurisdiction and ending in a jurisdiction confined in its terms, without coming to the conclusion that it was their determination that the jurisdiction should be circumscribed and limited."
>
> It is here averred, and the evidence is positive, that from the progress of the deliberations of the Convention, the opposite conclusion is the only one to come to.

Addition to second note on page I, 131, ante.

The question of the power to suspend the President is discussed in speeches of December 13, 1867, February 24 and 29, 1868, in the House of Representatives. (See *Congressional Globe*.)

Addition to third note on page I, 131, ante.

On these citations from the Federalist Hon. John C. Hamilton remarks:

> This quotation exhibits three most important facts: first, that the subjects of the jurisdiction "of the court for the trial of impeachments" are those offences which proceed from the misconduct of public men, or, in other words, from the abuse or violation of some public trust. Second, that in the delineation and construction of those offences the nature of the proceeding—

Mark the words, "nature of"—

> can never be tied down by the strict rules which, in common cases, limit the discretion of courts; that the discretion of the court for the trial of impeachments, thus unlimited in its proceedings, is "an awful discretion," and that its exercise was contemplated to be applied toward the most confidential and the most distinguished characters of the community.

And how high the discretion of this national inquest it was expected might reach is seen in these words, vindicating the constitution of the executive department from popular distrust:

> The President of the United States would be liable to be impeached, tried, and, upon conviction of treason, bribery, or other high crimes or misdemeanors, removed from office.

Addition to third note on page I, 136, ante.

In England and the United States there are different systems of law, each with its appropriate *tribunals, jurisdiction,* and mode of *procedure* established. The *judicial courts* have a jurisdiction and procedure well understood. They are governed by the Constitution, statutory and common law. *Military law* is a branch of the law of nations recognized in and adopted by the Constitution; has its *tribunals,* with their appropriate *jurisdiction and procedure.* They try and punish offences relating to the army and navy and the military and naval service defined mainly by common, unwritten military law, and only to a limited extent by statute. *(Attorney General Speed's opinion of July,* 1865, *on the trial of the assassins.)* Parliamentary law has its *tribunals,* with legislative, and, for some purposes, a judicial power, including the right to summon witnesses before committees of investigation, punish and even imprison for contempt of its powers or privileges, expel or otherwise punish its members, and with the power of *impeachment.* These different tribunals do not administer *the same law* nor for the same purposes. Each has its own independent law, governed by its own principles and reasons.

The same reasons which enable military tribunals to try offences undefined by statute authorize impeachment for misdemeanors defined by no written law. The Senate administers the common parliamentary law of impeachable misdemeanors, and establishes its *procedure* on principles peculiar to its organization and objects, uncontrolled by the powers of either judicial or military tribunals.

Additional note to page I, 141, ante.

The following charges, among others, were drawn up by Hon. John Minor Botts against John Tyler, in 1842:

I charge John Tyler with a gross usurpation of power and violation of law.

I charge him with the high crime and misdemeanor of endeavoring to excite a disorganizing and revolutionary spirit in the country, by inviting a disregard of and disobediency to a law of Congress, which law he has himself sworn to see faithfully executed.

I charge him with the high crime and misdemeanor in office of withholding his assent to laws indispensable to the operations of government.

I charge him with gross official misconduct in having been guilty of a shameless duplicity, equivocation, and falsehood, with Congress, such as has brought him into disgrace and contempt with the whole American people, and has disqualified him from administering this government with advantage, honor, or virtue.

I charge him with an arbitrary and despotic abuse of the veto power, to gratify his personal and political resentment, with such evident marks of inconsistency and duplicity as to leave no room to doubt his total disregard of the interests of the people, and of his duty to the country.

I charge him with the high misdemeanor of arraying himself in open hostility to the legislative department of the government, by the publication of slanderous and libellous letters over his own signature, with a view of creating false and unmerited sympathy for himself, and bringing Congress into disrepute and odium with the people, by which means that harmony between the executive and legislative departments, so essential to good government and the welfare of the people, has been utterly destroyed.

I charge him with pursuing such a course of vacillation, weakness, and folly, as must, if he is permitted to remain longer at the head of the government, bring the country into dishonor and disgrace abroad, and force the people into a state of abject misery and distress at home.

I charge him with being utterly unworthy and unfit to have the destinies of this nation in his hands as Chief Magistrate, and with having brought upon the representatives of the people the imperious necessity of exercising the constitutional prerogative of impeachment. (Congressional Globe, vol. 12, p. 144, third session 27th Congress.)

Additional note to page I, 142, ante.

Only two of the acts charged against West W. Humphreys could be deemed treason. The authorities which define that crime are conclusive on that subject.

A mere conspiring and a mere assemblage is not treason. (4 Cranch, 75; 1 Dallas, 35; 2 Wallace, jr., 139; 2 Bishop, Crim. Law, 1186 and 1204.)

The overt act must be one which in itself pertains to warlike operations. It must in some sense be an act of war. (23 Boston Law Reporter, 597, 705.)

If a convention, legislature, junto, or other assemblage, entertain the purpose of subverting the government, and to that end pass acts, resolves, ordinances, or decrees, even with a view of raising a military force to carry their purpose into effect, this alone does not constitute a levying war. (Sprague, J., charge to grand jury; 23 Law Reporter, 705; *ibid.*, 597, 601.)

If war be actually levied, that is, if a body of men be actually assembled for the purpose of effecting by force a treasonable purpose, all those who perform any part, however minute or however remote from the scene of action, and who are actually leagued in the general conspiracy, are to be considered traitors. (Per Marshall; 4 Cranch, 75, 126; Burr's Trial, Coombs's ed., 322; 1 Bishop, 54.)

Additional note to page I, 145, ante.

In the case of *The State of Mississippi* vs. *Andrew Johnson, President of the United States*, before the Supreme Court of the United States, April 11, 1867, a motion was made for leave to file a bill praying for an injunction to restrain the President and his military officers from executing the "reconstruction acts" of Congress. Henry Stanbery, then Attorney General, (but now of counsel for the President on the impeachment trial,) appeared on behalf of the President to resist the motion for leave to file the bill, and in argument said:

The President of the United States is above the process of any court or the jurisdiction of any court to bring him to account as President.

There is only one court or *quasi* court that he can be called upon to answer to for any dereliction of duty, for doing anything that is contrary to law or failing to do anything which is according to law and that is not this tribunal, but one that sits in another chamber of the Capitol. There he can be called and tried and punished, but not here while he is President; and after he has been dealt with in that chamber and stripped of the robes of office, and he no longer stands as the representative of the government, then for any wrong he has done to any individual, for any murder or any crime of any sort which he has committed as President, then, and not till then, can he be subjected to the jurisdiction of the courts. (The Reporter, Washington, 1867, vol. 3, p. 13.)

Additional note to page I, 146, ante.

It has been said that—

If a law passed by Congress be equivocal or ambiguous in its terms, the Executive, being called upon to administer it, may apply his own best judgment to the difficulties before him, or he may seek counsel of his advisers or other persons; and acting thereupon without evil intent or purpose, he would be fully justified, and upon no principle of right could he be held to answer as for a misdemeanor in office.

But this standing alone and unqualified is *not sound law*, if construed to mean that the President is not guilty of an impeachable misdemeanor in case he honestly misinterprets a law and executes it according to *his construction* in a mode subversive of some fundamental or essential principle of government or highly prejudicial to the public interest.

It is a very plausible view that punishment should not be inflicted on any person who, in good faith, does what he believes the law authorizes. But such a rule has never been applied in any court or tribunal—civil, criminal, military, or parliamentary—except in certain cases for the protection of judges of courts. At common law he who violates any civil right of another is liable to an action, no matter how much the violation may have resulted from the mistaken belief that it was justified by law. In the criminal jurisprudence of every country it is no excuse for a party indicted that his act is only criminal by the construction given by the court to a statute "equivocal or ambiguous in its terms." To hold otherwise would be to make the law depend on the opinion of the accused, and not on the determination of the court. The court is the sole judge of what the law is, and the rule applies—

Good faith is no excuse for the violation of statutes. Ignorance of the law cannot be set up in defence, and this rule holds good in civil as well as in criminal cases. (1 Sedgwick, 100.)

(See Kent's Com., 529; 3 Greenleaf's Evidence, 15.)

And this is so in parliamentary impeachments, as has already been shown.

The power of impeachment may frequently be exerted not for any purpose of *punishment*, but as *protection to the public*. If the President should err in the assertion of a constitutional power, or in the interpretation of a statute, so as to establish a principle dangerous to the public interests, impeachment is a mode, and often the only one, of correcting his error, and of protecting the rights of the people.

If the Supreme Court should, however, honestly interpret the Constitution or laws, even upon words "equivocal or ambiguous," so as to settle a principle dangerous to public liberty, there is a remedy by impeachment, employed not for punishment, but for protection, exercised in the nature of a *writ of error*, to reverse a decision subversive of civil liberty and republican government. The Supreme Court is not a court of *last resort*. The high court of impeachment is the only court of last resort, and its decisions can only be reviewed and reversed by the people in the selection of a Congress holding different views; so that at last the Senate, as the Constitution declares in effect, is "the sole judge of the law and the facts" in every case of impeachment, subject to reversal by successors chosen in the constitutional mode.

If a public officer should misinterpret a law in a case where adequate remedy could be had without resort to impeachment, or on a question not vital to any fundamental principle of government or of the public interests, the House of Representatives would never prefer articles to invoke the judicial powers of the Senate.

The House of Representatives in some sense and in proper cases may exercise a pardoning power by withholding articles, or by a failure or refusal to demand judgment after conviction when its purposes may be practically accomplished, but it never can be tolerated that the high conservative power of impeachment, so essential to finally settle great questions of constitutional law, can be stricken down or its jurisdiction destroyed by the *state of mind* or the *mental idiosyncracies* or *mistaken opinions* of an officer who violates the Constitution or laws as construed by the sole and final judges thereof in the high court of impeachment. The words of Pym, on the trial of Strafford, may be well applied:

To subvert laws and government—they can never be justified by any intentions, how good soever they be pretended.

This view of the law of impeachment popularizes our institutions, and makes the people at last the great depositaries of power, clothed with the ultimate right of interpreting their own Constitution in their own interests, and herein rests the greatest security for popular liberty.

While any citizen upon whom a statute is to be executed may rightfully take measures to test its constitutionality, the executive officer of the law can never be permitted to do so, because as to him the presumption of the constitutionality of a law is incontrovertible and conclusive, at least until reversed by a court of competent authority, if such there be.

DEBATE

ON THE

RIGHT OF SENATOR WADE TO SIT AS A MEMBER OF THE COURT.

IN SENATE, *March* 5, 1868.

[For the proceedings see volume 1, page 11.]

The CHIEF JUSTICE. Senators, the oath will now be administered to the senators as they will be called by the Secretary in succession. (To the Secretary.) Call the roll.

The Secretary proceeded to call the roll alphabetically, and the Chief Justice administered the oath to Senators Anthony, Bayard, Buckalew, Cameron, Cattell, Chandler, Cole, Conkling, Conness, Corbett, Cragin, Davis, Dixon, Drake, Ferry, Fessenden, Fowler, Frelinghuysen, Grimes, Harlan, Henderson, Hendricks, Howard, Howe, Johnson, McCreery, Morgan, Morrill of Maine, Morrill of Vermont, Morton, Norton, Nye, Patterson of Tennessee, Pomeroy, Ramsey, Ross, Sherman, Sprague, Stewart, Sumner, Thayer, Tipton, Trumbull, and Van Winkle.

The Secretary then called the name of Mr. Wade, who rose from his seat in the Senate and advanced toward the Chair.

Mr. HENDRICKS. Before the senator just called takes the oath I wish to submit to the presiding officer and to the Senate a question. The senator just called is the presiding officer of this body, and under the Constitution and laws will become the President of the United States should the proceeding of impeachment, now to be tried, be sustained. The Constitution providing that in such a case the possible successor cannot even preside in the body during the trial, I submit for the consideration of the presiding officer and of the Senate the question whether, being a senator, representing a State, it is competent for him, notwithstanding that, to take the oath and become thereby a part of the court? I submit that upon two grounds—first, the ground that the Constitution does not allow him to preside during these deliberations because of his possible succession, and second, the parliamentary or legal ground that he is interested, in view of his possible connection with the office, in the result of the proceedings—he is not competent to sit as a member of the court.

Mr. SHERMAN. Mr. President, this question, I think, is answered by the Constitution of the United States, which declares that each State shall be entitled to two senators on this floor, and that the court or tribunal for the trial of all impeachments shall be the Senate of the United States. My colleague is one of the senators from the State of Ohio; he is a member of this Senate, and is therefore made one of the tribunal to try all cases of impeachment. This tribunal is not to be tested by the ordinary rules that may apply in cases at civil law; for the mere interest of the party does not exclude a person from sitting as a member of the Senate for the trial of impeachment, nor does mere affinity or relation by blood or marriage. The tribunal is constituted by the Constitution of the United States, and is composed of two senators from each State, and Ohio is entitled to two voices upon the trial of this case. It seems to me, therefore, that the question ought not to be made.

If this were to be tested by the rule in ordinary civil tribunals the same objection might have been made to one other senator, who has already taken the oath without objection, being connected by ties of marriage with the person accused before us. It is, therefore, perfectly clear that while the rule might exclude the senator from Ohio in deciding in ordinary cases, or he might retire from exercising his right to vote, that is a question for him alone to determine. So far as the court is concerned he is entitled to be sworn as one of the triers in this case as senator from the State of Ohio, without regard to his interest in the result of the trial.

I have, as a matter of course, as the colleague of the senator who is now proposed to be sworn, looked into this matter, and I have no doubt of it. I was prepared, to some extent, for the raising of this question, though I hoped it would not be presented. How far the senator from Ohio, my colleague, may participate in the proceedings of impeachment, how far he shall vote, when he shall vote, and upon what questions he shall vote, are matters that must be left to him, and not for the tribunal or any senator to make against him. His right as a senator from the State of Ohio is complete and perfect, and there is no exclusion of him on account of interest, affinity, blood relationship, or for any other cause.

Mr. HOWARD. Mr. President, I do not suppose that under the Constitution any senator is to be challenged, even for cause, upon the trial of an impeachment. I concur entirely with the view presented by the honorable senator from Ohio [Mr. Sherman] which he has just expressed. The objection raised by the honorable senator from Indiana [Mr. Hendricks] is in the nature of a challenge, if I understand it properly, upon the ground of interest in the question about to be decided by the Senate sitting for the trial of an impeachment. Now, sir, as has been very justly remarked, each State has the right to send to the Senate two members, and the Constitution declares, whatever may be the character of those members, whatever may be their relation to the accused or their interest in the question involved, that they shall be component parts of the body trying the impeachment. If an objection upon the ground of interest is tenable an objection upon the ground of affinity must also be available. The Senate has already seen one member of its body proceed to take the oath prescribed in our rules who is known to be related by affinity to the accused. I can see no distinction between an objection resting upon interest and one resting upon affinity.

Besides, sir, the honorable senator from Ohio who now offers to take the oath is but the President *pro tempore* of the Senate. It is possible, and merely possible, that he may remain in that capacity until the conclusion of these proceedings; but at the same time it is not to be overlooked that it is but a possibility. The Senate has in its power at all times to choose another President *pro tempore* to preside over its proceedings. I cannot, therefore, see any such interest in the question as would seem to justify the objection which is taken by the honorable senator from Indiana. I hope the senator from Ohio, the President *pro tempore* of this body, will proceed to take the oath.

Mr. JOHNSON. Mr. President, the question is a purely legal one, and is to be decided upon principle. I have no doubt that the honorable member from Ohio will, as far as he may be able under the temptations to which he may be subjected unknowingly to himself, decide upon the issues which are involved in the impeachment trial with as much impartiality as any of us. It is not, therefore, any objection to the honorable member which induces me to say a word to the Senate on the subject.

The general rule, we all know, is applicable to a jury as well as to a court, that no one should serve in either tribunal who has a clear interest in the result of the trial. The honorable member from Ohio [Mr. Sherman] and the honorable member from Michigan [Mr. Howard] tell us that the Constitution provides that the court in this instance is to consist of the senators of the several States. That is true; but that does not prove that a senator may not be in a situation which should exclude him from the privilege of being a member of the court.

The Constitution of the United States provides that the Supreme Court shall consist of a Chief Justice and associate justices; the law from time to time has regulated their number; but I never heard it questioned that, although by the Constitution and the laws cases within the jurisdiction of that tribunal are to be tried by them, a judge would not be permitted to sit in a case in which he had a direct interest. It by no means follows, therefore, that because the honorable member from Ohio [Mr. Wade] is a senator, and as such entitled to be a member of this court, he is not as liable to the objection of interest in the result which your honor, the Chief Justice of the Supreme Court, would be liable to in a case before your high tribunal in which you had a direct interest in the possible result.

This is, as the honorable member from Ohio [Mr. Sherman] says, the only tribunal to try such a case as is now before us. That is true; but if the honorable member and the Senate will look to the sixty-fifth number of the Federalist they will find why it was that the court was constituted when the President is to be on trial as it is constituted by the Constitution. It was because of the manner in which impeachments are tried in the mother country. There they are tried in the House of Lords. And I have a recollection, not altogether distinct—I did not know that the question was to be raised to-day, or I should have refreshed my recollection—that when in the case of the senator from New Jersey, Hon. Mr. Stockton, who had been received as a senator on this floor upon his credentials, and it was proposed to exclude him, which required a majority vote, the honorable member from Massachusetts, [Mr. Sumner,] and I think several other members, but particularly the honorable member from Massachusetts, in order to satisfy the Senate that Mr. Stockton had no right to vote in his own case, cited many instances in the House of Lords in which it had been held that a member of the House of Lords was not competent to decide in a case in which he had an interest. It was upon the authority of those cases, as well as upon the general ground which runs through the whole of our jurisprudence and the jurisprudence of the mother country, and is founded in the nature of things, that Mr. Stockton was denied the privilege of voting in his own case.

Now what was his case compared in point of supposed influence to the case of the honorable member from Ohio? He was to have a temporary seat in this body, invested only with that proportion of the power of the legislative department of the government which one member of this body has in reference to the whole number composing the body and the numbers which compose the House of Representatives. His voice, therefore, would be comparatively unimportant. And yet it was adjudged by the Senate, as well as I remember, and almost with unanimity, especially by those who thought Mr. Stockton was not entitled to his seat, that he should not be permitted to vote upon that question. How does his case compare with that of the honorable member from Ohio? The honorable member becomes, in a contingency which this impeachment seeks to bring about, a judgment of guilty, the President of the United States, invested with all the executive power of the government. Is it right, would anybody desire, to be subjected to such a temptation, which might lead him, unknowingly to himself, into an erroneous judgment? The whole executive powers of the United States, to say nothing of the pecuniary compensation belonging to the office $25,000 a year, are to be his in a certain result of the prosecution; and his vote may produce that result.

I submit, then, and certainly without the slightest feeling of disrespect for the honorable member from Ohio, that it is due to the cause of impartial justice, it is due to the character of the Senate, in its management of this proceeding, that there should not be established a precedent which may in the end produce excitement and bring into disrepute the Senate itself. The reason why it is, Mr. Chief Justice, that you are here to preside over the deliberations of this court, shows that, in the judgment of our fathers, it was improper that any man should be placed in the situation in which the honorable member from Ohio will be placed if he is admitted to be a member of this court and exercise that function. Our fathers thought, and they have incorporated the thought into the Constitution, that he who is to be benefited by the result should not be permitted even to preside over the deliberations of this court when the President of the United States is on trial; that the Vice-President of the United States, who is entitled only to vote in case of a tie, of an equal division of the Senate, should not be permitted even to be a member of a court to preside over its deliberations. It was, Mr. Chief Justice, because our fathers were deeply versed in the history of the world, perfectly acquainted with the frailties of man's nature, as exhibited in the history of all political bodies, that they denied, in a case of this description, to the Vice-President of the United States the privilege even of presiding over the deliberations of such a court, much less of voting, and by his vote bringing about the judgment which was to make him President.

Mr. President, I do not know that we are able to decide this question at once. My impression is such as I have stated; but it is a grave question, an important question. It will be considered a grave and important question in the eyes of the country, and it should be by the Senate of the United States so esteemed. It is a new question; and I submit to you and the Senate whether it is not better to postpone the decision of it in this case until to-morrow, above all for the purpose of ascertaining what are the precedents of the House of Lords. Should they prove to be what I think they are, then, unless we are disposed to depart from the model upon which was formed this high tribunal, I am sure the Senate ought to decide—and I have no doubt the honorable member from Ohio will acquiesce cheerfully in that decision, and will himself see the propriety of so acting—that he is not entitled to take his seat as a member of this court. I move, therefore, that the question be postponed until to-morrow.

Mr. DAVIS. Mr. President, I will make a remark on this question before the vote is taken. If the senator from Ohio [Mr. Wade] asks to be excused from taking any part in this trial, it must be upon some principle established by the Constitution. The Vice-President presides in every case of impeachment, except upon the trial of the President, and there he is expressly excluded by a provision of the Constitution—upon what reason? Because of his interest in the question from the fact that if there is a judgment of a motion from office against the President the Vice-President is to succeed to his place. The Constitution thus establishes a principle, and that principle is this: that when the President of the United States, whether he has been elected by the electoral vote or has succeeded to the office by the amotion of the President from office—when a President who actually holds the office is under trial, the man who is to take the place, if he be removed upon that trial by the judgment of the court which is to try him, is disqualified from forming a part of the court. That is the principle. Now, can the senator from Michigan or any other senator adduce any principle that would require the exclusion of the Vice-President from presiding over a court of impeachment of the President of the United States that will not apply to the President *pro tempore* of the Senate when there is no Vice-President, when the President *pro tempore* is presiding officer of the Senate, and when by the Constitution and laws of the United States, if the acting President, as he is sometimes called, is removed, the President *pro tempore* of the Senate is to take his place?

Mr. President, my argument is that the Constitution itself, in relation to this court, has established a principle, and that principle is that any man standing in a position where he is to succeed to the office of the President in the event of his conviction cannot form a part of the court of impeachment that is to try whether the President shall be removed or not. It seems to me clearly that, although the exclusion of the President *pro tempore* of the Senate does not come within the strict letter of the Constitution, it does plainly and unequivocally within its principle and spirit. To every lawyer it is a familiar principle that where a law by its language and express terms does not include a case, but that case comes clearly within its principle and meaning, the law shall be extended by force of its spirit to comprehend the case that it is not strictly within its letter but is clearly and undeniably within its principles.

It seems to me, therefore, clear as a constitutional principle that the President *pro tempore* of the Senate, on the occasion of the impeachment trial, occupies the same position in relation to the office of President that the Vice-President would if he was here and was the presiding officer of the Senate; and the Vice-President being excluded for the reason and upon the principle that he is to take no part in the trial because he is to succeed to the vacant place if there be a judgment of amotion from office, the same principle, clearly, undeniably, in its full force and reason, applies to the President *pro tempore* of the Senate, and therefore he is excluded by the spirit and by the principle of the Constitution.

Mr. MORRILL, of Maine. Mr. Chief Justice, it strikes me that the whole proceeding is premature, for the obvious reason that there is no party here to take the objection. If this is a court there is no party before the court to raise this objection. It certainly does not lie in the mouth of any member of this court, of any senator, to raise the objection of disqualification against any other senator; and, therefore, there is no party here properly to raise the objection against the administration of the oath. Whenever the proper parties appear here on the one side and the other, either for the people or for the respondent, then the court will be in a condition to hear objections to the constitution of the body; then the people will be represented, and may put the inquiry as to the constitution of this court, and then, also, the respondent may institute the same inquiry. It may turn out that we are so constituted that it will be necessary to raise this question and to determine it; but at the present moment it seems to me that there is no option and no discretion but to administer the oath to all those who, by the Constitution, are senators representing the States.

Mr. HENDRICKS. Mr. President, I do not propose at this time to protract the debate; but I wish to reply to the technical point made by the senator from Maine. It is inherent in a court to judge of its own organization; it is a power necessarily possessed by the court itself; and it is not for the suitors to present the question whether a party claiming a seat in a court composed of more than one member is justly and legally entitled to that seat. It is for the court itself to decide whether a member proposing to exercise the right to sit in that court is entitled to that right. Therefore, sir, the question is not prematurely presented.

To the point made by the senator from Michigan, which is not upon the merits, I have just this to reply; that the possibility that the senator now proposing to be sworn may cease to be President of the Senate *pro tempore* is not an answer to the objection. He is now the presiding officer of the Senate, and as such will become the President of the United States if the impeachment be sustained and he continue to be the President *pro tempore* until the termination of the trial. If he ceases, during the progress of the trial, to be the presiding officer of this body, then he becomes competent, and under the second rule which has been adopted, if the rules should be recognized by the court, he will be sworn in as a member of the court. The point I make is, that now being the presiding officer of the Senate, and now being competent to become the President in case impeachment be sustained, he is now incompetent to participate in the trial.

The substantial merits of this question were settled in the case referred to by the senator from Maryland—the case of Senator Stockton, from New Jersey. There the Senate decided that a member of the body could not be a party to a decision in the Senate in which he is interested; and the possibility of holding an office was regarded as an interest by the Senate.

Nor do I think the point made by the senator from Ohio [Mr. Sherman] a good one, that, being a senator from a State, the presiding officer has the right to participate in all the proceedings of the Senate. The standing rules of this body as a Senate contradict that argument. One of the standing rules of the Senate is that a senator shall not vote when he has an interest in the result of the vote; so that the Senate itself has restricted those general rights and powers which the senator from Ohio thinks belongs to each senator as a representative of a State. The Senate has said, by its standing rules, that neither one of us can vote if we have an interest in the result of that vote. But, sir, in my judgment, the constitutional ground is higher than this ground of interest. The presiding officer has an interest in the result of an impeachment trial; he shall not even preside; he shall not even maintain order and decorum in the body during the progress of the trial; he shall vacate his seat that the Chief Justice may preside; and what does that mean? It means something, sir. It means that the relation which the Vice-President of the United States sustains by possibility to the office of President of the United States is such that he shall take no part in the great trial. That is what the Constitution means. It is not a matter of form and ceremony and dignity that the Chief Justice shall preside here. It is of the very substance that he who, by possibility, can fill the office if the Senate shall make it vacant, shall not sit here even to preserve order and decorum while the great proceeding is going on.

I hope, sir that I need not disclaim any personal feeling in this matter. I make the point now because I think that the Constitution itself controls the organization of this court. I think that the Constitution itself does settle it, that no man shall help to take from the President his office when that man is to fill the office if the proceeding succeed. There is no analogy between this and the case suggested by the senator from Michigan. Affinity does not of itself by common and universal law exclude a man from presiding in court; it must be done by express statute, and it is so provided in the codes of the different States. But here the Constitution itself says that no man shall preside who may succeed to the office. I hope, sir, in view of the importance of this question, that the motion made by the senator from Maryland, to postpone its consideration until to-morrow, will prevail.

Mr. WILLIAMS. Mr. Chief Justice, I submit that the motion or question made by the senator from Indiana is altogether premature, for this reason: it is either addressed to the Senate of the United States or to the court for the trial of an impeachment. If it be to the Senate, then I respectfully submit that the presiding officer of the Senate should occupy the chair; if to a court, then there is no court organized competent to pass or decide upon this question. Some of the members here have been sworn, others have not. Am I to be called upon to decide on this question which, perhaps, relates to the merits of the case to be determined, without having had an oath administered to me like other members? Is this question to be decided at this time? Is there any court organized that can decide this question? I do not know exactly what the question is. Is it a challenge that has been submitted by a senator to a fellow-senator? If that be so it is an extraordinary proceeding. I never heard that one juror could challenge another juror; I never heard that one judge could challenge another judge. When the necessary preparations are made for the trial, it may be that the managers on the part of the House of Representatives and the accused will be willing and desire to have the senator from Ohio participate in this trial. Is it not their privilege? Suppose they both agree to that and to waive all objections? Then I am confident that they have the right to make this question, and not any senator.

The senator from Indiana suggests that no judge who is interested in a question was ever known to preside when that question was considered. Is not that altogether a matter left to the judge? Did the honorable senator ever know a court to adopt a rule and declare that a member of that court should not participate in any decision? Whenever a question is presented to a court, the judge decides for himself as to whether or not it is a case in which he can take any part? If he decides that he cannot participate in the trial, he withdraws from the bench; but the court never undertakes to prescribe the rule for his action, to say that he shall or shall not participate in the decision. But I do not propose to discuss the question. I make this point, however, that at this time this body, with a part of the members sworn and a part unsworn, cannot decide the question, because it is a question that relates to the rights of the country and of the accused; and before I am called upon to pass upon this question, it is necessary, it seems to me, that I should be sworn as well as the other members who have not been called upon to take the oath.

Mr. DAVIS. Will the honorable senator answer me a question?

Mr. WILLIAMS. Certainly.

Mr. DAVIS. Suppose this was a trial of articles of impeachment against the President of the United States when there was a Vice-President in being, and suppose that Vice-President was to present himself here and offer to become a part of the court, could not the senators exclude him from that position?

Mr. WILLIAMS. Mr. Chief Justice, I do not propose to argue that question; but the case propounded by the senator is not parallel to the case before this body, because the Constitution expressly excludes the Vice-President from any participation in this trial, but it provides that each senator shall vote.

Mr. DAVIS. The honorable senator suggested that it rested with the senator himself whether he should form part of the court or not, and that the residue of the body could not make the exception. I presented that example for the purpose of showing that under that state of case the body of the court itself would exclude the Vice-President, though he even offered to become a component part of the court.

Mr. WILLIAMS. What I said was simply in response to the suggestion of the senator from Indiana, that the senator from Ohio could not participate in these proceedings because a judge who was interested in a case could not participate in the hearing of it. I say it is always in every case left for the judge to decide for himself as to whether he will or will not participate in the trial, and the court itself does not undertake to exclude him.

It does not follow, as it strikes me, because this court is organized as the Constitution requires, each senator taking an oath, that every senator will necessarily participate in the trial and vote upon the questions involved. He may take the oath; he is required to take the oath; and then, after he is qualified to act, it will be for him to determine whether or not he will participate in the trial, and not for the senator to say now before the court is organized that he shall not be allowed to take the oath. He is a senator, and the Constitution says that each State shall have two senators, and that each senator shall have one vote. The Constitution gives to each senator a right to vote upon every question in the Senate. That is a constitutional right; but if he is interested in any way, then he may not participate in the decision if he sees proper.

Mr. JOHNSON. What becomes of our rule on that point?

Mr. WILLIAMS. That rule is not one that can override the Constitution; and if any senator, notwithstanding that rule, upon any question should insist upon his right to vote, I maintain that he can vote notwithstanding the rule, because the Constitution says that every senator shall have a right to vote upon every question. It may be indelicate and improper for a senator to vote upon many questions; but as I said I did not intend to argue that question and was drawn off from the point which I intended to make, which is, that at this time it is not competent for this body to decide as to whether or not the senator from Ohio can take the oath.

Mr. FESSENDEN. Mr. President, I do not design to discuss the matter. I merely rise to make the suggestion which would follow from what has been said by the senator from Oregon, that it would be better to organize the court fully before deciding the question, if we are to decide it at all. There is no difficulty in postponing the administration of the oath to the honorable senator from Ohio until all have been sworn except him, and then the court will be properly organized so far as to enable all gentlemen to act as members of the court. I would suggest, therefore, that the administration of the oath to the honorable senator from Ohio be merely passed over until it has been administered to other gentlemen whose names come after his upon the list, and then the question can be decided.

Mr. CONNESS. My only objection to the proposition now made is that in my judgment the Senate have no such right. They have no right to pass directly or indirectly, in my opinion, any reflection upon the right of any senator to participate in the proceedings that are taking place. The question as it seems to me is settled. It was settled when the credentials of the senator were presented, and he was admitted to his seat. It is not competent for the Senate, in my opinion, to attempt to deprive a senator of his vote; and, so far as the suggestion or proposition casts doubt upon the question, it does not meet the approbation of my judgment. I prefer very much that a vote shall now be taken, not upon the direct question, as suggested by the senator from Indiana, but that it take the form of a motion. I think the question whether a senator has an interest in these proceedings such as would prevent him from voting and acting as such pending the trial is a question for himself alone, and that no other senator nor the Senate combined can impose any restriction upon his legitimate participation in these great proceedings.

Mr. FESSENDEN. I desire simply to say that, in making the suggestion, I did not mean to be understood as expressing the slightest opinion in any way, but to avoid the difficulty suggested by the honorable senator from Oregon. He says he is not yet a member of the court; he has not been sworn. If we are to take a vote upon this question directly, are we all to vote or not? Certainly the larger number have been sworn, but some have not been sworn. There is nothing in the shape of reflection or even the intimation of an opinion, one way or the other, in simply suggesting that it would be well to have all those who are to vote upon the question sworn, inasmuch as part have been sworn, before the vote is taken. That is all; and I see no difficulty such as has been suggested by the honorable senator from California. The honorable senator from Ohio can be presented again; there is nothing in any rule that requires the oath to be taken alphabetically as the names are called; that is a mere matter of convenience. Certain gentlemen are absent now from their seats; they will be allowed unquestionably to take the oath when they come in. My suggestion went to that extent and no further, that we who are to act upon the question, if we are to act at all, should be placed upon a level before we proceed to act, and that the court should be duly organized as a court, which it is not yet. If the suggestion is not agreeable to gentlemen, it makes not the slightest difference to me; I care nothing about it one way or the other. I have no opinion to express at present upon the subject.

Mr. HOWARD. Mr. President, we are now sitting in a judicial capacity for the trial of a particular impeachment. We are organizing ourselves for the purpose of proceeding to consider the facts of the case; but this must be regarded, I think, as a part of the trial. Otherwise, Mr. President, we should not expect to see you presiding over us. Now, sir, the Constitution declares that "each senator shall have one vote;" and it further declares that "no person shall be convicted without the concurrence of two-thirds of the members present." There may be absentees—no matter how many—so be that a quorum of the body remains present and voting.

The honorable senator from Ohio is present, not absent. He is now ready to take the oath prescribed by the Constitution, to participate in the trial like the rest of us. I do not understand upon what ground it is at this stage of the proceeding that an objection can be sustained to his taking the oath. Certainly it will not be claimed that we are now acting in our ordinary capacity as a Senate; but we are acting in a judicial capacity as a Senate; or, in other words, if you please, for brevity's sake, as a court, What right, I beg to inquire, have the members of the Senate, who do not yet under the Constitution constitute a part of the court, to say that a particular member of their body shall not take the oath prescribed by the Constitution? How are we to get at it? Who are the persons authorized to vote on this objection which is raised, and declare that the senator from Ohio shall not take the oath? Is it right of the court, or, to speak more accurately, of the comparatively few members of the court who have by their oath become such, to exclude a senator? That is a very strange view to take of the question. Of what interest is it to us, let me inquire, even if we were organized as a court, that the senator from Ohio should not take the oath prescribed by the Constitution? If there be an interest anywhere, that interest is only available on the part of the accused, who is not yet before us. He can avail himself of it only in the nature of a challenge for cause, which I do not now propose to discuss; at the same time, however, denying the right of any such challenge. But, as the Senate are now situated, it is entirely clear to my mind that we have no right whatever to pass a resolution or order prohibiting the honorable senator from Ohio, or any other senator, if he sees fit, from taking the oath prescribed by the Constitution, and which we are now in the act of taking. It is an act *coram non judice*, without jurisdiction or color on our part to perform.

I would suggest, therefore, that this objection should, for the present, be withdrawn. The honorable senator from Indiana must of course see that at the proper time, after a proper organization, all he seeks to obtain now by his objection will be raised by learned counsel upon the trial, fully discussed by them, and considered and decided by ourselves sitting in our judicial capacity.

Mr. MORTON. Mr. President, if it should now be determined that the senator from Ohio shall not be sworn it would be an error, a blunder of which the accused would have just right to complain when he should come here. If a judge is interested in a case before him, or if a juror is interested in the result of the issue which he is called upon to try, it is an objection that the parties to the case have the right to waive; and they have always had that right under any system of practice that I have known anything about.

As was suggested by the senator from Maine [Mr. Morrill] and the senator from Oregon, [Mr. Williams,] it is not an objection to be made by a fellow-juror, by another member of the court, or by anybody except the parties to the case; and if we now, in the absence of the accused, say that the senator from Ohio shall not be sworn, the President, when he comes here to stand his trial, will have a right to say, "A senator has been excluded that I would willingly accept; I have confidence in his integrity; I have confidence in his character and in his judgment, and I am willing to waive the question of interest. Who had the right to make it in my absence?" The senator from Indiana, my colleague, and the senator from Kentucky have no right to make the question unless they should do it in the character of counsel for the accused, a character they do not maintain.

Mr. President, I desire to say one thing further, that this objection made here, in my judgment, proceeds upon a wrong theory. It is that we are now about putting off the character of the Senate of the United States and taking upon ourselves a new character; that we are about ceasing to be a Senate to become a court. Sir, I reject that idea entirely. This is the Senate when sworn; this will be the Senate when sitting upon the trial, and can have no other character. The idea that we are to become a court, invested with a new character, and possibly having new constituents, I reject as being in violation of the Constitution itself. What does that say? It says that "the Senate shall have the sole power to try all impeachments. The Senate shall have the sole power to try; it is the Senate that is to try, not a high court of impeachment—a phrase that is sometimes used—that is to be organized, to be created by the process through which we are now going; but, sir, it is simply the Senate of the United States. The Senate, "when sitting for that purpose, shall be on oath or affirmation." That does not change our character. We do not on account of this oath or affirmation cease to be a Senate, undergo a transformation, and become a high court of impeachment; but the Constitution simply provides that the Senate while, as a Senate, trying this case, shall be under oath or affirmation. It is an exceptional obligation. The duty of trying an impeachment is an exceptional duty, just as is the ratification of a treaty; but it is still simply the Senate performing that duty. "When the President of the United States is tried the Chief Justice shall preside." Preside where? In some high court of impeachment, to be created by the transformation of an oath? No, sir. He is to preside in the Senate of the United States, and over the Senate; and that is all there is of it. "And no person shall be convicted without the concurrence of two-thirds of the members present." Two-thirds of the members of the Senate.

Mr. President, if I am right in this view, it settles the whole question. The senator from Ohio is a member of the Senate. My colleague has argued this question as if we were about now to organize a new body, a court, and that the senator from Ohio is not competent to become a member of that court. That is his theory. The theory is false. This impeachment is to be tried by the Senate, and he is already a member of the Senate, and he has a constitutional right to sit here, and we have no power to take it from him. As to how far he shall participate, as to what part he shall take in our proceedings, as has been correctly said, that is a question for him to decide in his own mind. But, sir, he is already a member of this body; he is here; he has his rights already conferred upon him as a member of this body, and he has a constitutional right to take part in the performance of this business as of any other business, whether the ratification of a treaty, or the confirmation of an appointment, or the passage of a bill, which may be devolved on this body by the Constitution of the United States. Because he has been elected President *pro tempore* of the Senate, does that take from him any of his rights as a senator? Those rights existed before, and he cannot be robbed of them by any act of this Senate.

But, sir, aside from this question, which goes to the main argument, this entire action is premature. There is nobody here to make this challenge, even if it could be made legitimately. The senators making it do not represent anybody but themselves. The accused might not want it made. He might, perhaps, prefer the senator from Ohio to any other member of this body to try his case. It is always the right of the defendant in a criminal proceeding and of the parties in a civil action to waive the interest that a juror or a member of the court may have in the case.

Mr. JOHNSON. Mr. President, the motion that I made to postpone the question now before the Senate till to-morrow was made with no view to impede at all the organization of the court, so far as it can be organized by swearing all the other members; and I withdraw the motion now and put it in another form, namely, that the question lie on the table until the other members are sworn.

While I am up permit me to say a few words in reply to the honorable member from Indiana, [Mr. Morton.] He tells us it is for the President of the United States—applying his remarks to the case which is to be and is before us—himself to make the objection, and that he may waive it. With all due deference to the honorable member, that is an entire misapprehension of the question. The question involved in the inquiry is what is the court to try the President? It is not to be such a tribunal as he chooses to try him. It is a question in which the people of the United States are interested, in which the country is interested; and by no conduct of the President, by no waiver of his can he coustitute this court in any other way than the way in which the Constitution contemplates; that is to say, a court having all the qualities which the Constitution intends.

The honorable member tells us that we are still a Senate and not a court, and that we cannot be anything but a Senate and cannot at any time become a court. Why, sir, the honorable member is not treading in the footsteps of his fathers. The Constitution was adopted in 1789. There have been four or five cases of impeachment, and in every case the Senate has decided to resolve itself into a court, and the proceedings have been conducted before it as a court and not as a Senate. To be sure, these component elements of which the court is composed are senators, but that is a mere *descriptio personarum.* They are members of the court because they are senators, but not the less members of a court. The Constitution contemplated their assuming both capacities. As a Senate of the United States they have no judicial authority whatever; their powers are altogether legislative; they are to constitute and do constitute only a portion of the legislative department of the government; but the Constitution for wise purposes says that in the contingency of an impeachment of a President of the United States or any other officer falling within the clause authorizing an impeachment they are to become, as I understand, a court. So have all our predecessors ruled in every case; and who were they? In the celebrated case of the impeachment against Mr. Chase, who was one of the associate justices of the Supreme Court of the United States, there were men in the Senate at that time whose superiors have not been found since, nor at any time before, and they adopted the idea and acted upon the idea that the Senate in the trial of that impeachment acted as a court and not as a Senate.

I submit, therefore, that the honorable member from Indiana [Mr. Morton] is altogether mistaken in supposing that we are not a court. But look at the power which we are to have. We are to pronounce judgment of guilty or not guilty; we are to answer upon our oaths whether the party impeached is guilty or not guilty of the articles of impeachment laid to his charge, and having pronounced him guilty or not guilty, we are then to award judgment. Who ever heard of the Senate of the United States in its legislative capacity awarding a judgment?

But besides that, why is it, Mr. Chief Justice, that you are called to preside over the court, or the Senate when acting as a court to try an impeachment? It is because it is a court. You have no legislative capacity; your functions are to construe the laws in cases coming before you; and the very fact that upon the trial of an impeachment of the President of the United States the Vice-President is to be laid aside, and the ordinary presiding officer, if the Vice-President himself does not exist, and you are to preside, shows that it is a court of the highest character, demanding the wisdom and the learning of the Chief Justice of the United States.

The honorable member says, and other members have said, that a question of interest or no interest is not involved in an inquiry of this description. Does the honorable member mean to say that if the honorable member from Ohio had a bill before the Senate awarding to him a sum of money upon the ground that it was due to him by the United States he could vote upon the question of the passage of the bill? Why not if the honorable member from Indiana is right? He is a senator. If he is right that the Constitution intends that each State shall have two votes upon every question coming before the body, then in the case supposed the honorable member from Ohio would have a right to vote himself, and by his own vote to place money in his own possession. Who ever heard that that was a right that could be accorded anywhere?

Mr. President, courts have gone so far as to say that a judgment pronounced by a judge in a court of which he was the constitutional officer in a case in which he had a direct interest, was absolutely void upon general principles; not void because of any statutory regulation on this subject, but void upon the general ground that no man shall be a judge in his own case. Does it make any difference what may be the character of the interest? If the honorable member from Ohio was the sole party under the Constitution to try this impeachment, could he try it? Would not everybody say it is a *casus omissus*? There can be no trial as long as he continues to be the sole member of the court, because he has a direct and immediate interest in the result; because the judgment would be absolutely void as against the general principle founded in the nature of man, that no man should be permitted to adjudge a question in which he has a direct interest.

I propose to say nothing more. I will suspend the motion I before made, and move now that the question of right of the honorable member from Ohio be laid aside until the other members of the Senate are qualified.

Mr. SHERMAN. Mr. President, I certainly do not appear here to represent my colleague on this question; but I represent the State of Ohio, which is entitled to two senators on this floor. The Constitution declares that each senator shall have a vote, and the Constitution further declares that each senator shall take an oath in cases of impeachment. The right of my colleague to take the oath, his duty to take it, is as clear in my mind as any question that ever was presented to me as a senator of the United States. The Constitution makes it plainly his duty to take the oath. He is a senator, bound to take the oath, according to my reading of the Constitution; and every precedent that has been cited, and every precedent that has been referred to, bears out this construction. If after he has taken the oath as a member of the Senate of the United States, for the purposes of this trial, anybody objects to his right to vote on any question that may be presented to this court or to the Senate hereafter, the objection can then be made and discussed; but his right in the preliminary stages to take the oath, and his duty to take it, is made plain by the Constitution itself. If, hereafter, when the impeachment progresses, his right to vote on any question is challenged, the question may be discussed and decided.

The case cited by my honorable friend from Maryland is directly in point. Mr. Stockton came here with a certificate from the State of New Jersey in due form; he presented it, and was sworn into office. Did anybody object to his being sworn? At the same time other papers were presented to the Senate challenging his right to be sworn, saying that the legislature of New Jersey had never elected Mr. Stockton; but because of that did anybody object to the oath being administered to Mr. Stockton? No one; although his right to take the oath was challenged, and a protest, signed by a very large number of the members of the New Jersey legislature, against his right to the seat, was presented. He was sworn in and took his seat here by our side, and voted and exercised the rights of a senator. When the question of the legality of his own election came up the Senate decided that he was not legally elected, and the question referred to arose upon his right to vote in that particular case. The question was whether he could vote, being interested in the subject-matter. The senator from Massachusetts made the objection, and offered a resolution that he had not a right to vote in the particular case; and after debate that was decided in the affirmative, although by a very close vote. My own conviction then was, and is yet, that Mr. Stockton as a senator from the State of New Jersey had a right to vote in his own case, although it might not be a proper exercise of the right.

So, sir, this question has been decided two or three times in the House of Representatives. In the celebrated New Jersey case, where a certificate of election was presented by certain members from the State of New Jersey and they were excluded, public history has pronounced their exclusion to have been an unjustifiable wrong upon the great seal of the State of New Jersey. I believe that action is now generally admitted and conceded to have been wrong. Those men presented their credentials in the regular form, and they had the right to be sworn. So in many other cases, where the right of persons to hold office is in dispute, those who have the *prima facie* right are sworn into office, and then the right is examined and finally settled. I had a matter presented to me once in which I was personally interested, and where I was sworn into office. I was directly and personally interested; but I took the oath of office, and I discharged my duties as a member of the House of Representatives; and when the question came up whether I should vote on the election of a particular officer, I being a candidate for the office, I refused to vote. But it was my refusal which prevented my vote from being received. If I had chosen to vote, I had the right as a member from the State of Ohio, even for myself. I have no doubt whatever of that. It is the right of the State; it is the right of the people; it is the right of representation. The power of the State and the power of the people must be exercised through their senators and through their representatives.

In the particular case here I do not suppose, I do not know, at least, whether the question will ever arise. My colleague is required to take this oath as a member of the Senate of the United States. You have no right to assume, nor have senators the right to assume, that he will vote on questions which may affect his interest. That is a matter for him to decide; but the right of the State to be represented here on this trial of an impeachment is clear enough. Whether he will exercise the right, or whether he will waive it, is for him to determine. You have no right to assume that he will exercise the right or power to vote for himself where he is directly interested in the result.

It seems to me, therefore, that no senator here has the right to challenge the voice of the State of Ohio, and the right of the State of Ohio to have two votes here is unquestionable, unless when the question is raised in due form it shall be decided against my colleague. In the preliminary stages, when we are organizing this court, he ought to be sworn, and then if he is to be excluded by interest, unfitness, or any other reason, the question may be determined when raised hereafter; but no senator has the right now to challenge his authority to appear here and be sworn as a senator from Ohio. His exclusion must come either by his own voluntary act, proceeding on what he deems to be just and right according to general principles, or it must be by the act of the Senate upon an objection made by the person accused in the trial of the impeachment. It seems to me that is clear, and therefore I object to any waiver of the matter. I think my colleague has a right to present himself and be sworn precisely as I and other senators have been sworn. Then let him decide for himself whether in a case in which his interest is so deeply affected he will vote on any question involved in the impeachment. If he decides to vote when his vote is presented, then, not the senator from Indiana, but the accused may make the objection, and we shall decide the question as a Senate or as a court, for I consider the terms convertible; we shall then decide the question of his right to vote.

Sir, several things have been introduced into this debate that I think ought not to have been introduced. The precise character of this tribunal, whether it is a court or a Senate, has nothing to do at present with this question. The only question before us is whether Benjamin F. Wade, acknowledged to be a senator from the State of Ohio, has a right to present himself and take the oath prescribed by the Constitution and the laws in cases of impeachment. He is not the Vice-President; he is not excluded by the terms of the Constitution. He is the presiding officer of the Senate, holding that office at our will. You have no right to take away from him the power to take the oath of office and then to decide for himself as to whether, under all the circumstances, he ought to participate in this trial.

Mr. BAYARD. Mr. President, I incline to the opinion that the objection made by the honorable senator from Maine [Mr. Morrill] to the motion of the honorable senator from Indiana, [Mr. Hendricks,] and also that made by the honorable senator from Oregon, [Mr. Williams,] is correct. I cannot see how a senator is to object to another senator being sworn in, although I think there may be some doubt raised on the question for this reason: the Constitution provides that in a case where the President of the United States is tried under an impeachment the Chief Justice of the United States, not the Vice-President, shall preside; and though that was intended originally to look to the Vice-President alone, yet if another person, from the death of the Vice-President, or from his absence or his acting as President, stands in precisely the same relation to the office of President under the law and the Constitution, whether he be a senator or not, ought not the principle equally to apply?

It certainly excludes the Vice-President from being a member of the court. Does it not equally exclude the presiding officer of the Senate? It does not make him, being a senator, less a senator of the United States in his legislative capacity; but the clause of the Constitution prevents and is intended to prevent the influence of the man who would profit as the necessary result of the judgment of guilty in the case. It supposes that he cannot be or may not be sufficiently impartial to sit as a judge in that case, or to preside in the court trying it. That is the object, as I suppose.

But, sir, there is great force in the objection that that point must come by plea or motion, if you please, from the party accused; and I should not have thought for a moment of embarking in this discussion had it not been for the renewal by the honorable senator from Indiana [Mr. Morton] of the endeavor to disprove the idea that the Senate must be organized into a court for the purpose of a judicial trial. Now, sir, whether it is to be a high court of impeachment or a court of impeachment, or to be called by the technical name court, is, in my judgment, immaterial; but the honorable senator's argument did not touch the Constitution. The Senate is to constitute the court; the Senate is to try. Is there nothing in the provisions of that article which gives the judicial authority—for it is not legislative, it is judicial authority conferred, a judicial authority in special cases—is there nothing in that article which, of necessity, makes the body a judicial tribunal whenever it assumes these functions, and not a legislative body? Otherwise, how comes the presiding officer who now fills the chair to be in the seat which he occupies? When the Constitution says that the Senate shall have the sole authority to try impeachments is it necessary that it should say that the Senate shall be a court for the purpose of trying impeachments if every clause of the Constitution shows that it must be a judicial tribunal and must be a court, or else the language is meaningless which is applied to its organization? The members of the body are to be sworn specially in the particular case as between the accused and the impeachers. Is not that the action of a court? They are to try an individual in a criminal prosecution. Is not that judicial action? Is not the entire judicial power of the United States vested in the Supreme Court and the inferior courts, with that exception, by the very terms of the Constitution?

But, further, the body is to give judgment, to pronounce judgment, a judgment of removal from office always as the result of conviction; and if they please to carry it still further, they may pronounce judgment of disqualification from hereafter holding any office. Do not these terms of necessity constitute a court? Did the Constitution mean, taking all its language, that the Senate in its legislative capacity, or as a Senate of the United States without any change whatever, should participate in the judicial power of the government; or did it mean to give judicial power? And if it gave judicial power, and prescribed the mode of its exercise in such a manner that it necessarily converted it into a court, why should it not be called a court?

But, sir, the precedents are conclusive. I cited the case of Blount on a former occasion in the Senate. He was impeached in 1798, nine years after the Constitution went into operation. Many of the members of the Senate at that time had been members of the convention which formed the Constitution, and all of them were conversant with its history and meaning. It was the first case of impeachment, and yet in that case there is conclusive evidence that no one interposed the idea that the body was not organized into a court, a judicial tribunal, and accordingly the defendant appeared—he had been expelled by the Senate under their other powers—and he pleaded to the articles of impeachment, and the case was argued at length on both sides, and the Senate determined to dismiss the articles, and in announcing their decision to the House of Representatives the presiding officer of the Senate said in terms "the court after consideration have adjudged" or "determined"—I forget the exact language; but it spoke of the court. This was the communication of the presiding officer of the Senate in the presence of the Senate, to the managers of the impeachment, that the court had determined to dismiss the articles, and the defendant was discharged. Is the precedent of no worth? Does the honorable senator from Indiana say that the men of that day, the Hillhouses and Tracys, and other men who then constituted the Senate, did not understand the language in which the Constitution was adopted as well as we do now? They were able lawyers. The case was one perfectly free from the bias of political excitement of every kind. And from that day to this, until this idea is now suggested that you are to try as a Senate, and not as a judicial tribunal, the President of the United States on an impeachment for high crimes, no one has ever doubted that the Senate must be resolved into a court for the purpose of performing such functions.

Sir, it is against this, which I consider a heresy, that I desire to protest. For my own part I cannot conceive on what ground such an idea should be thrown into this case, or what effect it can have, unless it be to let loose partisan passion by escaping from judicial responsibility. No one doubts that the court is to be composed of the Senate of the United States. Why it should not be called a court, in the face of the precedents, the face of the provisions of the Constitution, all of which confer on it judicial power and the modes of action which belong to a court, is to me inscrutable.

The question is collateral, I admit, because I think this is not the time to object to the honorable senator from Ohio being sworn in. My mind is somewhat in doubt; but my opinion inclines that way, that the objection must come from the party arraigned, unless, indeed, the honorable senator, looking to the particular circumstances of the case, should ask to be excused from being sworn. That is a question which is not for me to decide; but it is for him to decide to that extent, I admit. But, sir, I cannot admit the doctrine I have heard enunciated here, that the great, eternal principle, that no man shall be a judge in his own cause, does not apply to this case whenever the question is properly raised. What is the state of facts? The Senate of the United States is constituted into a judicial tribunal; that cannot be denied. They have the powers not only of judges, but of jurors; and if there be one principle more sacred than another it is as to the juror, who finds facts that he must be *omni exceptione major*. The great, general principle that a man shall not be a judge in his own cause applies everywhere, and commends itself to the universal sentiment of mankind. Now, what is the case here? The Senate are the judges of the facts, as well as of the law, when organized into a court for the trial of an impeachment. If the case was presented of the trial of the most ordinary misdemeanor in a court of justice by an unquestionably qualified juror in all other respects, if it was shown that that juror had a direct interest in the conviction or the acquittal of the defendant, would it not be a sufficient objection? Can there be any doubt about the directness of the interest here? Your judgment, if the accused is convicted, must be removal from office. It must go that far. The effect, then, of a judgment rendered by this court, were it rendered by the aid of the honorable senator from Ohio sitting as a judge, would be to elevate him to the position of the executive head of this great nation. Is not that an interest?

It is the necessary result of such a judgment when it is rendered that he has a right to the office, and is entitled to the office. Whether he choose to relinquish it or not would not alter the case. The interest is direct; and if there ever was a case in which the principle that a man shall not be a judge in his own cause applied, it surely must apply to the case where the members of the tribunal which is organized are judges, not only of the law, but also of the facts. Human nature is not to be trusted that far; that is the foundation of the principle, and no man who knows his own heart, no man who knows how delusive and how deceptive are the illusions of humanity, could for a moment tolerate any other principle. It has universally obtained as a great general truth.

I trust, sir, that whenever the case comes properly before us there can be no question as to what must be the decision of the Senate. As I said before, I hope, however, that we shall be relieved from the necessity of any decision in a case like this, as we can be relieved by the action of the honorable senator from Ohio. He must, of course, decide that question for himself in the first instance; but, for my own part, I can only say that if I stood in the same position the wealth of worlds could not tempt me for an instant to think of sitting as a judge in a case where my interests were so directly personally involved.

Mr. SUMNER. Mr. President, I shall not attempt to follow learned senators in the question whether this is a senate or a court. That question, to my mind, is simply one of language and not of substance. Our powers at this moment are under the Constitution of the United States; nor can we add to them a tittle by calling ourselves a court or calling ourselves a senate. There they are in the Constitution. Search its text and you will find them. The Constitution has not given us a name, but it has given us powers; and those we are now to exercise. The Senate has the sole power to try impeachments. No matter for the name, sir. I hope that I do not use an illustration too familiar when I remind you that a rose under any other name has all those qualities which make it the first of flowers.

I should not at this time have entered into this discussion if I had not listened to objections on the other side which seem to me founded, I will not say in error, for that would be bold when we are discussing a question of so much novelty, but I will say founded in a reading of history which I have not been able to verify. Senator after senator on the other side, all distinguished by ability and learning, have informed us that the Constitution intended to prevent a person who might become President from presiding at the trial of the President. I would ask learned senators who have announced this proposition where they find it in the Constitution? The Constitution says:

When the President of the United States is tried the Chief Justice shall preside.

This is all; and yet on this simple text the superstructure of senators has been reared.

The Constitution does not proceed to say why the Chief Justice shall preside; not at all; nothing of the kind. Senators supply the reason and then undertake to apply it to the actual President of the Senate. Where, sir, do they find the reason? They cannot find the reason which they now assign in any of the contemporary authorities illustrating the Constitution. They cannot find it in the debates of the national convention reported by Madison, or in any of the debates in the States at that time, nor can they find it in the Federalist. When does that reason first come on the scene? Others may be more fortunate than I, but I have not been able to find it earlier than 1825, nearly 40 years after the formation of the Constitution, in the commentaries of William Rawle. We all know the character of this work, one of great respectability, and which most of us in our early days have read and studied. How does he speak of it? As follows:

The Vice-President, being the President of the Senate, presides on the trial, except when the President of the United States is tried. As the Vice-President succeeds to the functions and emoluments of the President of the United States whenever a vacancy happens in the latter office, it would be inconsistent with the implied purity of a judge that a person under a probable bias of such a nature should participate in the trial, and it would follow that he ought wholly to retire from the court.

Those are the words of a commentator on the Constitution. They next appear ten years later in the commentaries of Mr. Justice Story, as follows. After citing the provision "when the President of the United States is tried the Chief Justice shall preside," the learned commentator proceeds:

The reason of this clause has been already adverted to. It was to preclude the Vice-President, who might be supposed to have a natural desire to succeed to the office, from being instrumental in procuring the conviction of the Chief Magistrate.

And he cites in his note, "Rawle on the Constitution, page 216," being the very words that I have already read. Here is the first appearance of this reason which is now made to play so important a part, being treated even as a text of the Constitution itself. At least I have not been able to meet it at an earlier day.

If you repair to the contemporary authorities, including the original debates, you will find no such reason assigned—nothing like it; not even any suggestion of it. On the contrary, you will find Mr. Madison, in the Virginia convention, making a statement which explains in the most satisfactory manner the requirement of the Constitution. No better authority could be cited. Any reason supplied by him anterior to the adoption of the Constitution must be of more weight than any *ex post facto* imagination or invention of learned commentators.

If we trust to the lights of history, the reason for the introduction of this clause in the Constitution was because the framers of the Constitution contemplated the possibility of the suspension of the President from the exercise of his powers, in which event the Vice-President could not be in your chair, sir. If the President were suspended the Vice-President would be in his place. The reports will verify what I say. If you refer to the debates of the national convention under the date of Friday, September 14, 1787, you will find the following entry, which I read now by way of introduction to what follows at a later date, on the authority of Mr. Madison himself:

Mr. Rutledge and Mr. Gouverneur Morris moved that persons impeached be suspended from their offices until they be tried and acquitted.

Mr. MADISON. The President is made too dependent already on the legislature by the power of one branch to try him in consequence of an impeachment by the other. This intermediate suspension will put him in the power of one branch only. They can at any moment, in order to make way for the functions of another who will be more favorable to their views, vote a temporary removal of the existing magistrate.

Mr. King concurred in the opposition to the amendment.

The proposition was rejected by the decisive vote—eight States in the negative to three in the affirmative. We all see in reading it now that it was rejected on good grounds. It would obviously be improper to confer upon the other branch of Congress the power, by its own vote, to bring about a suspension of the Chief Magistrate. But it did not follow, because the convention rejected the proposition, that a suspension could take place on a simple vote of the House of Representatives—that, therefore, the President could not be suspended. When the Senate was declared to have the sole power to try impeachments, it was by necessary implication invested with the power incident to every court, and known historically to belong to the English court of impeachment, from which ours was borrowed, of suspending the party accused. All this was apparent at the time, if possible, more clearly than now. It was so clear that it furnishes an all-sufficient reason for the provision that the Chief Justice should preside on the trial of the President, without resorting to the later reason which has been put forward in this debate.

But we are not driven to speculate on this question. While the Constitution was under discussion in the Virginia convention, George Mason objected to some of the powers conferred upon the President, especially the pardoning power.

This was on June 18, 1788, and will be found under that date in the reports of the Virginia convention. This earnest opponent of the Constitution said that the President might "pardon crimes which were advised by himself," and thus further his own ambitious schemes. This brought forward Mr. Madison, who had sat, as we all know, throughout the debates of the national convention and had recorded its proceedings, and who, of all persons, was the most competent to testify at that time as to the intention of the framers. What said this eminent authority? I give you his words:

There is one security in this case to which gentlemen may not have adverted. If the President be connected in any suspicious manner with any person, and there be grounds to believe he will shelter him, the House of Representatives can impeach him; they—

Evidently referring to the Senate, or the Senate in connection with the House—

can remove him if found guilty; *they can suspend him when suspected*, and the power will devolve upon the Vice-President.

Mark well these words: "they can suspend him when suspected." If only suspected the President can be suspended. What next? "And his power will devolve upon the Vice-President;" in which event, of course, the Vice-President would be occupied elsewhere than in this chamber.

Those were the words of James Madison, spoken in debate in the Virginia convention. Taken in connection with the earlier passage in the national convention, they seem to leave little doubt with regard to the intention of the framers of the Constitution. They were unwilling to give to the other House alone the power of suspension, but they saw that when they authorized the Senate to try impeachments they gave to it the power of suspension if it should choose to exercise it; and the suspension of the President necessarily involved the withdrawal of the Vice-President from this chamber, and the duty of supplying his place.

I submit, then, on the contemporary testimony, that the special reason why the Chief Justice is called to preside when the President is on trial is less what learned senators have assigned than because the Vice-President under certain circumstances would not be able to be present. It was to provide for such a contingency, being nothing less than his necessary absence in the discharge of the high duties of Chief Magistrate, that a substitute was necessary, and he was found in the Chief Justice. All this was reasonable. It would have been unreasonable not to make such a provision.

But this is not all. There is an incident immediately after the adoption of the Constitution which is in harmony with this authentic history. The House of Representatives at an early day acted on the interpretation of the Constitution given by Mr. Madison. The first impeachment, as we all know, was of William Blount, a senator, and in impeaching him the House of Representatives demanded "that he should be sequestered from his seat in the Senate." This was in 1797. The Senate did not comply with this demand; but the demand nevertheless exists in the history of your government, and it illustrates the interpretation which was given at that time to the powers of the Senate. The language employed, that the person impeached should be "sequestered," is the traditional language of the British constitution, constantly used, and familiar to our fathers. In employing it, the House of Representatives gave their early testimony that the Senate could suspend from his functions any person impeached before them; and thus the House of Representatives unite with Madison in supplying a sufficient reason for the provision that on the trial of the President the Chief Justice shall preside.

In abandoning the reason which I have thus traced to contemporary authority you launch upon an uncertain sea. You may think the reason assigned by the commentators to be satisfactory. It may please your taste, but it cannot be accepted as an authentic statement. If the original propositions were before me I should listen to any such suggestion with the greatest respect. I do not mean to say now that, as a general rule, it has not much in its favor. But I insist that so far as we are informed the reason of the commentators was an afterthought, and that there was another reason which sufficiently explains the rule now under consideration.

I respectfully submit, sir, that you cannot proceed in the interpretation of this text upon the theory adopted by the learned senators over the way. You must take the text as it is; you cannot go behind it; you cannot extend it. Here it is: "When the President of the United States is tried the Chief Justice shall preside." That is the whole, sir. "The Chief Justice shall preside." No reason is assigned. Can you assign a reason? Can you supply a reason? Especially can you supply one which is not sustained by the authentic contemporary history of the Constitution; and particularly when you have authentic contemporary history which supplies another reason. Unless I am much mistaken this disposes of the objections proceeding from so many senators that the senator from Ohio cannot take the oath because he may possibly succeed to the President now impeached at your bar. He may vote or not, as he pleases, and there is no authority in the Constitution or any of its contemporary expounders to criticise him.

This is all, sir, I have to say at this time on this head. There were other remarks made by senators over the way to which I might reply. There was one that fell from my learned friend, the senator from Maryland, in which he alluded to myself. He represented me as having cited many authorities from the House of Lords, tending to show in the case of Mr. Stockton that this person at the time was not entitled to vote on the question of his seat. The senator does not remember that debate, I think, as well as I do. The point which I tried to present to the Senate, and which, I believe, was affirmed by a vote of the body, was simply this: that a man cannot sit as a judge in his own case. That was all, at least so far as I recollect; and I submitted that Mr. Stockton at that time was a judge undertaking to sit in his own case. Pray, sir, what is the pertinence of this citation? Is it applicable at all to the senator from Ohio? Is his case under consideration? Is he impeached at the bar of the Senate? Is he in any way called in question? Is he to answer for himself? Not at all. How, then, does the principle of law, that no man shall sit as a judge in his own case, apply to him? How does the action of the Senate in the case of Mr. Stockton apply to him? Not at all. The two cases are as wide as the poles asunder. One has nothing to do with the other.

Something has been said of the "interest" of the senator from Ohio on the present occasion. "Interest!" This is the word used. We are reminded that in a certain event the senator may become President, and that on this account he is under peculiar temptations which may swerve him from justice. The senator from Maryland went so far as to remind us of the large salary to which he might succeed, not less than $25,000 a year, and thus added a pecuniary temptation to the other disturbing forces. Is not all this very technical? Does it not forget the character of this great proceeding? Sir, we are a Senate, and not a court of *nisi prius*. This is not a case of assault and battery, but a trial involving the destinies of this republic. I doubt if the question of "interest" is properly raised. I speak with all respect for others; but I submit that it is inapplicable. It does not belong here. Every senator has his vote, to be given on his conscience. If there be any "interest" to sway him it must be that of justice and the safety of the country. Against these all else is nothing. The senator from Ohio, whose vote is now in question, can see nothing but those transcendent interests by the side of which office, power, and money are of small account. Put in one scale these interests so dear to the heart of the patriot, and in the other all the personal temptations which have been imagined, and I cannot doubt that if the senator from Ohio holds these scales the latter would kick the beam.

Mr. POMEROY. I suggest that this question lie on the table, as we cannot take a vote until all the members are sworn. I cannot make that motion, because no motion can be acted upon, as we are partly sworn and partly not. I think by unanimous consent, and by consent of the senator from Indiana, his proposition may lie on the table until the oath be administered to the remaining senators.

Mr. HOWE. If the senator will indulge me in a remark, as this is the first time I have felt called upon to make one on this occasion, it seems to me he has presented the most conclusive argument, if he is right, against the objection that is taken here. An objection is taken which the senator says he cannot vote upon, and his proposition is that we ignore it, go around it, lay it on the table. Suppose we do not choose to go around it; then this proceeding stops, if the objection is well taken. It seems to me it cannot be well taken unless here is a tribunal which can pass upon it, and pass upon it now, dispose of it in some way. It seems to me the objection cannot be well taken if we are obliged to run away from it, because, whether we be a court or a Senate within the meaning of the Constitution, both are dissipated necessarily by the raising of a single objection to administering an oath to a single member.

One word further, as I am up. It seems to me that this would not be a difficult question to determine, and by this very tribunal, if we were willing to read what is written and abide by it, for it is written that "the Senate of the United States shall be composed of two senators from each State." That is written, and it is elsewhere written that Ohio is a State; and nowhere is anything written to the contrary; and if Ohio is a State and this—the Constitution—is law. Ohio is entitled to two senators on this floor at this time. It is also written that "the Senate," composed in this way, "shall have the sole power to try all impeachments." The Senate shall have the sole power to try all impeachments—nobody else—and I cannot understand why that is not the end of the law. If there were elsewhere in this instrument any qualification or modification of either of those provisions then we should be bound to attend to them; but if there is none I do not see why this is not the end of the law. Whatever may be the impropriety or indelicacy of the senator from Ohio, whose right to take the oath is now questioned, acting here—gentlemen are at liberty to entertain their own opinions upon that point—the law of the case is here; he is a senator; he is a member of the tribunal which tries impeachments; or we must wipe out one or the other of these clauses from the Constitution for the time being.

Sir, this being the language of the Constitution, if that were all of it, would there be any doubt that upon the trial of a President upon impeachment the Vice-President would sit where you now sit? If there were no other provisions of the Constitution but these, and a President were to be put upon trial on impeachment, would any one suggest that the Vice-President should leave his chair and the Chief Justice of the Supreme Court be placed in it? But the impropriety of the Vice-President sitting there would be just the same if the Constitution had taken no notice of it as it is now, and just the same as is the impropriety of this oath being administered to the senator from Ohio. The men who made the Constitution foresaw that and provided for it, and therefore said that in case the President be impeached the Vice-President shall not preside, as the Constitution had before declared he should, but the Vice-President shall leave his chair and the Chief Justice shall preside during that trial; and it is because the Constitution says so that the Vice-President does leave his chair on such an occasion. But here, in reference to this question, there is no such direction in the Constitution.

Now, as to the objection which is taken and as to the time of taking it. It seems to me if anything is plain which is not written in the Constitution it is the objection taken by the senator from Maine, [Mr. Morrill.] If there is any objection to the qualifications of the senator from Ohio to try this question it is an objection which one of the parties to this litigation has a right to urge, and nobody else in the world; and, so far as I know, neither of the parties to that litigation are here. If both were here would they not have a right to waive the objections, if there were any? Could we exclude a member of this Senate against the protest of both the parties to the litigation and say, when they were consenting, that this man or that should not be a member of the Senate? Clearly not.

But, then, what is the objection itself? That he is interested, is it? And how interested? Why, that in a certain contingency, if the issue of the trial be in one way, the senator whose right to take this oath is objected to would cease to be President of the Senate and would become President of the United States. It was well replied by the senator from Michigan that that is not certain; that that is not an inevitable consequence; that is a *non sequitur*. It does not follow that he would become President of the United States. If he continued to be President of the Senate up to the time when the judgment of amotion was pronounced, I suppose, by the terms of the Constitution, he would be President; but if he should not continue to be President of the Senate up to that time he would not be. Admit that he is now in possession of the office, which would give him the succession under the Constitution in case of amotion; but the office, the condition, the predicament which is his position to-day may be the reversion of any one of us to-morrow; we are remainder-men if he should happen to retire from that office by the judgment of the Senate.

Mr. FRELINGHUYSEN. And consequently all of us are interested.

Mr. HOWE. All his interest would thus be removed, and that same interest would be vested in some one of the rest of us; I do not know exactly who; but the same possible interest, contingent interest, which is objected to to-day in him is an objection which can be urged against every one of us, because we are liable to be, before the termination of this litigation, placed in precisely the same predicament, and no one of us can be fit, because of this possible interest, to try this question.

Mr. President, I believe, by a rule of the body governing this proceeding, the remarks of the senators are limited to ten minutes. I have said all I care to say upon the question.

Mr. DRAKE. Mr. President, I do not propose to go over any of the grounds that have heretofore been taken by other senators on this subject; but there are one or two questions which seem to me to lie in the foreground of this matter, and to which I should like to call the attention of those gentlemen who insist upon this exception at this time. If the objection has any vitality, any legal validity whatever, it is one that requires to be passed upon affirmatively or negatively by some body; and I should like to know who is to pass upon it at this stage of the proceeding? Is it addressed to the presiding officer of the Senate, as if he had the right to pass upon it? I imagine not. I suppose it will hardly be contended that so grave a question as this can be passed upon by that officer, even if any question in this trial can be passed upon by him at all. If not to be passed upon by the presiding officer of the Senate, then what body is to determine the question affirmatively or negatively? The Senate is not yet constituted for the trial of the impeachment.

Besides the honorable senator from Ohio, there are no less than four other senators in their seats on this floor at this time waiting to have the oath required by the Constitution administered to them. They are entitled to vote upon all questions which may arise in the Senate sitting in the matter of impeachment. Are you going to stop the proceedings of the Senate at this point and exclude four of the senators here that are ready and waiting to take the oath? If you are, then if it had so happened that the first name on the roll had been that of the president *pro tempore* of the Senate, all the remainder on the roll after him might, before being sworn, have undertaken to adjudge that he should not be sworn. It just so happens that the name of the senator from Ohio is low down on the roll of the Senate, alphabetically taken. If it had been the very first one the objection could have been just as well taken and decided by a Senate not one single member of which had yet been sworn in the matter of impeachment.

Mr. President, for these reasons, aside from all others, I hold that there is no person here who can pass upon this question; the President of the Senate cannot pass upon it; or even if he, in virtue of his presidency, could pass upon questions in the course of this trial, the court, if you call it so, is not yet organized; it is only in the process of organization. There are members of the court here, if you call it a court, waiting to be sworn; and you stop the whole thing here and vote, do you, upon this question, when the vote of those four members that are waiting to be sworn might change the determination one way or the other.

Sir, the whole thing resolves itself at last into a question of order, of entertaining this proposition at all. I will venture to say that if the court had been organized and the present incumbent of the presidency of the Senate had been accustomed, as he is in another tribunal, to announce the decision upon questions of order, he would instantly have decided that this question was out of order at the time it was raised. These are the views about this matter which have led me to participate for these few minutes in the debate on this subject.

Mr. THAYER. Mr. President, it seems to me that this question might with propriety be asked, what is there in a name? With all due respect for the honorable senators who have by argument attempted to convince the Senate that this is a court, I am compelled to think that it is a waste of words. It is true that in the earlier trials of impeachment the term "high court of impeachment" was used; but it was, in my judgment, a matter of taste or of form. We are, after all, obliged to come back to the plain, pointed, explicit language of the Constitution—

The Senate shall have the sole power to try all impeachments. When sitting for that purpose—

Sitting as a Senate for the trial of an impeachment—

they shall be on oath or affirmation.

Could language be plainer? Could meaning be more apparent than this? If we have passed into a "high court of impeachment" when did that transposition take place? This Senate was sitting as a Senate to-day from 12 o'clock till 1. It did not adjourn. What became of it? Where is it if we are here as a court to-day? The Senate does not die. The Senate is in existence. It is here in this body, or is this body sitting as a Senate to try a question on a case of impeachment?

But, after all, that is not material. I have risen more for the purpose of noticing the objection raised by the honorable senator from Indiana, [Mr. HENDRICKS.] The question of interest is made against the taking of the oath by the honorable senator from Ohio, [Mr. Wade,] upon a rule of law in the courts that a person having an interest in the verdict which may be rendered is excluded from sitting upon that jury. If that rule is to prevail here I am surprised that the honorable senator from Indiana did not raise the question at an earlier stage in the progress of these proceedings to-day. There is another rule of law, or the same rule applicable with equal force, which excludes from the jury a person related by blood or marriage to the accused. If the objection is good in one case, is it not equally good in the other? If it should exclude the honorable senator from Ohio, why should it not exclude the honorable senator from Tennessee, [Mr. Patterson?] I cast no imputation upon that senator; I do not question his determination to try this case justly and fairly according to the Constitution, the law, and the evidence. I make no objection to the senator from Tennessee; but I desire to say that if this objection is to be raised in the case of the honorable senator from Ohio, it ought, by the same rule of law, and of evidence, and of construction, to be applied to the honorable senator from Tennessee.

But, sir, in regard to the question of interest, if that objection is valid against the senator from Ohio, it lies against every member of this body, only one degree more remote. If, by the verdict to be rendered in this trial, the senator from Ohio should pass from that chair into the more exalted position of President of the United States, it devolves upon this Senate to elect one of the senators sitting here to fill that vacancy. Human life is in the hands of One who is above all human tribunals, and in the course of human events the honorable senator from Ohio, elevated to the position of Chief Magistrate of this nation, may pass away, and that senator sitting here on this trial who has been elevated to the position of presiding officer of this body may become the successor of him to whom objection is made to-day in the office of President of the United States. I repeat that the interest lies with every senator here, only one degree more remote.

But, Mr. President, it has been said repeatedly this afternoon, and it is not necessary for me to dwell upon it, that we are here as a Senate of the United States. The honorable senator from Ohio is here as a senator of the State of Ohio, clothed with the rights and all the power possessed by any other senator on this floor. He is the equal in every particular of every senator who is now sitting as a member of this body. I challenge the honorable senator from Indiana or the honorable senator from Maryland to point me to one iota in the Constitution which recognizes the right of this body to deprive any individual senator of his vote. No matter what opinions we may entertain as to the propriety of the honorable senator from Ohio casting a vote on this question, he is here as a senator, and you cannot take away his right to vote except by a gross usurpation of power. He is here as a senator in the possession and exercise of every right of a senator until you expel him by a vote of two-thirds of this body. Then he ceases to have those rights, and not till then.

Again, on this question of interest, suppose some 10 or 15 senators were related in some way to the accused; if the rule holds good you might reduce this body below a quorum, and thus defeat the very object which the Constitution had in view in creating this as the tribunal to try questions of impeachment.

Again, in course of law, if objections are made to any one sitting upon a jury, and he is excluded, an officer is sent out into the streets and the highways to pick up talesmen and bring them in to fill up the jury. Can you do that here? Suppose you exclude the honorable senator from Ohio, can you send an officer of this Senate out into the lobbies or into the streets of Washington to bring in a man to take his place? By no means. I need not state that.

Thus I come back to the proposition that we are a Senate, composed of constituent members, two from every State, sworn to do our duty as senators of the United States; and when you attempt to exclude a senator from the performance of that duty you assume functions which are not known in the Constitution and cannot for a moment be recognized. When you attempt to exercise the power, and do exercise it, are you any longer the Senate of the United States? The Senate, no other parties or bodies forming any part of it, is the only body known to the Constitution of the United States for this purpose, and the Senate is composed of two senators from each State.

Mr. HOWARD. I do not rise to prolong the debate, and I entertain the hope that we may be able to dispose of this question very soon. I rise more for the purpose of calling the attention of the Chair to the real matter before us, and of inquiring whether the proposition now made to us is in order. I believe the motion is, that other senators shall be called to take the oath, and the senator from Ohio be passed by for the present, until other senators are sworn in. If I am mistaken about that, I should like to be corrected.

The CHIEF JUSTICE. The senator from Ohio [Mr. Wade] presents himself to take the oath. The senator from Indiana [Mr. Hendricks] objects. The question then is, Shall the senator from Ohio be sworn? Pending that proposition, the senator from Maryland [Mr. Johnson] moves that in administering the oath to senators the name of the senator from Ohio [Mr. Wade] be omitted in the call until the remaining names on the roll shall have been called. That is the question now before the body.

Mr. HOWARD. Yes, Mr. President, I so understood; and that is a question, allow me to say, which I suppose to be entirely within the competency of the Chair. There is no rule requiring the members to be called alphabetically to take the oath. If the Chair should see fit upon his own responsibility to call them in reverse order, undoubtedly he could do so. I do not see, therefore, any necessity of spending further time in the discussion of this particular motion; but at the same time I must confess, on reflecting upon this objection, that it seems to me to resolve itself into a pure question of order. The Senate of the United States are endeavoring to assume their judicial functions in a particular case, and are sitting, or endeavoring to sit, upon the trial of an impeachment. Therefore, it seems to me, it must be held that the trial has commenced. If I am correct in this, it appears to me that but one conclusion can be arrived at by the Chair.

The Senate shall have the sole power to try all impeachments. When sitting for that purpose, they shall be on oath or affirmation.

The Constitution is mandatory; it is imperative in its very terms. When a senator offers, therefore, to take the oath, it becomes the duty of the Chair, under the Constitution, to administer the oath to him, and any objection to his taking the oath such as is made here seems to me to be out of order, because it implies that we may, or somebody here may, disobey and disregard this imperative mandate of the fundamental law. That will be a question, I apprehend, for the President of the Senate to decide.

Mr. BUCKALEW. I should like to inquire of the senator from Michigan if his own rules, for the adoption of which he has asked our assent some days since, do not provide that the presiding officer may submit any question to the Senate for decision? Having called upon us to adopt such a rule, and we having assented to his request, I think it very extraordinary that he endeavors to place upon the Chair the entire responsibility of deciding this question in any of the varied forms which it may assume, even assuming it to be (which I do not) a question of order, pure and simple.

Gentlemen read to us a section of the Constitution which says that the Senate shall be composed of two members from each State, and that each senator shall possess one vote. I suppose, if we were to be curious upon a point of constitutional history, we might ascertain that that last clause was put in the Constitution with reference to the previous practice in the Congress of the Confederation, where the votes were taken by States. This clause, declaring that each member of the Senate, representing a State under the new system, should give a single direct vote, was to exclude, I suppose, the practice which had previously obtained of voting by States. A fundamental idea in constituting bodies consisting of more than one person is that the members shall be equal; that each shall possess an equal voice in its proceedings. I take it, therefore, that upon principle each member of the Senate ought to possess one vote; and that this declaration in the Constitution found its way there simply because the practice previously in the government which preceded our present one had been to vote by States. I suppose that that clause of the Constitution has no other office or meaning. Most certainly it does not bear any such signification as that attempted here to be assigned to it, to oblige us upon every possible question, whether we be acting in a legislative, executive, or (as now) in a judicial capacity, to admit every single member to vote upon every single question which can arise. That is simply the rule by which votes shall be given in the Senate—"each senator shall have one vote"—but the Constitution does not attempt to define the cases where each member can vote. It does not attempt to exclude cases where his vote would be improper or might be excluded by law or by rule. In conformity with this view the Senate has already adopted a rule for excluding votes in particular cases. It is the practice of this body—and I believe in that respect our practice conforms to that of all other bodies of similar constitution—it is a rule founded in natural propriety and justice, that no man shall express his voice, although he be a representative, in a case where he shall have a direct personal interest in the decision to be made.

Gentlemen seem to feel great difficulty of mind, because, as they say, without the swearing in of the senator from Ohio the court will not be fully constituted; that we are at present in an imperfect condition; that the taking of an oath by him, and the taking of a place among us by him in the new capacity which we are assuming, is necessary and essential to the constitution of the body. That argument has no weight with me in determining the question which has been raised by the objection of the senator from Indiana. Sir, this is a difficulty which may arise in the organization of any body made up of many members. It may arise in a judicial, legislative, or in a popular body anywhere; a question with regard to the membership of the body in its organization. Questions of this kind have been continually occurring from the foundation of the government in the two houses of Congress. Formerly, in the Senate, the practice was that a member who presented his credentials was sworn, and afterward, in case there was objection to his right, his case was investigated and determined. Recently, however, the Senate seem to have fallen into a different practice. Upon one or more occasions recently, one notably in my mind, the recent case from Maryland, a member appearing in the Senate and claiming a right to a seat, with regular credentials from his State, upon an objection made was not sworn. The objection was sustained. The case was sent to a committee of this body and investigated through many months, and the case was, in fact, acted upon at a subsequent session of the Senate, when a decision was arrived at and the judgment of the Senate was pronounced.

Now, sir, in what respect does this case differ in principle from that? Here the Senate is about to organize itself into a court; its members to be put under oath. The Chief Justice of the Supreme Court is called to preside over the proceedings, and we have to proceed as judges of law and of fact to decide the gravest question which may be presented to any tribunal in this country. The senator from Indiana, when the senator from Ohio appears, suggests—not as a challenge in the ordinary way, or upon ordinary principles—that under the Constitution of the United States the member from Ohio cannot sit in this court. Now, sir, that question involves the question of his right to be sworn, and it is made at the proper time, for it is made when the question arises legitimately in the course of our proceedings. If the objection be well grounded in the Constitution of the United States this is the time to make it for a very plain reason. If it be not now made, assuming it to be a just objection, what will be the consequence? That a member not qualified to act will become a member of the court and take part in its proceedings; and he will remain a judge in the case, entitled to vote upon all questions which may arise, until at some future time, perhaps days, weeks, or months hence, a manager for the House or an attorney for the accused may raise the question of his right to sit by a motion or challenge. Then only (according to the argument) can our power of action upon this question be duly exerted.

The argument has been made by a member in debate that perhaps the counsel who come in here will not make the objection to this particular member; and what then? The Senate is to be unable at any time during the trial to relieve itself from an incompetent member! Then an unlawful member may continue to sit from the beginning to the end of the proceeding! At all events it is insisted that some attorney-at-law or manager must raise the question in order that we may assume jurisdiction over it and decide it. Can anything be more absurd than that?

When you pursue this argument to its consequences, I think it becomes manifest that this is the time to raise the question; and I believe that it is not only within our power to raise the question now, but that it is our duty to determine it. We are acting under the Constitution of the United States. Most of us have already been sworn by you, sir, to obey that Constitution; and if, indeed, it be true that by that provision of the Constitution which calls you here to preside over our proceedings—not to give dignity to them merely, but for the other and better and higher purpose, to give purity and a disinterested character to those proceedings—if, indeed, it be true that by that provision the member from Ohio (our presiding officer) is disqualified, we cannot shirk our duty of declaring his incompetency on the first occasion when the question is made.

Now, sir, upon what ground is it that gentlemen would deprive us of that ordinary power which exists in the nature of things, to decide upon the constitution of our own body? As I said before, this is not a question of challenge for partiality, nor even for interest under some law which gives it to a party in a court of justice. It is a question which arises under the Constitution as to the organization of our own body—who shall compose it; and we are to meet that question, and decide it, in the very outset of our proceedings.

The senator from Massachusetts has read to us what Judge Story wrote about 1830, in which he stated an opinion similar to that which was contained in a communication from yourself, sir, to the Senate yesterday; and that was, that when the President of the United States is on trial upon articles of impeachment the Chief Justice is called to preside because the presiding officer of the Senate is a party in interest, and it would be a scandal to have him preside in a case where his own possible accession to the office of President of the United States was involved. I am content for the present to take the opinion of the present Chief Justice of the Supreme Court of the United States, and the opinion of the most eminent commentor upon American law, in preference to the opinion of the Senator from Massachusetts pronounced here in debate. I think it would be an impropriety, if nothing worse, for the Senate to proceed at this moment, upon the strength of his opinion and of his argument against the highest authorities, to pronounce that the senator from Ohio is entitled, as a member of the Senate sitting as a court of impeachment, to try the present case.

In the courts of justice I understand that challenges are to be made to jurors before they are sworn. If that time has passed by, and the juror is charged, under oath, with the trial of the case, it is too late to object; and, undoubtedly, if, during the progress of this trial, an objection should be made to the competency of one of the members of the court to sit in the case, the answer which would be made before us and pressed upon our attention would be that the objection came too late, that the member had already been sworn.

Mr. FRELINGHUYSEN. I should like to ask the senator from Pennsylvania whether he considers that the respondent, the accused, has waived his right to challenge, if any such right exists, as to all those members of the Senate who have been sworn; and if he has not waived that right, is not that conclusive proof that this is not the time to interpose the objection, but that the challenge, if a challenge can be made, must be made to giving the vote, not to taking the oath?

Mr. BUCKALEW. I am not arguing the question of a challenge which may be presented during the trial. All that I was alluding to at the moment the senator interrupted me was the point that the particular argument I mentioned would be made. I am not treating this as a question of challenge by a party before us. I am not arguing on that ground. The question has not been put upon that ground by the senator from Indiana or the senator from Maryland. A right of challenge is a right given by a statute to a party in court to interpose in a particular manner and raise a particular question. We have nothing of that kind here. It is not involved in the present debate. The question now before us and for our decision is this: in proceeding to constitute ourselves into a court, an objection being made that a particular senator is not qualified to sit in that court at all, is it not our duty to meet the question and decide it? The practice that I was going to point out of both houses of Congress, at least in recent times, would seem fully to sustain this course. I have already mentioned the case of the senator from Maryland. In the House of Representatives, when members have appeared there in the present Congress, the whole delegation from a State have had their cases referred. Their being sworn in was deferred for the time until some investigation took place. It is an ordinary mode of proceeding, and it is a power which may be assumed by any body, unless there be some statute or constitution to prevent it, in deciding upon the qualifications of its own members. The Senate has a general power to decide upon the qualifications of its own members. Now, when we come to act in a particular capacity and under oath, have we not the power to decide upon the qualifications of the members of the Senate who are to act in this new capacity, and if there be any incapacity to declare it?

One point more, and I will leave the debate. The senator from Massachusetts informs us that in 1798, when the House of Representatives presented articles of impeachment against Senator Blount, they made a demand on the Senate that he should be sequestered from his seat. Like the senator from Ohio, he was a member of this body, as it was then constituted, sitting here under oath, speaking the voice of a State, having, one would suppose, as much authority and power as any of his colleagues. What did the House of Representatives do? They asked the Senate, for the purposes of the trial and during the whole trial, to sequester him from his seat; that is, to remove him from it; to say he should not sit and take part in the proceedings. That was the demand of the House of Representatives at a time when the House was composed of giants in intellect, who had participated in the formation of the very Constitution under which this proceeding takes place. They made that demand of the Senate. Was it repelled? Was it supposed to be an unreasonable or an impertinent demand? Was it supposed that the House of Representatives asked the Senate to do an unreasonable and unlawful thing? That was done in the very beginning of the proceedings, before the members of the Senate were sworn at all—earlier than the senator from Indiana now interposes in the present case upon this question of swearing the senator from Ohio. The Senate did not resent that demand of the House of Representatives. They made no objection to it. Subsequently, however, for good reasons, which I need not now recite, they did what was more effectual: they expelled Blount from membership by virtue of the constitutional power which they possessed. By a two-thirds vote they not only sequestered him from the Senate during the trial, but deprived him of his seat during his whole term. That was the action of the Senate.

Now, Mr. President, if the House of Representatives has a right to ask the Senate to remove or to sequester a member from this body because he is interested in the trial which is to take place, it must be upon an affirmance of the very point in this debate, that is, that the Senate, in constituting itself into a court, has a right in a proper case to omit a member from being sworn, from becoming a part of the body as reorganized for the special purpose. I insist, therefore, that this case, to which the senator from Massachusetts has referred as authority, will instruct us that it is our duty now to act upon this case, and, by omitting to swear the senator from Ohio, leave him to his general rights as a senator; but, for a particular constitutional reason, not to permit him to act with us in this particular trial, when the result of the trial, if conviction takes place, will be to place him in the office of President of the United States.

I repeat, sir, from my point of view, this is not in the nature of a challenge by a party. Nor is it an objection made as a matter of favor to either party in this proceeding. It is made as a constitutional objection, as a question of membership, as a question upon the organization of the Senate into a court of impeachment.

As to the capacity in which the Senate act, it seems to me there is no difficulty. The old writers and the old commentators used clear language—"the Senate of the United States sitting as a court of impeachment." That was the description of bodies like the one we are about organizing, in olden times, and the uniform language applied to them down to this day. It is still the Senate of the United States, but it sits as a court; for the time being it must act upon judicial rules, and must administer the laws of the United States which are applicable to the particular case. Its legislative powers and functions are left behind it. It has taken on a new character and is performing a new function, judicial in its nature and judicial only. That is the whole of it.

Mr. MORTON. I respectfully submit that the latter part of the argument of the senator from Pennsylvania does not accord well with the first part. The distinguished senator from Pennsylvania started out by saying that we were now organizing a court. He then used the words, "We are about to constitute a court." He talked a great deal about the creation or constitution of a court. He proceeded upon the theory, as did my colleague in his first argument, that we were about to constitute a court which was to be selected from the members of the Senate. Mr. President, the error of this whole argument is right here. The Constitution has constituted the tribunal itself. We have no right to organize a court. We have no right to constitute a court. The tribunal is constituted by the Constitution itself, and is simply the Senate of the United States.

The remark was made, I believe, by the senator from Ohio, and perhaps by the senator from Massachusetts, that it was immaterial whether you call it a court or a Senate. It is not very material what you call it; but it is material that you shall proceed simply on the idea that it is a Senate and nothing else. That is material; for if you abandon that plain and simple idea and adopt the theory that this tribunal is yet to be constituted, you will wander from the Constitution itself. The Constitution settles the whole question in a few words. It says, "the Senate shall have the sole power to try all impeachments;" and when it has said that, it has itself constituted the tribunal. The Senate is the tribunal. Who compose that tribunal? The senator from Ohio [Mr. Wade] is one of the men who now compose that tribunal, and we cannot get away from that conclusion.

It may be said that while the Senate is trying an impeachment it is exercising judicial powers. That makes no difference. Why, sir, when we come in here to counsel as to the confirmation of an appointment of the President we are not acting as a legislative body; our functions are decidedly executive in their character; but still we act not as an executive body, or as part of the presidency of the United States, but we act simply as the Senate. Our duties are then executive in their character; but we are performing them simply as the Senate. So when we exercise what may be called judicial power in this case, we do not do it as a court; we are doing it simply in the character of the Senate of the United States, performing certain powers or duties that are imposed upon us by the Constitution.

All this talk about organizing a court; all this talk, in the language of my friend from Pennsylvania, of constituting a tribunal, it seems to me, is idle. The Constitution has done that for us. It only requires that when this tribunal shall act in this capacity it shall be sworn. We have no right to refuse to be sworn. If I were to refuse I should violate my duty. If the senator from Ohio should refuse he would violate his duty. It seems to me this is the whole of it. The simple idea is, that it is a Senate, and the tribunal is already formed—is not to be formed, but is formed now; and the Constitution says it shall be under oath. The senator from Ohio had no choice but to take the oath. As to what he shall do hereafter on the challenge of the accused is a question that I will not discuss now. It is enough to say that all this talk about a high court of impeachment, about a tribunal yet to be constituted, yet to be organized, is outside of the Constitution. We are sitting simply as a Senate, as much so as when we pass a bill or as when we ratify a treaty. The Constitution says so, and there is nobody that is authorized to say no.

Mr. DIXON. Mr. President, the President of the United States is about to be tried before this body, either as a Senate or as a court, upon articles brought against him by the House of Representatives, charging him with high crimes and misdemeanors. In case of his——

Mr. GRIMES, (to Mr. Dixon.) Will you give way for a motion to adjourn?

Mr. DIXON. If the Senate wish to adjourn I will not take up the time of the Senate now.

Mr. GRIMES. I understand that the Chief Justice of the United States has been sitting in the Supreme Court and in this chamber since 11 o'clock this morning without an opportunity to leave his chair. I think it is due to him and to the Senate that we should now adjourn, and settle this question to-morrow morning. I therefore make that motion.

Mr. HOWARD. What is the motion?

Mr. GRIMES. To adjourn until to-morrow.

Mr. HOWARD. To adjourn what until to-morrow?

Mr. GRIMES. This court.

Mr. HOWARD. We have a rule by which the Senate, sitting for the trial of an impeachment, may adjourn itself, and still the ordinary business of the Senate continue, so that we may relieve the Chief Justice without adjourning the Senate.

Mr. GRIMES. My motion is that the court adjourn until to-morrow at 1 o'clock.

Mr. ANTHONY. I think the proper motion would be that the Senate proceed to the consideration of legislative business.

The CHIEF JUSTICE. The court must first adjourn. Senators, you who are in favor of adjourning the court until to-morrow at 1 o'clock will say ay, and those of the contrary opinion will say no.

The question being put, the motion was agreed to.

The CHIEF JUSTICE thereupon declared the court adjourned until one o'clock to-morrow, and vacated the chair.

IN SENATE, *March* 6, 1868.

The CHIEF JUSTICE. The Senate will come to order. The proceedings of yesterday will be read.

The Secretary read the "proceedings of the Senate sitting on the trial of the impeachment of Andrew Johnson, President of the United States, on Thursday, March 5, 1868," from the entries on the journal kept for that purpose by the Secretary.

The CHIEF JUSTICE. At its adjournment last evening the Senate, sitting for the trial of impeachment, had under consideration the motion of the senator from Maryland, [Mr. Johnson,] that objection having been made to the senator from Ohio [Mr. Wade] taking the oath, his name should be passed until the remaining members have been sworn. That is the business now before the body. The senator from Connecticut [Mr. Dixon] is entitled to the floor on that motion.

Mr. DIXON. Mr. President——

Mr. HOWARD. Excuse me one moment. Mr. President, I rise to a question of order.

The CHIEF JUSTICE. The senator from Michigan will state his point of order.

Mr. HOWARD. By the Constitution the Senate sitting on the trial of an impeachment is to be on oath or affirmation; each member of the Senate, by the Constitution, is a component member of the body for that purpose. There can, therefore, be no trial unless this oath or affirmation is taken by the respective senators who are present. The Constitution of the United States is imperative; and when a member presents himself to take the oath I hold that as a rule of order it is the duty of the presiding officer to administer the oath, and that his proposition to take the oath cannot be postponed; that other members have no control over the question, but that it is a simple duty devolved upon the presiding officer of the body to administer the oath.

Further, sir, the Senate, on the second day of the present month, adopted rules for their government on proceedings of this kind. Rule 3 declares that—

Before proceeding to the consideration of the articles of impeachment, the presiding officer shall administer the oath hereinafter provided to the members of the Senate then present—

Mr. Wade is present and ready to take the oath—

and to the other members of the Senate as they shall appear, whose duty it shall be to take the same.

The form of the oath is also prescribed in our present rules, and is as follows:

I solemnly swear (or affirm, as the case may be) that in all things appertaining to the trial of the impeachment of ———— ————, now pending, I will do impartial justice according to the Constitution and laws: So help me God.

That is the form of the oath prescribed by our rules. It is the form in which the presiding officer of this body himself is sworn. It is the form in which we all, thus far, have been sworn. And so far as the rules are concerned, I insist that they have already been adopted and recognized by us, so far as it is possible during the condition in which we now are of organizing ourselves for the discharge of our judicial duty. I, therefore, made it a point of order that the objection made to the swearing in of Mr. Wade is out of order; and also that the motion of the senator from Maryland, to postpone the swearing in of Mr. Wade, is out of order under the rules and under the Constitution of the United States; and I ask most respectfully, but earnestly, that the President of the Senate, the Chief Justice of the Supreme Court of the United States, now presiding in the body, will decide this question of order, and without debate.

Mr. DIXON. Mr. President——

Mr. HOWARD. I object to any further debate.

Mr. DIXON. The very question before the Senate is whether under this rule the senator from Ohio can be sworn.

Mr. DRAKE. Mr. President, I call the senator from Connecticut to order.

The CHIEF JUSTICE. The senator from Connecticut is called to order. The senator from Michigan has submitted a point of order for the consideration of the body. During the proceedings for the organization of the Senate for the trial of an impeachment of the President the Chair regards the general rules of the Senate as applicable, and that the Senate must determine for itself every question which arises, unless the Chair is permitted to determine it. In a case of this sort, affecting so nearly the organization of this body, the Chair feels himself constrained to submit the question of order to the Senate. Will the senator from Michigan state his point of order in writing?

While the point of order raised by Mr. Howard was being reduced to writing at the desk,

Mr. DIXON. I rise to a question of order.

The CHIEF JUSTICE. A point of order is already pending, and a second point of order cannot be made until that is disposed of.

Mr. DIXON. I submit to the presiding officer whether a point of order can be made with regard to that question, and, with the consent of the Chair, I will state——

The CHIEF JUSTICE. The Chair is of opinion that no point of order can be made pending another point of order.

Mr. Howard's point of order having been reduced to writing,

The CHIEF JUSTICE. Senators, the point of order submitted by the senator from Michigan is as follows: "That the objection raised to administering the oath to Mr. Wade is out of order, and that the motion of the senator from Maryland, to postpone the administering of the oath to Mr. Wade until other senators are sworn, is also out of order, under the rules adopted by the Senate on the 2d of March instant, and under the Constitution of the United States." The question is open to debate.

Mr. DIXON. Mr. President, as I understand——

Mr. DRAKE. I call the senator from Connecticut to order. Under the rules of the Senate questions of order are not debatable.

Mr. DIXON. I would remind the senator that when questions of order are referred to the Senate for their decision they are always debatable.

Mr. DRAKE. I do not so understand the rules of the Senate. There can be a debate upon an appeal from the decision of the Chair; but there can be no debate in the first instance on a question of order, as I understand the rules of the Senate.

The CHIEF JUSTICE. The Chair rules that a question of order is debatable when submitted to the Senate.

Mr. DRAKE If I am mistaken in the rules of the Senate on that subject I should like to be corrected, but I think I am not.

The CHIEF JUSTICE. The senator from Missouri is out of order unless he takes an appeal from the decision of the Chair.

Mr. DRAKE. Well, sir, if it is according to the rules of the Senate debatable, I have nothing to say.

Mr. POMEROY. The senator must be aware that when the Chair makes a decision it is to be decided without debate; but when it is submitted to the Senate our custom is that it is debatable.

Mr. JOHNSON and others. Always.

Mr. POMEROY. But it is not always submitted to the Senate.

Mr. HOWARD. I ask leave of the Senate to read the sixth of the general rules of the Senate:

If any member, in speaking or otherwise, transgress the rules of the Senate the presiding officer shall, or any member may, call to order; and when a member shall be called to order by the President or a senator he shall sit down, and shall not proceed without leave of the Senate. And every question of order shall be decided by the President without debate, subject to an appeal to the Senate, and the President may call for the sense of the Senate on any question of order.

Mr. DIXON. I understand the sense of the Senate to be as I supposed, and I take it I have a right to proceed. How far I have a right to discuss the general question I am somewhat uncertain. I suppose that the question is now presented merely in that different shape alluded to by the senator from Michigan yesterday when he reminded the Senate that, after all, this was, in his opinion, a question of order, and ought to be so discussed. I take it, Mr. President, the question now before this body is, whether as a question of order of the orderly proceedings of this tribunal the senator from Ohio [Mr. Wade] can be sworn; and it is upon that question that I now propose to address this body.

Mr. President, when I had the honor yesterday of addressing this tribunal, and gave way to a motion to adjourn, I was remarking that the President of the United States was about to be tried before this body in its judicial capacity, whether called a court or not, upon articles of impeachment presented by the House of Representatives. If upon the trial he be convicted the judgment may extend to his removal from office and to his disqualification hereafter to hold any office of profit or trust under the United States. How far the judgment would extend in case of his conviction it is of course impossible for any one now to say. In all human probability it would extend at least as far as to his removal from office; and, in that event, the very moment that the judgment was rendered the office of President of the United States, with all its powers and all its attributes, would be vested in the senator from Ohio, now holding the office of President of this body. The office would vest in the President of the Senate for the time being. And the question for this tribunal now to decide is, whether, upon the trial of the President of the United States, the person holding the office of President of the Senate, and in whom the office of President of the United States, upon the conviction of the accused, will immediately vest, can be a judge in that case. That, sir, is the question before us.

Mr. SHERMAN. I very rarely call a senator to order, but I feel it my duty on this occasion to do so in regard to the senator from Connecticut. I think he is not in order in the discussion he is now pursuing. The point submitted to the Senate by the Chair, and to be settled by the Senate, is whether or not it is in order to proceed with this discussion. While that matter is being submitted to the Senate the senator from Connecticut goes on and discusses the main question that was discussed yesterday. It seems to me that in a tribunal like this each senator should observe strictly the rules of order. I therefore make the point of order on the senator from Connecticut, and hope the discussion will be confined to the point of order which is submitted now to the Senate.

Mr. DIXON. If I may be permitted, I beg to say to the Senate that I am attempting to discuss the question of order in what seems to me a proper manner.

The CHIEF JUSTICE. The senator from Ohio makes the point of order that the senator from Connecticut, in discussing the pending question of order, must confine himself strictly to that question, and not discuss the main question before the Senate. In that point of order the Chair conceives that the senator from Ohio is correct, and that the senator from Connecticut must confine himself strictly to the discussion of the point of order before the house.

Mr. DIXON. Mr. President, I commenced by saying that it was somewhat uncertain in my own mind how far it would be proper to go into the general merits of this question upon the point of order; but that I supposed it would be proper to discuss the general question. And I will now take the liberty to say to the presiding officer of this body that if I were now commencing this debate without the example of those senators before me who have already in the fullest manner discussed the pending question, who, up to the time when I was permitted the privilege of the floor, made no objection to a full discussion— if I had commenced before that example, I should perhaps consider myself more strictly limited in the course of my remarks than I feel myself to be with that example before me. If permitted to proceed without interruption, I will say frankly to the Senate that I propose to go into the general merits of the question whether the President *pro tempore* of this body can be sworn in as a judge in this case—the same question which has been discussed by other senators. If it is the opinion of the Senate that I cannot go into that question, I certainly have not that desire to force myself upon the attention of the Senate that I should insist upon attempting to evade a rule. I should prefer, therefore, that senators would inform me, or that the Chair would inform me, how far I may proceed, and I certainly shall not willingly be guilty of any impropriety. But I beg leave again to remind the Senate that this strict rule is applied to me after ten senators at least have fully discussed this question; and the senator who raises the question himself has spoken, I think, at great length not less than three times. Now, sir, if it is the will of the Senate tha

I may proceed, I certainly shall be gratified to do it. As I have already said, I have no desire to proceed with constant interruptions upon questions of order.

Mr. JOHNSON. I believe the questions of order raised by the honorable member from Michigan are, that the senator from Ohio has a right to be sworn and that the Senate have no right to ask that it should be postponed even for a day. He places it upon the ground that, being a senator of the United States, he is by the Constitution of the United States made a member of the court. The argument yesterday on both sides was an attempt to show the affirmative and the negative of that proposition. Whether it is in order to object to his being sworn necessarily involves the question whether, under the Constitution, he has a right to be sworn. The honorable member made another question of order, or, rather, made it part of his first question of order, that these points are to be decided without debate. You, Mr. Chief Justice, have held that, as you have submitted the questions to the deliberation and decision of the Senate, they may be debated. All questions of order, when submitted by the presiding officer himself to the Senate, or when they are brought before the Senate by an appeal from his decision, are always open to debate. Then what is to be debated under the question of order, which is, that there is no right to object to the honorable member from Ohio taking the oath as a member of this court? I suppose whether he has that right. The objection that the right is a matter which cannot be disputed assumes the whole controversy. If it was admitted by every member of the Senate that the honorable member from Ohio had a right to be sworn there would be no question before the Senate. Some of the members of the Senate think that, for reasons stated in the debate yesterday, he has no right to be sworn as a member of this court. Whether it is in order to make that objection necessarily involves the question whether he has a right to be sworn. I do not see that there can be any other question discussed upon the question of order raised by the honorable member from Michigan but the question whether the honorable member from Ohio has under the Constitution a right to be sworn.

Mr. HENDRICKS. I ask for the reading of the point of order.

The Secretary again read the point of order submitted by Mr. Howard.

Mr. DIXON. I think I shall be able to discuss that question of order.

Mr. HENDRICKS. All that I desired to say was this, that the discussion——

Mr. HOWARD. If the senator from Indiana will allow me one word, I desire to call his attention to the 23d rule that we have adopted. Possibly it may have escaped his attention:

All orders and decisions shall be made and had by yeas and nays, which shall be entered on the record, and without debate.

Mr. JOHNSON. The honorable member will permit me to make a suggestion upon the effect of that rule. I was aware of the existence of the 23d rule, but that goes into force only after we have become a court. The question now is as to the manner in which we are to organize ourselves as a court. After we are organized all questions of order are, by force of the 23d rule, to be decided without debate.

Mr. SHERMAN. I should like to ask the senator from Maryland if there is any doubt of the power of the Senate to prescribe the mode and manner of organizing the court preliminary to the final organization? There can be no doubt of it. The last clause of the third rule adopted by us the other day provides that—

Before proceeding to the consideration of the articles of impeachment the presiding officer shall administer the oath hereinafter provided to the members of the Senate then present, and to the other members of the Senate as they shall appear.

Now, I will ask any senator whether another senator may stop the execution of this imperative order of the Senate while it is going on, and give rise to a long debate when the presiding officer, in obedience to this rule, is executing the order of the Senate? He might just as well stop the calling of the roll when the yeas and nays were being taken upon a motion and begin a discussion upon the right of a senator to vote on a pending motion as to stop the execution of this order of the Senate, while the presiding officer, in pursuance of the rule, is executing it. It cannot be done. The presiding officer is bound to execute the rule of the Senate in the ordinary way. Nothing can interrupt the execution of the order when once adopted.

Mr. DIXON. With the consent of the Senate I propose now—if the honorable senator from Ohio (Mr. Sherman) calls me to order I can proceed only by consent—to discuss this question as a question of order, under the Constitution of the United States and the rules of this body, as specified in the written statement of the question of order, as made by the senator from Michigan. Before proceeding I will request the Secretary to read the point of order once more. I wish to know precisely what I may be permitted to say.

The Secretary read as follows:

That the objection raised to administering the oath to Mr. Wade is out of order, and that the motion of the senator from Maryland, to postpone the administering of the oath to Mr. Wade until other senators are sworn, is also out of order, under the rules adopted by the Senate on the 2d of March instant, and under the Constitution of the United States.

Mr. DIXON. The question presented by the point of order is whether, under the Constitution——

Mr. HOWARD. Mr. President——

Mr. DIXON. If the senator calls me to order I will yield.

Mr. HOWARD. Well, I call the senator from Connecticut to order, and ask the Chair if it be in order now to take an appeal from the decision of the Chair?

Mr. DIXON. I submit that is not such a question of order as the senator has a right to raise. The only question of order that he can now raise upon me is that I am out of order.

Mr. HOWARD. Very well; I raise that question distinctly.

Mr. DIXON. If the senator claims that I am out of order he can call me to order.

Mr. HOWARD. I call the senator to order.

The CHIEF JUSTICE. The senator from Connecticut is called to order, and will take his seat until the point of order is stated.

Mr. HOWARD. Mr. President, the twenty-third rule, adopted by the Senate on the 2d of March, declares that—

All the orders and decisions—

Of course, decisions of the Senate—

shall be made and had by yeas and nays, which shall be entered on the record, and without debate, except when the doors shall be closed for deliberation, and in that case no member shall speak, &c.

The senator from Connecticut, in defiance, as I think, of this rule, persists in his right to address the Senate and discuss the question of order. I hold that to be out of order, and upon that question I ask a ruling.

Mr. DIXON. I respectfully submit that an appeal is debatable.

The CHIEF JUSTICE. The Chair will decide the point of order. This point of order is not debatable. The twenty-third rule is a rule for the proceeding of the Senate when organized for the trial of an impeachment. It is not yet organized; and in the opinion of the Chair the twenty-third rule does not apply at present.

Mr. DRAKE. I take an appeal from the decision of the Chair on that point.

The CHIEF JUSTICE. The senator from Missouri appeals from the decision of the Chair.

Mr. DRAKE. I do not feel disposed to argue the question at this time, consuming time upon it. I take the appeal and ask for a decision upon it by the Senate, if we are in a condition to decide anything until all the senators are sworn.

The CHIEF JUSTICE. Under the general rules of the Senate, as the Chair understands, an appeal being taken from the decision of the Chair, it must be decided without debate.

Mr. GRIMES. Oh, no; it is debatable.

The CHIEF JUSTICE. The Chair ruled that an appeal taken must be decided without debate under an erroneous impression as to the rules of the Senate. Every appeal taken from the decision of the Chair on a question of order is debatable, and this must necessarily be debatable. ["Question!" "Question!"] Senators, are you ready for the question? The question is, Shall the decision of the Chair stand as the judgment of the Senate? and upon that question the yeas and nays will be called.

Mr. FESSENDEN. I think the yeas and nays are not called for.

Mr. GRIMES. They must be called.

Mr. MORRILL, of Maine. Why? On what rule?

Mr. GRIMES. On some rule of the Senate.

Mr. FESSENDEN. They are not always taken, necessarily.

Several senators. Call the roll.

Mr. POMEROY. The point of order is not understood. I do not know what we are to vote upon. I do not understand the point of order of the senator from Missouri.

Mr. FESSENDEN. It is an appeal from the decision of the Chair.

The CHIEF JUSTICE. The Chair decides that the twenty-third rule is not applicable to the proceedings of the Senate when in process of organization for the trial of an impeachment. From that decision the senator from Missouri appeals. The yeas and nays are not demanded.

Mr. FERRY. I call for the yeas and nays.

The yeas and nays were ordered.

Mr. DRAKE. The form of the question, if I understand it, is, Shall the decision of the Chair stand as the judgment of the Senate?

The CHIEF JUSTICE. As many senators as are of opinion that the decision of the Chair shall stand as the judgment of the Senate will, when their names are called, answer yea; as many as are of the contrary opinion will answer nay. The Secretary will call the roll.

The question being taken by yeas and nays, resulted—yeas 24, nays 20; as follows:

YEAS—Messrs. Anthony, Buckalew, Corbett, Davis, Dixon, Fessenden, Fowler, Frelinghuysen, Grimes, Henderson, Hendricks, Johnson, McCreery, Morrill of Maine, Norton, Patterson of Tennessee, Pomeroy, Ross, Saulsbury, Sherman, Sprague, Van Winkle, Willey, and Williams—24.

NAYS—Messrs. Cameron, Cattell, Chandler, Cole, Conkling, Conness, Drake, Ferry, Harlan, Howard, Morgan, Morrill of Vermont, Morton, Nye, Stewart, Sumner, Thayer, Tipton, Wilson, and Yates—20.

ABSENT—Messrs. Bayard, Cragin, Doolittle, Edmunds, Howe, Patterson of New Hampshire, Ramsey, Trumbull, and Wade—9.

The CHIEF JUSTICE. On this question the yeas are 24 and the nays are 20; so the decision of the Chair stands as the judgment of the Senate. [Manifestations of applause in the galleries.] Order! Order!

Mr. DIXON. Perhaps it will not be improper for me to say, with the consent of the Senate, that it was my intention to speak very briefly and in good faith to the question before the Senate. I have not come here to delay proceedings; I have not come here to violate the rules; and I propose now, so far as I can, to confine myself to the proprieties of discussion in attempting to show that under the Constitution and the rules of this body, as expressed in the questions of order, it is not proper for the presiding officer of this body *pro tempore* to be sworn in as a judge in this case.

When interrupted, I was saying that in the event of the conviction of the President of the United States upon the charges brought against him, and his removal from office, there was a direct, apparent interest in the senator from Ohio, the President *pro tempore* for the time being of this body, which rendered it improper for him to act as a judge. In saying that, I beg leave to say, in the first place, that I am not unmindful of the high character of that senator. I acknowledge most cheerfully that he is as much raised above the imperfections and the frailties of this weak, depraved, corrupt human nature of ours as any member of this body.

Mr. CONNESS. I rise to a question of order.

The CHIEF JUSTICE. The senator from California rises to a question of order. He will state the question of order.

Mr. CONNESS. I understand the decision of the Chair to be, that under the general rules of the Senate the senator from Connecticut must confine his discussion to the question before us. I submit that a discussion of the personal qualifications or qualities of the senator from Ohio forms no part of such an argument; and I ask the Chair that the senator, if he proceed, shall be confined within the limit prescribed by the decision of the Chair.

The CHIEF JUSTICE. The Chair required the senator from Connecticut to proceed in accordance with the rules, confining himself strictly to the point of order raised by the motion of the senator from Michigan. But the Chair is greatly embarrassed when he attempts to ascertain the precise scope of debate to be indulged upon the point of order which is taken. He is therefore not prepared to state that the senator from Connecticut is out of order.

Mr. DIXON. Mr. President, I thought that I could, without violating the rules of this body, do justice to myself so far as to disavow any personal objection to the honorable senator whose taking the oath has been objected to. I could not conceive that such a statement from me, under the circumstances, could be considered by the senator from California or by any senator as being an infringement of the rules of order.

Now, Mr. President, what is the question before this body? Is the senator from Ohio so interested in the result of this trial that he cannot properly, under the Constitution and under the rules, be sworn in as a member of the tribunal? That is the question to which I propose to address myself. If the Chair shall inform me that I have no right to discuss it, I shall, of course, not proceed with my remarks.

I was speaking of the nature of the interest and of its effect upon any human mind. Now, sir, may I be permitted to ask this tribunal what is this interest? What is the question which is to be presented to the senator from Ohio as a judge, and to all of us? If any advantage or profit is to accrue to that honorable senator by any vote he may give in this body, what is it? What is the nature of the interest? The Senator from Massachusetts [Mr. Sumner] has spoken of it as a very slight character, a very slight degree of interest, a matter of trifling consequence. Sir, if any advantage is to accrue to this honorable senator, it is that which he is to receive in a certain event which may be influenced by his vote. It is nothing less than the high office of President of the United States, the highest object in this country, and perhaps in the world, of human ambition; an object of ambition which the very highest in the land may properly and laudably aspire to.

Mr. STEWART. I call the senator from Connecticut to order.

The CHIEF JUSTICE. The senator from Nevada calls the senator from Connecticut to order.

Mr. STEWART. It is not in order to discuss the main question as to whether the senator from Ohio is entitled to sit in these proceedings. Nothing further than this can be in order, as I understand the ruling of the Chair: to discuss the point whether now is the time to decide the question.

The point of order submitted by the senator from Michigan is, that this is not the time to dispose of the question whether the senator from Ohio shall sit in our deliberations on the question of impeachment. Certainly it does not involve the main question. It only involves the question of whether this is the time to dispose of the main question. My point of order is, that the senator from Connecticut is discussing the main question and not the question of determining that point at this time.

The CHIEF JUSTICE. The Chair has already said that it is very difficult to determine the precise limits of debate upon the point of order taken by the senator from Michigan. The first clause of the point of order is, "that the objection raised to the administering of the oath to Mr. Wade is out of order;" that is, the objection raised by the senator from Indiana is out of order. The nature of that objection and the validity of that objection, as the Chair conceives, must necessarily become the subjects of debate in order to the determination of the point of order. The Chair, therefore, repeats that he is unable now to decide the senator from Connecticut out of order.

Mr. DIXON. I was upon the question of interest. The objection made to the honorable senator from Ohio, as I understand it, is that he is interested in the result of this decision. It became necessary for me, therefore, to consider what was his interest, and in order to ascertain that it was necessary to consider what was the advantage or disadvantage that he was to receive or to avoid by the result of his action. I was considering the question, what is this office of the President of the United States, which is the matter in controversy? I was saying that it was an object worthy of the ambition of the highest and most distinguished senators in this body or of the most distinguished citizen of the United States, not because of its dazzling surroundings, its vulgar trappings; not because a man in that position breathes the atmosphere of adulation, so dear to human nature; not because he has an opportunity, which is still more dear to a generous mind, of doing favors to his friends, or even (which might be equally dear to men of ignoble character) punishing his enemies, but because it is a position in which the occupant of this great office can do immense good to his country; he may benefit the human race; he may at this time imagine that he might restore a dissevered and disunited country to prosperity and to Union; and for that reason a man of the very highest character and of the purest motives might properly aspire to this lofty position; and I venture to say that with that motive operating upon a human mind it would be nothing short of miraculous if he could be impartial. Nothing short of the power of Omnipotence, operating directly upon the human heart, could, under those circumstances, make any human being impartial.

Then, sir, such being the interest, what is the manner in which this subject is treated by the Constitution of the United States? It may be said that the objection does not come within the letter of the Constitution. Nor am I here to say that the Constitution of the United States expressly prohibits a member of the Senate, acting as presiding officer *pro tempore*, from sitting as a judge in this or a similar case. I am not prepared to say that there is within the letter of the Constitution an express prohibition. But, sir, is it within the spirit of the Constitution? I take it we are here to act, not merely upon the letter, but upon the spirit of that instrument. I take it, at least, that when we are under oath to act impartially, according to the Constitution and the laws, in a criminal proceeding, the spirit of that Constitution and the spirit of those laws are to govern our action. What is the language of the Constitution on this subject?

The Vice-President of the United States shall be President of the Senate, but shall have no vote unless they be equally divided.

The Senate shall choose their other officers, and also a President *pro tempore* in the absence of the Vice-President, or when he shall exercise the office of President of the United States.

The Senate shall have the sole power to try all impeachments. When sitting for that pur pose they shall be on oath or affirmation. When the President of the United States is tried the Chief Justice shall preside; and no person shall be convicted without the concurrence of two-thirds of the members present.

Judgment in cases of impeachment shall not extend further than to removal from office and disqualification to hold and enjoy any office of honor, trust, or profit under the United States, &c.

Now, sir, there is no provision in the Constitution of the United States that the acting Vice-President of the United States, the President *pro tempore* of the Senate, upon a trial of this kind shall not vote. It seems to have been, possibly, strictly speaking, an omitted case. The provision is, that the Vice-President of the United States, under those circumstances, shall not even give the casting vote which he is entitled to give when the Senate is equally divided. That is his sole power in this body; he can only give a casting vote; and he cannot proceed to give a casting vote in a trial of this kind. And why? What was the reason of that provision? The reason of that provision has already been discussed in this body. The senator from Massachusetts attempted to explain it. Other senators gave a reason. It seems to me the reason is obvious. It needs no explanation; and I might say, further, that it is not the custom and the habit of the Constitution to give reasons for its provisions. The senator from Massachusetts says that the Constitution gives no reason for this provision. The Constitution gives a reason, I believe, for very few, if any, of its own provisions. But in this case the reason was so palpable, so manifest, that it was not necessary, even in contemporaneous construction, to give a reason for the provision. The reason was perfectly plain. It was because there was so direct an interest in the Vice-President of the United States that it was deemed improper that he should act; or, in the language of the present presiding officer of this body, the Chief Justice of the United States:

It was, doubtless, thought prudent and befitting that the next in succession should not preside in a proceeding through which a vacancy might be created.

That undoubtedly was the reason of this provision. I have no doubt that the framers of the Constitution went further back. They acted upon principle. They knew that in the very nature of things, in common justice, a man could not be a judge in his own case. They knew that the provisions of the common law prohibited a man from being a judge in his own case. They probably remembered what has been said by one great commentator, (Blackstone,) that the omnipotence of Parliament was limited in this respect, and that body could not make a man a judge in his own case. Probably without that provision in the Constitution the Vice-President would have been prevented from acting under those circumstances. The Constitution provides that the two houses may make rules for their own action; and the House of Representatives has proceeded to make a rule that no member shall cast a vote in which he is interested. This body has not as yet made such a rule, I suppose, because it was thought impossible that any senator should offer or attempt to vote in a case in which he himself was interested. But, sir, this body has made particular rules applying to particular cases; and when the interest has arisen, this body has decided that the party having that interest could not act, as in the case of Mr. Stockton, of New Jersey.

This being the constitutional provision with regard to the Vice-President of the United States when he sits in that chair as the presiding officer of this body, and the President of the United States is tried for an offence which will deprive him of an office which will fall by his removal upon the Vice-President, what is the character and meaning and spirit of the Constitution in a case like that before us? Why, sir, the reasons exist as strongly in this case as in the other. If it would shock humanity, if it would violate every feeling of justice throughout the world, for a man to act in his own case in the first instance, would it not in the latter? I happen to have before me an extract from the speech delivered a few days ago by the honorable senator from New York, [Mr. Conkling.] He gives in his own forcible and striking language the reason for the rule:

> The reason in the case of the impeachment of the President for calling in some one to preside in lieu of the Vice-President is obvious. The Vice-President being next to the President in the line of succession, the impropriety of his doing anything in a trial which, in one event, would result in his own advancement, is clear.
>
> It can hardly be said that such a case would be provided for by calling some senator to the chair, because the fact of a senator being selected to preside would tend in some degree to his advancement also in case of the conviction of the President.

And so careful, so particular, so scrupulous was the honorable senator from New York, that it seemed to him that the reason of the rule applied to any senator called to the chair of this body, being selected to preside, as that would tend in some degree to his advancement in the case of the conviction of the President.

He proceeds to say:

> A senator made President of the Senate *pro tempore* even during a trial of impeachment might expect to continue such President in the event of the advancement of the regular presiding officer to supersede the President of the United States. These and other considerations of safety and decorum indicated the propriety of going outside the Senate for an officer to occupy the chair when the President should be brought to the bar, and nothing could be more natural or dignified than to select the head of one of the three branches of the government. The Chief Justice, being separated from both the political departments of the government, was deemed the person most fit, by reason not only of his disinterestedness, but of his learning and the great consideration of his position. These reasons might well have suggested the propriety of asking of the head of the bench that he should discharge, upon a great and solemn occasion, duties with which the highest subjects of England have ever been invested.

It is impossible for me, in stronger language than the senator from New York has used, to depict the impropriety of a member of this body, under the rules and under the Constitution, acting as a judge in a case which, in a certain event, is to place him in the presidential chair.

But, sir, it is said that this is not the time to raise the objection; that the objection may, perhaps, be waived by the party accused. If a President of the United States, chosen by the people, was actually on trial, and the Vice-President was in the chair, and proposed to sit and give the casting vote, and we objected to his being sworn, could it be said that possibly the President of the United States on trial might waive the objection? Can he waive the objection? He is not alone interested. The people of this whole country are interested in the decision of this question. The party nearest in interest cannot waive it. If he were the President of the United States, actually chosen as such, and the Vice-President, actually chosen, were sitting in that chair, he could not waive that interest. He could not say, as one senator has supposed he might say, "I prefer upon the whole that that distinguished officer, knowing his impartiality and his love of justice, should preside in this trial, and give the casting vote in my case; I think it would be for my advantage." That could not be allowed. If it is decided at all it is decided by the law and the Constitution and the general rules of right. Therefore, the objection that this point is made too early does not apply. It is an objection which, if it can be made at all, can be made here at this period, and should be made now, for it is perfectly evident that the distinguished gentleman now proposed to be sworn in as a judge, the moment he is sworn in, can decide important questions long before the accused party shall present himself here or shall be summoned to appear here. There is the question of notice, the question of time, and there are various questions on which he will be called upon to give a decision. If, therefore, the objection is to be made at all, it must necessarily or with great propriety should be made at this time.

But, sir, I do not desire to go further into this general question. I have attempted to look at this question as a judge. I have attempted, in considering in my own mind, whether it be proper for the honorable senator from Ohio to act as a judge in this case, to act myself as a judge, and it has seemd to me in the highest degree improper in every aspect of the case. Sir, if there is anything desirable in this great trial, it is, in the first place, that impartial justice should be done; and in the second place, that it should appear to be just that mankind should say that impartial justice was done. If it should so happen that, under the construction to be given to the rules of this body and under the Constitution of the United States, the Senate should decide that the honorable senator from Ohio should be a judge in the case, that the judge of the President is to be his successor in office, is there not danger that it may be said that there is doubt as to the fairness of this trial? If the future historian, in recording the fact that the President of the United States had been removed from his office by impeachment, should also be compelled to record the fact that his successor was his judge, such a record would violate the sense of justice of the nation and shock the heart of the civilized world.

Mr. HENDRICKS. Mr. President, with the indulgence of the Senate, I will add a very little to what I felt it my duty to say upon this question yesterday, and then, as far as I am concerned, I shall relieve the Senate from any embarrassment about it.

It was said by the senator from Nebraska [Mr. Thayer] and the senator from Ohio [Mr. Sherman] that the senator who now proposes to take the oath is, in all respects, the equal of any other senator, and that no objection can be made to his right to vote upon any question upon which other senators have the right to vote. The general proposition I do not question, that, as a senator, he is the peer of any other senator; but to both gentlemen my reply is this: that by his own act he has accepted an office above that of senator, if I may so express it, which disqualifies him from participating in this trial. It is his act, not the act of the Senate, if the State of Ohio upon this trial be not represented by two senators.

The objection is made by the senator from Missouri [Mr. Drake] that the Senate is not in a condition to consider the question, for the reason that it has not yet organized itself for the purposes of the trial, and, therefore, there is nobody competent to decide whether the senator from Ohio may participate in that trial. Sir, the question that is presented by me arises frequently in the organization of bodies composed of many persons. It must necessarily arise in the organization of such bodies. It frequently arises in the organization of the House of Representatives, and it matters not whether the question comes up on the call of the first or the last name. When an objection is made to the right of a representative or to the right of a senator when this body is being organized at the commencement of a new Congress, how is that question to be decided? If at the commencement of the 40th Congress it had been objected that some senator could not then take the oath required by the act of 1862, and that objection was made when the Secretary of the Senate was midway in the call, who would decide it? The Senate would not then be organized; and yet it is a question incident to the organization itself, and a question that must be decided before the organization can be completed. I say, therefore, as this is a question that may arise, that is likely to arise, in the organization of any body composed of many persons, it must be met here precisely as in other cases.

I am not going to discuss the question whether, organized for the purposes of this trial, the Senate be technically and in name a court. In substance, Mr. President, it is a court. It is to consider questions of law and questions of fact. It is not to consider legislative questions at all; and it cannot indulge in the considerations of public policy which may be indulged in in the Senate. The judgment of each senator is controlled altogether by questions of fact and of law. A body, by whatever name known, that has to consider only questions of fact and of law, and upon that consideration to pronounce a judgment, is a judicial body in its very essence and nature. It is no longer a legislative body.

Then, Mr. President, we propose (calling the body what you may) now to pass from the consideration of legislative questions to the consideration of the impeachment question; to cease to be a body for the consideration of legislative questions and to become a body for the consideration only of judicial questions. The first step in passing from the one character to the other is the appearance in the chair of the Chief Justice of the Supreme Court. The next step is the taking of an oath unknown to us as legislators, but binding us as judges—as judges of the questions of law and of fact that may arise. This is the step which we are now taking. We are now taking the oath to qualify us to discharge a peculiar and extraordinary duty—the oath that as judges we will be fair and just. The question arises during the organization of the Senate in that character and for that duty whether a senator is competent to participate in the adjudication. That question is incident to the organization of the Senate in its new character. I have not changed my opinion that that question properly arises in the administration of the oath.

I am not going to discuss further the merits whether the senator from Ohio, being now the President of the Senate and the possible successor should there be a vacancy in the presidential office, can participate in the trial, except to say this: that at one time I held the opinion that a senator having an interest in the result of a question might vote. I held that view in Mr. Stockton's case; but the Senate, by a deliberate vote, overruled that view, and established it as the law of the Senate that he who is to be benefited by the decision to the extent of holding an office or acquiring an office cannot help to decide that question. I was surprised yesterday that the senator from Massachusetts [Mr. Sumner] should occupy in regard to this question a very different position from that which he occupied when he helped to decide the Stockton case. Where is the difference? Mr. Stockton was a member of this body. He had credentials that *prima facie* entitled him to participate in our deliberations. He was entitled to cast a vote upon any legislative question that should come up to the very minute of the decision of the Senate against him. He was for the time being a senator from New Jersey. When the question was, shall he continue to hold that office, the Senate said, without an express rule on the subject and no general parliamentary law, but on a universal sentiment of justice, as it was claimed then, right, and propriety, that he could not vote when his vote helped him to hold an office. I am not able to see, when the vote of the presiding officer of this body may enable him to hold the highest office in the nation, the distinction in the two cases. The Senate deliberately decided in that case that the interest disqualified for the time being the party from voting in the Senate.

But, Mr. President, I find that some senators, among them the senator from Delaware, [Mr. Bayard,] who agree with me upon this question on the merits, are of the opinion that the question ought more properly to be raised when the court shall be fully organized, when the party accused is here to answer. I do not believe that he can waive a question that goes to the organization of the body; I believe it is a question for the body itself. But upon that I find some difference of opinion; and when I find that difference of opinion among those who agree with me upon the merits, upon the main point, whether he shall participate in the proceedings and judgment who may be benefited by it—while I find some senators, who agree with me upon that question, disagreeing with me upon the question whether it ought to be raised now or when the senator from Ohio proposes to cast a material vote in the proceedings, I choose to yield my judgment—my judgment, not at all upon the merits; my judgment not at all upon the propriety and the duty of the Senate to decide upon its own organization; but I yield as to the time when the question shall be made in deference to the opinion of others; and for myself, sir, I withdraw the question which I presented for the consideration of the President of this body and of the Senate yesterday.

Mr. POMEROY. The senator proposes to withdraw the point which he made, and I think it can be done by unanimous consent. I hope unanimous consent will be given, and let it be withdrawn, and let us proceed to swear in the other senators.

Mr. HENDRICKS. It does not require unanimous consent. I can withdraw it myself.

Mr. SHERMAN and Mr. GRIMES. The senator has a right to withdraw it.

The CHIEF JUSTICE. The Chair understands that the senator from Indiana has withdrawn his objection.

Mr. POMEROY. But an appeal has been taken.

Mr. GRIMES. That makes no difference.

The CHIEF JUSTICE. The senator from Ohio will take the oath.

Mr. HOWARD. I beg to inquire whether the withdrawal of this particular motion affects the motion that was made by the honorable senator from Maryland? [Mr. Johnson.]

Mr. FESSENDEN. That falls with it, of course.

The CHIEF JUSTICE. All the questions incidental to the main question fall with the withdrawal of it.

Mr. JOHNSON. My motion was founded upon the other motion. If the first motion is withdrawn mine falls as a matter of course.

Mr. HOWARD. Very well, if that is the understanding.

The Secretary called the name of Mr. Wade, who advanced and took the oath.

www.ingramcontent.com/pod-product-compliance
Lightning Source LLC
Chambersburg PA
CBHW030550300426
44111CB00009B/922